Power, Policy and Personality: The Life and Times of Lord Salter, 1881-1975

Power, Policy and Personality: The Life and Times of Lord Salter, 1881–1975

Sidney Aster

Copyright © 2015 Sidney Aster
All rights reserved

ISBN-13: 9781517179502
ISBN-10: 1517179505

For Isaac, Sam and Sadie

"Realise that whether you like it or not, your life will be written by someone."
Letter, Lionel Curtis to Sir Arthur Salter, 23 August 1950.

CONTENTS

	Introduction · xiii
1	"A Service Reputation," 1881-1914 · 1
2	"An 'Inner Circle' Reputation," 1914-1918 · 35
3	"One of the Apostles of the New Age," 1918-1922 · · · · · · · · · · · · · · · · 77
4	"Nations of the World are Together Building Up a New World," 1922-1930 · 123
5	"Public Tasks for a Private Person," 1931-1939 · · · · · · · · · · · · · · · · · · · 219
6	"I Am Glad on the Whole to be Inside Again," At War Once More, 1939-1945 · 366
7	Out of and In Office, 1945-1953 · 497
8	"The Less Exacting Chamber," 1954-1975 · 596
	Bibliography · 625

ACKNOWLEDGEMENTS

For permission to quote copyright materials, the author is grateful to the following:

Alexander Murray (Gilbert Murray)
Archives and Special Collections Research Center, Ball State University, A.M. Bracken Library, Muncie, IN (Norman Angell)
Baker Library Special Collections, Harvard Business School, Boston, MA (Winthrop W. Aldrich)
British Library Board and the Department of Western Manuscripts, British Library (J.A. Spender)
Department of Special Collections and Western Manuscripts, Bodleian Library, Oxford (Lionel Curtis)
William Douglas, John Douglas and Mary Felkin (Elliott Felkin)
Estate of Sir Winston S. Churchill (Sir Winston S. Churchill)
Library of Congress (Averell Harriman, Emory S. Land)
Literary Executors of the Estate of H.G. Wells (H.G. Wells)
Markham Estate (Violet Markham)
Master and Fellows of Trinity College, Cambridge (Sir Walter Layton)
Master, Massey College, University of Toronto (Vincent Massey)
Nigel Nicolson and the Library, Balliol College, Oxford (Sir Harold Nicolson)
Professor A.K. Lambton and the Department of Western Manuscripts, British Library (Lord Cecil of Chelwood)
Rare Books and Special Collections, Thomas Cooper Library, University of Southern Carolina (Lord Allen of Hurtwood)
Royal Institution of Cornwall and Special Collections, Old Library, University of Exeter (A.L. Rowse)
Royal Institute of International Affairs (Lionel Curtis and Chatham House)
The Controller of Her Majesty's Stationery Office (National Archives – UK)
Tomlin Coggeshall (Frances Perkins)
Trustees of the Liddell Hart Centre for Military Archives (Sir Basil Liddell Hart)

INTRODUCTION

There is hardly a historical biography or monograph dealing with the first half of the twentieth century which does not refer to Sir Arthur (Lord) Salter. Yet, this study represents his first biography, relying exclusively and uniquely on primary-source materials. The historical record reveals Salter had intimate, global access to the seats of power. He rose doggedly, through increasingly influential positions, national and international, political and economic. The record of this unprecedented journey reveals and elucidates Salter's influential and pioneering comprehension of the post-1918 world order, his personal impact on its evolution, and its eventual collapse.

Salter's was a privileged vantage point within the "inner and outer circles" of decision-making in British and international public life. Though mostly revered backstage, his influence can be traced in numerous decisive turning points in twentieth century history from Britain to the United States, Europe to the Far East. A multitude of milestone historical events unfolded with Salter's orchestration. As a prominent civil servant he was instrumental in shaping the welfare state. He was a pioneering administrator with the League of Nations and the United Nations. He was an original member and activist of the European Movement, a world recognized authority on economics and finance, an Oxford professor, an Independent MP and then a Conservative MP, and a cabinet minister in two of Sir Winston Churchill's governments, 1945 and 1951-53. He was, as well, an influential author, journalist, advocate and broadcaster.

Salter's historical impact begins with his work as a civil servant implementing the British National Health Insurance Act of 1911, and his leadership in the wartime Ministry of Shipping. He played a central role in establishing the convoy system, which enabled Britain to overcome the German U-boat campaign and thus avoid starvation. His creative role continued in the 1920s, as an international civil servant while at the Allied Maritime Transport Council, the Reparation Commission and crucially as the first Director of the Economic and Financial Section of the League of Nations. Throughout, he pioneered modern approaches to inter-allied cooperation, financial reconstruction, European integration and an international civil service.

In the 1930s Salter's popularity, resulting from his best-selling book, <u>Recovery: The Second Effort</u> (1932), outmatched that of John Maynard Keynes. As an Independent MP for Oxford University, he opposed appeasement and lobbied for the storage of raw materials for another world war he considered inevitable. His pivotal wartime experience was to head the British Merchant Shipping Mission to Washington from 1941-1943. There, he convinced the Americans to build ships to supply and feed a beleaguered Britain; his efforts saved Britain from starvation. Salter then assisted in the economic reconstruction of Britain and Europe, with his subsequent leadership of the United Nations Relief and Rehabilitation Administration, and in his roles as Chancellor of the Duchy of Lancaster, Minister of State for Economic Affairs, and Minister of Materials. During the entire period from 1922 to 1955, he also acted as economic and financial advisor to the governments of Austria, Hungary, Greece, Poland, India, China and Iraq.

Until the completion of this project, Salter's life has never been the subject of a biography. That deficiency is now remedied and we have a multi-layered portrait of the Edwardian Salter, the wartime Salter, the 1920s Salter, the Depression era Salter, and so on, down to the 1960s' elder statesperson. The primary sources for this biography include records of my interviews in London with Salter in the early 1970s, his personal papers, documents derived from almost 150 collections of private papers and research in archives/libraries located across the United States, Britain, Canada, France and Switzerland and South Africa. The biography also makes use of documentation about Salter's private life entrusted to me by a number of his female friends. These manuscripts include the 10 volumes of unpublished diaries of Mary Agnes "Molly" Hamilton, MP and biographer, correspondence with Renée de Lucy Fossarieu, who served as Salter's secretary in Paris and Geneva, and Katherine Arnold-Forster, better known as "Ka" Cox, former intimate of Rupert Brooke. These materials dispel the image, cultivated by Salter himself, of an abstemious person, with a frugal lifestyle, enamoured of nothing else but work and public service. What emerges is a refreshing portrait of a highly cultured individual, with acute sensitivities, a real genius for friendship and whose multi-faceted reputation deserves to be returned to public attention.

On a more personal note, and by way of background, I was first introduced to Lord Salter by the late Sir Martin Gilbert in April 1970. Salter and I agreed that I would visit him weekly for conversation and to study his personal papers. This was intended to be the basis of his biography which I would eventually write. This routine lasted until May 1975 when I took up a visiting professorship at Concordia University in Montreal. There I was notified on 27 June that Salter had died in his sleep, a result of an earlier stroke. On my return to London in late August I was shocked to discover that a portion of Salter's papers had been destroyed by Bonham's in the course of their removing, for auction, the contents of the Salters' residence, West House in Chelsea, London. Much of this material consisted of publications, official documents and the like. Thankfully, I had in my possession a massive number of Salter's papers on which I was working at my London home at the time. At that point I debated whether to abandon my promise to Salter, which I regarded as a moral obligation, or carry on, rebuild the archive and complete his biography. After my permanent return to Canada in June 1976, I came to the latter decision. Over the span of numerous years, even while I worked at my other publications, I gathered further documents for the Salter biography. The result is that the current collection of Salter papers and documents amassed during the research process, now deposited in the Churchill Archive Centre, Cambridge, is vastly greater than the original archive at West House.

Thanking those who have assisted me over the years, either with their oral and written reminiscences or providing documentary materials, is the greatest of pleasures. However, many individuals, who encouraged this project and looked forward to its completion, have sadly passed away. The individuals include Lady Allen of Hurtwood, Lady Aberdeen, Sally Adamson, Commander R.V. Adamson, Thanassis, Aghnides, Robert Alsop, Professor Stratis G. Andreadis, Mark Arnold-Forster, Jake Arnold-Forster, Countess Baldwin, Michael Barratt Brown, Professor James Barros, Professor Max Beloff, Sir Isaiah Berlin, Geoffrey D.M. Block, Lord Boothby, Lord Boyd-Carpenter, A.J. Brown, Pearl S. Buck, Lord Butler, Lady Catlin, Gertrude Caton Thompson, Harold Caustin, Sir Norman Chester, Thomas W. Childs, Viscount Chilston, Professor Patricia Clavin, Lord Clitheroe, Augusta Cobbold, Susanna W. Coggeshall, Dame Margaret Cole, Lady Conesford, Dame Margaret Corbett-Ashby, Captain Alex Danchev, Joseph S. Davis, Professor Roberta Dayer, Ruth Feis, Joyce Felkin, Douglas Fell, Sir Edward Ford, Renée de Lucy Fossarieu, Sir John Foster, Lord Geddes, Sir Martin Gilbert, Rosamond Gilder, Bernard L. Gladieux, Robert Grimm, Sir Noel Hall, Lord Harcourt, Jennifer Hart, Joanna Hirth, Sir J. Nicholas Henderson, Pat Hill, H.V. Hodson, David Hubback, Pamela Hurcomb, Elizabeth Clark Hutchison, Graham Hutton, Lord Inchyra, Sir Robert Jackson, Douglas Jay, Philip C. Jessup, M.L. Johansen, Aubrey Jones, Dr. Erin Jucker-Fleetwood, Jessica Katzenellenbogen, Sir William Keswick, Sir Charles Kimber, Mary D. Kierstead, Professor Stephen Koss, Lord Layton, Elizabeth Leach, Professor Christophe Le-Dreau, Donald Lowe, Ian Lowe, Lord Leathers, Kenneth Lindsay, Mary Lee Johansen, Sir Henry Lumby, Fred C. Lay, Lady Macadam, Malcolm MacDonald, Professor Norman MacKenzie, Sir Harold Macmillan, Sir Henry Mance, Dona Emilia de Madariaga, Nicholas Mansergh, Professor Arthur Marder, Robert de la Mare, A.D. Marris, Michael McGarvie, John McLennan, Rustin McIntosh, Professor J.E. Meade, Lord Molson, Jean Monnet, Sylvia Monnet, Aubrey N.

Morgan, Sir Jeremy Morse, Lord Muirshiel, Lord Nathan, Max Nicholson, Christopher Newton-Thompson, Professor Barry Nicholls, Lord Noel-Baker, Sir Frederic Osborn, Lithgow Osborne, Tonio Palmer, Stanley Payton, Lord Perth, Caroline Phybus, Sir Edward Playfair, Fred Poole, Sir John Pope-Hennessy, Reginald Pound, Sir Richard Powell, Johanna Preetorius, Sir Denis Rickett, Lord Robbins, W.A. Robson, Kenneth Rose, A.L. Rowse, John H. MacCallum Scott, Lord Segal, Lord Simon, Dr. Jean Siotis, Edward Sniders, John Sparrow, Elizabeth Spencer, Lord Stamp, Martin Strauss, Frank Swinnerton, Eva and W. Kenneth Thompson, John H. Shepardson, Dorothy Sackett, William Tyler, Rayner Unwin, Lady Vestey, Gillian Watson, Walter Muir Whitehall, Sir Harold Wilkinson, Freda Wint, Lowell P. Weicker, Dr. Simon Wenham, Dame Rebecca West, W.G. Weston, Lady Wheeler-Bennett, Professor Ralph White, Sir Duncan Wilson, and Sir Harold Wilkinson.

In the course of my entire research career I have worked personally in many libraries and archives and received wonderful assistance, both long-distance and on site. I am grateful to these individual librarians and archivists who assisted me and whom I hope will accept this general expression of thanks. I have also worked with several talented research assistants. My thanks to Amanda Beauchamp, Ariel Beaujot, Noah Belikoff, Jennifer Bonder, Mani Kakkar, Amy Legate-Wolfe, Jenevieve Mannell, Angela Petersen, Clara Rubincam and Scott Sleath. Finally, I wish to thank those institutions which over the years funded the research for this biography: Leverhulme Trust, Twenty-Seven Foundation, Social Sciences and Humanities Research Council, and the Research Board of the University of Toronto.

My ultimate debt of gratitude belongs to my wife, Joyce, who has shared in the Salter story and its final telling for a very, very long time. Her patience while I was distracted, her insight when required and advice over so many years were unmatched.

CHAPTER 1

"A SERVICE REPUTATION," 1881-1914

James Arthur Salter was born on the "Ides of March," 15 March 1881, in Oxford. Half a century later, when receiving an honourary DCL at the Oxford Encaenia on 22 June 1932, it was the Public Orator who informed him that he had been born in the parish of Speedwell, near Folly Bridge on the banks of the upper Thames.[1] Ninety-four years later, on 28 June 1975 he died, again just a stone's throw from the River Thames, but now as it runs through London near Chelsea.

Of the many themes that structure the life of James Arthur Salter, the Thames predominates. He was born into an Oxford boat-building family with premises on the Thames. His first civil service position was with the transport department of the Admiralty. During both World Wars he was involved at the highest levels in securing adequate shipping to guarantee Britain's survival. And his final years were concerned with both Oxford preservation and Thames Valley conservation. In the improbable context of Salter's Guide to the Thames, co-author James Arthur Salter paid homage to his river valley origins. Alone among the rivers of the world, he wrote, the Thames combines scenery, history and prosperity. If there is "no majesty there is no monotony," he observed, just "a wonderful series of ancient memories and monuments."[2] He remarked a typical great English career could run its course without ever leaving the rivers' environs: Eton and Oxford; followed by political involvement at Westminster; the rewards of high office in Whitehall; royal honours at Windsor; and the final tribute, a memorial service in Westminster Abbey. It was "the peculiar glory of the Thames," however, which most impressed him. The relatively short course of the river exhibited characteristics both ancient and modern:

> The monuments of the past, the placid and prosperous life of the present, the quiet pastoral beauty of meadow, woodland and silver stream, are all seen here, and all at their best. And one is inclined to say that if a visitor had only four days in which to capture a true impression of this country he would do well to spend two of them in the Thames Valley.[3]

Having had access to the Thames' intimacies at an early and impressionable age, Salter carried the memories throughout adult life. Little else would give him the same contentment.

The historical origin of the Salter family is obscure, partly because Salter and most other family members took little interest in the subject.[4] The Salter tree, however, is extensive, with likely late medieval origins. The Salters, first mentioned in the time of King John in the early thirteenth century, derived their wealth from the manufacture of salt in north Shropshire and south Cheshire. In the last quarter of the fifteenth century, the Salters sold their properties and dispersed throughout the country, some settling in London.[5] At the turn of the nineteenth century, some Salters found themselves living in the working-class neighbourhoods of London. In June 1836 Salter's great-grandparents James and Elizabeth Salter, and their very large family which included three sons, Henry, John and Stephen, moved from the borough of Fulham to Wandsworth across the River Thames. There the younger Salters grew up, taking advantage of the river to foster their interests in boats and rowing, and in time marrying and raising families.[6]

In 1858, at the height of the mid-Victorian boom, John and Stephen Salter left the south bank of the Thames and resettled with their young families in Oxford. There they took over Isaac King's boat building firm at Folly Bridge, establishing the presence of the Salter boatbuilding and steamer firm. At once tragedy struck, for in 1865 John Salter's wife Harriet died, leaving him to raise four sons and three daughters, one of whom died very young.[7] Despite such setbacks, the two enterprising students of Samuel Smiles' Self-Help concentrated on the boat-building business which they had taken over. They had chosen for their workshop the banks of the Thames, near Folly Bridge, a site where until 1779 had stood the study of Friar Roger Bacon, one of the most interesting intellectual figures of thirteenth century Oxford. Intensive work and the widening of the leisure market combined in a short time to turn the business into the foremost boat building enterprise on the Thames. Between 1858 and 1874 the Salter firm built an unprecedented number of racing boats. It also built the University Racing Eights, used by Oxford to beat Cambridge at the annual race on the Thames for nine years in succession. And with time, expansion led to a flourishing export trade in racing boats, punts and canoes to all parts of the world.[8]

As Stephen Salter approached his 40th birthday, business success had provided both him and his brother a small fortune. He then surprised all by announcing in 1874 his early retirement to "enjoy his remaining years."[9] An exceptionally active individual, Stephen Salter had never shirked the six-day, 18-hour work week. He had combined this with a successful career as a competitive oarsman. He could boast of a string of victories beginning in 1857, with the Coat and Badge, and Freedom of the Thames in the Royal Thames National Regatta, and the International Regatta at

Antwerp. The following year Stephen Salter's four-oared crew won both the champion prize and first and second prizes in pairs during the Royal Thames National Regatta. This was his crown of glory as an oarsman and boatman. By 1874, however, the strain of such activity was affecting his health and he retired from the business, a retirement that was to last 63 years. Having sold his share in the business to his brother John, Stephen Salter first retreated to Egrove, near Oxford, where he continued his interest in pigeons. He had first exhibited at the Crystal Palace in 1857 and in succeeding years had won numerous cups and medals for his home-bred pigeons, particularly turbits. He later added poultry, Collie dogs, Alderney cows and Berkshire pigs. In 1881, he moved to an impressive residence, "Pondwell," near Ryde, in the Isle of Wight. When he died in 1937 at age 103, he had lived through the reigns of six sovereigns, from William IV to George VI.[10] Such unprecedented longevity became a Salter tradition.

The boat-building business, now in the sole hands of John Salter, continued to prosper. High standards of craftsmanship, fixed to an enviable reputation and an enlightened policy for dealing with seasonal unemployment, ensured prosperity and a loyal labour force. A growing family needed as much attention as a thriving business. As each of the four sons – John Henry, the eldest, Thomas Alfred, James Edward, James Arthur's father, and George Stephen – came of age, they were sent to Crapper's School in Oxford for basic education until 14 years of age. As a self-made successful man, obsessed largely by business and shooting, John Salter thought that what had been good enough for him should be good enough for his sons. Each was given manual work in the boat-building shop at the age of fourteen.

However, if education was not highly prized, other virtues were ruthlessly inculcated. Thrift, as expected, was drummed into their minds, and each was paid an artisan's wage for labouring in their father's shop.[11] Religion was regarded as a living and active faith, particularly after the family left the Church of England and joined the Wesleyan Methodists. Their commitment found expression in practical work, from involvement with the Wesleyan Sunday school to active participation in the civic life of Oxford. But it was deep religious faith which formed the mainspring of both character development and community commitment. John Salter died on 21 January 1890, at his home in St Aldate Street, but a lifetime of hard and successful work left his heirs a very considerable estate. John Henry, James Edward and George Stephen inherited the boat-building facility, three small farms at Wootton and a personal estate exceeding £31,000. Fanny, the only surviving daughter, was given a legacy of £3,000, as was Thomas Alfred, the second eldest son.[12] Salter later recalled, with some bitterness, that his very wealthy grandfather's reluctance to properly educate his father convinced the latter his children "should have every advantage of education he could scrape together."[13]

The business which now passed into the hands of the three sons traded as the private company of "Salter Brothers." However, the character of the company changed with its second generation managers. John Henry inherited much of his father's drive and arbitrary character. He dominated the daily operations of the business, making it both unnecessary and difficult for his two younger brothers to participate on an equal footing. In addition, for the next 30 years, John Henry became a leading figure in Oxford's municipal life. He was chairman of the Thames Boating Trades Association, chairman of the City Finance Committee, and for much of his adult life he was a councillor or alderman, and served as mayor in 1902-1903. Civic commitment remained a firm Salter trait, as did religious devotion. As Wesleyan Methodists and confirmed Sabbatarians, the Salter brothers never placed profit before the Sabbath. In 1888 the Salters' steamboat service was inaugurated on the Thames. Although the fleet continued to grow, as did the numbers using the service, the Salter monopoly was finally broken with the company's refusal to operate services or rent river-craft on Sundays.[14] Only under the influence of the third generation of Salters was Sunday service instituted in 1933. By that time, however, the firm had lost its lead both in building racing boats and providing the pleasure boat service on the Thames.[15]

Under the shadow of a domineering older brother, and a business increasingly under pressure, James Edward diverted his energies into a combination of civic, religious, philanthropic and educational activities. He first entered the Oxford City Council as representative of the South Ward in 1896, until his election to the aldermanic bench in 1922. He also filled the positions of Sheriff and Mayor of Oxford from 1909-1910. His civic interests centred on the provision of playgrounds, open spaces, baths, swimming places and homes for "feeble-minded girls." His religion, the central fact of his life, found expression in a practical way. He was first teacher and then superintendent of the Wesleyan Sunday School from age 21 to 60. Simultaneously, he was one of the three founders of the Oxford YMCA, of which he was honourary secretary for 50 years, as well as a member of the board of governors of the Radcliffe Infirmary, and for a time president of the Oxford Association. Perhaps superseding all other interests was that of Poor Law work. Salter himself recalled: "from my boyhood I remember his discussions of relief problems as a principal topic of his conversation." In 1896 James Edward first became a member of the old Oxford Board of Guardians, continuing as vice-chairman for 28 years until the Board was abolished in 1930. Thereafter, and until his death on 31 March 1937, he remained a member of the Public Assistance Committee. "Boatbuilder and Friend of the Poor" was how The Oxford Mail headlined its 1 April 1937 obituary of James Edward Salter, and added, "He did much good among the poorer classes."[16]

To all his public duties James Edward brought qualities which endeared him to all. He combined humility, gentle courtesy and charity of judgement. On matters he considered vital, he exercised a tenacious will. His conscious dignity enhanced the status of any position he held or event over which he presided. In a tribute paid at the City Church, Oxford, the City Rector pointed to his "broad sympathies" and "conspicuous practical mindedness" as the hallmarks of a distinguished public career.[17] An almost saintly public character reflected a similar private person. Like his eldest brother, John Henry, James Edward chose another sister of the Oxford tailoring family, Julia Millin, as his wife. Small in stature, like James Edward, Julia was not striking, though beautiful to those who loved her, however, she shared few of her husband's intellectual interests. Modest musical abilities enabled her to sing to her children as she accompanied herself on the piano. Often she would take her young family boating on the Thames, stopping near a peaceful layby to read from Kenneth Grahame's Golden Age. Such experiences moulded the memories her sons retained in later years. To her husband she provided devoted companionship and a stable family life which ended on 17 April 1926 after almost 50 years of marriage.[18]

"Among the innumerable debts his sons owe him," Salter wrote on 5 April 1937, "I should personally put this first – in my view the greatest gift any father can give his children. He gave us an environment in which the scale of values was right." That environment and those values were fundamental late Victorian non-conformity. A good education was prized not for its career potential, but as the key to self-enrichment. Religion was both a faith and a practical way of life. Politics for the Salters had to be Gladstonian Liberalism, principled and consistent, yet also tolerant. Values were imparted not by words, but in a display of appropriate conduct, and the pleasures of the flesh were neither to be denied nor flaunted. James Edward was personally ascetic, living sparely, invariably self-denying, an abstainer, and until late in life a non-smoker; thereafter he allowed himself (except during Lent) an occasional cigar. Nevertheless, he was without the more forbidding qualities of the Puritan. Shakespeare and William Morris were as often read as the Bible. While money was limited, no restrictions were placed on the enjoyment otherwise of a rich life.[19] Left largely to their own devices, the four children were divided by no major incompatibilities. They had at their doorstep an enchanting river and all the means to enjoy its varied pleasures to the fullest. In winter there was skating on the Thames and once a year the entire family set out for a week to attend the Henley Regatta, sculling down in a large boat. From the bedrooms of their home, on a tongue of the river near Folly Bridge, they had a clear view twice a year of the college races, the Torpids and Eights, as the eight-oared boats reached the finishing line. Often in summer there were vacations at one of John Salter's farms. In 1897 came a lifelong memory, as a youth of 16 Salter was taken to London to witness from a platform in the Mall the Diamond Jubilee procession of Queen Victoria.[20]

The chief blemish in this otherwise typical late Victorian family lay in the emotional realm. "There was in all our family relationships an excess of silence except on trivial daily occurrences," Salter recalled in later years. James Edward could not share his intimate thoughts or feelings with his sons. Excessive reticence on the part of the father was matched by the distance felt by the children. These barriers fell only once when Julia Salter died in 1926. The family grieved openly; feelings of affection, suppressed for years, came to the surface – perhaps for the first time.[21] Looking back Salter admitted:

> My father is, on the whole, the chief figure in my childhood memories, as he was also the chief influence in my early development. Short, like myself, in stature; with (as far back as I can remember) a small beard, dark like his hair till age greyed it; slim and spare in age as in youth; physically active, liking to row when he was young and to walk in the country almost every day till his very last years, nothing in his physique or presence made him an outstanding figure in any company in which he might be.[22]

While Salter saw himself as a reflection of his father, the mirror image was not perfect. The latter was quite selfless, but Salter was growing into a shy, sensitive and introverted child, and quite selfish.

James Edward was determined that his sons would not be deprived of the educational opportunities he had been denied. At six, Salter was sent to a Dame's school, run by two spinster sisters. There he exhibited the excessively competitive spirit which was to characterize his later educational career. He hated to be beaten, either in the class or on the playing field. The prospect of defeat always motivated him to refuse participation rather than face a loss. In September 1890 James Edward began to enrol his sons in the recently founded City of Oxford High School for boys. It had been felt for decades that Oxford city did not possess an adequate grammar school for the majority of its citizens. Collegiate schools catered primarily to choristers, while Nixon's School founded in 1659 remained a preserve of the sons of Freemen. What Oxford required was a day school which offered a good liberal education and linked elementary school with university. It was to take a decade of fierce civic controversy before the City of Oxford High School opened its doors to welcome students on 15 September 1881.[23] The background to its inception is of relevant because the subject formed the basis of Arthur's earliest published writing. In June 1903 appeared the first issue of The Oxford High School Magazine. It contained, as did the subsequent issue, two outspoken articles by Salter, "T.H. Green and the High School," and "The Founding of the High School." The striking aspect of both is the evidence of research which informed the writing and the strong *parti pris* tone which sustained the argument. The first article warmly endorsed the Herculean efforts made by the Oxford philosopher, Professor T.H. Green, to promote a scheme "to establish a new Grammar School or High School for the City of Oxford." Between his first efforts in 1877 and his death in 1881, Green not only witnessed the opening of the school, but also the establishment of its endowment with substantial scholarship funds, some of which came from his own pocket.

What most impressed Salter when assessing the T.H. Green campaign were the ideals which inspired the effort, and with which he clearly identified. Referring to Green's address to the Wesleyan Literary Society on 19 December 1881, on the subject of the High School, Salter wrote:

At that time the ideal of a 'ladder of learning' had already become a fruitful one in English education; but many rungs were still missing. It was still true that the educational system not only expressed existing social divisions, but created new ones, aggravated the differences and made the barriers more impassable; that the few great schools which had adopted the name – and, incidentally, often the funds – which should have belonged to schools really open to the public, retained almost a monopoly in liberal education; for the great majority of English boys, and, till a few months before, notably for those of Oxford, there were neither means of access to these schools nor others to take their place.

The situation in Oxford, Salter's analysis continued, had been especially serious. The barrier to an Oxford citizen was no longer an entrance fee but an entrance examination – "the most fatal flaw in the ladder." The immediate objects of the school, therefore, were "to provide as liberal an education for those who were entering trades and professions as the ages to which they remained at school made possible; and to open a way to the University for all whom ability and interest qualified to use it." Finally, what Salter found most commendable about Green, characteristics the young writer was to emulate, was his ability "to connect near and remote ideals," link "the tangible to the intangible," and bring "the glamour of distant promise to the dullness of present purpose." The young Salter had clearly found his first public cause and his first great hero.

The original proposal had been to merge Nixon's School with a new grammar school. When such an amalgamation proved impossible, the scheme returned to the arena of political strife. The Conservative Council opponents were reluctant to spend public money to educate Oxford's middle class. The University authorities likewise saw no merits to the scheme. Early in 1878 a public meeting was held at the Town Hall attended by all factions concerned. The Corporation proved to be still divided against itself and the University. Only persistent lobbying by Green and a handful of dedicated aldermen enabled consensus. Graham Jackson, the noted Oxford architect responsible for designing the school, delayed his honeymoon for a fortnight to preside at the laying of the foundation stone on 13 April 1880 by Prince Leopold, Duke of Albany, the youngest son of Queen Victoria. Jackson also contributed the motto – *Nemo repente sapit* (no one suddenly becomes wise) – carved on the panels of the front doors of the building. The school's first decade proved a trying experience for all concerned. The Headmaster's house was never completed as anticipated, and instead he was forced to take boarders at his home. Although the original debt of about £2000 was finally cleared by a contribution from the Jubilee Fund, the city council continued to hedge on further funding. And time and again, the city council debated the direction the High School should take. Although fewer than 25% of the students studied the Classics, opponents argued the school should be a "Commercial School." After a decade, however, Green's "ladder of learning" approach seemed truly vindicated.[24]

The school which Salter entered in September 1890 was an obvious choice on the part of his father. It could give him an adequate preparatory education or equally it could prepare him for the business world. Only time, performance and possibly the influence of the staff would determine the direction he would take. "We were less instructed, but we were better educated," Salter wrote years later. His observation emphasized two unique aspects of his education. Firstly, there were fewer than 100 students at the school in the 1890s, leaving a high teacher-student ratio. Secondly, the staff tended towards a certain amateurishness. With slender financial resources, the school was forced to appoint young men who were paying their own way through an Oxford University education. As is often the case in such situations, the personalities of the young teachers surfaced in the class-rooms. Salter fondly recalled one master who would suspend the formal lessons to read famous passages from English or Greek literature. "A few of such days," he wrote, "probably did more than many months of more formal instruction to evoke whatever there was in us to respond." Another vivid memory was the Fifth Form Classics' master, H.G. Belcher. Despite his temper and impatience, Salter found himself drawn to the Classics by Belcher's passion for the subject and the attention paid to any student showing some aptitude and interest. Finally, there was the mathematics master and headmaster, Arthur Wilson Cave, known among the students as "Tubby." He had succeeded the first headmaster, A.T. Pollard, in January 1888 and was destined to remain head of the school until his retirement in 1925. Cave was zealously dedicated to the ideals, the staff and the students. He fought a continuous battle to protect its liberal traditions against the governors' utilitarianism. He allowed his staff considerable freedom, but within the rigid framework of a carefully constructed curriculum. And students were inspired by his evident love for his own subject, mathematics, with the results being reflected in an unusually large number of university entrance scholarships.

Salter's own performance at the school is revealing. It was only in 1893 that he first participated in the annual prize-giving ceremony. With his uncle, Councillor John Salter looking on, he accepted a scholarship for boys under 12. A year later he won the prize for the Fourth Form, and was recognized for the first time with Distinction in both Latin and Greek. His facility in the Classics was further evident in 1895, when in the Oxford Junior Locals he earned a sixth and third place in Latin and Greek respectively. The following year, with both his father and grandfather attending the prize-giving day in their capacities as Councillors, Salter walked onto the platform to receive prizes for the Fifth Form, Greek and a Senior School Scholarship. This excellent performance was matched during the following 18 months. He continued to excel in the Classics, and also maintained his distinction, one which he had earned since entering the high school, in Religious Knowledge. Finally, in November 1898 he won an Open Scholarship to study Classics at Brasenose College, Oxford. To this award, he added in October 1899 election to a Somerset Scholarship, raised from its usual value of £50 to £80 per year.[25] The T.H. Green "ladder of learning" approach had produced yet another success story.

The experience of Oxford High School had served to develop further Salter's character, maturing from adolescence to young adulthood. In the academic environment he found himself to be "excessively competitive," with the achievement of each year having to be bettered the next. Showing little aptitude for mathematics, he concentrated on the classics and excelled. His success was a combination of ability, hard work, and a taste of the carrot and stick approach. It was the custom of Oxford High School to send home with the students a report card for the week, with an order of merit attached. "I could not bear to be anywhere but at the top," Salter recalled. His parents fuelled this excessive competitiveness by increasing his pocket money whenever he emerged at the top of his form. The effect on his character, on his own admission, was "not good."[26] Outside the classroom, Salter had little time, and less inclination, to participate in extra-curricular activities. Nonetheless, he was for a short time captain of both the cricket and football clubs, accepting in 1899 the Earl of Jersey's Prize on behalf of his cricket club. But the standard of sports at Oxford High School was very low, and Salter owed his appointment more to academic performance than physical prowess. At a residential school his faults would have been the source of student derision, perhaps even correction. At Oxford High School he was regarded as very introverted, a commendable hard-worker, and generally ignored. Yet the school had served another purpose. "As time went on," Salter later wrote, "I became conscious of something growing in myself, a hardening fibre of will which began to lessen my earlier self-distrust; a sharpening of the mind."[27] A youthful daydreamer was on the verge of coming out of himself.

The first step in that intellectual direction was no doubt Salter's scholarship to the University, "at whose threshold, but outside whose gates," he had been born and raised.[28] At the time he entered Brasenose, founded in 1509 in the heart of Oxford, it was still a small college of about 100 students. Its reputation had for many years been based on its achievement in sports, ranging from boating to cricket. This "predilection for the exercises and amusements of out-door life" led to the result that its scholars, perhaps unkindly, were referred to as the "aborigines of Brasenose."[29] Arthur's contemporary at the college, John Buchan, later Lord Tweedsmuir, observed that a college which gave Lord Haig to the British army, and Lords Carnock, Bradbury, Askwith and Salter to the public services, had little reason to be ashamed. "But its chief produce was the commoner, healthy, sane, adventurous, who had 'no call to be bonny' but got through his day's work. It was a cross-section of all that was most vigorous in English society, and in distant parts of the Empire it proved its quality. There is nothing in the land more English than Brasenose."[30]

Indeed, Brasenose was a pioneering institution at Oxford. Its programme of entrance scholarships was designed to attract a cross-section of social classes. And a newly designed number of graduate scholarships, one of which Salter was later to receive, was intended for those who did particularly well in their finals. Initially, however, whatever fears may have plagued the young man were dissolved in the prospects of the university education denied his father. The charm of Oxford, as it presented itself to Salter in the autumn of 1899, was its mixture of the "constellations" and the "companionship of the ordinary man."[31] The principal at the time was Dr. Charles Buller Heberden, who began his association with the college when he was appointed a Fellow and lecturer in 1872. A gentle and gracious bachelor, with what Salter described as "a Red Indian nobility of feature," he shared the principal's lodging with his sister. While his gracious manner contrasted with the more robust atmosphere of the college, many appreciated only later his pervasive influence on college life. Among the dons were Alfred Joshua Butler, the bursar from 1884 to 1908 and a Greek and Latin scholar, whom many expected wrongly to succeed Heberden. Frederick William Bussell likewise impressed Salter for his wit, polymath learning and calculated eccentricity. This was hardly surprising. Bussell, who served as the college chaplain and vice-principal from 1896, lectured and published prodigiously in Classics, philosophy, theology, ancient and modern history and also composed music. He rejoiced in pronouncing he had no recreations, was proud of his conservatism, and on the eve of the First World War still controlled 13 votes to parliament. There were two dons in particular, however, whom Salter most adored during his years at Brasenose. Francis James Wylie, a lecturer, Fellow and tutor at Brasenose from 1891 to 1903, provided frequent guidance and counselling. His reputation was enhanced during the years from 1903 to 1931 when he was Secretary to the Rhodes Trustees and first Warden of Rhodes House. He served as mentor to the numerous Rhodes scholars from around the world. [32] Herbert Francis Fox, however, stood very much in the tradition of Oxford characters. Salter observed that Fox, a Fellow since 1889, "was a scholar in every fibre of his being," a man who divided his passions equally "between cricket, the Classics and a beautiful wife." He was not so much a teacher as someone who wished to share his love of the classics. A display of insight into some Latin verse from a student would give him pleasure only equal to a well-executed move on the cricket fields. His untimely death was mourned throughout Brasenose.[33]

If the "constellations" provided lifelong memories for Arthur, "the companionship of the ordinary man" unfortunately eluded him. "I became rather a recluse," he recalled, "with a small circle of not very intimate friends rather like myself." This self-imposed isolation derived from various influences. He felt very much the divisions between cliques and classes then evident at the college. Oxford High School was no match for Eton, and a boat-building background paled beside gentry origins. No doubt athletic prowess might have bridged the gap more effectively than scholarship. In fact, Salter could not be faulted for lack of effort, throwing himself into football, tennis and cricket, but with only moderate success. Then a weakening of his eyesight forced him to concentrate on rowing, a natural recourse accustomed as he was to the river, boats and oarsmanship since childhood. However, his career as an oarsman at Oxford was perhaps traumatic. Soon after registering at Brasenose, he had asked to qualify as a member of the rowing team for the spring Torpids. A special meeting of the college captains was called to discuss whether Arthur Salter, the son of the Oxford boat-building family, could qualify as an amateur and be eligible to compete for his college. Salter awaited their decision with trepidation. "I was myself, by temperament, exceptionally sensitive to any suggestion of rebuff," he later wrote. It was with enormous relief, therefore, that he welcomed the captains' positive response. In the spring Torpids of 1900 he rowed bow in the second boat, but soon afterwards, he found himself dropped. The reason for the abrupt rebuff was revealed to him in secret by the captain of the boat. His tutor, Wylie, had asked for the decision, fearing that a rowing career would affect Arthur's potential for an academic first. That latter result was eventually achieved. But the emotional impact on the young man trying to widen his circle of friends and interests at Brasenose was devastating.[34]

Rebuffed in his attempt to escape self-imposed seclusion, Salter retreated into himself and his books. His companions became the nameless and the studious; their evenings spent in their rooms. The weekly essay read to their tutors became the focal point of all activity. Determined to perfect the one skill which won him instant recognition and approval, Salter embarked on what he described as the "painful process of sharpening and shaping the instrument of the mind." He purposely refused to accept the glib, the superficial, or the easy catchword. When faced with a difficult question or problem, he struggled with himself. Often he would take long solitary walks in the Oxfordshire countryside, puzzling and thinking. He became an inveterate questioner, determined to find not the right answer but the original one. A combination of iron will and self-denial soon led to the desired results. "Little by little," he wrote, "my brain began to acquire edge and temper and to become a sharpened instrument for such work as I might give it." The penalty was also paid for such a monastic existence. Regretfully Salter recalled that while his mental abilities grew, his experience of life narrowed further.[35] Already his was a conventional personality within a determined will, shaped by a masterful brain.

On 23 April 1901 Salter gained a first in Classical Moderations, with its emphasis on the Greek and Latin languages, and still considered one of the most rigorous examinations in academia. Before him opened the prospect of what he called "that greatest of all schools," Literae Humaniores, which then consisted of ancient history and classical philosophy.[36] During the long summer holiday which followed, Salter joined his family for a vacation at Ilfracombe. His books came with him, and among these was a copy of Plato's Republic. Whereas his previous reading of the Classics had been for grades and approval, he now read for pleasure, and the results were gratifying. "I learned what philosophy, poetry and great literature, fused into a great work of art, could be and could give," he wrote and continued, "For me that summer brought something analogous to what, in religion, is called 'conversion'."[37] Unfortunately, Salter was already sufficiently monastic in temperament and personality.

For the next 18 months Salter threw himself with a vengeance into ancient history and classical philosophy. Day and night he lived with his Latin and Greek texts, to such an extent, that at the age of 94, in the last months of his life, he could still recite entire passages by heart. Nor did he confine his preparation for the final year of Literae Humaniores to the required materials. He read voraciously over the entire spectrum of English literature, law and economics, and on 30 July 1903 again took a first class. Thus ended, he recalled, "a respectable, though not an especially brilliant, Oxford record." His BA was posted on 18 March 1904 with the pro forma MA following on

29 June 1907.[38] Salter had won no athletic awards; had never spoken at the debating union; and earned no academic prizes. Yet his overall performance was sufficient for him to be offered a Senior Hulme Scholarship, an award that proved decisive to his education. These scholarships, established in the late seventeenth century by William Hulme, provided funds for outstanding graduates to extend themselves, reflect on their future, extending their horizons and reading widely. Salter therefore committed himself to a post-graduate programme, concentrating on ancient and modern history. At the same time, he dabbled in economics, and read widely in the area of English constitutional law.[39]

While savouring the pleasures of a graduate life, free of financial worries, and indulging every intellectual whim, Salter also gave some thought to his future. An academic career as an Oxford don offered intellectual rewards, but he realized he could not, in terms of personality, interact in an easy and informal way. He felt no calling either for the church or the life of a schoolmaster. Although the eldest son, and natural heir to the family boat-building concern, such prospects held no appeal, nor did his father encourage such a decision. On the other hand, he toyed with the idea of entering the legal profession. However, ever the realist even at the young age of 22, he calculated that with no proven forensic gifts nor without any independent income, and no personal connections among solicitors or at the Bar, his prospects were poor. With the choices so eliminated one by one, he decided reluctantly to try for the civil service.[40]

The three great civil services – Home, Indian and Colonial – had for several decades recruited through a joint examination every August. These were aimed, both in content and scope, at the graduates of the final honours schools of universities such as Oxford and Cambridge. In effect, therefore, a civil service career could be regarded as the final stage of the educational road Salter had travelled. Always fearful of rebuff or disapproval, he calculated that his chances of success in the civil service examination made this the best of all options. During a hot summer weekend in early August, Salter and his mother travelled by train to London, where they took rooms in a hotel near Whitehall for the final preparations. The examinations held at the offices of the Civil Service Commission in Burlington House proved to be a test of physical and intellectual resources. Salter sat, writing three-hour papers every morning and afternoon, for six days a week for two weeks. During this period, although he had placed near the top, he had continuously been affected by nervousness, compounded by increasing bouts of insomnia. By the third week he was not performing to his best abilities. The final stage of the examinations found an exhausted young man facing the board of oral examiners. Mercifully, the interview stage was perfunctory and immediately afterwards Salter and his mother returned to Oxford.[41]

When the results were calculated soon afterwards, Salter found that he had placed tenth, a respectable showing in a field of about 400 applicants for about 40 positions.[42] His performance, however, was not sufficient to gain entry into the two most sought after places in Whitehall – the Treasury or the Home Office. His choice was restricted therefore either to positions in the other domestic services or abroad in the Indian Civil Service. "I spent an agonizing night of indecision," Salter recalled, "and then plumped for staying at home, a choice which I often regretted in the next seven years, but never afterwards." He had rather quickly come to the conclusion, on the basis of considerable self-knowledge, that he had neither the temperament nor emotional range to deal with Indian affairs. Instead, he obtained a complete list of vacancies in government departments in Whitehall, and returned to London. Everywhere he was courteously received, even if with some amusement. A new recruit to Whitehall did not generally try and assess the prospects of career advancement. The results of this first-hand research finally pointed toward the Department of the Director of Transports at the Admiralty. The department anticipated the early retirement of two senior officials, leading to greater mobility in the junior ranks of the higher division clerks. Career advancement was uppermost in Salter's mind and at once he chose the Transport Department. A seemingly well-calculated decision, however, turned into a seven-year nightmare. On the first day in the Transport Department, 13 October 1904, his immediate supervisor invited the young recruit for lunch. During the course of the conversation, Salter was told that he had been misinformed after all. There had in fact been some recent recruitment to the Transport Department. "Your prospect of promotion is more than twenty years distant," was the essence of the revelation. Salter returned to work devastated, and as he later recalled, "My situation seemed hopeless."[43]

On 13 October 1904 Salter began his civil service career, Clerk Class 1, as an angry young man.[44] The manner in which he had learned of his fate smacked of incompetence. His dismal prospects for advancement clouded his first seven years in Whitehall. With little money and no London friends or connections, he was in a state of almost constant depression. Fortunately, he soon found a flat in Sydney Street, Chelsea, to share with others of similar occupation. The transient flatmates generally numbered about four, and included J.L. Brierly with whom Salter was to make his first continental tour, such later eminent civil servants as Basil Blackett, Edward John Harding, and a fellow graduate of Oxford High School, Cyril Hurcomb, with whom Salter was to share shipping responsibilities in both World Wars. Good company, good conversation and a common enthusiasm for Liberalism provided at least some compensation.[45]

To the young Oxford recruit, however, Whitehall loomed as a conglomeration of faceless buildings, staffed by an army of unfriendly bureaucrats. The ramparts and the hierarchy seemed impregnable. "One felt the smallest of worms at the base of the greatest of mountains," Salter candidly recalled, "it was like entering a prison with a long-term sentence – a prison bearing on its portals the inscription 'Abandon hope all ye who enter here'."[46] Tucked away near the Admiralty Arch were the offices of the Transport Department of the Admiralty, mainly concerned with organizing merchant shipping for naval uses. The Director of Transports was a position offered as a sinecure to those whom the Admiralty regarded as second-rate officers. The conditions under which the higher division clerks worked were abysmal, even by early twentieth century Whitehall standards. Salter joined two other clerks and three other superintending clerks in a small office. The one typewriter was in constant use, the ceiling was within easy reach, especially for the short-statured new recruit, and the office so dimly lit that even in summer electric lighting was required.[47]

An undisturbed backwater branch of the Admiralty, the Department of the Director of Transports functioned best when it functioned least. Years of routine procedure had hardened into principles and rules. Enterprise was never rewarded; yet equally penalties were rarely levied. Salter's seven years of service in the Transport Department gave him adequate time to experience and digest the meaning of both. One of the numerous instances which left an indelible mark on him concerned the hospital ship *Maine*. A relic of the Boer War, it had been assigned to peacetime service, conveying victims of Maltese fever back to Portsmouth. Salter noticed one day that the ships were returning from Malta empty because a cure for the fever had meanwhile been found. When he alerted of the Director of Transports, Vice-Admiral Robert T.H. Boyes, he was informed that the contract with the mixed English-Maltese crew required a return voyage. To Salter's suggestion that the contracts might be altered, the reply was, "Oh, we cannot disturb the practice." The *Maine* continued on its Malta-Portsmouth run, until the First World War forced it into a new role. As for Salter, he quickly concluded that initiative would receive no encouragement.[48] On another occasion, Salter was following the progress of colliers, hired by his department to attend the fleet on manoeuvres. A telegram from the master of one collier informed him that the ship could not sail to its newly designated point, as this was outside his charter-party limits. Horrified by the prospect that a part of the fleet would be immobilized due to a lack of coal, Salter immediately left his office, took a taxi, and after some effort managed to find the ship's owner who wired the necessary permission to the collier. When he returned to his office, he found that his claim for taxi fare would not be refunded. No official of his inferior rank could incur such expenses without prior authorization. Salter protested that his actions had saved possibly thousands of pounds and ensured that the fleet manoeuvres would proceed without interruption. Several months later, a refund duly arrived.[49] But the moral of his experience was also digested: enterprise would go unnoticed, but a breach of regulations could lead to endless trouble.

"Boredom, if it doesn't lead to drink or dissipation," Salter observed, "can be quite a powerful, and some times useful, incentive to finding a personal life somewhere else."[50] It drove him in fact into trying to build a life away from his stultifying civil service career. His flatmates over the years, young, congenial and all from Oxford or Cambridge, helped to provide some diversion. Like-minded political enthusiasts tend to gather together, and the Sydney Street flat attracted ardent Liberals, readers of the <u>Westminster Gazette,</u> and all eager to see the Liberals return to power in the January 1906 election. Evenings generally were spent in conversation, with occasional visits to the Court Theatre in nearby Sloane Square to watch the most recent production of George Bernard Shaw's plays. For some time Salter also explored the newer Fabian politics. He regularly devoured Fabian Society publications, adding extensive comments in the margins of his copies. He often attended meetings of the society and was clearly enthralled by the brilliant debates which from time to time featured Sidney and Beatrice Webb, George Bernard Shaw and H.G. Wells.[51] On 24 September and 5 October 1907 he contributed, for the first time, to the letters to the editor columns of <u>The Times</u>. In these, he made a spirited defence of the case for old age pensions, and answered the charges that he was merely expressing the views of his "Socialist friends."[52] Salter was in fact more deeply influenced by this period of Fabian involvement than he was later prepared to admit. He eventually became personal friends with both the Webbs and H.G. Wells. And while never a socialist, Fabian collectivist thinking was central to Salter's Liberal politics and economics in the 1930s.

Some times, finding the noise and dirt of London traffic unbearable, and his flatmates talked out, Salter would drive his new bicycle to Richmond Park. There he would spend a lazy day, reading, thinking and watching the people. As his meagre salary improved, rising by £15 increments from £150, he ventured back to the Thames, renting a houseboat near Goring for two successive and summers. Each day after work Salter, and some of his fellow office workers or flatmates, would journey to Goring for a late dinner, a swim in the Thames, and an early morning train for a return to Admiralty Arch.[53] These were brief interludes, however, in an increasingly painful existence. His "narrow and arid life" seemed to envelop his soul both in the office and outside. For a time he tried to escape London by journeying regularly to Oxford. His weekends there were mainly domestic and quite pleasant. Yet personality problems still plagued him. "A mixture of shyness and envy," he recalled, prevented him from taking advantage of the university society he had only recently left.[54] Such shyness was also leading to problems in other directions. With few friends and no relations in London, Salter's opportunities for informal social contact were limited and narrowing year by year. "We might almost have been in a monastery as far as feminine society was concerned," he observed. Indeed, as he approached his late twenties he was not on Christian name terms with any woman outside his relations. His situation may also have been more complicated. The lack of feminine contact, he recalled enigmatically, "was the more regrettable because of a long emotional experience which offered no hope at any time of a happy result."[55] Evidence of such a possible liaison suggests that he was intimately involved with Joyce Nettlefold who later went on to marry and move to South Africa.[56] Be that as it may, the experience was sufficient to leave him a bachelor until the age of fifty-nine.

Driven to desperation, and in a search for alternative company and intellectual stimulation, he gravitated towards Toynbee Hall, the University Settlement in East London, founded in 1884 and regarded as "the mother of all settlements."[57] In its focus on civic leadership, education and social research, Salter found scope for his growing sense of social activism. Initially, Salter's status at Toynbee Hall was as a "visitor." However, as his Sydney Street flat was gradually abandoned as the young men, one by one, married and moved away, in the fall of 1912 he became a "resident" for the first time.[58] This period of residence helped him to cement acquaintances with a remarkable generation of Toynbee men, including Frank Wise, J. Reeve Brooke, H.D. Henderson, William Beveridge and Llewellyn Smith.[59] The atmosphere, described by a later warden, J.J. Mallon, as one "of animation and liveliness and of certain residents in genial and continuous controversy," suited Salter's intellectual hunger. During one of Toynbee Hall's weekly public debates, he spoke against women's suffrage, while his friend and later colleague, E.F. (Frank) Wise advocated the issue.[60] With the encouragement of Warden Canon Samuel Barnett, he assisted in the activities of the "Enquirers' Club," originally named the "Club for Social Enquiry," intended "for the purpose of considering and discussing questions of social importance."[61] He recalled the members "were for the most part young civil servants. We would invite someone of distinction, and special knowledge of social problems, to be our guest for the evening and, after an opening exposition (all being comfortably seated in arm-chairs in the drawing room), submit himself to comment and cross-questioning." Among the visitors Salter managed to bring to Toynbee Hall were Ramsay MacDonald and the Webbs.[62] His experiences there led to the publication of his first article "Citizenship in Stepney." In this he addressed the issue of the lack of "civic pride," its causes, including a large and changing immigrant population and the lack of natural boundaries, and urged a greater "cross-fertilisation of interests and ideas" so as to begin building "channels of social communication" and make public opinion effective.[63] In the early 1930s Salter himself was to address the Club and in 1945, along with Beveridge, Edward Lascelles and George Booth, helped in its revival.[64]

Toynbee Hall provided a temporary respite, not an answer, to Salter's desperation with his career prospects. He often reflected that for seven long years he had been the ideal bureaucrat: never late, never on special leave, absent for only one day and showing just enough initiative to be noticed, but never pressing his viewpoint. His salary rose only by the predetermined minute increments and promotion came in negligible grades. He grew increasingly bitter, and in early 1911 unabashedly obstreperous. He deliberately began to make himself a nuisance to his superiors in the Transport Department. Some times he pressed for changes which stood no chance of acceptance. On other occasions he deliberately tried to embarrass his seniors in the office and "started agitating." He went so far as to organize an informal grievance society among his fellow higher division clerks.[65] Despite this, a colleague at the time praised Salter as having "a toughness of fibre, and an ingenuity and subtlety in debate," as well as "ingenious force."[66]

Perhaps just in time, Salter decided in September 1911 to take a rare holiday on the continent. His traveling companions were a former flat mate, J.L. Brierly, and the latter's sisters. The party left England in early September and headed straight for Spain. It was an inauspicious time for an English group to be vacationing there. England's industrial unrest was being imitated in the Spanish railroads. The Spanish press was alerted that "a short dark-haired English agitator" was being sought by the police, a description which bore a remarkable resemblance to Salter. Nonetheless, in an ill-advised attempt to see something of the countryside, Salter booked a third-class ticket. The train he boarded was guarded by an armed soldier, and packed with peasants and troops. As he alighted at Seville, he was at once arrested. Only the intervention of the British vice-consul secured his release. After parting from the Brierlys, Salter traveled by train to Lisbon, for the return voyage to England. His misadventures were not yet over. At sea he discovered that the boat, from South America, carried a case of black-jack fever aboard in the cabin next to his. Despite his fears, Salter returned in good health to London, back to his hated office.[67] The continental interlude left Salter with a blind determination to leave the Department of the Director of Transports. Within days of his return to Whitehall, the opportunity presented itself. Without hesitation, he took the plunge and overnight changed the course of his career and life.

Given his interest in social issues and Liberal politics, it was not surprising that Salter had been following with fascination the social service legislation introduced into parliament since the return of the Liberals to power in 1906. The pace quickened on 4 May 1911 when David Lloyd George, the Chancellor of the Exchequer, introduced the National Insurance Bill in the House of Commons. A more daring innovation than the 1909 old age pensions scheme, the National Insurance Bill (National Health Insurance, Part I) was designed to provide protection against sickness and disability for workers between the ages of 16 and 65 not covered by other insurance schemes. The plan was to be administered through "approved societies," such as Friendly Societies, Trade Unions and Industrial Assurance Companies, and financed by contributions from employers, the government and the insured person. The latter's contribution was to be paid through revenue stamps, purchased at the post office, and affixed on a card. Throughout the following months the bill became the target of bitter dissension in parliament and nationwide. Even while it continued on its course through parliament, provision was being made to set in motion the vast apparatus which would be necessary to administer the scheme.[68] The Treasury accordingly canvassed all government departments for candidates to staff the initial organization.

When the Treasury circular reached the Admiralty, there was no difficulty in recommending Salter as a suitable case for transfer. The department viewed him as eminently expendable, and in turn Salter did not hesitate for a moment. He later wrote:

> My chance had come. For seven years I had been unhappy, regretted my entry into the Home Civil Service, envied my contemporaries, saw no opportunities of interesting work or a career for myself. For the next twenty years I had no such feelings. I found in the public service work that offered development and expression for everything I had in me; and no other career, whatever it might have meant in wealth or position, could have brought to me such happiness as this one which had begun so inauspiciously.[69]

It was with little regret and an overwhelming sense of excitement that Salter arrived at 55 Whitehall on 30 October 1911 to begin the first significant phase of his career. The nucleus of civil servants whom Salter joined that day was already at work on the numerous clauses of the National Insurance Bill as Lloyd George guided it by stages through the House of Commons. The real work of research and preparation, drafting and revising, however, was in the hands of the secretary of the Insurance Commission for England, William J. Braithwaite, formerly an assistant secretary at the Board of Inland Revenue, and a mine of information on social insurance. The price of such expertise and the hectic pace, however, was that by the end of 1911 he was on the verge of collapse.[70]

"I worked harder than I had ever done in my life," Salter afterwards confirmed. "I was intensely interested in the Bill itself; had an inspiring leader; and was conscious that my personal future depended upon my now making good." Always terrified by the prospects of personal failure, he mastered every minute aspect of the bill. After the rigours of his Oxford self-imposed discipline, and after the long years of dull work at the Admiralty, he flourished. Although not trained as a lawyer, his mind could master legal argument. His memory, while not retentive in breadth, could recall facts needed for immediate action. He quickly developed a natural facility of expression and could muster persuasive arguments in pointed minutes and memoranda. He began to apply a constructive imagination suitable for his work at hand. He was not, and never proved, capable of long-term imaginative thinking. His strength was in an ability to perceive the next practical step, and perhaps the one after that. He was also finding at last that his short, tough and wiry physique was perfectly suited to his work: long, intensive hours into the early morning, a quick refreshing nap, and he could be soon back at his desk.[71] "The tradition of the office," a colleague later commented, "was that he worked twenty-four hours round the clock, without any trace of sleep."[72] Salter was determined that his talents and strengths would prevail over his inexperience, shyness and social diffidence.

The National Insurance Bill finally received royal assent on 16 December 1911, while a similar scheme had taken the German government 25 years to complete. "We were asked to complete a far more complicated scheme in six months," C.F.G. Masterman, the responsible minister, wrote, "Half the clauses were highly technical, many contradicted each other, some rendered necessary action obviously illegal. There was no office, no staff, no address, and no telephone." Another participant in those pioneer months was the Chief Registrar of Friendly Societies and later the legal adviser, Claud Schuster: "Haste was so necessary," he wrote that the ordinary methods of government office, minutes from one officer to another up the hierarchical scale and down again, were impracticable."[73] Yet another recalled that such a vast national scheme was "devised and perfected for the most part by a mere handful of officials working alone or together and burning midnight oil." Such were the circumstances and atmosphere in which Salter began "to make a service reputation."[74]

The machinery ultimately approved by the National Health Insurance Act provided for separate Commissions for England, Scotland, Wales and Ireland as well as a coordinating Joint Committee. The chairman of the Joint Committee, which first met formally on 30 December 1911, was indeed C.F.G. Masterman, a remarkably important individual in Salter's life. Masterman had been asked by Lloyd George to take charge of the coordination of the four Commissions in order to guarantee uniformity in procedure and policy throughout the United Kingdom. According to Braithwaite, who was appointed secretary to this Joint Committee, it was due to his personal recommendation that Salter was promoted as of 1 January 1912 to the additional position of private secretary to Masterman. "[R.W.] Harris and I knew a good man when we saw him," Braithwaite later wrote, and observed that Salter "was rightly made a private Secretary and went on to great promotion."[75] Harris confirmed that "Braithwaite and I may fairly take credit for having found him for Masterman. He worked like a slave at all hours of the night."[76]

Salter realized his appointment constituted the first real promotion he had ever secured, and he noted "it made perhaps more difference than any other single success in my later career." An increase in his salary, from £255 per year to £400 and an additional allowance of £150 for serving as private secretary, added to his evident elation. Membership in the Reform Club welded status to financial security.[77] And his position as private secretary to a leading politician and chairman of a major new social agency admitted Salter for the first time into the corridors of power. There is no doubt that he became personally devoted to Masterman. It was a relationship, the first of several which later included Lord Cecil and Winston Churchill, in which Salter willingly played humble disciple to a respected elder. Reverence, however, was matched by compatibility. Masterman faced a horrendous task in managing the affairs of the Joint Committee and overseeing the implementation of the Insurance Act. The two critical deadlines were 15 July 1912 when collections of contributions would begin and then 15 January 1913 for benefits to be payable. The volume of almost daily parliamentary questions on the controversial legislation reached epidemic proportions during February and March. Masterman, troubled by ill health and frequent absences from the office, allowed Salter increasing responsibility for dealing with parliamentary business. The latter responded knowledgeably and with enthusiasm. "I knew his mind well, and could with some confidence discern what would be his decision, and was quite ready to give it as his, in full assurance that he would not let me down, if an urgent decision was needed and he was away," Salter wrote, and added: "For me it had the enormous advantage of giving me a habit of initiative and responsibility, and a liking for it, as well as a general standing among my colleagues in the Service which was of great value when he had gone."[78]

Masterman was not destined to stay at his job, given the intrinsic difficulties of his task. The medical profession, the Friendly Societies, the commercial insurance companies, and the working class all had to be mollified or coerced. In addition, the new administrative structure had been attracting an astonishing *corps d'élite* of future luminaries of British public life, as well as some of the outstanding personalities of the civil service. At the beginning of 1912, John Anderson, Frank Wise, J. Reeve Brooke, and Alfred Watson were already among the younger talent involved with National Insurance. Sir Robert Morant, permanent secretary to the Board of Education since 1903, and Sir Robert Chalmers and Sir John Bradbury from the Treasury also joined. Masterman had in fact been responsible for urging the transfer of Morant to national insurance. However, he got more than he bargained for. Salter, as a witness to the ensuing bureaucratic imbroglio, has left this picture of Masterman, just prior to his eclipse:

> I remember many scenes in which he was surrounded by people like Bradbury and Morant, Schuster, Alfred Watson and John Anderson discussing some particular aspect of Insurance. All of these men were exceptional in their power of articulate expression and their intellectual subtlety; and after a quarter of an

hour's discussion, the problem would look almost too complicated for human solution. Meantime, C.F.G.M[asterman], bunched up in a big overcoat drawn up over his ears, dabbing his nose with a handkerchief against Hay Fever, and with that characteristic black lock of hair trailing over his forehead, would have sat silent, and apparently confused by the scintillation all around him. Then he would suddenly intervene and put his finger exactly on the one central point that mattered and the one real solution, which everyone then realized, though he had not done before, to be at once diagnosis and solution.[79]

No doubt, Masterman had relevant experience in the area of health insurance and an abiding interest in social reform. In many ways, too, he was the intellectual equal of those who, like Bradbury and Morant, offered alternative views. However, while Masterman possessed what Salter described as "flair, eloquence, the faculty of inspiring devotion, a sure instinct for the essential, good judgement as to what was practical, decision and authority," he also lacked something of the politician's killer instinct. Exceptionally sensitive to the feelings of others and fearful of personal rebuff, Masterman hid behind a shell of cynicism and wit.[80] These proved no defence, however, against the strong personalities of such seasoned politicians and bureaucrats as Lloyd George and Morant. Eventually, in 1914 Masterman's floundering political career led to his abandonment by Lloyd George. On this Salter observed: "Lloyd George's great qualities did not include loyalty or tolerance for colleagues who seemed to be faltering."[81]

The clash of personality and the storm of controversy centred most heatedly around Sir Robert Morant, appointed chairman of the National Health Insurance Commission for England, in effect the chief executive of the entire scheme. He had left the position at the Board of Education with a reputation which emphasized in equal measure his undoubted talents for administration with wildly unorthodox methods. To his detractors, Morant was vilified as a "Demon King, a scheming and unscrupulous arriviste." To his few defenders he was respected as the "supreme Civil Servant," and even loved for his "energy, vision and courage."[82] Whatever the case, his future colleagues on the National Health Insurance Commission were forewarned: "You must remember that for years he has led the life of a hunted animal."[83] Salter's views on Morant combined respect, "the most remarkable civil servant of his day;" with reservations, "neither politically nor personally sympathetic."[84] Of Morant himself, Salter has left this description:

A man of majestic presence; very tall, with a good figure, crowned by a leonine face and impressive white hair. He was excitable, some times in manner and mood almost hysterical. There was nervous excitement but also unusual nervous force at the service of his purpose. With this temperament he was, by nature and by habit – in the better and the worse sense – an intriguer, always advancing on his goal by several devious personal channels. But he was undoubtedly both sincere and creative; and he left his mark on health insurance (as he had done on education) as he could if his methods had been more orthodox. In retrospect, however, one can see that his creative and dynamic qualities made him after all a great man.

Salter understood that, having arrived late in the day, Morant would have "some natural prejudice" toward the existing staff that had drafted the bill and overseen its passage into law. As well, Morant would have wished to surround himself with his own people. Salter continued:

I myself, however, escaped the consequences of any such prejudice. I had some of the qualities that appealed to Morant. I soon found myself indeed working on close and intimate terms with him, and developing a great admiration for his energetic and able administration of the considerable part of the Act which he was deeply interested in, which was not, however, by any means all of it.[85]

In turn, Morant admired such loyalty and, even if guarded, devotion. He could often be heard speaking "with almost paternal pride of the qualities and talents of his younger men: "my Brock, my Salter, my Vivian." [86] Nonetheless, it was hardly surprising that deep differences soon arose between Morant and the minister and colleagues concerned with National Insurance.

The first and most contentious of these rifts concerned Braithwaite, the real architect of the insurance bill. Suffering from nervous exhaustion and the inhuman effort of shaping a revolutionary parliamentary bill, he and Morant experienced an immediate clash of temperaments. In Salter's view there was more: "Morant had no mercy for a possible rival." By the end of 1912 Braithwaite had been totally outmanoeuvered and on 21 December he left to accept a position as Special Commissioner of Income Tax, "unhonoured, unthanked and bitterly resentful."[87] For several decades afterwards, Salter and others went on record to emphasize that the National Insurance Bill was largely Braithwaite's creation. It was never Salter's opinion, however, that Braithwaite should have been given Morant's job. "There was good reason for not appointing him to the principal position," Salter wrote, "but every reason for recognizing what he had done by an appropriate honour."[88] It was not until Braithwaite's own memoir,

<u>Lloyd George's Ambulance Wagon</u>, was published post-humously in 1957 that his vital contribution was at last publicly recognized.

In the fall of 1911 and the early weeks of 1912, the issues of immediate concern were recruitment, organization and office space. The latter was finally solved with the move from 55 Whitehall to space created by the conversion of a former hotel into Wellington House in Buckingham Gate. New staff began to arrive, including Salter from the Admiralty, John Anderson from the Colonial Office and Henry Bunbury from the Treasury. But the recruitment drive in earnest began with Morant's efforts. To acquire the necessary staff to implement the act, Morant cajoled the government to make available to him the brightest and most talented. Morant regarded the situation as critical and the task of applying the new Insurance scheme to 12 million men and women as a recipe for potential disaster. On April 22 he temporarily panicked and urged postponement of the July deadline when he foresaw only "chaos and confusion."[89] Instead, Warren Fisher was sent from the Treasury with a mandate to recruit and impose a semblance of order and organization. This he did successfully and just in time, thereby rescuing the reputation of the civil service. Fisher recruited another group of brilliant young administrators with so called "return tickets."[90] Most in fact did not stay with National Insurance, but their ranks originally included Aubrey Symonds, Sylvanus P. Vivian, D.O. Malcolm, Alexander Maxwell and G.M. Young. Fisher and his team, according to Salter, proved "a triumphant success."[91] At the time the staff was a genuine "ministry of all the talents" and, as has been often noticed, "a veritable forcing-ground of future great reputations."[92] The younger men certainly fulfilled their mandate. In particular, it was later noted that "the storm-tossed Morant at last found the ballast that he so sorely needed in the level-headed sagacity of the two younger men who are now Lord Waverly [Sir John Anderson] and Lord Salter."[93]

"They were happy days, of intense but inspiring toil," Salter afterwards wrote.[94] Yet he was emphasizing not the back-stabbing of ambitious civil service empire builders, but rather his exhilaration at being part of a novel experiment which was to transform the fundamental basis of British society. Under Fisher's reorganization, Salter was promoted on 22 May 1912 from first class clerk to junior clerk with an accompanying increase in salary from £350 to £400. This promotion, among others, accompanied the transfer of almost the entire clerical staff of the Joint Committee to the English Commission; a clear indication of the shift of the balance of power away from Braithwaite to Morant.[95] Among Salter's numerous tasks in the early months of 1912 was firstly to oversee the procedure for the granting of "approved society" status. Eventually some 23,000 of these "approved societies" were to administer insurance benefits.[96] At stake was particularly the pressure of the 12 main industrial insurance companies, such as the giant Prudential, with its millions of individual policies and its army of some 70,000 door-to-door collectors. Determined to protect their financial stake in death benefits policies, Friendly Societies and the industrial insurance interests fought the government's proposed plans. At last, a compromise was reached; with national insurance becoming a matter simply of sickness benefit. This was to be administered through the "approved societies," namely, trade unions, insurance companies and Friendly Societies. The question of procedure, however, proved contentious. As early as 24 January, the National Health Insurance Joint Committee discussed issues such as the steps necessary to obtain approval, the form of application for approval and a set of model rules. A sub-committee on which Salter served as secretary was organized to thrash out these complex issues. In succeeding weeks the Joint Committee went ahead in approving societies and the first lists appeared on 7 June.[97]

It was part of Salter's work, secondly, to help organize and train the large number of government publicists required to explain the scheme. It had been decided at the very first meeting of the National Health Insurance Joint Committee on 30 December 1911 to appoint "lecturers to go about the country and explain the provisions of the Act." The lecturers who were hired were to meet in London for instruction in their tasks. This "work of propaganda" was to be completed in three months.[98] With speed of the essence, by the end of January 1912 more than 100 lecturers had been trained by a team which included Salter and some twelve other members of the Health Insurance administration.[99] The pace of preparations accelerated yet further as the 15 July deadline approached. Salter and his other colleagues worked at a fever pitch to complete the explanatory pamphlets which the post office agreed to distribute as well as the form and printing of insurance stamps and cards. As the appointed hour approached, Salter "sat up until midnight and licked the first stamps," Braithwaite later recalled, and added, "I went to bed. The Act was in operation."[100]

The most potentially serious objections to national health insurance, however, came from the medical profession and the British Medical Association [BMA]. The doctors' lobby strongly objected to any hint of lay control over its activities. By the fall of 1912 a full scale "doctors' revolt" threatened the implementation of the act. Salter found himself in the centre of the ensuing controversy. The issue at stake concerned the doctors' confusion between the payment of a fee for potential patients, and fees for actual patients. "The BMA was new to serious work of the kind which forms the normal business of Trade Unions," Salter wrote, "and it was not easy to conduct reasonable negotiations through them and get anything like a balanced description of the new system through to the individual doctor." On 21 December the British Medical Association broke off its negotiations with the government.[101]

In the meantime Salter and his colleagues implemented their own contribution to the negotiating process. As the deadline of 15 January 1913 for the implementation of medical benefits approached, they began to compile a simple and comprehensive description of the act as it directly affected the doctors, and planned to distribute copies of the document to all general practitioners throughout the country. Given his precise knowledge of the provisions of the act, Salter played a key role in its compilation. "We simultaneously drafted the different chapters of the necessarily long pamphlet," Salter recalled, "working far into the night and welding our separate contributions together as best we could. I have a vivid memory of Morant's massive form crawling on the floor and collecting sections of the draft. Printing went on throughout the night." During the course of the following weekend, every doctor received an individual description of his position under the act. When the Lloyd George government followed this with several concessions, notably medical benefits were to be administered by local insurance committees, opposition withered. The threatened strike never materialised, and the medical provisions of the scheme duly came into force on 15 January. There was visible jubilation in Salter's office.[102] The new insurance system in the following months became woven into the fabric of British society. Several amending bills, designed to iron out anomalies or toughen existing provisions, made their way through parliament. Resistance, as Masterman told an audience on 13 April 1913, was limited "to a few faddists and a few farmers" who still objected to being insured. Otherwise, over 96% of the insured population had already selected an approved society.[103]

In the spring a dinner was held, as Braithwaite put it, "to celebrate promotions and the success of the Act."[104] The former was partly occasioned by the return of Warren Fisher and some of his recruits, by then termed the "loan collection," to their previous departments.[105] In the subsequent reorganization, Salter was appointed on 10 April to one of the three positions of assistant secretary to the National Health Insurance Commission for England, with an accompanying generous rise in salary to £800.[106] Salter's rapid rise through the ranks occasioned comment at the time, not always favourable. One colleague, R.W. Harris, observed, "he had certainly well earned his exceptional promotion, however disappointing it may have been for one or two of us, a good deal his senior, who had been slogging away in responsible positions for some time."[107] But from others there were only praise and congratulations. On 13 April Salter wrote to Braithwaite:

> Very many thanks for your congratulations, which have given me more pleasure than any others I have received. I have only two regrets as I take over my new job, one that I must leave Masterman (and parliamentary work) and the other that I am not still, as I began, working under you. It is indeed extraordinary what a difference the Insurance Act work has meant to me. Before, I

had (& had had for seven years) dull work without interest, responsibility or prospects. I have never enjoyed anything in my life as I have the last eighteen months, & though it will scarcely be possible to retain the 'first fire frenzy' I see some years of extremely interesting work ahead in C. I shall never forget that I owe the difference to you and to the chance you gave me at the Treasury.

The appointment was an absolute surprise to me, as I knew nothing of the separation of Legal Adviser & Secretary, & had looked upon it as quite certain that the only two new appointments would be Anderson & Vivian as Assistant Secretaries. I believe everyone recognizes that Anderson is the best man in the office for the new post.[108]

The heady atmosphere of earlier days, as Salter pointed out, was indeed giving way to routine administration. In its own way, this had positive benefits for Salter. He had developed a close, and what was to prove, lasting friendship with Morant's private secretary, J. Reeve Brooke. This friendship helped to smooth relations with Morant. Equally important, it enabled Salter, in the company of Brooke, to leave London on weekends for walks on the Southern Downs, to spend time at the Brooke home at Bushey, with a wide circle of Brooke relatives and friends, or join J. Reeve Brooke's weekly lunchtime gathering in his rooms in Mitre Court in the Temple.[109] On other occasions he joined the Mastermans for evening concerts in London. Lucy Masterman recalled in 1939: "It was about this time that he heard Brahms' Requiem at Westminster Abbey when Mr. (now Sir Arthur) Salter came with us."[110] A growing love for music developed from this early introduction to the classical repertoire. But above all Salter reveled in the sheer delight of daily contact with the best of Westminster and Whitehall. As Masterman's private secretary, he was brought "into relations of real, though limited, intimacy" with Lloyd George, Winston Churchill, then in charge of unemployment insurance, Augustine Birrell, the Secretary of State for Ireland, cabinet ministers such as Lord Reading and Lord Haldane, and, on occasion the Prime Minister, Herbert Henry Asquith.[111] Such acquaintances left lasting memories for Salter. "A face in which there was something at once of the lion, the sheep and the goat'" was his impression of Lloyd George. Asquith himself was a remote personality, "only emerging on rare occasions either to restrain or support." Augustine Birrell was indeed a "rich and humorous personality," but unsuited for his office. At one point, when Churchill had the occasion to speak publicly on national insurance, Salter recalled that he personally prepared the brief. "It was instructive to see the amended copy, the way in which a phrase here, a striking analogy there, a brilliant passage and an apt anecdote, would transform a pedestrian memorandum into a notable speech, vivid and convincing."[112]

By the beginning of 1914 the pioneer days of the National Insurance Act were over. According to Morant, "the administration of the Insurance Act has sunk absolutely to the level of a political machine. Masterman stands as the exponent of methods which would flatter the effrontery of a party wire-puller. The demoralisation of the staff, almost wholly composed of young men, is extreme, and the office exists for little more than the progressive debasement of the Civil Service."[113] Although Salter would have disputed Morant's harsh words about Masterman, he shared somewhat the sense of demoralisation. "After years in a stagnant office I had tasted the joys of a new, adventurous, constructive task, and of the camaraderie it brings," he wrote.[114] Yet in the previous months his principal concerns were hardly adventurous. He continued to have responsibility for approved societies, adding membership of the Standing Committee on Amendment of Rules to his duties. Much of his time was also devoted to investigating the status of insured persons who emigrated, and pitching in with the framing of the 1913 National Insurance Amending Act. On this last item, Salter commented to Braithwaite:

> We have been getting suggestions together for the amending Bill & discussing them; & I wish you were here to see how the 'mountain' of imperfections disappear to nothing when it's looked at closely. You will at any rate see what a 'ridiculous mouse' emerges when the Bill is produced. What is constantly appearing is the way all sorts of queer remote difficulties were foreseen & guarded against.[115]

With the Insurance Act thus a running concern, the great creative period was over. Salter found himself prey to a strong urge to leave, attracted by the anticipation of yet other challenges. The outbreak of the First World War gave him the desired opportunity.

Endnotes

1. Lord Salter, Memoirs of a Public Servant (1961), 15. Unless otherwise indicated all places of publication are London.
2. J.H. Salter and J.A. Salter, Salter's Guide to the Thames (Oxford, 40th ed., 1938), 3-4.
3. Salter and Salter, Salter's Guide to the Thames, 6.
4. Dorothy E. Sackett (Salter's cousin) to the author, 5 Sept. 1979, author's archive.

5. Information on the Salter pedigree derived from The Rev. A.T. John Salter to the author, 8 July 1975, author's archive. He pointed out that when James Arthur Salter was raised to the peerage, he took as the basis of his coat of arms the ancient arms of Salter, in use in the 13th century in Oswestry.
6. Additional valuable information, including a Salter family tree dating back to the early 19th century, was provided by Dorothy E. Sackett. Sackett to the author, 14 July 1975, 5 Sept. 1979, author's archive.
7. http://www.oxfordhistory.org.uk/mayors/1836_1962/salter_john_1902.htm.
8. Salter, Memoirs, 15, Simon Wenham, "Salters' of Oxford: A History of a Thames Boating Firm over a Century of Evolution (1858-c.1960)," Oxoniensia, 71(2006), 111-143.
9. Salter, Memoirs, 15-16.
10. The Times, 17 Sept. 1937, The New York Times, 17 Sept. 1937, Pigeons and Pigeon World, 24 Sept.1937, The Isle of Wight County Press, 22 Sept. 1956.
11. Salter, Memoirs, 19.
12. Will of John Salter, 25 Feb. 1890, Somerset House, London.
13. Entry of 5 Jan. 1931, Elliott Felkin Papers, AEF/1/1/8, King's College Archive Centre, Cambridge.
14. The Times, 8 Aug. 1904, Salter, Memoirs, 17-18, 20.
15. See Wenham, "Salters' of Oxford," 111-143.
16. Letter to the editor, The Times, 15 June 1910, The Oxford Mail, 1, 5 Apr. 1937.
17. The Oxford Times, 2, 9 Apr. 1937.
18. Salter, Memoirs, 20-21, The Times, 20 Apr. 1926.
19. The Oxford Mail, 5 Apr. 1937.
20. Salter, Memoirs, 21.
21. Salter, Memoirs, 20.
22. Salter, Memoirs, 18.
23. Salter, Memoirs, 23. Information about the City of Oxford High School for Boys, as it was originally named, is taken from The City of Oxford High School Magazine, 40(Dec. 1947), 45(July 1953), 56(Mar. 1964), 58(Apr.1966). I am grateful to Frederick C. Lay, headmaster of Oxford High School, 1944-1962, for drawing this material and additional information to my attention.
24. Salter's articles "T.H. Green and the High School" and "The Founding of the High School" first appeared in the Oxford High School Magazine, 1(June 1903), 2(July 1903). These were reprinted in The City of Oxford High School Magazine, 57(July 1966), 62-68.
25. Salter, Memoirs, 23-25, The Register of the City of Oxford High School, 1881-1925, E.A. Bowen, ed., (Oxford, 1938), 32. Salter's academic record at the City

of Oxford High School was collated by Fred C. Lay, in letter to the author, 18 Oct. 1974, author's archive. Salter's contemporary at Brasenose College, John Drinkwater, in his <u>Inheritance: Being the First Book of an Autobiography</u> (1931), 17-28, also praised Belcher and Cave.

26. Salter, <u>Memoirs</u>, 25-26.
27. Salter, <u>Memoirs</u>, 26.
28. Salter, <u>Memoirs</u>, 26.
29. <u>The History of the University of Oxford</u>, vol. 4, <u>Nineteenth Century Oxford</u>, Part I, M.G. Brock and M.C. Curthoys, eds., (Oxford, 1997), 269, John Buchan, <u>Memory Hold the Door</u> (1940), 50.
30. Buchan, <u>Memory Hold the Door</u> (1940), 51.
31. Buchan, <u>Memory Hold the Door</u>, 50.
32. Salter, <u>Memoirs</u>, 28, Dorothy Allen, <u>Sunlight and Shadow</u> (1960), 44-46, <u>The Dictionary of National Biography: The Concise Dictionary</u>, Part II (Oxford, 1982), 741.
33. Salter, <u>Memoirs</u>, 28-29.
34. Salter, <u>Memoirs</u>, 29.
35. Salter, <u>Memoirs</u>, 29-31, Oxford University, <u>Brasenose College Register, 1509-1909</u>, 2 vols. (Oxford, 1909).
36. <u>The Times</u>, 24 Apr. 1901, Salter, <u>Memoirs</u>, 31.
37. Salter, <u>Memoirs</u>, 31.
38. Salter, <u>Memoirs</u>, 31-32, <u>The History of the University of Oxford</u>, vol. 4, <u>Nineteenth Century Oxford</u>, Part II, M.G. Brock and M.C. Curthoys, eds., (Oxford, 1997), 817. Salter's university results, along with other Oxford Colleges, were posted in <u>The Times</u>, 31 July 1903, 19 Mar. 1904, 1 July 1907.
39. Barry Knowles, Principal of Brasenose College, Oxford, to the author, 5 Feb.1981, provided details of Salter's record at the College, author's archive. See also Oxford University, <u>Brasenose College Register, 1509-1909</u>, 2 vols. (Oxford, 1909).
40. Salter, <u>Memoirs</u>, 32-33.
41. Salter, <u>Memoirs</u>, 34-35.
42. "Personnel File, Salter, J.A.," Ministry of Health, Establishment Division, National Archives, United Kingdom [NA-UK], MH 107/11.
43. Salter, <u>Memoirs</u>, 39, Lord Salter, <u>Slave of the Lamp: A Public Servant's Notebook</u> (1967), 2-5.
44. "Personnel File, Salter, J.A.," Ministry of Health, Establishment Division, NA-UK, MH 107/11.
45. Salter, <u>Memoirs</u>, 44-45, Salter, <u>Slave of the Lamp</u>, 4-5, author's interview with Lord Salter, 21 Sept. 1970.

46. Salter, Memoirs, 39.
47. Salter, Memoirs, 39-40.
48. "The Transport Department," Salter Papers, File 1, Anecdotes and Incidents, unpublished typescript, completed January 1956.
49. Salter, Memoirs, pp. 39-41.
50. Salter, Slave of the Lamp, 8.
51. Salter, Memoirs, 44-45.
52. Letters to the Editor, The Times, 24 Sept., 5 Oct.1907.
53. Salter, Memoirs, 45.
54. Salter, Memoirs, 46.
55. Salter, Memoirs, 45.
56. Violet Markham to Joyce Nettlefold, 26 Dec. 1915, Joyce Newton Thompson Papers, BC 643 B18.7, University of Capetown Libraries, Capetown, South Africa, Salter to Joyce Nettlefold, 14 Oct. [1915], Newton Thompson Papers, BC 643 B22.1, entry of 8 Feb. 1931, Elliott Felkin Diary, AEF/1/1/8, King's College Archive Centre, Cambridge.
57. Werner Picht, Toynbee Hall und die Englische Settlement-Bewegung (Tübingen, 1913), 27, (die 'Mutter der Settlements').
58. See The Toynbee Record, 14(Nov. 1911), 19, The Toynbee Record, 24(Feb. 1912), 63.
59. Salter, Memoirs, 46-47. Salter spoke at the 50th anniversary of the opening of the East London University Settlement. The Times, 1 June 1935.
60. J.A.R. Pimlott, Toynbee Hall: Fifty Years of Social History, 1884-1934 (1935), xi, 190, 233.
61. Picht, Toynbee Hall, 73, "A Club for Social Enquiry," The Toynbee Record, 17(Nov. 1904), 23, "The Enquirers' Club," The Toynbee Record, 17(Jan. 1905), 55.
62. "The Enquirers' Club, 'Wages Boards,' J. Ramsay Macdonald," The Toynbee Record, 20(Feb. 1908), 58, "The Enquirers' Club, 'The Poor Law Reports,' Mrs. Sidney Webb," The Toynbee Record, 21(June 1909), 141.
63. "Citizenship in Stepney," The Toynbee Record, 14(Dec. 1911), 33-36.
64. Salter, Memoirs, 46, Standish Meacham, Toynbee Hall and Social Reform, 1880-1914: The Search for Community (1987), 124.
65. "Personnel File, Salter, J.A.," Ministry of Health Establishment Division, NA-UK, MH107/11, Salter, Memoirs, 42, 47-48, William J. Braithwaite, Lloyd George's Ambulance Wagon (1957), 281.
66. Memoir of Sir Basil Kemball-Cook, Kemball-Cook Papers, PP/MCR/310, pp. 105-106, Imperial War Museum, London.

67. Salter, Memoirs, 49, "Personnel File, Salter, J.A.," Ministry of Health, Establishment Division, NA-UK, MH107/11, "Some Incidents in the Peninsula," Salter Papers, File 1, Anecdotes and Incidents.
68. See Bentley B. Gilbert, The Evolution of National Insurance in Great Britain: The Origins of the Welfare State (1966), and R.W. Harris, National Health Insurance in Great Britain, 1911-1946 (1946). Harris was one of the drafters of the bill.
69. Salter, Memoirs, 48. Part II of the Act, the unemployment provisions was not of direct concern to Salter. For a copy of the Treasury circular letter see NA-UK, MH78/55.
70. The Times, 29 Nov. 1911, Braithwaite, Lloyd George's Ambulance Wagon, *passim*, Salter, Memoirs, 59.
71. Salter, Memoirs, 52, Salter, Slave of the Lamp, 13.
72. Lucy Masterman, C.F.G. Masterman: A Biography (1939), 262.
73. Quoted in Masterman, C.F.G. Masterman, 223.
74. R.W. Harris, Not so Humdrum: The Autobiography of a Civil Servant (1939), 145, Salter, Memoirs, 52. Another early participant Alexander Gray, Some Aspects of National Health Insurance (1923), 11 described the Act as "of a complexity positively dementing."
75. The Times, 2 Jan. 1912, Minutes, National Health Insurance Joint Committee, 30 Dec. 1911, NA-UK, PIN2/1, Braithwaite, Lloyd George's Ambulance Wagon, 280-281.
76. Harris, Not So Humdrum, 175. On appointments to the Commissions, see Salter to Wheeler-Bennett, 23 June 1959, in John W. Wheeler-Bennett, John Anderson, Viscount Waverley (1962), 35.
77. Salter, Memoirs, 52-53, "Personnel File, Salter, J.A.," Ministry of Health, Establishment Division, NA-UK, MH107/11.
78. Salter, Memoirs, 64-65, Masterman, C.F.G. Masterman, 230-231.
79. Quoted in Masterman, C.F.G. Masterman, 239-240.
80. Salter, Memoirs, 63.
81. Salter, Memoirs, 64.
82. Quoted in Violet Markham, Friendship's Harvest (1956), 177, 190.
83. Quoted in Harris, Not So Humdrum, 161.
84. Arthur Salter, Personality in Politics: Studies of Contemporary Statesmen (1947), 46.
85. Salter to Lynda Grier, 3 Dec. 1947, Sir Michael Sadler Papers, MSS Eng misc. c552, ff. 243-245, Bodleian Library, Oxford.
86. Markham, Friendship's Harvest, 203, Bernard M. Allen, Sir Robert Morant (1934), 267-272.

87. Harris, Not So Humdrum, 160, Salter, Memoirs, 59, The Economist, 184(7 Sept. 1957) 753-754.
88. Salter, Personality in Politics, 49, Braithwaite obituary, The Times, 18 Mar. 1938.
89. Allen, Morant, 273-274.
90. Wheeler-Bennett, Anderson, 32.
91. Braithwaite, Lloyd George's Ambulance Wagon, 281, Salter, Memoirs, 72, Markham, Friendship's Harvest, 191-192.
92. Harris, Not So Humdrum, 170, Wheeler-Bennett, Anderson, 31-32, Allen, Morant, 273.
93. The Economist,184(7 Sept. 1957), 754.
94. Salter, Memoirs, 65.
95. "Personnel File, Salter, J.A.," Ministry of Health, Establishment Division, NA-UK, MH107/11, Masterman to Braithwaite, 8 May 1912, NA-UK, MH107/11.
96. Masterman, C.F.G. Masterman, 391.
97. Gilbert, The Evolution of National Insurance in Great Britain, 423, Minutes, National Health Insurance Joint Committee, 23, 24 Jan. 1912, NA-UK, PIN2/1. Salter further described this effort in Hansard, Parliamentary Debates, 5th Series [H.C. Debs.] vol. 436, 25 Apr. 1947, cols. 1426-1428.
98. Minutes, National Health Insurance Joint Committee, 30 Dec. 1911, NA-UK, PIN2/1.
99. The Times, 19 Feb. 1912.
100. Braithwaite, Lloyd George's Ambulance Wagon, 289. The majority of the lecturers were released from their duties in July. See Minutes, National Health Insurance Commission, England, 26 July 1912, NA-UK, PIN2/20.
101. Salter, Memoirs, 66.
102. Salter, Memoirs, 67-68. Cf., Alfred Cox, Among the Doctors (1950), 84-102.
103. Masterman, C.F.G. Masterman, 386, 389.
104. Baithwaite, Lloyd George's Ambulance Wagon, 302.
105. Masterman, C.F.G. Masterman, 236.
106. Minutes, National Health Insurance Commission, England, 10 Apr. 1913, NA-UK, PIN2/21.
107. Harris, Not So Humdrum, 176.
108. Salter to Braithwaite, 14 Apr. 1913, William J. Braithwaite Papers, Section 1c [Pt. III, p. 80 of typescript], British Library of Political and Economic Science [BLPES], London. A small part of this letter was quoted in Braithwaite, Lloyd George's Ambulance Wagon, 302, but is incorrectly dated.
109. Salter, Memoirs, 65, Mary Agnes Hamilton, Remembering My Good Friends (1944), 133.

110. Masterman, <u>C.F.G Masterman</u>, 258.
111. Salter, <u>Memoirs</u>, 69.
112. Salter, <u>Memoirs</u>, 69-70, Salter, <u>Personality in Politics</u>, 97.
113. Quoted in diary entry, 25 Nov. 1913, Sir Almeric Fitzroy, <u>Memoirs</u>, vol. 2 (6th ed., n.d.), 527-528.
114. Salter, <u>Memoirs</u>, 72.
115. Minutes, National Health Insurance Joint Committee, 11 July 1913, NA-UK, PIN2/2, Salter to Braithwaite, 14 Apr.1913, Braithwaite Papers, Section 1c [Pt. III, p. 80 of typescript].

CHAPTER 2

"AN 'INNER CIRCLE' REPUTATION," 1914-1918

On Armistice Day, 11 November 1918, the editor of the Daily News, A.G. Gardiner, and his companion, Andrewes Uthwatt, legal adviser to the Ministry of Food, left the Reform Club together. "'Well,' Gardiner said, 'it's over.' 'Yes,' said Uthwatt, 'it's over; and if I asked you to name the man who has done most towards winning it you wouldn't get it right in a hundred guesses.' 'Come,' said Gardiner, 'that sounds interesting. Not a soldier?' 'No.' 'Nor a politician?' 'No.' 'A civil servant?' 'Yes,' replied Uthwatt, showing some signs of surprise that Gardiner was getting 'hot,' so soon. 'Salter,' Gardiner plunged. 'Yes. Salter. But how on earth did you get it?' 'Ah, well,' said A.G.G., 'I know Salter and the work he's been doing'."[1] Gardiner and Uthwatt were referring, among other things, to the seminal role which Salter had played as Director of Ship Requisitioning and as one of the organizers of the convoy system at a moment of the most intense submarine warfare. Not least they were also complimenting the fine service reputation which Salter had so quickly built in the course of the First World War.

In August 1914 and again in November 1915 Salter volunteered for army service. On the latter occasion he wrote, "I am 34, physically fit, unmarried, without ties or obligations of any kind."[2] His first decision was based as much on boredom as on patriotism. Following the declaration of war, the National Health Insurance Commission found itself mainly concerned with the problems of adopting the Insurance Act for military purposes. For example, the respective medical needs of the armed forces and the civilian population had to be equitably met. It was necessary also to determine which doctors could be released for service at the front and which could remain to cater to domestic needs. Such problems were solved in direct negotiation between the medical profession and the Insurance Commission.[3] On the other hand, a wartime footing served to galvanise other government departments with a high proportion of talented and now experienced administrators. Within a short time as much as 80% of the staff – by then known as "Morant's young men" – transferred from civilian to military life. The remainder were to be slowly drawn upon for crucial positions in different war departments, such as munitions, shipping and food.⁴ Eventually Salter was to hear, ironically from the Director of Transports, that his services would again be required in his old department, rendering military duty out of the question.⁵

Before returning to the Admiralty, however, Salter spent several months in an unusual, and some times embarrassing, position. The outbreak of war in August 1914 had been followed by a temporary increase in women's unemployment, partly the result of the rush of volunteers for "war work." On 20 August, Queen Mary, after consultation with the trade unionist Mary Macarthur, established the Queen's Work for Women Fund which ran "workrooms" for the unemployed. It was part of the National Relief Fund, on which Salter assisted, already set up to accept contributions for relief purposes resulting from wartime conditions.⁶ Out of the former emerged the Central Committee on Women's Training and Employment, the brainchild of Mary Macarthur, who became its first Secretary, with Lady Crewe as Chairman.⁷ The Committee consisted of women representing all shades of interested opinion, including such members of the Labour movement as Margaret Bondfield, Dr. Marian Phillips and Susan Lawrence, as well as Mrs. Austen Chamberlain, Lady Askwith, and Violet Markham. Mary Macarthur was passionately committed to the idea that relief for women should consist of gainful employment rather than the dole.⁸ The Central Committee on Women's Training and Employment got off to a chaotic start: "the atmosphere the hectic muddle of the early war days." Its first location was the ballroom of Wimborne House, "a vast room lit only by artificial light, blocked with candidates for jobs and piteous applicants for work; the candidates at first with little qualification save good intentions, the applications with no industrial training whatever." Workrooms had to be organized, pay rates fixed, goods marketed and new trades, such as fruit bottling and toy making, encouraged.⁹ Mary Macarthur shortly found herself with a successful national scheme on her hands but without the organizational facilities to back her up.

When rumours of this state of affairs began to circulate, several civil servants arrived on 29 September to impose a semblance of order. A witness to their first appearance, Violet Markham, later wrote:

> I looked up as a door opened and across the top of the room three men passed in single file, casting glances of dismay as they did so on the scene before them. The first, a short sturdy figure, stepped out with the air of the proverbial small boy whistling in the graveyard, but horror was writ large on the faces of his two companions…. The third, and that day the most unhappy-looking of the trio, has been for more than forty years one of my best friends.¹⁰

The third of the government watch-dogs was in fact Salter who had joined with Henry Bunbury and Michael Heseltine to impose a semblance of civil service procedure. For not only were the working conditions unorthodox, but the personalities of Mary Macarthur and Lady Crewe were often used as negotiating tools. Mary Macarthur had a tendency to burst into tears to strengthen her arguments. Lady Crewe's techniques were later described by Salter:

> I was young, innocent, shy and easily shocked, feeling anyhow awkward at having for the first time to work in a feminine organization. At the first meeting I attended some question of policy was raised which required some favourable concession from the President of the Local Government Board, Sir Herbert Samuel. It was decided to send a deputation, upon which Lady Crewe coolly observed, 'I'd better lead it. Herbert knows I'm going to have a baby and he'll find it hard to say no to me.'[11]

Although "baffled and horrified" at the outset, a process of mutual education soon served the interests of all concerned. Civil service procedure brought some order into the chaos; while admiration and affection soon dominated attitudes towards Mary Macarthur and her executive. By January 1915 over 9,000 women had passed through the workrooms, with an additional 4,000 juveniles.[12] The success of the scheme, as well as an improvement in the employment situation, enabled Salter to leave the Central Committee on Women's Training and Employment on 11 January 1915. Its Interim Report, presented to parliament in March 1915, was the first such document prepared by a group of women.[13]

Salter's return to the National Health Insurance Commission was brief. He soon received word from the Director of Transports, Graeme Thomson, that his services were now needed in his old department. His previous experience there from 1904 to 1911, coupled with the expertise gained from association with Masterman, Braithwaite and Morant, led to his return on 12 April 1915 to the Admiralty.[14] It was a move that placed him in a position to play a more central role in the nation's wartime effort. In his definitive 1921 study, <u>Allied Shipping Control: An Experiment in International Administration</u>, Salter argued that the First World War had been as much "a war of competing blockades, the surface and the submarine, as of competing armies." Behind the blockades, he contended, the economic systems of countries at war struggled for survival. And on several occasions, the threat of starvation almost achieved the ends which deadlocked land armies and immobilized navies could not.[15] At the centre of Britain's economic warfare, and its ultimate success in the blockade, lay initially the Transport Department of the Admiralty. In August 1914 the Transport Department was structured only to pursue its peacetime functions, chartering passenger ships for the transport of British troops around the world, and colliers to supply the fleet and overseas bases. As well, it arranged for the transportation and supply of the British Expeditionary force, and for the ships needed for general use under specific naval war plans. As the "Cinderella of the Service," the pre-war Transport Department had been small in size and smaller in status. Its personnel numbered about a dozen, with a total salary budget in 1913 of only some £14,000.[16] From such humble origins grew the organization in which Salter was to play a crucial role and which was central to the final achievement of victory.

The tradition of the Transport Department had been to appoint as its head a retired naval officer, above the rank of captain, for a period of three years. As soon as the term of the then Director of Transports, Rear Admiral Herbert W. Savory, came to an end on 30 November 1914, the First Lord of the Admiralty, Winston Churchill, broke with tradition. He appointed a civilian director, Graeme Thomson, whom he had described in the House of Commons, as "one of the discoveries of the war."[17] Among Thomson's first moves was to recall Salter to the Admiralty. The department which Salter joined on 12 April 1915 was divided into four main branches: the Naval Executive Branch handled Admiralty shipping requirements; the Military Executive Branch catered to the needs of the War Office; the Naval Assistant's Branch outfitted ships for specific requirements; and finally, the Financial Branch dealt with the department's accounting and finances. Salter was placed in charge of this last branch with the title of Superintendent of Finance.[18] It was the rapid extension of ship requisitioning for war purposes which put Salter into the centre of a process which was ultimately to lead to his appointment as Director of Requisitioning in a newly created Ministry of Shipping.

Upon the declaration of war, the British government had authorised the Admiralty to requisition all shipping needed for defence purposes. This allowed the government to instruct shipowners where to send their ships, the nature of the cargo, and to fix payment and adequate compensation for loss or damage. The immediate problem facing the Transport Department was how to determine the rates of payment for requisitioned vessels, and resolve any disputes which arose about compensation. An Arbitration Board was set up, therefore, and through its sub-committees agreement was reached on a scale of rates for various classes of ships. These rates, published in a Blue Book in October 1914, became known as the "Blue Book rates." With some minor modifications, these remained the standard rates for all tonnage engaged by the government throughout the war.[19] Salter observed in retrospect that "they proved a fair arrangement for both the Government and the shipowners. They were considerably lower than in any other country. On the other hand they gave higher net rates of profit than had been current, except for short and brief periods, in peacetime."[20] Yet such a judgement appears short-sighted in light of actual wartime developments.

As Superintendent of Finance, Salter played a key role in the questions of compensation for shipowners and arbitration cases as they arose. As well, he was responsible for the general financial policy of the department and for recruiting a rapidly expanding staff, including for the first time women in the Admiralty.[21] This was then followed with the introduction of a scheme which was later to have far-reaching consequences. The Transport Department of the Admiralty in peacetime received its information as to the availability of shipping from only two sources, the customs authorities and Lloyd's of London. Even before the outbreak of war the Transport Department had been on the verge of instituting a card index system to monitor the movements of all vessels suitable for military purposes in British waters. Nothing however was done to implement this project. Salter recognized the pressing need in wartime for such a shipping intelligence system. What was required, he argued, was a system which would obtain, collate and maintain up to the minute information as to the type, position and use of every British, ocean-going vessel in the world. In addition, the system's structure would have to allow instant access to every item recorded. As a result, a card index expert was hired to implement the scheme which was simple and totally reliable.[22] "Each ship had its own card on which every item of information about it was concentrated. The colour of the card distinguished its type and a movable metal clip its approximate position." Consequently, any ship could be picked out at once, its position and employment noted, and provision made for its fullest use. The information sources for the card index system were expanded to include telegrams from owners and merchants, the customs department, admiralty officials at home and abroad, naval boarding and patrolling ships. By the end of the war, the card index system on which Salter lavished so much attention was supplying some 5,000 items of information to government departments interested in sea transport, ranging from the Admiralty to the big supply departments, and even allied and neutral powers.[23] In effect the system proved to be the major cog in the supply side of the sea war, and ensured the demands made on the Transport Department would be adequately fulfilled. This would prove especially vital when merchant shipping would be brought to the forefront of wartime grand strategy. The dawning realization of its importance soon contributed to a series of major innovations which led, by 1916, to the virtual nationalization of the British shipping industry.

Throughout 1914 and the first half of 1915 government demands for supplies and shipping were evenly balanced, and met the needs of a wartime economy. In other words, shipping was fulfilling its obvious role as the servant to the transport of cargo. However, by mid-1915 the cruelest dilemma to face the government began to make itself apparent. Later Salter himself recalled the crisis:

> Now when those in charge of shipping have plenty of ships their task is an easy one. They have only to select the right ship for the right cargo. But when there aren't enough ships to go round, you have to decide which needs shall be met first and which shall give way – how far munitions shall be carried at the expense of food, and so on. But it was never possible to make a complete plan in this way, and in the meantime those who controlled shipping had to do the best they could, never knowing quite certainly, if they refused ships asked for food in order to carry munitions, that the result would not be starvation at home, or, if they refused ships asked for munitions in order to carry food, that the result would not be disastrous at the front. It was a terrible responsibility.[24]

The process whereby shipping was transformed from servant to master and back again was to preoccupy Salter over the next 18 months. It was a process that proceeded in two distinct phases, in which Salter was to play a critical role.

During the first months of the war, government shipping requirements for transport and supply were limited to about 20% of British ocean going tonnage and Blue Book freight rates were slightly in excess of the open market. By the beginning of 1915, however, the situation began to change. Open market rates inched steadily upwards, due to the combined impact of war losses, delays in loading and discharging, and steadily increasing wartime demands. Shipowners began to protest the burden of requisitioning, seeing higher profits on the open market. At the same time, rising freight costs led to public indignation at increases in the cost of living. The shipping industry was soon being accused of earning excess profits.[25] While the Transport Department of the Admiralty, with an "overworked and overburdened staff," struggled to balance the conflicting demands between trade and the needs of the fighting services.[26] On 15 February 1915 in the House of Commons, Andrew Bonar Law, leader of the Conservative Party, castigated the poor performance of the Transport Department. He also called for the appointment of Sir Joseph Maclay, a Glasgow shipowner, as head of the Transport Department.[27] Maclay was eventually to get the position for which he was already being picked. Yet at this early point in the war such far-reaching solutions found no favour with the H.H. Asquith government. For his part the First Lord of the Admiralty, Winston Churchill, as well, had already urged Asquith "to take over the whole British mercantile marine for the period of the war for national purposes." Excess profits, not efficiency, were the motive for Churchill's novel suggestion.[28]

Faced with such diverse criticism, the Transport Department concentrated on making its limited powers fall as equitably as possible on all concerned. For example, Salter fixed his attention on trying as "to keep the proportion of requisitioning fair as between different owners." His approach was governed by the clear understanding that at this early stage in the war full-scale requisitioning of all British shipping was out of the question. Such a step, requiring fixed and controlled rates, would have meant accepting responsibility as well for usage and allocation of all cargoes. He knew his department did not yet have either the personnel or the organization to implement such a drastic solution.[29] And finally, the Asquith administration was not yet prepared politically or ideologically for what, in effect, could amount to nationalizing the shipping industry.[30]

Nonetheless, Salter did follow the lead, demonstrated by Churchill in the cabinet, of advocating control by way of taxation on shipowners' profits. In the early months of the war, on 23 December 1914, Salter had already gone on record in favour of the principle "that the remuneration of requisitioned ships should be such as to secure a limited rate of profit and should not be based upon the current market rates, which are themselves determined by war conditions and by the action of the Government itself in requisitioning." He proposed therefore "a narrow margin of profit," leaving the shipowners free to argue the case for additional money. The proposal was rejected as premature by the Transport Department's Finance Committee.[31] In July 1915 Salter again returned to the charge, still troubled by what he described as "the scandal of the preposterous profits" earned by shipowners. With the help of Sir Thomas Royden, at the time deputy-chairman of the Cunard Steamship Company, Salter prepared a "Memorandum as to Limitations of Shipowners' Profits," for submission to the Board of the Admiralty. His 14-page document showed the vast savings possible with a cap on excess profits. Salter was no more successful with the Admiralty Board than Churchill had been with the Asquith cabinet.[32] Stymied in his first efforts at influencing policy making, Salter refocused his attention on further streamlining the work of his department. He advocated, for example, the centralization of all requisitioning in a "central executive branch." Such an organization, Salter argued, would avoid the duplication and inefficiency of the existing system whereby separate executives dealt with the transport needs of either the army, navy or civilian requirements.[33]

Salter embodied these thoughts in a memorandum which he circulated on 20 October. They were implemented in two stages. In the first, a new Information Branch was formed, with Salter as its head, "to centralise the whole business of shipping intelligence and classification." Based on a previously organized Shipping Intelligence Section, the main duty of the Information Branch was to maintain a complete card index to British shipping worldwide, and have ready at a moment's notice information as to the size and type of any free ships available for requisitioning. By December 1915, in its second stage and with sufficient experience, the functions of the Information Branch were extended. Its name was changed to Requisitioning Branch, Salter was appointed Assistant Director of Requisitioning, and its functions were widened to include actual requisitioning. "In this way the new Branch became a clearing house for all information relating either to requisitioned tonnage or tonnage available for service, while the actual process of requisitioning was centralised to a much greater extent than ever before."[34] To facilitate the enlarged executive functions of the Requisitioning Branch, Salter extended the card index to cover all ships available or running on requisitioned service. The card index was accordingly rearranged in alphabetical order under ship names and continuously updated. This facilitated administrative decisions as well as policy questions.[35]

In the second year of the war, the government was reluctantly forced into further measures of control over both shipping and supplies. "Day by day my branch was faced with a balance sheet of shipping and pressing demands always in excess of what was available," Salter recalled.[36] This second phase of "control by committee" was soon upon the country. On 10 November 1915, under Orders in Council, the Board of Trade had appointed two committees with drastic powers. The first, the Ship Licensing Committee, was designed to regulate the use of steamers for the carriage of cargoes between ports outside the British Empire. The committee continued to control shipping by its system of licensing until it was wound up a year later. The second committee, the Requisitioning (Carriage of Foodstuffs) Committee, with Salter appointed joint secretary, proved to be equally short-lived. The Requisitioning Committee made little use of its considerable powers, but focused instead on providing additional shipping for the North Atlantic food trade, particularly wheat. Unfortunately, Salter observed, "As an experiment in dealing with the problem created by shortage of tonnage, the Committee was not a success." Assessing the lessons of "control by committee," he continued: "To be effective, control over commodities once begun must be comprehensive in its range as well as complete in its character."[37]

It was clear by mid-1916 that growing pressures from a variety of sources would soon force the government to take more drastic action. The more he turned his mind from executive to policy making areas, the more Salter addressed this precise problem. Finally, in December 1916 his contribution to the discussion was complete. His 177-page document, "High Freight Rates and Government Control," addressed the problem of how "increasing demands with diminishing numbers" was affecting mercantile shipping. While Salter concentrated on the problem of high freight rates, the question he focused on was the issue of competition versus control. He first analysed the causes of the prevailing shortage of tonnage, and followed that with a thorough analysis of the various forms of control and methods of limiting freight rates. Finally, he turned to the question of "possibilities of further control." Of the various schemes under consideration, which included the chartering of neutral tonnage or a complete system of licensing imports, Salter singled out the "complete requisitioning of the mercantile marine." While there were administrative difficulties in such a drastic solution, he pointed out several advantages. Complete requisitioning, he argued, would end the excess profits earned by shipowners and the Transport Department would be relieved of the nightmare of "proportionate requisitioning," a solution which he preferred.[38] As was to be his habit in future years, Salter gave his memorandum the widest possible distribution. He was never deterred by potential charges of impinging on other people's jurisdiction. If a problem demanded solution, and if Salter felt he could make a definite contribution, little would deter him.[39] Thus, after completing his memorandum on the problem of freight rates and government control, he made copies available to key civil servants both in his department and outside. Recipients, for example, ranged from Thomas Lodge, secretary to the Ship Licensing Committee to Josiah Stamp (later Lord Stamp) of the Inland Revenue Department, to the various shipowners then advising the Transport Department. Reaction ranged from qualified agreement to outright hostility, hardly surprising considering the volatility of the issues involved.[40] The issue was to be soon resolved with the raising of the excess profits duty up to 80% from 1 January 1917.

At the time Salter was circulating his memorandum, the country was in the middle of a cabinet crisis which resulted in the formation of the second wartime coalition, led by David Lloyd George as Prime Minister. Among the numerous issues which had led to Asquith's resignation was the question of the higher direction of the war. "The normal economic system, based upon competitive individual enterprise," Salter later observed, "was breaking down in every direction." Even from the shipping perspective, it was clear that the Transport Department, for example, was exercising responsibility in the free market in excess of its authority. How this had come about was explained as follows by Salter:

> It is important to remember that control was extended step by step by the compelling force of circumstances. It was already almost complete before it was adopted as a deliberate policy. Each new extension was normally undertaken reluctantly as the only method of meeting an immediate emergency.[41]

On 6 December 1916, with the formation of the Lloyd George coalition, such hand to mouth methods became a thing of the past. Among the first steps taken by the new Prime Minister were a series of restructuring moves which completely transformed the shipping situation in Britain with profound effects on the course of Salter's career. On 19 December Lloyd George met the rising demand for action against shipowners' excessive profits and in favour of nationalizing the shipping industry. Speaking in the House of Commons, he declared that shipping "is the jugular vein, which, if severed, would destroy the life of the nation, and the Government felt that the time has come for taking over more complete control of all the ships of this country .... so that during the War shipping will be nationalized in the real sense of the term."[42] Under a New Ministers and Secretaries Act, which received royal assent on 22 December, a Ministry of Shipping was established. It was headed by a Shipping Controller, the Glasgow head of Maclay and McIntyre, Sir Joseph Maclay, who was to serve for the remainder of the war in an unpaid capacity. His appointment, in the words of the Act, was "For the purpose of organizing and maintaining the supply of shipping in the national interests in connection with the present war" – a phrase which gave the controller wide and very vague powers.[43]

For a brief time, the Ministry of Shipping consisted only of the Shipping Controller, and his private secretary, Salter's former colleague on the National Health Insurance Commission, John Anderson. However, responding to a request earlier in the New Year from Maclay, the cabinet agreed on 9 February to transfer the over 500 personnel and the equipment of the Transport Department of the Admiralty to the Ministry of Shipping, thereby giving it an administrative nucleus.[44] By the end of February the organization of the Ministry was complete, one which was to last throughout the war with only minor modifications. The Department of the Director of Transports and Shipping constituted one of three administrative divisions of the new ministry. The new department consisted of seven branches, with Salter transferred from the Finance Branch and named as Director of the Requisitioning Branch.[45] His position as Director of Ship Requisitioning placed him at the centre of Britain's wartime efforts and made his reputation. As he faced his new tasks, he also looked back on his career. "During this time my working week was one of seven days and my working day ended late at night," he wrote, "I became an inhuman machine, scarcely conscious of anything outside my work and incapable of any sensation or emotion that was not related to it." The habits so assiduously cultivated when he was still an undergraduate were meeting his needs. The death of friends and relatives, at sea or on the western front, played heavily on his mind, but hardly on his emotions. On hearing of the death of a cousin, Salter recalled, "I found myself incapable of deep feeling. Something, though happily only a fraction, of this defect remained in later years."[46] The war years served in a decisive way to confirm his character and determine his career.

Salter also found some of his pre-war experience with the National Health Insurance Commission was being repeated. He rejoiced in a sense of power, its exercise and the ability to use his considerable talents. Once again there were friendships with colleagues, a demanding and absorbing task, and what he called "a kind of 'inner circle' reputation."[47] He was in daily contact with a wide array of colleagues, enjoying the company of men participating in common goals. The most notable of such contacts was an informal group which became known as "the Family." Besides Salter, this consisted of among others J. Reeve Brooke, at the time with the War Office, Frank Wise, a civil servant and economist, E.M.H. Lloyd of the War Office, J.J. Mallon with the Board of Trade, Ralph Enfield from the Ministry of Munitions and Thomas Jones, newly appointed assistant secretary to the War Cabinet. This informal group of civil servants met for dinner on a weekly basis, to discuss items of common interest, based on shared political sympathy.[48] Salter struck one as "a little pale man with dark hair; but possessing a mathematical brain which without effort tackles any statistical problem and reduces it to order."[49] "Official intimacy is a curious thing," Salter later observed, "it has depth without necessarily having breath." He was conceding in effect that he could know little about his colleagues' private lives and interests. Nonetheless, he did regard such relationships as "a good and stable basis for friendship," if not of intimacy.[50]

In his daily routine during the first half of the war, Salter's official contacts were almost exclusively in the Transport Department and then the new Ministry of Shipping. He developed a particularly high regard for the abilities of Sir Joseph Maclay, and the two successive chairmen of Cunard Steamship Company, Sir Thomas Royden and Sir Percy Bates. What impressed Salter about Maclay was his "curiously detached attitude to his political colleagues, with a judgement of their personal qualities which was little affected by the dignity of their official positions."[51] As for Bates, Director of the Commercial Services Branch, Salter found him a thorough professional, with "great industry and a boyish zest in his work; and a strong will, expressed in a forceful chin which most of us probably remember as the most characteristic feature in a striking presence." Bates' deputy, Cyril Hurcomb, was another colleague with whom Salter was to share responsibility for shipping in the next World War. In his own department, Salter worked closely with two "exceptionally able " shipbrokers, Norman A. Leslie, head of the Convoy Section, and Arthur Eugene O'Neill, head of General Allocation, both knighted after the war for their services in the Ministry of Shipping. The former Salter described as "competent, patriotic, devoted, and industrious, with good judgement in the practical making and implementing of merchant shipping policy under war conditions." In addition, there was Sir Kenneth Anderson, a manager of the Orient Steam Navigation Company, and Sir Lionel Fletcher, an expert marksman, with interests in Australasian trade, both working in the Liner Requisitioning Section. There were also the less well-known personal assistants, on whom Salter depended for the smooth functioning of his branch. Leonard Browett, a later secretary to the

Ministry of Transport during the Second World War, was chosen to be Salter's deputy. G.V. Howell was given full responsibility for the card index system. Shipowners and civil servants were welded, therefore, into an interdependent, respectful team, submerging any conflicts of interests for purposes of winning the war.[52]

As his personal assistant, and later sharing the same office as himself, Salter chose Gertrude Caton Thompson, who later made her reputation as an archaeologist with East African interests.[53] More than 60 years after the war, she recalled details of her association with Salter:

> I first met J.A.S. in the late winter of 1916 at dinner at the house of Mr and Mrs. Eustace Davies in London. He was then about 35. Eustace Davies was a fairly senior civil servant, and he had already mentioned J.A.S. to me as 'a man to be reckoned with.' At first sight he was not physically prepossessing in appearance, with broad shoulders out of proportion to his short height. His pleasant voice and penetrating glance seen through spectacles when we were introduced, combined with controlled movements, left me with an impression of great energy of mind and body.
>
> J.A.S. had heard well of me from the Davies' and I imagine our meeting was prearranged. Anyhow, he asked me to become an assistant member of the staff. I was put into a room occupied by Mr (later Sir) Norman Leslie, a ship-owner; Mr (later Sir) Eugene O'Neill, a Director of Stricklands; a young wounded officer named (Lieutenant R.T.) Hinde, son of a shipping man; and a lower grade civil servant to keep us disciplined. They were all charming to me, and Leslie in particular, busy as he was, took trouble with my education, and absorbed me into the task of requisitioning ships – from great liners to colliers, despite the passionate pleas from some owners for exemption – a job I was usually deputed to handle as tactfully as a resounding 'no' could be.
>
> During those twelve months I worked for them I hardly set eyes on J.A.S. who lived in a much grander room with a carpet, which he shared with a personal secretary. Shortly before Christmas 1917 a message came that he wanted to see me. Full of apprehension, I went along to be told that he was dissatisfied with his secretary, the Hon. Fanny (E.M.) Farrer (later to become a D.B.E. for social work). Would I take her place? My workmates spoke well of me.
>
> Thus I became his personal assistant for the next 12 months, cooped up with him and much too busy to establish any contact with his real being. It was a gruelling time for him, and I learnt to marvel at his capacity to keep an even keel. He was, at that time, convinced that the awful ship-sinkings, with their precious cargoes, which were daily reported to him confidentially, could

only be met by bringing all allied merchant shipping under a single control, in spite of powerful opposition.[54]

By the end of February 1917 the Ministry of Shipping was already well installed in its new quarters. Temporary wooden buildings had been erected on the drained bed of the lake in St. James's Park. To these new offices were transferred the whole staff of the new Ministry of Shipping from its constituent parts previously housed in the Admiralty Arch and the Cunard offices in Cockspur Street.[55] The switch to centralized control of British shipping had come just on time to meet the gravest crisis yet faced by Britain in the course of the war. On 1 February 1917 unrestricted German submarine warfare had been resumed against British shipping, with devastating impact. In just the one month of April total losses of British Empire ships, of all classes, amounted to a wartime high of 526,447 gross tons, compared with a loss of 1,231,867 gross tons for the entire previous year. One quarter of the ships leaving Britain that month were sunk.[56] It was widely rumoured during April, and the shipowners' association made representations to the government, that continued losses of such magnitude would have meant Britain having to capitulate because of scarcity of tonnage.[57] The twin dangers of starvation and surrender were real.

The ferocity of the German submarine campaign affected all aspects of shipping, from building to requisitioning to cargo, and Salter found himself intimately involved. The main burden of his work during the first four months of the year lay in the complex area of liner requisitioning. By the end of 1916, it had become clear that the Transport Department could not fulfil the demands for shipping without tapping the liner fleets. Consequently, on 12 February 1917 the government extended requisitioning to liners at Blue Book rates "so as to make it general and as nearly as possible universal."[58] As a result "an ingenious and novel form of requisition" was devised.[59] A Liner Requisitioning Section was formed in Salter's Branch, under the direction of Sir Lionel Fletcher who largely masterminded both the conception and implementation of the scheme. All liners were to be formally requisitioned and compensated at Blue Book rates. However, ownership would remain in the hands of owners who would operate the ships, and would be able to offer surplus space on the open market. The accounting for the liners' operation, however, would be done by the government, the shipowners crediting the government with gross earnings and debiting net charges. By the end of May only a few "local services in distant seas" were exempt from requisitioning.[60] By November 1918, more than four-fifths of British imports were being transported under the new scheme.[61]

At each stage of the liner requisitioning scheme, Salter was intimately involved. As Director of Ship Requisitioning, he oversaw the Liner Requisitioning Section and its six-member Committee whose policy was then implemented by the requisitioning section. While not a member of this committee, Salter was instrumental maximising shipping and limiting imports. In December 1916 when the new Lloyd George administration had decided to restrict non-essential imports, Salter's Requisitioning Section was brought into play. It estimated a shipping deficit for 1917 so alarming that on 21 December Lord Curzon, a War Cabinet member, was named to head a committee whose mandate was "to consider and report on the question of the restriction of imports." Salter then sat as the Admiralty representative on an inter-departmental sub-committee to work out a detailed programme of restrictions.[62] At the same time a new Tonnage Priority Committee was appointed in February 1917 to draw up monthly lists of priorities for the importing departments. The work of the former led on 31 March to the prohibition, except by license, of a large number of commodities. The latter continued to meet throughout 1917, with little effect, but a firm recognition that choices between commodities be determined by a supply organization.[63] As the liner requisitioning scheme was implemented, Salter helped draft and authorise the requisitioning terms for the country's shipowners. As well, he assisted in ironing out the complexities involved in guaranteeing that requisitioned vessels should be covered by War Risk Insurance.[64] On 7 April he forcefully argued the case, after consultation with the Head of the Commercial Branch, Sir Percy Bates, that a more systematic approach should be adapted to the problems of shipment of non-governmental requirements. Salter suggested, and it was approved, that the whole problem should be brought under the control of the Commercial Branch.[65]

Such activity paled, however, in comparison with the immediate threat posed by the German submarine campaign "to sink without distinction and without warning." In Salter's view, "The whole war effort of the Allies was soon threatened with disaster; and all the main European Allies were in imminent danger of starvation."[66] As so often in future years, Salter stood at the periphery of major executive action, yet his hand could be discerned in its formulation. The British response to submarine warfare, when it finally came, proved one of the most decisive acts of the war. The situation from February 1917 was evidently desperate. Commander Reginald G.H. Henderson, of the Anti-Submarine Division of the Admiralty, proposed a solution. He had organized a system of "controlled sailings" for the French coal trade, and the excellent results led him to consider the practicality of ocean convoys.[67] The Board of Admiralty, however, argued that the shortage of destroyers and cruisers made ocean convoys impossible. In addition, it was Salter's view, that the First Sea Lord, Admiral Jellicoe, played a seminal and delaying role. Salter later observed:

> I have always been convinced myself that the principal reason for the delay in the introduction of convoy was that Admiral Jellicoe was very exhausted and

very disinclined to take over any further responsibility. To him convoys and their protection would mean a very definite additional responsibility, and one which he did not feel for the loss of dispersed vessels not in convoy.[68]

And finally, Admiralty figures mistakenly inflated the number of voyages which would require protection, estimating as many as 2,500 arrivals and a similar number of departures every week. In reality, as Salter noted, "the real number was anything like as small as 140."[69] As Lloyd George described it, this was "the fateful error in accountantship which nearly lost us the war."[70] However, initially nothing would alter the Admiralty opposition to convoys. At this point Henderson approached the Ministry of Shipping for precise information and Salter, impressed by the young naval officer, was very receptive. Salter nominated Norman Leslie, a member of the Baltic Exchange, and with the shipowners firm of Law and Leslie, then volunteering with the Requisitioning Branch, to head a new Convoy Section and act as Henderson's opposite number. In Salter's view Leslie "was competent, patriotic, devoted, and industrious, with good judgement in the practical making and implementing of merchant shipping policy under war conditions."[71] For his part, Leslie recalled: "I suppose Salter had learnt that I knew something about ships; anyhow he threw me at Henderson like a bone to a dog, and very indignant was I, because I was quite satisfied with my work and did not know what Henderson was after. When I found out what this extraordinary young man had in mind I caught fire with enthusiasm at once and worked out my side of it eagerly."[72] In Salter's Requisitioning Branch, Henderson discovered, by means of the ubiquitous card index, that the weekly totals of arrivals of ocean-going vessels at British ports indeed numbered no more than about 120 to 140, with similar figures for outward voyages. Such figures instantly made ocean convoys "a manageable problem." Even more, Henderson's proposals received an enthusiastic hearing at the Ministry of Shipping, where Salter "was convinced by the fact that all the younger officers who had seen the submarine war against merchant ships at sea and at close quarters were united and confident, and that the opposition came from those who had no such recent experience." In typical fashion, he then decided to take the initiative. He brought Henderson's case in favour of convoy directly to the Prime Minister, using what he himself described as "methods which, by the strictest code of departmental procedure, were perhaps open to criticism, but were, in the circumstances, I thought – and think – justifiable."[73] In turn, Lloyd George in his post-war memoirs was extremely generous in his praise of Salter's work on convoys.[74]

While the convoy controversy simmered in Whitehall, Henderson continued his research at the Ministry of Shipping and he thus acquired all the information necessary to organize a convoy system. Salter also went further in his determination to assist Henderson's plans. He ordered that a special section of the card index be set up "in which ships were arranged in groups of ports and routes, so that it was possible to state on any given day the numbers and names of all ships in any given port, or on passage on any given trade routes." A small staff was also organized at the Ministry of Shipping to collate all this information received from the card index, in order to transfer the data at once to the Admiralty or any other interested body. Such information enabled plans to be drawn up for the grouping of ships as to speed, arrangements for collecting vessels at loading ports, and dispersing them at ports of arrival.[75] Writing in 1921 about the convoy crisis, Salter paid adequate tribute to the "energy, initiative, and ability" of Henderson, and to the dedication of Leslie. Salter concluded, "little as it was known to the public, their work proved of capital importance in the conduct of the war."[76] In actual fact, Salter's receptiveness to Henderson's convoy ideas, and his opening the resources of the Requisitioning Branch to this officer, proved to be his primary contribution to a resolution of the crisis.

Throughout what Salter described as the "black fortnight of April," the convoy question was under intensive consideration by all concerned.[77] By early May Admiralty opposition was weakening under the combined pressure of the Prime Minister, most of the cabinet and the Ministry of Shipping. Finally, on 17 May the Admiralty organized a Convoy Committee to plan a scheme for ocean convoys. Leslie, representing the Ministry of Shipping, gave the committee the full benefit of the revised Ministry of Shipping card index, fully up to date in all respects. The Convoy Committee presented its report on 6 June, paying tribute to Henderson's initiatives, and proposed the establishment of a system of convoys on selected routes, beginning with "ocean-going Atlantic Trade."[78] Two days later an experimental trans-Atlantic convoy of 12 merchant ships arrived from Hampton Roads. Except for two vessels which had been forced to drop out because of their slow speed, all 10 ships had safely arrived. On 14 June Admiral Jellicoe, himself the most hardened opponent of the innovation, formally approved the Convoy Committee report, which was implemented and fully operational by September.[79] By the end of that month 2,095 merchant ships in 138 convoys had been escorted on the North Atlantic, South Atlantic and Gibraltar routes, with only 20 lost.[80] Although improvements were to be made during the course of the war, the recommendations of the Convoy Committee were still being carried out as they were written when convoys were discontinued on 12 November 1918. As for the results, with over 99% of nearly 17,000 ships escorted in ocean convoy arriving safely by the time of the armistice, Salter summarised the general elation noting, "The success of the new convoy system in protection was as striking as that of the new submarine campaign in its opening attack."[81] Later Salter wrote to Leslie that "The work of Henderson and yourself was certainly one of the crucial factors in the War though its importance was only recognized by a few who knew enough of the situation to see what it meant."[82]

It was ironic that Salter, who had so enthusiastically supported Henderson, was not at his desk in St. James's Park for the final approval of the convoy system. Instead, with the United States now a co-belligerent, having declared war on 6 April 1917, he found himself, in the company of Royden, on a shipping mission to Washington from June to August. Their mandate was to urge upon President Woodrow Wilson and his administration greater co-operation on shipping related questions, and particularly to convince American officials to increase shipbuilding capacity.[83] Although convoy protection was reducing shipping losses, there was still a shortage of replacement tonnage which had to remedied, partly by purchase abroad. In several memoranda prepared by Salter and Royden, and later brought to Wilson's attention, the seriousness of the tonnage shortage was detailed.[84] American entry into the war, however, convinced a strong lobby in Washington to argue for the retention under the American flag of all vessels, including some being built for Britain. The British dilemma, as Salter later wrote, was that "while America's entry into the war brought no substantial new tonnage immediately available for war service, her military effort began very soon to increase the general strain on the tonnage of the world."[85] In an effort to sort out such difficulties and generally plan for future wartime cooperation, the War Cabinet had agreed on 6 April that a special mission to Washington was required. Arthur J. Balfour, the Secretary of State for Foreign Affairs, was asked to head a multi-departmental delegation.[86] Among its numerous tasks was to argue the case both for pressing into service enemy tonnage interned in American ports, including 500,000 tons of German shipping, and "the need of developing to the full the shipbuilding capacity of the United States of America."[87] Accompanied by representatives of various ministries, Balfour arrived in Washington on 22 April and returned to London on 9 June.[88] It had been decided that, as Ministry of Shipping representatives, Salter and Royden would join the Balfour mission at a later stage and their departure was announced in the press on 2 June. The Times pointed out that "The decision to spare at the present time one of the chief advisors of the Controller [Royden] and one of the most able of the executive officers [Salter] is proof of the desire that the United States should be offered the very best assistance available in dealing with tonnage problems."[89] Despite their well laid plans, the departure of Salter and Royden proved eventful. Salter recalled:

> We started off in the evening from Liverpool in an American passenger ship, the Philadelphia, Royden and myself having two adjacent cabins on the boat-deck. In the early hours of the morning we were awakened by an enormous crash. We thought, of course, that it was a torpedo, though it was very early

for that. But in fact one of H.M. Cruisers had collided with us, striking just between Royden's cabin and mine and then smashing the boats all along the deck. We had to return and wait till hurried repairs could be effected.

The rest of the trans-Atlantic voyage, except for a brief submarine scare off the coast of Ireland, was uneventful.[90]

When Salter finally arrived in Washington on 6 June he could hardly have realized how significantly the American connection would figure in his life.[91] Ultimately, he would marry an American woman and count among his friends and colleagues a wide circle of Americans from all walks of life. Indeed, in the 1930's his reputation as an economist was second to none there, and hardly a year passed when he did not visit the United States to lecture or consult. This first visit, however, was relatively short and only partially successful. At the time Washington seemed, at least to Salter, "a chaotic scene." After three years of war, the British could at least pride themselves on some sort of organizational efficiency. In contrast, committees in Washington, springing up almost overnight, were ill defined and with unclear duties. "It was difficult in the extreme to discover," Salter observed, "what they were really doing beyond talking and where, if anywhere, was the official authority which, on any particular question, for a long time seemed always 'nothing', and to the second 'nowhere'."[92]

If organizational problems posed one form of difficulty, policy and personality conflicts made their task virtually impossible. The Wilson administration was gripped in "a heated controversy" about the nature of the American shipbuilding programme. Proponents of a revived wooden shipbuilding programme were opposed by advocates of steel construction. In addition, the chairman of the United States Shipping Board, William Denman, a lawyer from San Francisco, although soon replaced by the businessman Edward N. Hurley, was known to favour complete requisitioning of all British ships, some 150 vessels, being built under contract in American shipyards. By an executive order on 11 July, however, Wilson empowered the rival body, the Emergency Fleet Corporation, to requisition and oversee the construction, management and disposal of all American ships.[93] For a short time Salter was hopeful he might yet negotiate the delivery of the ships already ordered by Britain and under construction for British use. This became an option when both he and Royden gained a rare personal interview with President Wilson on 26 July. Salter and Royden stressed "the necessity for shipbuilding by America on a scale much larger than any hitherto indicated" and Britain's urgent need to obtain "American tonnage suitable for trans-Atlantic trade." They made a specific appeal to Wilson, without success, to avoid the requisitioning of British ships under construction. In conclusion, Wilson expressed his "personal interest" in the shipbuilding requirements, but also outlined the difficulties involved in expanding the programme, including the scarcity of raw materials.[94] Salter later observed that given Wilson's tendency to be "withdrawn, reserved and shunning personal discussion," he was pleased to know that he was afterwards know "as one of the select number of foreign visitors who had 'talked with the President.'"[95] In his first ever appearance before the War Cabinet on 22 August, Salter spoke about this interview. He stated:

> The President was at that time in favour of requisitioning the ships, but had come to that conclusion under pressure from Mr. Denman, the ex-head of the American Shipping Board, and on grounds that were not really relevant, and he had promised to reconsider the question. It must be remembered that there was an element in the United States of America that was very jealous of our Mercantile Marine, and also that the United States Army and Navy were anxious to carry their troops and stores to France in their own ships.[96]

Indeed, throughout July and early August both Salter and Royden had put up, what Lord Northcliffe, the newspaper proprietor who headed the British War Mission in Washington after Balfour's return, described to Lloyd George as a "splendid fight" to save the British ships.[97] Northcliffe added that the two shipping experts were "essential to this Mission" and urged Lloyd George not to recall them.[98] Nonetheless, on 3 August the requisitioning order was issued, which confiscated all vessels either contracted for or under construction. On 22 August the cabinet contemplated various approaches to avoid the requisition, including allowing the Americans to retain ownership after the war. As well, an appeal based on the American "sense of justice and goodwill" was made.[99] It proved useless and Britain eventually lost 150 ships of 960,800 tons deadweight.[100] Nonetheless, Salter and Royden were successful in their meetings with Denman and Frank Polk, counsellor to the State Department, in negotiating a reduction of the high steamship rates, and the eventual inclusion of all vessels flying allied flags world-wide.[101]

If one part of the mission had proved a failure, the loss of the replacement tonnage, there still remained what Salter later described as "the principal objective of persuading America to organize a vast ship-building programme." After careful study of needs and resources, he and Royden concluded Britain required from the Americans a yearly target of six million tons deadweight.[102] The Americans had never before built ships on this scale, producing for example in 1913 a mere 276,000 tons gross of merchant ships, as compared with Britain's 2,000,000.[103] But Salter and Royden were convinced the figure was realistic, particularly if a new facility for prefabricated ships was built at Hog Island on the Delaware River south of Philadelphia. Salter recalled:

We had at first a sceptical though friendly reception, but at last a sympathetic hearing, and in the end the always latent American enthusiasm for aiming high if you aim at all was fired. After many soundings we came to the conclusion that if the British Cabinet made a formal appeal for this figure, it was likely to succeed.

With Royden remaining in New York until the end of the year to carry on negotiations with Hurley, Salter returned to London where he had argued this case before the War Cabinet on 22 August. As a result, and following a personal appeal by Lloyd George to Wilson, the United States did commit itself to build up to the Salter-Royden figures.[104] The Hog Island yard soon became known as "the eighth wonder of the world," and Hurley noted soon after the end of the war that it "constituted the most remarkable achievement in shipbuilding that the world has ever seen."[105] Originally a desolate swamp, the first keel was laid at the yard as early as 12 February 1918, with the first ship launched on 5 August. Eventually serviced by 80 miles of railway track, 250 buildings, 3,000,000 feet of underground wiring, and a hospital, the 900-acre yard could hold 78 ships under construction at once. At peak periods, a keel could be laid every five and one-half days. The full figure of six millions tons, had the war lasted, would have been reached by 1919.[106] Failure in the short term to safeguard replacement tonnage, therefore, was more than outweighed by success in the long term. The latter guaranteed, as Salter put it "that the war would not be lost for want of shipping."[107]

Salter returned from the United States relieved to be escaping "the sleepless nights in the airless sticky heat of the old Shoreham Hotel." He later reflected that he was certainly much better briefed on American matters and customs than before his mission. "It was to a novice a disturbing, exhausting, but exciting and fascinating environment in which to work," he noted. He had made the acquaintance of Raymond B. Stevens, a former Congressman and vice-chairman of the United States Board, Frank Polk, later a close friend and legal advisor to the future Lady Salter, and Franklin D. Roosevelt, then assistant secretary to the Navy. In early August Salter left Washington with an appreciation of "the combination of generosity and suspicion"' which formed the backdrop to all the future Anglo-American negotiations he was to engage upon.[108] His return to London also coincided with the end of the third year of World War for Britain. It led him to a series of conclusions, in which he argued:

(1) that for a long-continued war America's shipping contribution would be decisive; (2) that her building resources were such as to make a building programme of 6,000,000 tons [deadweight, i.e., about 4,000,000 tons gross] a year, a practicable proposition, and that building of these dimensions, once attained, should

be an effective counter to the submarine campaign on the rate of losses at that time; (3) that no alleviation of the Allied problem in shipping could be expected from American ships at any rate until the spring of 1918; (4) that it was of the utmost importance, therefore, that a renewed effort should be made to enforce such restrictions on the British imports as would give a margin for the now desperate needs of France and Italy, and that for this purpose the continuous work of a committee with Cabinet authority was necessary; and (5) that once this had been achieved, national action required to be supplemented by an Allied organization to deal with both shipping and supplies.[109]

It was a series of short-term problems, however, which were to lead to the significant long-term solutions formulated by Salter after his American visit, particularly the need for an allied organization to co-ordinate shipping with supply requirements. The "ominous and menacing" fact, he later observed, was that the actual pressure on shipping was at a wartime high. More tonnage was lost in the first ten months of 1917 than in the previous two and a half years of war. This pressure was all the more dangerous as it coincided with anticipated food shortages throughout the coming months in Britain, France and Italy. This combination of reduced tonnage capacity and "a real danger of starvation in the European Allied countries," he added, had a momentous impact on allied supply programmes in general, and his career in particular.[110] The emergence of this tonnage and supply crisis spurred closer and better co-operation between the Allies. Both Britain and France maintained national organizations designed to relate tonnage to requirements. As well, the habit of weighing the comparative value of different supplies, of munitions against wheat, was already ingrained. The remaining problem was that inter-allied co-operation was "very tentative and incomplete."[111] No central authority existed which was charged "with the general adjustment of tonnage to the requirements of the Allies as whole."[112] Finally, the entry of the United States into the war, and the inevitable heavy demands which followed on assistance from the United States by Britain, Italy and France, demanded organizational co-ordination.[113]

The necessity to convert separate national control systems into an inter-allied organization became an obsession for Salter. This is not to suggest he had a pioneering vision, not usually part of his character, of allied cooperation applicable in a post-war economic or political arena. Rather he realized a short-term problem demanded a short-term and effective solution. This was the sort of situation to which he could apply all his organizational and administrative talents and he set to the problem with energy and determination. So impressive would be his success, that it was later suggested "that the great progress made in the direction of co-ordination was due, in large measure, to the appointment of Mr. J.A. Salter, Director of Requisitioning, as Secretary to the Allied Maritime Transport Committee, and Chairman of the Executive."[114] The shape of inter-allied cooperation stemmed from a series of meetings and initiatives in which Salter played a decisive role. Working closely with Sir Percy Bates, Director of the Commercial Services Branch, Salter attempted on 30 September a complete analysis of the tonnage position for the next six months. His purpose was that of "directly assisting immediate executive action." Similar estimates were made in France and Italy in advance of upcoming Allied consultations.[115] Early in October he was in almost continuous consultation with Sir John Beale, Chairman of the Wheat Executive, the sole existing inter-allied committee, established on 11 October 1916 to purchase, allocate and transport all cereals, John Anderson, then secretary to the Ministry of Shipping, Bates, and most importantly, a young Frenchman, Jean Monnet.[116] The latter, London representative of the Commission internationale de ravitaillement, established on 18 August 1914 to co-ordinate allied purchases of military supplies, recalled these early days of an association which was to last into the 1970s:

> Salter was the same age as myself, and he had the same attitude towards what we both regarded as common problems. At that time, the problems were those of organizing the Allied war effort; later, those of organizing the peace at Geneva; and later those of war again, in 1940. It was through Salter's conception of public service, which he made the subject of his memoirs after having held high political office, that I came to understand the quality of the British civil service.

In turn, Salter recognized a kindred soul in Monnet, and both sensed in the other the "inner circle" of reputation syndrome. At an informal dinner soon afterwards, Monnet, Anderson and Salter determined "that the thing could be done, and that we would do it."[117] Together they sketched out a plan for an "Allied Maritime Transport Committee" (AMTC) with its own executive (AMTE). Such executives for wheat, oils, sugar and meats already existed. But, according to Monnet's account, "a transport executive would be something altogether more ambitious: it would supervise all Allied and neutral ships, their specifications, their movements, and their cargoes. A continuing inventory of this sort was only imaginable by means of the extensive information network that was at Salter's command, and which he would bring to the AMTE if we could succeed in getting him appointed Secretary-General." Most important was the fact that such an executive would centralise supply programmes and adjust them in the light of available shipping.[118]

Throughout October discussions were carried on between British officials, Italian representatives and a French delegation led by Étienne Clémentel, the Minister of Commerce from 1915-1919 and a passionate advocate of inter-allied economic co-operation.[119] Agreement was at last reached on 3 November whereby the three Allies consented "to accept the responsibility of providing the tonnage that may be required *proportionally to their respective means of transport* with or without the help of the United States."[120] Although the agreement was in fact limited to tonnage for the carriage of food, the principle hinted at "an Allied examination of all Allied demands and Allied tonnage."[121] "Today's agreement is a beginning," Clémentel said to Monnet at the conclusion of the meeting. "Go and see Salter, and work out proposals for a first Allied body to deal with transport. Then we'll gradually enlarge its scope."[122] Salter, too, set his sights on what he regarded as the agreement's wider significance. In fact, such a body already existed on paper, having been planned at the dinner between Salter, Monnet and Anderson. They held further consultations and made additional refinements, bringing in Bates as well. By 17 November an historic document was completed above the signature of Salter. Simply entitled, "Note as to Form of Co-operation Between the Allies, November 17th 1917," Salter argued firstly that there was in practice no workable distinction between food and other inter-allied requirements. Secondly, preliminary thought was given to the actual machinery of inter-allied co-operation. He suggested the model of the Wheat Executive be extended to cover all essential imports. Once such inter-allied executives were operational, they should be closely integrated with a clear programme for the allocation and direction of available shipping, in turn attuned to a programme of essential requirements.[123] Leading members of the British government, including Lord Reading, Winston Churchill, Lord Robert Cecil and Lord Milner were immediately given copies of the note. Although the note was pessimistic with regard to American participation, this soon proved unwarranted. Colonel Edward M. House, Wilson's close advisor, and Bainbridge Colby, a member of the United States Shipping Board, were at that time on a mission to London. To the delight of all concerned, the note was found generally acceptable on 20 November on behalf of the United States.[124]

Encouraged in his efforts, Salter continued to further elaborate on his proposed inter-allied organization. On 21 November he completed another part of the proposal, entitled "The Shipping Situation and American Assistance." This began with the appropriate emphasis on the "gravity" of the shipping situation, which, he carefully argued, only the United States could alleviate. With regard to the form of allied co-operation, he enumerated three precise objectives:

(a) to make the most economical use of tonnage under the control of all the Allies;
(b) to allot that tonnage as between the different needs of the Allies in such a way as to add most to the general war effort; and

(c) to adjust the programmes of requirements of the different Allies in such a way as to bring them within the scope of the possible carrying power of the tonnage available.

This was the stage which Salter's thinking had reached on one of the most pressing questions regarding "a new Allied control organization."[125] Once again his views received maximum exposure. They had been intended for use by the Ministry of Shipping at a forthcoming Allied conference, scheduled for Paris from 29 November to 3 December. Nonetheless, Sir Joseph Maclay sent the memorandum to Lloyd George on 23 November, citing Salter as the author and commending it as "a remarkably able document."[126] As well, it subsequently formed the basis of discussions throughout the Paris meetings. Salter himself related what in fact transpired:

I attached myself to the British party, taking my memorandum with me. And then came a great stroke of luck. On the journey from London I got into conversation with Lord Reading, and full of my problem poured out my heart to him. He listened with sympathy and the quick apprehension which was so characteristic of him. 'I think you're right; how are you going to put it through; would you like me to handle it at the conference?' I jumped at the offer, and when the time came he steered it through with the consummate skill of a great advocate.[127]

It was Salter's impression that the Paris conference, at which 15 powers were represented, proved to be "perhaps the most impressive expression the war had seen of both the range and unity of the Allied effort."[128] The conference divided into two main sections, military and economic, and into several specialised committees. The most important of the latter was the "Special Committee for Maritime Transport and General Imports," on which Salter represented Britain, along with delegates from Italy, France and the United States. According to the "Official Report" of the three-day conference, the discussions proceeded smoothly on the basis of Salter's 21 November memorandum, and it was agreed the United States should aim at increasing its annual shipbuilding programme from six million to nine million tons deadweight. The three objectives of Allied co-operation, as previously outlined by Salter, were also endorsed. The question of how this might be achieved proved more contentious. Giving executive power over a common pool of tonnage to an international board was ruled out as too complicated. Instead, this statement of principle was adopted: "The problem of the allocation of tonnage is largely a problem of securing that the different requirements which make demands upon tonnage should be adjusted in the fairest and best way, and these requirements can only be restricted by the experts in each class of commodities." Fortunately, the committee then went further into the pioneering field of inter-allied organization. It declared that each Allied country should designate one or two ministers, with one or two special delegates from the United States, who would be "responsible towards their respective Governments for the execution of the agreements arrived at and who will meet in conference as Allied representatives as may be necessary from time to time," in Paris or London, "either on their own motion or at the request of the Executive Departments." It was further resolved that the appropriate ministers and representatives of Britain, France, Italy, and the United States, "shall take steps to secure the necessary exchange of information, and co-ordination of policy and effort, establishing a permanent office and staff for the purpose." On 3 December, at the conclusion of the Paris conference, all the recommendations of the "Special Committee" were adopted. The mandate to appoint "Ministers and delegates" and organize a "permanent office and staff" gave birth to the Allied Maritime Transport Council and its Executive. It was to prove, as Salter later noted, "a novel, notable and successful experiment in the technique of Allied administration."[129]

Immense as was the significance of the Paris conference, the situation early in the New Year with regard to shipping remained anxious. To officials like Salter, "disaster was indeed within a few days." As early as 2 November 1917, in a memorandum, he had cautioned that "the estimated importing power of the ships available for 1918 was 8 million tons less than for 1917," and advised severe cutbacks in imports. Indeed, during this period, central stocks of sugar in Britain were reduced to a mere ten days' consumption, while France had only eight days' supply of steel. January 1918 proved the cruelest month. Poor harvests in Britain, France and Italy held out the prospect of starvation. Munitions required for upcoming military campaigns had been ordered from the United States, but with little hope of the required shipping. As Salter put it, "there were no more ships for food at the expense of munitions, or for munitions at the expense of food."[130] After a lengthy discussion during a cabinet meeting on 24 January, attended by Salter, his proposals to reduce munitions imports in order to maintain the flow of cereals were reluctantly accepted. As Lloyd George stated, "Food was our first line of defence."[131] This decision was later to be confirmed by a further cabinet meeting on 19 February.[132] Another option for relief was to try and increase the supply of wheat from the nearest source, the United States. To achieve this objective, Salter, Beale and Bates crossed the Channel to Paris to arrange a joint appeal from Allied ministers. The agony of the situation remained vividly embedded in Salter's mind:

> Paris and Versailles, as we arrived, were beautiful as in the days of peace in the splendour of sun and brilliant weather; most of the comforts of life seemed

still available; there was little to suggest the hidden stress except the darkening of the streets in the early evening. But coming to find some relief for food, we were at once met with a new crisis: a threatened shortage of the coal on which transport for military operations depended. In the meantime ships had to be allotted to one service or another with results that those taking the decisions could not possibly forecast. Any one of the current decisions of the day's work might be the one that would bring the crash. It was like hearing the tapping of the sappers constructing a hostile mine which the rest of those who were threatened failed to detect and waiting for the last ominous silence before the explosion.

That appeal was finally worked out, sent to Washington, and generously answered by the United States.[133]

As far as Salter was concerned, however, the formation of the proposed inter-allied transport organization could not come soon enough. On 15 February an informal meeting of representatives of Britain, France, Italy and the United States was held at the Foreign Office. Lord Robert Cecil, Minister of Blockade, and Salter represented Britain. Acting as chairman, Cecil explained that he had called the meeting to plan the opening session of the new Council, discuss preliminary questions and arrange staffing. The name Allied Maritime Transport Council was adopted and its primary function, it was agreed, was "to watch over the general conduct of Allied transport." To this end the AMTC, later nicknamed the "Shipping Commissariat," would secure relevant information from the four major Allies, enabling it to adjust "programmes of imports to the carrying capacity of the available tonnage ... and in making the most advantageous allocation and disposition of the tonnage under their control in accordance with the urgency of war needs." It was further agreed that the permanent executive organization, the Allied Maritime Transport Executive, should consist of four national divisions, French, Italian, American and British, and that the secretary of the Council should also be the head of one of these four sections, a position Salter later filled. To assist with co-ordination, two further international committees were formed, for tonnage and for imports. As well, 20 additional committees were eventually formed on the model of the Wheat Executive. Their purpose was to collate the programmes of import requirements and advise on reductions in imports or the acquisition of further tonnage. Separate committees were formed for such commodities as wool, cotton and paper. An inter-allied Food Council oversaw the work of committees for such commodities as sugar, cereals and meats, while the Munitions Council concentrated for example on nitrates, chemicals and steel. Finally, "Mr. J.A. Salter, on the proposal of M. de Fleuriau [the French representative], was asked to undertake the duties of Secretary, this arrangement being provisional and subject to confirmation by the Council at its first meeting." Salter's first task for the next meeting scheduled for early March was to draft a press release, outlining the function of the Council.[134]

Salter's appointment as secretary of the Council, and then chairman of the Executive, was due to a combination of factors. He was in the first place eminently qualified to fill both posts. His experience with shipping questions, and his recognized ability to fashion consensus out of divergence, were necessary talents for inter-allied work. Secondly, he had crucial French approval. Monnet recalled that the Transport Executive, first conceived and even named during the November dinner party, was an enormously ambitious project, whose success depended on getting Salter appointed.[135] It is not surprising, therefore, that the French representative proposed Salter's name. The first meeting of the Allied Maritime Transport Council, originally scheduled to take place in Paris, met and was formally constituted at Lancaster House, in London on 11 March and continued in session until the 14th.[136] Besides the members of the Council – ministers from Britain (Cecil and Maclay), France (Clémentel and M. Loucheur), Italy (Signor Crespi and O.S. Orlando), and an American representative (Raymond B. Stevens) – some 30 other officials were present. In the course of the sessions, chaired by Cecil, the recommendations of the 15 February meeting were approved, and Salter was officially appointed secretary to the Council and head of the British Division. The new discussion centred on consideration of a provisional balance sheet of Allied import requirements versus tonnage under their control, revealing the serious nature of the shipping tonnage deficit. It was left to the new permanent Secretariat of the Council to examine in detail the import programmes of the Allies in view of the drastic reductions required by this deficit. A press notice, prepared by Salter, provided details of the new organization and its first meeting. This emphasized that the purpose of the new Council was "to supervise the general conduct of Allied transport, in order to obtain the most effective use of tonnage for the prosecution of the war, while leaving each nation responsible for the management of the tonnage under its control."[137] Summarising this historic meeting, Salter recorded: "By the middle of March, therefore, the new organization, though undeveloped and incomplete, was already plunged into the midst of the main problems which were to occupy it during the following six crucial months."[138]

During this period Salter worked in a dual capacity, with a double work load, in two separate offices. He continued to preside, as Director of Ship Requisitioning, at the Ministry of Shipping in St James's Park. At the same time, as secretary to the AMTC and chairman of its Executive, he had an additional office in Lancaster House, a private mansion requisitioned by the government. Later acquired by Lord Leverhulme, Lancaster House was given to the nation and was used for a short time as the home of the London Museum. Salter then discovered in conversation with Lord Leverhulme that he had almost missed being invited to the dedication ceremonies.[139] By July Lancaster House became home to the permanent organization of the AMTC, and its four national divisions – British, French, Italian and American. However, the American division remained directly responsible only to the American delegate, Raymond B. Stevens, soon joined by George Rublee, who worked in Lancaster House. The other three national divisions were controlled by officials who were responsible to their national representatives on the AMTC. In the particular case of Britain, there was no clear line between British officials in the AMTC and the adjacent Ministry of Shipping. In fact, the entire Shipping Intelligence Section was transferred to Lancaster House, thereby allowing Allied access to the card index system. For practical purposes each division was separate with its own staff for private communication with its government. A central secretariat, composed of all four nationalities, and divested of any national point of view, acted in a secretarial capacity to the AMTE.[140] The entire organization was unified, and all adjustments of policy and action made, by the creation of the AMTE. This was composed of the heads of the Italian (Professor Bernardo Attolico) and French (Jean Monnet) divisions, together with the second American delegate, George Rublee. Salter now acted simultaneously as Chairman of the Executive and Secretary of the Council, in addition to being head of the British division. The Council itself was only to meet four times before the Armistice, in March, April and August, and in October. The AMTE met much more frequently, and always acted as liaison between the various governments on shipping questions. This Executive was in a short time to prove a remarkably novel form of international co-operation.[141] Its members had to perform the difficult and delicate task of working, in Salter's words, in a "dual personal capacity, international in relation to their own country, national in relation to other countries."[142] It was a situation which made partners out of competitors and formed a successful experiment in international administration.

By late March 1918 the Executive machinery was already running smoothly. But only a handful of officials, Salter among them, realized how precarious was the central balance sheet. The existing tonnage deficit, already severe, was further aggravated by the success of a German offensive on the Western Front launched on 21 March. The German advance hindered the output from the Pas-de-Calais mines, France's principal coal supply, and its transport by rail to Paris. Salter privately described the situation as "a serious one." The AMTE immediately decided to arrange for 100,000 tons of British coal to be diverted to Italy to make up for the deficit caused by the shortage of promised French coal.[143] When the AMTC met on 23 April for its second session, therefore, the general situation had changed for the worse. Paris was chosen as the venue because French Ministers were reluctant to visit London in view of the deteriorating military situation. Some of the British representatives to the session, Salter included, had to reach Paris by road from Boulogne, while others took 30 hours to travel by rail from the coast to Paris.[144] This was an appropriate preface to the major problems facing the Council. It had before it a report, dated 20 April and signed by Salter, on the recent activities of the AMTE. The first item of discussion was the urgent French and Italian coal situation in light of the German advance. Additional supplies, which Britain could provide, depended unfortunately on providing additional tonnage. This latter question, in turn, hinged on the revised balance sheets of imports and tonnage for 1918 prepared by the AMTE. This starkly revealed a deficit of eight and a half million tons of imports for which there was no shipping capacity. Restoring the equilibrium between tonnage and imports required at the minimum a "drastic revision of the import programmes." The Council, therefore, directed its attention to this urgent situation, at the same time trying to safeguard supplies of vital military requirements. To facilitate import reductions, it was agreed that so-called Programme Committees, modelled on the Wheat Executive, should be appointed for other essential commodities. Where requirements exceeded capacity, the AMTC would thus be able to discuss reductions with the committees before making recommendations to the Allied governments. The Council also entrusted the AMTE with direct control of some 500,000 tons of neutral shipping which the Allies had been able to charter, and responsibility for finding additional shipping for the Belgian relief programme. Finally, the most serious new factor in the shipping position for 1918 was considered, namely, the shipping requirements of the United States army. At the end of 1917 the AMTC had anticipated that the United States would be able to supply the tonnage to meet deficiencies in European imports. This judgement was based on the expectation that only one million American troops would be transported to France by the end of 1918. As a result of the March offensive, however, that figure would eventually double. The additional burden of transporting and supplying such a force was a challenge of which the Council was forewarned in April.[145] The second session of the AMTC thus adjourned, with the AMTE given the task to get on as best it could. The Times noted that "the proceedings were entirely unanimous, and showed that in all respects the associated Governments and their representatives were moved by a common purpose."[146]

Salter returned to Lancaster House in London in a mood of grim desperation. "I was with him the whole of that terrible time," Gertrude Caton Thompson recalled. "He, of all men, knew the knife-edge between victory and defeat, but remained as calm and determined as in earlier days. I was proud to serve with."[147] On the basis of military assessments which he had gathered in Paris, Salter believed that the German offensive would soon place the Channel ports in enemy hands, "in which case we should have to feed London by sending ships round the north of Scotland. I hurried back," he wrote, "to work out what that would mean for all our shipping programmes, and to make a hurried and desperate scheme which happily it was never necessary to put into force."[148] There still remained, however, the tasks of the Council's Executive, under Salter's guidance, to implement the decisions of the AMTC. This was to prove so successful that it was found unnecessary to summon another full Council meeting until August. Among Salter's priorities was the recommendation to form Programme Committees, one which the Cabinet approved on 23 May.[149] These were to remain firmly rooted in the respective national control systems of Britain, France, Italy and the United States. However, as Salter explained, the work was now "co-ordinated and infused with an international spirit." The Programme Committees varied a great deal in their powers and got to work slowly and unequally. Ultimately, there were to be established nine committees for such imported commodities as wool, petroleum and cotton; a further seven committees essential in the manufacture of munitions were grouped in April under a Munitions Council; and four further committees were established in July under an umbrella organization known as the Food Council. Neither the Programme Committees, nor the Food and Munitions Councils, were as such subordinate organs of the AMTC. But the dominant position of the AMTC was reinforced by its central role in balancing supplies and shipping.[150] This was precisely the problem faced in supplying fuel to continental Allies. Despite the German advance, the AMTE managed to secure shipments of coal to Italy which almost equalled the total originally contemplated of 600,000 tons a month. As well, every ton of coal produced in Britain and destined for France reached its destination. With regard to Belgian relief, both Britain and the United States shared the responsibility for shipping additional emergency cargoes of miscellaneous stores. The total tonnage almost equalled the full programme. The problem of how to allocate the neutral pool tonnage was also resolved. Between May and August, 176 such ships were allotted in accordance with an elaborate plan designed to satisfy all concerned. Finally, the AMTE was forced to pay considerable attention to the ramifications of the transport of United States troops to Europe. The increasing demand by the Allied military authorities for American troops, however, was beginning to have repercussions for the AMTE. It was understood that the ultimate size of the United States army in France, given the limits to American shipping, would increasingly depend upon the release of tonnage designated for imports. Salter directed, therefore, that a survey be made of this problem in anticipation of future supply difficulties.[151]

As the fourth year of the World War drew to a close, Salter attempted, for the benefit of the forthcoming third session of the AMTC, to assess the general shipping position. At the heart of any analysis, he pointed out, was the military situation in general, and the American army programmes in particular. As a rough indication of what this meant, he had calculated on 23 July that "For every 5,000 tons of imports to which we agree, we must face the fact that we thereby reduce the number of American troops in France by 1,000." He could not help but conclude that the tonnage situation for the rest of 1918 remained "very uncertain," with the import programmes showing "a large excess over carrying power." What he emphasized equally was that the ability to handle both shipping and commodities was now highly developed, and emergencies, as they arose, could be controlled.[152] "The corner was turned. Safety was in sight, though not attained," was how he summarised his experiences after four years of wartime administration.[153] Salter was indeed looking towards the end of hostilities. Rarely did he speculate, at least on paper, far in advance of problems at hand. Yet that is precisely what he began to do amidst his other activities. On 19 April he had analysed the prospective shipping position after the war. He first enumerated the factors – the need for reconstruction, the revival of emigration and the tourist trade, large-ship repair contracts and a revival of consumption – which would stimulate the shipping industry. Against this he warned that it would be mistaken to assume that the economy as a whole would "jump rapidly back to peace standards of consumption and peach methods of supply." Shipping specifically would be affected by the immediate release of numerous vessels from wartime duties. By the end of the war building would exceed losses of ships. For this reason, he put it on record that "there is likely to be an immense and immediate decline in freight rates as soon as peace is declared, and a decline, though not so sensational, in value of ships." Salter concluded, "I have been of this opinion for some years, although until recently I believe I have been in a minority."[154] The situation in the long term was to develop, in fact, precisely as he had anticipated.

The AMTC met for its long-delayed third session, this time at Lancaster House in London, from 29-30 August. The meeting was primarily designed to deal with an impasse which threatened the organization so carefully constructed since March, leaving the AMTE, as Salter termed it, was in "serious shock."[155] The newly created Food Council had submitted its food requirements for the 1918-1919 cereal year (which ran from 1 September to 31 August) and had asked for the additional import of almost four and a half million tons of cereals and the requisite shipping, for a total of 13.5 million tons. The AMTE for its part had anticipated a substantial reduction after the improved harvests of 1918. Salter undertook the delicate task of negotiating the matter with the Food Council, asking on 30 July for a policy of no increase in consumption. The Food Council refused to budge, arguing that Salter's recommendations would harm civilian morale. He again replied that the choice was simple, guns or butter, but he also suggested a compromise solution, involving a division of food requirements into priority and non-priority commodities.[156] That was the position which Salter took before the AMTC on 29 August. The potential shipping deficit was further compounded by additional requests for commodities and military supplies advanced by France, Italy and the United States. The combination of all such demands would have paralyzed the war effort. Not surprisingly the AMTC chose to accept the Salter compromise on the demands of the Food Council but to ask for further study on the allocation of shipping.[157] Salter afterwards summarised the general outlook: "with 2,000,000 tons less of shipping, the shipping authorities were asked to carry more food, more munitions, and the supplies of a new army. The position, therefore, was very grave and might have seemed hopeless."[158]

The AMTE was thus left to deal with the various issues on which the AMTC had deferred making decisions. At the heart of the situation was the fact that projected imports continued to exceed available tonnage. The difficulties were further compounded by the United States demand for help with the transportation of its troops and military supplies. In effect, by the summer of 1918 the United States "had become a debit rather than a credit item in the tonnage balance sheet."[159] The provision of transport, simple carrying power, was the last obstacle that stood between the Allies and victory. The climax of the authority and usefulness of both the AMTC and the AMTE was reached in the autumn of 1918. Between the end of the third session of the AMTC and the opening on 30 September, at Lancaster House, of the fourth and final peacetime session, the AMTE worked on its "Memorandum as to Policy to Govern the Allocation of Tonnage in Cereal Year 1918-1919." In preparing its proposals for the fifth year of the war, the AMTE was in fact working at its best, in a well-developed manner, with a trained and experienced secretariat and staff at its disposal. In addition, the statistical departments of the four national divisions now presented a unanimous estimate as to the imports which the Allies could transport. After an exhaustive analysis, the AMTE recommended what it termed, "Munitions in Winter: Food Afterwards." It was argued a general preference should be given to the transport of munitions and army supplies, with that order of priority being reversed by the spring when there would be a substantial improvement in the whole allied tonnage position.[160] When the issue was debated in the Cabinet on 6 September no firm decision could be reached other than leaving the "13.5 million standard" for the time being while plans for a reduction were being implemented.[161] In preparation for a cabinet discussion on 1 October both the Food Controller and the Shipping Controller submitted papers arguing their respective cases.[162] Salter attended that cabinet, but made no recorded comment and the meeting ended with a compromise of 10 million tons of shipping allocated each to food and munitions for the first 6 months of the coming cereal year.[163]

The focus of attention at the fourth session of the AMTC, from 30 September to 2 October, fell naturally on the AMTE memorandum. It was a tribute indeed to the AMTE's work that the recommendations were approved virtually without change and America's allocation of tonnage was increased. This was clearly done on the understanding, given by the United States Secretary of War who attended the session, Newton D. Baker, that his country would co-operate fully with the AMTE and abide by its decisions. It was further agreed that the United States would repay the assistance given in supplying its armies, by the allocation of new American ships to the allied import programmes. This confidence in American co-operation made it feasible to accept the major recommendation of the AMTE to give priority to munitions over food. The AMTE was instructed finally to issue a public statement explaining the need for civilian sacrifices during the coming winter, in order to allow maximum American troops to be transported to France for the 1919 military campaign.[164] It was then Salter's duty to inform the respective authorities, the Food Council and the Transport Council that until the spring of 1919 munitions would take priority over food.[165] Even as the AMTE made plans to implement these decisions, the Central powers showed signs of collapse. A request for an armistice was advanced on 6 October and signed on 11 November. The AMTE shelved its public statement in the knowledge that no further wartime sacrifices would be required. In his usual report on the work of the AMTE, Salter already looked towards post-armistice issues, including "the need for feeding liberated areas, etc., and possibly enemy countries, and the repatriation of troops."[166]

The war at sea, of the submarine against the merchant ship – the battle with which Salter was so intimately connected – had in fact been over since early October. It was a struggle which had been waged and won independently of the wider conflict. In Salter's estimate, the success of the struggle at sea was due to a combination of factors. These included the introduction of the convoy system, the expansion of American shipbuilding, and of course the economies in transport effected by inter-allied control systems and their integration into the AMTC. Yet, while in its short existence the results achieved by the AMTC "sufficiently striking," the armistice ironically "exempted the Allied organization from its final test."[167] This was a factor which would have a decisive impact on Salter's post-war prospects. In the meantime, Salter could look back and write, "This last year has been the most interesting & (in spite of the anxiety) one of the most enjoyable I've ever had."[168]

Endnotes

1. Quoted in Wilson Harris, <u>Life So Far</u> (1954), 101-102. The anecdote was also recounted in <u>The Star</u>, 14 Nov. 1918, in an article entitled "The Man Who Won the War." It was written by "Alpha of the Plough," a pseudonym for A.G. Gardiner, according to Stephen Koss, <u>Fleet Street Radical: A.G. Gardiner and</u>

the Daily News (1973), 7. A similar view was expressed in Harold Nicolson, Dwight Morrow (1935), 224-225.
2. Salter to Anderson, 3 Nov. 1915, "Personnel File, Salter, J.A.," Ministry of Health, Establishment Division, NA-UK, MH107/11.
3. Salter, Memoirs, 74.
4. Harris, Not So Humdrum, 194-195, Allen, Morant, 290.
5. Salter, Memoirs, 74.
6. The Times, 19 Aug. 1914.
7. Mary Agnes Hamilton, Mary Macarthur: A Biographical Sketch (1926), 136-137, Kathleen Woodward, Queen Mary: A Life and Intimate Study (1928), 178-188.
8. Hamilton, Mary Macarthur, 138-139, Markham, Friendship's Harvest, 90-91, Lord Riddell, Lord Riddell's War Diary, 1914-1918 (1933), 12-13.
9. Hamilton, Mary Macarthur, 138-139.
10. Markham, Friendship's Harvest, 92-93.
11. "Feminine Technique in Administration," Salter Papers, File 1, Anecdotes and Incidents.
12. Hamilton, Mary Macarthur, 139. See also Salter to Violet Markham, 24 Jan. 1915, Violet Markham Papers, 25/73, BLPES, London.
13. Central Committee on Women's Employment, Interim Report Cd. 7748 (1915). 1-42, Irene Osgood Andrews and Margarett A. Hobbs, Economic Effects of the World War Upon Women and Children in Great Britain (1921), 23-27.
14. "Personnel File, Salter, J.A.," Ministry of Health, Establishment Division, NA-UK, MH107/11.
15. Arthur Salter, Allied Shipping Control: An Experiment in International Administration (1921),1, 39-40, Salter, "A Civil Servant's Career," The Listener, 16(19 Aug. 1936), 346. Allied Shipping Control was a volume in the Carnegie Endowment for International Peace's economic and social history of the World War.
16. Salter, Allied Shipping Control, 40-41, C. Ernest Fayle, History of the Great War Based on Official Documents, Seaborne Trade, vol. 2, From the Opening of the Submarine Campaign to the Appointment of the Shipping Controller (1923) 44-46.
17. H.C. Debs. vol. 69, 15 Feb. 1915, col. 925.
18. L.F. Goldsmid, "Report on Shipping Control, 1914-1918," part VI, chapter I, 10-11, NA-UK, MT25/87/1921, which also contains parts IV-V. Parts I and III are in NA-UK, MT25/86/1921 and part II is in NA-UK, MT25/67/29597. This massive typescript is an authoritative account by a former member of the Transport Department.
19. Salter, Allied Shipping Control, 43.

20. Salter, Memoirs, 77.
21. Salter, Memoirs, 74-75.
22. Salter, Memoirs, 75, 81-82.
23. Ministry of Shipping Minute, 31 Mar. 1920, NA-UK, MT25/37/30382/1920, Salter, Allied Shipping Control, 55-56.
24. "Sea Power: The Direction of Shipping in Time of War," The Listener, 16(28 Oct. 1936), 795.
25. Salter, Allied Shipping Control, 43-48.
26. Fayle, Seaborne Trade, vol. 2, 46.
27. H.C. Debs., vol. 69, 15 Feb. 1915, cols. 939-947.
28. Martin Gilbert, Winston S. Churchill, vol. 3, 1914-1916 (1971), 282-284.
29. Salter, Memoirs, 77-79.
30. Gilbert, Churchill, vol. 3, 284-285.
31. "Memorandum as to Limitations of Shipowners' Profits," July 1915, reprinted as Appendix B to his "High Freight Rates and Government Control," in NA-UK, MT25/66/42831/1921, 132.
32. "Memorandum as to Limitations of Shipowners' Profits," July 1915, reprinted as Appendix B to his "High Freight Rates and Government Control," in NA-UK, MT25/66/42831/1921, 132-145.
33. "Limitations of Shipowners' Profits," July 1915, reprinted as Appendix B to his "High Freight Rates and Government Control" in NA-UK, MT25/66/42831/1921 132-145.
34. Fayle, Seaborne Trade, vol. 2, 239-241.
35. Salter, Memoirs, 80-81. The information in the card index system was made available to Britain's Allies during the war. For a detailed description by Salter of the card index system, see "Shipping Intelligence Section, AMTC – Note of Records and Work," "AMTC, 1918," NA-UK, MT25/1021068.
36. Salter, Memoirs, 85.
37. Salter, Allied Shipping Control, 49-53, C. Ernest Fayle, The War and the Shipping Industry (1927), 217.
38. "High Freight Rates and Government Control," NA-UK, MT25/66/42381/1921.
39. Arthur Salter, The United States of Europe and Other Papers, W. Arnold-Forster, ed. (1933), 7.
40. See e.g., Salter to Lodge, n.d., NA-UK, MT25/66/42381/1921, Salter, Memoirs, 79, Sir Josiah Stamp, Taxation During the War (1932), 191-194.
41. Salter, Allied Shipping Control, 62, 68.
42. H.C. Debs., vol. 88, 19 Dec. 1916, col. 1345.

43. The Times, 18 Dec. 1916, L.F. Goldsmid, "Report on Shipping Control, 1914-1918," part VI, chapter II, 18, NA-UK, MT25/87/1921.
44. Memoranda (A.) (C.) (D.) by Maclay, 30 Jan. 1917, Minutes, War Cabinet 60, 9 Feb. 1917, NA-UK, CAB23/1.
45. L.F. Goldsmid, "Report on Shipping Control, 1914-1918," part VI, chapter II, 16-17, NA-UKMT25/87/1921, C. Ernest Fayle, Seaborne Trade, vol. 3, The Period of Unrestricted Submarine Warfare (1924), 11-12.
46. Salter, Memoirs, 91.
47. Salter, Memoirs, 126.
48. Entries of 28 Dec. 1916, 12 Jan., 10 Sept., 31 Dec. 1917 in Thomas Jones, Whitehall Diary, vol. 1, 1916-1925, Keith Middlemas, ed. (1969), 17, 20, 36, 41,
49. Entries of 28-30 Dec. 1916 in Joseph Davies, The Prime Minister's Secretariat, 1916-1920 (Newport, Mon., 1932), 52-54, 56-57.
50. Salter, Memoirs,127.
51. "Maclay and Downing Street," Salter Papers, File 1, Anecdotes and Incidents.
52. Salter, Memoirs, 91-93, "Ministry of Shipping, Distribution of Business, 1917, 1918," NA-UK, MT25/62/37310/1921, Fayle, War and the Shipping Industry, 216-217.
53. "Ministry of Shipping, Distribution of Business, November 1918," NA-UK, MT25/62/37310/1921.
54. "Some Memories of Lord Salter," 9 pp. MS, encl. in Gertrude Caton Thompson to the author, 23 June 1979, author's archive. She added that she had kept "a fairly complete set of diaries of the First War Years," some of which she used in her Mixed Memoirs (Gateshead, 1983), 64-80.
55. Fayle, Seaborne Trade, vol. 3, 12.
56. Salter, Allied Shipping Control, Table No. 6, 355-358.
57. Salter, Allied Shipping Control, 70, Fayle, War and the Shipping Industry, 285. The figures for gross tonnage destroyed in April are marginally different in Sir Archibald Hurd, History of the Great War, Based on Official Documents, The Merchant Navy, vol. 3 (1929),17, 367. *Gross Tonnage* will be taken to be a vessel's entire internal cubical capacity. *Net Tonnage* is gross tonnage less deductions for space occupied by engines, crew, etc., giving a rough measure of a ship's capacity for cargo or passengers. *Deadweight* capacity is the actual weight in tons which can be carried. See W. Palin Elderton, Shipping Problems, 1916-1921 (1928), 3-4. Likewise a *liner* implies a ship providing a fixed service, at regular intervals, between named ports. A *tramp* is a ship hired as a whole, by voyage or time period, to load and carry cargo between ports. See C.

Ernest Fayle, <u>A Short History of the World's Shipping Industry</u> (1933), 253-254. American shipping usage is somewhat different. See Edward N. Hurley, <u>The New Merchant Marine</u> (New York, 1920), 274-275.

58. Maclay to Lloyd George, 2 Feb. 1917, Minutes, War Cabinet 62, 12 Feb. 1917, NA-UK, CAB23/1.
59. Salter, <u>Allied Shipping Control</u>, 71-72.
60. Fayle, <u>War and the Shipping Industry</u>, 228-229, Fayle, <u>Seaborne Trade</u>, vol. 3, 112-113.
61. Salter, <u>Allied Shipping Control</u>, 72.
62. L.F. Goldsmid, "Report on Shipping Control, 1914-1918," part VI, chapter IV, 92, NA-UK, MT25/87/1921.
63. Minute by Salter, 7 Apr. 1917, NA-UK, MT25/7/72717/1917, Salter, <u>Allied Shipping Control</u>, 75-76, Fayle, <u>War and the Shipping Industry</u>, 212-213, Fayle, <u>Seaborne Trade</u>, vol. 3, 9-10, 17-20.
64. See correspondence by Salter in NA-UK, MT25/7/72717/1917.
65. "Non-Government Requirements and Liner Shipments," 7 Apr. 1917, NA-UK, MT25/7/72717/1917.
66. Salter, <u>Allied Shipping Control</u>, 76-77.
67. L.F. Goldsmid, "Report on Shipping Control, 1914-1918," part IV, chapter IV, 155, NA-UK, MT25/87/1921.
68. Salter to Arthur J. Marder, 17 May 1968, quoted in Arthur J. Marder, <u>From the Dreadnought to Scapa Flow, The Royal Navy in the Fisher Era, 1904-1919</u>, vol. 4, <u>1917: Year of Crisis</u> (1969), 137.
69. Salter, <u>Allied Shipping Control</u>, 123. These reduced figures were accepted in Fayle, <u>Seaborne Trade</u>, vol. 3, 128-129.
70. David Lloyd George, <u>War Memoirs</u>, vol. 1 (2 vol. edition, 1938), 682.
71. Quoted in Marder, <u>From the Dreadnought to Scapa Flow</u>, vol. 4, 155.
72. Sir Norman Leslie to Lord Maclay, 14 Feb. 1933, Sir Norman Leslie Papers, LESL3, Churchill College Archives, Cambridge.
73. Salter <u>Memoirs</u>, 88, Salter, <u>Allied Shipping Control</u>, 123.
74. Lloyd George, <u>War Memoirs</u>, vol. 1, 687-689, 735, 746.
75. L.F. Goldsmid, "Report on Shipping Control, 1914-1918," part IV, chapter IV, 157-162, NA-UK, MT25/87/1921.
76. Salter, <u>Allied Shipping Control</u>, 124.
77. Salter, <u>Allied Shipping Control</u>, 125.
78. Atlantic Trade Convoy, Report of Committee, 6th June 1917, copy in Leslie Papers, LESL1.
79. Fayle, <u>Seaborne Trade</u>, vol. 3, 129-131.

80. Henry Newbolt, History of the Great War, Based on Official Documents, Naval Operations, vol. 5, From April 1917 to the End of the War (1931), 139.
81. Salter, Allied Shipping Control, 125, 128. For a more detailed account see Ministry of Shipping, The System of Convoys for Merchant Shipping in 1917 and 1918, copy in Leslie Papers, LESL1.
82. Leslie to Maclay, 14 Feb. 1933, Leslie Papers, LESL3. In a letter to the editor, The Spectator, 143(20 July 1929), 82, Salter modestly gave full credit to Henderson for "the initiation, advocacy, and execution" of convoys.
83. Salter, Slave of the Lamp, 62, Salter, Memoirs, 94-95.
84. See The Papers of Woodrow Wilson, vol. 43, June 25-August 1917, Arthur S. Link, ed., (Princeton, NJ, 1985), 9-11, 45-46, 140-142.
85. Salter, Allied Shipping Control, 80.
86. Minutes, War Cabinet 115, 6 Apr. 1917, NA-UK, CAB23/2, Lloyd George, Memoirs, vol. 1, 993.
87. Minutes, War Cabinet 116, 9 Apr. 1917, NA-UK, CAB23/2, John J. Broesamle, William Gibbs McAdoo, A Passion for Change, 1863-1917 (Port Washington, NY, 1973), 215.
88. The Times, 23 Apr., 11 June 1917.
89. The Times, 2, 9 June 1917.
90. Salter, Memoirs, 94.
91. The New York Times, 7 June 1917.
92. Salter, Memoirs, 95.
93. Fayle, Seaborne Trade, vol. 3, 214-216.
94. "Note as to Discussion of Certain Shipping Questions Between President Wilson and Mr. T. Royden and Mr. J.A. Salter on July 26th 1917, in Sir Cecil Spring-Rice to A.J. Balfour, 26 July 1917, NA-UK, FO368/1836/158310.
95. Salter, Slave of the Lamp, 65.
96. Minutes, War Cabinet 222, 22 August 1917, NA-UK, CAB23/3. Lloyd George, Memoirs, vol. 1, 1011-1012 refers to Salter's comments in cabinet but without quotation marks.
97. Quoted in Lloyd George, War Memoirs, vol. 1, 1011.
98. Reginald Pound and Geoffrey Harmsworth, Northcliffe (1959), 545.
99. Balfour to Walter Page, 16 Aug. 1917, G.T. 1740, NA-UK, CAB24/23, Minutes, War Cabinet 222, 22 Aug. 1917, War Cabinet 223, 24 Aug. 1917, NA-UK, CAB23/3.
100. Fayle, Seaborne Trade, vol. 3, 216.
101. The Times, 24 July 1917.
102. Salter, Slave of the Lamp, 65-66.
103. Salter, Allied Shipping Control, 84.

104. Minutes, War Cabinet 241, 28 Sept. 1917, Minutes, War Cabinet 246, 8 Oct. 1917, NA-UK, CAB23/4.
105. Quoted in Edward N. Hurley, The Bridge to France (1927), viii, 82.
106. Hurley, The Bridge to France, 78-82, Hurley, The New Merchant Marine, 79-80, The Times History of the War, vol. 18 (1919), 263-267.
107. Salter, Slave of the Lamp, 66.
108. Salter, Memoirs, 97, 99.
109. Salter, Allied Shipping Control, 80-81.
110. Salter, Allied Shipping Control, 144.
111. Salter, Allied Shipping Control, 147.
112. Fayle, Seabourne Trade, vol. 3, 237.
113. "Allied Maritime Transport Council, 1918" ["AMTC, 1918"], 5, NA-UK, MT25/10/21068. This 322 page document contained a chapter, "Formation and Objects of Council" by Salter, as well as relevant minutes, documents and statistics. A selection of these documents was reprinted as appendices to Salter, Allied Shipping Control, 281-369.
114. Fayle, War and the Shipping Industry, 281-282.
115. Minute by Salter, 30 Sept. 1917, NA-UK, MT25/22/61759/1918.
116. The Times, 11 Oct. 1916, Salter, Slave of the Lamp, 79.
117. Jean Monnet, Memoirs (1978), 55-56, Salter, Memoirs, 113.
118. Monnet, Memoirs 68-69, Wheeler-Bennett, Anderson, 41-42.
119. Etienne Clémentel, La France et la politique économique interalliée (Paris, 1931), 167-195. Salter read the manuscript for Clémentel and provided comments. Salter to Clémentel, 19 Mar. 1930, League of Nations Archives, [LNA], Box S115.
120. Quoted in Salter, Allied Shipping Control, 148. Italics in original. The text of the agreement of 3 November 1917 was reproduced in "AMTC, 1918," 18, NA-UK, MT25/10/21068.
121. "AMTC, 1918," 17, NA-UK, MT25/10/21068.
122. Quoted in Monnet, Memoirs, 68.
123. "AMTC, 1918," 20-22, NA-UK, MT25/10/21068; Fayle, Seaborne Trade, vol. 3, 241.
124. "AMTC 1918," 17, NA-UK, MT25/10/21068, Salter, Memoirs, 113.
125. "AMTC, 1918," 23-29, NA-UK, MT25/10/21068, Salter, Allied Shipping Control, 150.
126. "The Shipping Situation and American Assistance," "Form of Cooperation between the Allies," 22 Nov. 1917, encl. in Maclay to Lloyd George, 23 Nov. 1917, David Lloyd George Papers, F/35/2/33, House of Lords Record Office, London.

127. Salter, Memoirs, 113, Graeme Thomson to Sir M.P.A. Hankey, 1 Dec. 1917, G.T.2835, NA-UK, CAB24/34.
128. The Times, 29 Nov. 1917, Salter Allied Shipping Control, 151.
129. "AMTC, 1918," 35-37, NA-UK, MT25/10/21068, Salter, Slave of the Lamp, 83.
130. Salter, Allied Shipping Control, 156-157, memorandum by Salter, "Ministry of Shipping," 18 Jan. 1918, NA-UK, MT25/22/61503/1918. This memorandum became the Cabinet Paper, "Tonnage for Cereals," G.T. 3388, NA-UK, CAB24/39.
131. Minutes, War Cabinet 330, 24 Jan. 1918, NA-UK, CAB23/5.
132. "Priority for Shipments of Foodstuffs in February and March," 14 Feb. 1918, G.T. 3621, NA-UK, CAB24/42, Minutes, War Cabinet 349, 19 Feb. 1918, NA-UK, CAB23/5.
133. Salter, Allied Shipping Control, 157-158.
134. "Minutes of Meeting Held at the Foreign Office," 15 Feb. 1918, "AMTC, 1918," 38-38A, NA-UK, MT25/10/21068, Fayle Seaborne Trade, vol. 3, 293-294, Alfred Zimmern, The League of Nations and the Rule of Law, 1918-1935 (1936), 145.
135. Monnet, Memoirs, 68-69.
136. See Minutes, War Cabinet 360, 6 Mar. 1918, NA-UK, CAB23/5.
137. "Minutes of First Session at Lancaster House, London, March 11-14, 1918," "AMTC, 1918," 41-51, NA-UK, MT25/10/21068. Salter's press notice which appeared in The Times, 14 Mar. 1918 was reprinted as Appendix 2 in "AMTC, 1918," 50-5l, NA-UK, MT25/10/21068.
138. Salter, Allied Shipping Control, 164.
139. "Lancaster House and Lord Leverhulme," Salter Papers, File I, Anecdotes and Incidents.
140. Salter, Allied Shipping Control, 176-179.
141. "Notes as to Permanent Organization," Appendix 12 in "AMTC, 1918," 66-67, NA-UK, MT25/10/21068;
142. Salter, Allied Shipping Control, 179.
143. Salter to Cecil, 6 Apr. 1918, Viscount Cecil Papers, ADD MSS 51113, vol. 63, fol. 3, British Library, London, "Report of Action Taken March 15th to April 15th, 1918," "AMTC, 1918," 63-66, NA-UK, MT25/10/21068. This was also circulated as G.T. 4367, NA-UK, CAB24/49.
144. Clémentel, La France, 253, Salter, Allied Shipping Control, 167.
145. "Minutes of Second Session at Paris, April 23-25, 1918," "AMTC, 1918," 68-110, NA-UK, MT25/10/21068. On the development of the Programme Committees, see AMTE memorandum, 25 May 1918, in Salter, Allied Shipping Control, 301-304.

146. The Times, 30 Apr. 1918.
147. "Some Memories of Lord Salter," 9 pp. MS, encl. in Gertrude Caton Thompson to the author, 23 June 1979, author's archive.
148. "Sea Power: The Direction of Shipping in Time of War," The Listener, 16(28 Oct. 1936), 796.
149. Minutes, War Cabinet 415, 23 May 1917, NA-UK, CAB23/6.
150. Salter, Allied Shipping Control, 181-182, Salter to Hurcomb, 13 Sept. 1918, NA-UK, MT25/11/23971.
151. Salter, Allied Shipping Control, 183-185, 190-194, "Report of Action, April 16th - July 15th, 1918," 111-134, "Report of Action, July 16th Aug. 15th, 1918," 135-150 "AMTC, 1918," NA-UK, MT25/10/21068.
152. Minute by Salter, 23 July 1918, NA-UK, MT25/22/61759.
153. Salter, Allied Shipping Control, 196.
154. "Note as to Prospective Shipping Position Immediately After the War, 19 Apr. 1918," Appendix 59, "AMTC, 1918," 237, NA-UK, MT25/10/21068.
155. Salter, Allied Shipping Control, 198.
156. "Report of Action, April 16th to July 15th, 1918," "AMTC, 1918," 112-134, NA-UK, MT25/10/21068, Salter, Allied Shipping Control, 198-199, 304-310, Fayle, Seaborne Trade, vol. 3, 377-379.
157. "Minutes of Third Session at Lancaster House, August 29-30, 1918," "AMTC, 1918," 151-172, NA-UK, MT25/10/21068
158. Salter, Allied Shipping Control, 200.
159. Fayle, Seaborne Trade, vol. 3, 381.
160. Salter, Allied Shipping Control, 204, 310-315.
161. Minutes, War Cabinet 470, 6 Sept. 1918, NA-UK, CAB23/7.
162. J.R. Clyne, "Food Imports," 25 Sept. 1918, Minister of Shipping, "Note on Food Controller's Memorandum of 26 Sept. 1918," NA-UK, G.T. 5788, G.T. 5799, CAB24/64.
163. Minutes, War Cabinet 480, 1 Oct. 1918, NA-UK, CAB23/8.
164. "Draft Minutes of the Fourth Session held at Lancaster House, September 30th, October 1st and 2nd, 1918, "AMTC, 1918," 185-206, NA-UK, MT25/10/21068, AMTC, "Full Association of the United States Government," 12 Oct. 1918, G.T. 6005, NA-UK, CAB24/67.
165. Salter to Food Council, 4 Oct. 1918, Salter to Munitions Council, 10 Oct. 1918, in AMTC, "Report of Executive, September 16th to Oct. 15th,1918," G.T. 6168, NA-UK, CAB24/68.
166. AMTC, "Report of Executive, October 16th to November 15th, 1918," NA-UK, G.T. 6447 CAB24/71.

167. Salter, <u>Allied Shipping Control</u>, 239, 242.
168. Salter to Dwight Morrow, 17 Feb. 1919, Dwight W. Morrow Papers, microfilm reel 80, Amherst College Archives and Special Collections, Amherst, MA. In Morrow's <u>The Society of Free States</u> (1919), 117-118, he described Salter's <u>Allied Shipping Control</u> as "an accurate history" of the AMTC.

CHAPTER 3

"ONE OF THE APOSTLES OF THE NEW AGE," 1918-1922

At the end of the war in November 1918 Salter was still in his thirties, vigorous, confident, and enjoying a considerable "inner circle" reputation. "If reputation is not to be lost," he observed later in life, "it has to be re-won in different work." With the return to private life of numerous wartime colleagues, therefore, he worried that his own reputation was in danger of being eroded.[1] Nor was there any certainty as to where it might be re-won or re-established. At the time, whatever status Salter continued to enjoy was based increasingly on his position within the Allied Maritime Transport Council and its Executive. The Council had been spared what could be called its final test because of the armistice. It ceased to exist as an independent body on 7 April 1919 and its Executive was terminated on 7 February 1920. By that time the entire organization had "shrunk and shrivelled" to a shadow of its former self.[2] For the final eight months of the war, however, the AMTC and the AMTE, with Salter as its secretary and chairman respectively, had stood at the heart of the Allied transport and supply organization. The system had its limitations; it was an advisory not an executive body. As well, some members of the AMTC, such as Britain whose tonnage by late 1918 was more than adequate for its requirements, were more equal than others. Nevertheless, as Salter later argued, the results achieved by the Council and its Executive were striking. By September 1918, Allied food supplies were purchased in common using American credits, divided by agreement and with Britain supplying the shipping. Distribution was effected through measuring the relative needs of each ally. It remains a remarkable tribute to the system's efficiency that at the time of the armistice, although the Allies had two million tons less of shipping and a new army to transport from the United States, food stocks were greater than in 1917. Similar successes could be measured in the areas of Belgian relief, coal supplies for France and Italy, and Allied munitions' programmes.[3]

The success of the AMTC and its executive can also be assessed in the areas of international administration and co-operation. In an experiment unique to that date, the AMTE pioneered the way towards an international civil service. Its members were forced to act in "a double capacity, partly national and partly international, representing the views of other countries to their own and of their own to others." This was described by Salter as "the discovery of the war administration, neither parallel, nor superior, but essentially intermediary in character."[4] To effect such co-operation required complete mutual confidence among members of the secretariat. "Friendship for me," Jean Monnet recalled, "is the result of joint action rather than the reason for it."[5] What in fact provided the continuity was the formation of a "non-national" secretariat, headed by Salter and responsible to the AMTE. Its functions were described by Salter:

> Each of the members of this secretariat, who were in fact of all the four nationalities, was required to divest himself of any national point of view and to give effect to any agreed policy with an absolute impartiality; and in view of the character of its duties, the secretariat was organized under a secretary, on ordinary administrative principles, and not under a committee.[6]

Indeed, among the members of the secretariat of the AMTC were several with whom Salter became life long friends. André Simon, formerly associated with the French winery of Pommèry, specialised in munitions requirements. Simon, whom Salter described as having done "perhaps more than any other single man to educate the Englishman into a civilised appreciation of good wine and food," hosted an end of war banquet which Salter remembered for years afterwards.[7] J.F. Henderson, later a member of the Reparations Commission, was another congenial colleague. In fact, Salter befriended the entire Henderson family, taking a close interest in their affairs. When Marian Henderson died on 2 December 1936, Salter mourned the loss "of an intimate friend of many years."[8] Another was Joseph S. Davis, an American in charge of the Statistical Branch of the secretariat.[9] Although their official collaboration ended soon after the war, Davis remained in life long contact with Salter and recorded these impressions:

> Salter was short of stature, slender, quick, intense, nervous in manner, and sharp. He smoked incessantly when I knew him best, and often talked with a cigarette dangling from his lips. He had amazing endurance, initiative, and skill in expressing, after a controversial discussion, a position on which all could agree. He also was resilient in defeat and modest in success, never arrogant nor condescending, clearheaded under pressure, delightful when at leisure.[10]

Most important in terms of personal friendships, however, was the only woman on the secretariat, Mrs. Will Arnold-Forster (Katherine "Ka" Cox). She and the more public figure of her husband, Will Arnold-Forster, then working in the Ministry of Blockade, were for almost 20 years at the heart of Salter's circle of select friends. In the summer of 1918 Ka Cox became Salter's personal secretary in matters relating to the AMTC.[11] He profoundly admired "her personality – which was distinctive in every form of expression, in gait and bearing, in manner and speech, in dress, in action, and the interchange of personal relations." [12] Another person in close contact with Ka Cox at the time, and also working under Salter's supervision, was Gertrude Caton Thompson. She observed of Ka Cox:

> Her physical appearance was not impressive. She was large in body, and loose in movement, with nothing notable in her features except the immediate impression she gave of warm-heartedness, lively intelligence and calm vitality. The timbre of her speaking voice was clear, soft and attractive. There was nothing of the purposeful 'good-doer' about her; she was simply herself.

There is no doubt that Salter found himself very much drawn to Ka Cox.[13]

Many years later, sharing an intimate moment with Elliot Felkin, also a friend of Ka Cox and his assistant at the League of Nations, Salter revealed that he "nearly married her. He was going to propose to her in 1917, & he said he remembered that one of the reasons why he put it off was his rooted disapproval of mixing up official with private relations. He'd made up his mind definitely to propose at the end of the war." But by then she had married Will Arnold-Forster.[14] Her son, Mark Arnold-Forster, in whom Salter always took a warm interest, noted, "I think it is likely that Arthur Salter was in love with my mother or thought that he was. Several people thought that they, too, were in love with my mother." His acquaintance with her dated from the World War, was always intimate, and persisted until her death on 23 May 1938.[15] His wartime experiences, he recalled, created a kind of "hothouse" atmosphere in which friendship and intimacy flourished, overcoming his inherent shyness. And more generally, Salter always remained proud of the achievements of the AMTC. He believed that it proved its merits in the course of the war, influenced international organization in the inter-war period, and was copied in the Second World War. He was the first to admit, however, that in peace time international co-operation was "normally a delicate plant of slow and precarious growth."[16]

The armistice of 11 November 1918 had raised the question whether inter-allied control should continue into the post-war era? The situation was particularly unclear with regard to the future of the AMTC and other forms of inter-allied co-operation. It was certainly the case that the Wilson administration largely opposed any post-war, inter-allied economic co-operation. There was also the difficult question of what to do with the German and Austrian mercantile fleets. As well, available tonnage had increased dramatically due to the winding up of convoys, the end of war losses, and the release of ships required to transport American troops. In strict terms, the AMTC had no economic powers, however, shipping would still be demanded to supply liberated areas and for troop repatriation.[17] In fact, for some time prior to the armistice, Salter had been considering precisely such problems. On 7 October he had met privately with a group of colleagues, including E.M.H. Lloyd, J.J. Mallon, E.F. Wise, John Maynard Keynes, J. Reeve Brooke and Lord Eustace Percy. The group, mostly involved in some aspect of Allied co-operation, agreed that enemy shipping should be placed into an "Inter-Allied Pool." As well, it was suggested that control over shipping and food supplies should be maintained into the post-war period.[18] Then on 28 October the AMTE, meeting with the Food Council, recommended that a clause should be inserted into the terms of the armistice providing for "the immediate surrender" of "all German and Austrian merchant vessels [which] should be placed under the direction of the Allied Maritime Transport Council." In addition, supplies of food and other commodities should only be dispersed to the Central Powers "through the instrumentality of the existing Allied organizations." A member of the AMTE was sent to Paris that very same day to press for the adoption of this recommendation by the armistice negotiators but to no avail. Salter recalled that the proposal was rejected as "not strictly relevant" to an armistice agreement. And no provision was made in the armistice for the surrender of German and Austrian tonnage. Salter was convinced that the immobilisation of nearly one million tons deadweight of shipping – the delivery of ships was not to begin until 22 March 1919 – had "a substantial effect on the world shipping position and in particular increased seriously the difficulties of relief."[19] However, when the issue was discussed by the War Cabinet on 4 November, it "was not considered practicable that the German merchant ships should be handed over to the control of the Allied Maritime Transport Council, as a condition of the armistice."[20] A further discussion in the War Cabinet on 13 November linked the supply of food to Germany and Austria with the placement of German and Austrian mercantile shipping under the AMTC. Lord Robert Cecil was given the task of meeting with the AMTC to discuss "the utilisation of enemy shipping and the conditions on which relief could be given to enemy countries."[21] During this time, as well, Salter had been attending meetings of the Economic Defence and Development Committee (EDDC) of the War Cabinet. On 15 October the EDDC, led by Cecil, had approved his suggestion that the AMTC should be expanded and become "a supreme Inter-Allied Economic Authority."[22] At a following meeting on 22 October, the EDDC had further recommended that the AMTC become a "General Economic Council" with a mandate to deal with reconstruction of war devastated territories, distribution of foodstuffs and other essential commodities. Salter preferred the title "Council for Transports and Imports."²³ At a further meeting on 5 November, again attended by Salter, the recommendation was approved with the support of both Churchill and Maclay, forwarded for approval to the War Cabinet and "communicated unofficially" by Salter to Stevens and Morrow.²⁴

General Economic Council was the name adopted and it received War Cabinet approval on 13 November, followed soon by the concurrence of the French and the Italian governments. Unfortunately, the United States administration refused to prolong the life of any wartime organization into the post-war world. It preferred instead "American control over American resources," and setting up new machinery for economic reconstruction.²⁵ Both at the time and afterwards, Salter could not restrain his regret at the failure to follow through in November with the recommendation for a General Economic Council. He pointed out that this resulted in a four-month delay before a million tons deadweight of German shipping were put at the disposal of the Allies, among other things for relief work. Further, he stated this had led to unnecessary delays because it was not until February 1919 that a new organization, the Supreme Economic Council (SEC), was formed, in structure, function and personnel matching the body for which Salter had lobbied. "There can be little doubt," he wrote in 1921, "that if the proposals made by the Transport Executive before the armistice had been adopted the economic position in the spring of 1919 and possibly afterwards would have been substantially better."²⁶

The armistice, in the words of Maclay, "brought with lightning speed an entire change of conditions." At the same time, Maclay recommended "the discontinuance of the system of general requisitioning," a move approved by the War Cabinet on 8 January 1919.²⁷ Denied the opportunity to play a central role in the armistice or post-armistice negotiations, and thus no longer preoccupied with shipping requisitioning, Salter and the AMTC pressed ahead but without clear direction. On 5 December Salter had chaired a conference at Lancaster House of representatives of the Programme Committees. The question of commodity controls was thoroughly discussed with the recommendation they be extended into the post-war period and handled by an inter-allied organization, such as the proposed General Economic Council.²⁸ These and other inter-allied discussions finally led to the establishment on 11 January, in Paris, of the Allied Supreme Council of Supply and Relief (SCSR). It was to concern itself only with victualling of Allied, neutral and enemy countries.²⁹ However, once again Salter returned to the attack. On 27 January he circulated a memorandum arguing again that the AMTC should be made into the one "supreme authority" on questions of enemy tonnage, possibly under the umbrella of the SCSR which should be extended to cover all economic questions, including food and raw materials.[30] The SCSR, according to Salter, poorly led by Lord Reading who resigned very quickly, proved quite "ineffective."[31] Its short life ended on 8 February when it merged with the newly created SEC.

During this post-armistice period, the question of supply depended as always on available tonnage. This now included the repatriation of prisoners of war, the return of Allied troops to their home countries, and the transportation of food for relief purposes. The latter aspect was now more complex due to the problems derived from the acquisition, management and allocation of former enemy ships. Some immediate relief had in fact been afforded by the requisitioning of almost three-quarters of a million tons of Austrian shipping anchored in Adriatic ports occupied by Italy.[32] It was arranged on 21 December that this tonnage would be provisionally managed by the AMTC and would fly its blue, white and blue flag. Salter attached "considerable political importance" to this gesture.[33] Far more complex was the acquisition of three million tons of German shipping, lying in German or neutral ports. These latter negotiations proved to be, in Salter's recollection, "long and difficult," involving various Allied organizations, and with the AMTE and himself throughout playing an active role.[34] The negotiations came to a head at the renewed armistice talks which opened at Trèves on 15 January. Salter, John Anderson and Beale formed the British contingent of a large group of inter-allied experts. On the third day Salter was among the ten Allied signatories of an agreement placing the entire German merchant fleet "at the disposal of the Associated Governments, with a view to increasing the world tonnage required for the supply of foodstuffs to Europe, including Germany."[35] The agreement signed at Trèves, however, was sufficiently general and ambiguous that it was not immediately implemented. Further difficulties arose when, denied the option of paying for food with gold earmarked by the French for reparations, Germany refused to surrender the ships despite the blockade. It was clearly desirable that the AMTC, the only inter-allied agency with the relevant experience, should meet for discussion of such outstanding issues.

The fifth, extended session of the AMTC opened in Paris on 1 February. It was firstly announced by the chairman, Clémentel, that Cecil had resigned from the AMTC. Salter later noted that the resignation of Cecil, "whose authority had been throughout a tower of strength in all our work," added further to the diminishing authority of the AMTC.[36] The main concern of the AMTC, as explained at the outset of the meeting, was "the necessary arrangements for acquisition, management, and utilisation" of surrendered enemy tonnage. The Trèves agreement of 17 January had designated the AMTC as one authority which might administer the surrendered German fleet, subject to the exemption of certain categories of vessels. After preliminary meetings on 1 and 4 February, the AMTC appointed four representatives to proceed immediately to

Spa. During the discussions, Salter made a strong case "that the general principle to be adopted should be allocation in proportion to net losses." He was then made head of the British delegation with instructions "to complete arrangements for the acquisition of German tonnage."[37]

The conference at Spa, Belgium, held at the Grand Hotel Brittanique from 6 to 8 February, proved to be Salter's first experience at the centre of the international affairs. The 30 pages of minutes of the proceedings indicate the leading role he took as interrogator, trying to outmanoeuvre the stalling tactics of the German delegation. At the third meeting, on 7 February, for example, Herr Seeliger, a shipping expert with the German Foreign Ministry, argued that the German fleet could not be surrendered before details of the proposed compensation were settled. The minutes record:

Admiral [George W.] Hope: A contract has already been signed on January 16th by Marshal Foch. We are here therefore to explain and make our position quite clear as to the compensation which has been fixed by the Allied Governments.

Herr Seeliger: It is correct that we concluded the agreement in this way. There is, however, a clause in it which makes our point of view appear justified. This clause is that all details should be determined by a special agreement. Under these details which are to be settled by special agreement is also included the special compensation which should be given us. Therefore we consider that we are entitled to receive these details in the morning, as I have said.

Mr. Salter: Details will be given to you but the question of the amount of remuneration is fixed by the Allied Governments and is not a matter for discussion.

Herr Seeliger: The German delegation cannot accept this point of view because according to the text, the details remaining were also reserved for the special agreement.

Mr. Salter: The compensation is not a detail. It is a condition.

Herr Seeliger: Another question ....?

In what amounted to an ultimatum at the fifth and final meeting on 8 February, Salter asserted that what was required by 12 February was a note from the German government, relating to all ships over 1600 tons gross, confirming "that the vessels are definitely handed over to us." The Spa conference was then adjourned *sine die* without any resolution of several outstanding questions, including the removal of German crews from German ships allocated for Allied operation, and the fate of ships under construction.[38]

The Allied representatives reported back to the reconvened session of the AMTC on 11 February. Salter gave the AMTC an account of the futile negotiations and tabled a note of the proceedings. Despite the lack of progress, the AMTC continued discussion on the question of the allocation of enemy tonnage. It was decided that this would be used primarily for the relief of liberated territories and the repatriation of troops, prisoners and refugees. The AMTC also made one recommendation of some importance to Salter personally. It was learned at Spa that a first batch of 53 cargo vessels had been made ready for allocation by the German government. The AMTC decided that Salter would "be authorised in cases of urgency to give orders as to the use of individual ships."[39] For a short time, Salter later recalled, "apart from my continuing power over British ships, I had a direct executive authority over a large merchant marine with no responsibility except to a rarely meeting composite Allied Council. It soon came to an end, but it was an interesting experience while it lasted."[40]

Despite this brief, satisfying interlude, this was not a happy period in Salter's career. The hothouse atmosphere of wartime co-operation was over, and the creative days of the AMTC had passed. The vexatious question of the surrender of German shipping was eventually settled in the course of two further conferences, the first at Spa from 4 to 5 March and the second at Brussels from 11 to 14 March. Two million tons of shipping were exchanged for Allied agreement to begin sending foodstuffs to Germany. Salter played no direct part in these final negotiations. The peace-making process was in the hands of the "Big Four" already in session in Paris. Writing to his former colleague on the AMTC, Dwight Morrow, Salter observed on 28 January:

Our work generally has been in a state of suspended animation since you left, & the future is still obscure. However the League of Nations (thanks to Pres. Wilson, Ld. Robert Cecil & Gen. Smuts) seems to be going better than any of us hoped for. I hope all the old lot, including yourself, may find ourselves some day & somehow connected with its work.

And again on 17 February he wrote:

I expect to be living in Paris the next few months – I wish very much that you were too. The AMTC work has been falling to pieces since Nov. 11, but we're getting the Supreme Economic Council started now, and the League of Nations appears to be going better than one had dared to hope for.[41]

Salter was clearly anxious to move on to other work and abandon the crippled AMTC and his opportunity came sooner than expected.

On 8 February, on the basis of a proposal made by President Woodrow Wilson and prepared by the U.S. Food Administrator Herbert Hoover, the SEC was established. It was intended to "absorb or replace" such existing bodies as the AMTC, the Programme Committees and the Inter-Allied Food Council. Designed to co-ordinate all inter-governmental economic activity during the armistice, it was made up of delegates from Britain, the United States, France and Italy and held its first meeting at the French Ministry of Commerce on 17 February.[42] Cecil was persuaded to head the British delegation, a position he undertook after personally requesting from Lloyd George the assistance of Salter as secretary to the delegation. Salter's appointment was confirmed by the War Cabinet on 6 March.[43] It was Salter's subsequent impression, confirmed by the first meeting of the SEC, that the new organization "was too tardily commenced, too hurriedly improvised, and insufficiently equipped with a personnel accustomed to corporate work."[44] Nonetheless, he threw himself into the tasks at hand. At the AMTC meeting in Paris on 10 March, he announced his resignation as secretary of the AMTC to take up his new duties on the SEC. Otherwise, the session was devoted to considering another of Salter's periodic executive reports and planning the allocation of German tonnage.[45] The life of the AMTC, however, was shortly to be terminated. On 24 March a "special conference" of Allied representatives, with Cecil in the chair and Salter attending as one of the two British delegates, agreed that the AMTC "should terminate its existence," with the SEC assuming responsibility for major decisions regarding shipping. The AMTE was to be reconstituted in London, and be responsible to the SEC which in turn would be advised by a newly organized Allied Shipping Committee in Paris. These recommendations were adopted by the SEC on 7 April and the AMTC ceased to exist.[46] On that same day, 24 March, the SEC further approved of Salter's additional appointment as General-Secretary of the Shipping Section of the SEC, "in view of his past experience of and signal success in the work."[47] Reflecting on the fate of both the AMTC and the AMTE, so significant in his career, Salter later wrote that they had "been drained of their life and power, long before their formal dissolution."[48]

On the basis of past performance, Salter was not one to have much patience with an organization with its future in doubt. Nonetheless, he found it convenient, if nothing else, to be associated with the SEC and hoped thereby to influence policy. In the meantime, there was the exhilaration of an extended stay in Paris. "At that time Paris was at its unsurpassed best in a fine spring," Gertrude Caton Thompson recalled. "Even J.A.S. felt spring in the air, and the bliss to be free of all the home restrictions was intoxicating."[49] In his Memoirs, Salter confirmed these impressions: "Paris, intact and beautiful, a city of light and colour, the more vivid to eyes accustomed to the drab and darkened streets of London, was an incomparable setting for a pageant of victory."⁵⁰ Salter himself took no part in the peace-making process which unfolded around him. His concerns stemmed from the executive work attached to the SEC, namely, tasks related to food, raw materials, shipping and, above all, blockade questions. Yet these were heady days for him, as Gertrude Caton Thompson confirmed. She had been asked to continue as his personal assistant in Paris and described what followed when she arrived early in March 1919:

> He met my train at the Gare du Nord, helped me with the douane and took me in a large official car to my headquarters. He explained that the Majestic Hotel was overcrowded owing to the lavish retinues of the Big Four. He himself was there but he had personally engaged a room for me in a nearby hotel. There I stayed until early July. I had expected hard work but in fact he was perpetually at meetings and conferences, with only occasional visits to the stuffy little office near to, but detached from, the Majestic. There he would give me hurried instructions and rush off to some palatial meeting well served by professional highly-geared staff. I seldom had more than half a day's work, so I was enabled to sample the august company of secondary importance always to be found in the couloirs of the Majestic, and learn what was afoot with the leading figures of Woodrow Wilson, Lloyd George, Clémenceau, Poincaré, Orlando and Smuts. In this way I became acquainted with such persons as T.E. Laurence, Keynes, Gertrude Bell, McMahon, and Will and Ka Arnold-Forster, close friends of J.A.S. and from then on mine too.⁵¹

Salter described his own role in Paris as "a privileged spectator rather than a participant." Yet from his vantage point he was in close touch with many of the leading personalities and *au courant* with much of the peace-making process. On a daily basis his immediate superior was Cecil, "Tall, slim, aquiline in feature, with the face of a Savonarola." Salter had Cecil's complete confidence and carried on with the SEC while Cecil busied himself with helping to draft the Covenant of the League of Nations. Occasionally, Salter shared with Sir Maurice Hankey the task of providing secretarial assistance at meetings of the Big Four. He had a chance to observe, at close quarters, "the unusually silent" Orlando, Wilson arguing "with a cold precision," Clémenceau with his "concentration and realism," or Lloyd George intervening with "consistent purpose." There were meetings with Colonel House, conversations with Smuts and Lloyd George, a dinner which Salter hosted for the "tantalizingly secretive" T.E. Lawrence, and close contact with many leading advisors, including John Maynard Keynes, Thomas Lamont, Norman Davis, Walter Layton and Bernard Baruch.⁵²

There were times, too, when Salter was able to turn from intense activity to socialising in the company of close friends. Gertrude Caton Thompson recalled some of these occasions:

> His capacity for relaxed enjoyment was visible in Paris when Violet Markham and her husband [James Carruthers] and Will and Ka Arnold-Forster went with J.A.S. and me to the Longchamp races. We all backed horses and I won 3,000 francs. It was a perfect spring day and we decided to have supper in a Bois de Bologne restaurant. The day passed into a perfect evening amongst the trees, uncrowded and with a superb meal. We were all happy and voted it an entirely delightful day. The only other relaxation amongst many was an invitation from Violet Markham and her husband to Mounet-Sully's production of <u>Oedipus Rex</u> in French. It was a stupendous performance of that incomparable actor, and J.A.S. was deeply impressed, apart from the fact that his classical education at school and Oxford aroused his memories of the Greek text.[53]

Such diversions helped in some ways to assuage Salter's increasing feelings of restlessness and his conviction that his abilities were not being used to the fullest. There was some recognition of past performance for he had been made a Companion of the Order of the Bath (C.B.) at war's end.[54] Then on 26 April Cecil wrote to Lloyd George recommending Salter for a knighthood. Cecil pointed out that Salter "has had here a most important and exacting task, and he has throughout worked most untiringly and has been in a large measure responsible for the organization and smooth working of the Council." The knighthood in fact had to await the 1922 honours list.[55] But Salter saw no future for himself with the Supreme Economic Council, a temporary appointment with a limited usefulness and largely preoccupied with the controversial question of blockade.

Increasingly, Salter concentrated his thoughts on an emerging area of post-war interest, the League of Nations. At the time Paris was awash with plans for the future League's Covenant, structure and functions, and rumours as to its first secretary general. The position was first offered to Sir Maurice Hankey who deliberated for two months and then declined.[56] Sir Eric Drummond, a career Foreign Office official since 1900, was then approached and he accepted.[57] Salter later learned that he was next on the list. He confirmed that he would have refused an offer:

> I'm quite sure that it was very much better from the point of view of the League that Drummond should have been appointed rather than myself. I'm not speaking with modesty now but simply from the fact that my experience

in great affairs had been under the conditions of war where one acted with a ruthlessness and scrupulousness of power. This would have been quite impossible as between different and competitive and rather jealous nations during peacetime. Drummond was free from that particular, what would have been curious, defect of mine.

Such reasoning in 1919 did not prevent Salter from foreseeing a personal role in the League of Nations. Defects of temperament or personality might have made him unsuitable as secretary general.[58] This, despite the fact that Morrow wrote to him on 25 March, "You are the candidate of those Americans who worked in London for the exalted job of Secretary-General."[59] But Salter did have an unblemished reputation for executive ability, not to speak of his leadership of the first international secretariat, the AMTE. It is not surprising, therefore, that he focused on the future structure of the League of Nations. As early as 19 December 1918 he had put on paper his view "that the establishment of an effective League of Nations is infinitely the most important test that confronts this generation – that it is the only thing which could make this war worthwhile, and that it is a test by which all of us who are now alive will have failed or succeeded." The supreme difficulty in his view was how to devise machinery for the peaceful settlement of disputes particularly those arising from competing commercial interests. He argued, therefore, that a future League of Nations should pursue a policy of complete world free trade and develop "machinery only for the enforcement of an economic boycott where necessary as the League's weapon."[60]

After giving the issue much further thought, Salter completed on 10 May a memorandum, "Note on the Organization of the League of Nations." He began by arguing for an ambitious structure that was "effectively international," and not one merely concerned with such innocuous matters as postal conventions and waterways. He foresaw that the League, in its more ambitious guise, would face a mixture of "national and separatist feeling," indifference and the handicap of being located in Geneva. "The great danger of the League, in a word," he observed in the event incorrectly, "is that it will die of dullness. Geneva will be a suburb, not a centre, in the world's government." Applying his wartime experience, he suggested the organization aspire to "the developed stage of international administration," and for the application of the tactic of working "by direct communication of expert with expert and not by means of the formulation of a general national policy subsequently communicated from one country to another." In essence, he urged a League machinery where policy "would be subject to real international consultation while still in the actual process of formation." Finally, he turned his attention to the economic work of the League:

I believe the ultimate causes of war are mainly economic; that the fundamentally wrong thing in government is to use the instrument of government to give a commercial advantage either to a section of a community or to one community in competition with others and I, therefore believe that in the end the economic division of the League should be the most important part of the organization, it may ultimately have the biggest task to perform.

He then followed this with several administrative suggestions. Some proved simply not realisable, such as provision for separate "National Departments of the League." Others, such as the formation of an "Intelligence and Research Division," especially for economic matters, were soon implemented. And one soon involved him personally. He stressed that personnel should be recruited from "a few of the best people in each country," preferably with wartime international experience.[61] Salter gave his memorandum the widest possible circulation in Paris and London, with copies going to Cecil, Drummond, Lloyd George, Monnet, Gordon Auchincloss, House's secretary, and Raymond B. Fosdick, among many others. Unlike similar schemes under review, for example those variously drawn up by Hankey, Philip Baker, Lord Eustace Percy and Jean Monnet, Salter's memorandum drew heavily on his wartime experience of Allied administration.[62] And his views were soon widely echoed, including the ideas which Drummond himself committed to paper.[63]

Early in May Salter met with Drummond and was offered a position on the projected international secretariat of the League. His acceptance was then communicated to the Organization Committee of the League at its first meeting on 5 May and approved on 9 June.[64] Drummond was determined to keep the number of appointed officials to a minimum, pending the signature of a peace treaty. Afterwards he wanted to secure "men and women of great experience in official international affairs." The early appointment of Salter, along with Monnet, Raymond B. Fosdick, Erik Colban and Joost van Hamel, as assistant secretary general, were the first steps in this direction.[65] After Professor Bernardo Attolico accepted an invitation to join the secretariat, it is interesting to note that among the chief officers planning the new League of Nations were three principal members of the AMTE.

Salter officially took up his appointment as the Director of the Economic and Financial section of the League on 13 June for a five year term.[66] The general thrust of public opinion toward the new organization did not inspire his confidence. "Most of us are rather gloomy after the experience of the last few months in Paris," he wrote to Morrow. "Allied affairs have not been going as well as they did in our day, and the League of Nations starts off with many handicaps."[67] Despite these reservations, Salter and the other appointed heads of sections, made their way to London to take up their temporary offices in Curzon Street at Sunderland House, "a pretentious, ugly, uncomfortable and inconvenient mansion."[68] Until the League would begin to function officially, that is, after the ratification of the Treaty of Versailles, Salter pursued there what he called his "humble preparatory tasks" with typical energy.[69] He laid great emphasis on developing the areas of economic research, intelligence and statistics. Secondly, he envisaged close economic ties between the League and other international economic bureaux. Thirdly, he was concerned with thorough preparations for the projected first meeting of the League. Fourthly, he was very much concerned with the famous article 16 of the League Covenant. This envisaged a series of escalating sanctions against any member of the League that went to war in violation of the Covenant. Salter was determined his section would have prepared the information and plans to implement the economic sanctions if required. Finally, he began to tackle the question of personnel for his section. Despite his attempts to recruit internationally from the United States, France, Belgium and Scandinavia, his early efforts tended to favour British appointees, such as E.M.H. Lloyd and Alexander Loveday.[70] As was to be his habit in future years, Drummond treaded carefully with Salter. Indeed, Salter later commended Drummond because he "rode with a light rein, delegating generously to those he trusted" and that included Salter.[71] On the question of sanctions, Drummond advised extreme caution and warned of the widespread revulsion against "international control." Otherwise Salter's proposals with regard to personnel and salaries received quick approval.[72]

The subject of international co-operation in statistical matters might not appear to have been of great significance in the early post-war period. Nonetheless, the Council of Four had recommended the SEC set up some sort of International Statistical Committee to produce a monthly bulletin of economic statistics. The British section of the SEC was already producing a <u>Monthly Statistical Bulletin</u>. Salter's skeletal Economic and Financial Section appropriately took the matter in hand. Salter had the relevant experience derived from his wartime card index system. As well, it was thought that the League would ultimately be the prime producer of such material.[73] Planning went ahead in early August, and invitations were sent, for example, to the International Institute of Agriculture in Rome, established in 1905, and the Hague-based International Institute of Statistics.[74] The Conference on International Co-operation in Statistics opened in London, on 14 August, at 117 Piccadilly. In his remarks as chairman of the two-day conference, attended by 24 government and institutional representatives, Salter outlined his main objectives. He encouraged discussion of the relation between the League and existing statistical bodies, and how the League might develop greater co-operation in this area. He also emphasized that there were both gaps and overlapping in the treatment of current statistical information. The general tenor of the discussions revealed, however, considerable opposition "against excessive concentration in Geneva." That same reserve was echoed in one of the conclusions reached by the conference, namely, that there be formed "a Central Advisory Council on Statistics to meet normally at the seat of the League." The real measure of agreement was echoed in the exhortation to all concerned to rationalize and increase the efficiency of world production of statistics.[75] Despite the failure to agree on a monthly publication, as far as Salter was concerned "we had a very successful conference."[76] And within the modest limits he had outlined on the first day, the conference represented a boost to what was to become a major concern of Salter's section of the League. The League eventually took over sponsorship of the <u>Monthly Statistical Bulletin</u> from the SEC. And throughout the 1920s the work of statistical collation and publication became among Salter's proudest achievements.

As the embryonic secretariat proceeded with its work, the limitations of the organization could not be ignored. For example, the question of a League intelligence service seemed at the time pressing. It raised the issue as to the future effectiveness of the secretariat in tendering advice to the Council and Assembly. Drummond had come to the conclusion that no government would pass on to the secretariat "information of a really confidential kind."[77] Fosdick feared that the League would become "a step-child" of the Foreign Offices of members. Salter intervened on 9 October but only to apply the discussion to his own section. He hypothesised, correctly, that when matters were in dispute self-interest would encourage governments to supply the League with information. He did not want to see any concrete rules laid down, but he did envisage that in the future the League would be privy to a vast amount of privileged information.[78] The League never did formally establish its own intelligence office. Nonetheless, Drummond had access to British confidential documents. Salter likewise kept in intimate touch with the Treasury and the Bank of England, exchanging confidential information. Given the fact, as Drummond pointed out, "that we are the Secretariat of a League of Nations, and not of a supranational body," the compromise was as efficient as it was inevitable.[79]

Not all organizational questions in which Salter was involved proved as interesting as that of a separate League intelligence division. For example, he arranged that the secretariat should have its own reference library by acquiring documentation used by various states at the Paris Peace Conference. He pioneered the system for the internal distribution of League correspondence and brought some uniformity, namely, calculations in Swiss francs, into the payment of salaries and disbursements.[80] For a short time he was in charge of liaison between the League and the organising committee for the future International Labour Office.[81] Such questions, of which there were dozens to be handled every day, held inherent fascination for Salter. They appealed to the rational, methodical and fact-oriented part of his character. And to all problems he brought initiative and energy when most needed in these pioneering days. This is not to suggest that he neglected larger, some times more intractable issues which excited the executive aspects of his personality. In fact, he regarded certain articles of the League Covenant as giving him ample authority to deal with all questions of international significance in the area of economic affairs, and even beyond. On 17 September Salter directed one of his lengthy memoranda to the secretary general on the subject of disarmament. He wished to see the issue raised at the upcoming first meeting of the Assembly. Arguing that "the boldest course is certainly the best," he observed that the issue would be "the criterion by which the world will judge the League as a whole."[82] Not only did the first Assembly discuss the issue, but Salter's views added to the pressure which led to the establishment of a disarmament section within the secretariat.

More strictly within the confines of his own area of expertise, Salter became absorbed with international economic affairs. Problems of production, distribution, and standards of living, he noted, had become global concerns, and hence of prime importance to the League. In early September, he completed another memorandum on the economic and financial questions which he wished the first Assembly of the League to debate. He also envisaged possible courses of action which the League could oversee. These ranged from what he termed "Economic Councils" to commissions to consider specific problems of currency reform and tariff disputes.[83] This task was to preoccupy Salter until his first resignation in January 1920. Ultimately, it would lead in September to the summoning of the Brussels Conference on the world economy. There is no doubt that during the fall of 1919 Salter was placing his authority behind what he had described in May as the more ambitious view of the League. Consequently, he turned his restless energy to the heart of the League Covenant, the weapon of the international economic and financial blockade as contemplated in the sanctions provisions of Article 16. On 22 September he completed the first of several drafts simply entitled "The Economic Weapon of the League." After making a case for effective economic sanctions, implemented after careful preparation, Salter wrote:

> Many people think that the League is founded more upon good intentions than upon a cool consideration of the stern realities of international trouble. It is, therefore, desirable on general grounds that while the first meetings of the Council and of the Assembly should give the world the positive hope of removing misunderstandings and promoting international co-operation, they should also show quite clearly that the Members of the League as a whole are

determined, if necessity arises, to enforce their will by effective action on any particular country which in the circumstances contemplated by the Covenant defies the general verdict of the world.[84]

The document, with modifications by Drummond, was approved and printed for submission to the Council. Further second thoughts on the subject from Drummond unfortunately led to the document being shelved.[85]

Throughout September and October, the provisional League secretariat laboured under a cloud of uncertainty. The delay in the American ratification of the peace treaty, consequently putting doubt on the legality of the League itself, led to most secretariat decisions being delayed.[86] On 7 November Salter unburdened himself in a letter to Morrow. With evident sadness, he wrote that the debates over ratification in the United States had "the effect of both postponing our work and also reducing it, because the character of what will be required has become so uncertain." Despite this, he saw a variety of urgent tasks that confronted the League, not the least being the provision of financial credits for countries desperate to reconstruct their economies.[87] In this climate of uncertainty, and at his own initiative, Salter undertook his first European trip on behalf of the League.[88] He addressed the SEC, meeting in Rome from 21 to 23 November, where he was very cautious not to suggest that the League, still unofficially constituted, and the SEC collaborate too closely. However, he did state that it would be "convenient" if the SEC were to continue temporarily to ensure "some form of international co-operation." As well, he equally foresaw the need for both organizations to concentrate on general problems of relief, the provision of international credits for "non-indemnity countries," and currency reform. The SEC in fact concluded with the recommendation that further study be given to the future relations between it and the League.[89] After the SEC meeting, Salter spent the next five days studying the Institute of Agriculture in Rome. He came away extremely critical of "the most top-heavy institution" he had ever studied. Nonetheless, he recommended reform of the Institute, particularly if the League could get effective control over its operations, a development which was finally achieved in May 1929.[90] On his return to London he reported to a Directors' meeting on 10 December, in blunt terms, that the SEC remained "with very little power for the reason that it had no money at its disposal."[91]

By early December Salter was well aware, as were so many others, that the deadlock in the Senate of the United States over ratification would not be broken. It was a heart breaking time to be involved with an organization in which he so thoroughly believed but one with an uncertain future. Still, Salter and the secretariat pressed ahead on both new and continuing problem areas. For a time the question of moving the League temporarily to Brussels, until permanent buildings were available in Geneva, was discussed. Salter, as others, counselled against the move and the plan was dropped.[92] Relations with the International Labour Organization [ILO] were also a cause of confusion and concern. Salter proposed the eventual solution, namely, the ILO would be regarded as "part of the League of Nations," but also parallel in terms of organization and constitution.[93] The question of another auxiliary agency of the League, that of a permanent transit organization, had a smoother development. The League's interest in this area stemmed from article 23(e) of the Covenant, which obliged member states "to secure and maintain freedom of communications and transit." In December 1919 the Ports, Waterways and Railways Conference at Paris drafted a convention for a permanent transit organization under the League. The question arose as to the degree of autonomy to be given to such a permanent authority, and its relation to the League. Deep differences surfaced as the secretariat pondered the problem. Salter weighed in with arguments in favour of tight links between the new organization and the League. Most of these found their way into the final convention, including provision for association for non-member states of the League, which were developed during the course of two conferences in 1921 and 1922 at Barcelona. What emerged was a transit organization whose secretariat was the Transit and Communications Section under the authority of the secretary general.[94] For a short time in 1923 Salter acted as interim head of this section before the permanent appointment of Robert Haas, with whom so much of the creative work of this section is associated.

The first six months of the provisional League drew to a close in a mood of frustration and despair widely shared by secretariat officials. The situation in the United States was particularly upsetting. As he surveyed the post-war European world, Drummond predicted "disaster in Europe of a most appalling kind" unless American co-operation was forthcoming.[95] For his part Salter was equally frustrated by problems ranging from European economic reconstruction to which nations would sit on the governing board of the ILO.[96] The Council of the League of Nations finally did meet on 16 January 1920 at the Quai d'Orsay in Paris, six days after the entry into force of the Versailles Treaty, and hence the League Covenant, but without American ratification.[97] In a post-mortem on the proceedings, one of the questions debated was the degree of publicity which should be accorded the proceedings.[98] Salter argued the merits of maximum publicity concomitant with maximum efficiency, best achieved by a mixture of open and closed meetings. By the time the Council reconvened in London on 11 February for its first public meeting, a variation of the Salter compromise had been adopted.[99] By that time, too, Salter was already at work in Paris as the newly appointed secretary general of the Reparation Commission, set up under the Versailles Peace Treaty and mandated to determine the extent of German reparations for war damages.[100]

In early January Salter's name had been advanced for the position by Sir John Bradbury, the British representative on the Reparation Commission. Support for this nomination, in exchange for a French chairman, came from Sir Austen Chamberlain, the Chancellor of the Exchequer. On 8 January he wrote to Salter:

> It is with some hesitation that I invite you to undertake this work, because I recognize that it would involve the abandonment of the important work on which you are at present engaged in connection with the League of Nations – in fact I should not ask you to relinquish that work unless I felt that it was in the interests of the public service that you should do so. It is hardly necessary for me to emphasize the importance attaching to the post which I now offer, as you would be the first to recognize it, or the need for securing as Secretary General to the Reparation Commission a Civil Servant whose experience and qualifications leave no doubt as to his ability to perform the work successfully. I know of no one who possesses the necessary qualifications to a greater degree than yourself, and I earnestly hope that I may have your permission to approach the Foreign Office with a view to ascertaining whether your transfer could be arranged.[101]

This quite unexpected offer caused Salter a great deal of soul-searching which included consultations with friends and associates. To Keynes who had recommended rejection, Salter replied on 13 January:

> Both Lord Robert Cecil & Drummond took the view that, having regard to the poor present prospects of an active economic policy by the League, & the great & immediate powers of the Commission, I should accept the offer. This I have now done &, if the British nomination is accepted by the Commission, I shall be starting work practically at once.[102]

On the same day Chamberlain wrote to Prime Minister David Lloyd George, recommending Salter as "quite the best man available." Warren Fisher, the head of the civil service and who was consulted about the position, was quoted as having described Salter as "*persona grata* with all the Allies," possessed of "a first rate mind," knowledgeable about financial matters, and with a forceful imagination. Besides, Drummond felt that Salter would be more usefully employed with the Reparation Commission.[103] Salter's nomination was presented and quickly approved by the Commission on 24 January, the same meeting which approved the recommendations of the Committee for the Organization of the Reparations Commission.[104] Prior to taking up his new appointment, Salter wrote at length to Drummond. He explained that he had accepted with diffidence, and only because of the delays in developing the secretariat. "My real interest is in the League," Salter wrote, "and in such general principles and development of policy as I understand the League to stand for." Hence, he offered to return at a suitable time in the future. Drummond responded, "your decision was right," and accepted Salter's offer of a future return to the League.[105] By the first week of February Salter was already at work in Paris, engaging staff for several departments and for the tasks ahead.[106]

The fact remained that Salter left the League, to which he had dedicated six months of intensive work, and on the eve of its official and legal existence. He did so only reluctantly and under pressure from Chamberlain, who presented the work as serving both national and international interests. In addition, status and salary were both increased with the move to the Reparation Commission. The overriding consideration, however, was that during 1919 Salter was obsessed with European economic and financial reconstruction. His ambitions presupposed naturally American inclusion and a League commitment to innovation and intervention. Neither was being fulfilled early in 1920 when he was approached with this new offer. He was convinced that the Reparation Commission would give effective scope to his views and ambitions. "It was rightly foreseen," he later observed, "that reparation would occupy a central position in the relations between Great Britain and France in the years immediately ahead, in the relations of both to the new Germany, and in the general economic recovery of Europe."[107] No doubt, too, he shared Keynes' widely publicized view that the Reparation Commission would "yet be transformed from an instrument of oppression and rapine into an economic council of Europe."[108] The two, however, differed on other issues, in particular the latter's <u>The Economic Consequences of the Peace</u>, which Keynes had read to Salter in manuscript. On 14 October 1919 Salter urged Keynes to tone down the criticisms of Wilson and American diplomacy which he thought would harm the efforts to bring the United States into the League of Nations. In response, Keynes wrote that he was "recasting my story to some extent," but still expected some American "resentment."[109] Many years later Salter observed that the book, brilliant as it was, "probably did more harm than good."[110]

While officially on a leave of absence from the League, Salter left London in the last week of January to travel once more to Paris. He was soon installed in what he described as a "palatial" office on the first floor of the Astoria Hotel, at 131 Avenue des Champs-Elysées. The room, in fact, had been earmarked for Kaiser Wilhelm to watch the victorious German troops marching along the Champs-Elysées through the Arc de Triomphe. Within two months, with the growth in personnel and tasks, he received authorization to rent a second building in rue Bassano.[111] Private accommodation proved more troublesome. At an exorbitant rent, he secured a small apartment but one plagued by continuous squabbling between landlord and tenants. To this he remained an amused, though untroubled, witness.[112] "These are crowded days," he wrote. "I start with a French lesson at 8.30, get to the office about 9.30, leave about 8 & more often than not have a shop dinner & shop talk for the rest of the night. So I've had no time so far for a gay life."[113]

The Reparation Commission, of which Salter was now the first secretary general, had its origins in Part VIII, Reparation, of the Versailles Peace Treaty. The Allied and associated powers had been unable to agree upon the amount of compensation Germany would owe for "loss and damage." Consequently, Article 233 of the treaty authorised its determination by an "inter-Allied Commission to be known as the Reparation Commission." It was to have a five-member commission, with delegates from the United States, Britain, France, Italy and generally Belgium, with Japanese or Serbian officials attending on specific matters. Once appointed, the delegates were to act autonomously and independent of government instruction.[114] The Reparation Commission formally came into existence with the ratification of the Versailles Treaty on 10 January 1920. Salter later observed that two erroneous assumptions doomed the Commission to failure from the outset. The first was that the expert delegates would succeed where the Big Four had failed. In the event, the total damages assessed by the Reparation Commission at the deadline of 1 May 1921 were "hopelessly beyond Germany's capacity." The second assumption, that an odd number of delegates would always ensure a majority vote, proved equally erroneous. Thus with the final failure on 19 March of the United States Senate to ratify the peace settlement, American representation became ambiguous at best. With only four permanent members, in cases of deadlock the Commission had to fall back on Article 437 of the treaty which provided for a double vote from the French chairman. Under such disabilities, Salter wrote, "the Commission, instead of being all-powerful, independent and united, was in fact, impotent, dependent and divided; its powerful personalities a source of disruption rather than strength, its internal organization founded on what one member described as 'the sacred principle of international distrust.'"[115] Such strictures did not reflect merely wisdom after the event. Certainly, Salter went to the Reparation Commission hopeful about the constructive work that he might help succeed. However, he soon fell under the general gloom associated with the intractable question of reparation. The fact remains that he made little lasting contribution to the Reparation Commission.

In the short term, it was symptomatic that reparation related issues appeared to occupy only part of Salter's time. For a period after arriving in Paris he was, as he called it, "rushed off my feet."[116] Thereafter he kept up a lively correspondence with members of the League secretariat. He pressed Drummond to appoint an Advisory Committee on International Statistics to realize the conclusions of the August conference. A Council document on the subject was prepared and approved by him during a visit to London in the last week of February.[117] On this same visit, Salter also helped organize another project in which he was greatly interested. Since November he had been lobbying for the summoning of a major financial conference, attended by leading bankers and others, to plan a European-wide programme of economic reconstruction. With the approval of the British Treasury, the League went ahead with more detailed planning to which Salter contributed.[118] Finally, in London he signed the preface of one of the earliest publications by the League, <u>Currencies after the War: a Survey of Conditions in Various Countries</u>. In this Salter pointed out that the book, whose contributors included leading bankers and economists from eight countries, was designed to offer information on which to base future currency policy. It was urged that an economic conference should indeed be summoned to deal with worldwide problems of inflation. Continued currency depreciation, it was stated, would lead to "bankruptcy and anarchy in Europe."[119] The larger project was making progress and the publication, one of the most concrete achievements of Salter's first period at the League, became a model of numerous similar surveys produced by the Economic and Financial Section. Interestingly, on his return to Paris, Salter received an invitation which was to lead to his own first publication. He was asked to contribute a volume on "Inter-allied Control of Shipping" to the <u>Economic and Social History of the World War</u>, sponsored by the Carnegie Endowment for International Peace. The American editor-in-chief, James T. Shotwell, later described the venture as "the greatest co-operative history ever written." By the time the series concluded in March 1937, 152 volumes had appeared, many written by individuals with relevant wartime experience.[120] Salter was an obvious choice to analyse Allied control of shipping. Replying to the chairman of the British Editorial Board, Sir William Beveridge, Salter agreed to write on the theme, which he regarded as important, of "an experiment in international administration." He also promised an early completion date, the end of the year which the Board found acceptable.[121]

During his first months as secretary general of the Reparation Commission, Salter turned his attention to various organizational matters. The structure of an international secretariat was familiar to him and he set about building a new one. So, for example, he expanded the translation services, particularly those from English into French.[122] He was at great pains to establish an intelligence service for the Commission, which he regarded as part of the mandate authorised by the Peace Treaty. Eventually, Maurice Frère, later President of the Bank of Belgium, took responsibility for this activity.[123] Salter also worked out how to co-ordinate the relations between the Reparation Commission and its "General Services," such as Finance, and Restitution and Reparation in Kind, and the Maritime, given that he was the conduit for any such communication.[124] In several instances, Salter in fact called on the League secretariat for assistance. This intimate contact, though quite unofficial, had wider purposes as well. Firstly, Salter intended to make his position one with some influence on reparation policy. He saw his own role as "designed to suggest a possible criterion for the maximum annual sum which could be taken from Germany supposing she were nursed back to pre-war activity." Secondly, he was quite determined to arrange "an officially recognized liaison between the two Secretariats," at least in connection with the forthcoming international financial conference. And finally, it was his intention to implement "a policy of generous publicity" for the work of the Reparation Commission.[125] None of these expectations unfortunately were to be fulfilled in the long term. As Salter later pointed out, "the legal authority of the Commission to adjust current demands to capacity did not include the right to scale down the total bill."[126]

Salter's correspondence at this time illustrated his short-term gloom combined with long-term hope. In what he described as "a black letter" to Violet Markham on 18 March, he wrote:

> I'm in the middle of a very difficult, unsatisfying & I'm afraid hopeless job here – the general international distrust & suspicion is worse than anything I've ever seen even in Paris last year & renders efficient work – or indeed progress at all – practically impossible. The things we want – the spirit & policy in the world's affairs – that we've both wanted before & through the war will have to struggle through more slowly & painfully than we had thought in 1918. I believe & hope that we shall both live to see them at least substantially advanced. I feel and have felt through all this last year that the whole top layer of government, of administration & entrenched power, is unworthy of the real people of the world – the spirit we saw at the beginning of the war is not dead but only lethargic & crushed – at no very distant date we shall find people in many countries to evoke it.

Several weeks later he again affirmed to Violet Markham that he did not regret his decision to come to Paris. "I am confident it is right," he wrote, "though the way ahead looks longer & less pleasant than ever. We have I'm afraid to resign ourselves to losing the quick progress & visible results that seemed possible after the armistice, but the only thing is to plod if we can't run." Besides, he still remained "doubtful" about any alternative prospects, particularly at the League of Nations.[127]

Salter never found the two and a half years he was to spend in Paris "either unhappy or unfruitful." Not least, for the first time since 1911 he began to slow down. Status, substantial salary and staff, and a life free from daily crises enabled him to become expansive. He even found some pleasure in entertaining, noting little as there was "in either my experience or my temperament to fit me for it."[128] He grew to enjoy the company of the French representative on the Reparation Commission, Raymond Poincaré – "the most perfect human machine." He acquired a deep affection for the American delegate, Roland Boyden, and a mixture of fear and admiration for Sir John Bradbury, whose "foibles added spice to many conversations in Paris."[129] In particular, he embarked upon one of the most intimate friendships of his life that centred upon Royall (Peter) Tyler and members of the family. Royall Tyler, an American and three years younger than Salter, was an individual with eclectic tastes and friendships. By the time he was to meet Salter in 1919, he was already an editor of the Spanish Calendar of British State Papers, an intelligence officer in the United States army and a member of the American delegation to the Paris Peace Conference. "Never has a career owed less to planning than his," recalled his son, William R. Tyler, "but he succeeded in everything to which he turned his hand." His eventual achievements in the areas of history, art history and international finance were, according to his son, the products of "exceptional intellectual powers, a strong character graced with extraordinary sensitiveness, and a natural drive and vitality. He was by temperament the opposite of ascetic."[130] In 1920 Salter appointed him to the Reparation Commission with responsibility for personnel questions.[131]

Outwardly, there could hardly be anything more opposite than these two individuals. Yet they recognized the distinctiveness in each other, and sought to supplement respective weaknesses. Immediately nicknaming him "little Arthur," Tyler consciously widened Salter's circle of acquaintances and areas of interests away from the narrowly political and economic. As early as 4 May 1920 Tyler was already entertaining Salter at his home, where the latter met the Italian born Elisina Tyler. She remained an intimate confidant of Salter's for years to come. During the following months, Salter and Royall Tyler frequently toured the French countryside, with the latter acting as the expert guide to French ecclesiastical architecture. Salter, too, benefited from Tyler's knowledge of fine food and wine, acquiring tastes which lasted a lifetime.[132] Among the numerous individuals whom Salter met through the Tylers was the American novelist, Edith Wharton. Royall Tyler described their first meeting on 9 August at Wharton's home at St Brice-sous-Forêt:

Yesterday evening I took Salter out to Jean Marie [Edith Wharton's home, twelve miles north of Paris, which Elisina Tyler had found for the novelist]. It was a lovely evening and no one else was there. Edith was very nice indeed, and quiet. We all enjoyed it very much, I think. Edith liked him and understood him at once, and I think they will be great friends. His quickness delighted her, of course. We told stories and laughed a great deal.[133]

Edith Wharton had a different initial impression of Salter, noting that he was "a sort of 'roll-top desk person'" and a "statistician." Later she came to value Salter's "attractive and imposing qualities," though the anticipated friendship never blossomed.[134] For his part, Salter introduced the Tylers to Violet Markham and her husband James Carruthers, at the time chief demobilisation officer for the British army on the Rhine. Immediately afterwards, Tyler wrote:

Mrs. Carruthers I liked enormously, as I think you would. She expresses herself beautifully, is full of vitality and cares for all sorts of things. Bodily she is a plain stoutish woman of about fifty, but a very vivacious expression at once warns one that there is something unusual about her, and whatever subject comes up she handles it in a masterly way – masterly because adapted to the degree of her knowledge or ignorance of the subject.[135]

In her memoir Violet Markham referred to the Tylers as "remarkable and gifted." She paid tribute to the fact that Royall Tyler had introduced her to the world of early Christian and Medieval art and architecture which led to her publishing in 1929 a popular tourist guide, Romanesque France.[136] Recalling his long association with Royall Tyler, Salter described him as "the closest to a male friend I ever had."[137]

From a personal and social point of view, these were happy times for Salter. Despite some residual shyness, an overly serious demeanour, and a fondness for informative rather than informal conversation, he was opening himself to his surroundings. His writing career was also beginning to occupy much of his time. At the end of April he had completed, in the course of a weekend, his contribution, "Economics and Finance," to The League of Nations Starts: An Outline by Its Organizers.[138] His chapter described the work of the secretariat, the influence which inter-allied wartime co-operation had exerted on the organization of the League, and concluded with some warnings. Then from the perspective of his recent knowledge of reparations, he cautioned that the economic foundations of European reconstruction were "insecure." He continued, "There is the weight not of a large indemnity, which might be payable and possible, but what is much more serious, the crushing weight of an unknown and uncertain indemnity."[139]

In fact, Salter was holding out little hope that the Reparation Commission could play any constructive role in the economic rehabilitation of Europe. Its authority as defined by the Versailles Peace Treaty was already being eroded.[140] In a series of high level meetings, beginning at San Remo on 19 April and encompassing that at Spa on 5 July, no progress was reached on reparation payments. The Spa conference could only agree on the proportion of payments due for the six month period from 1 August. It was among Salter's post-conference duties, which he regarded as an "urgent necessity" to execute these decisions.[141] There were, however, impediments as far as Salter was concerned in achieving these ends. These he summarised in a 41-page memorandum, entitled "The Reparation Commission from the Point of View of Administrative Efficiency." He restricted the circulation of the memorandum to delegates and assistant delegates, hoping thereby to achieve complete frankness in expressing his views. He argued that the achievements of the Commission were "very small in relation to its size and expense" and that it was "cumbrous and expensive." The three most important duties given to the Commission, evaluating damages, drawing up a schedule of payments and planning how to modify the schedule with reference to Germany's capacity to pay, had not even begun. Describing the situation as "urgent," and not least the fact that the Commission would likely cost about a million pounds a year, he went on to make numerous detailed suggestions for administrative reform in the interests of greater efficiency.[142] But he was hardly sanguine. "I contemplated two years when I came," he wrote to Violet Markham on 18 August, and continued, "I've done little except learn my job since." He confided that he had "just put forward a biggish reform scheme which won't have much chance of success now but will have a better chance next year."[143]

On 24 September one of Salter's long held ambitions was achieved. An International Finance Conference, the first organized by the League of Nations, opened in Brussels. He had lobbied for months for such a gathering, as a prerequisite for European reconstruction. Then on 23 June he had obtained permission from the Reparation Commission to exchange information with the League, and on 17 August Drummond agreed to attendance by the Reparation Commission.[144] In late August Salter visited London to keep abreast of pre-conference planning by the League secretariat.[145] On 7 September the Reparation Commission, after much discussion, agreed to send Salter to Brussels largely as an observer.[146] Once in Brussels, he officially followed the deliberations as the representative of the Reparation Commission, but he also contributed to the proceedings, albeit behind the scenes. Much had been prepared "very carefully with Salter, Blackett, Walter Layton and Robert Brand," Monnet later recalled. As well, Salter was glad, as he put it, to "give a hand to my old League friends."[147] In fact, he took an active part in drafting the final resolutions approved by the conference. In this respect, he was applying his talents "in the interesting art of divining from the discussions the wording on which it is possible to secure agreement and then 'putting it over'."[148] It was a talent he was to apply on numerous occasions in coming years. Salter left Brussels on 8 October satisfied, though not euphoric. Admittedly, the conference resolutions were "a compendium of financial orthodoxy," including the balancing of budgets, measures to combat inflation, a return to the gold standard and greater freedom for international trade. Its immediate value, in Salter's opinion, was that 86 delegates from 39 countries, representing 75% of the world's population, had been assembled for discussion under the auspices of the League. This educative function, in the view of the League secretariat a decade later, helped bring the international economy back to the "narrow path of saving and solvency."[149] The uncertain factor at Brussels, as previously, lay with the reparation issue. On 26 October discussion at the Reparation Commission centred on the concern that "the time limit would arrive without the Commission having done its work," under Article 235 of the peace treaty, in assessing Germany's reparations.[150] Indeed, progress continued to be painfully slow, confined largely to occasional inter-allied conferences. At such "pleasure-resort" gatherings, Salter observed, "an international official had no real place, and was indeed not only a novel but little understood creature."[151] In fact, he did not even attend the next stage in the reparation discussion, the Conference of Finance Experts which opened at Brussels on 16 December and continued in Paris in the New Year. What finally emerged was a provisional rather than a complete reparation plan.[152] This envisaged a schedule of payments, beginning on 1 May 1921 and extending over a period of 42 years. However attractive these so-called Paris Resolutions of 29 January 1921 were for the Allied powers, they clearly overrode and seriously weakened the authority of the Reparation Commission.[153]

Increasingly subject to a "sense of futility and frustration," which ultimately led to his leaving the Reparation Commission, Salter diverted his attention and energy elsewhere.[154] He turned enthusiastically to the task of completing his book on Allied shipping control, having signed on 22 September the final contract which provided for an honorarium of £300.[155] By the middle of November, writing during the late evenings and on weekends, always in longhand, the manuscript was complete except for the important final section. Here Salter discussed what he termed "the principles" of Allied wartime administration, and he attempted to forecast the administrative development of the League.[156] The more the Reparation Commission failed to fulfil its mandate, the more Salter seemed determined to press home his views on international administration. Thus on 17 December he lectured on "Some Problems of

International Administration" to the Society of Civil Servants in London. Here he analysed the mechanics of his subject, but drew the strands together with a conclusion that focused on the League of Nations. He admitted that the League "suffers from both extravagant hopes and excessive despair." He continued:

> The League of Nations, however, can only be the medium through which the desire of the world may express itself. International co-operation can be effected if, but only if, the world desires it. If the League is to succeed it must not forget the essential principle of international administration that was discovered in the war. It must proceed by trying to link together the international administrations of the world. It must proceed by attempting to penetrate within the national administrations. It must assume, not the role of a super-Government, but the role of a co-ordinating secretariat.[157]

During the following days in London, Salter worked non-stop on his manuscript.[158] Returning to Paris on 30 December, he triumphantly wrote to Beveridge: "I have now finished my book 'Allied Shipping Control' in accordance with the promise to get it done by the end of the year." His primary anxiety as the year closed was that the book should be published as soon as possible, given the topical nature of the "conclusions for the future of international administration."[159] Beside the completion of the manuscript, Salter derived further satisfaction as the year drew to a close. Public recognition of his work was never paramount in his mind. However, he must have derived some satisfaction that his public service and work in the area of international administration was receiving some recognition. On 28 February 1919 he had received from the Belgian King the Croix d'Officier de l'Ordre de la Couronne. This was followed on 21 September 1920 by the French Commandeur dans l'ordre de la Légion d'Honneur and within four days by the Commandatore del Suo Ordine della Corona d'Italia.[160] The knighthood recommended by Cecil in April 1919, however, still eluded Salter.

Following the Paris Resolutions of 29 January 1921, Salter returned to London from 1 to 7 March to attend yet further Allied meetings at Lancaster House. Having proposed a reparation figure and a schedule of payments in Paris, it was hoped that Germany would respond in London. When that finally came, it proved unsatisfactory and led to the imposition of military and economic sanctions. Afterwards, as a leading German negotiator wrote, "chaos reigned in reparations questions."[161] The failure of the London Conference resulted in a period of intensive work in the Reparation Commission. Time and again Salter replied to letters making demands on his time with the refrain, "I'm so overwhelmed with Reparation work, May 1st is our crucial date under the Treaty."¹⁶² Finally, the Reparation Commission completed its primary task. Meeting in London on 28 April, the Commission notified the German government of its liability for damages amounting to "132 milliard (billion) gold marks." The "Schedule of Payments," prescribing the time and manner for securing and discharging the entire obligation of Germany for reparation under Articles 231, 232 and 233 of the Treaty of Versailles, followed on 5 May.¹⁶³ The London Payments Plan, which in reality amounted to an ultimatum accepted by the German government, ended the long struggle over fixing the figures for reparation debt.

From the vantage point of his writing career Salter was grateful for the respite from reparation questions. Besides his numerous official duties, he was also keeping a close eye on the pre-publication progress of his manuscript _Allied Shipping Control_. The most serious of his concerns with the Carnegie Endowment related to the final part of his book dealing with "International Administration." The editors of the series baulked at its inclusion on the grounds that it was personal reflection rather than history. Salter retorted that this section "includes what I'm anxious to preach a little this year about the League." He reinforced this moral fervour with threats to withdraw the manuscript.¹⁶⁴ At one point he complained, "I'm sorry to be so troublesome but you realize how irritating it is for a writer to have more time taken over the publishing of a work than it took him to write it (even though it was written in the evenings & on Sundays on the top of an office life)."¹⁶⁵ A combination of tact, flattery and constructive criticism from Beveridge finally managed to assuage Salter. The offending section of the book was included, but with a disclaimer that it represented the views of the Carnegie Endowment.¹⁶⁶ Shotwell's final comment about Salter was that as "a man who has moved the merchant navies of the world during the war he is not likely to accept a setback readily."¹⁶⁷ _Allied Shipping Control_ finally appeared in the first week of July at the same time as Salter settled in at the Reform Club for a month to oversee publication and reviews. As would be his practice with future books, he actively solicited reviews and publicity. In particular, he was anxious to elicit "candid criticism from those who can speak with authority." The reviews which followed were indeed "full & favourable, much better than I expected," he noted on 30 July.¹⁶⁸ _The Times_ wrote of the book as a "full and illuminating account," while _The Economist_ thought it "a fascinating tale."¹⁶⁹ The _Times Literary Supplement_ noted "the accomplishment was great. The achievement has worthily been put on record by Mr. Salter in his highly interesting contribution to the history of the war."¹⁷⁰ Further praise was forthcoming from friends and wartime colleagues. Sir Percy Bates observed that "As an accurate record of the facts and events described it is almost impossible that the book will be surpassed."¹⁷¹ J. Reeve Brooke wrote of his "great satisfaction in hearing the chorus assigning to you the position you ought to have in world affairs." H.G. Wells noted that it was a book "from which I have much to learn."[172] It was not until September, however, that Allied Shipping Control came in for some acute criticism on points of detail and proportion in the letters to the editor columns of the New Statesman.[173] After seven weeks the editor ordered a stop to the correspondence.

With Allied Shipping Control now part of the public domain, Salter turned his attention to reparation and related problems, including the work of the League. With regard to the latter, he never for a moment abandoned the closest scrutiny of its activities. He was frequently consulted, asked for advice and kept *au courant*.[174] So for example, on 25 August he set out to tour the Saar basin in the company of Royall Tyler who left the following record:

> Little A. and I enjoyed our trip very much, and it was most interesting to see the League of Nations' experiment in governing the Saar Basin. Lambert and Moltke took us about in their cars and showed us the whole of their little principality, which is the most autocratic state in the civilized world at present. They have power of life and death, taxation etc. etc., and I must say their people look very happy and contented.[175]

For his part, Salter thought that the League had "competently discharged" its administrative tasks. However, he considered it "quite out of line" with the League's advisory and consultative functions, and therefore "the worst possible test of the League."[176] On the other hand, nothing quite so engrossed Salter at this time as the Upper Silesia boundary dispute. Unable to reach a decision on the demarcation of the Polish-German frontier in Upper Silesia, the Allied Supreme Council on 12 August had referred the problem for arbitration to the Council of the League of Nations. Salter shared the view that this was the organization's first real test. He was also aware that the dispute would affect Germany's abilities to pay reparation, as Upper Silesia contained one of the largest industrial complexes in Europe. At last, meeting in its permanent home in Geneva on 12 October, the Council announced its recommendation in favour of partition with full economic guarantees for all parties.[177] "I've been very rushed, both here, Geneva & in London in connection with the Upper Silesian question," Salter wrote in the aftermath of the Council announcement.[178] In fact he was very intimately involved behind the scenes, especially when the danger loomed of the economic arrangements being shelved. "Whether or not the League's solution is satisfactory," he urged, "it must be accepted and put fully into practice." He then worked out a legal ploy, described by Hankey as "very sound," to guarantee acceptance of both the frontier and economic provisions.[179] Thus the Council recommendations were accepted by all concerned, with details eventually confirmed on 15 May 1922. While complaints from both sides of the new frontiers persisted for years to come, the League had indeed passed its first major test.

Attention in the fall of 1921, in the meantime, had turned to the question of "deliveries in kind." The Wiesbaden agreement of 6 October, never fully implemented until 31 March 1922, had been intended to stimulate such deliveries from Germany to France to help with reconstruction.[180] Yet it was Salter's belief at the time, and subsequently, that reparation using German "men, materials and management" offered a solution. Employing such resources to repair the war devastated regions of France and Belgium, he argued, would have involved no strain on the German mark, provided work for the German building trades, and offered relief for hard-pressed French contractors.[181] At the time Salter attempted to gather additional support for such a policy, but unfortunately his efforts ended in failure. From that point in the fall of 1921 reparation work held little attraction. Indeed, on 14 December Germany had asked for a moratorium on payments as prescribed by the London Schedule of Payments. The question was taken out of the hands of the Reparation Commission and discussed instead at an Allied meeting at Cannes which opened on 11 January and which Salter attended.[182] A provisional postponement was in fact agreed upon, with another rescheduling of Germany's obligations slated for 31 May 1922.[183]

All this time, Salter continued to distance himself from the Reparation Commission. As far back as the fall of 1920, just months after he left the League, Drummond was already asking for Salter's return.[184] Drummond wrote to him on 24 October 1920 urging that he return to active service at the League. Drummond was unhappy with Walter Layton, Salter's replacement, and lobbied unsuccessfully to have Salter leave the Reparations Commission.[185] On 3 November Salter responded that the Reparation Commission was still in its "formative stage" and he felt obliged to continue with his work in Paris, a decision really taken by the British government.[186] There the matter rested until January 1922 when he confidentially advised each of the delegates to the Reparation Commission that he felt "reluctantly obliged to resign," effective 30 June 1922. This was even as he accepted his annual re-appointment to the Commission, accompanied with praise for his "competence and scrupulous exactitude."[187] On 27 January the Reparation Commission approved his appointment to a British sub-committee to prepare documentation for the upcoming Genoa Conference on European financial and economic questions. Salter was recommended by Sir John Bradbury as someone who had "considerable experience of international meetings of this character."[188] In fact, Salter was determined to return to what had become his real passion – the financial and economic reconstruction of Europe. Already he was involved in Austria's financial difficulties which by February 1922 had become catastrophic. A year earlier, in March 1921, the Reparation Commission had agreed to release Austria from some of its reparation obligations.[189] Collapse was only averted by a pooling of credits advanced by Britain, France, Italy and Czechoslovakia. Salter's interest in the matter was observed by Royall Tyler, who wrote, "You may imagine that we are following with great interest the news about progress being made towards the granting of the 2½ million credits [i.e., Britain's share] to Austria, and surmising as to how it is being engineered. Little A's eye twinkles over it."[190]

With Austria now part of an international financial rescue operation, Salter decided on a tour of inspection. He took Royall Tyler with him to Vienna, where on 20 February Tyler recorded:

> We had quite a comfortable journey and arrived on time, to find most of the R.C. people waiting for us in the snow. At the hotel there were letters from the Chancellor asking us to lunch today. I liked [Johann] Schober very much indeed, and so did Salter. We found them all very cheered about the credits, and stoutly decided to do their best to make the utmost of the opportunity. A very much better atmosphere than when I was here last. I'm only rather nervous about their executive. Schober doesn't seem at all apprehensive of the political situation, and he certainly does radiate strength and confidence. Tonight he's given us his box at the opera, & we are hearing Ariadne auf Naxos, with Strauss conducting.[191]

While in Vienna, one of Salter's tasks was to close down what he described as "the indefensible scandal" of maintaining there a vast and expensive Reparation Sub-Commission. This he accomplished, reducing a staff of over 200 to about 20 hand-picked individuals who were transferred to Paris on 1 May. From Vienna Salter and Tyler travelled briefly to Budapest and then returned to Paris. They presented their report which was approved by the Reparation Commission on 18 April.[192]

Throughout March and April Salter busied himself with the forthcoming conference at Genoa. He sensed that if the ambitious reconstruction schemes being prepared for discussion at the conference were realized, including free trade and a return to the gold standard, the League would at last find its proper role in the economic life of Europe, and on his return to Geneva he could play a role in that reconstruction.[193] The Genoa Conference proved to be a complete failure, with the delegates merely reiterating many of the conclusions of the earlier Brussels' Conference. There remained one glimmer of hope for Salter. On 28 March Bradbury had proposed to the Reparation Commission a novel solution to prevailing reparation difficulties. It was agreed to set up an international committee of expert bankers. Its mandate would be to examine the possibility of the German government raising foreign loans to be applied against the partial redemption of the capital of the reparation debt.[194] A distinguished Bankers' Committee was convened, with Salter acting as secretary, and which met for the first time in Paris on 24 May. Its members included J. Pierpont Morgan (United States), Sir Robert Kindersley (Britain), Jean Sergent (France), Carl Bergmann (Germany), D'Amelio (Italy), Léon Delacroix, as chairman (Belgium) and Gerald Vissering (Holland).[195] A successful outcome to the deliberations of this committee might have changed Salter's determination to turn his back on reparations.[196] Unfortunately, the committee was at once faced with a question of competence. With the exception of the French representative, the bankers argued that the question of a German loan demanded a discussion of reparation in general, and its possible reduction. When the committee decided nonetheless to enquire whether Germany's reparation debt was negotiable, it was brought into conflict with official French views. The bankers were irreparably split and on 10 June adjourned indefinitely.[197] In its penultimate hours, Salter had struggled to make one final contribution to the reparation question. "Poor little Arthur worked all night last night, and may have to again," Royall Tyler wrote on 9 June.[198] The following day, the final report was completed, found acceptable and presented, without a French signature, to the Reparation Commission.[199] In accepting the report, Bradbury praised Salter's "valuable assistance," and confessed that "the reparation problem, unfortunately, was one of the most baffling problems which had ever confronted the intelligence of mankind."[200] One of the committee members, J.P. Morgan, wrote to Salter in gratitude for "the extraordinary ability and conciseness of the report." Morgan was still confident that it would have far-reaching results.[201] Salter did not quite share this unremitting optimism. He believed that but for French opposition, "we might have gone far towards settling the reparation problem (though it can never be settled until inter-allied debts can also be dealt with)." Salter later explained that the Bankers' Committee was forced:

> to suspend operations. I was then very anxious that we should leave behind us a manifesto which would win public opinion to some extent & help to make it possible for the Committee to meet again later. In this I had some luck. Most of the delegates had contemplated a short 'non possimus' reply of a few lines. But I sat up through the night & wrote a full report & got it through the next morning with hardly any change. It was quite a good stunt to finish with, & I hope may really be of some use. If the Committee does meet again in the autumn or winter I shall come back for a month or two.[202]

As The Times commented the Bankers' Committee had "replied both in the negative and in the positive." Namely, the report suggested that a loan was only possible if France reduced the amount of Germany's liability, but this could only be achieved if inter-allied indebtedness was likewise reduced.[203] The Bankers' Committee never reconvened and immediately afterwards Salter submitted his formal resignation to the Reparation Commission.

Salter's departure was the first item on the agenda when the Reparation Commission convened on 16 June. He began by pointing out that his acceptance of the secretary general position had always been a conditional one. He reminded delegates of his promise to the League that he would return if needed after two years and that time had now arrived. "I leave with feelings of real and deep gratitude," he concluded, adding that "one of the most interesting has also been one of the happiest periods of my life." Following this brief statement, there occurred an outpouring of tributes to Salter personally and the work he had done. The chairman, Louis Dubois, praised Salter's "high sense of duty" and "tireless activity." The task of setting up the secretariat "had been so rapidly and efficiently carried out," Dubois continued, "that from the first moment the General Secretariat had been able to fulfil all that the Reparation Commission could require of it with a regularity that was little less than astonishing." He concluded: "His well-considered judgement and his conciliatory and impartial mind made him the model of what the secretary general of an inter-allied organization as important as the Commission should be." What then followed from Bradbury was as effusive as it was measured. He stated that Salter's "most pre-eminent quality was that he possessed the spirit of the New Age." The minutes of the meeting record Bradbury continuing in the same vein:

> Quite recently a form of international civilisation had been introduced whose apostles had been regarded as citizens of the world – a position which was some times regarded as incompatible with good citizenship of their own country. Public opinion had now come to recognize that a man might at the same time show loyalty to his family and his country and would, Sir John Bradbury hoped, in the near future come to the conception that the fact that a man was a good citizen of the world did not prevent his being a loyal citizen of his own country. To Sir John Bradbury's mind, Sir Arthur Salter was one of the apostles of that New Age. In all the circumstances of the case, however, Sir John Bradbury did not think that he could pay a higher tribute to Sir Arthur Salter than to say that good cosmopolite as he was, he had never ceased to be a good British citizen.

In response to this and the additional tributes which followed, Salter expressed his "deep gratitude." His resignation became effective on 30 June.

The praise Salter heard in the Reparation Commission was echoed in his private correspondence. James A. Logan, an unofficial American delegate to the Commission, wrote of Salter as an "international citizen."[204] Another, more substantial form of recognition, at last came Salter's way. On 24 May Lloyd George had informed Salter, to the latter's "immense amazement," that he had been appointed a Knight Commander of the Order of Bath (KCB).[205] It was an honour which pleased his intimate circle of friends. Frank Wise wrote from London that "the family" felt he had "earned it years ago." Anderson acknowledged that "on personal grounds you care little for these things but I am sure that you do care for the opinions of those who know you and your work."[206] In reality, Salter relished his KCB, as he explained to Violet Markham: "The one thing I did rather feel from the personal-official point of view was that I might be losing status for future opportunities & this quite alters that."[207]

The final two weeks of June were unusually hectic for Salter. "I have been overwhelmed with work and correspondence," he bemoaned on 26 June.[208] As well, there was an intensive round of farewell dinners which Royall Tyler arranged. Together they paid a farewell visit to Edith Wharton, driving out to St. Brice in Salter's "enchanting toy," a newly purchased Fiat automobile. Tyler went about these activities with a heavy heart. Finally, on 1 July he noted: "This is the first day of the new regime, you know how I grieve for Arthur; the perfume of that little flower is a thing one will not soon forget."[209] For his part, Salter left the Reparation Commission with no regrets for what he later termed its "follies and failures."[210] In a contemplative letter to Violet Markham on 22 June, he wrote:

> I go to Geneva tomorrow week, the 30th: and in spite of the personal friendships I'm leaving here, which will be a really serious loss, I am going with no kind of hesitation, & very gladly. I've been more and more sure that the decision was right ever since I took it. I think there is a chance – a real one though not a big one – that the tide may turn. And if so I've got much more opportunity of contributing something than I have here. If the chance is only 1 in 10 it's worth it. The work & the life will be more interesting, as I shall have not only my proper section (economic & finance), but some responsibility also for the other technical work (health, etc). In addition I shall understudy Drummond for liaison with London (which much needs improving) on all subjects.

Salter concluded his ruminations on a more personal, revealing note:

> Well, my dear Violet, this last seven years – just the period I have known you, have been incomparably the best in my life. All that is best, in personal friendship or in work, has come or came to its best fruition in that time. And you

know how large a part of your friendship, affection & support have been to me in that time. There were moments in the war when I nearly went under, and what you were to me then is more than I can ever express. It is curious that till I was over 30 the only people I knew intimately were men. Since then you & Margaret Brooke (whom I much want you to meet some time) & Marian Henderson have given me a more intimate friendship than I think I have with any man. It confirms me in my choice that, while many men I know think I'm foolish to leave here, you all three think I'm right to go.[211]

Salter was truly coming home to the League of Nations.

Endnotes

1. Salter, Memoirs, 127-128.
2. Salter, Allied Shipping Control, 230.
3. Salter, Allied Shipping Control, 231-234, 241-242.
4. Arthur Salter, "Problems of International Administration," in The Development of the Civil Service: Lectures Delivered Before the Society of Civil Servants, 1920-1921 (1922), 222-223.
5. Monnet, Memoirs, 76.
6. Salter, Allied Shipping Control, 180.
7. "Who Won the First War," Salter Papers, File 1, Anecdotes and Incidents.
8. Salter to Joseph S. Davis, 23 Dec. 1936, copy in author's archive, The Times, 3 Dec. 1936.
9. Davis to E.F. Gay, 13 Aug. 1918, copy in author's archive.
10. "Three Outstanding Men I Have Known," 29 pp. unpublished MS by Davis, 15 Feb. 1963, copy in author's archive. Davis also added, "Notes for Sidney Aster's Work on Lord Salter," 5 pp. MS, author's archive.
11. Ministry of Shipping, Distribution of Business, November 1918," NA-UK, MT25/62/37310/1921.
12. Obituary tribute, The Times, 28 May 1938, signed "A.S."
13. "Katherine Cox, 1887-1938," encl. in Gertrude Caton Thompson to the author, 5 Aug. 1979, author's archive.
14. Entry of 5 Jan. 1931, Felkin Diary, AEF/1/1/8.
15. Mark Arnold-Forster to the author, 24 July 1979, author's archive.
16. Salter, Allied Shipping Control, 243.
17. "Report of Executive, October 16th to November 15th, 1918," AMTC, 1918, 2, NA-UK, MT25/10/21068.

18. Minutes, Meeting at 3 Cranley Place, London, 7 Oct. 1918, Sir Alfred Zimmern Papers, Bodleian Library, Oxford.
19. "AMTC, 11th November, 1918 to April 6th, 1919," 1-4, 5, NA-UK, MT25/62/37344/1921, Salter, Memoirs, 131.
20. Minutes, War Cabinet 496, 4 Nov. 1918, NA-UK, CAB23/8.
21. Minutes, War Cabinet 501, 13 Nov. 1918, NA-UK, CAB23/8.
22. Minutes, EDDC 11th Meeting, 15 Oct. 1918, NA-UK, CAB27/44.
23. Minutes, EDDC 12th Meeting, 22 Oct. 1918, Draft Resolution, Inter-Allied Supply and Transport Organizations," 26 Oct. 1918, EDDC 55, NA-UK, CAB27/44.
24. Minutes, EDDC 15th Meeting, 5 Nov. 1918, Cecil to Sir Richard Crawford, 9 Nov. 1918, NA-UK, CAB27/44, "Communication by Salter to Permanent Representatives of France, Italy, and United States on the AMTE," 13 Nov. 1918, AMTC, November 1918-April 1919 [AMTC 1918-1919] 17, NA-UK, MT25/62/37344/1921.
25. Minutes, War Cabinet 501, 13 Nov. 1918, NA-UK, CAB23/8, House to Balfour, 1 Dec. 1918, Foreign Relations of the United States, 1919, The Paris Peace Conference, vol. 2 (Washington, DC), 648.
26. "AMTC, 11th November, 1918 to April 6th, 1919," AMTC 1918-1919, 2, NA-UK, MT25/62/37344/1921, Salter, Allied Shipping Control, 222.
27. "Note by the Shipping Controller on the Tonnage Situation in Relation to Future Shipping Policy," 13 Dec. 1918, G.T. 6470, CAB24/71, "Future Shipping Policy," 23 Dec. 1918, G.T. 6544, NA-UK, CAB24/72, Minutes, War Cabinet 514, 8 Jan. 1919, NA-UK, CAB23/9.
28. "Conference of British Representatives on Programme Committees," 5 Dec. 1918, AMTC 1918-1919, 18-23, NA-UK, MT25/62/37344/1921.
29. "Memorandum as to Constitution of an Inter-Allied Council to Deal with the Victualling and Supply of Allied, Neutral and Enemy Countries," 12 Dec. 1918, AMTC, 1918-1919, 50-52, NA-UK, MT25/62/37344/1921.
30. Salter, "Note as to Questions Not Adequately Covered by Existing Allied Authorities," 27 Jan. 1919, Lord Reading Papers, NA-UK, FO800/222.
31. Salter, Allied Shipping Control, 221.
32. Fayle, Seaborne Trade, vol. 3, 421, Salter, Allied Shipping Control, 224.
33. Salter to Captain C. Hardy, 4 Jan. 1919, NA-UK, MT25/23/62784/1918, "Memorandum of Meeting of AMTE at Lancaster House, January 6th, 1919," AMTC, 1918-1919, 110, NA-UK, MT25/62/37344/1921.
34. Salter, Allied Shipping Control, 223.
35. "Minutes of the First Session of the Allied Supreme Council of Supply and Relief, 13 Jan. 1919," in The Blockade of Germany After the Armistice, 1918-1919, Selected Documents, Suda Lorena Bane and Ralph Haswell Lutz, eds., (New York,

repr. 1972), 37-39, "The Trèves Agreement of 17th January 1919, in Respect of Relief Arrangements and the Employment of German Tonnage," AMTC, 1918-1919, 53-54, NA-UK, MT25/62/37344/1921, Hurley, Bridge to France, 276-281.
36. Salter, Memoirs, 132.
37. "Minutes of the Fifth Session Held at Paris, February 1st to 11th, 1919," AMTC, 1918-1919, 112-125. NA-UK, MT25/62/37344/1921.
38. "Minutes of Conference at Spa, 6-8 Feb. 1919," NA-UK, MT25/36/R337/1919.
39. "Minutes of the Fifth Session Held at Paris, February 1st to 11th, 1919," AMTC, 1918-1919, 112-125. NA-UK, MT25/62/37344/1921, The Times, 13 Feb. 1919.
40. Salter, Memoirs, 136.
41. Salter to Morrow, 28 Jan., 17 Feb. 1919, Morrow Papers, microfilm reel 80.
42. Hoover, An American Epic, vol. 2, 295-296, "First Meeting of First Session Held at the Ministry of Commerce, 17th February, 1919," Foreign Relations of the United States, The Paris Peace Conference, 1-3, http://digital.library.wisc.edu/1711.dl/FRUS.FRUS1919Parisv10.
43. Cecil to Lloyd George, 8 Feb. 1919, Lloyd George Papers, F/6/6/9, Minutes, War Cabinet 535, 24 Feb. 1919, Minutes, War Cabinet 542, 6 Mar. 1919, NA-UK, CAB23/9.
44. Salter, Allied Shipping Control, 221-222.
45. "Minutes of the Sixth Session Held at Paris on 10th March 1919," AMTC, 1918-1919, 126, NA-UK, MT25/62/37344/1921.
46. "Memorandum as to Conference in Paris on March 24th on Organization of Allied Shipping Work under the Supreme Economic Council," AMTC, 1918-1919, 136-237.
47. Tenth Meeting of the Supreme Economic Council, 24 Mar. 1919," Foreign Relations of the United States, The Paris Peace Conference, 88, http://digital.library.wisc.edu/1711.dl/FRUS.FRUS1919Parisv10.
48. Salter, Allied Shipping Control, 230.
49. "Some Memories of Lord Salter," 9 pp. unpublished MS, encl. in Gertrude Caton Thompson to the author, 23 June 1979, author's archive.
50. Salter, Memoirs, 138.
51. "Some Memories of Lord Salter," 9 pp. unpublished MS, encl. in Gertrude Caton Thompson to the author, 23 June 1979, author's archive.
52. Salter, Memoirs, 139, 143-146, Salter, Slave of the Lamp, 85, 89.
53. "Some Memories of Lord Salter," 9 pp. unpublished MS, encl. in Gertrude Caton Thompson to the author, 23 June 1979, author's archive.
54. The Times, 3 June 1918.
55. Cecil to Lloyd George, 26 Apr. 1919, Lloyd George Papers, F/6/6/35.

56. Lord Hankey, The Supreme Control at the Paris Peace Conference 1919 (1963), 103-105.
57. James Barros, Office Without Power: Secretary-General Sir Eric Drummond, 1919-1933 (1979), 13-14.
58. Salter, Memoirs, 146-147, Transcript of Interview between Lord Salter and M. Jean Siotis, 4 Jan. 1969, 2-3, author's archive. I am grateful to M. Siotis for having given me a copy of these interviews, conducted on 4, 22 Jan., 11 Feb., and Mar. [sic] 1969.
59. Morrow to Salter, 25 Mar. 1919, Morrow Papers, microfilm reel 80.
60. Salter to Waldorf Astor, 19 Dec. 1918, Markham Papers, 25/73.
61. "Note on Organization of League of Nations," 10 May 1919, encl. in Salter to Drummond, 15 May 1919, Salter Papers, File 4, League of Nations, Organization and Administration, 1919-1939. Also in LNA, Box R1357, 1919: 25/263/11, and reprinted with Salter's additional comments in The United States of Europe and Other Papers, 13-31.
62. For these contributions, see files in LNA, Boxes R1455, R1357, and Raymond B. Fosdick Papers, Box 2, Department of Rare Books and Special Collections, Princeton University Library, Princeton, NJ.
63. Memorandum by Drummond, 31 May 1919, NA-UK, F0608/242. For a lengthy analysis of the impact and significance of Salter's 10 May 1919 memorandum, see Martin David Dubin, "Transgovernmental Processes in the League of Nations," International Organization, 37(1983), 469-493.
64. Minutes by Drummond, 9 Apr., 7 May 1919, LNA, Box R1455, 1919: 29/266/255, 29/267/255, Minutes, Organization Committee of the League of Nations, 5 May 1919, NA-UK, F0371/4310 W39/72492/1362, Drummond to Salter, 29 May, 14 June 1919, Salter to Drummond, 16 June 1919, Sir Arthur Salter Personnel File, LNA, S874/3100.
65. Draft Resolutions by Drummond, 7 July 1919, LNA, Box R1455, 1919: 29/115/38.
66. Salter to John Anderson, 18 June 1919, NA-UK, MH107/11.
67. Salter to Morrow, 5 June 1919, Morrow Papers, microfilm reel 80.
68. Frank P. Walters, A History of the League of Nations (Repr. 1969), 79.
69. Salter, "Economics and Finance," in The League of Nations Starts: An Outline by its Organizers (1920), 172.
70. "General Note as to Immediate Work and Requirements of Economic and Financial Section," 10 July 1919, LNA, Box R291, 1919: 10/243/243.
71. Salter, obituary tribute to The Earl of Perth, The Times, 19 Dec. 1951.
72. Minute by Drummond, 11 July 1919, LNA, Box R291, 1919: 10/243/243.
73. Minute by E.M.H. Lloyd, 31 July 1919, LNA, Box R289, 1919: 10/213/80.

74. Minutes by Salter, 7 Aug., 13 Aug. 1919, LNA, Box R289, 1919: 10/654/80, 10/696/80, The Times, 15 Aug. 1919.
75. League of Nations, Conference, International Co-operation in Statistics (1919), 1-41.
76. Salter to Attolico, 20 Aug. 1919, LNA, Box R289, 1919: 10/213/80.
77. Drummond to Monnet, 18 Aug. 1919, Paul Mantoux Papers, LNA.
78. Minutes by Drummond, 4 Oct., Fosdick, 3 Oct., Salter, 9 Oct., 1919, LNA, Box R552, 1919: 11/1169/1169.
79. Minute by Drummond, 4 Oct. 1919, LNA, BOX R552, 1919: 11/1169/1169. Cf., Drummond to Curzon, 8 July 1919, NA-UK, FO371/4310, W39/103323/1362.
80. "Method of Communication from and to National Governments through the Medium of the League Secretariat," LNA, Box R1457, 1919: 29/1367/1367.
81. See Minutes in LNA, Box R1191, 1919: 15/1151/245.
82. Minute by Salter, 17 Sept. 1919, LNA, Box R1358, 1919: 26/1181/861.
83. "Suggestions for Agenda of First Meeting of the Assembly," 30 Aug. 1919, "Economic and Financial Questions," 5 Sept. 1919, Morrow Papers, microfilm reel 80.
84. Salter, "The Economic Weapon of the League," 29 Sept. 1919, LNA, Salter Papers, Box S121. This memorandum was reprinted in Salter, The United States of Europe and Other Papers, 144-157.
85. Minutes by Salter, 23, 24 Sept., 13, 25 Oct. 1919, and Drummond, 22 June 1920, LNA, Box R289, 1919: 10/1196/16.
86. Minutes of a Meeting Held in the Secretary General's Room, 24 Sept. 1919, LNA, Box R1569, 1919: 40/1252/854.
87. Salter to Morrow, 7 Nov. 1919, Morrow Papers, microfilm reel 80.
88. Minute by Salter, 15 Oct. 1919, LNA, Box 1026, 1919: 13A/1475/1308, Drummond to Salter, 21 Nov. 1919, LNA, Box R293, 1919: 10/2101/2101.
89. "Resume of Mr. Salter's Remarks on the Relations of the Supreme Economic Council with the League of Nations and the Reparation Committee," 662, http://digital.library.wisc.edu/1711.dl/FRUS Salter to Drummond, 24 Nov. 1919, LNA, Box 293, 1919: 10/2179/2101, Salter, "Present Position with Regard to the Supreme Economic Council and Economic Co-operation Under the League," 10 Dec. 1919, LNA, Box R293, 1919: 10/2390/2101.
90. Salter, "Report of Visit to International Institute of Agriculture, Rome," 30 Dec. 1919, LNA, Box R1026, 1919: 13A/2594/1308. See also "Memorandum sur l'Organization Statistique de la Société des Nations," Jan. 1921, LNA, Box R291, 1921: 10/15519/80.
91. Minutes, Directors' Meeting, 10 Dec. 1919, LNA.
92. Minute by Salter, 17 Dec. 1919, LNA, Box R1568, 1919: 40/2493/527.

93. Minute by Salter, 2 Jan. 1920, LNA, Box R1191, 1919: 15/2471/245.
94. Minute by Salter, 10 Dec. 1919, LNA, Box R1089, 1919: 14/2352/229, minute by Salter, 17 Dec. 1919, LNA, Box R1089, 1919: 14/2454/229. See also The League of Nations Starts, 185-200, and Secretariat of the League of Nations, Ten Years of World Co-operation (Geneva, 1930), 207-218.
95. Drummond to Fosdick, 15 Dec. 1919, in Raymond B. Fosdick, Letters on the League of Nations (Princeton, NJ), 83.
96. Salter, "Note as to Constitution of Governing Board of the Labour Conference," 1 Jan. 1920, LNA, Box R1217, 1919: 16/2565/1892, Minutes of a Meeting Held in the Secretary-General's Room, 6 Jan. 1919, LNA, Box R1217, 1920: 16/2675/1892.
97. The Times, 16 Jan. 1920.
98. Gilchrist, "Memorandum on the First Council Meeting, 22 Jan. 1920," LNA, Box R1431, 1920: 27/2822/2822.
99. Salter, "Publicity and the Council of the League of Nations," 21 Jan. 1920, LNA, Box R1431, 1920: 27/2822/2822.
100. The duties and responsibilities of the secretary general were approved at Proceedings of the Committee on Organization of the Reparations Commission, Minutes of Meeting, 19-20 Dec. 1919, NA-UK, FO801/1.
101. Chamberlain to Salter, 8 Jan. 1920, Salter Papers, File 2, Miscellaneous Political Correspondence, 1916-1950.
102. Salter to Keynes, 13 Jan. 1920, John Maynard Keynes Papers, King's College Archive Centre, Cambridge.
103. Chamberlain to Lloyd George, 13 Jan. 1920, Lloyd George Papers, F/7/3/1.
104. Reparation Commission, Minutes of Meeting, No. 1, 24 Jan. 1920, NA-UK, FO801/4. Reparation Commission, Annex B. 252, NA-UK, FO801/3 detailed the responsibilities of the secretary general and the Commission as whole.
105. Salter to Drummond, 23 Jan., Drummond to Salter, 24 Jan. 1920, Sir Arthur Salter Personnel File, LNA, S874/3100.
106. See Reparation Commission, Minutes of Meeting No. 11, 11 Feb., No. 13, 16 Feb. 1920, NA-UK, FO801/4.
107. Salter, Memoirs, 152-153
108. John Maynard Keynes, The Economic Consequences of the Peace (1919), 204.
109. Salter to Keynes, 14 Oct., Keynes to Salter, 18 Oct. 1919, in The Collected Writings of John Maynard Keynes, vol. 17, Elizabeth Johnson, ed., (1977), 5-7, Salter, Personality in Politics, 141.
110. "Maynard Keynes, II, His Influence in World Affairs," Britain To-day, no. 144(Apr. 1948), 12.

111. Reparation Commission, "Request for a Second Building," Annex 137, 13 Mar. 1920, NA-UK, FO801/13.
112. "A Conflict of Wills," Salter Papers, File 1, Anecdotes and Incidents.
113. Salter, Memoirs, 159, Salter to Violet Markham, 21 Feb. 1919, Markham Papers, 25/73.
114. Reparation Commission, V, Report on the Work of the Reparation Commission from 1920 to 1922 (1923), 4-5.
115. Arthur Salter, Recovery: The Second Effort (1932), 131-133, Étienne Weill-Raynal, Les réparations allemandes et la France, vol. 1, Novembre 1918-Mai 1921 (Paris, 1947), 143-154.
116. Salter to Lloyd, 4 Feb. 1920, E.M.H. Lloyd Papers, Section 3/5, BLPES, London.
117. Salter to Drummond, 14 Feb. 1920, Lloyd to Drummond, 20 Feb. 1920, LNA, Box R289, 1919: 10/2951/80.
118. Lloyd to Salter, 17 Feb. 1920, Lloyd Papers, Section 3/5.
119. The International Secretariat of the League of Nations, Currencies After the War: A Survey of Conditions in Various Countries (1920). The preface was drafted by Lloyd with corrections by Salter. See Salter to Lloyd, 14 Feb. 1920, Lloyd Papers, Section 3/5.
120. James T. Shotwell, The Autobiography of James T. Shotwell (New York, 1961), 134-139.
121. Salter to Beveridge, 8 Mar. 1920, Shotwell to Salter, 25 Mar. 1920, James T. Shotwell Papers, Butler Library, Columbia University, New York.
122. Salter to Lloyd, 27 Feb. 1920, Lloyd Papers, Section 3/5, Reparation Commission, Salter, "Proposed Rules for the Choice of Language," Annex 162, NA-UK, FO801/4.
123. Reparation Commission, Minutes of Meetings, No. 26, 17 Mar. 1920, NA-UK, FO801/4, No. 44, 5 May, No. 50, 19 May 1920, NA-UK, FO801/5.
124. Reparation Commission, Salter, "On Points of Organization in Relation to the General Services," Annex 164a, NA-UK, FO801/4.
125. Reparation Commission, Minutes of Meeting No. 25, 15 Mar. 1920, NA-UK, FO801/4, Salter to Lloyd, 15 Mar. 1920, and encl., "Scheme of Information Desired," Lloyd Papers, Section 3/5.
126. Salter, Memoirs, 156.
127. Salter to Violet Markham, 18 Mar., 8 May, 18 Aug. 1920, Markham Papers, 25/73.
128. Salter, Memoirs, 165.
129. Salter, "The Letter of Resignation," Salter Papers, File 1, Anecdotes and Incidents.
130. "Royall Tyler, 1884-1953, A Summary Biography," 8 pp. MS, by William R. Tyler, Aug.1972, author's archive. William R. Tyler to the author, 30 July 1979 added to this "Personal Recollections of Arthur Salter," 3 pp. MS, author's archive.

131. Salter, Memoirs, 161.
132. Royall Tyler to Elisina Tyler, 28 Apr., 24 July, 1920, Royall Tyler Papers, author's archive. From 1973-1981 their son William Tyler copied a massive number of such letters for the author's use in this biography. He also gave the author dozens of letters exchanged between Salter and Royall and Elisina Tyler.
133. Royall Tyler to Elisina Tyler, 9, 10 Aug. 1920, Tyler Papers.
134. R.W.B. Lewis, Edith Wharton: A Biography (New York, 1975), 482. Salter, Slave of the Lamp, 91-94 provides an extensive appreciation of Royall Tyler.
135. Royall Tyler to Elisina Tyler, 26 July 1920, Tyler Papers.
136. Markham, Return Passage, 176-177, Royall Tyler to Elisina Tyler, 24 July 1920, Tyler Papers.
137. Author's interview with Lord Salter, 9 Nov. 1973.
138. The book was organized by Huntingdon Gilchrist. See Salter to Gilchrist, 20 Apr. 1920, Gilchrist to Salter, 27 Apr., 25 May, 16 July 1920, Huntingdon Gilchrist Papers, Library of Congress, Washington, DC.
139. Salter, "Economics and Finance," in The League of Nations Starts, 170-184.
140. Reparation Commission, Minutes of Meeting No. 27, 19 Mar. 1920, NA-UK, FO801/4.
141. Weill-Raynal, Les réparations allemandes, vol. 1, 562-578, Salter to the British, French, Belgian and Italian Governments, 8 Aug. 1920, NA-UK, F0801/97.
142. Salter, "The Reparation Commission from the Point of View of Administrative Efficiency," 13 Aug. 1920, Bradbury Papers, NA-UK, T194/6.
143. Salter to Violet Markham, 18 Aug. 1920, Markham Papers, 25/73.
144. Reparation Commission, Minutes of Meeting No. 61, 23 June 1920, NA-UK, FO801/5, Reparation Commission, Drummond to Salter, 17 Aug. 1920, Annex 380a, NA-UK, FO801/116.
145. Drummond to Salter, 17 Aug. 1920, LNA, Box R294, 1920: 10/5945/2845; Royall Tyler to Elisina Tyler, 17 Aug. 1920, Tyler Papers.
146. Reparation Commission, Minutes of Meeting No. 84, 7 Sept. 1920, NA-UK, FO801/5.
147. Monnet, Memoirs, 95-96, Sir Frederick Leith-Ross, Money Talks: Fifty Years of International Finance (1968), 76-77.
148. Salter, Memoirs, 166, Recueil de documents sur l'histoire de la question des Réparations, 1919-5 mai 1921, Germain Calmette, ed., (Paris, 1929), 321-331.
149. League of Nations Secretariat, Ten Years of World Co-operation (Geneva, 1930), 180-182, Salter, Allied Shipping Control, 275-277.
150. Reparation Commission, Minutes of Meeting No. 97, 26 Oct. 1920, NA-UK, FO801/5.
151. Salter, Memoirs, 159-160.

152. Reparation Commission, Minutes of Meeting No. 122, 4 Jan. 1921, NA-UK, FO801/6.
153. Reparation Commission, Minutes of Meeting No. 129, 21 Jan., No. 130, 25 Jan., No. 132, 28 Jan. 1921, NA-UK, FO801/6, The Times, 21 Jan. 1921, Weill-Raynall, Les réparations allemandes, vol. 1, 582-607.
154. Salter, Memoirs, 164.
155. Salter to Beveridge, 22 Sept. 1920, Shotwell Papers.
156. Salter to Beveridge, 13 Nov. 1920, Shotwell Papers.
157. "Some Problems of International Administration," in The Development of the Civil Service, 214-227.
158. Royall Tyler to Elisina Tyler, 8 Dec. 1920, Tyler Papers.
159. Salter to Beveridge, 30 Dec. 1920, Shotwell Papers.
160. Salter Papers, File 3, Honours and Decorations, 1919-1922, The Times, 19 June 1920, French Embassy to Curzon, 28 Dec. 1920, NA-UK, FO372/1546, T14883/10748/317D, Italian Ambassador to Curzon, 25 Sept., 16 Dec. 1920, NA-UK, FO372/1561, T11137/11137/322D.
161. Carl Bergmann, The History of Reparations (1927), 69.
162. Salter to Beveridge, 19 Mar. 1921, Shotwell Papers.
163. Reparation Commission, I, Statement of Germany's Obligations Under the Heading of Reparations, etc., at April 30th, 1922 (1922), 5, Reparation Commission, III, Official Documents Relative to the Amount of Payments to be Effected by Germany Under the Reparations Account (1922), 4.
164. Salter to Beveridge, 10, 31 Jan. 1921, Salter to Shotwell, 14 Jan. 1921, Shotwell Papers.
165. Salter to Shotwell, 20 May 1921, Shotwell Papers.
166. Shotwell to J.B. Scott, 14 May 1921, Shotwell Papers, Salter, Allied Shipping Control, 243.
167. Shotwell to G.A. Finch, 9 Mar. 1921, Shotwell Papers.
168. Salter to Zimmern, 4, 30 July 1921, Zimmern Papers.
169. The Times, 22 July 1921, The Economist, 93(27 Aug. 1921), 328.
170. The Times Literary Supplement, 28 July 1921, 475.
171. "A Note on Mr. Salter's Allied Shipping Control," The Economic Journal, 31(Sept. 1921), 412-414.
172. Brooke to Salter, n.d., H.G. Wells to Salter, 6 July 1921, Salter Papers, File 2, Miscellaneous Political Correspondence, 1916-1950.
173. Salter to the editor, New Statesman, 17(24 Sept.1921), 673, 18(8, 22 Oct.1921), 12, 73, Leo Chiozza Money to the editor, New Statesman, 17(17 Sept., 1, Oct.1921), 645, 700-701, 18(15 Oct., 5 Nov. 1921), 44, 131-132.
174. See e.g., F.H. Nixon to Salter, 4 June, 1921, LNA, Salter Papers, Box S116.

175. Royall Tyler to Elisina Tyler, 30 Aug. 1921, Tyler Papers.
176. "A Few Notes on the Saar Position," Salter Papers, File 4, League of Nations, Organization and Administration, 1919-1931.
177. Walters, History of the League of Nations, 153.
178. Salter to Shotwell, 21 Oct. 1921, Shotwell Papers.
179. Balfour to Salter, 17 Oct. 1921, Salter Papers, File 2, Miscellaneous Political Correspondence, 1916-1950, Salter, "Note on Upper Silesian Question," n.d., minute by Hankey, 17 Oct. 1921, NA-UK, FO371/5929, C19997/92/18.
180. Reparation Commission, I, Agreements Concerning Deliveries in Kind to be Made by Germany Under the Heading of Reparations (1922), 3-11, Reparation Commission, Minutes of Meeting No. 229, 18 Oct. 1921, NA-UK, FO801/8, Reparation Commission, V, Report on the Work of the Reparation Commission from 1920 to 1922, 127-128.
181. Salter, Recovery, 128-129, Étienne Weill-Raynal, Les réparations allemandes et la France, vol. 2, Mai 1921-Avril 1924 (Paris, 1947), 29-67.
182. Royall Tyler to Elisina Tyler, 12, 14 Jan. 1922, Tyler Papers, Reparation Commission, Minutes of Meeting No. 255, 13 Jan. 1921, NA-UK, FO801/8.
183. Reparation Commission, III, Official Documents Relative to the Amount of Payments to be Effected by Germany Under the Reparations Account, 51, 55, 140-141, Reparation Commission, Salter to the Secretary-General, German Delegation, 13 Jan. 1922, Annex 1226, NA-UK, FO801/27.
184. Drummond to Sir Warren Fisher, 28 Oct. 1920, Sir Arthur Salter Personnel File, LNA, S874/3100.
185. Entry of 7 Jan. 1921, Per Jacobsson Diary, no. 9, 82, BLPES, London.
186. Salter to Drummond, 3 Nov. 1920, Drummond to Balfour, 4 Nov. 1920, Sir Arthur Salter Personnel File, LNA S874/3100.
187. Reparations Commission, Minutes of Meeting No. 256, 20 Jan., No. 297, 16 June 1922, NA-UK, CAB801/4.
188. Reparation Commission, Minutes of Meeting No. 258, 27 Jan. 1922, NA-UK, CAB801/4.
189. Reparation Commission, V, Report on the Work of the Reparation Commission from 1920 to 1922, 167-170.
190. Royall Tyler to Elisina Tyler 28 Jan. 1922, Tyler Papers.
191. Royall Tyler to Elisina Tyler, 20 Feb. 1922, Tyler Papers.
192. Salter, Memoirs, 161, Reparation Commission, Minutes of Meeting No. 156, 30 Mar., Meeting No. 174, 18 Apr. 1921, NA-UK, FO801/6, Reparation Commission, "Staff Proposals by Mr. Salter and Mr. Tyler," 14 Apr. 1921, Annex 826a, NA-UK, FO801/23.

193. See T. Quinton-Hill to Hankey, 29 Mar. 1922, Lloyd George Papers, F/26/1/27, and the recommendations of the Financial and Economic Commissions, Genoa Conference, in NA-UK, FO31/8-9.
194. Reparation Commission, Minutes of Meeting No. 275, 28 Mar. 1922, NA-UK, FO801/8.
195. The Times, 25 May 1922.
196. Salter, Memoirs, 167-168.
197. Bergmann, History of Reparations,130-138, Weill-Raynall, Les réparations allemandes, vol. 2, 166-180, The Times, 12 June 1922.
198. Royall Tyler to Elisina Tyler, 9 June 1922, Tyler Papers.
199. Reparation Committee, "Report of the Loan Committee to the Reparation Commission," 10 June 1922, Annex 1478, NA-UK, FO801/29.
200. Reparation Commission, Minutes of Meeting No.294, 10 June 1933, NA-UK, FO801/8.
201. Morgan to Salter, 19 June 1922, Salter Papers, File 2, Miscellaneous Political Correspondence, 1916-1950.
202. Salter to Violet Markham, 22 June 1922, Markham Papers, 25/73.
203. The Times 12 June 1922, which also reprinted the "Report of the Bankers' Committee."
204. Logan to Salter, 17 June 1922, Salter Papers, File 2, Miscellaneous Political Correspondence, 1916-1950.
205. Lloyd George to Salter, 24 May 1922, Salter Papers, File 3, Honours and Decorations, 1919-1922, Salter to Violet Markham, 29 May 1922, Markham Papers, 25/73.
206. Wise to Salter, 7 June 1922, Anderson to Salter, 16 June 1922, Salter Papers, File 3, Honours and Decorations, 1919-1922.
207. Salter to Violet Markham, 29 May, 22 June 1922, Markham Papers, 25/73.
208. Salter to Shotwell, 26 June 1922, Shotwell Papers.
209. Royall Tyler to Elisina Tyler, 19, 21, 23, 24, 27, 30 June, 1 July 1922, Tyler Papers.
210. Salter, Memoirs, 172.
211. Salter to Violet Markham, 22 June 1922, Markham Papers, 25/73.

CHAPTER 4

"NATIONS OF THE WORLD ARE TOGETHER BUILDING UP A NEW WORLD," 1922-1930

For a brief moment in July 1922 Salter's confidence faltered. "Had I been wise to leave a great capital and a position which after all had considerable attractions, for the idleness in a suburb?" This was the question that plagued him as he arrived in Geneva. F.H. Nixon, who had served for a short time as Salter's replacement, was about to step aside – a disappointed man. His parting memorandum had advised contracting the Economic and Financial Section, so poor did he consider its future prospects.[1] Such temporary doubts passed, because Salter's return to the League soon proved to be well timed. After his resignation from the Reparation Commission and a further two-week stay in Paris, he travelled to England on leave. On 8 August, after an enjoyable drive across France, he finally joined the secretariat in Geneva.[2] There he found that his section had burgeoned from two members in 1920 to 34 officials in both Geneva and London.[3] As well, it had been intimately involved in the preparation and the implementation of the resolutions of the Brussels and Genoa Conferences. It had carried through with the Salter-inspired scheme for international statistical collaboration, publishing among other things, the <u>Monthly Bulletin of Statistics</u>. Further publications on economic and financial matters had begun to appear under the guidance of Alexander Loveday, the head of the Economic Intelligence Service. In addition, following the resolution of the League Council on 27 October 1920, a Provisional Economic and Financial Commission had been appointed, with wide-ranging responsibilities.[4] It ceased to be provisional in 1923 and became the Economic and Financial Committees respectively. It was the Economic and Financial Section that provided the secretariat for these committees and the conferences summoned in connection with their work.[5] In short, Salter returned to a secretariat that was already maturing in terms of organization, staff and responsibility.

Initially, Salter made a few changes to his section. He called on the Central European expertise of the French financier, Pierre Quesnay, for advice on questions relating to Austria. He also secured as his personal secretary, Renée de Lucy Fossarieu, formerly with the Reparation Commission. She was to further serve Salter, faithfully and efficiently, until his departure from the League in 1930.[6] Finally, he recruited Elliot Felkin from the Finance Section of the Reparation Commission. Throughout the next 10 years, Felkin was Salter's personal assistant for both official and personal duties. The latter began with Felkin securing for Salter his first Geneva flat at 27 Quai de Mont Blanc, a welcome change from the room at the Hotel des Bergues into which he had moved on first arriving in the Swiss capital.[7]

Salter settled back into his position as head of the Economic and Financial Section and was personally welcomed back at the Directors' Meeting on 10 August.[8] Immediately, he found himself at the centre of a crisis that was to lead to the first exercise in financial reconstruction undertaken by the League. The ideas that Salter had helped develop during the Brussels and Genoa conferences were to be applied with successful results. These included the reduction of inflation through balanced budgets, reconstruction assistance through international loans to bridge the periods of budget deficits, and responsible monetary policy through a Central Bank of Issue were to be applied with very successful results. The financial measures taken early in 1922 to assist Austria, which Salter had followed so closely, proved inadequate. The foreign credits, which had been advanced, were not subject to central control and were "consumed for current needs." Austria's financial collapse proceeded at an alarming rate. By August 1922, the Austrian crown was worth only 1/15,000th of its pre-war gold value. "The country," Salter observed, "lived on a combination of inflation and charitable aid." Austria, he continued, "has been in the unhappy position of knowing that she could not stop inflation until her budget balanced, and could not balance her budget while inflation continued." Some assistance had already been offered by the Reparation Commission, which agreed to release liens on some Austria assets as security for a new Bank of Issue. Still, Austria was desperate, without any standing in international money markets, and faced with the prospects of having to feed its population with a currency which was unacceptable for foreign purchases of food and coal. The Austrian government appealed to the Supreme Council, then meeting in London. On 15 August, the conference chairman Lloyd George replied that the Allied governments could offer no further financial assistance. However, he advised the Austrian situation should be referred to the League of Nations "for investigation and report." If the League would then propose a reconstruction programme, with firm guarantees that additional credits "would not be thrown away like those made in the past," then further assistance might be available.[9] On 28 August, after extensive consultations in London, Salter returned to Geneva to report his findings to the League Council.[10]

By the time the Council of the League met on 31 August to discuss the Austrian situation, a political dimension had been added to the financial crisis. Social distress and civic disturbances in Austria were regarded by many as a threat to European stability. On 6 September Austria appealed to the League for assistance, followed at once by the formation of a League Austrian sub-committee to co-ordinate an enquiry. It consisted of five members with Balfour in the chair, and met 12 times before announcing its conclusions on 4 October. The strategy, which was followed during the lengthy discussions of September, had its origins in the following event. According to Salter, and corroborated by two other accounts, he, Jean Monnet and Sir Basil Blackett, a member of the Financial Committee and Controller of Finance at the British Treasury, had retreated for a Sunday picnic and a motor boat ride on Lake Geneva. From their discussions emerged a scheme designed to keep Austria independent, ensure its financial well-being, and rebound to the credit of the League.[11] Thus the four weeks between Austria's appeal to the League and the announcement of a solution were among the busiest of Salter's career. On 7 September he alerted the members of the Financial Committee that they had been placed at the disposal of the Austrian sub-committee and their presence in Geneva would be needed for another week. Two days later, at the Economic Committee, Salter advised its members that they would be required "to consider urgently certain questions" relating to Austria. Thereafter, Salter attended all meetings of both committees and acted in close liaison with Balfour. The preliminary research work of Salter's section on the situation, as well as his personal familiarity with Austrian finances, considerably facilitated discussions. He was also persuasive in influencing the Financial Committee. On 15 September, for example, he advised members they might have to move beyond "a simple enquiry" and "make proposals relating to the credits and to the control to be imposed." With several government representatives in Geneva, Salter asked that the Financial Committee "negotiate with them especially concerning the guarantees." This unusual suggestion, which aroused some opposition, was finally accepted. The meeting concluded with emphasis on the necessity for "rigorous control" and "guarantees from the foreign governments in order to obtain loans." By 25 September, the outlines of a reconstruction scheme had emerged in the Financial Committee. Suggestions were already being voiced that the League itself might act as the control committee for the anticipated loans. Three days later, the Financial Committee concluded its work with a complete plan for the financial reconstruction of Austria. It also approved Salter's suggestion that "the Provisional Committee of Control" should hasten to Vienna within ten days.[12]

After approval by the League Council and the Assembly, three "Geneva Protocols" were signed by British, French, Italian and Czech representatives on 4 October. The first contained a declaration of respect for Austrian independence and territorial integrity. The second authorised Austria to float a loan of 650 million gold crowns on international money markets to cover the projected budget deficit over the next two years. It also included the conditions of the guarantee of the loan. The final protocol set out Austria's obligations under the scheme and the functions of the commissioner-general. Salter summarized the programme as one:

> of financial reform extending over two years; provision to meet the deficit during this period by guarantee loans; the arrest of the collapse of the crown; the supervision of the Austrian Government's execution of the scheme within carefully defined and restricted limits.[13]

Salter's personal role in the negotiations earned him congratulations from many colleagues for "pulling the thing through at Geneva."[14] Salter himself was under no illusions. The task of implementing the scheme, he wrote on 4 October, "will be an immensely difficult one, but it is certainly, I think, in a much more advanced stage than has ever been reached in the course of any previous attempts."[15] As well, he was at pains to emphasize why the League had succeeded where other attempts had failed. "It was a great piece of luck," he wrote, "that the request came at a moment when the Assembly and the Council were in Geneva for other purposes, and when, therefore, we were able to secure a concentration of authority for the long period of negotiations without which any scheme is impossible." It was in effect another successful application of the principle of direct contact so cherished by Salter. Understandably, he observed that the resolution of the crisis as "a real triumph for the League." Some time later, he looked back at this period and described it as "the great game of bluff played in the last months of 1922."[16] At the time he even anticipated that "we may have a shot at the reparation problem through the League machinery."[17] Such exuberance, however, did not abate and in the New Year Salter was again ruminating "that the League ought to come in on reparations at once."[18]

During October and November, however, other issues took priority. The foremost was the task of selecting a commissioner-general, as much a political as an administrative choice. Besides having to be acceptable to Britain, France, Italy, Czechoslovakia and Austria, he would also have to walk carefully between the Socialist municipality of Vienna and the Christian Socialist government of Austria. After casting his net widely, and after a personal meeting in Paris on 16 October, he secured the services of Roland Boyden, the unofficial American delegate to the Reparation Commission. Boyden agreed to the task, observing that in going to Vienna "I should feel that I was putting my head in a lion's mouth."[19] However, the appointment proved to be too vital to be left to Salter's devices alone. In London, the

Governor of the Bank of England, Sir Montagu Norman, had for some time taken an interest in Austrian financial affairs. Indeed, without his "active aid," Salter believed, "the whole venture might have fallen through." As soon as the Geneva Protocols had been signed, Norman went over the whole problem with Salter in London. On the advice of the Dutch banker, C.E. ter Meulen, Norman strongly supported A.R. Zimmerman, a former anti-socialist mayor of Rotterdam, as commissioner-general. Norman also advocated the appointment of a neutral president for the new Austrian Bank of Issue.[20] In addition, Blackett had his own reservations and notified Salter in the strongest terms that Boyden was "insufficiently forceful" and that Zimmerman should get the position.[21] The possibility of any conflict over the former's appointment was resolved by Boyden's inadvertent misreading of the State Department's acceptance of his wish to go to Vienna as a veto.[22] This was a "stunning blow" to Salter, who now saw no option but to proceed with the appointment of Zimmerman, which he did only reluctantly.[23] Based on Salter's own soundings in London, Paris and Geneva, Zimmerman emerged as "notoriously very anti-democratic." His appointment might have been regarded as a direct challenge to Viennese left wing opinion. Nonetheless, Zimmerman finally took up his position, arriving in Vienna on 15 December. The same day the Reparations Commission agreed to the release of all foreign liens against Austrian assets.[24]

The League of Nations Provisional Delegation, in the meantime, comprised of members of the Financial Committee, Salter, Quesnay and a small staff, had arrived in Vienna in mid-October. Salter noted, after this first visit, that "the task here is, of course, urgent, vital and complicated, and I am sure we were right to be here." A colleague wrote to him underlining the fact that Austria "is really the biggest thing the League has done."[25] Initially Salter was "not particularly pleased with the way things are going," noted the British Chargé d'Affaires Edward Keeling.[26] However, after some considerable pressure on the Social Democratic Party to co-operate, the Provisional Delegation's first report detailed an impressive list of recommendations already passed in parliament. The austerity measures included provisions for the dismissal of 100,000 civil servants, the reorganization of state enterprises including the possible privatisation of the railroads and the tobacco industries, an increase in revenue from customs, excise and direct taxation, and the cancellation of all state subsidies. As well, on 18 November an internal loan floated for public subscription was favourably received, thus giving the government temporary credits.[27] In the last week of November, Salter was twice able to report to the meetings of League Directors the "satisfactory progress being made in the work of Austrian reconstruction."[28] Finally, on 4 December the subscription was opened for the initial capital of the new Bank of Issue, the National Bank of Austria. Salter, installed on 15 December for the second visit at the Imperial Hotel in Vienna to assist with all these arrangements, had been particularly struck with the widespread misery which he encountered. He found the Viennese:

> in a state of destitution and indeed starvation such as, in a civilized city, I have never seen before or since. The people you met, including scholars of European reputation, very often visibly starving. The commerce and industry of the city were dead. On the wide and normally crowded Ringstrasse I once watched for some time and saw only one old woman pushing a kind of wheel barrow. The situation was desperate; but as we used to say, 'desperate, but not serious.' With any momentary relief from suffering and the sight of its gaiety would return.[29]

With so much visible hardship, Salter was at least pleased that government cutbacks had spared the Opera. It was his friend, Violet Markham, at the time visiting with him in Vienna, who later revealed "that Vienna among other things owed Arthur Salter a great debt at the time for not allowing the Opera to be sacrificed to economic necessity."[30]

Salter was generally pleased that the League's reconstruction plans for Austria were progressing well. As he had put it on 27 November, "Austria is giving us an infinitely difficult and very anxious time, but so far we have got over our different stiles one by one."[31] Nor was this without some personal expression of fatigue and anxiety. Writing to Violet Markham on 3 December, he noted, "There is something much more trying about these interminable detailed anxieties, sprung from individual folly or vanity & petty national spite, than the single big anxiety in the war itself which by its very gravity made people work together & behave decently."[32] Among the final hurdles was the news that greeted Salter at his breakfast table on 25 December. The Austrian government, acting unilaterally, had that morning appointed Dr. Richard Reisch, a former Austrian Minister of Finance, as President of the new central bank, the National Bank of Austria The move was a blatant rebuff to Salter, Zimmerman and the British and French ministers in Vienna, who all agreed that the post required a foreign central banker. As well, according to Salter's memoirs, Montagu Norman was so "incensed" by Austria's action that he cabled Salter to "count him and the Bank of England out." Salter feared that such a threat would adversely discourage Zimmerman. However, he also surmised that Norman was too committed to Austrian reconstruction to pull out so abruptly. Consequently, he related, "I took a match, burnt the telegram, made no reply, and said nothing, then or thereafter, to anyone."[33] A copy of Norman's telegram cannot be traced in the archives of the Bank of England.[34]

Salter carried on nevertheless and cabled at once to Sir Otto Niemeyer, at the Treasury in London, trying to explain, though not to excuse, the Austrian choice. "We all regret decision but confident you will agree that since it is irrevocable we must make every effort to diminish disadvantages." Salter continued:

> We find it difficult to understand how the very extreme character of the communication you state you have made to Austrian Government is justified. If any rumour escapes result will be serious for last week of internal loan which otherwise shows every prospect of reaching 20 millions. We hope you do not mean that effort now ceases. If so reason being decision which though regrettable is not inconsistent with engagements responsibility to Austria and to League very serious. Z[immerman] as well as myself feel this very strongly. Suggest you show this Norman adding that Z would greatly appreciate visit from him here.[35]

Salter concluded by asking Niemeyer to show the cable to Norman. In reply, Niemeyer dismissed Austria's reconstruction efforts as "heroics." But his main invective was reserved for Reisch's appointment which he described as a "piece of idiocy." Niemeyer also added his own explanation of the event:

> Everyone here knows why the Austrian banks (who are at the back of all this) want one of themselves. What therefore has happened (and everyone here and in the United States of America knows it) is that the Vienna Jews in their own interest have secured that the bad old traditions of inflated credits will go on in Austria and that there will be no sound money policy. I am afraid that you will think this unduly violent. But I want you to realise, as I think from your letter you do not entirely, the devastating effect of this last bêtise. Norman for instance thinks it ends the whole Austrian business and I feel very little doubt that his judgement is right, so far as the effect on world finance goes. At present I see no way out other than Reich's [sic] early decease![36]

In the event, Reisch survived, and what Niemeyer described as "the whole Austrian business" turned out well. Inflation had in fact been decisively stopped on 18 November with the cessation of unrestricted note issuing. The exchange value of the Austrian crown was stabilized on international money markets, while the general level of prices showed a decline, for the first time since the armistice. At the same time, savings markedly increased. Finally by 16 January 1923 the internal loan floated for public subscription had yielded a healthy 30 million gold crowns from banks and a further 21 million from the public. All the while plans went ahead for the new Bank of Issue that took over from the former Austro-Hungarian Bank on 2 January 1923.[37] It was not until June 1923 that the long-term loan was issued, raised by public subscription in the markets of ten different countries, and guaranteed by eight European states. By then Austria was indeed on the road to financial stability, a prerequisite to economic recovery.

The striking success enjoyed by the League in these initial phases of Austrian reconstruction undoubtedly raised its public profile. This was a development which Salter both encouraged and ruminated upon. In a letter to Violet Markham on 8 February 1923, he ranged over the canvass of world affairs, but with particular emphasis on the place of the League. "We have to face the fact (about which personally I've never had any doubt since America refused to ratify)," he wrote, "that the League cannot prevent any first class country from doing anything it is determined to do." However, he continued:

> From the fact that the League cannot handle the most important job to the belief that it's not worth while for it to tackle the less important ones in its power is a step against which I protest with the utmost vigour. Face the facts of the world position & temper & what is the right conclusion? Clearly that the League must be built up till it has an adequate power for the biggest tasks; & clearly that it should be built up, in the only possible way, on the basis of the tasks which it can & does accomplish.

Among the latter Salter listed the settlement reached in Upper Silesia and the successful reconstruction of Austria "which would certainly have been in a chaos of rioting at this moment, with very probably a war of partition round it." He concluded: "The League can foster, exploit, realize & give permanent effect to the maximum potential co-operation of its members (& thereby achieve immensely more cooperation that would happen of itself) – but here it stops." Attached to this letter was his note suggesting, again, that if requested the League would hold itself ready to play a role in resolving reparation issues.[38]

Such was the basis of Salter's League credo, and in affirmation of this he was determined to give maximum publicity to League activities. Already in October 1922 he had circulated to European and North American newspapers, for possible publication, a memorandum he had written on Austrian reconstruction, which reviewed events up to 4 October.[39] Further progress was detailed in an interview for <u>The Financial Times</u> on 13 February 1923, where he emphasized the "remarkable growth of public confidence" in Vienna.[40] However, the major platform for publicity derived from an invitation that he received to address the Rome meeting of the International Chamber of

Commerce, founded in June 1920. In accepting the invitation from the former French Finance Minister, Georges Clémentel, he agreed to speak about Austrian reconstruction, a process he described as without precedent in history.[41] In his speech on 24 March, Salter observed the "experiment" at once combined "national self-help and international cooperation." In its wider implications, he argued that the progress of reconstruction was living proof that "Austria is essentially viable." On the other hand, and for the first time, he also admitted that increased unemployment and some rise in the cost of living accompanied financial reform.[42] A lavish reception hosted by the Italian government in a vast ballroom gave Salter and other delegates an opportunity to meet Benito Mussolini. He recalled, that "Suddenly the large closed doors, hitherto closed, on a side wall were thrown open. The most astonishing spectacle burst on our gaze. In the centre was Mussolini himself, in civilian evening dress, with decorations and the wide green band of an Order on his shirt. There was the Fascist glare in Mussolini's eyes and his chin was thrust out." As were many others, Salter was granted an interview with Mussolini the following day but seemed more impressed by the spectacle surrounding the Duce than anything of substance.[43] On his return to Geneva, Salter informed the League's Directors that the Rome visit had been useful and he recommended further visits by League officials.[44]

During this time Salter took every opportunity to specifically brief American colleagues and friends on progress in Austrian reconstruction. This was partly to dispel what he termed "the present American ignorance of what is happening in Austria" and partly to prepare the ground for United States participation in the long-term loan. But it was also his impression that "this piece of reconstructive work is exactly along the lines of America's own views of the way Europe should proceed with her economic recovery." Writing to Dwight Morrow on 31 March to enlist his assistance with some publicity, Salter underscored that Austrian reconstruction was "the most interesting and significant piece of economic work that has been done in Europe since the war. So far it has been astonishingly successful." Morrow's reply was to press for an immediate visit from Salter to the United States, one the latter regretfully declined because of the burden of his reconstruction activities.[45] However, final details of American participation in the long-term loan were ironed out by Thomas Lamont, representing J.P. Morgan and a syndicate of other interested American banks, during his visit to London and Paris. Salter met with Lamont in Paris in early May and these talks were decisive, in the opinion of observers, of having cleared up numerous difficulties and contributed "to our American success."[46] At one point, Royall Tyler recorded Salter lamenting his having "the most tremendous difficulties and troubles." Nonetheless, it was Tyler's view that "there'll be a waiting list of patients wanting the same treatment by the time Arthur has finished with his present victim."[47] At long last, American participation in the long-term loan was secured which, along with other lender countries, produced a net yield of 585 million gold crowns or about 90% of the total originally contemplated. By the summer of 1923 Salter wrote afterwards, "the sum estimated as necessary to carry the scheme through had been obtained, and all anxieties under this head were at an end."[48] Privately, he exulted about "the most ambitious, & the most fruitful, piece of work the League has yet undertaken."[49] He wrote of the long-term loan as "much the biggest piece of international constructive work undertaken anywhere."[50] In interviews with the American press he stated that Austria was "loyally" carrying out its obligations to the League of Nations.[51]

After such a long period of intensive work, Salter left for a month's vacation, spent partly with the Tylers who had just purchased their new home Antigny-le-Chateau in Burgundy.[52] However, by 8 August, he was back at the League, at once immersed in current problems. One priority was involvement with the resettlement of Greek refugees. As early as 22 October 1922 Salter had been unofficially approached as to whether the League could offer the Greek government financial assistance.[53] The request became more urgent by 1923 as the result of a mutual agreement with the Turkish government, after the end of Greek-Turkish hostilities, on the exchange of populations. As a consequence, some 1,400,000 refugees from Asia Minor flooded into Greece, a country with less than five million people. This constituted one of the largest movements of population in so short a period. While Greece had the land to resettle the refugees, it was very short of capital to feed and house such numbers. On 13 November, Salter had replied, "Regret regard practically impossible."[54] Nonetheless, after Greece appealed to the League of Nations for help in February 1923, Salter threw himself into the task of facilitating financial assistance. After a lengthy investigation by League officials, a resettlement scheme was eventually discussed in the Financial Committee on 25 June, and initially approved by the Council of the League on 5 July.[55] The plan that was adopted, and successfully applied from 1923 to 1930, did not involve League intervention in the general financial affairs of Greece. Nor was a commissioner-general needed to supervise the scheme on the spot. Instead, an interim advance from the Bank of England, followed by a monthly commitment from the Greek government, was arranged for immediate purposes of resettlement. These advances were to be placed at the disposal of a new Refugee Settlement Commission, responsible to the League. The Commission would also be charged with the dispersal of the projected long-term loan of 10 million pounds.[56] The entire scheme was approved by the Council on 29 September, and the protocol signed the same day by the Greek government.[57]

Salter played little part in these more general negotiations. His main contribution was in the area of recruitment for the Refugee Settlement Commission, to which the League was to appoint one of the four members. Salter preferred a suitable Englishman with relevant experience as the League representative, especially in light of "the initiative and risk" taken by the Bank of England.[58] As well, he lobbied personally for the inclusion of the American chairman for the commission, trying to overcome what he called the "shyness" of the US in being associated with League work. Salter's first choice was Henry Morgenthau Jr, formerly American ambassador at Constantinople and already familiar with his government's relief efforts in the Middle East.[59] Morgenthau eventually accepted and took up his appointment, while an Englishman, Colonel John Campbell of the Indian Civil Service, became the League nominee. The Greek government with the approval of the League Council appointed the remaining two members. By 9 October, with the commission members finalized, Salter wrote with satisfaction about its "strong personnel."[60] Morgenthau began his appointment as chairman with a visit to London and then to Paris where he met with Salter. The latter made a strong impression on Morgenthau who wrote, "Like many another high-minded British patriot, he has made the welfare of his country his sole aim in life. He has gone about this purpose without noise or display, but quietly has made himself an expert on international affairs." Morgenthau noted that Salter's "particular skill lies in the power of analysis of conditions in other countries, and of devising practical financial measures to relieve their necessities." He was also keen to show that Salter, "the financial wizard of the League," was "most solicitous" that the US should play a greater role in international affairs. Finally, he provided this description of Salter: "Below medium height, Sir Arthur yet gives an instant impression of competence and power. His keen eyes, behind the spectacles, are penetrating yet kindly. The firm jaw indicates decision and power."[61]

The plan for the resettlement of the Greek refugees was, in the words of the League secretariat, "a new example of the same methods" used to prepare the scheme for the financial reconstruction of Austria. Faced with a problem that had political, legal, technical and financial aspects, the League Council worked directly with all the principals concerned, thereby guaranteeing co-ordination and eventually cooperation.[62] To all those involved, the work of the Resettlement Commission proved a source of pride. The Governor of the Bank of Greece, A.N. Diomède, later thanked Salter "for the wonderful zeal and devotion" with which he laboured on behalf of the resettlement scheme.[63] After the first of two visits to Greece to watch the progress, Salter wrote:

> The refugees, instead of being an intolerable burden, soon proved a source of strength and wealth. The grain of Macedonia greatly reduced the food deficit of Greece, which had always been a wheat-importing country; and the skilled

carpet-makers and other craftsmen from Asia Minor brought the same gifts as the Huguenots had brought to England in the time of Louis XIV. Increased prosperity helped to restore social, and even political, stability.[64]

No sooner was this project in motion, than the League was involved in another programme of financial reconstruction in Hungary, a situation quite unlike Austria. Whereas the latter had experienced a period of relative political stability after the war, Hungary had undergone a Bolshevik revolution in 1919, a brief occupation by a Romanian army, and with power finally being concentrated in a strong right-wing government. Hungary, however, had a productive agricultural base, making it at least self-sufficient in necessities. Nonetheless, in its broad outlines, Hungary's financial problems paralleled those of Austria, "a rapidly depreciating currency, an unbalanced budget, and the inability of the country to achieve unaided recovery." As Salter immersed himself in the issues he discovered, as he put it, that "if the problem was technically easier, it was politically more difficult."[65] As well, before financial reconstruction could begin, Hungary's frontier disputes with its Little Entente neighbours, including Romania, Czechoslovakia and Yugoslavia, would have to be conciliated. When that was partially achieved in July at a conference at Sinaia, Hungary was ready to approach the League for financial help, which it did in September. Salter was involved in framing the resolution presented to the Assembly, which approved it, and then worked on the protocols to govern the loan.[66] Initially he was not overly optimistic, advising the League Directors on 17 October that "The moment was a very difficult one for the raising of money." Privately he added, "We have a very difficult and perhaps impossible task of negotiation both political and financial before we actually get to a loan."[67] The practical aspects of the task began with a League fact-finding delegation, consisting of Salter, Avenol and Stoppani, visiting Budapest from 6 to 17 November. At its conclusion Salter stated that "he saw promising signs for the chances of a loan."[68] The resulting report, largely the work of Salter, was examined and revised by the Financial Committee, meeting in London on 22 November, which then drew up a reconstruction scheme.[69] This was submitted to the Council when it met in Paris between 10 and 20 December. There followed several months of negotiations, between the Little Entente, the Reparation Commission and the League. Finally on 14 March 1924 the protocols were signed at Geneva and the League accepted full responsibility for the scheme. Of the many aspects of the plan, Salter was particularly pleased that Hungarian reparations had been reduced and fixed. The plan, which did not entail governmental guarantees as in the Austrian case, went into effect on 1 May and thereafter the Hungarian experience closely followed that of Austria. The League Commissioner-General, Jeremiah Smith, Jr, a Boston banker, the preferred choice for the position by J.P. Morgan but not of Salter, was appointed, with Royall Tyler as Assistant-Commissioner.[70] Despite some difficulties earlier in June, the loan was floated by the end of the month, and with American participation, stability soon returned to Hungary.[71] Assessing the experience afterwards, Salter wrote, "For negotiations so important in their results, so intricate in their character, so involved with the separate policies and interests of so many countries, a period of six months was not excessive."[72] Certainly, others were effusive in their praise for Salter's work, including Smith, members of the Hungarian government and the press.[73] The Observer summed up opinion by crediting Salter with "a singularly successful piece of reconstructive work."[74]

Hectic though these six months had been for Salter, it was hardly the extent of his extraordinarily busy schedule. There was a never ending round of speeches, including one for the League of Nations Union, in Cambridge on 28 November. Then there was the Geneva-Paris-London circuit that kept him in touch with financial and economic officials in all three capitals. Occasionally, there was even time for friends. In early October, Salter enjoyed a weekend with Tyler at Coppet, "in a glorious sun, in and out of the lake." A week later they dined with Mildred Bliss, who, according to Tyler, "was very dear and we all felt comfortable and happy, and little A. was so good, his limpid soul open to our enraptured inspection, and his exquisitely balanced expressions of opinion following one another as easily as the bird sings. He is a marvel – the more I see of him the more I wonder at his nobility of mind and delight in his humanity."[75] Another guest at Coppet described his visit:

> Before and after dinner we strolled along the lake front, on his own territory, enjoying the moonlight, the lapping of the little waves, the goodnight twitters of the birds, the odor of the woods and blossoms, and the light on the water and the hills beyond. We had time for a good chat before turning in early. Next morning, after part of breakfast in bed, we went down to the shore for a sunbath and a plunge in the lake, brief but tinglingly delicious, then returned for the rest of breakfast, a lazy respite in the soft morning sunshine following.[76]

As well, the success of the Austrian experiment and the emergence of the Hungarian reconstruction plans were enhancing the reputations of both the League and Salter personally. Thus Portugal had made sounding at the League early in the New Year for a similar possible plan.[77] At the same time, Salter was asked to brief the Dawes Committee of Experts sitting in Paris. The goal was to find a solution to Germany's financial problems, balance its budget and stabilize its currency. Commenting on the announcement of his visit to Paris, The New York Times described Salter as "the League's leading expert on the financial rehabilitation of nations" while The Times wrote that his experience with Austria would prove helpful.[78] On 28 February, according to Dawes, Salter briefed the Committee on the recovery of Austria, "to which his own genius has so much contributed. His report was a model of clearness and condensation."[79] Salter returned on 25 March and again, as noted by both Dawes and Sir Josiah Stamp, one of the experts representing Britain, he assisted in the large-scale redraft and edit of the report's first 100 pages.[80] Indeed, when meeting with some members of "the family" on 2 May at the Reform Club, Salter revealed he personally had been responsible for entirely rewriting Part One of the Committee's Report.[81] +During this time as well, there was an increasing number of invitations to speak and to write for newspapers and journals. A letter from the editor of Foreign Affairs led to his first contribution to that journal, an article on the financial rehabilitation of Austria. In accepting, Salter promised to deal with "some of the important criticisms" of the scheme.[82] Then on 23 April, St George's Day in the UK, he made his first BBC broadcast, "The British Empire and the League." He emphasized the two complemented each other's needs, which were the pursuit of peace, because "under modern conditions of war the victor is only one degree better off than the vanquished;" and secondly, prosperity, because the empire stood to benefit by the economic recovery of Europe. It had no reason to fear the League, which was not a "super-state."[83] On 22 May he addressed the British Institute of International Affairs in London to help publicize the progress made with Hungarian reconstruction.[84] The topic was already so familiar to Salter that he gave the impression that he had spoken without notes.[85]

Even as his publicity work expanded, ongoing League responsibilities for Salter continued unabated. On 7 May, the Greek Committee of the League Council met in London, on Salter's initiative, to map out the future work of the Refugee Resettlement Commission. The pressing problem was financial, the initial loan of one million pounds was almost exhausted and the need remained to consider some long-term funding for the refugees.[86] The major complications were fears, raised by Salter at the meeting, that the Greek government, dependent on the support of the military, would make armaments' expenditure a priority over refugee resettlement. When his fears were assuaged by the British Foreign Office, the results seemed assured.[87] Thus two resolutions Salter had prepared, providing for another one million pounds of short-term funding from the Bank of England and confirming the pressing need for a long-term loan, were adopted.[88] As the Greek scheme progressed, the Austrian situation also had to be continually monitored. On 10 March the Austrian government had asked for the release of a portion of the reconstruction loan, not to meet a budget deficit, but rather for economic investment. This was not part of the original contractual obligations. After leaving London, Salter reported to Zimmerman that the financial situation in Austria "was being watched with great interest and indeed anxiety." Niemeyer, Strakosch and Norman were "inclined to take a rather serious view of the situation." Salter too was troubled by the fact that "the progress of reform [had] slowed down and the will to effect drastic economies seemed to have evaporated."[89] Thus, he advised, a co-ordinated and well-researched report should be made to the Council, meeting in Geneva in June.[90] The Financial Committee, however, in its report to the Council on 14 June vetoed any but the strict application of the original terms of the loan, describing this as "a breach of faith." Further enquiry was called for with a reconsideration scheduled for the fall.[91] In an interview which he gave to the Geneva correspondent of the Neue Freie Presse on 22 June, Salter stressed "the amazing contrast between the present Austria and the Austria of 20 months ago." While hardships and anxieties might continue, it was well to be reminded of a worse scenario that might have enveloped Austria but for the intervention of the League.[92]

For some time Salter had been urged from several quarters to pay a visit to the United States.[93] This made good sense given the increasing US participation in the humanitarian and technical work of the League and the need to publicize the League's efforts at financial reconstruction. Indeed, on 14 February Salter had accepted an invitation to participate in the fourth session of the Institute of Politics at Williams College, Williamstown, Massachusetts. The Institute had a reputation as an important think tank with membership restricted to those in academic, political and economic circles or related professions such as the military and journalism. It would thus provide Salter with a ready-made forum for an extensive dissemination of his views. He agreed, therefore, to attend for the better part of August, offer two public addresses, and contribute to roundtable discussions. The platform of the Institute, therefore, loomed prominently as a vehicle to foster the relationship between the League and the United States.[94]

Salter sailed to New York on 23 July aboard the *Olympic*, arriving on 29 July for a dinner in his honour given by the League of Nations Non-Partisan Association at the Hotel Astor.[95] While concentrating on the Austrian and Hungarian reconstruction schemes, he also addressed the issue of German reparations, praising the Dawes plan which among much else, recommended the scaling back of German reparation payments. He forecast that if this "last of the great treaty problems" were resolved, "the League would enter upon a new era of usefulness."[96] On 2 August, promptly at 9 a.m., Salter began the first of his eight roundtable sessions on "Reconstruction in Europe and the League's Contribution." He spoke broadly on economic cooperation, the League and its workings, reconstruction across Europe, and German reparation.[97] On the evening of 4 August, Salter delivered the first of his two official addresses, on "The Economic Recovery of Europe." He asserted that the resolution of the German reparation question would provide the basis for a complete return to equilibrium. He believed steady progress had been made and that the two most desperate European countries, Austria and Hungary, were on the road to recovery. He outlined his view that the roots of current economic problems were "a misdirection of effort, a maladjustment of supply and demand, a sense of insecurity, diminishing savings, disorganization of the system of credit and a restriction of the range of international commerce."[98] The following day, in his roundtable, he contrasted the League's success in financial rehabilitation with other efforts, such as conferences of ambassadors or prime ministers. "The League is no super-state or separate state," he said, but worked by consensus, and managed in so many cases to bring "order out of chaos." On 6 August, The New York Times editorial commended the fact that Salter had made "no extravagant claims" for the League and congratulated what it called these "islands of hope."[99]

On 7 and 10 August, continuing with his contributions to the roundtables, he emphasized that League members in no way sacrificed their sovereignty, and discussed several articles of the League Covenant. His major emphasis was again on European reconstruction. He argued that only the League had the requisite "elastic machinery" to tackle problems that were both political and economic in origin.[100] On 11 August, during an open session on "International Finance in the Commercial Policies of Nations," Salter weighed in with a discussion of the Dawes plan which he titled "The Four Gulfs and the Four Bridges." Here he drew on his experience of "the principles of the League system of controlling assigned revenues in Austria and Hungary," noting that these were replicated in the Dawes plan. The next day, in a long editorial on the subject, The New York Times found his analogy of gulfs and bridges "helpful, though a bit confusing." At the same time it described the League as "an international economic engineering company bridging gulfs thought impassible and showing the way to others."[101] A debate on 13 and 14 August on the League and the issue of American membership was described as "the most crowded and interested gathering yet held." When called upon to field questions, Salter tactfully tried to assuage questioners' fears that the US would be drawn into wars or economic sanctions of which it did not approve.[102] On 15 August, for his second major address, "Economic Conflicts as the Causes of War," his approach was more pessimistic than usual. He cautioned that if war was used as an instrument in economic competition, then he foresaw "the ruin of civilization." The next day he expanded on this theme by indicating how the League worked through its Economic Committee to mediate disputes. He emphasized that questions were not negotiated by politicians as part of national policy, but "by experts from the different countries meeting in an international committee. Thus is the basis of international relations broadened."[103] The New York Times, carefully following these discussions, praised Salter's achievements and noted "The flowing tide is with the League."[104]

Controversy and fierce debates were not unknown at the Williamstown Institute of Politics. This unfolded on 19 August when Salter felt compelled to reply "as an Englishman" to charges that Britain was using the League to maintain the superiority of its navy and merchant marine. However, his main contribution that day was to offer the view that as Europe settled down the reconstruction work of the League would be replaced with more regulatory activity such customs, railway conventions and trade markets.[105] Similarly, the following day, he argued, that the requirement of all members was to maintain the freedom of communication, transit and treatment for the commerce of all nations. He described this as "the policy of 'safety valves' designed to prevent the economic strains and stresses of the world from developing an explosive force." Summing up the conference on 22 August, The New York Times used Salter's contributions for commentary. It praised his "apocalyptic statement" about the future and the need for "a continuous economic league" and concluded with a strong appeal for American participation.[106]

Salter had noted that he found the Institute "interesting, but very strenuous" and at its conclusion "a very valuable experience."[107] Part of that fatigue was due to the ongoing League work he carried on, even at Williamstown. Felkin, as usual, served as his conduit, informing him of developments at Geneva and elsewhere.[108] One of the additional duties Salter accepted was to write a long memorandum, at the invitation of Prime Minister Ramsay MacDonald, on the possible admission of Germany to the League, and policies to achieve security and the reduction of armaments.[109] Salter finally sailed from New York on 23 August, but not without a flurry of the publicity he so assiduously shunned. He chastised Walter Lippmann, editor of The World, about a misleading headline above an interview that he had given to that newspaper. He wrote to Lippmann, "Really, you know, your head-liner is a public danger," and the latter was forced to issue a *démenti*.[110]

A daunting array of problems and prospects awaited Salter on his return to Geneva. The fifth assembly of the League opened on 1 September in a spirit of optimism and with ambitious plans to reinforce the Covenant by compulsory arbitration. This "Protocol for the Pacific Settlement of International Disputes" was designed "to translate into a formal system the formula, Arbitration, Security, Disarmament."[111] Among the accompanying recommendations was for the expert committees of the League to work on implementing this measure. Salter worked assiduously to fulfill this mandate, believing that League action against an aggressor under the Covenant and Protocol "must be immediate, simultaneous, and impressive in character." [112]

The Geneva Protocol for Security and Disarmament, approved on 2 October by the League Assembly, was abandoned in March 1925, much to Salter's disappointment.[113] In other respects, however, the fall session proved more productive for Salter's other concerns. A committee, appointed by the Financial Committee to further investigate the Austrian situation, visited Vienna in August and September. Its results were embodied in a final report on 15 September which recommended a series of amendments to the original protocols. The Council of the League unanimously adopted these recommendations.[114] As for Hungary, events unfolded smoothly, a process which Salter described "as one of rapid and unvarying progress." The Council approved on 13 September the appointment of three trustees to represent the interests of the bond holders. From then onwards the budget was in equilibrium and no more demands were made on the reconstruction loan.[115] At the same time other European nations were paying attention to the League work of reconstruction. In early October Estonia signaled that it wished to host a League deputation to discuss financial and economic concerns. This was later followed as well by other ""minor currency reforms" in Danzig, but with no further major financial reconstruction.[116]

As the year ended Salter felt enormous satisfaction, even as ongoing issues persisted. He made plans to visit Athens, while working on details of the long-term refugee loan[117] On 23 October, accompanied by Violet Markham and James Carruthers, he visited Vienna where the question of the number of government officials to be dismissed was still unresolved. He also found Zimmerman's handling of affairs, as previously, was causing concern.[118] From there, joined by Thannasis Aghnides of the Political Section of the League, they visited Athens and Crete after which Violet Markham recorded her impressions for the Fortnightly Review.[119] Salter then returned to Geneva, "deeply impressed both with strength of securities of loan and with the great reconstructive value of work."[120] For his part Salter recorded his thoughts in Headway, the journal of the League of Nations Union, describing his admiration for "Greece's remarkable powers of absorption."[121] However, as the year was drawing to a close, he admitted that he was getting "rather tired."[122] His recent travelling companion, Violet Markham, wrote to a mutual friend that Salter was "very far from well – the strain of years of overwork is beginning to tell on him." [123] Concerned as always for her friend, she then confided to Felkin that Salter's "health is not sufficiently consolidated for him to assume that he can go on without further rest or treatment." She revealed that he had had "a very anxious and trying time," adding "that never during the darkest days of the war have I seen him so tired and rattled and depressed as he got in Athens." She finally observed, "Of course one has to realize frankly about Arthur that he has lived for so many years in such a state of strain and excitement that he actually misses the stimulus if life and work become in any way normal."[124]

Cognizant of this, and heeding the advice of friends, Salter travelled on 3 December to vacation for three weeks in Grasse, in the company of Marian Henderson and her family.[125] Later he admitted that at this time he "began to feel the strain" of his last 13 years and in future planned more extensive breaks.[126]

As the New Year began Salter welcomed Charles P. Howland as chairman of the Refugee Settlement Commission, a successor to Morgenthau. Salter shared his relief that, with the long-term loan raised and approved by the League the previous December, "you start at a happy moment."[127] All the while Salter kept up a blistering pace of publicity work for the League. On 12 January 1925 he addressed the League of Nations Union in London, and during this time he completed an article for The Times, on "Reconstruction in Europe." In this he suggested that if peace prevailed, Europe would reap "the fruits of the combined and complementary efforts of individuals, of certain national Governments, and of the League."[128] In another article for The Manchester Guardian Commercial on "The Financial Work of the League of Nations," he acknowledged that the League had "substantially contributed" to European economic recovery by targeting financial reconstruction through currency stabilization and balanced budgets. However, he was not prepared to sanction the League's intervening directly for economic reconstruction or development. As for the future, he suggested that the League's work in financial reconstruction might have run its course, but there remained the necessity to remove the economic causes of conflict and friction between nations.[129]

After the rejection of the Geneva Protocol by the British government in March 1925, Salter continued to study the problem of how to implement financial and economic sanctions and achieve the cooperation envisaged in the Geneva Protocol and the Covenant. On 3 April, while in London, he continued to press forward with his own vision of the Protocol. In a conversation with Alexander Cadogan, responsible for League affairs at the Foreign Office, Salter stated that, while the British government clearly "would not sign a general pact based on compulsory arbitration," other countries continued to show interest in local agreements for purposes of mutual guarantee. He proposed, therefore, that there be some advantage in evolving through the League "a uniform model" for such pacts:

> His idea seemed to be that it might be possible thus eventually to build up a solid structure of peace, brick by brick, avoiding the mistake which the last Assembly made of building castles in the air, and the structure would be easier to build if the bricks were made in one mould.

> He also suggested "that a growing number of such regional 'pacts,' of strong family likeness, might one day be united under the parental authority of the League."

Privately, Cadogan expressed his reservations but considered the proposal deserving of further study.[130] Over the next few months, Salter's template began to circulate and arouse interest, a development which he followed with some satisfaction.[131]

In the spring of 1925 Austria again aroused concern in the League as unemployment rose, bankruptcies increased and the trade deficit mounted. The viability of Austria was widely discussed in the European press. Questions were raised whether these economic difficulties would compromise the work of reconstruction.[132] The information Salter received indicated that the Bank of England was not content with Austrian financial management, although he regarded fears about Austria's viability and economic future as exaggerated.[133] However, he let it be known on 27 March that he favoured the dispatch of two economists for a fact-finding mission to Austria. The idea immediately found favour.[134] Shortly afterwards Salter approached Layton, who agreed, despite the fact that since 1922 he had been fully occupied as editor of The Economist.[135] Finding another economist proved more difficult, as Salter wanted someone unconnected with Austria and preferably a labour specialist.[136] The search became more complicated when leaks were made about the mission's alleged secret agenda, namely, to investigate "the 'economic barriers' question," and this raised the question of the Anschluss of Austria and Germany.[137] Salter was annoyed, but argued that leaks were inevitable "when we have to consult five different governments."[138] On 9 June the Council approved both the mission and the appointments of Layton and his co-investigator, selected by Salter, Professor Charles Rist of the University of Paris.[139] After consulting with Salter in Paris on 26 June, they arrived in Vienna on 30 June to begin their economic mission. The work, expected to take six weeks, extended into a ten-week investigation.[140]

Salter next turned his attention to Brussels where on 23 June he addressed, for the second time, the International Chamber of Commerce. His subject, "Recent Progress in European Reconstruction," was a natural follow-up from his talk the previous year in Rome. While he acknowledged Austria had economic difficulties, he cautioned against undue pessimism, arguing that the financial under pinnings were "firmly secured." Turning to Hungary, he described progress as "remarkable," in particular because the current surplus enabled much of the original loan to remain unspent and that it had now been targeted towards capital investment. As for Greece, he reminded his audience that reconstruction there was of a different character. Namely, it required the resettlement of 1.5 million refugees from Asia Minor, and all evidence confirmed the scheme was moving ahead. When Salter turned to the Dawes plan he described it as "the greatest event in the economic sphere" in the previous year. It was his view that it was rooted in the spadework of reconstruction strategy achieved by the League schemes. "Principles that in 1922 were regarded as paradoxes, or at the best as economic theories untried as a remedy for the unprecedented disorganization caused by the war," Salter asserted, "had in 1924 become the axioms of proved experience – so completely accepted as to be regarded almost as platitudes." Finally, while acknowledging such problems as unemployment and depressed industries such as coal, he argued the overall picture was one of a Europe rebuilding its prosperity. If political security could show such equivalent progress, he concluded, Europe's future would be secure.[141]

As was his habit during the summer months, Salter tried to spend some time in London, renewing associations with colleagues and friends, and in Oxford where he visited with his parents. "Having an interesting time here, with just enough work but not too much" he wrote.[142] On 29 June, he attended a discussion by the Economic Group at the British Institute of International Affairs and followed up on a long delayed meeting with Howland and others regarding the Greek question.[143] On 6 July he addressed the League of Nations Parliamentary Committee at the House of Commons. After reviewing the progress of European reconstruction, he also emphasized that a major achievement of the previous two years was the stabilization of European currencies, leading to an increase in exports of almost all European countries.[144] He also continued with a favourite lobbying effort, meeting with Morrow in London on 9 July to plan strategy to firm up American support for "efforts to attain stability, conciliation and security in Western Europe," including the admission of Germany to the League.[145] During a brief return to Geneva, Salter was able to catch up on European developments, sufficient for him to confide that he now had "certain anxieties" regarding Austria and "a great deal of anxiety" about the political situation in Greece.[146] Returning to England in early August, he spoke to the Liberal Summer School, first held in 1921, in Cambridge on 4 and 5 August.[147] There he suggested that economic causes, particularly the struggle for markets and for oil, would be a major cause of future wars. He then attended the Independent Labour Party's Summer School at Easton Lodge, held at Lady Warwick's estate in Essex, for a discussion on "World Economic Organization."[148]

The report from Layton and Rist reached Salter's desk on 18 August and helped inform his thinking about the Austrian situation.[149] While Zimmerman signaled an attenuation of control as of 1 September, Salter favoured, in light of the report and a conversation with Layton, "a more extensive transformation." Hence, he described Zimmerman's move as "meaning practically nothing at all."[150] In a closely argued and confidential memorandum, Salter explained his reasoning, including the facts that budget equilibrium had prevailed for 18 months and the currency had been stable for three years. He also valued the conclusions reached by Layton and Rist that the economic situation would not impact negatively on the financial one. Most importantly, he argued that as long as the commissioner-general continued, he and the League would be blamed and make the Austrians "think of the Anschluss as a sort of Eldorado."[151] He thus favoured action by the end of the year, however, with "special safeguards." He wished to see some sort of "League Information Officer" remain in Vienna to report back to Geneva, and have the right to re-impose control in the event that financial stability was endangered.[152] Drummond responded to Salter: "The case made out seems to me to be overwhelming."[153]

At the same time, Salter disseminated the disturbing news that Howland had conveyed regarding the situation in Greece. In letters to Salter on 12 and 20 August, Howland had detailed the numerous problems that the Refugee Settlement Commission had been experiencing. These included a reduction in the amount of land covenanted by the Greek government for resettlement, problems in communication, personnel difficulties, the lack of land surveys, and the frequent changes of administration in Greece. Howland cautioned that "the situation here is worse than we had supposed."[154] He then alerted Greek officials that the work of the Commission would be a subject of discussion at the next session of the Council of the League. By the end of August he was warning Salter that, if outstanding questions were not settled by the end of September, "the Commission, if it goes on at all, will be a cripple and will be subject to further encroachment upon its powers." He then urged "prompt vigorous action" from the Council.[155] As September began Salter observed that "Both the Austrian position and also the Greek will want very serious consideration."[156]

After due deliberation, the League Council on 10 September approved the recommendations regarding Austria, including the conditions for budget control, to be modified at an early date and then terminated. The two primary conditions, ones first enunciated by Salter – the possibility of re-establishing the control and the continuance of a bank adviser – were adopted.[157] In the following weeks Salter lobbied vigorously for the manner in which the Austrian government would accept and adopt these alterations. He confessed to having been "anxious" about the post-League phase of Austria's financial life. Indeed, he urged Layton to publicize the need for a "stiffening element" to the Austrian government after the departure of the commissioner-general.[158] Salter continued his lobbying while in London in early October. On the third anniversary of the 4 October 1922 signature of the protocols for Austrian reconstruction, he reviewed its history and its significance in two articles in <u>The Times</u>. He wrote, with evident satisfaction, that "the financial stability of Austria is assured."[159] He also held discussions with Strakosch and Niemeyer about the legal requirements to extend control and the role of the bank adviser.[160] Their recommendations were adopted by the Council on 9 December and approved by the Austrian government in the New Year.[161] As for the Greek situation, Salter was pleased to report that the Greek government had relented on a variety of difficulties that had impeded the work of the Resettlement Commission. He was firm in his recommendation to Howland to guarantee a more frequent distribution of information on the work of the Resettlement Commission, thereby ensuring future roadblocks were overcome before they became intractable. Within a short time, Howland was able to report an improvement in relations with the Greek government.[162]

It was at this time that Salter focused on a more ambitious proposal, a plan for a World Economic Conference. He had been an early proponent, having produced a memorandum on the subject on 25 August. He addressed the criticism that, while the League had proved its competence with schemes for financial reconstruction, it had never addressed related economic issues. He pointed out that governments could address financial issues such as budgets and currency, and establish Banks of Issue. Economic reconstruction, on the other hand, entailed more complex problems, such as production, and supply and demand, and these activities could not always be legislated by central governments. Nonetheless, given the progress made with financial reconstruction, he endorsed the call for an Economic Conference. He further detailed his vision of the gathering as "a forum of responsible world opinion." The mandate would be to examine the obstacles to economic recovery, and discuss policies which might provide remedies to mitigate economic conflicts that threatened war.[163] The French delegate to the Sixth Assembly of the League, Louis Loucheur, took up the suggestion on 15 September and proposed that preparations for such a conference should be set in motion.[164] At once, Salter drew up an 11 page memorandum endorsing the proposal and expanding on "the opportunity, character and purpose of such a conference."[165] The Assembly endorsed the proposal on 24 September and in December the League Council appointed a Preparatory Committee which then met in April and November 1926.

In the meantime, Salter began to explore and promote the idea. After noting that the British delegation was the only one that initially hesitated, he wrote to Layton on 24 September. "I do not know of course whether the kind of conference that ultimately emerges will be the kind I want. I shall, of course, do what I can to secure it in the year of preparation that is before me."[166] Layton replied that he would consult with others and respond on the scope and methods he would endorse for the conference.[167] As well as targeting specific individuals to work on the projected, he broadcast on the BBC, noting that the Economic Conference would be a further step in Europe's economic recovery.[168] He also continued to circulate his own memorandum, although he was not certain to what extent the Preparatory Committee would adopt it and preferred a widely drawn agenda.[169] On 15 October, while at the end of an extended stay in London, he spoke to the Political and Economic Circle of the

Liberal Party and tested out the notion of what such a conference could realistically achieve.[170]

On 19 October 1925, an exchange of shots at a remote area of the Bulgarian-Greek frontier quickly led to troop movements by both sides. Bulgaria officially appealed to the League on 23 October, invoking Articles 10 and 11 of the Covenant. The sequence of events surrounding these developments was clarified in a note Salter later wrote about his own role:

> At 11.15 p.m. (10.15 London time) I put on my wireless at Founex to hear the 'General News Bulletin.' I heard a statement phrased so as to appear authentic, that a message in the nature of an ultimatum had been sent by Greece to Bulgaria over the frontier incident that had occurred on the 19th. I at once rang up the S.G. and in agreement with him rang up the Greek Legation at Berne and asked that a telegram should be sent to [the Greek Prime Minister General Theodoros] Pangalos [requesting confirmation of the ultimatum]. I believe this telegram was sent by the Greek Legation to M. Pangalos about midnight. In the early hours of Friday the 23rd an official appeal came from Bulgaria. The S.G. at once, after telephonic communication with M. Briand [the President at the time], summoned the Council meeting for the 26th at Paris. It occurred to those of us who were discussing with him at the time (M. [Joseph] Avenol, [Major G.H.F.] Abraham and myself) that much might happen before the 26th. We therefore drafted telegrams in the name of the President calling on both sides to abstain from military action pending the deliberations of the Council. The telegrams were approved by telephone by M. Briand, sent out the same morning, and the Greek telegram reached M. Pangalos the same day (23rd).

Salter continued that Briand's telegram stopped a planned Greek offensive. He wrote:

> It may be that the earlier telegram sent on the 21st had a useful effect in preparing M. Pangalos to act at once on the second telegram, but the second telegram was the decisive one. The really important thing was the initiative taken by the Secretariat in drafting the President's telegram and getting his approval without a moment's delay.[171]

He might have added that it was his good fortune to be listening to his wireless at an opportune moment. Somewhat later Salter added, "we have great reason to congratulate ourselves in the Secretariat on the dramatic timeliness of the 'Briand' telegram of October 23rd, which was in fact devised and written in the office, telephonic authority being obtained for its despatch."[172] So pleased was he about his role, that he was uncharacteristically immodest in sharing this with friends.[173]

Salter then attended the emergency session of the Council that met in Paris from 26 to 31 October. The deliberations resulted in a resolution for a ceasefire, the withdrawal of troops within 60 hours and the dispatch of a Commission of Enquiry. The Council meetings, he later wrote, "went off extremely well," and he felt confident that the Council's intervention was effective and had increased the prospect for peace in the Balkans.[174] For his part, Salter had several conversations should sanctions, perhaps in the form of a naval blockade, have to be applied under Article 16.[175] In addition, he also prepared a detailed analysis memorandum on the merits and demerits of the League applying various forms of pressure under Articles 10, 11 and 16. In this he emphasized the duty of the League to do all in its powers to prevent war before the outbreak of hostilities.[176] Salter also attended a meeting on 4 November, convened by Drummond, to discuss the work of the Commission of Enquiry and particularly how to avoid such incidents from occurring and escalating in the future.[177] The League Council, which reconvened on 7 December, heard the Commission's report, accepted its recommendations, including an indemnity to be paid by Greece to Bulgaria, and plan for its implementation. On 17 December, the government of Greece notified its acceptance and the indemnity was finally paid in full by March 1926.

Two further items of business on this Council agenda concerned Salter. On 9 December the Council agreed on several measures intended to wind up the financial reconstruction of Austria. These included control of the Austrian budget that ceased on 31 December and the termination of the office of commissioner-general effective 30 June 1926.[178] On 15 December, the Council also decided on the composition of the Preparatory Committee for the Economic Conference, although the actual list was to be kept secret pending acceptances. However, Salter at once wrote to Layton, stating "that to my great joy" the Council had invited him, even though English representation had thereby exceeded the norm of three representatives.[179] The next day Salter wrote to Owen Young, along with others, encouraging them to accept a forthcoming official invitation of membership, even though the "general character" of the conference had not yet been determined. He enclosed his 25 August note describing his personal vision of what the conference might achieve. In this, he was covertly attempting to secure advance agreement on the composition of the committee.[180] For the remainder of the year, Salter stayed in Geneva, with a renewed burst of writing. He continued to contribute book reviews, for example, praising Maurice Fanshawe's analysis of reconstruction under the League.[181] He also began to write an article for the 13th edition of the Encyclopaedia Britannica, "League of Nations: The Work of the First Six Years," and was also asked to contribute another on "Control:

Inter-Allied."[182] Little wonder that he noted on 21 December, "I've been absolutely worked off my feet."[183] The pace did somewhat slacken for Salter in the New Year. He spent the second week of January in London, completing his two articles for the Encyclopaedia Britannica, with long distance assistance from Felkin.[184]

The beginning of February brought a letter from Norman which described Poland's financial position as "desperate," due to its high bank failure rate, high interest rates and lack of credit. Although the Polish Central Bank was searching for capital from abroad, Norman thought this would be impossible until "some comprehensive plan is adopted." By this he meant League sponsored reconstruction and control, and he asked for Salter's advice.[185] The latter replied on 5 February that the Poles had never asked for assistance and without a formal application and approval by the Financial Committee of the League, nothing could be done. Salter believed that Poland considered League control "would hurt her dignity as a new sovereign nation aspiring to the first rank" and that she had an unclear idea of the application process. He followed this with a personal analysis of Polish finances in which he suggested that a revival of domestic confidence was not possible without external support. Finally, he revealed that in anticipation of a Polish referral to the League, he had in fact devised a draft scheme for financial reconstruction under the auspices of the League. In terms of the broader picture, Salter pointed out that, as Poland was pressing to become a permanent member of the League Council in March, any move on the financial front was unlikely.[186]

Despite the advance preparations needed for meetings of the League Council and Financial Committee in March, Salter continued his busy schedule. He arrived in Brussels on 18 February and then went on to Amsterdam on 23 February for an ongoing round of discussions with officials involved in the Preparatory Committee.[187] From there he went to London to attend a meeting of the Balkan Group at Chatham House on 1 March, returning to Geneva on 3 March for League meetings.[188] So hectic was his current schedule that he had to write "in great distress" to Tyler that he could not provide his usual hospitality at Coppet. Tyler explained to Elisina Tyler that Salter had written, "The Council is going to be a very heavy one – other powers beside Germany will make a desperate attempt to get permanent seats on the Council – and it's an extremely critical moment for the League. A. wants to, & must have his flat & his time entirely free for parleys."[189]

On 8 March, the League Assembly and the Council were both convened and met until 17 March. The major item of business was the expected admission of Germany, following on logically from the signature of the Locarno Pacts the previous December. However, some "formidable political complications" emerged with a growing campaign by Poland and its supporters for permanent membership on the Council.[190] As early as 3 February Salter had put his mind to the impending difficulty, arguing in a confidential note to Drummond that such a move "would substantially change the character of the Council." It was originally conceived as limited to the great powers, thereby, making the Council "manageable in size, and thus efficient for current executive work." The experience of the past six years, as exhibited by the Greek-Bulgarian incident, had "confirmed the wisdom of this conception." With regard to Poland, he wrote, "No one would, on plain merits, think of classifying her as a great power or as being entitled to permanency on the original conception of the League." Nor did Salter hesitate about from writing critically of French support for the Polish campaign. French motives were derived from the advantageous situation to be created when Germany became a permanent member "and a desire to assure extra strength in the Council for non-German policy." France already had two Allies, Czechoslovakia and Belgium, on the Council and thus threatened to have an influential pro-French bloc. Finally, Salter warned that the developing situation could convince Germany to remain outside of the League. Another scenario he dreaded even more would be the brief period when, although not yet a permanent member of the Council, Germany would be in the invidious position of blocking the possible applications of Brazil and Spain for permanent Council membership. In conclusion, Salter offered a larger perspective on the issue:

> We have now reached the most crucial point of the League's development. The danger that the League would be either destroyed, or relegated to a secondary position, is past. It is now evident that it will be the main instrument of international negotiation of the future. The rather impotent idealism of the first years has been reinforced by the incorporation of the forces of real politics. The doubt of the future is not as to the strength but as to the character of the League. Those forces and politics of the world which it was the hope of the Covenant to replace or transform will not kill the League but they may capture it. The issue is still uncertain. It is of vital importance that the constitution of the League should be 'fairly worked' in the spirit as well as the letter of the Covenant.

For this reason, Salter opposed the election of the two unanticipated permanent members. But for the same reason, he continued, "The first entry of the great 'ex-enemy' state marks the crucial point, and places the League at the cross-roads, of which one leads to the gradual modification of national policies and the building up of a world system through which all nations collaborate, and the other to deformation into another 'Holy Alliance'." [191]

The objections and reservation voiced by Salter and others proved futile.[192] The obstruction of Brazil and to a lesser extent Spain led on 17 March to an Assembly meeting which postponed until September any action on Germany's application.[193] In a confidential memorandum, Salter condemned Brazil's action as an attempt "to extort" for itself a seat on the Council. He was also critical that the issue had never been publicly discussed by the Council and only for one day by the Assembly. Instead, the "Locarno Powers" met on 16 March and agreed to stay the issue. Salter contended that this was not a League failure, but that "League methods were never applied. The League machinery was never used, except at the last moment to record a failure announced to the world the day before." As to the future, he foresaw the very same difficulties and secret negotiations recurring. He was hopeful, however, that over the next six months the seriousness of the recent crisis will allow for clearer thinking to prevail.[194] In a further confidential memorandum on the "Composition of the Council," he again laid out his objections both to any enlargement of the Council. In conclusion, he returned to "the great wisdom of the original framers of the Covenant." He recounted the ongoing alterations to the original constitution of the League and argued "this process of meeting a temporary political difficulty by making a breach in the constitution can only lead to disaster." A set of "positive proposals" then followed, the primary one being the election of Germany as a new permanent member. In the following months, Salter lobbied strenuously for German entry into the League, a move finally achieved on 26 September 1926.[195]

Not for the first time did Salter use Violet Markham as a sounding board, in a long letter he wrote to her on 26 March. "This has indeed been, & is, a bitter time. In a moment we have lost – for the time & till we can retrieve it – the fruits of several years of patient & painful progress. And it need not, & ought not to have happened. It was not, I believe, in the first instance, a plot by France." But in turn, he castigated Poland for pushing the permanent seat agenda, Britain for not making clear its position in advance, and France which "jumped at the chance of redressing the balance against Germany." In addition, Brazil was "pressing her outrageous claim," assisted by a divided League, while Italy and Spain maneuvered secretly against German admission. Salter believed that by March 16 Brazil had been successfully isolated. But then Briand, under attack from all quarters, "came to the conclusion that he would prefer adjournment to the solution he had accepted." And supported by Chamberlain, the two saw the Germans who agreed because they did not want Brazil to resign. This news was allowed to leak and was then supported by the Locarno powers. When the Assembly met for the first time on the subject, it was faced a *fait accompli*. "The greatest League defeat had been assured – without any of the League powers & League machinery ever having been allowed to be used." Salter went on: "It is a bitter thought that a single man, in two single hours of folly & weakness, has done such harm. In any case we are practically impotent till September; the dangers of this year are terrifying. The League may remain weak for years." Salter then turned to other projects such as the Economic Conference which he regarded as proceeding, but slowly, "for the moment it's like a pricked bubble." He would continue with the Bulgarian refugee settlement scheme, which required "concessions from reparation powers under League influence." But that was now in doubt because after 16 March "what influence can the League exercise on reluctant reparation creditors this summer!" In conclusion, he decried Chamberlain's "state of mind. He seemed to me to have got his head in the clouds, & his feet off the ground. It is this that has led him to disaster."[196] In later years, Salter admitted that while Chamberlain had a tendency to "put a brake upon the League's idealism, in retrospect we can most of us see to have been wiser than we thought it at the time."[197]

The Bulgarian situation was, in fact, as Salter had anticipated. With the League's prestige, "sadly injured," he wrote, it would be difficult to arrange for a refugee loan to take priority over payment of reparations.[198] However, Salter was relieved to hear from Niemeyer that the latter had encouraged the Bulgarians to go ahead with their application. Thus he wrote to Niemeyer on 8 April, "we must now all put our backs into it and put it through."[199] Nor did the ongoing problems of the Refugee Settlement Commission provide any good news. Greek requests for a new loan roused little interest in Salter or Howland. Salter preferred that the Refugee Settlement Commission should continue to act as the collection agency, and that the problem be allowed to simmer until September.[200] By that time, thankfully, Howland was able to complete and publish a glowing report on the success of the Greek refugee settlement, one that Salter endorsed in a feature article in <u>The Times</u>. "The difficulties have been great," he wrote, but "the prospects for the future are promising."[201] Meanwhile, Salter pressed on with his primary focus, and that was the Preparatory Committee for the Economic Conference. Thus, he journeyed to Berlin on 10 April, conferring with the German members of the Preparatory Committee for several days.[202]

On 16 April, Salter departed suddenly to London and then on to Winchester. The following day, his mother Julia Salter died, while visiting with her son the Reverend George Herbert Salter, precentor of Winchester Cathedral. On 17 April, Salter wrote to Felkin, "My mother died this afternoon." Royall Tyler noted, "It is a relief, I think, that his mother should suffer no longer."[203] Julia Salter had been ill for two years, when she had a cerebral hemorrhage and "died peacefully and without pain three hours after the attack." Her obituary reminded readers that she was a native of Oxford, where she had lived all her life, regularly attended Wesley Memorial Church, and was interred at Wolvercote Cemetary.[204] As was the case so often, Salter shared his feelings with Markham. He wrote that losing his mother had been "a very painful & wearing" experience, especially when told that earlier in the month she had been asking for him. "My mother's life was certainly a singularly happy & fortunate one. These last three years she has been failing, with periods of distress. She had herself a happy & sunny temperament which made her really loved by all those who knew her." Salter's thoughts then turned to his father:

> I wish very much I could help him to recover a real life – which has been filched away from him by his selfless devotion during the strain of the last three years. He is I think the most 'selfless' man I have ever known. His own father was narrow & tyrannical, & though quite well-to-do by Oxford standards, & though my father had every natural aptitude & intense desire for a full education, sent him as a workman to the shops as a boy and when he married kept him at a workman's wage, so that I was born in little more than a slum tenement. On a different nature this might have meant disaster for the next generation of us as well. In my father it meant a definitive resolve that his sons should have the chances he had been denied: & to give them there was no length to which he was not prepared to go in denying himself.

He concluded with the thought that "a period like this last week turns the mind for the moment from the daily immersion in the days' affairs," adding, "It is a real consolation that a period in which one realizes what has been lost is also one in which one is more vividly conscious of what remains in friendship."[205]

As Salter returned to London, the League's work awaited him. He met there with Bulgarian Minister Hadji Misheff to review questions of procedure, namely, that the League was the proper channel for Bulgaria to get approval for the loan and the information needed regarding the settlement of refugees.[206] On his return to Geneva on 22 April, Salter successfully pushed for a prior visit by René Charron, Loveday's assistant, to Sofia to survey the ground and assist the Bulgarian government to expedite funding[207] He followed this with a personal note to Charron on 3 May, explaining why the League was eager to pursue a Bulgarian settlement scheme. He emphasized that "the need of the refugees is very great" but that the obstacles remained to get concessions from the reparation creditors. Thus information was urgently needed to present to the forthcoming Financial Committee and Council meetings in early June, without it appearing that the Secretariat had gone ahead on its own.[208] Explaining his commitment to the project, Salter wrote on 7 May:

We all feel very strongly here that the existence of these destitute refugees is the most important source of the political difficulties, both internal and external, of Bulgaria. They constitute a danger of Bolshevism, and by reaction of the extreme right of Governments; and the impulse their destitution gives to migration means a continual risk of disturbance in the relations with Bulgaria's neighbours.[209]

By 14 May Salter noted that Charron was "making good progress" in Sofia.[210]

Salter had anticipated that June would be a busy month in Geneva and so it was. The Financial Committee met on 3 June and Salter led off the discussion with an analysis of the Bulgarian situation and its request for a loan to resettle refugees. He pointed out that Bulgaria had acquitted itself well concerning both pre-war debts and reparation payments. On the recommendation of the Financial Committee, the Council approved the project on 10 June and at the same time agreed to terminate the functions of the commissioner-general in Hungary.[211] While the latter was achieved on 30 June, no such progress attended the Bulgarian loan, nicknamed Salter's "Bulgarian stepchild." While there appeared to be all-round agreement in principle, the French, Italian and Balkan neighbouring countries were suspicious.[212] In practice, however, Salter foresaw no problems in relation to the reparation schedule of payments of June 1924, which he believed, could remain untouched. In his view the only security needed was a first charge against customs revenues from such items as salt and alcohol, and protection against a possible depreciation of the Bulgarian "leva." Indeed, he foresaw that the adoption of the proposed refugee scheme would help pacify much potential Bulgarian turmoil, including "the danger of internal political trouble, Bolshevist movements, etc."[213]

On 30 June a momentous day began in the history of the League's financial reconstruction programmes. On that day both the Austrian and Hungarian control ended, on the grounds that "financial stability is assured," and both Dr. Zimmerman and Jeremiah Smith simultaneously left their posts in Vienna and Budapest respectively.[214] While Salter noted that "Bouquets have been flying about," he paid special tribute to Monnet's role regarding Austria. He thought it had been "literally indispensable" and added "without you the scheme could not have gone through." He wrote similarly to Blackett, recalling the essential role the latter had played in drafting the scheme "on that Sunday early in September 1922."[215] In an article in <u>The Times</u> on 9 July, Salter reviewed "the character and significance of the achievement." Despite a few setbacks, he noted that Austrian recovery was much more rapid than was expected. Reconstruction in Hungary was "technically easier" though the political difficulties were greater. Both schemes, however, with currency stabilization preceding budget balancing, had influenced the Dawes plan. The League, he concluded, had no other plans for financial reconstruction, however, the task of refugee resettlement was proceeding in Greece, with a similar scheme being planned for Bulgaria.[216] He brought a different message on 26 July when addressing the League of Nations Parliamentary Committee in the House of Commons.[217] While he mentioned that the currency of those countries, assisted by the League with reconstruction, had remained stable, others such as France had experienced a recent fall. However, he did predict that France had the necessary resources to return to prosperity.[218]

Further progress on the question of Bulgaria was delayed in early July because the Reparation Commission adjourned without deciding on the pre-war debt question. Salter continued to work behind the scenes to speed the agreement of the Reparations Commission and that finally did come on 23 July.[219] Meanwhile, a special meeting of the Financial Committee to authorise an advance loan to Bulgaria had gone ahead in London on 19 and 20 July. Salter led the discussions, suggesting that as the necessary agreements would be reached, he wished to go ahead and examine the conditions of the loan and the system of control. The Financial Committee fully endorsed his approach.[220] Thereafter, Salter pressed ahead in the coming weeks, touring European capitals and reassuring Bulgaria's neighbours about the focus of the loan.[221] By 21 August, he noted that "the advances have been practically arranged" and suggested, with the support of Niemeyer, that Charron visit Sofia and "spend some of them – a little and very cautiously – but some."[222] In the event, Charron's visit to Sofia had to be cancelled and Salter had to accept the fact that "a little judicious expenditure at Sofia" had to be put off. For his part, Salter continued to negotiate for the agreement of the "pays voisins."[223] This hectic activity, unlike on previous occasions, seemed to trouble him little. Tyler wrote on 29 August that, along with Fischer Williams and Howland as house guests, he found Salter "looking very brown and well" and that they all had enjoyed a swim and spending "a lazy day."[224]

As a result of the decision by the League Council on 7 September, Salter's "Bulgarian stepchild" finally was put into play. An advance of £400,000 was made in the form of a loan from the Bank of England to the Bank of Bulgaria, with a forthcoming loan of £2,250,000 to be issued for refugee relief. Charron was appointed as the League Commissioner and on 11 September Salter authorised him to begin releasing money for "immediate needs," such as seed for planting.[225] The scheme rapidly took shape, with Salter exhorting Charron, for example, on 24 September to settle the refugees "on land suitable to their habits and method of culture." At the same time Salter cautioned Charron to keep in mind the anxieties of the neighbouring states, particularly Romania and Greece, and not settle refugees within 50 kilometres of their borders.[226] The Bulgarian scheme thereafter was never far from Salter's mind and he wrote again to Charron on 5 October. He emphasized the need for "quick action" from the Bulgarians on their negotiations with the pre-war creditors prior to issuing the loan later in the year. He was anxious to meet the scheduled meetings in December of the Financial Committee and the Council and confessed, "I'm rather anxious about delay." It is not surprising, therefore, that he and Major Abraham decided to visit Bulgaria with the intention of spending four days in Sofia and then visiting some of the proposed resettlement areas (the Danube, Provadia-Varna, Burgas and Mastanly regions). Salter asked that the visit "be as practical, informal and 'unconvivial' as possible."[227]

On his way to Bulgaria, Salter spent from 5 to 8 November in Bucharest. He had been asked to provide "a personal and informal" assessment of Romania's monetary and financial situation. The visit included an extensive round of meetings with leading officials in the ministries of Finance and Foreign Affairs and the governor of the National Bank, all widely reported in the Romanian press. Salter demurred on the invitation to visit the resort of Sinaia, but on 7 November he attended "a festive and sumptuous lunch" in his honour.[228] His "Rough Notes" indicate Salter regarded the overall situation as too uncertain for a stabilization scheme.[229] In due course, he returned a very discouraging response to the Romanians, pleading that he was not in a position to offer "an individual opinion."[230] He then journeyed on to Sofia and the contentious frontier districts. His first impression was of "the extraordinary mingling of types and races." He wrote afterwards:

> Peoples from all the Balkan lands, Slavs, Mongol and Tartar types; shepherds, with sheepskin coats and fur caps; blue-sashed peasants in richly painted carts; wagons drawn by Asiatic yak-like oxen; trains of transport camels; Bulgars (Pomaks); black-robed and silken-bearded Orthodox priests, or Mahomedan dervishes, pass in endless succession. But dominating every other impression is that of the overwhelming effect on the whole of the Near East of successive wars and unending apprehension.

As for the refugees, he found that many were impoverished and in distress. "It will be long before I shall forget a desolate medley of hovels near Burgas," he wrote, "with their desolate malaria-stricken inmates, lacking the barest necessities and having to fetch every drop of water in hand-carried pails from over a mile away." Nonetheless, he also found others "reasonably well off" and "industrious and skilled." Salter anticipated transforming the refugees into productive farmers, and increasing political and social stability for the Bulgarian state.[231] On 6 December, after his strong intervention, the Financial Committee approved a loan of £2.25 million. This was then approved by the Council and successfully floated in December. The difficult task of enumerating the refugees, their whereabouts, requirements and finding available land for their settlement thus went ahead.[232]

Never one to court personal publicity, Salter's trans-Atlantic profile nevertheless continued to grow. In early December, Roland W. Boyden recommended Salter's name to Harvard University for an honourary degree, noting "that his constructive work all over the place has been extraordinary." Boyden enlisted Thomas Lamont to write the recommendation, which in fact was drafted by Morrow.[233] The letter to the Committee on Honorary Degrees at Harvard University on 11 December emphasized the behind the scenes influence Salter had exerted:

> As the Secretary of this Council [AMTC], he practically ran the work of the Council, always modestly and never himself appearing in any of its prominent work, although he was preparing the material used by men like Lord Robert Cecil and Clémentel (later French Minister of Finance), and some times by the Prime Ministers. After the War, he was Secretary of the Reparations Commission, and on that body was always a most tolerant influence. I think he has been the backbone of the Economic Section of the League. The awarding of a degree upon him would be a marked case of choosing a man who has done very real work of the greatest importance, for which he has received relatively little recognition.[234]

Knowledge of this recommendation would have pleased Salter at the time, as he so regretted the movement in US opinion away from collaboration with the League. Thus he was eager to explain to any American contact what US membership in the League would entail and enlisting that country's participation in the Economic Conference.[235] As preparations for it raced ahead and as the year drew to a close, Salter wrote, "For myself, I'm much as before, alternating between periods of what you call 'madhouse' activity and lethargy (the latter on the whole I think getting shorter and less frequent)."[236]

After a brief vacation on the Riviera and a further stay in London, Salter returned to Geneva on 10 January. Tyler wrote that Salter "needed his holiday in the south, but feels very fit now."[237] In reality, however, Salter's grueling pace of work was beginning to affect him and would later in the year force him into a protracted leave. To Mildred Bliss he confessed, "This year is likely to be a heavy one with me."[238] In the meantime, there were numerous ongoing concerns, including his lobbying campaign to ensure American participation in the Economic Conference, which he regarded as critical;[239] as well as embarking on a vigorous series of engagements to publicize the forthcoming conference. On 19 January he spoke to the British branch of the International

Chamber of Commerce, followed on 28 January with a speech to the Manchester Chamber of Commerce, and on 8 February he attended a meeting at Chatham House to discuss the conference.[240] Everywhere he stressed that the conference was not intended to be an isolated event, but an extension of the League's work.[241] He did not return to Geneva until 12 February and then left for another speech at Vienna on 16 February to the Austrian League of Nations Union. The occasion, in fact, was the receipt of an honourary degree from the University of Vienna. In his speech, Salter first dwelt on the League's efforts in the financial reconstruction of Austria. He then spoke, according to the British ambassador, Viscount Chilston, "in a rather optimistic manner" about the forthcoming work of the Economic Conference. Chilston went on to note:

> Sir Arthur Salter told me one of the things which struck him most on his visit was the little appreciation the Austrians showed of the great improvement in the situation since the League of Nations reconstruction scheme was begun. He has not been here for several years, and when he said to Austrian acquaintances: 'There is a great change here since 1922,' as often as not he was answered by the question: 'Do you mean for the better or for the worse?'[242]

This initial acquaintance led to a lifelong friendship with two generations of the Chilston family.[243] From Vienna, Salter's next stop was Paris to attend a meeting of the International Chamber of Commerce. It was actively campaigning for the abolition of "the wall of trade barriers," an important component of the Economic Conference's agenda.[244]

By early March the extensive agenda for the conference was completed as well as much of the documentary materials. Salter was delighted to learn that the US was sending "a powerful delegation." Equally, he valued that items of major public interest had been included, particularly tariff policy and "the organization of industry and cartelization." The latter he anticipated could be developed "to the benefit of producers and of consumers."[245] With almost everything in place, he continued to promote the event which he profoundly believed would shape the future of the League and the global economy. In the March issue of Round Table, he anticipated that one of the results would be "a much stronger impulse toward international cooperation." The conference, in his view, was only for purposes of general consultation, and not aimed at any immediate conclusions. Nonetheless, he argued, as he was to do for many years, that the most serious and permanent of all dangers threatening peace were "economic conflicts and divergence of economic interest." He anticipated that the personal contacts, the possible emergence of a code of recognized economic principles, and agreement on the restrictive nature of tariffs and cartels would all contribute towards greater international economic collaboration.[246] In a contribution to Headway, he singled out ongoing tariffs, as well as international cartels as hindering full recovery from the effects of the First World War.[247] Finally, he wrote about the conference in The Europa Year-Book where he struck a more cautious note, suggesting "immediate definite results cannot be great," but more specialized work would in time lead to change.[248]

Even with his attention focused on the upcoming conference, Salter pursued his other concerns. Earlier in the year, he had written to H.G. Wells, regretting they had not been able to meet while in the south of France, but inviting Wells to stay with him again on a future visit. Salter enclosed a memorandum, "Notes on the Present Position of Liberalism," that he was circulating privately. "That Liberalism and the Liberal Party are in grave danger needs no arguing," he wrote, admitting that divisions about the leadership and the absence of a "constructive and accepted" programme had done great damage. Instead, he recommended a combination of "continuity of principle and living adaptability," namely, that the new guiding liberal principle to capture moderate opinion must be the "public interest" at the expense of private or class interests. The first condition for revival was new policies and programmes, in the spirit of *res publica*. He conceded that Lloyd George was the only possible leader in the near future. "He has the magnetic qualities of a leader, the power of presentation and advocacy, the vivid sense of what the public wants, of what the situation demands, of what is politically possible." However, a future leader would have to accept new policies and programmes, being developed by people such as E.D. Simon, Keynes and Layton. As for the economy, he supported a case by case, middle of the road analysis of what industry, trade or even profession would be best served by private enterprise or nationalization. In international affairs, he urged support for the League of Nations, arbitration agreements and disarmament. "Constructive liberalism," Salter concluded, must engage with "fearless and radical reform." A combination of "Industrial reconstruction and the interests of the consumer" would reinvigorate the appeal of the Liberal Party in a distinctive manner and enable it once again to win elections.[249] This was Salter's first real foray into British domestic politics, but one that would completely absorb him in the 1930s.

Another matter also captured Salter's restless attention. Sir Austen Chamberlain suggested at the League's Council meeting in March that the number of such annual meetings be reduced from four to three. This was his response to a growing body of opinion that argued the presence of foreign ministers could not always be guaranteed, and hence reduce the number of Council meetings. Salter, in contrast, tried to convince Drummond that such a move was premature, and that the direct contact of foreign ministers "at a common neutral meeting ground and at regular periodical meetings, has such decisive advantages that it ought to be secured wherever practicable."[250] Drummond responded by complimenting on a "very able paper," but added, "we probably must be content to differ."[251] Privately, Salter regarded the British Foreign Office's negative attitude towards the League's financial reconstruction schemes, as well as the effort to reduce the meetings of the Council, as evidence of an attempt "to restrict and cripple our work."[252] The 10th Assembly of the League in September 1929 did reduce the number of annual Council meetings to three.

On 20 March the New York Times featured a profile of Salter with the startling news, quite unfounded, that he was "soon to retire." The journalist, Robert Neville, credited Salter as "the man who, perhaps, more than any other is responsible for its [the League's] success." After reviewing the League's work of financial reconstruction, Neville turned to the substance of his interview with Salter. When asked about his career, Salter advised consulting Who's Who. "He was a little bit amused that anything more might be interesting." The article concluded:

Unlike the other British members of the Secretariat, he is in no sense a sportsman. He does not keep dogs and he does not fish. Though he is a member of the Golf Club, he has never seen the course. In twelve years he has played just twelve sets of tennis. His automobile is a conveyance to carry him to his office. Though he accepts dinner invitations as a part of his day's work, his secretary has standing orders to refuse all invitations to balls. He collects nothing except facts. His only obvious British trait is his reserve. And that apparently is the result only of atmosphere. His brain is Latin.[253]

The official photograph of the opening session of the International Economic Conference on 4 May showed Salter on the right hand of the President, Georges Theunis, with Drummond to the left. Almost two years after having first suggesting the event, Salter had the pleasure of seeing it finally open. As The Times reported, "it was indeed a world conference in the fullest sense, in its composition, the scope of its task, and its outlook." The Observer noted that on 4 May the League begins "a grand inquest, ranking, ultimately, in importance before any other work it has attempted."[254] On opening day Salter wrote in The Times that the event was "a world conference in the fullest sense," that participants were experts but not officials, and that a year's preparatory work provided an "unequalled picture of the general world situation."[255] Indeed, the mandate of the Preparatory Commission, also chaired by Theunis, had been approved by the League Council on 14 December 1925. It comprised 35 people of 21 nationalities, and included among its members, "industrialists, merchants, agriculturists, financiers, officials of experience of commercial policy, economists and representatives of workers' and consumers' organizations." In March 1927 the Council had approved the agenda and the massive documentation, more than 60 papers of several thousand pages, which had been prepared. Similar representation was reflected at the conference, which consisted of 194 delegates and 226 experts from 50 member and non-member states. Salter described the event as "distinguished from all earlier conferences by the length, the elaboration and the international character of the previous preparation." He emphasized that the disruption of the war had led to worldwide changes in tariffs and commercial policies that were higher, and more complicated and unstable than prior to 1914. That one problem, he wrote, was "of special importance."[256]

The first four days of the conference were devoted to general discussions in plenary sessions. It then broke into three commissions – commerce, industry and agriculture – and reconvened from 21-23 May for discussion of the commissions' reports, resolutions and recommendations.[257] Salter himself took no formal part in the conference, although he helped draft the opening speech by Theunis, and planned its timetable and order of procedure.[258] Halfway through he wrote that the "conference is going quite well; it means of course a terrific amount of work and numerous difficulties." He had anticipated a stressful period and had even asked Arnold-Forster to come to Geneva to assist.[259] However, among the final resolutions, which likely most heartened him, was that from the Commission on Commerce. Under the heading of "Liberty of Trading," the Commission set out a detailed agenda on how to free international commerce from "prohibitions and restrictions." It suggested ending increasing tariffs by individual state action, bilateral commercial treaties and collective action through the League.[260] As Salter termed it, the recommendation was "not free trade but 'freer trade'," and this he regarded as the crucial theme of the conference's recommendations. He further reported to the League Directors on 25 May, "The Conference had been on the whole, he thought, a success. Its work on commerce was its most important result." Despite the difficulties and obstacles ahead, he believed world opinion would "prevail over every obstacle of vested interests, fallacious doctrine and national sentiment which obstructs the road to increased prosperity and a more stable peace."[261]

On 3 March Royall Tyler had noted that "Poor A. is very tired, and he has a long row of exceedingly busy weeks to look forward to before he can hope to get any rest – after the June Council." On 11 June Tyler further wrote:

> A. is very tired after the Econ. Conf. but he scored a very great success there, opening the door on several years of work that will be wholly worth while, &

so he's on the crest of the wave. But when the Council is over he may have a slump – people who watch him here all the time expect it. It is quite on the cards that he may very seriously require a rest. He is as sweet and dear as you can possibly imagine, most angelic; one loves him tenderly and only wishes that one could make him feel the tenderness of one's sentiments for him. He has plenty of anxieties connected with the work here and with outside things, but everything is made right by his passion of the hour, the Econ. Conf., & until he has had his fill of that beauty's charms, & made an honest woman of her by marrying her off to someone else, he will be walking on air. [Tyler continued on 14 June]. I'm afraid Arthur won't take any holiday before the end of July. The new beauty whose charms he is feeding gluttonously on at present – the Econ. Conf. & its possible developments – holds him in her silken thrall, & it's no good talking to him about anything else. He is awfully tired, though physically better than I have previously seen him when tired.[262]

The League Council on 16 June approved the recommendations and resolutions of the Economic Conference. Not surprisingly, Salter wrote the next day that the conference "was, in my opinion, more successful than I had hoped."[263]

The end of the conference did not provide Salter with the rest he required. Instead, he pondered, "How is practical effect to be secured to the recommendations and what are the prospects of success?"[264] He embarked on an ambitious publicity campaign to influence this result. On 8 June he accepted invitations to address in Stockholm a meeting of the International Chamber of Commerce, to contribute an article about the Economic Conference to The Times, and to speak at Toynbee Hall.[265] Five days later he had completed and submitted a 5,000-word article on the Economic Conference for the July issue of Nineteenth Century and After.[266] One of his first post-conference speaking engagements was to the International Council of Women at Geneva, but his first major speech, widely covered by the press, was on 1 July to the International Chamber of Commerce.[267] He stated that a concerted effort was needed to implement those recommendations of the Economic Conference relating to trade barriers and tariffs. While the obstacles to reform were great, it was encouraging that the consensus at the conference was that "the process of increasing barriers had gone too far and must be reversed." He hoped that other governments would adopt the conference's recommendations, as already signaled by Belgium, Czechoslovakia and Germany. Finally, he made a plea that peace depended on the adoption of the conference's economic recommendations.[268] According to The Economist, the one topic that dominated discussion was "the movement for a reduction in trade barriers and especially customs tariffs."[269] From Stockholm Salter traveled to London for his

Toynbee Hall engagement and returned to Geneva. There he continued his furious writing pace, completing a 2000-word preface on the Economic Conference for a forthcoming issue of the Europa-Year Book, as well as similar articles for the American Academy of Political and Social Sciences and the Revue de Genève.[270] Likely, his most widely read contribution appeared in The Times on 14 July, titled "The 'New Era'." Salter admitted that the path to removing trade barriers was long, but progress in the "new era" of commercial policy would depend on the support of public opinion and governments. Turning to the British response, he noted that Sir Austen Chamberlain had declared the government was "'in agreement with by far the greater number of them [resolutions], if not with all'." Salter was heartened by the "very promising and encouraging reception" thus far accorded the conclusions of the conference. He anticipated that by the autumn a clearer picture of prospects would emerge.[271]

In the immediate aftermath of the Economic Conference, Salter also focused his attention on the future of both the Economic and Financial Committees. He pointed out that with Europe's financial reconstruction complete or in progress, and with new directions towards freer trade highlighted by the resolutions of the Economic Conference, the work of both these committees needed to be rethought.[272] The Economic Conference had anticipated, and the Council approved this in June, that the League's Economic Committee would meet in extraordinary session on 12-14 July to study the question of tariffs and also redesign its structure and place within the League. These changes were to be approved by the League Council on 28 September.[273] Secondly, Salter was actively lobbying to add an American member to the Economic Committee of the League, following its "strong delegation" to the conference, and another on the Financial Committee. He wrote in this vein to Morrow to sound out the US President, and spoke similarly with Owen Young and S. Parker Gilbert.[274] For a short time it was contemplated that Salter should visit the US to lobby further. Morrow encouraged the idea, noting that "there are so many good friends of yours here that would be glad to help you that I know your trip would be profitable."[275] That proved unnecessary, as in early September it was announced that Jeremiah Smith Jr was appointed as the American representative on the Financial Committee. He attended his first Financial Committee meeting on 29 November.[276]

At the end of August Salter wrote another of his clarification memoranda, titled "Economic Organization of the League of Nations." He focused on the history of the Economic Committee, originally a provisional one, its tasks and composition. However, the Economic Conference had made recommendations, particularly in the area of tariff reform that required "some strengthening and adaptation." After reviewing several proposals put forward since May, which he termed "impaired," he offered his own recommendations. These included a committee limited to 15 with a three-year term, reservation of a place for an American member, and the addition of several "corresponding members."[277] These were among the recommendations for the restructured Economic Committee approved by the Council on 28 September.[278] This also contained provision for a new Economic Consultative Committee that Salter later described as "a kind of annual Economic Conference in miniature."[279]

In an unusual move at the end of September, Salter signaled that "it was impossible for me to take any new work for this year."[280] Indeed, he had a grueling schedule ahead, travelling to London in early October to fulfill a series of engagements. These included, besides private consultations on a myriad of matters, talks to the League of Nations Union on 12 October and to the National Council of Women, in Bournemouth, on 13 October, both of which were broadcast on the BBC.[281] On 18 October he addressed the Royal Institute of International Affairs on the prospects of practical results from the Economic Conference and traversed mainly familiar grounds. Given the nature of the audience, however, he provided greater details on the vexed question of tariffs and their complexity. As for prospects, he detailed the number of international organizations and individual countries that had accepted the principles of the conference, and pointed, as a hopeful sign, to the Franco-German Commercial Treaty of 17 August, *inter-alia* removing French discrimination against German goods.[282]

On 28 October Felkin wrote, "Salter is away, having been ordered a month's rest by his doctors. Nothing serious, but he ought to get it while he can."[283] Such fatigue after a grueling year of activity was not surprising, even given his sturdy constitution. Indeed, among the people Salter had seen in London, Niemeyer observed that Salter "was looking very ill and said something about having all his teeth out."[284] The situation in fact was serious, as Salter revealed to Felkin on 19 October. He wrote that "after x-rays & 3 opinions it seems clear that I shall have to have my mouth completely stripped. This means I'm told that I shall be unfit for work for from three weeks to a month." He deliberated as to whether he should be treated in London or Geneva, the latter being preferable from a work point of view. He realized, however, "wherever it is I fear I'm not going to be much use for at least three weeks. I'm told I shall probably be under the weather most of the winter, but ought afterwards to be much fitter than I have been for years." Fearing that he would be regarded in Swinburne's phrase as "'an aged and toothless baboon'," Salter asked Felkin to state only that he was "rather run down" and taking a rest."[285] On 2 November, Salter wrote from Paris, "The teeth came out without much difficulty. But I was very run down before, & I am still feeling rather weak & am likely to for a bit." Salter took advantage of an invitation from the Arnold-Forsters to spend some of his recovery at their home, Eagles Nest, Zennor, near St Ives in Cornwall.[286] By 23 November Salter was back in

Geneva and following a meeting with him, Tyler wrote: "Arthur isn't looking very well, poor pet. There were abscesses at the roots which were draining off into his system. I'm not much pleased with his looks, and there's something in the sound of his voice that doesn't ring right." Indeed, within a few days Tyler reported: "Arthur dashing about like a mad thing," while Salter himself confessed, taking a moment away from the meetings of the Financial Committee, that "Things are interesting here but rather exhausting."[287]

Among Salter's primary ongoing concerns were to secure representatives to fill the position reserved for an American on the reorganized Economic Committee and two on the newly established Economic Consultative Committee. With regard to both, he enlisted the help of Jeremiah Smith Jr, to find candidates who were "at once suitable, acceptable to the American Administration and able and willing to come."[288] Salter also lobbied unsuccessfully to have an Indian representative on the Consultative Committee, in order to make it "less purely European and less Occidental in character."[289] However, all of these issues were overshadowed when on 26 November the Finance Minister of Portugal requested that the League study the possibility of a large loan to assist the government "to carry out a complete scheme of financial reconstruction, currency stabilization and economic development." On 7 December the Financial Committee recommended a League delegation be sent to Portugal, as had been done in the Bulgarian case, to study the situation first hand.[290] On 21 December Salter noted that "the whole Portuguese problem has arisen" and that he was scheduled to leave to Lisbon on either 11 or 13 February 1928.[291] After taking a vacation at Vence in the south of France, Salter returned to Geneva in the middle of January.[292] In the following weeks, he completed an article for The Spectator, on "Economic Policy – the Next Stages." After reviewing familiar ground, he emphasized his view that economic conflicts were the root of war, and described the new Economic Consultative Committee as "a kind of annual Economic Conference in miniature."[293] He was also busy finalizing the membership of the delegation to Portugal, its itinerary and agenda.[294] As well, he spent what he called "two very heavy days" in Paris, consulting with Felkin, Drummond, Avenol and Stoppani at the end of January on arrangements for the forthcoming Economic Consultative Committee. He then journeyed to London to attend a League of Nations Union meeting on 8 February, and returned to Geneva for final preparations.[295]

Salter and other members of the delegation – Strakosch, Melchior, Dubois, Count de Chalender, Janssens and Count Montefuerte – gathered for their first official session at the Avenida Palace Hotel in Lisbon on 15 February.[296] In the evening Salter and Strakosch met with the new Portuguese President, General Oscar Carmona. Salter then shared some of his impressions with Ka Cox:

This is a very beautiful place – seen at its best in the most heavenly weather. I remembered it as attractive – but I hadn't expected to find it clean, orderly and to all outward appearance very prosperous. We shall have a most enjoyable time here I think – certainly very interesting, but I mustn't go into details, as letters are probably opened. The two days journey on the train, with Strakosch as companion, was <u>most</u> enjoyable & a real rest, and I'm very fit and fresh. It was quite like the old Vienna days to be met by the faithful [Per] Jacobsson and de Bordes [in the advance party] & to go straight on to midnight discussions.[297]

Over the next several days, extensive consultations were held on such issues as currency stabilization, balanced budgets and infrastructure improvements. <u>The Times</u> noted that League officials "have received every possible assistance from the Portuguese authorities."[298] Salter was certainly pleased with everything, writing on 20 February:

This has been a most enjoyable week, the most amazing weather – brilliant early summer, warm but the air light & fresh. Everywhere in Portugal you see that there is the same instinct for tidiness & cleanliness as in Switzerland. We are working steadily & I feel much more hopeful now that we may make a good job of it. I have been extremely well all the time, & much enjoying myself. We are a considerable party here – 18 including the typists – & we are making a pretty thorough enquiry.[299]

The day before, however, Salter revealed to Ka Cox that he had almost been killed. "Strakosch & myself had a rather narrow escape yesterday (Sunday)," he wrote. "We were motoring near Cintra when our driver, racing another car, failed to get round a corner & crashed into a tree. The car was smashed up, but we were not hurt at all." The driver's response was to say: "Well, there's an experience for you gentlemen. I'll charge nothing extra." In fact, the incident convinced Salter to purchase a small two-seater Renault, in addition to his Fiat, and he promised Ka Cox to drive her from Paris to Geneva during her visit in May.[300]

On 22 February the League delegation left Lisbon, but with Salter, Strakosch, Janssens and Montefuerte adding an extra in Oporto. Salter regarded this as important because of the city's economic significance and its reputation for producing anti-government movements.[301] From there they returned to Geneva, where the Financial Committee, which met intermittently from 27 February to 6 March, wrestled with aspects of the Portuguese loan. These concerned the political stability of the new

Portuguese government and its financial institutions. The questions were debated at length, and most vigorously pursued by Salter, who concluded that a League loan would legitimize a government which, while recognized by the majority of League members, had come to power after a *coup d'état*. He suggested, therefore, that strict control and conditions be applied if the loan were to go forward.[302] During this time, in fact, several loan agreements were drafted, intending to establish budget equilibrium, stabilize the currency and reduce the state debt to the Bank of Portugal.[303] However, on 10 March the Financial Committee reported to the Council that it had not been possible to complete discussions of the stabilization loan. The Portuguese representative to the League, Ivens Ferraz, more accurately reported "there were clauses concerning control by the League which Portugal could not accept."[304] Then on 6 June the Portuguese government concluded that the control clauses drafted by the Financial Committee were unacceptable and withdrew its request for financial reconstruction.[305] Salter afterwards wrote that the Portuguese government "with as it proved, justified confidence in its own stability, carried through the rest of the plan successfully on its own responsibility." He also mused that it "marked the last chapter in the League's work of reconstruction."[306]

In mid-March, accompanied by a member of his section, Per Jacobsson, Salter visited Rome at the request of the Italian government. The purpose was to further explore the relationship between the League and the International Institute of Agriculture. The Institute had never been recognized by the League under the provision of Article 24 of the Covenant as had so many other international organizations. However, given the fact that the Economic Conference had passed resolutions on agricultural matters, and that these were to be raised at the forthcoming Economic Consultative Committee on 14 May, the visit offered an opportunity for consultation. In a report prepared afterwards, Salter provided a scathing critique of the Institute he regarded as "expensive and cumbrous," producing poor quality statistical studies. However, with the League expanding its involvement in agricultural questions, he recommended that the Institute be brought under the League's umbrella. This would make it "the official international authority for agricultural questions," subject to some structural reform. He also laid out a schedule that would lead by stages to the Council's approval of the entire scheme.[307] During the course of the visit, Salter had an opportunity to meet with Mussolini, his second such encounter. After his return to Geneva, he wrote to Mussolini on 30 March, thanking him for the hospitality, and indicating that the mission had "been very useful and will bear fruit in the future."[308] However, progress proved extremely slow.[309] It was not until September 1932 that final arrangements were put in place, establishing the Institute as the League's advisory body on agricultural matters.

Over the next weeks, Salter completed a new article for the 14th edition of Encyclopaedia Britannica on "Allied Maritime Transport Council" and updated his article on the League of Nations.[310] On 21 April he wrote that "the whole Bulgarian position remains uncertain and Portugal shows no sign of coming back." The problem with the projected Bulgarian reconstruction loan concerned the thorny issue of assigning specific securities for a public loan.[311] Immediately after a meeting of the Supervisory Financial Commission on 27 April, Salter left, yet again, for a series of visits to Paris, Brussels and London where he lingered from 1-10 May. He returned to Geneva for the first meetings of the Economic Consultative Committee from 14 to 19 May. It is not surprising that the question of tariffs dominated the discussions. Some delegates, Layton for example who had also been previously briefed by Salter, favoured proposals to induce countries to lower their tariffs, while others argued that such a League initiative was dangerous and should be abandoned.[312] Not surprisingly, F.L. McDougall, an advisor to the Australian delegation at the League, observed that "There is no doubt that Sir Arthur Salter carries a very considerable number of guns among political people in England."[313]

Although successful at insuring American representation to the Economic Committee and the recent Economic Consultative Committee, Salter tried to extend that relationship. On 25 May, for example, he had a long conversation with Governor Benjamin Strong, head of the Federal Reserve Bank of New York. Salter proposed calling a bankers' conference to deal with the fluctuating purchasing value of gold and examine the role of central banks in affecting price levels by monetary policy. Strong replied that he was against central banks maintaining any given price level. He believed that the public was being misled into an exaggerated view of the powers of central banks. He preferred to see the League study only questions such as the supply and use of gold, and that its Financial Committee should in future provide "advice not control" as with Austria.[314] In two follow-up conversations on 25 June and 7 July, Salter found Strong even more opposed to both any League fact-finding enquiry and any measure of monetary policy which would affect the gold standard. As for the Federal Reserve Bank, Strong added, he would never put it in a position of being outvoted at a conference made up of borrowers. Salter seemed resigned to the fact that any League action would have to be taken without "the good-will of the Central Banks."[315] After attending the last of these meetings, Jacobsson recorded that Salter was convinced that Strong's opposition was based on his fears that the "theoreticians," like Keynes and Cassel, "would overshadow the 'practical' bankers."[316] Indeed, it made Salter reflect that perhaps the programme of the Economic Consultative Committee might be curtailed "because certain countries and certain interests are beginning to fear the effect of a successful development of the policy of the Conference of last year."[317] Even further, if the League's economic activity and structure could not find new areas to explore, as he was endeavouring to do, was there much reason for him to stay on?

A major political catalyst for Salter was two earthquakes which had struck on 14 and 18 April 1928 in the Maritza valley in southern Bulgaria. The devastation spurred him into action, even if not officially sanctioned. Royall Tyler wrote, "Charron overflows with gratitude to Arthur for immediately saying he would take responsibility for using interest on loan monies to rebuild earthquake-destroyed houses. The legal section at Geneva did not consider it admissible under the protocol to do so – and Arthur's way of disregarding the letter on such occasions is one of his great qualities."[318] Further symptomatic was the fact that the summer of 1928 appeared to fly by quickly for Salter, with little League related work. On 11 July he completed the revisions for the Encyclopaedia Britannica of his article and Lord Robert Cecil's on the League of Nations.[319] He also committed himself to speaking on Liberal policy in foreign affairs at the Oxford Summer School and delivering the Richard Cobden Lectures at the London School of Economics in November.[320] The situation in Bulgaria required continuous monitoring, but he was reluctant to encourage any future League intervention in Yugoslavia because of too many complications.[321] In August he made his third and final contribution to the Geneva Institute of International Relations. He surveyed developments since the holding of the World Economic Conference and declared himself satisfied by the almost universal acceptance of the many recommendations, as well as a perceived "stability of tariffs." As for future prospects, Salter stated, "There is matter for hope, but not for complacency."[322] The main item of business was the ongoing question of the League's link with the International Institute of Agriculture. On this subject, Salter was the target of a rebuke from the Italian ambassador in London for insisting on replacing the Italian President of the Institute with a British official. Salter, however, remained very much a hardliner on the issue of reform at the Institute prior to its association with the League.[323]

After a period of vacation in London and Oxford in August, Salter's final effort at the end of the summer was a major article on 2 September in The New York Times. He explored how the League had contributed "a new method" to the dynamics of negotiations between states. The League, he pointed out, was "not a super-state but an inter-state organization," its actions required not a majority but unanimity; and "the basis of every method is not compulsion, but persuasion." What distinguished League action was careful preparation by a permanent international staff and follow-up by a network of specialized committees. The result, Salter maintained, was that "the world is governing itself through the League, not being governed by the League." The effect of this "method of penetration, persuasion, permeation" led to the process of thinking internationally."³²⁴ The timing of the article could not have been more opportune. On 4 and 5 September <u>The Times</u> carried articles by Salvadore de Madariaga that cautioned against an encroaching nationalism in the character of the League and its secretariat. Several days later <u>The New York Times</u> picked up the story with a headline: "Usefulness of League Seen As Imperiled."³²⁵

September as usual brought the meetings of the League Assembly and Council. At least one observer, William Lyon Mackenzie King, who formed a lasting friendship with Salter, found the proceedings "uninteresting." However, when dining with Salter on 21 September, Mackenzie King pressed the case for England adopting a policy of free trade for its great staple industries, such as steel, coal and shipbuilding.³²⁶ Of additional concern for Salter was to press ahead with new work recommended by the Financial Committee, including an enquiry into the purchasing power of gold. Thus he gave instructions to Loveday, J. van Walre de Bordes and Jacques Rueff to begin research on the relationship between the supply of gold, monetary policy and general level of prices.³²⁷

In early October Salter, accompanied by Charron, began an extensive tour of Central and Southern Europe. Salter's first stop on 4 October in Prague was to address the Economic Conference of the International Federation of League of Nations Societies, called to explore the ramifications of the World Economic Conference. In his remarks, Salter emphasized that while the League of Nations was accepted as a part of the "recognized machinery of the world's government," as he then put it, "where there is no issue there is no interest." Hence, he exhorted all representatives to lobby in favour of the recommendations adopted by the World Economic Conference. He singled out for greater attention the close relationship between economics and the prospects for peace.³²⁸ From Prague Salter and Charron arrived in Budapest the next day. They were greeted by Tyler, and went on to a meeting with the Hungarian Prime Minister Count Bethlen to discuss financial and economic conditions. From there on 7 October, and again joined by Tyler, they set out for Sofia and Salonika. In his letters to Elisina, Tyler recorded some impressions:

[5 Oct. 1928] Arthur and Charron arrived this morning. Arthur very dear and angelic. He urges me to make the trip to Salonika with him. Charron is sending him by car from Sofia all the way, through the Macedonian mountains, and it will be a marvelous trip.

[6 Oct. 1928] Arthur has decided me to go with him. We'll spend a day at Sofia & probably see the King, & do the trip to Salonika in two bits, sleeping at the Rila monastery on the way. I am rushing about with Arthur – very interesting and very useful to have him here. Charron goes back by train & isn't taking the Salonika trip, so Arthur & I will be alone together. I get enormous profit from these talks with him. Everyone has been extremely nice to Arthur & I think the country now realizes what he has done for it. He's so dear.

[7 Oct. 1928] We are leaving in an hour or two. Arthur is in high spirits, enjoying everything here in addition to our more serious preoccupations. Arthur is in a great state of excitement about the news in today's papers that the Chinese govt. has now officially requested the League that Avenol go out there on an advisory mission. There's a prospect that the whole Chinese question may come to the League. It's a most interesting trend things are taking. You may imagine Arthur's feelings.

[10 Oct. 1928, Sofia] Arthur has had a very busy & tiring day talking with people. Arthur is in splendid form, & full of ideas. He is a continual treat, & so very dear.

[13 Oct. 1928, Salonika] I've just bid good-bye to Arthur, almost tearfully: it is so sad to part from that bright little eye.[329]

Salter as well recorded some impressions, writing to Ka Cox on 12 October:

Peter Tyler & myself arrived here [Salonika] this morning after two days of the most wonderful motor run from Sofia through S. Bulgaria to Salonika. A most beautiful & romantic journey – in perfect weather – & the more interesting because it took us over the ground of the Greco-Bulgarian affair of Oct. 1925. The next four days I shall be touring western Macedonia with Hope Simpson. Yes, I shall take extra care – mosquito nets, etc. I am in the best of health & spirits & greatly enjoying myself.[330]

Both in Sofia and Salonika, where Salter toured refugee settlements, he mediated between the two countries regarding compensation for the value of properties due to population exchanges. A convention having been agreed at the League earlier in the year, full details of the Bulgarian stabilization had been published on 3 October and this led successfully to final ratification on 18 December.[331]

On 22 October Salter returned to Geneva but soon travelled to London where he stayed from 7 to 14 November.[332] There, amid his usual round of discussions, he gave the Richard Cobden Lectures at the London School of Economics on 7 and 8 November, on "The Future of Nationalism in Economic Policies" and "Economic Policies as a Factor in Prospects of Peace." The latter certainly echoed much of what he had presented in Prague on 4 October.[333] Among the more important conversations that Salter had was with Strakosch, a strong supporter of analyzing the question of undue fluctuations in the purchasing power of gold.³³⁴ On his return to Geneva Salter wrote to Strakosch suggesting that a committee be appointed to examine the non-contentious aspects of gold in relation to supply and demand, without a commitment to proceed further. Salter believed this cautious procedure would assuage the suspicions of, among many others, the Banque de France.³³⁵ For his part, Strakosch wrote to The Times on 3 December suggesting that the League was best suited to undertake the investigation.³³⁶ Salter must have been delighted when the Financial Committee on 8 December agreed to proceed with his strategic approach to establish such a committee, a decision quickly then approved by the Council. As he admitted later, he hoped the limited terms of reference would "result in the Central Banks regarding it as useful rather than embarrassing."³³⁷

Salter ended the year by returning to the ongoing question of Liberal Party policy, which he had last addressed with H.G. Wells. This time, writing to Layton and with the warning "keep authorship absolutely confidential," he offered a cogent argument for the Liberal Party to publish a brochure outlining its main principles of foreign policy. He made suggestions on issues ranging from disarmament and the League to the Kellogg Pact and the USSR. Naturally, he argued for greater support for the League of Nations, "in spirit as well as letter of the Covenant," and particularly for the resolutions of the World Economic Conference. Some time later, he again returned to the subject. "The need of the time," he wrote, "is to build a new world order" upon what he termed "seven corner stones." These included support for the League Covenant, disarmament, avoiding the dangers of alliance diplomacy and comprehensive international cooperation in every sphere of human activity.³³⁸

There were increasing signs of a certain restlessness and discontent in Salter as the New Year began. Since returning to the League in 1922 he had worked with undiminished vigour, imagination and dedication to increase the profile of the League, both in his own area of finance and economics and others. Financial and economic reconstruction work had changed the face of Europe. Now he was trying, with limited success, to reach into new areas for League activity. Questions such as League intervention into the gold question or tariff reform were complicated and meeting resistance. In contrast, he was taking an increasing role in the formulation of Liberal Party policy in England. He was also spending a good portion the year away from Geneva, on both League and other business. And finally, he continued to press with vigour another resolution approved by the World Economic Conference, and endorsed by the first meeting of the Economic Consultative Committee. This concerned a proposal for the League to initiate research and discussion among economists and universities on the relationship between economics and war.³³⁹ Salter later admitted that the significance of this resolution was hardly understood or appreciated at the time. Nonetheless, he continued to work on the proposal with an eye to its implementation.[340]

As long ago as 21 January 1926, when negotiating an extension of his appointment with the League, he noted, "Personally I feel more, as time goes on, the measure of expatriation which League appointments involve."[341] His feelings of disassociation later emerged in a letter to Violet Markham on 9 January 1929. He confessed that separation from friends, such as herself, "has made me feel, as I have increasingly these last few years, the disadvantages of exile. I feel much cut off from English news." However, he added that "I cannot feel that is right for me yet to turn from international to national things." He continued:

> The English situation is so difficult & complicated that it's no use for anyone to touch that without continuous work & concentration. My qualifications & experience, such as they are, are much more for international work – where the situation is no less serious. I'm not thinking of reconstruction of countries like Austria – a line of business where we've perhaps nearly finished our job – but general League & peace work. For the last 3 years we've been, in my view, drifting in to wrong lines [?] in a number of ways – ways which may ultimately mean war & short of that increased, instead of diminished, armaments competition.
>
> I am overwhelmed at present & I no longer unhappily have the margin of spare energy I had some years ago. Indeed I've felt almost continuously overtired for some years & want if I possibly can to get something like a real rest in England this summer. If not, if there should as there may be a situation favourable for international advance by the end of the year, I shall be unable to take any effective part in it. This is to explain why I don't think its possible for me to try my hand in English national questions.[342]

On 2 February 1928 Yale University had informed Salter that he was to receive the Henry E. Howland Memorial Prize. The first award had been made posthumously in 1916 to Rupert Brooke and later consisted of a medal and fifteen hundred dollars.[343] Salter's award, the "first made in the field of government," was publicly announced on 19 January.[344] Ramsay MacDonald congratulated him, writing, "You very richly deserve it."[345] Salter sailed from Cherbourg aboard the *Homeric* on 16 January 1929. Rough Atlantic weather delayed his crossing for two days, a situation hardly welcome to him as he had had asked for a few days interval before the ceremony. This was, as he wrote, "to get my bearings more clearly, and partly also to allow for the possibility that a bad sailor, after a winter crossing, may not be at the top of his form."[346] However, he finally managed to arrive at New Haven on 25 January, the same day as the prize-giving at

Yale. After being introduced to the audience as "the real reconstructor of Europe," Salter spoke that evening on "Economic Interdependence as Opposed to Political Nationalism." He stated that the great danger to peace came from the trend of world markets becoming increasingly competitive and that the movement towards greater protection should be weighed against the benefits of competition. Finally, Salter reiterated the mandate ordered by the World Economic Conference to embark on a programme of research and public discussion which alone would lead to an international trade etiquette" to avoid economic friction which could lead to war.[347]

Salter's itinerary, planned with Charles P. Howland, with whom he stayed while in New Haven, included several informal talks at Yale and catching up with former colleagues including Boyden and Norman H. Davis.[348] On 30 January the Council on Foreign Relations hosted a dinner for Salter, chaired by Howland and attended by prominent American bankers, politicians and academics.[349] Thereafter, he traveled to Washington for further consultations, and stayed with Ethel and Arthur Bullard, who had recently left Geneva to spend some time in Washington.[350] Finally, he returned to New York to speak at another luncheon on 16 February, hosted by the Foreign Policy Association at the Hotel Astor. Addressing the topic, "Prosperity, Economic Nationalism or Internationalism," Salter suggested that an international economic system, though short of free trade, must replace what he termed "excessive nationalism." He regarded this as a key to world prosperity and a certain way to avoid war rooted in economic conflicts.[351] After almost a month's absence, Salter sailed from New York on 22 February aboard the *Olympic*.[352]

On his return to Geneva, Salter reported to a meeting of League Directors on 15 March that he had conferred with "a number of people who were close to the [new Hoover] Administration," and concluded that American policy toward the League would not be changed. He continued, "From the League point of view the tariff situation was bad, and a furious wave of protection was passing over the country."[353] He also privately shared some impressions of a trip which he described as "a continuous whirl." He wrote that the "Amazing, bounding prosperity – the cheerful assumption that everything's going to go on increasing all the time – are such an extraordinary contrast both to the facts & the psychology of this side of the Atlantic." To be in New York, he continued, "is to be stimulated & fascinated – the efficiency, greater energy & the accumulated power are terrific. And then you go to Washington & say here is the wisdom that must direct that, or at least largely determine its impact on the outside world! And you are depressed accordingly. Everywhere efficiency tends to outshine wisdom but never quite so hopelessly." Salter conceded his impressions were "so complex it seems almost hopeless to try to write about them."[354] To several others he briefly noted that he had spent an enjoyable month in America.[355]

The project that clearly inspired Salter on his return was the proposal for the Bank for International Settlements. The Committee of Experts on Reparations (Belgium, Britain, France, Italy, Japan and Germany), set up during the September 1928 session of the Council and chaired by Owen D. Young, had been given the task of drawing up a new plan for reparations. During its meetings in Paris in February and March, the Committee discussed draft schemes for such a bank. It was initially intended to take over the functions previously performed by the Agent General for Reparations in Berlin.[356] However, Salter immediately focused on its possible non-reparation functions. "I am convinced myself," he wrote on 18 March to Stamp, a British member of the Committee and the principal drafter of the final report, "that as the economic and financial operations of the world cut more and more across frontiers, and still more as they are reflected in institutions that are not confined within national boundaries, the international relations of the world are placed on broader and less precarious foundations." He preferred to see the bank as a complement rather than an alternative to the League's work of financial reconstruction and its Financial Committee, but he urged close collaboration between the two. As "a new and untried experiment," Salter certainly anticipated opposition, for example from commercial banks, but anticipated support from "those who think 'internationally'." As to the organization of the bank, he wished to see its aims clearly stated, and the bank situated in Switzerland, mainly because of the country's long history of neutrality and sound financial experience and traditions.[357] Stamp believed that the proposed bank should develop into a genuine international one, handling inter-governmental debts and acting as a lender of last resort to central banks. Salter followed this up with a direct intervention with Owen D. Young. Writing on 26 March, he singled out the question of most concern to him, namely, the relations between the proposed International Bank and the Financial Committee. The central issue, he noted, was that the "non-reparation functions" were likely to increase and bring into question relations with the League. At this early stage, he could offer no specific suggestions on how to address the issue. He simply asked that the point should be addressed in the Committee's final report, to the effect that the new bank was "a complement and not an alternative" to other League action.[358] This was an issue Salter was to keep a sharp eye upon throughout the period of the proposed bank's establishment. Confidentially he wrote from Paris, "Here for the moment I'm back in 'reparation' – in among though not of the experts – a pleasant position as one can have insight into their work & some influence without all their worries."[359]

Salter's other concern was the upcoming meeting on 6 May of the Economic Consultative Committee. In a survey of the previous year, he admitted "that there has been a setback to the progress visible soon after the Economic Conference."

Most notably, he pointed to "a wave of furious protectionism" in the US. Salter urged Layton, when at the Economic Consultative Committee, to bring this out "quite frankly and clearly" by emphasizing the benefits of freer trade, and condemning duties protecting industries with large export markets, guilty of dumping.[360] Indeed, this was also the subject of Salter's Ludwig Mond Lecture which he delivered in Manchester on 25 April. He first surveyed the success of reconstruction in post-war Europe, but then argued that "excessive and unstable trade barriers" were the real obstacles to world prosperity.[361] This and similar issues were thrashed out by the Committee with final recommendations to simply work harder at stimulating public interest in the recommendations of the 1927 World Economic Conference. In reality, considerable opposition was emerging to the League's pursuit of "freer trade."[362] Nonetheless, it was Salter's expectation at this time that the Economic Consultative Committee would "become more and more the pivot of the international consideration of economic problems."[363]

As the Committee of Experts on Reparations continued its deliberations, on 29 May Salter again wrote to Stamp who had provided him with a draft report. He expressed himself satisfied that the two issues which had previously concerned him – possible overlap with the League's loan work and the location of the bank – were no longer mentioned and therefore not an issue. What troubled him was the monopoly that the Governors of the Central Banks of the seven founding reparation countries, forming the future Board of Directors, would have on the functions of the bank. He suggested a more flexible system of governance, including members from non-reparation countries. Secondly, he was worried that the proposed bank would be beyond any form of governmental or other control.[364] On 7 June the Report of the Experts on revised German reparation payments was signed in Paris, including the draft constitution of the new Bank for International Settlements. As many noted, the report converted a political debt into a commercial obligation. The Economist observed that "the ultimate ideal of a central bank of central banks" was on the horizon.[365] Salter's concerns would have to await the resolutions of the Hague Conference in August to set up a definitive plan for the Bank.

Salter was clearly aware that the Bank for international Settlements posed a possible challenge to the League's Financial Committee. On 5 June he had produced a lengthy memorandum, entirely unofficial and provisional, in anticipation of a possible call from either the Council or the Assembly for such a review. He admitted that the major focus of attention for the committee had been financial reconstruction and that was nearing its end. However, he argued that "the experience and reputation" of the committee could be "used for further practical work." Thus he suggested a formulation of principles of "international financial ethics" as a contribution to world peace.

Secondly, in what he termed "advice without 'League loans'," he envisaged the committee advising governments on particular questions, such as currency or central bank reform. More generally it would provide counsel on a country's financial situation, or act as a conciliator in disputes regarding loan contracts. Finally, he proposed a new kind of League loan, one for economic development. With such suggestions he hoped to breathe new life into the committee which he wrote was "the League's technical adviser."[366] In time, the Hague Conference which opened on 8 August approved the Report of the Committee of Experts and on 31 August recommended that the organizing committee mentioned in the Report draw up definitive plans.

Earlier in the year, when writing to Violet Markham, Salter had shared his wish to enjoy "something like a real rest in England this summer." To Elisina Tyler he also confessed his regrets about "being homeless & unanchored."[367] At the end of June, Salter's dream came true. He later wrote, "I have myself been 'rediscovering England.' It's the first time since I joined the League 7 years ago that I've taken leave in England & I've been motoring some 3,000 miles all over the country & immensely enjoying it."[368] At the start of his vacation, Salter might have been amused, as was his usual reaction, by a full-page profile of him which appeared on 6 July in The Spectator. The anonymous writer was clearly well-informed, particularly about the private life, mind and character of the subject, whom he termed "a great Englishman." The writer noted that Salter "excels in logical exposition, and has a crisp, pointed style. He thinks and talks like a two-page memorandum with numbered headings and sub-headings." As probably "the first international official," Salter's "quick mind, combined with a disarming frankness and modesty that win him instant confidence, explains the unique popularity and influence which he established with the Allies during the war and has maintained ever since." His success "is due as much to his transparent honesty and singleness of purpose as to his indomitable energy and belief in human nature." The article then turned to Salter's personality:

> He is of course an effective speaker and makes an ideal broadcast lecturer. Rhetoric and vague sentiment he abhors. He appeals to reason and good sense, and flatters men only by the implicit assumption that they are open to reason. He is consequently greater as a strategist than as a tactician.
>
> Salter was never athletic, is not interested in sport, and seldom plays games. He is notorious in Geneva as the only Englishman who has never been seen on a golf course. For exercise he prefers swimming in the Lake. He has also the reputation of being a dashing motorist. Salter has a way of passing swiftly to his goal without wasting much time in gossip or social intercourse by the way. Not that he is unsociable. He has a genius for friendship, and a keen sense

of humour; but you would not find him disporting himself with evident enjoyment either at a village pub or at a fashionable tea-party. He reads poetry but few novels. If these are limitations, Salter makes up for them by a complete absence of intellectual arrogance or personal vanity. International fame and the respect and confidence of statesmen and financiers have not affected the simplicity of his tastes or impaired his intellectual integrity and social idealism.[369]

No sooner had Salter returned to Geneva, than the outstanding question of "freer trade" suddenly took on a different complexion. In June 1929 when the League Council had met in Madrid, Aristide Briand, then French President and Foreign Minister, had floated the idea of a pan-European initiative. Some time later at the Quai d'Orsay, he spoke about a "United States of Europe," hinting that he would raise the issue at the League Assembly in September.[370] The revival of the pan-European idea had its short-term roots in 1923 when Count Coudenhove-Kalerghi published Pan-Europe. He persisted with his campaign and personally broached the issue with Drummond in July 1925, following up with a memorandum on 2 August, titled World Organization and Pan Europe, A Memorial to the League of Nations. Drummond remained unconvinced, partly because the plan involved a reorganization of the League along larger regional lines rather than upon existing states.[371] Nonetheless, the plan attracted Salter's attention. He observed that "This memo which I have already read in the Review of Reviews is extremely able and interesting. It is packed with ideas, which deserve careful study and some of which are likely to prove of great importance. I recommend anyone whom this reaches to read it."[372] The pan-European idea clearly resonated with Salter who on numerous occasions had lobbied for the internationalization of the traditional nation-state.

It is not surprising that with the Briand initiative in the summer of 1929 beginning to make news, Salter followed up with one of his memoranda. He noted that "There has been a strong increase in the feeling that Europe must do something to make itself an economic unit, or to secure units within itself, more comparable in resources with America." His great fear was that the project might take a purely anti-American form.[373] He then produced an extended analysis titled "The United States of Europe," circulated privately on 2 September, but soon leaked to several delegations at Geneva. He admitted that the recommendations of the 1927 World Economic Conference regarding the reduction of tariffs had not been very successful. He went on to suggest that a United States of Europe obviously meant "complete free trade within Europe: a Zollverein of the countries of Europe." However, he pointed out that a Zollverein was only practicable within a system "little short of a political federation of Europe." Unconditional "Most Favoured Nation" clauses, he found, had their limitations. The remaining possibility, therefore, was an inter-state association to arrange "by common agreement for lower tariffs *inter se* than with the rest of the world, or some part of the rest of the world." While recognizing that this might be condemned "as both retrograde and dangerous," he elaborated a step-by-step approach, based on "differential tariffs" to achieve this objective, which he regarded as a vital counterpart of political *rapprochement*.[374] On 4 September, Salter had a conversation with the new British Prime Minister, Sir Ramsay MacDonald, where he expressed his concerns that the new International Bank, despite his own best efforts and provisions of article 24 of League Covenant, was not as yet tied in any way to the League. In the event, this kind of lobbying ultimately proved unsuccessful.[375]

On 5 September, in what The Times called one of Briand's many "oratorical triumphs," the League Assembly heard for the first time, without much detail, about a "federal bond" between European states.[376] Given that the British response overall was reserved, Salter pressed his views in an article for Round Table and directed his thoughts specifically to the ambiguous position of the UK. While reiterating some of the ideas in his 2 September document, he suggested that "the United States of Europe cannot, in the full sense, be an economic reality without also being a political one." However, he now went further, providing a scheme within which he foresaw a conference, scheduled in fact for February, to arrange a tariff truce leading to the removal of economic barriers *inter se*. The implication for a free-trading Britain, according to Salter, was that it could be granted "unconditional most-favoured-nation treatment" while remaining outside any new association. Thereby, he concluded, Britain could "escape the dilemma of being either included or excluded."[377]

Salter continued to be preoccupied with his ongoing critique of the proposed Bank for International Settlements. As he wrote to Layton on 12 September, he was convinced that the consensus at Geneva was for an effective connection between the Bank and the League, even as he doubted that the League would make a compelling case. Indeed, he remained critical of the work of the Committee of Experts particularly in its push for total autonomy for the new bank.[378] With Layton, along with Sir Charles Addis appointed on 21 September as British members of the Organization Committee of the new bank, he might have been more optimistic.[379] In fact, when Salter addressed the Second Committee of the Assembly on the subject, on 23 September, he was witness to a procedural dilemma. This led to the withdrawal of a resolution about the relationship between the League and the proposed bank under article 24.[380] However, he remained committed to his position; his overriding concern was that the new bank's responsibilities would inevitably extend beyond reparations into issues of international commerce and finance. If so, Salter demanded assurances that "public interests" would be safeguarded against the powers of all central banks, but especially the new bank, whose independence he feared as "irresponsible." When invited to comment by the Labour Parliamentary Under-Secretary for Foreign Affairs, Hugh Dalton, Salter returned to what he described as "the most reasonable basis of a reasonable relationship between the League and the Bank." He suggested several basic principles, including the provision of reports on the bank's activities to the League, referral to the League of certain classes of loans to governments, for advice and technical assistance, and some "organic link," such as having the Governor becoming an ex-officio member of the League's Financial Committee.[381] A charter for the new bank was adopted at the second Hague Conference on 30 January 1930, based at Basel, but without any connection to the League.[382]

Even as the League Assembly was meeting, Salter was saddened to hear of the premature death, on 10 September, of Arthur Bullard at age 49. Described at his memorial service as "a citizen of the world," Bullard had a chequered career as a journalist, author of several books on international affairs, a novelist under the pseudonym Albert Edwards, a State Department official and a prominent American internationalist. In July 1924 he became the permanent representative in Geneva of the Non-Partisan League of Nations Association. He also served as a member of the Information Section of the League in 1926 and 1927. He once observed that he had difficulty deciding "to be a novelist or a publicist."[383] Bullard had married Ethel Mather Bagg on 30 July 1918 at the leased summer estate of the future President Herbert Hoover.[384] Born in 1883, Ethel Mather Bagg was the daughter of Louisa [Leonora] L.S. Bagg, widow of Dr. John Sullivan Bagg of Springfield, Massachusetts, a naval surgeon who had taken his own life in 1887. Ethel's sister, Louise Mather Bagg, born in 1873, was a painter, sculptor and medalist. She was married before the First World War to an Italian sculptor of Spanish origin, Marchese Emanuele de Rosales, whom she divorced in 1923. The mother and the two daughters led a very cosmopolitan life, travelling between Massachusetts and European capitals such as Rome, Paris, Geneva and London, and living at times in each. At the turn of the century Ethel attended Newnham College, Cambridge, but never took her degree.[385] In New York and Washington the Baggs became prominent socialites with their movements and attendances often noted by the press.[386] In 1905 Ethel made an extended visit to South Africa which she later wrote about for a popular travel magazine, <u>Revue Le Tour du Monde</u>.[387] During the First World War Louise served with the Italian Surgical Dressing Committee on the Italian-Austrian border.[388] Ethel returned to the US from London on 6 July 1916, shortly after Bullard himself also decided to go home.[389] Ethel busied herself in several ways, acting as the American representative of the Royal Horticultural Society and, from 1917 to 1919, involved in the work of the United States Food Administration.[390] Throughout this period, Bullard had kept in close touch with the Bagg family, often turning to Louisa L.S. Bagg for advice, assistance and introductions to prominent individuals on the continent.[391] After their marriage Arthur and Ethel Bullard formed both a personal and professional partnership, based from their home, at 2326 California Street Washington, purchased in October 1921, and the Baggs' Geneva home at 43 Quai Wilson.[392] In the 1920s, Salter had become acquainted with the Bullards, and had stayed with them when he visited Washington in November 1928. Soon after Arthur Bullard's death, Salter sent his condolences, addressed to "My dear Ethel." He wrote, "I do hope you are finding it possible to re-start life. I know that after such a terrible blow the realization is often more painful some time afterwards than just at first. I am glad you intend to keep alive and real the interests and activities which you and Arthur shared."[393] Such was the beginning of a more personal friendship and eventual marriage between Ethel Bullard and Salter, as she joined his small but intimate group of friends. In turn, he was to benefit from her network of prominent contacts both in Europe and the US. The freedom to cultivate these networks, travel extensively, and enjoy a lavish life-style came the Bagg sisters' way on 2 February 1930. While visiting the Bullard home in California Street, Washington, Louisa L.S. Bagg died from bronchial pneumonia.[394] She left an estate valued at $2,223,080, a veritable fortune at the time, with the proceeds of this and her shares in the Bagg family owned Parsons Paper Company, the largest of its kind in the US, going to her daughters.[395]

Salter was in fact writing from London, where he had arrived on 10 October for a fortnight's stay. He had already expressed his concern, given the recent onset of the Depression, that "Things are rather grim & dark here in England, with the shadow of this hideous & demoralizing unemployment getting if anything blacker."[396] Unemployment was the focus of a speech, which he gave on 25 October to a joint conference of the Marshall Society and the League of Nations Union Conference at Oxford. The reasons for Britain's unemployment, he contended, were foreign tariff barriers, the "unelastic system" of British production that was unresponsive to world conditions and prices, a high rate of taxation and the effects of the World War. He went on to argue that "We should avoid thinking of cooperation and competition as rival principles, one of which must be right and the other wrong. Competition must continue, but must be directed and controlled so that extravagant waste, intolerable injustice or uncontrollable friction were not caused, but that there should be a general increase in prosperity which all would share."[397] Thinking along such lines helped to shape Salter's views as the worldwide Depression deepened over time. On this same visit to London, he also attended a League of Nations Union meeting to discuss the proposed autonomy of the International Bank. Opinion here clearly favoured that the bank, he noted, "should be organically related to the League."[398]

During this time Salter seemed perpetually on the move. From London he returned to Geneva, via Paris, from where Royall Tyler wrote on 28 October, "Little Arthur was very dear last night. I met him and gave him dinner & saw him off to Geneva."[399] Salter intended to return to Paris in mid-November, but a crisis surrounding the National Bank in Bulgaria, albeit shortly resolved, forced him instead to hasten back to London for consultations with several members of the Financial Committee.[400] He was back in Paris, however, from 18 to 26 November, traveling afterwards to Copenhagen and Berlin for consultations, before returning to Paris on 2 December.[401] There Salter reported to Drummond on his travels and fixed the date for the next meeting of the Financial Committee. Most importantly, he committed to paper his thoughts on the upcoming Tariff Truce Conference, based on his extensive consultations in Europe's capitals during the previous weeks. Salter emphasized that the primary objective of the conference was to arrange a tariff truce, before proceeding to any subsequent detailed negotiations. His soundings had found both hesitation and opposition, however, he remained hopeful.[402]

Part of Salter's sense of urgency was his fear that the concurrent failures at the League to pass the draft Convention on the Treatment of Foreigners as well as the Convention for the Abolition of Import and Export Prohibitions and Restrictions would have serious consequences. In fact, in a meeting of the Economic Committee on 10 January, he was personally criticised for "errors" in procedure. He admitted to some problems, but cited a lack of prior co-ordination and the choice of Paris as the venue, rather than Geneva, as major causes. He noted that future important meetings, for purely practical reasons, should be held at the home of the League of Nations with the necessary supporting infrastructure in place. Drummond agreed the situation was serious enough to warrant distributing Salter's views throughout the Secretariat.[403]

Equally worrying for Salter was the exceptional amount of work he anticipated in the next few years because of numerous international conferences dealing with economic issues. He pointed out that since 1927 he had been obliged to be absent from Geneva on League work for more than one third of the year, including extended preparatory work in London.[404] Such second thoughts continued to occupy him as the year drew to a close. Writing on 20 December, he suggested that future crises, such as threats of war or pressing financial issues with political implications, would likely be settled outside the League. Although the League remained a useful meeting place for foreign ministers to consult and for the disarmament issue to be pursued, he confessed that "we are having a set-back" in the area of economic work. He continued, "It is certainly true that we have aimed for the last months at more than we are able to pull off for the present. The attitude disclosed particularly at the Prohibitions Conference makes it difficult to conceive that we can achieve success at the Tariff Conference and we are therefore in an extremely difficult dilemma." Cancellation, he added, "would spread the evil results very much wider." Factoring in as well the American financial crash and the resulting economic Depression, Salter predicted "that we shall fail substantially over our tariff truce and that we are in for a set-back of a year or two." It was best to accept the fact that the US preferred to stand aloof from the League, but attempts should be made to build instead greater co-ordination between the League and the Kellogg-Briand Pact. This he concluded would result "in a universal world instrument for securing peace."[405] Indeed, this became British policy when the League Council opened on 13 January 1930.[406]

A similar mood was reflected in one of Salter's last letters in 1929. Writing to Felkin on 28 December, while on vacation in Vence, he noted, "Alternate days of brilliance & rain – a restful & enjoyable holiday – with some work which I'll show you when I return." He reflected on their 10 year association at the League, "which for me has immensely added both to the pleasure & the value of my work. But I've often thought with concern of the paucity of prospects at the League." Salter had in mind Felkin's career, though it might as easily been his own at the time. He also completed Felkin's annual review, noting that "To the quick & subtle intelligence he always possessed, experience has added a sound & sure judgment."[407] Felkin's reaction was to admit that he had no real natural grasp of the "new economic work." He continued, "I feel Arthur grows more attached to me & in spite of my laziness, I do feel (as I nearly wrote to him) that one element which makes of my work one of the happiest factors in my life, is that one of my greatest satisfactions in life is if & when I have the sense that he is pleased with me & relies on me."[408] The fact was that Felkin increasingly had become part of Salter's inner circle. When Ka Cox visited Salter in early January, Felkin was included, and his diary recorded several conversations. Among them was one about "psychoanalysis & modern sex morals," to which Salter contributed:

> a whole exposition of his view of civilization – a crust – just thick enough to hold people in. In the case of the Irish or the Balkans the crust is very thin; & a little scratch & you come down to the 'brutal' instincts. He thought this crust consisted of the rules of conduct which people followed often unreasoningly. This part of man you could extend & develop indefinitely; (this being the real answer to people who said human nature will never change, therefore, it's no good attempting a League); & 'underneath' the essential 'brutish' nature of man the central forces of the earth go on burning. But once you removed that crust, you don't know where you wouldn't be landed.[409]

On one such occasion, Ka Cox confided to Felkin that he "was one of the few people Arthur was really attached to & that he saw only out of the corner of his eye with an almost pathetic admiration of the intimacy I achieved with people & the help I gave them & wd like to do the same e.g. with Margaret Brooke." On another occasion, Felkin recorded Salter as saying "he wanted neither power nor money, but he was tired of committees & he wanted leisure to study 2 or 3 questions. 'I'm not ambitious, I think.' I said of course you're too big for your job & he wd. not deny it. But he does feel the point about power."[410]

1930 was to prove a decisive landmark in Salter's career, as he was already suggesting to his intimate circle of friends. Closely related was the reality that he was also absorbed in discussions surrounding the possible reform of the League Secretariat. In order to achieve "a real League corporate sense," he wrote on 13 January, everything must be done to secure the international character of the Secretariat. While aware it was not possible to eliminate "national advocacy," he admitted it had its place in the debates that went into the League decision-making process. However, he rejected any suggestion of having resident national representatives at Geneva, stating that this would "destroy the essential League spirit." It was only in 1931 that Salter's section was divided into two, an Economic Section headed by Pietro Stoppani and the Financial Section headed by Loveday. It was not until the 13th Assembly in 1932 that some of the higher positions at the League were earmarked for nationals of a particular state.[411] In the meantime, League business continued with the focus on the Tariff Truce Conference, the unfulfilled part of the agenda of the 1927 World Economic Conference. Salter was "extremely doubtful" of a truce and foresaw a long negotiating process, extending possibly into May or June.[412] The League Council's meeting, beginning on 13 January, approved the opening of the Tariff Truce Conference for 17 February. For Salter the upcoming gathering was unique in one respect. In contrast to previous League meetings and economic activities, this was to be an "essentially Ministerial Conference," and the resulting work would involve ministerial negotiations.[413]

Ever since the Labour Party came to power in Britain in May 1929, Salter had kept in touch with several of its members, such as Foreign Minister Sir Arthur Henderson and his parliamentary secretary, Philip Noel-Baker.[414] One of their subjects of discussion concerned President Hoover's proposals to allow the free passage of food ships in wartime. On 20 December 1929 Salter had sent to the Foreign Office a memorandum on the matter which would have preserved the League principles of blockade, yet conceded something of Hoover's intentions. This was regarded as providing "a rather neat solution." On a related issue, that of "Freedom of the Seas," Salter also weighed in, arguing that League members had to abide by Article 16 of the Covenant to impose a blockade. This included the stoppage of food ships, unless exceptions were agreed to beforehand by a conference of signatories of the Kellogg Pact and League members.[415] In late January Noel-Baker urged Salter to visit London during the Naval Conference, which opened on 21 January, to lobby specifically Morrow and Rublee on these subjects.[416] Salter duly went to London and had several inconclusive discussions on these issues. Of interest was that he paid his first, consecutive weekend visits, in early February, to the Astors at their home in Cliveden. Writing to thank Lady Astor, Salter noted that "It isn't often that I've combined the useful with the enjoyable," and added that the many talks he had there had been "extremely useful."[417] Salter was to become an infrequent visitor to Cliveden, for example, returning again in October, but he was never associated with the later controversies surrounding the pro-appeasement mentality of the "Cliveden set."[418]

After returning to Geneva, Salter wrote on 17 February, "We are all plunged here into the midst of the Tariff Truce Conference – as difficult as but less exciting that the [Naval] Conference in London."[419] The conference, opened that same day, was never regarded with much hope by Salter, even though he remained convinced that tariff reduction held the key to global prosperity. However, prospects for an effective truce were grim, with the United States sending only an observer, with most delegates coming from Europe, and with widespread fears of the deepening effects of the Depression. After its general discussions, the conference on 20 February broke into two committees, one to discuss the draft convention for a tariff truce, the other to draw up a programme for the subsequent negotiations.[420] Neither was he able to make much progress over the following weeks. Discovering that the French delegation had "instructions to have nothing to do with a tariff truce," Salter could only anticipate "a hopeless position."[421] To Lord Lothian he wrote that, as he looked into the economic future, all he could see was "a painful and discouraging prospect."[422]

Salter's generally gloomy outlook led him to a decision which he shared in confidence with Felkin. In his diary on 9 March, Felkin referred to "Arthur's projected resignation," and noted that he has been "showing me quite an astonishing burst of affection & frankness." Felkin further wrote that Salter admitted "he himself was getting stale and wished to leave soon in any case," that "he had not been pulling his weight, [and] since 1927 he had done nothing. He was the sort of person to take up & throw himself into a quick job, not to carry out a long-distance policy." Salter noted that he felt "the hindrances of a growing hierarchy at the League. He had never been intimate with Drummond; he was not consulted on questions of general policy until it was too late." Finally, he confessed "He felt a growing distrust of his own judgement. He felt he would be a better man if he went away (writing a book, an occasional letter to The Times) & a worse one if he stayed." Felkin observed that "In all of this business of his going there is both something quixotic & some wounded pride & pique, though he would deny this." Felkin reluctantly concluded that if Salter's heart was no longer in the work, "then he ought to go."[423]

On 16 March, Felkin again expressed in his diary his conviction that Salter "will go: also that at the back of it all is a strong resentment against Drummond's treatment of him." By that point, in fact, Salter had written to Drummond about his possible resignation, prior to the expiry of his contract on 31 December, 1931. According to Felkin's diary, Salter was pressing for resignation by the end of the year.[424] When Salter and Drummond met, according to Felkin's diary entry of 26 March, their talk was based on the premise "that Arthur's going was settled." Drummond "gave Arthur, who is of course disappointed, surprised & hurt – the sense that he wants Arthur to go." At bottom, Felkin recorded, Salter stated "he could not face another three years here."[425] Felkin then went further, writing a long letter to Drummond, but never sent, describing Salter's predicament. Another aspect Felkin addressed was the coming reorganization of the League, with the prospect that Salter might lead the disarmament section. This prospect Felkin dismissed, as he put it, because of Salter's strong personality and because "he isn't colourless enough." Nonetheless, Felkin did add that Salter "becomes more moderate & temperate every year, now."[426] Privately, Salter wrote on 28 March that "I'm a bit fatigued by ten years of this kind of life abroad, & I am meditating having a year away from official life, & probably mainly in England, next year. After a time a real change of environment is desirable from many points of view."[427]

Even as Salter struggled with his future prospects, the ongoing Tariff Truce Conference wound up on 24 March with the signature of a Commercial Convention, binding the signatories to prolong existing commercial arrangements for a year.[428] In Salter's view the results were "modest" and provided "a certain temporary stabilization." On 27 March, he admitted, "We did not make a particular success of our Tariff Truce."[429] To Ka Cox he wrote: "Well, that's that, a half failure, which can be dressed up to look like a two-thirds success. It leaves a large part of the fight ahead." In this despondent mood, he lobbied successfully to cancel the next meeting of the Economic Consultative Committee, scheduled for 2 May. As well, the campaign for a tariff truce was soon abandoned.[430] Likely needing a break from Geneva, and wishing to follow the continuing Naval Conference in London at first hand, Salter spent most of April in England. On 11 April he paid a farewell visit to Norman at the Bank of England and informed him that he was leaving the League at year's end and would take a year's holiday.[431] On the same day he wrote to Ka Cox:

> I'm having an enjoyable – though as regards naval conference questions not fruitful – time in London. Every day I rejoice more at the prospect of being

more in England. London is crowded with interesting things. On Wednesday night there were five separate things I wanted to do – the one I did was to attend a little dinner with Stamp, A.G. G. [Gardiner], J.A. Spender, Arnold Bennett, H.G. Wells, J.A. Hobson & a few others, which proved one of the most enjoyable evenings I've ever had.

He also revealed to Ka Cox that he had received an invitation, "which greatly excites me," to visit India to advise the government. "I've wanted to go to India for many years – but not to stay too long."[432] Besides that, however, Salter already found himself in London being offered a variety of positions – from going into politics to editor of Round Table – to all of which he demurred.[433] In some English circles, his reputation was such that he and Keynes were regarded "as the two men who could save the country if they were given a free hand to organize the unemployment situation."[434]

The London Naval Conference, which had its closing session and treaty signing on 22 April, held a special interest for Salter. This was partly because he had an *entrée* behind the scenes due to his friendship with Dwight Morrow who chaired the committee drafting the final terms of the treaty. "Had it not been for Morrow," Salter later wrote, "there would never have been an agreement."[435] Somewhat indirectly, however, another matter concerned Salter during his stay. The London Naval Conference had highlighted the ongoing relationship between disarmament and security, an issue of major concern to a country such as France. Of further relevance was the upcoming meeting at Geneva, still unscheduled, of the Preparatory Committee for the Disarmament Conference. Some in the Foreign Office were inclined to weaken the application of sanctions under Article 16 from a requirement to a recommendation that would be contingent on consultation with the US. Others, such as Dalton, worried that there was a growing "flight from the Covenant." A long memorandum on the subject by Cadogan, advocating revision and the "weakening" of Article 16, found its way to Salter who responded from London on 15 April. He argued against any amendment to the Covenant, such as inviting American approval prior to the application of sanctions. To do so, he contended, would be "to put to the Administration just the question they don't want to have put to them." Drummond also shared Salter's reservations and in fact was responsible for forwarding Salter's views to the Foreign Office.[436]

On his return to Geneva, Salter confronted what he regarded as an even greater challenge to the League. On 17 May the French government finally circulated its formal memorandum on European Federal Union, originally proposed in the summer of 1929, and requested responses by 15 July. The so-called "Briand Memorandum" was to prove extremely important for Salter's reputation and influence. Within three days he had completed his own 13-page memorandum, clarifying his thinking and intended for private circulation and discussion. In "The French Memorandum on a European Federal Union," and shortly dubbed by the press as "Reply No. 27," following those of the 26 members of the League, Salter pointed out that "While the fundamental conception is political, the programme of work is predominantly economic." He agreed that closer European economic cooperation, as envisaged in the memorandum, was desirable. However, he emphasized that such activity was already within "the methods and machinery" of the League. Turning to questions of organization, he pointed out that, while the memorandum promised to avoid diminishing the League's authority, the actual proposals were "inconsistent with these intentions." He foresaw that the projected annual Conference, the Permanent Executive Committee and a possible separate Secretariat would inevitably lead to an "external and parallel organization," without any linkage to the League, leaving it as a "mere shell." Salter feared that regional clusters, such as Europe, Pan-America and the British Empire could erode the authority of a genuinely universal League and endanger future peace. His response was to elaborate a scheme, within the framework of the League, to solve regional, that is European questions, unrelated to larger League issues such as the prevention of war. This provided for close integration between what Briand envisaged but channeled through what Salter termed "a European Committee of the Council." Salter continued, "'Regionalizing,' therefore, as far as it is desirable, should, I suggest, be within the League, not outside it." Lastly, he advocated British association with any new form of European Union. Great Britain, he pointed out "is the indispensable intermediary between the European and the world point of view." He concluded by emphasizing that none of his observations should be interpreted as criticism of the main idea of a more united Europe. He considered it obvious that for both economic and political purposes "a greater solidarity between the countries of Europe is of the utmost possible importance."[437]

Salter gave copies of his memorandum to Drummond, members of his own section and other League officials. All were categorically notified as to its "personal and confidential character." Indeed, on 21 May Drummond advised all League Directors that the Briand proposals were "most delicate" and to "refrain from expressing any official opinion on them." Salter later responded that "Personally he regretted that there had been no discussion of the Briand Memorandum."[438] In the short term, however, the copy he sent to Noel-Baker on 22 May was to have wide and unexpected ramifications.[439] On receipt of the French memorandum, the Foreign Office engaged in an extensive round of consultations on its future reply. Initial comments by its officials suggested a response of caution and sympathy. This was certainly reflected in a 30 May memorandum prepared by Allen Leeper of the Foreign Office.

On the one hand, Leeper found Briand's thinking "permeated by a vague and puzzling idealism." On the other hand, he focused on the negative impact the proposals would have in Geneva, sufficient to "certainly destroy much of the League's authority." His advice, echoing Salter's, advocated opposition to any proposals "which in practice may damage the prestige and authority of the League," and for any new machinery to "be built into the existing framework of the League."[440] There was no doubting the impact of Salter's approach to the project of European Union on Britain's response. On 26 May, for example, echoing Salter's reservations, Noel-Baker cautioned that Briand's proposals overlapped with work already begun in Geneva and would be "a dangerous rival to the League."[441] On 1 June Lord Robert Cecil suggested that future European cooperation "should be under the full control of the organs of the League." Equally, on 5 June a Foreign Office minute noted, "When the S of S. [Henderson] read this paper [Salter's memorandum], I understand that he considered that the memo prepared by Mr Allen Leeper should be revised in the light of Sir A. Salter's criticisms."[442] The reality was that Salter had galvanised his contacts, especially, Noel-Baker and Lord Robert Cecil, to influence the British response to Briand's memorandum. The outcome was eventually reflected in Henderson's draft response, finalized on 8 July, approved by the cabinet on 16 July and published the following day.[443]

On 25 May Salter arrived for a week's visit to Vienna, at the end of which he came away "impressed at the character of the achievement of the Socialist administration."[444] After his return to Geneva on 2 June, he no longer kept his intended resignation a secret. He confided to Felkin that Gilbert Murray had asked him to take on an Oxford Chair. Felkin noted in his diary on 11 June, "an ideal appointment as he recognizes. He is hesitating." Felkin urged Salter to discuss this with Murray in person when next visiting London. "Yes," Salter responded, "but in talking there's a danger of steering away from one's resolutions." Salter had also notified J.A. Spender, the Liberal journalist, that he was leaving the League at the end of the year.[445] In mid-June Salter returned to London for two weeks. One of his few commitments, and indicative of how he was gradually removing himself from League duties, was a meeting on 19 June with Lloyd George, the industrialist Seebohm Rowntree and Lothian. The subject of the discussion was a note Lothian had drawn up on various Liberal measures to meet the worsening economic crisis.[446] Some further discussion with Gilbert Murray confirmed that Salter would not take the Oxford position. "It means too much working up," Felkin noted on 1 July.[447]

Another prospect almost immediately came Salter's way. On 3 July he received a telegram enquiring whether he would be able to visit China in October. Felkin was delighted to have Salter invite him along.[448] In fact, the League, with Salter at the helm, had been investigating the nature of "national economic councils," and believed these might "have a considerable future ahead of them."[449] On 22 July Sir Frederick Whyte, advisor to the Chinese Nationalist Government, sounded out Salter as to whether he personally would be available to visit. The objectives were to survey the economic situation and advise on the best use of financial resources for economic development. On 14 August Salter replied, cognizant of the importance of the mission, modest about his qualifications and reserved about prospects for "ambitious schemes of reconstruction." Despite his concern regarding the civil war, being fought between the Nationalist government and the Communists, he understood that the mission would enhance the League's reputation. On 14 August Salter responded he would "certainly accept with eagerness and interest" an official invitation.[450]

Salter had left Geneva in early July for a leisurely motoring holiday in Austria and Germany with an old acquaintance, G. Lowes Dickinson. Salter reported on 13 July, "All going well & both enjoying ourselves immensely." Five days later he wrote, "This has been an extremely successful holiday – car running splendidly and weather cool (though with rather too much rain)." Throughout the journey, Salter kept in touch with Felkin regarding League matters, few as these were.[451] The real news, however, came even as he holidayed, when the media carried reports of his resignation. "Nearly all my letters refer to my resignation having been mentioned on the wireless & in the press," Salter wrote. "I presume this is only a repetition of the statement which had already appeared in the D[aily] H[erald], & that nothing has been communicated by the League. The latter would be regrettable & incorrect as I have not yet officially resigned (although of course I'm going to) & the date may be affected by China or India."[452] On 12 July The Manchester Guardian also wrote that Salter had resigned, describing him as the League's "financial wizard," while The New York Times on 17 July noted that Salter would resign by year's end. The latter's Geneva correspondent, the well-informed Clarence K. Streit, wrote more accurately that Salter's departure was the result of the diminishing need for the League's financial reconstruction work. The Economist on 19 July reported that Salter had already resigned.[453] For his part, Salter wrote of his "considerable annoyances arising from the fact that my coming resignation had been (unhappily) announced in the Press, & all sorts of people with all sorts of jobs thought that here's an idle fellow on whom we can put something. Well, they didn't."[454]

If that was not sufficient exposure for the normally publicity-shy Salter, The New York Times once again focused on him. On 19 July, four days after the deadline for responses to the Briand Memorandum, the newspaper observed, "It is known that the British reply is derived directly from a report recently made to the Foreign Office by Sir Arthur Salter." That same day <u>The Manchester Guardian</u> similarly reported on the Salter influence in the British response.[455] On 4 August Streit returned to the subject, quoting at length from the Salter memorandum, in particular from the section he devoted to "Britain's Attitude," and pointing out that paragraphs 5 to 10 of the British response were essentially a summary of Salter's memorandum.[456] With regard to the publicity Salter's resignation was receiving, he was privately confirming that he had "already resigned officially," albeit without a fixed date. In his private correspondence, he ruminated that his resignation was not because of "a change in interest, or outlook, about international affairs, or in any diminished belief in the League, or any kind of personal trouble at Geneva." He explained that he had never desired to be away from England "for more than the first constructive period, and I feel that the particular kind of work for which I had some special personal contribution to make, has reached a stage which makes it easier for me to leave." He continued that the era of European financial reconstruction was more or less over, that the milestone Economic Conference of 1927, a first stage, was over, and that "the second stage of slowly changing commercial policy by successful conferences and conventions is a patient work of many years for which I am not specially qualified, either by experience or temperament." Finally, he added that he had long wanted a period of "leisure and liberty" to write about international and League affairs without constraints of official position. Almost as an afterthought he noted, "Affairs in the world are not too happy, and the world's mood has not been good this last year."[457]

On 2 August Cecil sang Salter's praises in <u>The Nation & Athenaeum</u>, credited him for being "the brain" behind the schemes for financial reconstruction and refugee resettlement and for help in "creating an atmosphere of international confidence." In a follow up letter to the editor, Salter modestly paid tribute to such colleagues as Monnet, Blackett, Layton and Stamp for their roles in financial reconstruction. He emphasized that League initiatives were "essentially collective," and this resulted in their success. Salter finally confirmed that he intended to resign his position, not for any personal reason or a diminished belief in the League. Rather he had concluded that he could "work more effectively through some other medium than that of a position in the Secretariat."[458] On the morning of 20 August, Salter sent Drummond his official letter of resignation, effective 31 December. In response, Drummond accepted the resignation with regrets. He thanked Salter for his "untiring energy and whole-hearted devoted to the interests of the League."[459] Salter later commented: "I've been here much longer than I intended."[460]

September, as usual, found Salter engaged with the meeting of the League Assembly, where the main item of business continued to be the Briand Memorandum.

The unsolicited publicity attached to his note on the subject had forced him on 27 August to further address this issue. He provided recipients' names and, despite his emphasis on its confidential nature, his note was leaked to the press. "I did not depart by a hair's breadth," he wrote, from what he considered to be the appropriate conduct of an international official. Unless the Secretariat was to remain merely "clerks carrying out routine duties," he argued, it was "not only the right, but the duty" of an international official to express his views to his colleagues, the secretary general and, in the absence of disagreement, to member states. He expressed his relief that he was not accused of being the British government's instrument of policy. Rather, he pointed out, the British government and others "took some account" of his views and he regarded this as a credit. Finally, he regretted the leak, but thought its importance might be "greatly exaggerated."[461] However, given the impact of his memorandum on the British response to Briand proposals, events in Geneva during September were not surprising. After some discussion, the Assembly on 17 September approved a resolution to set up a "Commission of Enquiry for European Union," with Briand as its chairman. The Commission which was to report within a year held its first two preparatory meetings on 8 October and 20 November. Salter attended and expressed his continued reservations on the issue.[462] Shortly thereafter, he left his position at the League and in due course the Briand Memorandum passed into history.

Even as events in Geneva unfolded, Salter was already distancing himself. On 13 September, in a memorandum titled "A Lacuna in the League's Technical Organization," he provided what was, in effect, an assessment of the League after 10 years. He was convinced that the Briand proposal "on its organization side, is an implicit criticism, and in fact is largely founded on a feeling that the present League organization is too cumbrous." He acknowledged that there were deficiencies in the technical work of the League because of defects in the organization, but that increasing the number of permanent officials of the Secretariat was too expensive. Rather he urged an expansion of temporary experts to provide the required continuity and co-ordination. This suggestion became one of the recommendations for the reorganization of the Secretariat, adopted by the Assembly on 3 October.[463] With Salter's resignation both official and public, delegates paid tributes to his achievements at the League, along with regrets on his departure. One delegate stated Salter's "name will be forever linked with the financial reconstruction of Europe." Another praised him as "the ideal personification of the international official. He has kept before us a high ideal. He has shown great knowledge and unwearying energy. He has never allowed himself to be influenced by political considerations or personal sympathies."[464] As the Assembly session ended on 4 October, Salter reflected on its myriad discussions. "The situation is horribly difficult," he wrote, "and certainly a world Depression gives the least favourable atmosphere for the kind of policy we have been working on for some years. It makes everybody apprehensive and defensive."[465] On 8 October he observed that "a period of Depression such as the present was not suitable for the advance of that liberal economic policy with which the League had hitherto been associated."[466] In another vein, Felkin's diary recorded an epigram by Salter who observed: "There are four categories of Council members. The interested (big power) whom we must have; the disinterested whom we ought to have; the interesting whom we might have; & the uninteresting & uninterested (S. America) with whom the Council is being swamped."[467]

With his resignation looming, Salter had made no firm plans, other than promising himself he wanted at least a year "without any executive work."[468] However, he turned his attention to some writing plans, as invitations for his reflections on world events arrived almost weekly. Ramsay MacDonald wrote to him, asking "Have you anything in mind?"[469] In mid-October he spent a fortnight in England, and that now included his usual visit with the Astors at Cliveden. From them came an invitation to use a cottage at Cliveden for his future writing plans.[470] He had already committed himself to writing an article for Foreign Affairs, and in late September promised The Times three articles focusing on British economic policy in relations to the global situation.[471] On 30 October, while in London, he broadcast for the BBC on "Trade Within the Empire," a topic then under discussion at the Imperial Conference. He explored the implications of expanding the system of imperial preference.[472] His talk was published in The Listener and was the first of many such contributions throughout the 1930s to the early 1950s.[473] In Foreign Affairs he addressed the issue of "The Economic Organization of Peace." He conceded that the Covenant of the League, the Locarno Treaties and the Kellogg Pact provided some mechanism for the prevention of war. However, he suggested that this was only half the task, the other being to address the economic causes of war. He regarded economic competition as presenting the greatest dangers of conflict and urged that tariffs be rationalized and stabilized. Also he suggested that state assisted "dumping" (which he defined as "the fixing of prices for export at less than those for sale at home") only increased inter-state animosities and must be curtailed. Finally, he urged that more be done to inform governments and public opinion about the dangers of unregulated economic competition.[474] In The Spectator Salter noted that the League had some role yet to play in what he termed "the most severe general Depression that has ever been known." He highlighted the fact that the Financial Committee was studying the "gold problem" and its relation to the Depression. On the economic side, he noted that the League was beginning to provide expert advice alone, without any other financial commitments, though it could not enforce any specific policy to deal with the Depression.[475]

The Depression was a subject to which Salter was taking a cautious approach. He could offer, as yet, no confident explanation of its causes or cures. He was not entirely convinced that the collapse of commodity prices in terms of gold, and the scarcity of gold itself were primary causes. Nor did he think that tariff reform in itself, while necessary, was sufficient. Rather, he was working his way, issue by issue, towards a comprehensive analysis, which was to result in his 1932 book, Recovery: The Second Effort."[476] On 8 and 9 December he contributed articles to The Times, titled "A 'Frozen' Trade System," which aroused widespread interest. Looking beyond the current Depression, Salter argued that "there are certain defects in our system which neither palliatives, protection, nor our general attitude of optimism towards the future" could remove. He pointed out that since 1913 the UK's portion of world trade had declined. This was due to the fact that Britain's economic system was "more rigid, stiff and inelastic" than others. He accused British industry, the banking system, employers and trade unions of being antiquated, unresponsive and conservative." How then to make it "more elastic and more responsive to new methods, new prices, new conditions?" He then ranged over an array of reforms in the banking system, taxation laws and the labour movement. Ultimately he believed these would lead to a rise in the standard of living and increased prosperity.[477] Finally, Salter contributed to Round Table an article "Where is Europe Going?" He assessed some of the political repercussions of the Depression, in particular the "note of real anxiety" which had dominated the September meeting of the Assembly in Geneva. He was convinced that the future peace of the world depended on the choice between "the 'universal' [League Covenant] or the 'alliance' principle?" Adoption of the former, he believed, would guarantee peace; the latter would lead to war. However, he would not reveal his own view on what would prevail.[478]

On 21 November the India Office in London sent its formal invitation to Drummond requesting that Salter visit India. Beside encouraging greater Indian participation in the technical work of the League, Salter's mission was to assist in the creation of an Economic Advisory Council [EAC].[479] Felkin noted again how "delighted" he was to be asked to accompany Salter, and pleased to hear that Salter regarded him as "the ideal traveling companion."[480] Royall Tyler who was visiting with Salter, wrote:

> Arthur's delight in going to India is refreshing, & Felkin, whom he is taking along, is thereby saved from the immediate consequences of Arthur's leaving the League. The two of them are the only happy people I've seen here. Everyone else is deeply despondent, apprehensive, discouraged about the League's future. I've never known Geneva in such dumps. Arthur's going gives

an all-round impression that Geneva, somehow, has missed the mark and that the livest elements in it are seeking other fields. The press communiqué, issued on 1 December by the League, referred to Salter's 'special experience' as being of interest to the Indian government in setting up some organization to study economic questions and engage in purposive economic planning.[481]

On 4 December Salter left Geneva for Paris and London. He spent the final few days before his departure to India at Isis House, Oxford, in his father's company. On Christmas Eve, he wrote to Ethel Bullard about his mission:

> I get more excited as the time approaches when I shall see the painted East. I had a vivid account from Lady Blackett a few days ago of what it means for one who first passes East of the Mediterranean & the curtain goes up on the Orient & hope it may be for me what it evidently was for her. What I shall make of my job I can't yet guess. The framework into which any particular plan has to fit is still so uncertain. I went over to Chequers on Sunday & had an interesting account [of the Round Table talks on India] from the P.M. (there was no other visitor).[482]

That same evening he also wrote to Elisina Tyler in response to her annual Christmas letter. Again it was his forthcoming journey which dominated his reply. "I feel like a boy with a new adventure in starting for India, as I do tomorrow with Elliott Felkin. I expect like most jobs it will be largely dealing with papers in an office – but not all. I shall be seeing something of the painted East if only in glimpses."[483] On 25 December Salter left London to Marseilles, and the following day he embarked on the P&O liner *Rampura*, accompanied by Felkin. Marian Henderson turned up to wish them bon voyage.[484] The journey marked the beginning of a new career for Salter, one he had not much anticipated, as economic advisor, journalist, author, consultant, professor and then a member of parliament.

Endnotes

1. Salter, Memoirs, 174-175, transcript of interview between Lord Salter and M. Jean Siotis, 4 Jan. 1969, 2-3, author's archive.
2. Salter to Violet Markham, 27 July 1922, Markham Papers, 25/73, note by D.R.F.[sic], 14 Aug. 1922, Sir Arthur Salter's Personnel File, LNA, S874/3100.
3. League of Nations, "Staff of Secretariat," [1920], LNA, Box 696, "The Composition and Functions of the Economic and Finance Section," LNA, 1921:

29/12601/12601, League of Nations, "Staff List of the Secretariat," 15 May 1922, LNA, 1922: 29/21186/1083, "Staff List of the Secretariat," Apr. 1923, LNA, 1923: 29/28899/1083.

4. League of Nations, Proceedings of the First Session of the Provisional Economic and Financial Committee, Geneva, Nov.-Dec. 1920, LNA.
5. Second Assembly of the League of Nations, "Reports of the Provisional Economic and Financial Committee," 28 Sept. 1921, LNA, Box R293, 1921: 10/16303/2101.
6. Salter to Royall Tyler, 29 Aug. 1922, LNA, Box S116, McFadyean to Salter, 26 Sept. 1922, LNA, Box S107, Renée de Lucy Fossarieu, Esquisses de la vie d'une femme (Ambilly-Annemasse, 1969), 73-84.
7. Royall Tyler to Elisina Tyler, 8 Sept. 1922, Tyler Papers, Felkin to Salter, 21 Dec. 1922, LNA, Box S106.
8. Minutes, Directors' Meeting, No. 56, 12 Aug. 1922, LNA.
9. Salter, "General Survey," in The League of Nations, The Financial Reconstruction of Austria: General Survey and Principal Documents (Geneva, 1926), 9-85, Salter, "Preface" to Supplement to the Monthly Summary of the League of Nations, "The Financial Reconstruction of Austria," Oct. 1922, 1-8, "Austrian Reconstruction – Comparison of Results Anticipated and Achieved [by Salter]," n.d., LNA, Box S113.
10. The Times, 29 Aug. 1922.
11. Salter, Memoirs, 177, Monnet, Memoirs, 94, Erin E. Jacobsson, A Life for Sound Money, Per Jacobsson, His Biography (1979), 51, Blackett to Salter, 5 Oct. 1922, LNA, Box S107.
12. Minutes of the Provisional Economic and Financial Committee, Financial Committee, Eighth Session, First to the Eighteenth Meetings, 4-28 Sept. 1922, LNA, Minutes of the Economic Committee, Sixth Session, Fourth to the Fifth Meetings, 4-9 Sept. 1922, LNA, Salter to Balfour, 18 Sept. 1922, LNA, Box S107, Salter, "Notes as to Future Action," 26 Sept. 1922 LNA, Box S107.
13. Salter, "Preface" to Supplement to the Monthly Summary of the League of Nations, "The Financial Reconstruction of Austria," Oct. 1922, LNA, 1923: 1OB/27751/24461, 9.
14. Sir William Goode to Salter, 4 Oct. 1922, LNA, Box S107.
15. Salter to McFadyean, 4 Oct. 1922, LNA, Box S107.
16. Entry of 23 Jan. 1924, Jones, Whitehall Diary, vol. 1, 1916-1925, 267.
17. Salter to G. Lowes Dickinson, 18 Oct. 1922, LNA, Box S113.
18. Salter to Drummond, 16 Jan. 1923, LNA, Box S113, Salter to C.B. Fry, 24 Oct. 1923, LNA, S115.

19. Boyden to Salter, 12, 16 Oct., Salter to Boyden, 18 Oct. 1922, Salter to Monnet, 18 Oct. 1922, LNA, S107. See also Salter to Boyden, 21, 28 Oct. 1922, Roland Boyden Papers, MS Am, v. 7, 119-121, Houghton Library, Harvard University, Cambridge, MA.
20. Sir Henry Clay, Lord Norman (1957), 185-187, Norman to Salter, 19 Oct. 1922, LNA, Box S107.
21. Blackett to Salter, 23 Oct. 1922, LNA, Box S107. On Zimmerman see also Adrian Pelt to Salter, 31 Oct. 1922, LNA, Box S107.
22. Salter to Boyden, 10 Nov. 1922, LNA, Box S106, Edward Keeling to Lord Curzon, 17 Nov. 1922, Documents on British Foreign Policy, 1919-1939 [DBFP] Series 1, vol. 24, W.N.Medlicott and Douglas Dakin, eds., (1983), 413-414.
23. Salter to Monnet, 11 Nov. 1922, LNA, Box S106, Salter, Personality and Politics, 166-167.
24. Salter to Attolico, 20 Oct., Salter to Denis, 12 Dec.1922, LNA, Box S106, "A Christmas Letter in Vienna," Salter Papers, File 1, Anecdotes and Incidents.
25. Salter to Drummond, 13 Nov., Philip Baker to Salter, 22 Oct. 1922, LNA, Box S106.
26. Keeling to Curzon, 3 Nov. 1922, DBFP, Series 1, vol. 24, 386-388.
27. See Salter, "Note sur la mission a Vienne," 19 Dec. 1922, LNA, Box 505, 1919-1927: 10B/24095/24095, Austria, I, "Report by the Provisional Delegation of the League of Nations at Vienna," II, "Summary of Position on December 15th, 1922," LNA, Box S106.
28. Minutes, Directors' Meetings, No. 63, 24 Nov., No. 64, 29 Nov. 1922, LNA.
29. "Desperate but Not Serious," Salter Papers, File 1, Anecdotes and Incidents, The Observer, 17 Dec. 1922.
30. Markham, Return Passage,168.
31. Salter to Frank Wise, 27 Nov. 1922, LNA, Box S106.
32. Salter to Violet Markham, 3 Dec. 1922, Markham Papers, 25/73.
33. Salter, Memoirs, 180, "A Christmas Letter in Vienna," Salter Papers, File 1, Anecdotes and Incidents,
34. R.S. Sayers, The Bank of England, 1891-1944, vol. 1 (1976), 167-168.
35. Salter to Niemeyer, 22 Dec. 1922, LNA, Box S106.
36. Niemeyer to Salter, 27 Dec. 1922, LNA, Box S107, entry of 7 Dec. 1922, Sir Montagu Norman Diary, ADM34/11-1922, Bank of England Archive, London.
37. Austria, II, "Summary of Position on December 15th 1922," LNA, Box S106.
38. Salter to Violet Markham, 8 Feb. 1923, and encl., "Notes on Attitude of League of Nations Towards Present Reparation Position," 22 Jan. 1923, Markham Papers, 26/10.
39. Arthur Sweetser to Salter, 14 Nov. 1922, LNA, Box S106, Morning Post, 14 Oct. 1922.

40. The Financial Times, 13 Feb. 1923.
41. Salter to Clémentel, 10 Feb. 1923, LNA, Box S116, Clémentel to Salter, 20 Feb. 1923, LNA, Box S389.
42. Salter, "Austria," Speech to the International Chamber of Commerce, 24 Mar. 1923, LNA, Box S113. He provided further summaries of progress in Austrian reconstruction in "The Reconstruction of Austria," Young Men of India, 34(May 1923), 201-209, and "Austria: Saved or Duped?" The New Republic, 35(22 Aug. 1923), 359-361.
43. A Glimpse of a Dictator," Salter Papers, File 1, Anecdotes and Incidents.
44. Minutes, Directors' Meeting, No. 78, 28 Mar. 1923, LNA.
45. Salter to Morrow, 31 Mar. 1923, LNA, Box S116, Salter to Morrow, 31 May 1923, Morrow Papers, microfilm reel 80.
46. Salter to Quesnay, 9 May 1923, LNA, Box S116, Salter to Zimmerman, 11 May 1923, LNA, Box S109, F.H. Nixon to Salter, 14 May 1923, LNA, Box S108.
47. Royall Tyler to Elisina Tyler, 8 May 1923, Tyler Papers, F.H. Nixon to Salter, 14 May 1923, LNA, Box S108.
48. Salter, "General Survey," in League of Nations, The Financial Reconstruction of Austria: General Survey and Principal Documents, 43.
49. Salter to Fosdick, 30 May 1923, Fosdick Papers, Box 2.
50. Salter to Morrow, 31 May 1923, Morrow Papers, microfilm roll 80. Salter to Blackett, 6 July 1923, LNA, Box S115, contains Salter's estimate of the contributions by individuals to the Austrian loan.
51. The New York Times, 2 May 1923, The Wall Street Journal, 11, 24 May 1923.
52. Royall Tyler to Elisina Tyler, 1 Oct. 1923, Tyler Papers.
53. Phillip Baker to Salter, 22 Oct. 1922, LNA, Box S106.
54. Salter to Drummond, 13 Nov. 1922, LNA, Box S106.
55. See Salter to James Logan, 11 Aug. 1923, LNA, Box S115, The Times, 9 July 1923.
56. Salter to James Logan, 11 Aug. 1923, LNA, Box S115, League of Nations, Economic, Financial and Transit Department, The League of Nations Reconstruction Schemes in the Inter-War Period (Geneva, 1945), 74-78. This book was the work of Royall Tyler.
57. League of Nations, The Greek Refugees Settlement Scheme, Protocol with the Relevant Documents (Geneva, 1923), 3-5. Salter reviewed the early stages of the Greek resettlement in The Times, 3 Nov. 1926.
58. Salter to J. Murray and Sir Hubert Llewellyn Smith, 18 Aug. 1923, LNA, Box S115.
59. Salter to Niemeyer, 25 Aug. 15 Sept. 1923, LNA, Box S115, Salter to Morgenthau, 27 Oct. 1923, LNA, Box S115.

60. Salter to Montagu Norman, 9 Oct. 1923, LNA, Box 1764, 1923: 48/31413/29451.
61. Henry Morgenthau, I Was Sent to Athens (New York, 1929), 83-84, 180, 197-198.
62. League of Nations, The Settlement of Greek Refugees: Scheme for an International Loan (Geneva, 1924), 4-5.
63. The Financial Times, 7 May 1925.
64. Salter, Memoirs, 184.
65. Salter, "General Survey," in The League of Nations, The Financial Reconstruction of Hungary: General Survey and Principal Documents (Geneva, 1926), 9-10, The Financial Times, 9 May 1924.
66. See Salter to Lord Robert Cecil, 10 Sept. 1923, LNA, S115.
67. Minutes, Directors' Meeting, No. 96, 17 Oct. 1923, LNA, Salter to J.C. Maxwell Garnett, 18 Oct. 1923, LNA, Box S115.
68. The Manchester Guardian, 15, 19 Nov. 1923.
69. The Times, 23 Nov. 1923, Salter, Memoirs, 181-182, Salter to T.B. Hohler, 26 Dec. 1923, LNA, Salter to O.E. Niemeyer, 27 Dec. 1923, LNA, Box S115.
70. On Smith see Salter to Count Bethlen, 11 Apr. 1924, LNA, Box 298, 1924: 10/33315X/2920, The New York Times, 24 Apr. 1924. Tyler went on to serve as Trustee of the League Loan from 1926-1928, and then resided in Budapest from 1931-1938 as a representative of the Financial Committee.
71. Minutes, Directors' Meeting, No. 117, 12 June 1924, LNA.
72. Salter, "General Survey," in The League of Nations, The Financial Reconstruction of Hungary: General Survey and Principal Documents 15. One of Smith's assistants was Royall Tyler. Salter to Janssens, 12 May 1924, LNA, Box S110.
73. See correspondence in LNA, Box 413, 1924: 10/35939/35908, The Times, 8 May 1924, The Financial Times, 9 May 1924.
74. The Observer, 15 June 1924.
75. Royall Tyler to Elisina Tyler, 1, 10-13 Oct. 1923, Tyler Papers.
76. Joseph S. Davis to "Folks," 15 May 1924, Davis Papers, courtesy of Joseph S. Davis.
77. Dufour to Salter, 8 Jan., Salter to Dufour, 10 Jan. 1924, LNA, Box 411, 1924: 10/33219/33219.
78. The New York Times, 26, 28 Feb. 1924, The Times, 27 Feb. 1924.
79. Entry of 28 Feb. 1924, Charles G. Dawes, A Journal of Reparations (1939), 130-131, The Times, 29 Feb. 1924.
80. Entry of 25 Mar. 1924, Dawes, A Journal of Reparations, 179-180, J. Harry Jones, Josiah Stamp: Public Servant (1964), 222, 224-226. This was also confirmed by Léon Dufour to Jacobsson. See entry of 9 Apr. 1924, Per Jacobsson Diary, no. 9, 114.
81. Entry of 2 May 1924, Jones, Whitehall Diary, vol. 1, 1916-1925, 278-279.

82. Salter to A.C. Coolidge, 13 Mar. 1924, LNA, Box S113, "The Reconstruction of Austria," Foreign Affairs, 2(1924), 630-643.
83. "The Empire and the League of Nations," encl. in Vernon Bartlett to Salter, 29 Mar. 1924, LNA, Box R1333.
84. See correspondence in LNA, Box 297, 1923: 10/32508/2920, and "The Reconstruction of Hungary," Journal of the British Institute of International Affairs, 3(1924), 190-202.
85. Clement Jones to Salter, 24 May 1924, Royal Institute of International Affairs [RIIA] Papers, Chatham House, London.
86. Salter to Lord Parmoor, 12 Apr. 1924, NA-UK, FO371/9889, C6417/1900/19, Salter to Alexander Cadogan, 24 Apr. 1924, NA-UK, FO371/9889, C6820/1900/19.
87. Minute by Cadogan, 7 May 1924, NA-UK, FO371/9889, C7516/1900/19.
88. Cadogan to Salter, 8 May 1924, NA-UK, FO371/9889, C7227/1900/19.
89. Salter to Zimmerman, 29 Apr. 1924, LNA, Box S109, Salter to Zimmerman, 15 May 1924, LNA, Box S110.
90. Salter, "General Survey," in The Financial Reconstruction of Austria: General Survey and Principal Documents, 54-58. See also Salter to Niemeyer, 15 May 1924, LNA, Box S110.
91. Salter, "General Survey," in The Financial Reconstruction of Austria: General Survey and Principal Documents, 58-60.
92. Neue Freie Presse, 22 June 1924, LNA, Box S110.
93. See e.g., Gilchrist to Salter, 13 June 1924, Gilchrist Papers.
94. Salter to H.A. Garfield, 14 Feb. 1924, Salter to W.W. McLaren, 11 Apr., 3 June, 17 July 1924, Institute of Politics Collection, Williams College Archives and Special Collections, Williamstown, MA.
95. One of the first people Salter met with was Morrow, who afterwards cabled: "Tell Salter I found perfectly good Burberry coat in my car this morning. It shows some signs of Austrian and Hungarian wear. He may occasionally lose his ticket or his luggage or his coat, but so far I have not noticed that he has lost his head." Morrow to Boyden, 30 July 1924, Morrow Papers, microfilm roll 80.
96. The New York Times, 28, 30 July 1924, The Washington Post, 30 July 1924.
97. Syllabus, Round Table Conference by Salter, 31 July 1924, Williams College Archives.
98. The New York Times, 5 Aug. 1924, The Washington Post, 5 Aug. 1924.
99. The New York Times, 6 Aug. 1924. Both of Salter's speeches were included in the post-session collection, sponsored by the Institute, The Reawakening of the Orient and Other Addresses (New Haven, CT, 1925), 115-160. Some of his

comments were published by the League of Nations Non-Partisan Association, Europe's Recovery: What It Means to World Peace (New York, 1924).

100. The New York Times, 8, 10 Aug. 1924.
101. The New York Times, 12, 13 Aug. 1924. For a transcript of the discussion on 11 August see "Culbertson Conference," 11 Aug. 1924, Williams College Archives.
102. The New York Times, 15 Aug. 1924.
103. The New York Times, 16, 17 Aug. 1924. A copy of Salter's speech on "Economic Conflicts as the Causes of War" can be found in the Morrow Papers, microfilm roll 80.
104. The New York Times, 17 Aug. 1924.
105. The New York Times, 20 Aug. 1924.
106. The New York Times, 21, 22 Aug. 1924.
107. Salter to Morrow, 13, 14 Aug. 1924, Morrow Papers, microfilm roll 80, Salter to Dr. McLaren, 2 Dec. 1924, Williams College Archives.
108. See e.g., Felkin to Salter, 13 Aug. 1924, LNA, Box S110.
109. Salter to MacDonald, 11 Aug. 1924, encl. in Drummond to W.H.M. Selby, 22 Aug. 1924, NA-UK, FO371/10569, W7259/134/98.
110. Lippmann to Salter, 18 Aug. 1924, Lippmann Papers, Yale University Library, New Haven, CT, Salter to Lippmann, 2 Sept. 1924, LNA, Box R421, 1924: 10/37457.
111. Walters, History of the League of Nations, 272-274.
112. Salter, "Economic Sanctions," 30 Sept. 1924, LNA, Box S121. This paper was reproduced in his The United States of Europe and Other Papers,162-168.
113. See Minutes, Directors' Meetings, No. 129, 4 Feb., No. 130, 5 Mar. 1925, LNA.
114. Salter, "General Survey," in The Financial Reconstruction of Austria: General Survey and Principal Documents, 59-71.
115. Salter "General Survey," in The Financial Reconstruction of Hungary: General Survey and Principal Documents, 29, 131.
116. H.M. Grove to Leigh Smith, 6 Oct. 1924, NA-UK, FO371/10382, N8021/7329/59, Salter to Marcus Wallenberg, 24 Feb. 1925, LNA, Box S115, Salter, Memoirs. 182.
117. Felkin to Dufour, 23 Oct., T. Aghnides to Salter, 23 Oct., Salter to Commandatore Bianchini, 24 Oct. 1924, LNA, Box R1767, 124: 48/39545/38170.
118. Markham to Joyce Newton Thompson, 20 Oct. 1924, Newton Thompson Papers, BC 643 818.25, Pelt to de Bordes, 9 Oct. 1924, LNA, Box 513, 1924: 10B/39478/24461, de Bordes to Salter, 20 Nov. 1924, LNA, BoxS111. Zimmerman's performance was a continuing matter of concern. See Layton to Salter, 9 Feb. 1925, LNA, Box S113.

119. Thannasis Aghnides to the author, 2 June 1979, author's archive, Violet R. Markham, "Greece and the Refugees from Asia Minor," Fortnightly Review, 117(Feb. 1925), 176-184.
120. Salter to Speyer and Co., New York, 13 Dec.1924, LNA, Box 397, 1924: 10/40952/26389.
121. "Good Work in Greece," Headway, 7(Jan. 1925), 5.
122. Salter to Felkin, 20 Oct. 1924, Felkin Papers, AEF/3/1/75.
123. Markham to Joyce Newton Thompson, Dec. [sic] 1924, Newton Thompson Papers, BC 643 818.26-27.
124. Markham to Mrs. Henderson, 2 Dec. 1924, encl. in Markham to Felkin, 1 [sic] Dec. 1924, Felkin Papers, AEF/3/1/76.
125. Salter to Felkin, 3, 17, 18 Dec. 1924, Felkin Papers, AEF/3/1/76.
126. Salter to Joyce Newton Thompson, 24 Apr. 1925, Newton Thompson Papers, BC 643 822.2.
127. Salter to Howland, 28 Jan. 1925, LNA, Box S115.
128. The Times, 10 Feb. 1925.
129. The Manchester Guardian Commercial, 29 Jan. 1925.
130. Minute by Cadogan, 3 Apr. 1925, NA-UK, FO371/11065, W2964/9/98.
131. Felkin to Salter, 2 July 1925, LNA, Box S115, Salter to Denis, 3 July 1925, LNA, S115.
132. Salter, "General Survey," in The Financial Reconstruction of Austria: General Survey and Principal Documents, 64-65.
133. Felkin to Professor Andreades, 15 May 1925, LNA, Box S115, de Bordes to Salter,18, 20 Mar. 1925, LNA, Box S111.
134. Niemeyer to Zimmermann, 27 Mar. 1925, LNA, Box S111, Salter to Avenol, 31 Mar. 1925, LNA, Box S111.
135. Salter to Layton, 17 Apr. 1925, Lord Layton Papers, 44^{17}, Trinity College Library, Cambridge, Salter to Niemeyer, 20, 27 Apr. 1925, LNA, Box S115.
136. Salter to Frère, 17 Apr. 1925, LNA, Box S115.
137. Salter to Niemeyer, 20, Apr. 1925, LNA, Box S115, Salter to Niemeyer, 27 Apr. 1925, LNA, Box S104.
138. Salter to Layton, 27 Apr. 1925, Layton Papers, 44$^{19(1-2)}$.
139. Minutes of the Finance Committee, 18th session, 5 June 1925, LNA, Salter to Layton, 15 June 1925, Layton Papers, 44$^{28(1)}$.
140. See minutes by Salter, 27 June, 16 Sept. 1925, LNA, Box R521, 1925: 10B/44614/25461.
141. See Journal of the International Chamber of Commerce, April 1925, LNA, Box 389, 1925: 10/42952/2478. The text of Salter's speech is in LNA, Box S113.

Salter requested that Layton provide comments regarding the Austrian content of the speech. See Salter to Layton, 18 June 1925, Layton Papers, 44[16].

142. Salter to Denis, 3 July 1925, LNA, Box S115.
143. Felkin to Salter, 27 June 1924, LNA, Box S115.
144. The Times, 7 July 1925.
145. Salter to Morrow, 9 July 1925, Morrow Papers, microfilm roll 80.
146. Salter to Philip Baker, 2 Apr. 1924, Cecil Papers, ADD MSS 51113, vol. 43, fol. 31, Salter to Joseph S. Davis, 31 July 1925, LNA, Box S115.
147. On the origins of the Liberal Summer Schools, see http://www.libdemvoice.org/dlt-liberal-summer-school-now-keynes-forum-8062.html.
148. Salter to A. Fenner Brockway, 25 July 1925, LNA, Box S115, Salter to Niemeyer, 25 July 1925, LNA, Box S115, The Washington Post, 13 Sept. 1925.
149. See W.T. Layton and Charles Rist The Economic Situation of Austria: Report Presented to the Council of the League of Nations (Geneva, 1925).
150. Zimmerman to Salter, 14 Aug. 1925, LNA, Box S109, Salter to Zimmerman, 19 Aug. 1925, Salter to Leith-Ross, 19 Aug. 1925, LNA, Box S115.
151. Salter, "Note on Budget Level," 26 Aug. 1925, LNA, Box S109.
152. Salter, "Termination or Transformation of Control," 27 Aug. 1925, LNA, Box S109.
153. Minute by Drummond, 29 Aug. 1925, LNA, Box S109.
154. Howland to Salter, 12, 20 Aug. 1925, Charles P. Howland Papers, Yale University Library, New Haven, CT.
155. Howland to Salter, 25 Aug. 1925, with encls., Howland Papers.
156. Salter to Niemeyer, 26 Aug. 1925, LNA, Box S109.
157. The Times, 7, 11 Sept. 1925.
158. Salter to Layton, 24 Sept. 1925, LNA, Box S109, Salter to Jacques Seydoux, 15 Sept. 1925, LNA, Box S115, Salter to Zimmerman, 24 Sept. 1925, LNA, Box S109.
159. The Times, 6, 8 Oct. 1925.
160. Record of Conversation, 12 Oct. 1925, LNA, Box S109, Salter to Niemeyer, 23 Oct. 1925, LNA, Box S115.
161. Salter, "General Survey," in The Financial Reconstruction of Austria: General Survey and Principal Documents, 70-71.
162. Salter to Howland, 16 Sept. 1925, LNA, Box S115, Howland to Salter, 9 Oct. 1925, Howland Papers.
163. "Proposal for a General Economic Conference in 1926," Salter Papers, File 5, League of Nations, Economic, United States of Europe, 1925-1930. This was reprinted with some minor amendments in Salter, The United States of Europe and Other Papers, 33-43.

164. The Times, 16 Sept. 1925.
165. "Monsieur Loucheur's Proposal for an Economic Conference," Sept. 1925, Salter Papers, File 5, League of Nations, Economic, United States of Europe, 1925-1930.
166. Salter to Layton, 24 Sept. 1925, LNA, Box S109.
167. Layton to Salter, 30 Sept. 1925, LNA, Box S109.
168. "Europe's Recovery – Recent Progress," 9 Oct. 1925, BBC Written Archives Centre, Caversham [BBC WAC], Salter Scripts.
169. Salter to E.F. Wise, 4 Nov. 1925, LNA, Box S115. See also Salter, "Possible Lines of French Government Memorandum as to Composition of Preparatory Committee," 22 Oct. 1925, Salter Papers, File 5, League of Nations, Economic, United States of Europe, 1925-1930.
170. Salter to J. Henderson, 18 Sept. 1925, LNA, Box S115, The Manchester Guardian, 16 Oct. 1925.
171. Salter to H.R. Cummings, 13 Dec. 1926, LNA, Box S119. Salter later confirmed the sequence of events in his "The League of Nations in Action: An Actual Example of How a War was Stopped," The Highway, (Oct. 1930), 8-11. See also his accounts in The Manchester Guardian, 28 Oct. 1925, The New York Times, 20 Mar. 1927, and The Times, 27 Feb. 1932.
172. Salter to Baker, 21 Dec. 1925, LNA, Box S115.
173. Markham to Joyce Newton Thompson, 26 Nov. 1925, Newton Thompson Papers, BC 643 818.33.
174. Salter to Philip Baker, 8 Nov. 1925, Salter to Howland, 7 Nov. 1925, LNA, Box S115.
175. Salter to Loveday, 3 Nov. 1925, LNA, Box S115.
176. "The Greek-Bulgar Incident, Sanctions," Oct. 1925, LNA, Box 624, reprinted in Salter, The United States of Europe and Other Papers, 173-184. Frank Walters, Drummond and Van Hamel, Director of the Legal Section, responded to Salter's note. See LNA, Box S119, Box 624.
177. Note by Major G.H.F. Abraham, 5 Nov. 1925, LNA, Box S119. Drummond provided updates to the League Directors. See Minutes, Directors' Meetings, No. 150, 11 Nov., No. 151, 18 Nov. 1925, LNA.
178. Salter, "General Survey," in The Financial Reconstruction of Austria: General Survey and Principal Documents, 70-71.
179. Salter to Layton, 15 Dec. 1925, LNA, Box S115.
180. Salter to Young, 16 Dec. 1925, LNA, Box S115. Young refused the invitation. Salter to Young, 20 Jan. 1926, LNA, Box S115.

181. In <u>Journal of the British Institute of International Affairs</u>, 4(Nov. 1925), 313-314.
182. Salter to Margaret Bryant, 28 Sept., 16 Dec. 1925, LNA, Box S115.
183. Salter to Baker, 21 Dec. 1925, LNA, Box S115.
184. Felkin to Salter, 11 Jan. 1926, LNA, Box S115, "Control: Inter-Allied," <u>Encyclopaedia Britannica</u>, 13th ed., vol. 29(1926), 710-719, "League of Nations: The Work of the First Six Years," <u>Encyclopaedia Britannica</u>, 13th ed., vol. 30(1926), 680-688.
185. Norman to Salter, 1 Feb 1926, NA-UK, T176/23.
186. Salter to Norman, 5 Feb. 1926, Salter to Niemeyer, 3 May 1926, NA-UK, T176/23.
187. <u>The Times</u>, 19 Feb. 1926.
188. Curtis to Salter, 17 Feb. 1926, RIIA Papers.
189. Royall Tyler to Elisina Tyler, 19 Feb. 1926, Tyler Papers.
190. Walters, <u>History of the League of Nations</u>, 317.
191. "Poland," 3 Feb. 1926, Salter Papers, File 4, League of Nations, Organization and Administration, 1919-1931.
192. See Chamberlain to Cecil, 9 Feb. 1926, <u>DBFP</u>, Series 1A, <u>1925-1926</u>, W.N. Medlicott, et al. eds. vol. 1 (1966), 412-413.
193. Walters, <u>History of the League of Nations</u>, 319-323.
194. "Note on Completion of the Council," 1926, Salter Papers, File 4, League of Nations, Organization and Administration, 1919-1931, Minutes, Directors' Meeting, No. 159, 24 Mar. 1926, LNA.
195. "Composition of the Council," Apr.-May 1926, Salter Papers, File 4, League of Nations, Organization and Administration, 1919-1931, Salter to Cecil, 26 Feb. 1925, and encls., Cecil Papers, ADD MSS 51113, vol. 43, ff. 25-45.
196. Salter to Violet Markham, 21 Mar. 1926, Markham Papers, 26/10. Salter's P.S., "Please destroy this," thankfully was ignored.
197. Salter, <u>Memoirs</u>, 203-204.
198. [Felkin?] to John Fisher Williams, 22 Mar. 1926, LNA, Box S115.
199. Salter to Niemeyer, 8 Apr. 1926, LNA, Box S104.
200. Howland to Salter, 24 Mar. 1926, Felkin to Howland, 27 Mar. 1926, Salter to Howland, 1 Apr. 1926, Howland Papers.
201. <u>The Times</u>, 3 Nov. 1926.
202. Salter to B.W. von Bülow, 29 Mar. 1926, LNA, Box S115.
203. Salter to Felkin, 17 Apr. 1926, Felkin Papers, AEF/3/1/82, Royall Tyler to Elisina Tyler, 6 May 1926, Tyler Papers.
204. <u>The Oxford Chronicle</u>, 23 Apr. 1926, <u>The Times</u>, 20 Apr. 1926.

205. Salter to Violet Markham, 25 Apr. 1926, Markham Papers, 25/73. Salter had in fact anticipated his mother's early passing. See Salter to Violet Markham, Sunday [sic] Markham Papers, 26/10.
206. Memorandum by Major Abraham, "Proposed Loan for the Settlement of Bulgarian Refugees," 20 Apr. 1926, LNA, Box S104.
207. Salter to Jeremiah Smith, Jr, 24 Apr. 1926, LNA, Box S104.
208. Salter to Charron, 3 May 1926, LNA, BoxS104.
209. Salter to Seydoux, 7 May 1926, LNA, Box S104.
210. Salter to Niemeyer, 14 May 1926, LNA, Box S115.
211. Minutes, Finance Committee, 3, 5 June 1926, vol. 7, LNA, Salter to Reparation Commission, 14 June 1926, NA-UK, FO371/11370, C6976/443/21.
212. Sydney Armitage-Smith to Salter, 30 June 1926 LNA, Box S104.
213. Salter, "Note as to Relations between Reparation Interests and Conditions of Proposed Bulgarian Refugee Loan," 30 June 1926, LNA, Box S105.
214. Salter, "General Survey," in The Financial Reconstruction of Austria: General Survey and Principal Documents, 70-71.
215. Salter to Monnet, 1 July 1926, Salter to Blackett, 1 July 1926, LNA, Box S115.
216. The Times, 9 July 1926. For more complete assessments of the Hungarian experience see Salter, "The Reconstruction of Hungary," Foreign Affairs, 5(Oct. 1926), 91-102, and "The Progress of Financial Reconstruction in Europe," The Europa Year-Book, 1926, Michael Farbman, et al., eds., (1926), 90-95. In August, the League prepared two volumes, one on Hungary and the other on Austria, with prefaces by Salter. De Bordes to Buxton, 16 Aug. 1926, LNA, Box 519.
217. The Times, 22 July 1926.
218. The Times, 27 July 1926, The Financial Times, 27 July 1926.
219. See Minutes, Directors' Meeting, No. 169, 23 June 1926, LNA, Salter to Niemeyer, 17 July 1926, LNA, Box S104.
220. Minutes of the Financial Committee, 19-20 July 1926, vol. 6, LNA.
221. See e.g., Salter to V. Braf, 3 Aug. 1926, Salter to Charron, 23 Aug. 1926, LNA, Box S104.
222. Salter to Niemeyer, 21 Aug. 1926, Niemeyer to Salter, 24 Aug. 1926, LNA, Box S104. In the former letter, Salter noted that the Greeks were asking for a new loan, but concluded that this was "quite out of the question." Salter to Niemeyer, 27 Aug. 1926, LNA, Box S104.
223. Salter to Niemeyer, 27 Aug. 1926, LNA, Box S104.
224. Royall Tyler to Elisina Tyler, 29 Aug. 1926, Tyler Papers.
225. League of Nations, Bulgarian Stabilisation Loan, Protocol and Annexes (Geneva, 1928), 32, Salter to Charron, 11 Sept. 1926, LNA, Box S104.

226. Salter to Charron, 24 Sept. 1926, LNA, Box S104.
227. Salter to Charron, 5 Oct. 1926, LNA, Box S105. An attached memorandum outlined various measures to be taken by the Bulgarian government before the loan was finalized.
228. See press cuttings in LNA, Box S123.
229. Salter, "Romania: Rough Notes on Impressions During Visit, November 5th to 8th 1926," LNA, Box S123.
230. Salter to le Président, 13 Dec. 1926, LNA, Box S123.
231. The Times, 26 Nov. 1926.
232. Minutes of the Finance Committee, 6 Dec. 1926, LNA, Salter, "Preface," League of Nations, Bulgarian Stabilisation Loan, Protocol and Annexes (Geneva, 1928), 4.
233. Boyden to Lamont, 7 Dec. 1926, Lamont to Boyden, 10 Dec. 1926, Lamont Papers, 129-11, 1922-1931, Baker Library, Harvard University, Boston, MA, Morrow to Lamont, 8 Dec. 1926, Morrow Papers, microfilm roll 80.
234. Lamont to Committee on Honourary Degrees, Harvard University, 11 Dec. 1926, Lamont Papers, 129-11, 1922-1931.
235. Salter to Morrow, 16 Dec. 1926, Morrow Papers, microfilm roll 80.
236. Salter to Jeremiah Smith Jr, 15 Dec. 1926, LNA, Box S120. See also, Salter to Owen Young, 16 Dec. 1926, LNA, Box S115.
237. Royall Tyler to Elisina Tyler, 20 Jan. 1927, Tyler Papers.
238. Salter to Mildred Bliss, 24 Jan. 1927, Bliss Papers, HUGFP 76-8, Box 36, Harvard University Archives, Harvard, MA.
239. See e.g., Salter to Dr. Page, 13 Jan. 1927, LNA, Box S116, Morrow to Salter, 24 Feb. 1927, Morrow Papers, microfilm roll 80.
240. Salter to Stoppani, 20 Jan. 1927, LNA, Box 529, 1927: 10C/51057/46431, The Financial Times, 20 Jan. 1927, The Manchester Guardian, 29 Jan. 1927, Salter to Clement Jones, 15 Jan. 1927, RIIA Papers.
241. See "World Economic Problems and Trade Barriers," Manchester Chamber of Commerce Monthly Record, 38(Feb. 1927), 47-51.
242. Chilston to Chamberlain, 24 Feb. 1927, NA-UK, FO371/12076, C1857/490/3.
243. Viscount Chilston to the author, 4 June 1979, author's archive.
244. The Times, 26 Feb. 1927.
245. Salter to Salvadore de Madariaga, 3 Mar. 2007, LNA, Box S116, The Economist, 104(19 Feb. 1927), 383. Salter was at the time anxious to increase the number of women representatives at the conference. Salter to Theunis, 4 Mar. 1927, LNA, Box S116.
246. "The World Economic Conference," Round Table, 17(Mar.1927), 267-286.

247. "What's Wrong With the World? The League Tackles Tariffs and Cartels," Headway, 9(Apr. 1927), 67.
248. "The Economic Conference," The Europa Year-Book, 1927, Michael Farbman, et al., eds., (1927), 3-4.
249. Salter to Wells, 25 Jan. 1927, encl., "Notes on the Present Position of Liberalism," H.G. Wells Papers, Folder S-021, The Library, University of Illinois at Urbana-Champaign, Urbana, IL. See also Salter to Gardiner, 22 Jan. [1927], A.G. Gardiner Papers 1/32, BLPES, London.
250. Minutes, Directors' Meetings, No. 186, 16 Mar., No. 189, 7 Apr. 1927, LNA, "Three Councils or Four," 1 Apr. 1927, LNA, Box S118. Salter's memorandum was reprinted in The United States of Europe and Other Papers, 71-82.
251. Drummond to Salter, 6, 7 Apr. 1927, LNA, Box S118.
252. Salter to Niemeyer, 14 Apr. 1927, LNA, Box 123, Salter to Niemeyer, 4 May 1927, LNA, Box S116. See also Salter to Cecil, 28 Apr. 1926, Cecil Papers, ADD MSS 51113, vol. 43, ff. 46-47.
253. The New York Times, 20 Mar. 1927.
254. The Times, 4 May 1927, The Observer, 1 May 1927.
255. The Times, 4 May 1927.
256. Salter, "Note," League of Nations, Guide to the Documents of the International Economic Conference, Geneva, May 1927 (Geneva, 1927), 1-19.
257. League of Nations, Report and Proceedings of the World Economic Conference Held at Geneva, May 4th to 23rd 1927, 2 vols. (Geneva, 1927).
258. "Economic Conference April 1927," Salter Papers, File 5, League of Nations, Economic, United States of Europe, 1925-1930.
259. Salter to E.F. Wise, 17 May 1927, Salter to Arnold-Foster, 4 May 1927 LNA, Box S116.
260. The World Economic Conference, Geneva, May 1927: Final Report (Geneva, 1927), 20-34, League of Nations, Ten Years of World Cooperation (Geneva, 1930), 196-199, League of Nations, Report and Proceedings of the World Economic Conference Held at Geneva, May 4th to 23^{rd,} 1927, 2 vols. (Geneva, 1927).
261. "The League's Contribution," in The Economic Consequences of the League: The World Economic Conference, (1927), 5-8, Minutes, Directors' Meeting, No. 195, 25 May 1927, LNA. In The Times, 14 July 1927 Salter admitted that "A resolution in favour of *free trade* would probably have secured only a minority of votes; one in favour of *freer* secured unanimity."
262. Royall Tyler to Elisina Tyler, 3 Mar., 11, 14 June 1927, Tyler Papers.
263. Salter to J.H. Jones, 17 June 1927, LNA, Box S116.

264. "The World Economic Conference of May 1927," Nineteenth Century and After, 102(1927), 25.
265. Salter to Sir Alan Anderson, 8 June, Salter to Harold Williams, 8 June, Salter to J.J. Mallon, 1927, LNA, Box S116.
266. Salter to C. Romer, 13 June 1927, LNA, Box S116.
267. The Manchester Guardian, 24 June 1927, The Financial Times, 2 July 1927, The Times, 2 July 1927, The New York Times, 2 July 1927.
268. "The World Economic Conference of May, 1927, How to Secure Practical Results," Address Delivered to the Congress of the International Chamber of Commerce at Stockholm, July 1st, 1927, Stockholm, 1927.
269. The Economist, 105(2 July 1927), 5.
270. Salter to Farbman, 13 July 1927, Salter to E.M. Patterson, 26 Aug. 1927, LNA, Box S116, "The Economic Conference," in The Europa Year-Book, 1927, Michael Farbman, et al., eds., 3-4, "The Contribution of the League of Nations to the Economic Recovery of Europe," The Annals of the American Academy of Political and Social Science,134(1927),132-139.
271. The Times, 14 July 1927.
272. Salter to Norman, 2 June 1927, LNA, Box S123, entry of 7 Oct. 1927, Norman Diary, ADM34/16-1927.
273. "Statement by Salter," Minutes of the Economic Committee, 15 Dec. 1927, vol. 9, LNA.
274. Salter to Morrow, 9 July 1927, LNA, Box S123. Salter let it be known that he approved of Jeremiah Smith Jr as a potential US member of the Financial Committee. Salter to Morrow, 2 Aug. 1927, and Salter to Norman, 30 Aug. 1929, LNA, Box S116.
275. Morrow to Salter, 2 Sept. 1927, Morrow Papers, microfilm roll 80.
276. Salter to Norman, 10 Sept. 1927, LNA, Box S123, Salter to Moorhead, 29 Nov. 1927, LNA, Box S116.
277. Salter, "Economic Organization of the League of Nations," 30 Aug. 1927, LNA, Box S123.
278. League of Nations, "Work in the Economic Field," LNA, Box R2647, 1928-1932.
279. "Economic Policy – the Next Stages," The Spectator, 140(11 Feb 1928), 189.
280. Salter to V.C. Clinton Baddeley, 22 Sept. 1927, LNA, Box S116. Salter declined to revise his entry on the League of Nations for a new edition of the Encyclopaedia Britannica. He agreed, however, to revise his entry on "Allied Maritime Transport." See Salter to Sir Leo Chiozza Money, 28 Sept. 1927, LNA, Box S116.
281. See "Are We Getting Richer or Poorer?" Radio Times, 17(4 Nov. 1927), 239, Salter to M. Green, 12 Sept. 1927, LNA, BoxS116.

282. "The Economic Conference: Prospects of Practical Results," Journal of the Royal Institute of International Affairs, 6(1927), 350-360.
283. Felkin to Jeremiah Smith Jr, 28 Oct. 1927, LNA, Box S116.
284. Royall Tyler to Elisina Tyler, 15 Nov. 1927, Tyler Papers.
285. Salter to Felkin, 19 Oct. 1927, Felkin Papers, AEF/2/1/12.
286. Salter to Felkin, 2 Nov. 1927, Felkin Papers, AEF/2/1/12.
287. Royall Tyler to Elisina Tyler, 29 Nov., 6 Dec. 1927, Tyler Papers, Salter to Moorhead, 29 Nov. 1927, LNA, Box S116. Tyler further wrote: "Poor Elliot Felkin is invaded by half-a-dozen Finance Ministers all wanting to see Arthur." Royall Tyler to Elisina Tyler, 8 Dec. 1927, Tyler Papers.
288. See e.g., Salter to Smith, 12 Dec. 1927, LNA, Box S116, Smith to Salter, 29 Mar. 1928, LNA, Box S123.
289. Salter to Smith, 12 Dec. 1927, Salter to Sir Atul Chandra Chatterjee, 10 Dec. 1927, Salter to Sir Lewis Kershaw, 10 Dec. 1927, LNA, S116.
290. Minutes of the Finance Committee, 3, 7 Dec. 1927, LNA.
291. Salter to Rev. W. Allen, 21 Dec. 1927, LNA, Box S116.
292. Salter to Stoppani, 3 Jan. 1928, LNA, Box 2613, 1928-32: 10A/298/154.
293. "Economic Policy – the Next Stages," The Spectator, 140(11 Feb. 1928), 189.
294. Salter to Strakosch, 23 Jan. 1928, LNA, Box S115, Salter to Janssens, 28 Jan. 1928, LNA, Box S115, Felkin to L.G. Roussin, 7 Feb. 1928, LNA, Box S115, de Bordes to Marcus Wallenberg, 8 Feb. 1928, LNA, Box R2925, 1928-32: 10E/632/203.
295. Salter to Yeates Brown, 27 Jan. 1928, LNA, Box S115, Minutes of the Economic Committee, 8 Feb. 1928, League of Nations Union Papers [LNU Papers], IV,19, BLPES, London.
296. The Times, 17 Feb. 1928.
297. Salter to Ka Cox, 15 Feb. 1928, Salter Papers, File 7, Salter-Mrs. W.E. Arnold-Forster (Ka Cox) Correspondence, 1920s-1933.
298. The Times, 24 Feb. 1928.
299. Salter to Ka Cox, 20 Feb. 1928, Salter Papers, File 7, Salter-Mrs. W.E. Arnold-Forster (Ka Cox) Correspondence, 1920s-1933.
300. Salter to Ka Cox, 20 Feb. 1928, Salter Papers, File 7, Salter-Mrs. W.E. Arnold-Forster (Ka Cox) Correspondence, 1920s-1933. The episode was later recounted in "Illusory Instability," Salter Papers, File 1, Anecdotes and Incidents.
301. The Times, 24 Feb. 1928, de Bordes to de Makay, 10 Apr. 1928, LNA, Box 2925, 1928-1932: 10E/908/203.
302. Minutes of the Financial Committee, 27 Feb.-7 Mar. 1928, vol. 11, LNA.
303. See e.g., Niemeyer to Ivens Ferraz, 10 Mar. 1928, and "Financial Reconstruction of Portugal," 7 Mar. 1928, LNA, Box R2927, 1928-32: 10E/2644, 2565/203.

304. Minutes, 9th Meeting of the 49th Session of the Council, 10 Mar. 1928, League of Nations, Official Journal, no. 2154.
305. Alb. D'Oliviera to Drummond, 5 June 1928, LNA, Box R2927, 1928-32: 10E/4960/203.
306. Salter, Memoirs, 182, Salter, Slave of the Lamp, 105-106.
307. "Relations between the League and the Institute of Agriculture (Rome)," 29 Mar. 1928, LNA, Box R2800, 1928-1932: 10/3369/2016.
308. Salter to Mussolini, 30 Mar. 1928, LNA, Box S115.
309. Salter to Drummond, 1 Nov. 1928, LNA, Box R2800, 1928-1932: 10D/3369/2016, Minutes, Directors' Meeting, No. 280, 12 Nov. 1930, LNA.
310. Salter to the Editor, Encyclopaedia Britannica, 12 Apr., 11 July, 22 Oct. 1928, LNA, Box S115, "Allied maritime Transport Council," Encyclopaedia Britannica, 14th ed., vol. 1(1929), 652-657.
311. Salter to Rost, 21 Apr. 1928, LNA, Box S109, Salter, "Note on the Security for a New Bulgarian Reconstruction Loan in Connection with Bulgaria's Reparation Payments," 31 Mar. 1928, LNA, Box S104.
312. Salter to Layton, 13 Apr. 1928, Salter Papers, File 5, League of Nations, Economic, United States of Europe, 1925-1930.
313. http://www.info.dfat.gov.au/info/historical/HistDocs.nsf/vSearch/2BD921985B F90A28CA256D950 020EA83?openDocument&start=1&Highlight=2, Arthur, Salter&SearchOrder=4.
314. "Note of Conversation between Governor Strong and J.A.S.," marked "confidential and personal," 25 May 1928, LNA, Box S123. For Strong's record of this conversation, see Lester V. Chandler, Benjamin Strong, Central Banker (Washington, DC, 1958), 280-281.
315. Salter, "Notes of Conversations on Monday, June 25th, 1928," LNA, Box S123.
316. Entry of 7 July 1928, Per Jacobsson Diary, no. 10, 9-10.
317. Salter to Theunis, 11 June 1928, LNA, Box S115.
318. Royall Tyler to Elisina Tyler, 2 May 1928, Tyler Papers.
319. Salter to Baddeley, 11 July 1928, LNA, Box S115.
320. Salter to Wilson Harris, 28 July 1928, LNA, Box S115, Salter to J. Mair, 28 July 1928, LNA, Box S115.
321. Salter to de Bordes, 15 July 1928, Salter to Niemeyer, 16 July 1928, LNA, Box S115.
322. "The First Results of the World Economic Conference," in Problems of Peace, Third Series, Lectures Delivered at the Geneva Institute of International Relations, August 1928 (1929), 75-95.
323. Details in NA-UK, FO371/12956, C6124, C6770/921/22, Salter to Drummond, 1 Nov. 1928, LNA, Box S115.

324. Royall Tyler to Elisina Tyler, 10 Aug. 1928, Tyler Papers, The New York Times, 2 Sept. 1928.
325. The Times, 4, 5 Sept. 1928, The New York Times, 9 Sept. 1928.
326. Entry of 21 Sept. 1928, William Lyon Mackenzie King Diary, (J13) p. 5230, Library and Archives Canada, Ottawa, ON.
327. Minutes of the Financial Committee, 30 Aug.-5 Sept. 1928, Salter to Loveday, de Bordes and Rueff, 29 Sept. 1928, LNA, Box S115.
328. Speech by Salter to the Economic Conference of the International Federation of League of Nations Societies, 4 Oct. 1928, LNA, Box S115, The Times, 5 Oct. 1928, The Financial Times, 5 Oct. 1928.
329. Royal Tyler to Elisina Tyler, 5, 6, 7, 10, 13 Oct. 1928, Tyler Papers.
330. Salter to Ka Cox, 12 Oct. 1928, Salter Papers, File 7, Salter-Mrs. W.E. Arnold-Forster (Ka Cox) Correspondence, 1920s-1933.
331. The Financial Times, 4 Oct. 1928, The Times, 12 Oct., 19 Dec. 1928, Salter to Philip Kerr (Lord Lothian), 14 Oct. 1928, Lord Lothian Papers, National Records of Scotland, Edinburgh.
332. de Lucy Fossarieu to Margaret Cleeve, 22 Oct. 1928, RIIA Papers.
333. The Sunday Times, 4 Nov. 1928, The Times, 7, 8 Nov. 1928.
334. The Economist, 10 Nov. 1928 reprinted a memorandum by Strakosh circulated at the June meeting of the Financial Committee of the League.
335. Salter to Strakosch, 23 Nov. 1928, LNA, Box S123.
336. Letter to the editor, The Times, 3 Dec. 1928.
337. Minutes of the Financial Committee, 8 Dec. 1928, vol. 12, LNA, Salter to Governor Émile Moreau, 19 Dec. 1928, LNA, Box S115.
338. Salter to Layton, 27, 28 Nov. 1928 and attached memorandum, Layton Papers, $10^{72(1-3)}$, Salter to Violet Markham, 16 May 1929, Markham Papers, 25/73, copy, April 1929, also in Gilbert Murray Papers, vol. 206, ff. 100-102, Bodleian Library, Oxford. Salter continued his campaign the following year urging the Liberal Party to rethink its foreign policy. See Salter to Murray, 14 May 1930, Murray Papers, vol. 208, ff. 85-86.
339. For the extensive discussion of this issue, see Minutes of the Economic Committee, 15 Jan. 1929, vol. 13, LNA.
340. See "Economic Tendencies Affecting the Peace of the World," 5 June 1929, LNA, Box S118, Minutes of the Economic Committee, 8 Apr. 1929, vol. 16, and Minutes of the Finance Committee, 10 June 1929, vol. 13, LNA.
341. Salter to Drummond, 21 Jan. 1926, Sir Arthur Salter Personnel File, LNA, S874/3100.
342. Salter to Violet Markham, 9 Jan. 1929, Markham Papers, 5/8. Similar sentiments regarding his feeling "increasingly exiled," were expressed in Salter to Joyce Newton Thompson, 8 Jan. 1929, Newton Thompson Papers, BC 643 B22.4.

343. President, Yale University to Salter, 2 Feb. 1928, Salter to President, Yale University, 17 Feb. 1928, Secretary's Office Papers, Yale University, Record Unit [RU] 49, Box 651, Folder 861, Yale University News Release, 19 Jan. 1929, Yale University, RU 24, Box 105, Folder 1066, Salter to Howland and Fosdick, 20 Mar. 1928, LNA, Box S115.
344. The New York Times, 19 Jan. 1929.
345. MacDonald to Salter, 21 Jan. 1929, MacDonald Papers, NA-UK, PRO80/69/1439/3/1797.
346. Salter to Howland, 1 Nov. 1928, 21 Dec. 1928, LNA, Box S115, The New York Times, 19, 26 Jan. 1929.
347. "The Coming Economic Struggle," The Yale Review, 18(1929), 505-519.
348. Salter to President, Yale University, 29 Sept. 1928, LNA, Box S115, Davis to Salter, 6 Feb. 1929, Norman Davis Papers, Library of Congress, Washington, DC.
349. Salter Dinner Guest List, 30 Jan. 1929, Council on Foreign Relations Papers.
350. See Salter to Bullard, 1 Nov. 1928, LNA, Box S115.
351. Foreign Policy Association, Prosperity, Economic Nationalism or Internationalism, Discussed by Joseph M. Pavloff, David Friday and Sir Arthur Salter, February 16,1929 (New York, 1929).
352. The New York Times, 22 Feb. 1929.
353. Minutes, Directors' Meeting, No. 247, 15 Mar. 1929, LNA.
354. Salter to Violet Markham, 28 Mar. 1929, Markham Papers, 25/73.
355. Salter to Layton, 4 Apr. 1929, Layton Papers, 53[1].
356. The Times, 14 Mar. 1929.
357. Salter to Stamp, 18 Mar. 1929, Layton Papers, 97[50].
358. Salter to Young, 26 Mar. 1929, Layton Papers, 97[56(11-15)].
359. Salter to Joyce Newton Thompson, 29 Mar. 1929, Newton Thompson Papers, BC 643 B22.11.
360. Salter to Layton, 4 Apr. 1929, Layton Papers, 53[1].
361. The Manchester Guardian, 26 Apr. 1929.
362. The Times, 8 May 1927.
363. Minutes, Directors' Meeting, No. 249, 11 Apr. 1929, LNA.
364. Salter to Stamp, 29 May 1929, Layton Papers, 97[56].
365. The Economist, 107(15 June 1929), 1333.
366. "Note on Future Work of the Financial Committee," 5 June 1929, Salter Papers, File 4, League of Nations, Organization and Administration, 1919-1931.
367. Salter to Violet Markham, 9 Jan. 1929, Markham Papers, 5/8, Salter to Elisina Tyler, 24 Apr., n.d., Tyler Papers.
368. Salter to Elisina Tyler, 26 Aug. 1929, Tyler Papers.

369. "The League of Nations: Sir Arthur Salter," The Spectator, 143(6 July 1929), 15.
370. The Times, 13 July 1929, The Economist, 109(20July 1929), 107-108
371. Count Coudenhove-Kalergi, An Idea Conquers the World (1953),114, Coudenhove-Kalergi to Drummond, 2 Aug. 1925, minute by Drummond, 15 Oct. 1926, LNA, R1566.
372. Minute by Salter, 6 July 1925, LNA, R1566.
373. Salter, "Notes," Aug. 1929, Salter Papers, File 5, League of Nations, Economic, United States of Europe, 1925-1930.
374. "The United States of Europe Idea," LNA, R2868, reprinted in Salter, The United States of Europe and Other Papers, 84-104, Stoppani to Hugh R. Wilson, 19 Sept. 1929.
375. "Note of Conversation with the Prime Minister on Sept. 4th, 1929," Layton Papers, 97^{56}, memorandum by Philip Snowden, 26 Sept. 1929, CP 261 (29), NA-UK, CAB24/206.
376. The Times, 6 Sept. 1929.
377. "The United States of Europe," Round Table, 20(Dec. 1929), 79-99.
378. Salter to Layton, 12 Sept. 1929, Layton Papers, 97$^{56(1-6)}$.
379. The Times, 21 Sept. 1929. Salter also met privately with Sir Arthur Henderson to press his views. Entry of 16 Sept. 1929, Felkin Diary, AEF 1/1/5.
380. Extract from the Minutes of the Second Committee of the Assembly, Sept. 1929, copy in Layton Papers, 97^{63}.
381. Salter to Dalton, 1 Oct. 1929, Salter, "The B.I.S., The Public Interests Involved," Layton Papers, 97$^{63(1-7)}$.
382. The Times, 14 Nov. 1929, 20 Jan. 1930.
383. Bullard to Mrs. Bagg, 30 Nov. 1914, Arthur Bullard Papers MC008, Princeton University Library, Princeton, NJ. On Bullard see Ernest Poole, The Bridge: My Own Story (1971), Warren F. Kuehl and Lynne K. Dunn, Keeping the Covenant: American Internationalists and the League of Nations, 1920-1939 (1997) and Chris Hedges, Death of the Liberal Class (New York, 2010), 66-69.
384. The Washington Times, 30 July 1918, The New York Times, 31 July 1918.
385. Ethel M. Bagg to Marion Nichols, 21 Dec. 1903, Folder 131, Nichols-Shurtleff Family Papers, Schlesinger Library, Harvard University, Cambridge, MA.
386. The author commissioned an extensive genealogical study of the Bagg family by Noah Belikoff, 9 Jan. 2010, Gaia Research Services, Richmond CA. Author's archive.
387. Helena de Kay Gilder to Mrs. Bagg, 15 Jan. 1905, Helena de Kay Gilder Papers, I. Correspondence, Box 1, Lilly Library, Indiana University, Bloomington, IN, "Voyage Dans L'Afrique du Sud, I-II," Revue Le Tour du Monde, nos. 39-40, 27 Sept., 4 Oct,

1913. Her only other publication was "Mussolini's Program for Italy," <u>Our World</u>, 2(Oct. 1922), 113-115. One of the editors of <u>Our World</u> was Arthur Bullard.
388. See "Letters From the Italian Front: By Marchesa Louise de Rosales to Ethel Mather Bagg," <u>National Geographic</u>, 32(July 1917), 46-67.
389. Bullard to Mrs. Bagg, 25 June 1916, Bullard Papers, MC008.
390. See Ethel Mather Bagg to Sir Horace Plunkett, 30 July 1917, Sir Horace Plunkett Papers, BAG.1, Plunkett Foundation, Oxford.
391. See correspondence between Mrs. Bagg and Arthur Bullard, 16 Dec. 1907-23 Mar. 1929, Bullard Papers, MC008.
392. Bullard to Mrs. Bagg, 3 Oct. 1921 Bullard Papers, MC008
393. Salter to Ethel Bullard, 23 Oct. 1929, Salter Papers, File 8, Salter-Ethel Bullard Correspondence, 1929-1931.
394. <u>The Washington Post</u>, 3 Feb. 1930.
395. <u>The New York Times</u>, 6 June 1931, Last Will and Testament of Louisa L.S. Bagg, 18 Nov. 1929.
396. Salter to Ethel Bullard, 23 Oct. 1929, Salter Papers, File 8, Salter-Ethel Bullard Correspondence, 1929-1931.
397. <u>The Observer</u>, 13 Oct. 1929, <u>The Times</u>, 26 Oct. 1929.
398. Minutes, League of Nations Union Economic Committee, 22 Oct. 1929, League of Nations Union Papers, III.9.
399. Royall Tyler to Elisina Tyler, 28 Oct. 1929, Tyler Papers.
400. Niemeyer to Salter, 4 Nov. 1929, Salter to Charron and Melchior, 13 Nov. 1929, LNA, Box 105, Salter to Melchior, 6 Dec. 1929, LNA, 1928-32: R2655, 10A/14452/2697.
401. Salter to Felkin, 22 Nov. 1929, LNA, Box S123.
402. "Notes on Tariff Truce and Subsequent Negotiations," 4 Dec. 1929, and "Preparations for Tariff Truce Conference," 6 Dec. 1929, Salter Papers, File 5, League of Nations, Economic, United States of Europe, 1925-1930.
403. Salter, "Holding of League Conferences Outside Geneva," 20 Dec. 1929, LNA, 1928-1932, R3586, 50/16145/13346, LNA, Minutes of the Economic Committee, 10 Jan. 1930, vol. 16, Jan. 1930-Jan. 1931, LNA.
404. Salter, "Note as to Economic Work," 12 Dec. 1929, Salter Papers, File 4, League of Nations, Organization and Administration, 1919-1931.
405. Salter to Drummond, 20 Dec. 1929, Drummond Papers, LNA. See also "Annual Summary for 1928 and 1929," Felkin Diary, AEF 1/1/6.
406. <u>The Times</u>, 11 Jan. 1930.
407. Salter to Felkin, 28 Dec. 1929, Felkin Papers, AEF/3/1/96.
408. Entry of 29 Dec. 1929, Felkin Diary, AEF/1/1/6, "Annual Summary for 1928 and 1929," Felkin Diary, AEF/ 1/1/6.

409. Entry of 7 Jan. 1930, Felkin Diary, AEF/1/1/6.
410. Entry of 21 Jan. 1930, Felkin Diary, AEF/1/1/6.
411. "The International Character of the League Secretariat," 13 Jan. 1930, Salter Papers, File 4, League of Nations, Organization and Administration, 1919-1931, also reprinted in Salter, <u>The United States of Europe and Other Papers</u>, 125-138. These ideas were further developed in Salter to Drummond, 24 Jan. 1930, LNA, Box S115.
412. Salter to Theunis, 7 Jan. 1930, LNA, Box S115.
413. Salter to Theunis, 27 Jan. 1930, LNA, Box S115.
414. See Salter to Noel-Baker, 13 Jan. 1930, LNA, Box S115.
415. Minute by R.W. Makins, 24 Dec. 1929, memorandum by Salter, "President Hoover's Proposals," NA-UK, FO371/13541, A8687/279/45. Salter's memoranda, "Food Ships: President Hoover's Proposal for Immunity" and "Freedom of the Seas," were reproduced in his <u>The United States of Europe and Other Papers</u>, 252-270.
416. Entry of 28 Jan. 1930, Felkin Diary, AEF 1/1/6.
417. Salter to Lady Astor, 6, 17 Feb. 1930, Lady Astor Papers, MS1416/1/2/76, Special Collections, University of Reading, Reading.
418. See Salter to Lady Astor, 25 Sept. 1930, Lady Astor Papers, MS1416/1/2/76.
419. Salter to Lady Astor, 17 Feb. 1930, Lady Astor Papers, MS1416/1/2/76.
420. <u>The Times</u>, 20, 21 Feb. 1930.
421. Salter to Noel-Baker, 17 Feb. 1930, LNA, Box S115.
422. Salter to Lothian, 13 Mar. 1930, Lothian Papers, GD40/17/245.
423. Entries of 9, 12 Mar. 1930, Felkin Diary, AEF/1/1/6.
424. Entries of 16, 19 Mar. 1930, Felkin Diary, AEF/1/1/6, Drummond to Salter, 5 Feb. 1927, Sir Arthur Salter Personnel File, S874/3100. It has not been possible to trace the letter Salter wrote to Drummond in March 1930.
425. Entries of 26, 27, 29 Mar. 1930, Felkin Diary, AEF1/1/6.
426. Felkin to Drummond, n.d., Felkin Papers, AEF/3/1/98/142.
427. Salter to Joyce Newton Thompson, 28 Mar. 1930, Newton Thompson Papers, BC 643 B22.6.
428. <u>The Times</u>, 25 Mar. 1930.
429. Salter to Layton, 27 Mar. 1930, Salter to Theunis, 28 Mar. 1930, LNA, S115.
430. Salter to Theunis, 1 May 1930, LNA, Box S115, Salter to Ka Cox, 11 Apr. [1930], Salter Papers, File 7, Salter-Mrs. W.E. Arnold-Forster (Ka Cox) Correspondence, 1920s-1933.
431. Entry of 11 Apr. 1930, Norman Diary, ADM34/19-1930.
432. Salter to Ka Cox, 11 Apr. [1930], Salter Papers, File 7, Salter-Mrs. W.E. Arnold-Forster (Ka Cox) Correspondence, 1920s-1933.

433. Entry of 28 Apr. 1930, Felkin Diary, AEF/1/1/6.
434. Entry of 19 May 1930, Beatrice Webb Diaries, BLPES, London.
435. Quoted in Nicolson, Dwight Morrow, 377.
436. Minute by Dalton, 26 Apr. 1930, memorandum by Cadogan, 8 Apr. 1930, Salter to Drummond, 15 Apr. 1930, Drummond to Cadogan, 24 Apr. 1930, NA-UK, FO371/14958, W4384/31/98.
437. "Preliminary Note on French Memorandum on a "Union Fédérale Européenne," 20 May 1930, NA-UK, FO371/14982, W5805/451/98, reprinted in The United States of Europe and Other Papers, 106-122, The Sunday Times, 17 Aug. 1930.
438. Minutes, Directors' Meeting, No. 271, 23 May, No. 273, 11 June 1930, LNA.
439. Salter to Drummond, 20 May 1930, LNA, Box S115, Salter to Noel-Baker, 22 May 1930, NA-UK, FO371/14982, W5805/451/98.
440. See minutes by Leeper, 21 May, Sargent, 23 May and Vansittart, 27 May 1930, NA-UK, FO371/14980, W5111/451/98.
441. Minute by Noel-Baker, 26 May 1930, NA-UK, FO371/14981, W5585/451/98.
442. Cecil to Henderson, 1 June 1930, NA-UK FO371/14981, W5585/451/98, minute by Howard Smith, 5 June 1930, NA-UK, FO371/14982, W5805/451/98.
443. Minutes of the Committee on the Proposed Federal European Union, NA-UK, CAB27/424, Cabinet Conclusions, 41(30)8, 16 July 1930, NA-UK, CAB23/64, The Times, 18 July 1930. See NA-UK, FO371/14983, W7204/451/98 for the text of the British response. The seminal role played by Salter is analysed in Robert W.D. Boyce, "The Briand Plan and the Crisis of British Liberalism," in Antoine Fleury and Lubor Jilek, eds., Le Plan Briand d'Union fédérale européenne: Perspectives nationales et transnationales, avec documents (Bern, 1998),122-144, and Ralph White, "Cordial Caution: The British Response to the French Proposal for European Federal Union of 1930," in The Federal Idea: The History of Federalism from Enlightenment to 1945, vol. 1, Andrea Bosco, ed., (1991), 256.
444. Salter to Noel-Baker, 7 June 1930, LNA, Box S115.
445. Entries of 11, 13 June 1930, Felkin Diary, AEF1/1/7. Salter to Spender, 23 May 1930, LNA, Box S115.
446. Lothian to Lloyd George, 18 June 1930, Lloyd George Papers, G/12/5/23.
447. Entry of 1 July 1930, Felkin Diary, AEF/1/1/7.
448. Entry of 3 July 1930, Felkin Diary, AEF/1/1/7.
449. Salter, "Economic Councils, General Introductory Note," 23 May 1930, Salter Papers, File 5, League of Nations, Economic, United States of Europe, 1925-1930, Salter to Charron, 4 July 1930, LNA, Box 105.
450. A.F. Whyte to Salter, 22 July 1930, Salter to Whyte, 14 Aug. 1930, Felkin Papers, AEF/3/1/102/356[a-b].

451. Salter to Felkin, 11, 13, 18 July 1930, Felkin Papers, AEF/3/1/101.
452. Salter to Felkin, 18 July 1930, Felkin Papers, AEF/3/1/101.
453. The Manchester Guardian, 12 July 1930, The New York Times, 17 July 1930, The Economist, 19 July 1930.
454. Salter to Elisina Tyler, 19 Aug. 1930, Tyler Papers.
455. The New York Times, 19 July 1930, The Manchester Guardian, 19 July 1930.
456. The New York Times, 4 Aug. 1930.
457. Salter to Norman Davis, 1 Aug. 1930, Norman Davis Papers.
458. The Nation and the Athenaeum, 47(2, 9 Aug. 1930) 556-557, 587-588. Cecil likewise described Salter as "the architect" of European post-war reconstruction. Lord Robert Cecil, "Ten Years of the League," The Living Age, 337(15 Oct. 1929), 204.
459. Salter to Drummond, 20 Aug., Drummond to Salter, 20 Aug. 1930, Sir Arthur Salter Personnel File, LNA, S874/3100. Because of the scheduled visit to India and later to China, Salter's resignation date was delayed to 31 March 1931. Until 14 July 1931 Salter was on temporary appointment with his Director's salary. Drummond to Salter, 1 Dec. 1930, Sir Arthur Salter Personnel File, LNA, S874/3100.
460. Salter to Lady Astor, 25 Sept. 1930, Lady Astor Papers, MS1416/1/2/76.
461. "Note as to Publicity Given to My Note on the Briand Memorandum," 27 Aug. 1930, Salter Papers, File 5, League of Nations, Economic, United States of Europe, 1925-1930.
462. The New York Times, 10 Oct. 1930, The Times, 10 Oct. 1930.
463. "A Lacuna in the League's Technical Organization," 13 Sept. 1930, and Salter's further "Notes," n.d., LNA, Box 123, The Times, 4 Oct. 1930.
464. The Times, 3, 6 Oct. 1930, Discussion in the Second Committee of the Eleventh Assembly, 26 Sept. 1930, LNA, F.852, F/Gold/56, F/Fiscal/50.
465. Salter to Theunis, 10 Oct. 1930, LNA, Box S115.
466. Minutes, Directors' Meeting, No. 279, 8 Oct. 1930, LNA.
467. Entry of 13 Sept. 1930, Felkin Diary, AEF/1/1/7.
468. Salter to Sir John Campbell, 2 Oct. 1930, LNA, Box S115.
469. MacDonald to Salter, 13 Oct. 1930, NA-UK, PRO30/69/1440/625.
470. Salter to Lady Astor, 27 Oct. 1930, Waldorf Astor to Salter, 22 Oct. 1930, Lady Astor Papers, MS1416/1/2/76.
471. Salter to R.N. Barrington-Ward, 27 Sept. 1930, LNA, Box S115.
472. "Trade Within the Empire," The Listener, 4(5 Nov. 1930), 729-30, 762.
473. See correspondence in the BBC Written Archives Centre, Caversham [BBC WAC], R Cont. 1, Salter Talks, File 1, 1926-1948, File II, 1949-1962.

474. "The Economic Organization of Peace," Foreign Affairs, 9(Oct. 1930), 42-53.
475. "Word Finance and Economics: The Next Steps," The Spectator, 145(22 Nov. 1930), 770-771.
476. Salter to Noel-Baker, 21 Nov. 1930, LNA, Box S123, Salter to Drummond, 21 Nov. 1930, Murray Papers, vol. 209, ff. 58-59.
477. The Times, 8, 9 Dec. 1930, The Observer, 14 Dec. 1930. The articles elicited a number of critical responses on Salter's treatment of debentures. See letters to the editor, The Times, 11, 12, 13 Dec. 1930.
478. "Where is Europe Going?" Round Table, 21(Dec. 1930), 1-16.
479. Wedgwood Benn to Drummond, 21 Nov. 1930, Drummond to Salter, 24 Nov. 1930, Press Communiqué, 1 Dec. 1930, LNA, Box R2667, 1928-1932: 10A/24177/2417, The Times, 2 Dec. 1930, The Times of India, 24 Dec. 1930.
480. Entries of 26 Nov., 11 Dec.1930, Felkin Diary, AEF/1/1/7.
481. Royall Tyler to Elisina Tyler, 26 Nov. 1930, Tyler Papers.
482. Salter to Ethel Bullard, 24 Dec. 1930, Salter Papers, File, 8 Salter-Ethel Bullard Correspondence, 1929-1931.
483. Salter to Elisina Tyler, 24 Dec. 1930, Tyler Papers.
484. Entry of 28 Dec. 1930, Felkin Diary, AEF/1/1/7, The Times of India, 24 Dec. 1931.

CHAPTER 5

"PUBLIC TASKS FOR A PRIVATE PERSON," 1931-1939

As Salter sailed for the Far East, he was embarking on more than a final mission for the League of Nations. He was at the same time beginning almost a decade long journey of discovery and reinvention. He had resigned from the League with a reputation as an expert in financial reconstruction, reparations and currency issues and the cachet of being a pioneering international civil servant. That reputation had been enhanced by a growing body of journalism and numerous public lectures and appearances. His connections ranged through all the major European capitals and included European, American and British politicians, bankers, financiers and civil servants. However, he was leaving the League without any firm prospects or plans, beyond his often repeated wishes to write and be free of any institutional attachments. Financial considerations did not as yet weight heavily on Salter, as he had saved and invested wisely throughout the 1920s and had always lived abstemiously.[1] However, he was embarking on a freelance career at a moment of global and financial upheaval. This was the beginning of a path which shortly placed him among the most prominent and sought after analysts of the Depression and related economic, financial and social issues. That reputation he soon parlayed into several other paths which he either chose or fell to him. From author, commentator, lecturer and journalist, he traveled through the roles of economic advisor to the British government, Oxford University academic, Independent member of parliament and, in November 1939, parliamentary secretary to the Minister of Transport. By then the outbreak of war provided yet new horizons for Salter to explore and further enhance his reputation.

Before his departure, Salter had anticipated something of his schedule, writing, "As to my own plans, I expect to be on the Indian job till about Feb. 20. After that uncertainty because (this is very confidential) there is a possibility that the China affair may revive. Rajchman (Director of the Health Section of the League) & Zilliacus (Member of the Information Section of the League) are now there & I expect to hear from them soon after I reach Delhi. If it does I should go straight on & not get back to Europe till June."[2] In fact, even as Salter was at sea on the way to India, the President of the Chinese Republic, General Chiang Kai-shek and his brother-in-law, the Finance Minister T.V. Soong, jointly cabled on 7 January to Drummond. They enquired whether Salter could continue from India onwards to China, with the purpose of discussing the impact of the Depression on China and consulting on further areas of collaboration with the League. The Council of the League approved the visit on 19 January, including Salter's request that he be joined in China with Maurice Frère to provide additional financial expertise.[3] The Times referred to the mission as one of "economic reconstruction." The New York Times commended the choice of Salter – "No name stands higher in the list of tried public servants whom the Secretariat of the League provides than that of Sir Arthur Salter."[4] It was also regarded as significant, that with three League officials either in, or going to China, the Chinese would increase their interest in League affairs. Privately, Keynes wrote to Salter with regard to the China visit, "I am sure that there are immense possibilities in the situation which you will no doubt develop and bring to birth."[5] The Foreign Office as well followed the news of Salter's appointment with interest and approval, noting that Lionel Curtis might have suggested Salter's name to the Chinese.[6]

After short stops in Malta, Port Said and Aden, Salter and Felkin arrived on 9 January at Bombay, and the next day proceeded to Delhi to confirm their schedule for visits and consultations with representative people and institutions in India.[7] Salter, as he was shortly to discover, was scheduled to sail from Columbia on 15 February for consultations with the Chinese government. Time therefore was limited, but sparing himself no inconvenience, allowing little time for rest and even less for recreation or sightseeing, Salter and Felkin embarked on a formidable programme. Efficient prior arrangements, a willingness to cooperate, and advice given with candour enabled the most efficient use to be made of the time available. Besides Bombay and Delhi, Salter and Felkin visited Lahore, Cawnpore, Lucknow, Calcutta and Madras. They consulted representatives of the governments, legislatures and administrations, Chambers of Commerce and other institutions likely to be affected. Representatives of the governments of Bihar and Orissa and of Burma specially travelled to Delhi for the same purpose.[8]

There was another important, though less well publicized purpose to Salter's mission. The Indian delegation to the League Assembly had often spoken to Drummond, regretting the lack of collaboration between the League and India, especially in the technical field. Salter had also been instructed, therefore, to discuss this problem while in India. Thus, beside his consultations with officials, he also lectured to universities at Lahore, Lucknow, Calcutta, Bombay and Delhi. At Calcutta and Bombay he met prominent locals and, under arrangements made by the President, he addressed members of the Legislative Assembly at a special meeting at New Delhi. In a major speech in Bombay on 28 January, the first by a League official in that country, he suggested that India "had much to get from the League and had much to give to the

League."⁹ The results of his conversations with those concerned with League affairs gave Salter the impression of a measure of indifference, and even some hostility to the League. His reception at the universities he visited, he described as "one of critical interest and courtesy, without cordiality." Everywhere his impressions were that India was too deeply preoccupied with its immediate internal affairs to be able to give much consideration to the outer world.[10]

Despite his heavy schedule, Salter took time out to brief friends on his personal impressions. On 18 January he wrote to Ethel Bullard:

> This is a wonderful experience – the sun, the heavenly climate, the colours, the infinite variety of native dress – all this apart from the human & political interest & the actual problems of my job. The only bore is that I have so crowded a programme – as I must leave Colombo on February 15 – that there's no 'elbow room' – there will be no joy-riding. I am just dashing off to Cawnpore (5 hours & several deputations), Lucknow 1 day (a series of meetings & a public speech) & Calcutta (3 days), back to Bombay, then to Delhi again & down to Madras – some 5000 miles of running about inside the country. We're travelling in the greatest comfort & are both extremely well.[11]

To Violet Markham, he confided, "One's general impression is that, with the political forces as they have been allowed to develop – the pace of the advance to responsible govt. cannot be retarded & will have to be accelerated – but that is a tragedy - & an unnecessary tragedy in its origins – that the excessive pace should have become inevitable." Salter continued: "My job is interesting. I don't know if, under present conditions, it can be useful. Still more doubtful am I about anything coming out of my visit to China – but the potentialities there are so great that one daren't refuse a chance however small."[12] In another letter on 10 February, Salter thanked Ethel Bullard for her introductions to people in China, as well as the news that both Yale and Harvard Universities were planning to confer on him honorary degrees. "You must be spending a fortune on the cable services, but is extraordinarily pleasant to feel that one is in touch," he wrote and continued:

> I have had a terrific week of work here, trying to get myself reasonably clear by the time I reach Colombo; & even today, when I am snatching a little time to write this, is pretty full. I spent this morning discussing with members of the Government (Sunday is rather a good day for that) & I am just going to have a garden party of farewell for about 80 people – for we go on to Madras this evening. I am looking forward to China with great interest but considerable

trepidation. I cannot really believe that I can do much good. At the same time there will be the rather worrying feeling that perhaps a great opportunity is there to be seized if one knew how. My work here has been as satisfactory as it could be in the extraordinarily difficult conditions of this transition period. There can be nothing in the world quite like this life of the official in India: & we are getting an inside experience of it that is very interesting. There is so much that will almost certainly be lost as it goes, & yet there is so much that makes one understand the feelings of those who are calling for it to go. What a life it must have been to be a Viceroy or Governor in India in the spacious & comfortable days before the trouble began! There never was such a country for the pageant of life.[13]

When Salter and Felkin left Madras for Colombo on 15 February, the latter noted that they will have travelled about 5,000 miles from London to Bombay, nearly 6,400 miles in India, "or nearly ½ way around the world."[14] Salter was under no illusion that because of the limited time and knowledge of Indian affairs, his report could only be provisional, a point which he made at the outset of the 92-page document. This was completed on 20 February, with the assistance of Felkin, on the sea journey between Ceylon and China.[15] Salter tendered his advice, he wrote, with "considerable diffidence" and noted that his proposals could only be "tentative and provisional." A Scheme for an Economic Advisory Organization of India, published by the Indian government on 10 June, recommended the setting up of a Central Economic Advisory Council, with similar Provincial Councils. As to the composition of the Central Council, Salter recommended that its members, about 50, should represent various types of economic experience, interest or research, with certain precautions taken to assure a balance between different qualifications and types of special experience. The best method of work, with the Central Council meeting only once or twice a year, would be through small specialised ad hoc committees. The Central Council, especially during its earlier years, would devote itself to two main tasks: drawing up a programme for the examination of specific problems; and also reviewing the progress of the past year and recommending policy for the ensuing year. Salter emphasized that, especially in its early years, the Council "should devote its principle attention to subjects on which objective, and largely scientific, investigation is both practicable and valuable. If it embarks upon problems which are at present inextricably entangled with acute political controversy, it will establish traditions and a method of discussion which will seriously diminish its usefulness as an adjunct to the normal machinery of legislation and government." Success, he wrote, "cannot be achieved unless the Governments, both at the Centre and in the Province, not only take immediate and serious account of the recommendations, but also have at their disposal an official machinery which will enable them to take the required action quickly." Finally, he advised that so long as India was preoccupied by constitutional questions no attempt should be made to implement the proposals. The report was favourable received by the press in London, New York and India, but it was never implemented. Many years later Salter wrote of his mission that it "was a fascinating experience, but of more value, I fear, for myself than for India."[16]

On 20 February, still at sea, Salter wrote, "With the finishing of my report to-day, I must try to begin to think Chinese instead of Indian." Salter and Felkin had left India on 10 February crossing first to Ceylon, where they were joined by Maurice Frère. Salter wrote of his spending "two delightful days" and reveled in a two-hour drive at sunrise "through the most romantic scenery I've ever seen." Salter, Frère and Felkin arrived on 2 March in Shanghai from where Salter viewed his mission with a certain amount of trepidation. "I do not know what situation I shall find or what I shall be expected to do when I get to Hong Kong," he wrote. He thought that perhaps the League could act as "an intermediary between China & the Western world in some of its problems." To Violet Markham, he confided, "Here again, I expect an experience of great interest to myself, with not much hope of its being of any value to the country I am going to."[17] By the time Salter left China on 17 April, he had achieved more than his pessimistic approach to his mission might have justified. In the first place, if he was intrigued by India, he ended up enchanted with China. Both his volumes of memoirs digress about this part of his travels and his unpublished manuscript, <u>Anecdotes and Incidents</u>, has numerous vignettes of the people and places he encountered. Salter and his team were given the use of a country house a few miles outside Nanking. There he was visited daily by T.V. Soong for long discussions about economic affairs which were followed by horseback excursions. Among his other visitors were Chiang Kai-shek and Madame Chiang. The latter Salter described as "a remarkable woman, beautiful, courageous, in the first bloom of her beauty, with the slim grace of the Chinese lady of culture, exquisitely dressed and soignée, vivacious and animated."[18] He also made the acquaintance of the American novelist, Pearl Buck, with whom he made several car trips through the countryside. She recalled, "I think I had the only automobile in the city at that time and I drove it myself, much to the shock and surprise of the Chinese." She also confirmed Salter's account of their visit to "suicide rock" and that "he benefited me by his experience and wisdom, some times he came to my house for tea and lingered on to talk."[19] As his visit neared its half-way point, Salter confessed to being "rather dazed" by the conditions he witnessed, "especially at Shanghai & Nanking you are so completely in the West at one moment & then in the East the next."[20] He also wrote to Ka Cox on 11 April, describing his routine.

"Frère & myself discuss, dictate, write & see people from the Government, have walks before breakfast & dinner along the sides of the great amphitheatre which hold a great Ming tomb & the recent Sun-Yat-Sen memorial. I've seen nothing of China yet – apart from one day at Hangchow & haven't worked harder for many years. But it's fascinating work, perhaps all to end in nothing, but that is mercifully hidden. And it may not.[21]

Salter's pessimism about the outcome of his visit was certainly not shared by the Chinese government. T.V. Soong wrote to Salter on 16 April that he was satisfied with the general consultations on economic matters covered in the six weeks' stay. Furthermore, he informed Salter of the Chinese government's decision to pursue, as a result, "close and continuous collaboration" with the technical organizations of the League. In particular, he announced that the Chinese government had established a new National Economic Council as a result of the consultations, and hoped that the relevant economic and financial organs of the League would be at its disposal. Finally, Soong looked forward to "close, constant and fruitful" relations with the League, including the services of a League official to assist with economic planning. On 19 May the League Council approved this new, and very welcome, collaboration with the Chinese government.[22] The British Foreign Office likewise welcomed these developments, with the suggestion that Salter be consulted on these matters on his return.[23]

Salter's visit to China, despite operating within the confines of a League mission, did have wider implications. With his country in a state of civil war, T.V. Soong had focused on domestic economic reforms. In the background, however, hovered such questions as to whether China should retain its silver standard, or adopt the gold standard, and the related decisions about international financial assistance. Both these proved to be of enormous interest to the British Foreign Office, and by implication cast its shadow on Salter's visit to China. Some in the Foreign Office debated rumours, emanating from the United States, of a silver loan to China or even of India going back to a silver standard, a metal it had in abundance. Attached to this was a suggestion, again from the United States, that China should be given a loan along lines previously employed in Austrian reconstruction. It was thought appropriate to inform Salter of this. Ethel Bullard, at the time in the United States and a friend of President Herbert Hoover, discussed these questions with him. When she told him of Salter's forthcoming visit to China, Hoover allegedly replied, "if anyone was so foolish as to try to put the finances of China on a satisfactory footing, he was welcome to do so, and had his best wishes."[24] In addition, Salter was kept up to date by the Foreign Office on matters relevant to his mission. This included the recommendations of the newly formed Economic Advisory Council's report from its Committee on the Chinese Situation. The latter committee had recommended in December 1930, British financial assistance to rebuild the Chinese railway system.[25] The bottom line remained that the Foreign Office was at pains to ensure that Salter's visit remained a purely League affair, and that any outside intervention at that point would only endanger his mission. Nonetheless, there was some support for anything Salter could do to help T.V. Soong in his attempts at financial and economic reforms before considering plans for foreign loans to China.[26] The Foreign Office's view was that in Salter – "At last we have someone who sees things as they are." This was a response to a telegram from Sir Miles Lampson on 2 May who had observed that Salter opposed any large international loan and that T.V. Soong "has been greatly impressed by Salter whose visit has been most opportune and opened up hopeful field for League collaboration." Lampson later added that Salter had mentioned that "he was much impressed by the personality and capacity of Mr. T.V. Soong."[27]

All these cross currents of Salter's mission were discussed when he met with Lampson on 26 April who later described their "long and interesting conversation." Salter confirmed that the first part of his mission, to establish some measure of economic and financial collaboration between China and the League, had succeeded. As for the second objective, establishing personal relationships and offering advice, Salter noted that he had always spoken "frankly and fully" with the Chinese. Hence, he advised that the time was not ripe for an international loan to finance reconstruction and that the rehabilitation of the railway system could be secured by a modest loan, against the customs, for new construction. Lampson concluded his report by noting that Salter's visit had been very useful. Equally impressive is that Foreign Office officials uniformly agreed with Salter's recommendations, and desired to enlist his assistance, described as "a current of fresh air," to influence a change in British policy towards China.[28] Some months later, Salter further discussed his observations on China at the Foreign Office with Sir John Pratt. He emphasized that the entire situation in China depended on "the fundamental political and military position." He singled out those northern areas of China outside of Chiang Kai-shek's control, the challenge from "communist and banditry troubles" in several provinces, and problems within the Kuomintang itself. He gave the Chiang Kai-shek government only a 50% chance of overcoming its difficulties, and therefore he was reluctant to commit the League or approve any international reconstruction loan to China. He preferred to encourage the Chinese government to appoint foreign experts, preferably from the League, to provide advice and build the confidence needed for financial and economic reconstruction.[29] In fact, Salter himself firmly refused to return to China and advised caution regarding the dispatch of any League officials. However, on 19 May the Council of the League went ahead and approved a limited programme of technical cooperation with China.[30]

Even as he had prepared to leave China, Salter completed a final overseas commitment. Unable to attend the Biennial Congress of the International Chamber of Commerce, scheduled for 4 May in Washington, he prepared a speech which was distributed at the meeting. He took for his subject the world economic Depression and detailed what he termed its "special aggravating features," such as the "greater fickleness of modern demand," over-production, the speculative boom of 1929, investor timidity, agricultural over-production, and problems in the currency and financial systems. The latter enabled him to focus on the controversial problem of gold, or what he termed the "mal-distribution" of gold. He argued that there was an artificial scarcity of gold leading to a depression in world prices. He then returned to the recommendations on tariff reduction made by the 1927 World Economic Conference, and added his thoughts on what he termed "the fallacy of the trade balance," suggesting it received too much attention. Finally, he admitted that "the world still knows too little of its own economic processes to be master of its economic destiny." However, he offered hope that the work of the League and newly formed Economic Councils would help to restore confidence so necessary to recovery.[31] The New York Times singled out Salter's contribution as important for "stimulating thought" on the Depression, while The Economist praised the way he "deftly unraveled" such complicated issues as debts, tariffs and gold mal-distribution.[32]

Salter sailed from Shanghai on 28 April to Japan. At sea he reflected:

This has been a fascinating two months. If the present Govt. succeeds – it must be an 'if' though all of China's well-wishers hope that it will. I think we have laid the foundations of League collaboration well & soundly. I have been partly engaged on that & partly on giving personal and confidential advice on all the financial & economic problems they poured out before me. But I have not been negotiating a "League loan" in the ordinary sense, or even preparing the way for one. I have found the work here very much more congenial than in India. With the educated Chinaman one can work with no greater sense of difference of race (& often less) than with the people of the nationalities in Europe. I've not worked so hard for years! Or so satisfactorily I think, subject always to the overhanging political interrogative. Japan will I expect prove interesting – but a rush.[33]

Between arriving in Kobe 30 April and leaving on 7 May, he found Japan indeed to be a "rush." In the middle of his visit he wrote, "But what a programme – 7 days in Japan, 7 speeches, ten official meals, numerous official talks & some attempt to see Kyoto, Nara, Tokio, Nikko, to say nothing of landing at Kobe, speaking at Osaka & embarking at Yokohama."[34] His first speaking engagement was at Osaka, on 1 May, to the Liberty of Trading Association, before an audience of 1,500 people. His theme was the world Depression and the need for greater international collaboration. As always he was at pains to point out that the paradox of the Depression was "that we are poor, not because the world has not enough, but apparently because it has too much." From there Salter traveled to Tokyo for discussions with the Japanese ministers of finance, commerce and industry, foreign affairs and Prime Minister Baron Wakatsuki. With the latter, Salter took a somewhat optimistic view of the future stability of the Nanking regime. There followed further speaking engagements, including one to the League of Nations Union of Japan on 4 May where he drew on his experience of his 10 years with the League. His message was that the League had a continuing role to play if another great war was to be prevented. Most importantly, he argued was "the inter-penetration of the international point-of-view into national life." Thus, he noted that the League had and continued to have a vital role to play, through research and analysis and discussion of the world Depression. His final address was on 6 May to the Japan Economic Federation. On this occasion, Salter spoke again about the world Depression, relying largely on the comments he had sent to the International Chamber of Commerce.[35]

Despite the intensive public schedule, Salter took some time out for sightseeing. On Ethel Bullard's advice he visited Nikko, from where he wrote to her. "And here I am! And very good advice it was. We have had too a perfect day of sun, fleecy clouds & blue sky & the cherry blossom has not yet gone, & the azaleas are just beginning. The Temples are finer than anything I've seen since India. And what a change from dinginess & dilapidation to this spotless order, it is a new & unsuspected world for me." Salter wrote of his impressions of the Cherry Dance at Kyoto, "incomparably more beautiful than anything I've seen on the stage." To Ka Cox he wrote on 6 May, "What a country – six days - & insights & impressions more like a year. The mechanized efficiency on the one hand & aesthetic discipline on the other." Salter summed up his impressions thus: "the tortured and tortuous mind of the Hindu, the primitive vigour of China, the mechanical efficiency & aesthetic discipline of Japan – what a variety!"[36]

In fact, India, China and Japan had served to raise and some times lower Salter's spirits. At the beginning of the year he had written to Violet Markham that 1930

> was a rather bad year for me, feeling that I was no longer in my place at the Secretariat at Geneva – feeling too very much the wrench at breaking ties

that had been so strong, & all aggravated very much by the inevitable but not less painful realization that I am no longer capable of as much sustained intensity of work as I used once to pride myself on. I very badly needed a change & I could not in any case have plunged into affairs at home. I could of course have taken a routine sort of job, but I wouldn't have done any good at anything really exacting. The complete change of scene may I hope make a difference, though it's been far from a holiday so far."[37]

To Ka Cox he had written on 8 February, "I am greatly enjoying myself & am in splendid health. I was glad to find I could write for 9 hours on Friday without ill effects."[38] However, on 15 March, his 50th birthday, he wrote with some sadness to Ethel Bullard, "Today I enter my sixth decade & I fear (though I know this makes you angry) pass definitely <u>from</u> the stage of middle age in any real sense of the term. However I am hoping for a good sixth decade – the fifth has been very good … the time has come for gathering from fields already explored than embarking on new one. I <u>do</u> anyhow very much want to sit down for a bit & <u>reflect</u> & escape the hurry & bustle of daily action at least for a time."[39] Ethel Bullard wrote back stating, "I totally disagree with your middle-aged & self-reflection [sic] attitude. She continued, "You seem to enjoy putting on age – putting yourself on the shelf. I think that everyone should do exactly what they want to if they can, & I only wish you might choose your own way of living. But 50 with a man is just about bringing him to his fullest development. It <u>does</u> enrage me for you to talk in this 'shelf' manner!" For the rest she provided Salter with details of his growing renown in New York and Washington circles, including the arrangement of a meeting between Salter and Herbert Hoover.[40] As he set to leave Japan on 7 May, Salter reflected that "This is my annus mirabilis – or half of one. I'm more than ever sure I was right to leave the Secretariat."[41] As he crossed the meridian, he wrote to Violet Markham, "This has been – or will have been – a wonderful half year for me."[42]

After leaving Japan on 7 May, he arrived in San Francisco on the 20th for a series of engagements arranged by Howland. He had dinner at Stanford University with invited academics and spoke the next day to the Chamber of Commerce and urged greater American support for the League's economic research activities.[43] Although he had anticipated going directly to New York, for further conversations and consultations, he instead went first to Denver and then on to Chicago. On 25 May he spoke at a luncheon of the Chicago Council on Foreign Relations, addressing the issues of the Depression and urging once again a global perspective on events.[44] His New York stay began with a private dinner at the Knickerbocker Club on 26 May to meet with an influential group of bankers.[45] On 31 May, in the course of a radio broadcast, he emphasized his growing belief, confirmed by his travels, that the "Depression was conclusive proof of the economic interdependence of the world." He called for more knowledge of what should be done and better means of achieving this. "No country alone can find the causes; no country alone can find the remedies; no country alone can apply the remedies," he stated. "We need concerted research. We need a common policy; we need co-ordinated action." And the League alone could help secure all these.[46]

This was followed on 1 June with a luncheon in Salter's honour at the Hotel Astor, hosted by the Academy of Political Science and his many American friends. Salter was introduced by Lamont who, in glowing terms, praised his backstage accomplishments throughout the 1920s. Salter took as his subject the fall in the value of silver, a factor which many regarded as one of the causes of the Depression, but a subject on which he had not previously spoken in public. It was his view that the fall of silver had been a result rather than a cause of the Depression. As for causes, he suggested that the demand for silver, *inter alia* as coinage, had declined, while production had actually increased. Certain countries, such as China which was the only important country to use silver currency, and India which used silver as a medium of saving, had no doubt suffered, as had producers of silver. While it might be the case that China and India and other silver-using countries constituted nearly half the population of the world, Salter pointed out that China took only 2.5% of the world's exports. He thus argued that the fall in the value of silver was not the cause of declining Chinese imports or a major contributing factor to the Depression. Turning then to proposals for "amelioration," he dismissed the idea of a world conference, pointing out that this was not a remedy but only a procedure. Nor did he think it useful to try and restrict the supply of silver to raise demand and its price. As for the proposal to offer China a silver loan, he professed that he regarded this as too vague. He apologized for being "critical, destructive, negative," and ended on a more optimistic note, namely, that the danger of war was not imminent.[47] Somewhat later Salter wrote, "I have had an astonishing success over a 'silver' speech, which I made at what proved to be just the right psychological moment." He noted that that it "was greatly welcomed by Wall St., the Federal Reserve people & the Gov't (Hoover & Mellon) as saying what they wanted said but felt difficulty in saying themselves because of the silver producers." He even received a cable from T.V. Soong congratulating him on the speech and also found Keynes, then in New York, in complete agreement.[48]

During the following two hectic weeks Salter met with a large number of friends and admirers, including Howland, Morrow, Boyden and Lamont, each of whom assisted with his stay.[49] This was to be Salter's last meeting with Morrow and he spent some time in his company at Englewood where he also met Colonel Lindbergh. When Morrow later died on 3 October, Salter referred to him as "a great internationalist."[50]

On 2 June, Columbia University conferred on Salter the honourary degree of Doctor of Laws during its annual commencement exercises. He was commended as "always constructive, patient and thorough-going; a natural guide and leader of men." At the alumni luncheon, he suggested that in the battle between what he termed "the universal principle," embodied in the League and the Kellogg Pact of 27 August 1928, designed to renounce war, and the "national or alliance principle" expressed in arms and alliances, he foresaw the ultimate triumph of the former to preserve the peace. Rather rashly, given his aversion to prophesy, he suggested there would be no war in the coming decade, especially if there emerged a greater involvement of public opinion with the academic community. The following day The New York Times commended his views, especially his emphasis on the harmful effect inflicted by the ongoing cycle of pessimism and optimism.[51] From 3 to 7 June Salter visited Washington, staying with Ethel Bullard at her home in California Street. Previously, she had provided accommodation for Felkin on his return, via the United States, to England. She found his company enjoyable and described him as "one of the most attractive people I have ever know." For his part, Felkin noted that she "talked incessantly" of Salter and asked him to tell no one that she was returning to Europe together with Salter.[52] On 4 June Salter spent more than an hour in the company of President Herbert Hoover, a visit organized by Ethel Bullard, followed on 6 June with a visit to Stimson. On both occasions he discussed the missions to China and India and the option of a silver conference. The effect of Salter's views and influence became evident as early as 4 June when the US press reported that Hoover had ruled out a silver conference. Salter told Hoover that the news came as "a great relief."[53] From Washington Salter returned on 10 June to New York for further speeches and meetings. Among the most interesting was one to the New York Bond Club, advertised as "Collective Leadership in Finance and Industry." What the audience heard on 16 June, however, was a pitch for an American "modified form of supreme economic council" to pull the American economy out of the current Depression and prevent future ones. He also recommended this as an alternative to socialism.[54] Salter's next destination was Harvard University where he was honoured with another Doctor of Laws on 18 June. In his address he again spoke of the danger of war and the need for American participation in world events.[55]

After a global tour that had begun in late December 1930, Salter returned briefly to London on 29 June, for what he described as "some urgent conversations," before going on to Geneva. "I've had a wonderful time in America," he wrote, "everyone (outside Washington) in an exceptionally amenable & accessible & thoroughly subdued mood. If only one knew certainly what to preach." He continued, "Six months – in events & impressions it seems a century."[56] The fact is that Salter had in some way discovered his international reputation. He was then determined to keep closely in touch with what he described as matters which were "extremely interesting & important, & contemplate keeping in close touch with certain developments for the rest of this year."[57] His tour also had an impact on his personal life in which Ethel Bullard was playing an increasingly important role. He had used her home in Geneva at the end of December and had stayed with her, at her home, in Washington. She had provided him with contacts in China and helped in the arrangement of his Washington/New York itinerary. She was extraordinarily well-connected and her network spread far and wide across Europe and the United States. She began to co-ordinate her travel plans with his, and when apart they regularly corresponded. In a revealing letter of 8 July, addressed "Well, Arthur dear," she wrote, "I wonder whether life is really as simple for you as you try to make out? I _know_ it isn't for me." She admitted, that given her lifestyle and world-wide contacts, she was "utterly spoiled," but that the "foundations" of her life were missing. She wrote that during the past six weeks "I have shared so much with you that I will now go on to say – that I _am_ at sea as to how it will work further. There is no going back for me – what is – is – I know myself – when a thing has gone deeply below the surface it remains untouched." She concluded by writing, "we've got something which is rare and precious anyhow."[58] She asked Salter not to answer and he did not at the time, but waited for a decade before making up his mind. To some observers, it was evident that Ethel Bullard was "very much in love with Arthur."[59]

Salter remained in Geneva in early July as a guest at the Felkins' home, which he used as a base to catch up with various people. Thanking Joyce Felkin for her hospitality, he wrote, "My life these last ten years has been much more enjoyable than it would have been without Elliott's help and friendship."[60] In the same vein, he later observed that the decade he had spent at the League was "the greatest good fortune of his life."[61] After a short visit to stay with Ethel Bullard in Paris, he returned to England to participate in a conference, held at New College, Oxford on 11 to 12 July, to study the causes of the world Depression. Participants included some of Salter's former colleagues such as Blackett, Brooke, Henderson, Lloyd, Mallon and Wise. The discussion was a wide-ranging one, with the first day devoted to the "Condition of Great Britain." Salter for one urged greater co-operation as opposed to a rigid belief in competition. The following day, he briefed the group on his travels to India, China and the United States, and emphasized his belief that behind world problems lay the fear of war. This created "a crisis of confidence" which had forced investors to keep their funds liquid, not for economic reasons but for political ones. He saw the United States as the only power able to deter aggression and hence restore confidence. While this view garnered some support, for the most part the discussions were "rather inconclusive."[62] Another platform Salter used to air his views was his speech, on 15 July, at the Second Annual Dinner of The Royal Institute of International Affairs (RIIA). He began by announcing that he had "formally resumed residence in my own land" that very day. For the most part he reviewed his usual themes, including his view that China was not a cause of the Depression. However, free from his League duties, he was already taking a more historical and philosophical approach to his analysis. He predicted that China was capable of a "leap forward," that improved communications, such as the transatlantic telephone, were already having global repercussions, and that "remedial and constructive forces," such as the BIS, were capable of coping with the crisis. The key to recovery and to the future, he argued, was adherence to the "universal collective principle." He also suggested that continued crises demanded more research, such as was being done at Chatham. Finally, addressing the current banking crisis in Austria and Germany, he attributed it largely to panic, and in economic terms suggested as a remedy the slogan – "No income without responsibility."[63] Later, commenting on the Prime Ministers' Conference hastily summoned for a meeting in London on 20 July to deal with Germany's financial difficulties, including the withdrawal of short-term credits, he wrote, "This blessed Conference has done very little." He advocated, therefore, what he termed the strengthening of "the collective system" with greater cooperation between debtor and creditor nations.[64]

When Salter had looked towards his return to London, he noted, "I do want to settle down for a bit, & in England now. I hope I shall be allowed to. But an intention to study, reflect & write is I find a poor defence against importunities."[65] On the one hand, he was approached by the publisher Stanley Unwin for a manuscript, but demurred, writing that he had to delay any such plans for the autumn.[66] On the other hand, he remained actively engaged on several matters including the fall-out from his visit to China. Salter had been asked for his views on several recommendations made by the Economic Advisory Council on 29 December 1930 regarding railway rehabilitation in China. His response, contained in a long letter to Sir Victor Wellesley at the Foreign Office, was to dissent entirely from the EAC's recommendation. Instead, he argued that the Banking Consortium for China, despised by the Chinese, should be bypassed in favour of "an international loan issued in national tranches by the present Consortium houses who would thus continue to be associated with the development of China." The entire scheme, to be only implemented when political conditions in China improved, would also be drawn up in cooperation with the League. The Foreign Office recommended the adoption of Salter's approach.[67]

The Chinese question, however, was deferred as the financial crisis intensified for the British government. For his part, Salter used the month of August for mainly private activities. For example, he went on a long motoring tour with Margaret Brooke, spent some time with Violet Markham, lunched with Felkin and Frank Walters, and as usual visited his father in Oxford. He also found a London base, with the help of Marian Henderson, at 66 Cornwall Gardens which remained his home until March 1939. "Arthur is rather wanting to write I think, but one must have a 'room to oneself' to do it in," she wrote on 21 August. Even Lionel Curtis, when talking with Salter on 13 August, encouraged him to use the facilities of Chatham House for his writing plans, thereby building up its reputation as a research institution. Curtis observed that Salter "can show you better than any man alive how to build up an effective research organization."[68]

Public service, however, continued to intrude on Salter's personal plans. On 6 September he was officially appointed to represent Britain at the 12th session of the League Assembly which opened the next day. On hearing of his appointment, Ka Cox observed, "This must be a very odd business – this Assembly – Arthur – his bonds loosed – but his tongue tied – cries everywhere."[69] At the outset Salter likely expected a quiet return to Geneva. He had been briefed before his departure, including the intention of the government to maintain the pound on gold and at its existing parity. Thus on 18 September, at the League's Second Committee (economic and financial questions), he voiced his disappointment that the resolutions of the 1927 World Economic Conference regarding the elimination of tariffs had not been implemented, and resulting in the prevailing crisis.[70] However, he ended up at the centre of a financial storm which first broke on Sunday evening, 20 September. News had leaked that the newly formed National Government in Britain had decided to go off the gold standard. This proved a stroke of good luck for Salter for he had been originally scheduled to speak on Saturday and defend British financial policy of parity. In the event, his speech was rescheduled for Monday, 21 September, a move which he later recalled prevented him from becoming a complete "laughing-stock."[71] On receipt of the news Salter consulted with Cecil on a plan of action. Salter wanted to empower the Council to act and that the financial organs of the League should likewise be free to draw on League resources of staff and money. Cecil cautioned that he would first consult with the French delegation. However, on 21 September Cecil recommended the ideas as "reasonable" to the Foreign Office which saw no harm in them. It was gauged as a gesture more to do with the prestige of the League than any practical results. Consultations with the French the previous day on Salter's proposed comments, however, found the French opposed to their "sensational character," anticipating that it would have "a calamitous effect throughout the world and bring confidence tumbling down in every direction." Among the offending passages were Salter's predictions that the winter months would bring further repudiations of debt, with more countries abandoning the gold standard.[72]

On 21 September Salter went ahead and addressed the Second Committee of the League, reading from a prepared statement. He announced that Britain had abandoned the gold standard because of the massive withdrawal of gold and foreign currency held by the Bank of England.[73] He went on to analyse both the causes and remedies for the crisis. With regard to the former, he singled out debtor nations who were not able to meet their gold obligations and had borrowed "on short term, a very dangerous expedient." He offered three remedies: debtor countries should be allowed to increase their balance of trade in their favour; creditor nations should expand their credit structure; and a revision of intergovernmental debts. To restore confidence, he suggested further short-term credits made available either by private or governmental sources. Finally, he suggested that the financial organs of the League could "play an important part." A resolution, along these lines, including reference to the role of the League, was then submitted to the Assembly.[74] In a further speech to the Second Committee on 23 September, Salter insisted that Britain continued to be a major creditor nation and that "Her ultimate resources were immeasurably greater than her liabilities." With regard to the gap in the balance of payments between creditor and debtor nations, he called for a reduction in reparations and allied debts and suggested that the League could advise "on the principles which should govern public borrowing."[75] Salter himself may have drawn some satisfaction when Hugh R. Wilson took his seat on 21 September, as the first American official to participate in the work of the Third Committee (war and peace, disarmament and security).[76] He would have drawn further satisfaction from The Times which wrote that it was fortunate to have Salter in Geneva, on 21 September, "to make a firm and candid statement which had an instantaneously reassuring effect."[77] Other than providing a forum for discussion of the latest financial crisis, on 23 September the Assembly had ultimately more important issues to deal with, namely, the request of the Chinese government to consider, under Article 11 of the Covenant, the news of the Japanese invasion of Manchuria.

On his return to London on 28 September, Salter found himself without any firm commitments to public life. On a lighter note, and at the invitation of H.G. Wells, he contributed to Wells' series of radio broadcasts "What I Would Do With the World," if one was a dictator.[78] Salter broadcast on 1 October and stated that over the next 20 years he would work to purge the world of "war and the fear of war," establish a stable monetary system, pursue collective security, maintain the League, and direct human nature to serve the common good. He also foresaw a world of "perfected inanimate machines" tending to human needs.[79] All the while, however, he continued to comment on the fallout from the British abandonment of the gold standard. He was quite comfortable, he wrote to Layton, with the pound falling below four dollars, particularly because, in his view, this would not greatly affect domestic wage and price levels."[80] On 17 October in The Times he further developed his ideas about what he termed was "all a crisis of the pound" and his call to halt a further fall. He argued that abandoning gold now meant that "'purchasing power parity' replaces 'gold parity'." He was very much opposed to those who thought that sterling should be allowed to find its true value. He feared for its effect of increasing the cost of living, inviting the dangers of inflation and its potential to reduce Britain's balance of payments, both visible and invisible. He hoped that the pound would be stabilized at about four dollars and not depreciate further. The dominant consideration, he concluded, was to avoid any increase in the cost of living such as would then "force up the wages, costs and prices level."[81] Salter carried on his analysis in further publications. On 12 December he wrote of "The Future of the Pound" in The Spectator. Here he raised the question about what parity would stabilize the pound. The most important, in his view was general domestic price levels, determined by wages and costs of production. Again Salter cautioned against the "'vicious spiral'" which had gripped European countries in the 1920s. Hence, he contended that the first priority was to maintain the pound's internal purchasing value. And in general, he maintained that every effort should be made to prevent any "increase in the cost of living as would involve increases in the wage and cost of production level."[82] He also surveyed the entire period of the financial crisis since June for The Yale Review. He focused on a larger perspective, suggesting that the combined economic and financial crisis had the potential to erupt in "social revolution" but was "capable of human solution." The key requirement, he suggested, given the inability of debtor nations to meet their obligations without new credits, was a reduction of "the gap in the balance of payments between creditor and debtor countries" to prevent further defaults. While various remedies were available, such as lower tariff barriers, programmes of public works, increasing the supply of money and reductions in reparations and Allied war debts, "the heart of the whole problem" was the necessity to create new long-term lending and investment conditions. Salter also added his personal perspective, arguing that what was also required was an improvement in the climate of inter-state relations, rooted in the security that could be offered by the League Covenant and the Kellogg Pact. In the short term, however, he saw no general return to investor confidence and, hence, advocated extending moratoria in debtor countries and government guarantees for new foreign lending as was done for Austria in 1923. This article earned Salter The Yale Review award of $2000, announced on 19 September 1932.[83]

However immersed Salter was in this ongoing stream of publications, his overall focus still remained a larger scale writing project. In the autumn Stanley Unwin had returned to the charge, asking him for a manuscript. He had in fact already signed a contract with George Bell and Sons and the American publisher Century Company for a book on the impact of the Depression on finance and trade.[84] Distractions, however, continued to come his way. In early November the Foreign Office tried to recruit Salter, described as "well known English economist," to write an article for an American periodical on Britain's position on war debts. Salter responded that besides being unwell with flu, he had "so much already in hand that he cannot undertake to do anything more."[85] Ka Cox visited with at this time, finding him "far from well – <u>very</u> gloomy – about the world as one may well be, & about himself. I gather he is reassured about health, but this next 6 months is going to be very hard on him – I think. Marriage – you know – has its uses."[86] It was also interesting that the Foreign Office received reports that the government of Siam contemplated having Salter visit Bangkok to provide financial advice. It was understood that Salter did not have the time.[87] Salter's name was also one proposed by Cecil to join the forthcoming League Commission of Enquiry to Manchuria agreed to by the League Council on 10 December.[88] In the event Lord Lytton was appointed and took the chair, but Salter let it be known that he supported the Council's approach to the Far Eastern crisis, namely, that Japan must withdraw its troops prior to any negotiations. "War should not be used as an instrument of national policy," he wrote, and observed that such compliance would also have a positive effect on the economic and financial crisis.[89] Certainly, the RIIA took up some of his time. There he offered his views on "The Future of the Pound" as well as on silver, and also served on the Publications and Study Groups Committees.[90] And as always Salter was called upon to comment on European affairs. On 23 December the BIS at Basel issued its report on Germany's capacity to carry on with its reparations payments and this led to plans for a forthcoming conference on the subject. Salter's views received attention in <u>The Observer</u> on 27 December. During the course of an interview, he faulted Germany's for its financial policies of irresponsible foreign borrowing, but linked the question of reparations to war debts. He also wished the forthcoming conference to consider the relation of the world financial crisis debts and reparations, not an entirely popular view.[91]

On 31 December Salter wrote: "I have been & am working very hard on a book on the general situation, which I call 'Recovery: The Second Attempt' & hope to publish it in a couple of months. It has been fun doing it, but fatiguing."[92] "I am trying hard to write rather an elementary book on the general situation, but I find it very difficult, partly because events move so fast," Salter further observed in early 1931.[93] Yet even as he continued to finalize what was to become his best-selling book, he continued a hectic pace of lectures, talks and radio broadcasts. On 2 January the BBC carried his talk on "The Prospects of World Settlement." While he admitted the disastrous impact of the deepening Depression and financial crisis, he offered his prescription for "a second recovery," following on that of the post-1918 period. He looked forward to the upcoming Lausanne Conference to provide some solutions to the issues of both reparations and war debts. Solutions to these would also, Salter argued, assist in the related problems surrounding the gold standard, tariffs and foreign lending. Thus once again, as previously and in future, Salter looked to the world's material resources, technology and industrial skills as capable of providing a better life for all, if only mankind would turn to "the regulative wisdom to control and direct its specialized activities" and "sectional interests."[94] He also addressed the global economic crisis, in similar terms, in the annual Halley Stewart Trust lectures. Here he argued that theory and practice, doctrine and experience had to be brought together to search for a path to economic recovery. A "second effort" was needed to overcome what was a global economic crisis. He analysed the reasons for the intensity of the current Depression and suggested more "deliberate planning" would be required in the future. He also posited some "remedies," such as a long-term suspension and reduction of reparation and war debts, monetary reform, including "limited inflation" in France and the USA, a "managed currency," and last but not least, support for the League of Nations. He concluded, "And what man has made, man can reform." All that was required was for people to "think internationally."[95] The Economist, always partial to Salter's views, described his contribution as "masterly."[96]

Salter also found time to address the Lord Mayor of London's meeting in support of the Winter Distress League. He praised the principles of the League, particularly its employment schemes. As well, he lectured at Birkbeck College on 26 January on the subject of the League of Nations and the forthcoming Disarmament Conference, and also found time to speak to the Working Men's College on "Great Britain and World Traffic."[97] That month, too, he contributed to Foreign Affairs on the subject "England's Dilemma: Free Trade or Protection"? Here Salter targeted the recent election results and the emergence of a clearly protectionist movement in Britain. He surveyed policy since the 1927 World Economic Conference and the general failure to reduce tariffs, and attributed much of the current financial crisis to a gap in the balance of payments between creditor and debtor nations. He observed that loans from creditor to debtor nations or the cancellations of existing obligations might alleviate the situation. As to future British policy, Salter guessed correctly, that "a scheme of protective duties of a more permanent character" was in the offing.[98]

The high public profile that Salter was maintaining continued with a six-part series of BBC broadcasts on "The Problem of World Government," beginning on 18

February.[99] He posited the notion that the transportation revolution on sea, land and air created new challenges both for national and world governments, and for industry and trade. One special consequence of this global interdependence, Salter continued, was that tariffs, especially when unstable, created "conflict between world trade and national frontiers." Thus some sort of "world commercial policy" was required, but he conceded that the 1927 World Economic Conference, for various reasons, had not been able to secure any "agreed world policy about tariffs." What form of "world government," he asked, could prevent this "perpetual dislocation?" Salter admitted that ultimately a "World Federation" would supplement and complement but not abolish national sovereignty, with two areas of jurisdiction – tariffs and armaments. "If only these two sovereignties – the right to erect frontiers and the right to raise armies – could be thus restricted by agreement," he argued, then peace would be assured. He described this policy as neither utopian nor timorous but a practical one. He was convinced that world government would "ultimately" come, but only built up by stages. It would not mean, he continued, setting up some new external authority, but instead national governments for certain objectives would "act as a single world government," such as at the League of Nations, which he argued represented the beginning of a real world government. "Every stone in the world structure is a national stone," he suggested, but not all units could be equal in size shape or authority. He further explained that his notion of world government was "essentially international government, not super-state government." This required agreement at stages and no abandonment of absolute sovereignty, except by assent, for specific objectives and by unanimity, and movement towards what he termed "limited super-government." In his final broadcast, Salter looked into the future to predict what world government would look like in 1957. His vision, unduly optimistic, was of a world purged of war.[100]

For several years Salter had enjoyed the friendship of H.G. Wells and it appears to have been reciprocated. Questions of world government, addressed so thoroughly in the BBC radio talks, and also of enormous concern to Wells, had become a much debated issue between them. Wells had sent to Salter a copy of his recently published <u>The Work, Wealth and Happiness of Mankind</u>. In the introduction, Wells wrote, "I cannot say how much I owe in the correction and steadying of my ideas, to the conversation of my friend Sir Arthur Salter." Replying on 21 March, Salter referred to his ongoing work on his own manuscript and continued, "mine is much more a near and middle vision than a long vision like yours. I think I am a pretty loyal disciple to you as far as the ultimate goal [world government] is concerned. But, as you know, with my bias as a working official, I am always trying to build up with what we have rather than clear the ground for a completely new construction."[101] Some time later

Salter added, "I have regarded myself as one of your disciples for more than a quarter of a century."[102]

After visiting with Salter earlier in the year, Ka Cox had written that he was "tremendously full of the book & enjoying life very much in spite of general gloom – with all sorts of irons in the fire, making a good many new 'contacts' I hope – in spite of protesting he sees no-one!" Somewhat later she wrote "he seems to move in higher and higher circles."[103] This certainly reflected Salter's efforts throughout the winter. One of his ongoing concerns was the evolving Manchurian crisis, and the short-lived Japanese military threat to Shanghai, in which he took a close interest. Even as the Lytton Commission traveled to Manchuria, where it only arrived in April, Salter began to contribute to the debate. On 2 February he discussed the situation with the Foreign Secretary, Sir John Simon. Given Britain's military weakness, its over-reliance on its clout in the Far East and the hesitancy of the French, Salter urged "collective and identical pressure" on Tokyo, and a strong British lead at Geneva in support of the Covenant. The risk involved, he argued, would require working together with the United States. Opinion in the Foreign Office was not so certain of American readiness to cooperate to the point of war. Anthony Eden, then under-secretary of state for foreign affairs, thought that "Sir A. Salter would have us court disaster."[104] A short time later, in remarks at Chatham House, Salter professed to understand, though not condone, the economic motives for Japan's sweep through Manchuria. While suggesting some special economic status for Japan on the mainland, he condemned the Japanese military campaign. As for practical measures, Salter supported "collective world action," again including the United States, and non-recognition of "any settlements arrived at the point of the sword."[105] On 18 February he was one of the signatories of a letter to <u>The Times</u>. This condemned Japanese "atrocities," urged "joint action" in China, and suggested Britain secure the cooperation of the United States with the League to exert maximum economic and diplomatic pressure on Japan to respect "the collective system and the sanctity of treaties."[106] On 7 March Salter was among those who spoke at a mass meeting in the Royal Albert Hall organized by the League of Nations Union. What he emphasized, yet again, was that the vital need for "close and cordial cooperation between America and League members."[107]

Salter had in fact been energized by events in the Far East. "I'm hoping immensely the League will retrieve its position over this Shanghai business," he had written on 3 February and continued, "I'm doing everything I possibly can here, & have been having an exciting time."[108] As well, he had been enthused by the historic "Stimson doctrine" of non-recognition. On 8 January Stimson had addressed a note to the Japanese and Chinese governments stating that the United States would not recognize any changes in China which were contrary to the Kellogg Pact or the Nine Power

Treaty of 1922. The Foreign Office followed on 9 January with its own communiqué which acknowledged Japan's reaffirmation of support for the "Open Door." However, as Salter put it, "It was silent upon everything else," and "was the more unskillful – and not less disastrous in its consequences."[109] Throughout his League career Salter had lobbied for greater American participation in League affairs and other collective action. That seemed finally to have been bearing fruit since September 1931 when Americans, such as Norman Davies and Hugh Gibson, began to participate in the work of the League. Stimson then on 24 February, in a letter to United States William Senator Borah and made public, reiterated his warning to Japan and indicated to the League Assembly, then in session, that his doctrine of non-recognition, if adopted by the League, would deter any future act of aggression. The real intentions of Anglo-American foreign policy became a matter of intense controversy both at the time and later, based on the sense that the Americans had taken the initiative which the British obstructed. In fact, recriminations resulting from this contentious matter resurfaced in 1935, when it became known that Stimson was writing his memoirs. In a letter to Lord Stanhope, under-secretary of state for foreign affairs, written after a lunch at 10 Downing Street on 8 April, Salter described Britain's initial response to Stimson as "a direct snub to America," "as a casual mistake," and "a gaffe." On 3 May, in reply to a letter from Stanhope, he returned to the charge, noting that the British response had the effect of weakening the League and was inept. Salter went on to declare that the basis of British policy must be "the utmost possible co-operation with the U.S.A and the fullest support of the League system." In his final letter on 13 June, he urged a greater degree of understanding between the State Department and the Foreign Office.[110]

Even as he monitored events in the Far East, Salter continued his prodigious output and pace of activities. On 3 March he had addressed the London Commercial Club and argued the case for a reduction of German reparation payments. In March Lloyd's Bank Review issued a supplementary number on the Depression and Franco-German economic relations. In his contribution there, Salter again argued that the moratorium on German reparation payments should be continued and further scaled down.[111] On 3 April he broadcast from London to the United States, via the WABC-Columbia network, He reviewed his analysis of the causes of the Depression – the speculative boom in security values, war debts and reparations – but emphasized that greater American liquidity was the first step on the road to recovery. The following day he spoke to the annual Universities Congress at Rhodes House in Oxford, on the subject of Britain's economic future. Here he reiterated his now public views on "freer trade," and his call for a moratorium followed by a moderate payment of reparations and war debts.[112]

In the middle of this, the press reported on 2 April that Salter had accepted the position as chairman of the proposed Conference on Road and Rail, at the invitation of the Minister of Transport, Percy John Pybus.[113] In the House of Commons, Pybus later explained the choice, crediting Salter with the "impartiality and ability to handle conferences of this kind."[114] The participants were to be the four managers of the railways and four representatives of "Goods Transport by Road." The heart of the controversy between the two means of goods transport lay in the fact that roads were maintained at public expense, funded from the rates, while the owners of railways and canals, contributed to the rates but enjoyed no subsidy from public revenues. The result, in the eyes of the railway owners, was unfair competition worsened by the unprecedented growth in all types of road traffic, including transportation vehicles. Trade and industry thrived on these new methods of distribution, thus diverting traffic and business from the railroads. Salter had no direct experience of land transport, however, his candidacy had been strongly supported by Sir Josiah Stamp, chairman of the London Midland and Scottish Railway, and one of the railway representatives. Many years later, Cyril Hurcomb, at the time permanent secretary at the Ministry of Transport, recalled his own part in Salter's appointment:

> When I was attempting to persuade you [Salter] to accept this task, you put your objections to me more tersely. You walked to the window and said: 'Cyril, I am prepared to work for profit, for pleasure or for power. You offer me none of these things.' All I could say was that I should do my best to influence my Minister to put your recommendations on the Statute Book. This, with one exception, was eventually done, Oliver Stanley being the Minister in 1934.

The terms of reference of the inquiry was to establish "what would be a fair basis of competition" and to allow both sides of the industry "to carry out their functions under equitable conditions." The first of 18 committee meetings was held on 14 April with a report scheduled for the end of July.[115] At least at the early stages, Salter regarded the post as a challenge, one he termed "an entirely un-international piece of work."[116]

On 7 April Recovery: The Second Effort, with proofs completed in mid-January, was published in London and New York.[117] In many ways, Salter had been thinking, lecturing, writing and publishing about the issues for years. As well, he had been personally involved, as a national and international official, in grappling with the complexity of related economic, financial problems since before the World War. He candidly admitted in the preface to Recovery that he had no academic qualifications as an economist, nor any business experience. However, his career had brought him into close contact with both, and he wished to elaborate a coherent policy of what he termed a "second recovery." The theoretical basis, from which Salter launched his analysis, was his belief that the prevailing crisis derived from "defects in human organization and direction, from imperfect planning, from weakness in our financial and distributive systems – from essentially remedial evils and essentially removable causes." In his view, the Depression was the result of the decline of laissez-faire with its self-adjusting mechanisms and periods of boom and bust which had not yet been replaced with an alternative economy based on "collective guidance and planned direction." The task, as he set it out, was to find a new way to adjust "competition and individual enterprise with regulation and general planning." He went on to review both the short and long term causes of the economic Depression, and the financial crisis which followed in June 1931, much as he had been doing for the previous 24 months. With regard to the gold standard, Salter advocated an increase in world gold prices to the level of 1929 as a means to create more money and a measure which the Americans could take and thereby "pump" more money into the market. With regard to the world's credit system, he then singled out the negative impact of "ill-directed" foreign lending to governments, and proposed some much-needed reforms to restart a normal flow of investments. He then returned to the familiar territory of reparation and war debts, and argued for a continuation of the June 1931 Hoover moratorium for another four to five years. And again he reiterated his long standing conviction of the need to reduce tariffs on the road to "freer trade," before turning to solutions. "The world's economic mechanism has lost its self-adjusting quality," he wrote. "The defects of the capitalist system have been increasingly robbing it of its benefits." The prospects facing the world, he noted, were "the alternatives of collective leadership, collective control, or chaos." How then could the public interest best be protected, he asked? He then explored this question, beginning with state control. He took the British experience of the First World War to argue that certain enterprises "should be socialized" and that national economic councils should be further expanded. With regard to widespread fears of another war, he argued that security was essential and that Franco-German relations were the key. He warned against an emerging danger of the continent dividing into opposing camps which threatened the collective principle of the Covenant and the Kellogg Pact. He regarded the terms of the Versailles Treaty as "not just, but they were probably as good as the complexities of the questions left by the war allowed." As for the long term, in his view "The framework is there, but the building is incomplete." What he termed the "collective" system had to be fortified, especially by melding the League and the Kellogg Pact, and by America exercising its influence and support for the system. As for "the proposals for action," Salter argued for the restart of foreign lending, a multi-year moratorium or suspension of reparations and war debts, an increase in prices to 1929 levels, a concerted and managed currency policy for countries off the gold standard, and increased public works programs. He also advocated a reduction of tariffs, with gold prices brought back to their 1929 price levels, and most of all what he termed "political appeasement," namely, the re-establishment of the "collective system." He concluded by declaring his faith that humanity had the "material resources, technical knowledge and industrial skill" to achieve recovery.[118]

Recovery became, in Salter's words, "technically a 'non-fiction best-seller'," with over 20,000 copies sold in the first eight weeks. It was very widely reviewed, translated into Italian, Swedish, Dutch and Turkish, extensively advertised and reprinted seven times, with a revised, "cheap" edition appearing in February 1933. The first printing had sold out in the United States in 11 hours. Until August, in fact, it remained on The New York Times list of bestsellers. Salter admitted at the time that "The sales of the book have been very much greater than I ever anticipated when I wrote it." His publisher's response was to attribute part of the success to "a fertile-minded and most energetic and helpful author."[119] On publication day, 7 April, The Times praised the book as "masterly" and "brilliant," a view shared by much of the daily press and weeklies.[120] His enormous success in the United States, at least according to Salter himself, was due to a review by Walter Lippmann. This praised Recovery for its "perspective and proportion," its "liberal view of international relations," and for Salter's recognition "that we are living in a world economy." The New York Times Book Review lauded the book for its "insight and candour" and for providing a successful "general map" of the crisis.[121] Some rare discordant notes, however, were also struck. The Times Literary Supplement, while generally praising the book, suggested it "smacks strongly of Geneva." So too, Sir Basil Blackett, though complementing Salter's "flashes of brilliance," observed that Recovery read like "a series of brilliant memoranda" and that Salter's solutions were vague on details. Sir Ernest Benn considered Recovery "a catalogue of the failures of the Salter method."[122] A more private dissenter was among Salter's new and growing intellectual circle. Beatrice Webb appears to have been quite taken with him, though not always positively. In her diary she referred to "The old governing class, represented by men like Beveridge, Stamp, Cecil [and] Salter." Though she admired their hard work and experience, she was critical of their economic prescriptions. On 8 April Salter arrived to stay overnight with the Webbs, who were also joined by Bertrand Russell. The invitation had come with the comment: "(evening clothes unknown in our cottage; likewise bridge.)" Beatrice Webb afterwards recorded her impressions of Salter:

A short stocky figure, clean-shaven, well-formed hands, kindly bright eyes, curved nose, pleasant unassuming manner, 'classy voice,' good memory alike for personalities and arguments, open-minded, <u>ultra public</u> spirited, obviously self-controlled and hard-working without vanities or moods, he inspires liking and confidence among those with whom he works, whether as superior, an equal or a subordinate. Unmarried, with no 'silly pleasures', his work is his life.

With regard to the impact of <u>Recovery</u>, she wrote: "So far as we could make out he does not believe that his advice will be followed." However, she concluded he was "a collectivist Liberal and ardent internationalist (he began, it appears, as a Fabian.)"[123]

Salter was quite pleased of course with the reception of his book, and with the many complimentary letters coming to him.[124] He acknowledged that the book was "being very generously reviewed," and that comments had been "very full and favourable." However, he wavered between hope the book would have some influence, to admitting that "I don't delude myself that it will ever have any visible effect on action."[125] On 16 April he wrote to Joyce Newton Thompson, "After being a vagabond for ten years I'm now the most stationary of persons – never going many miles from London, in which I like living immensely. I'm having rather a success – at least a *success d'estime* – with my book both here & in America, & rather enjoying it." In another letter he commented, "I'm enjoying the freedom of my work & life in London immensely; & all the opportunities of making & renewing acquaintances."[126] Clearly, Salter now relished his leaving the League and his life in London. He admitted that on leaving Geneva he was really for the first time without a salary and wondered how he would fare as a freelance writer and consultant. He need not have worried. He had left Geneva with a comfortable pension and had substantial savings and investments. While much of the public work he undertook was unpaid, his writing career was already proving profitable, and he was certainly, between the two, as busy as he wanted. Finally, it is the case, as one of his friends observed, he had "made a lot of money by it."[127]

In one sense, Salter was being somewhat modest regarding the impact of <u>Recovery</u>. His views on foreign loans were discussed in the Foreign Office. He also pressed his views on the necessity for a moratorium in a meeting with British Treasury officials.[128] Perhaps most importantly was the impact in the United States. Walter Lippmann wrote: "Your book has made a great impression in this country. I see it everywhere and on all the best seller lists and portions of it have even been read into the Congressional Record by Senator Borah."[129] The impact went much further to the highest levels of government. On 8 August Stimson, addressing the Council on Foreign Relations in New York, discussed the implications of the Kellogg Pact for

American foreign policy. There was little doubt at the time that the analysis of this treaty in Recovery, and the suggestion that it was vital for the United States to confirm that it would consult with other signatories in the event of war, influenced the content of Stimson's speech. Particularly, this was evident in Stimson's reference to the fact that the pact did indeed carry with it "the implication of consultation."[130] The Living Age probably summed up American reaction best when it noted that Recovery "has caused the greatest international sensation" since Keynes' Economic Consequences of the Peace.[131]

As the work on the Road and Rail Conference continued, Salter had accepted another public task, one more to his liking. On 27 January 1930 the Labour government had established an Economic Advisory Council, composed largely of economists, to provide it with information and advice on a range of issues. The Economic Advisory Council did not survive the 1931 financial crisis and was largely superseded by the Committee on Economic Information, formed on 14 July 1931. Four days later Salter accepted MacDonald's invitation to join and from his first attendance until the committee issued its last report on 20 July 1939 he was present at all of its meetings, in the company of colleagues such as Keynes, Stamp, Henderson, Sir Ernest Simon and Sir Sydney Chapman. The issues considered by the committee varied over the years, but its earlier reports, largely influenced by the thinking of Keynes, Salter, Stamp and Henderson, argued that economic recovery required policies of cheap money, public works and relief for overseas debtor countries.[132] Looking back on the committee, Salter conceded that it "was an interesting experience. But in fact we had little practical effect. Our reports were secret, and could be, and were, rejected or ignored by any department which disliked them, without explanation in public, or even in private to ourselves."[133] He added that the main reason he continued to attend was that the participants enjoyed each other's company and exchanging ideas.[134] Despite Salter's views, the Committee on Economic Information was a pioneering British attempt to engage economists to provide expert advice to the government.

Even as the work of the Conference on Road and Rail and the Committee on Economic Information proceeded, Salter continued to be widely engaged. On 11 May he had received an honourary LL.D (Doctor of Laws) from the University of Manchester. Already the recipient of several honourary degrees on the continent and the United States, this was his first British honour. In his address, Salter renewed his plea for greater international co-operation to achieve disarmament and economic recovery.[135] A second one, a D.C.L., was bestowed on him at the Oxford Encaenia on 22 June. The Public Orator, Dr A.B. Poynton, introduced Salter as "the pride of the City and the University, born in Speedwell Street (in *vico Faustitatis*), brought up among Oxford's boats, educated in its High School."

After a review of his career, Salter was then complimented for exhibiting "that most welcome and salutary spirit which great men, like M. Briand, had infused into the counsels of nations." The Vice-Chancellor, Dr. F. Homes Dudden, then addressed Salter as "a man of utmost wisdom, most knowledgeable in economics and monetary matters, who has long worked at the League of Nations to solve the tortuous problems of international affairs." Several members of Salter's family attended, including his father.[136] Throughout most of June he was critical of what he regarded as "the dangers of excessive economy" with regard to both personal and public spending.[137] On 13 June he added to his commitments by joining a Bank of England committee set up to monitor the interests of bondholders of various League loans. The Financial Times commended his appointment, indicating he "has an unrivalled knowledge and experience of European reconstruction work." Privately, Salter revealed that his intentions, at least, were to secure "some recognition by debtor govts. of the special character of League loans."[138] In the meantime he continued to add his voice on a variety of issues. On 30 June he used The Times to suggest that what was required was a policy of "reflation," a word coined by him to mean "the increase of the general level of wholesale prices to a point not higher than that of 1929," in order to restart depressed economies and recovery. He lauded American attempts at reflation and urged the British government similarly to increase money supply, have the Bank of England further lower its discount rate to stimulate demand, and, of course tariff reductions. Most of all, he urged the British government to take a lead.[139] On the same day this article was published, Salter delivered the 1932 Burge Memorial Lecture at the Middle Temple Hall, one of the oldest of the Inns of Court. His focus was upon the political aspects of the Depression, which he first characterized as partly due to "unutilized productive capacity" not being translated into purchasing power, resulting in unemployment and Depression. The capitalist or "competitive" system, he suggested, was unable to operate effectively to deal with the breakdown of the gold standard and the ongoing problems of war debts and reparations. In his concluding remarks, he stated: "Planning, national and international, is required not to replace freedom and enterprise, but to save them from suicide."[140]

At the time, Salter had also turned his attention to two international conferences, dealing with issues in which he was deeply involved. On 9 July the representatives of Britain, Germany and France had concluded an agreement, subject to ratification, for a three-year moratorium on German reparations and subsequent annual payments of only one-tenth fixed by the Young Plan of 1929. Salter of course welcomed the outcome, which he hoped would lead to "world recovery."[141] He wrote to MacDonald that the political situation in Germany was still unsettled and "the chief risk of the Lausanne

Scheme is failure of ratification there and not elsewhere." He also included a draft statement to be made by MacDonald welcoming the Lausanne accords, one which the latter refused to use.[142] Speaking on the same subject at the Chatham House Annual Dinner on 15 July, Salter described the agreement as "the candle-light of new hope," and referred to reparations as "this ancient evil which has poisoned the life of the world" since 1919. He took the event as signifying a "landmark pointing to recovery."[143] In print, as late as October, Salter wrote that "the success was practically unqualified and complete." Part of his reasoning was that a moratorium accorded with the interests of France which would not have tolerated complete cancellation. As for war debt, Salter urged debtor states to negotiate separately with the US for a reduction rather than cancellation, an option he considered impossible given American opinion and the forthcoming presidential elections.[144] The other gathering to draw Salter's attention was the Ottawa Conference held between 21 July and 20 August. Writing on 11 June, Salter had singled out the looming question of Empire Free Trade or Imperial Preference, "as the most dangerous." He cautioned that some of the Dominions were extremely protection minded, despite their being exempted in the March 1932 Import Duties Act, and negotiations "may well lead to a deadlock." Alternatively, he feared that agreement in Ottawa might be based on Britain having to maintain high tariffs against foreign countries, on which British exports were highly dependent.[145] On the eve of the conference's opening, Salter returned to the subject in a major article in The New York Times. He argued that empire free trade was "a complete illusion" because the Dominions would never permit Britain to compete with their newly established industries. However, he suggested that a possible solution would be empire wide "reflation" to increase price levels to that of 1929. In time, he cautiously welcomed some of the results of the conference, such as the adoption of principles on the "reciprocal remissions of existing tariffs," but strongly criticised imperial preferences based on the most favoured nation principle and the British commitment not to reduce existing tariffs.[146]

When Salter undertook the chairmanship of the Road and Rail Transport Committee, he described the competition between road and rail as of "an embittered character." His primary mandate was to establish "what would be a fair basis of competition and division of function between rail and road transportation of goods." The committee was also directed to make further recommendations "to assist the two sides of the industry to carry out their functions under equitable conditions." Over a period of three and a half months Salter's negotiating and mediating skills proved to be up to the task. The unanimous report, drafted by Salter himself, was completed on 29 July. Pybus wrote to him on 9 August, commending his "skill of presentation" and his "gifts of Chairmanship."[147] Among the recommendations of the report, released publicly on 17 August, were proposals for the higher taxation and licensing of commercial motor-vehicles and some legal restrictions on the transfer of certain goods from railways to roads. The report also examined the questions of what it termed "Community Use" (those paying rates and taxes) and "Legacy from the Past" (the existing pre-motor age roads). After complex financial analysis, the report recommended ways to distribute equitably annual road costs between users. It went on to examine the regulations to be applied to the transportation of goods by road and rail and to make various recommendations, including the requirement for all hauliers to hold an operating license. In his conclusion, Salter emphasized that the report was an integral whole and had been arrived at by "concessions on both sides."[148] Reaction to the report was naturally mixed. MacDonald wrote to Salter that some relevant people he had seen were "loud in your praise."[149] Others lauded his "tact, ability, and impartiality." The Times termed the report "a remarkable document," lauding Salter and his colleagues for going about their work in a "thoroughly practical and businesslike manner," and looked forward to "a new era of collaboration between former rivals." The Financial Times described the report as "a remarkable achievement." The New York Times observed that the report had aroused "world-wide interest." However, while railroad interests praised the recommendations, not surprisingly the Road Haulage Association called the "Salter Conference," as it became known, a "betrayal of road transport to the railways." With a few minor changes the report was put into effect in the Road and Rail Traffic Act of November 1933 and remained the basis of the goods transportation system until 1939.[150] Years later Salter professed that "a financial amalgamation" of the road and rail services would lead to a monopoly which would then allot traffic between the two on some sort of scientific basis.[151]

With the report concluded, Salter again turned his attention to commentary and analysis of world affairs. Early September saw the publication of a collection of essays, The Causes of War, commissioned by the executive committee of the recent World Conference for International Peace through Religion. Salter contributed the introductory essay on "The Economic Causes of War," a subject on which he always wrote with conviction. He argued that economic competition, such as protective tariffs, or problems relating to credit, currency, raw materials and commercial policy, would ultimately constitute the greatest threat to peace. His conclusion echoed that of the 1927 World Economic Conference, namely, what was required was greater agreement by governments on the principles that should guide national and international economic policy.[152] Later in the month Foreign Affairs carried his contribution to the tenth anniversary edition, "The Future of Economic Nationalism." He began by boldly calling for a transformation of the capitalist, or as he preferred, the "competitive" system, by "deliberate planning." The choices the world faced "at one of the great crossroads of history," he argued, were between a system of "closed units," each aiming a self-sufficiency, or "building up world trade within a framework of a world order." In case of the former, major states and empires will move toward self-sufficiency with a minimum of external trade. If the latter option prevailed, he believed, this would not be the total elimination of tariffs. However, he did posit certain alternatives between the two extremes. The recent collapse of the credit system certainly held out the danger that some countries like the United States would retreat into isolation, while others such as Britain turned to protection. To continue along the path of economic nationalism, however, was to prolong the ongoing causes and impact of both the 1929 Depression and the 1930 financial crisis. As for the future, Salter returned to his theme of "collective control" and "collective wisdom." The world economy, he concluded, pointed towards greater world trade and world order and away from economic nationalism. That direction, he wrote, "is the greatest challenge ever given to the constructive and collective intelligence of man."[153]

The results of the Ottawa Conference continued to preoccupy Salter. In a full-page, feature article in The New York Times on 2 October, he turned his attention first to the significance of the conference for the future development of the British Empire. He suggested that various agreements on tariffs would have only a limited impact, but that the Dominions were now "completely masters of their commercial policy." The worst feature, he wrote, was the extension of imperial preference, in his view a retrograde move because it threatened the general principle of the "open door."[154] Finally, Salter expressed ongoing opposition to the growing movement towards "protection and preferences" which he believed threatened not only global trade but world peace. In a letter to the editor of The Times, he even questioned the constitutionality of the Ottawa agreements and suggested that imperial preference threatened the most favourite nation clause, a chief obstacle to tariff reduction. He specifically praised the recently concluded Belgian-Dutch Convention, providing "progressive reciprocal reductions of tariffs, within a regional context" as the road to take.[155] Some further comments on the Ottawa agreements appeared in The Spectator, where he derided a few "novel and regrettable principles" introduced into British policy. Among these he singled out the fact that the new agreements would hinder relations with such important trading partners as Argentina and Denmark. He also expressed a fear regarding the negative impact the agreements would have on non-self-governing British colonies whose trade might no longer be governed by the "open door."[156]

Salter's unrelenting campaign against the Ottawa agreements derived in part from his vision of global economics developed at the 1927 World Economic Conference. It was also driven, perhaps, by a kind of desperation. When dining with him on 6 October, Beatrice Webb quoted Salter as saying, '"We have to make one more effort to make the system a success." She went on, "Salter is a public spirited, puritanical, pleasant mannered and essentially kindly man, absorbed in the daily task, with an acute and cultured intellect …and he will defend loyally the status quo, as in duty bound, even to the last ditch."[157] Nonetheless, Salter realized that his views came at a price. On 10 October he confided to Violet Markham that he had "snapped any fragile links I may have had with the present powers that be. When they began to say it was a contribution to reduction of tariffs through a World Economic Conference, I thought I had to make some protest, as after all that's something on which I have some special experience. I shan't much regret being dropped from such consultations as they've been good enough hitherto to invite me to – for it's been increasingly clear that they were quite useless."[158] He wrote similarly to Royall Tyler who reported to Elisina Tyler that Salter "says he is quite out of official things now, having given offence for attacking Ottawa."[159]

There were sufficient other issues and engagements to capture Salter's attention. On 10 October he confessed that he was "very anxious" over the armaments' situation, particularly because of the British tactic of talking separately to the Germans and the French.[160] The World Disarmament Conference which had first met in February 1932, in Salter's view, had made very little progress.[161] A letter to the editor of The Times on 12 October, which Salter drafted and signed along with 24 other notable personalities, focused on trying to discourage the a growing trend to allow Germany a degree of limited rearmament. It argued that this would only lead to a new arms race. Instead, the signatories reaffirmed their support for a program of "qualitative disarmament," such as the prohibition of offensive weapons under international supervision, and renewed support for what was in Salter's phrase, "the collective system," including the Kellogg Pact.[162] Salter then broadcast on the BBC on the prospects for disarmament, or what he preferred to term, "a reduction and a limitation of armaments." However, how could this be achieved, he asked? He conceded that the system of "pooled security," including the Covenant, Locarno and the Kellogg Pact, had not provided the security needed to encourage disarmament. Given Germany's demand for equality, he concluded that the only feasible course of action was a measure of disarmament so as to make Germany's demand for re-armament "unjustifiable." He was hopeful that with British, Russian and even Italian and American opinion now in favour, disarmament stood a chance of success.[163] Meanwhile, economic questions continued to engage Salter. Responding to a request in The Times inviting economists to comment on the vexing question of private spending, Salter co-signed a letter which argued that encouraging private savings impeded economic recovery, reduced national income and restricted consumption. A follow-up letter from the same group had to point to the unemployment statistics as proof for their argument.[164]

Salter's growing high profile, particularly in the trans-Atlantic area, soon led to a return visit to the United States. On 2 October it was announced that he would head the list of speakers at a conference, hosted by New York University, from 15-17 November, on the subject of "The Obligations of the Universities to the Social Order."[165] Salter accepted the invitation because it would give him the opportunity to confer with colleagues and friends in New York and Washington. He had already indicated, "I am anxious for a number of reasons to make this visit one of conversations rather than speeches."[166] On his arrival in New York aboard the *Aquitania* on 2 November, he was met by reporters eager to have his views on war debts. Salter later explained: "I replied only 'On that subject my lips are closed. I can say nothing'." Unfortunately, the British United Press quoted him as saying that after the next war debt instalment due on 15 December, Britain would default on future payments to the United States. This misquote immediately reached the Chancellor of the Exchequer, Neville Chamberlain, who wrote to MacDonald that Salter's views were "likely to be accepted as having at least semi-official authority," and further lamented Salter's "mischief." On seeing the misquote, Salter telegrammed to MacDonald and Chamberlain that the statement was "a complete invention." On 4 November he wrote to MacDonald with the details, apologized for any trouble the incident may have caused the prime minister and concluded, "As you will see, however, I am innocent." MacDonald replied that he had never believed Salter had made the statement.[167] The same day MacDonald issued a statement, carried by the American press, clarifying the situation.[168]

With Thomas Lamont acting as his host, Salter embarked on a round of meetings with prominent individuals. The largest informal meeting, to which he had earlier agreed, was on 9 November when he dined with a group of leading members of the Council on Foreign Relations. The "Digest" of the discussion records Salter as stating that he had come "not to preach or set forth a creed, but to learn from you." He then set out three "headings" intended to shape discussion – ongoing cooperation between the United States and the League, United States monetary policy, and the question of tariffs.[169] A few days later, while in Washington, Salter recorded his initial impressions: "I'm having a hectic & interesting time here; plenty of gloom but not (as in June) panic. I always find New York so stimulating that it's difficult to realize their fears & anxieties." Among those with whom he lunched were Stimson and Senator Borah when economic recovery was the main topic of discussion.[170] On 16 November began his first formal engagement, addressing the New York University conference, attended by more than 1,000 representatives from academic and public life. Thomas Lamont, introducing Salter, described him as having served the public for 25 years but never having occupied public office, and "one of the exponents of that spirit of our modern days," dedicated to achieving "the conscious cooperation of men throughout the world." In response, Salter described himself as "an Englishman and a European," a non-academic, but one with certain views about the role of universities. He argued that universities must play a primary role in creating a new "framework of laws, customs and institutions," namely, a new form of governance to safeguard the public interest. This could only be achieved, given the shortcomings of the "competitive system," by "some form of collective planning." He regarded the role of the university as crucial, in producing good citizens, constructive leaders, fostering a sense of internationalism to overcome narrow historical perspective and favouring deliberative planning.[171] On 18 November the Academy of Political Science held its annual meeting which brought together bankers, economists and industrialists to discuss "Steps Toward Recovery." Speaking at the evening dinner, Salter risked voicing the view that the worst of the Depression had passed. After surveying current problems, such as disarmament and economic questions, he observed that world finance was now dispersed between headquarters in London, Paris and New York. Hence greater co-ordination was required, particularly in the world movement of credit with one central directing body, and he expected the United States to lead the way. Salter repeated his view that a key to recovery was "controlled reflation" to raise price levels and a reduction in tariffs. He concluded with an exhortation that "the constructive intelligence, the wisdom and the collective will of man" would rise to the challenge.[172] He later wrote that "I greatly enjoyed America, & am beginning to feel that for me a well-organized life would include one visit a year there."[173]

Salter sailed from New York aboard the *Europa* on 18 November.[174] On his return to London, he received an unexpected invitation from Yale University President, James R. Angell, to accept an academic post. Salter replied that he could not accept an offer which meant his leaving England, owing to his involvement in numerous activities and responsibilities. He was tempted enough to add that he would consider an annual visit to Yale to lecture and offer seminars, and suggested that the academy might one day appeal to him.[175] Among those issues which concerned him at once was the question of the upcoming payment on 15 December of war debts to the United States. On 6 December he sent a note both to MacDonald and the Treasury, suggesting that any settlement would require a "drastic reduction" and the fixing of a "final capital sum to be 'commercialised'." As for the 15 December payment, he recommended paying but reserving the right to claim it as part payment of a final settlement, and payment in gold from the gold reserve, advice which was in fact followed.[176] Speaking to a conference of the National Peace Council in London on 9 December, he pointed out that just as reparations at the Lausanne conference had commuted Germany's liability for a fixed capital sum, he hoped that acting on similar "enlightened self-interest" the same process would apply in the United States toward war debts.[177] At Chatham House on

20 December he took a somewhat different position, first emphasizing some of the weaknesses of British policy with regard to previous negotiations on war debts and reparations. He acknowledged that debt obligations had become "impossibly onerous" and made a case for drastic reduction, primarily because they impeded any economic recovery. He urged that negotiations with the United States take into account American psychology and maintain the maximum of good-will.[178]

Since returning from the USA, Salter felt "fearfully rushed," yet the pace hardly slackened.[179] In mid-December he completed a preface to a new book by a young economist, H.V. Hodson, praising the writer as "brilliant" and the book for its ability to explore emerging economic theories and challenges. In his own preface, Hodson acknowledged his debt to Recovery and his personal acquaintance with Salter.[180] At the same time, in an article for The Yale Review, Salter analysed the financial crisis since the summer of June 1931. He found some signs of recovery as a result of "collective action," such as the Lausanne Conference, the British "conversion operation," completed on 31 October, converting £2,000 million pounds sterling of internal war debt war from a 5% basis to 3.5% percentage basis and thereby securing a budget reduction and lower rates of interest. As for the year ahead, "the most critical in the history of modern civilization," he urged a settlement of war debts, "a world policy of controlled reflation," and a return to "freer trade."[181] Finally, the fallout from the report of 17 August on road and rail transport had continued for months to fuel public and private debate. On 31 October Salter met with Hurcomb and inconclusively discussed whether a response was needed. By mid-December Salter again pressed the case for a public response which resulted on 17 December with the members of the conference signing a 4000 word letter addressed to Phybus and immediately made public. This dealt with "certain misconceptions" that had been advanced, namely, that the road transport industry had not been adequately represented, or that there was to be an increase of license duties on passenger vehicles. In conclusion, the letter noted that the members "remain convinced of the justice of our unanimous recommendations."[182] Commenting on this latest development, The Economist reaffirmed the recommendations of the "Salter Conference" as "equitable and logical."[183]

"Since I came here [from Geneva]," Salter wrote on 31 December, "I've been full of dispersed activities, which have their own attraction & are more satisfying than anything but a really good single job, but not of course so satisfying as that. It is at least much better than Geneva had become for me. I'm very unhappy about developments there."[184] In the meantime the New Year, at least initially, offered more of the same. In his first radio broadcast directly to the United States, from Broadcasting House by way of the National Broadcasting Company, he looked forward to a year of continuing anxiety but with prospects of recovery. He cautioned that the upcoming World

Economic Conference should be carefully prepared beforehand, because "If we enter this conference without a plan we shall certainly come out of it without a remedy." He also digressed on his advice regarding "reflation," saying that it would stimulate business, the burden of debts would be lightened, and the dangers of widespread bankruptcy and default which threatened the credit system would be alleviated.[185] On 9 January The Times announced that Salter would deliver on 18 April the second annual lecture, under the auspices of the Massey Foundation, at McGill University in Montreal.[186] The invitation from Vincent Massey, who had met Salter in Washington three years earlier, had in fact been made on 26 October 1932. When accepting it on 5 November, Salter wrote, "I have long wished to make a visit to Canada." He added that instead of a formal lecture tour he preferred speaking at public and private lunches and dinners where he could engage in "extended conversation rather than formal speaking." As a result Massey advised appearances at the Canadian Clubs in Toronto and Ottawa, and branches of the Canadian Institute of International Affairs [CIIA], the counterpart of Chatham House.[187]

For the most part, however, Salter kept a low public profile in the winter of 1933. Much of his time was dedicated to lecturing, writing and broadcasting, including, for a short time, the BBC programme, "The Week Abroad."[188] He completed revisions to Recovery, with a new Preface, which appeared on 14 February in a cheap edition. At the same time, the League Loans Committee, constituted to frame policy regarding loans sponsored by the League but now in default, and of which Salter had been a member since 13 June 1932, met in London for two weeks at the end of January. It examined the position of defaulting countries, in particular Greece, and considered future policy. Its first annual report on 16 May suggested temporary adjustments in defaulted loans.[189] The continuing controversy of the "Salter Conference" recommendations still commanded public attention. On 7 February, in answer to a question in the Commons on the "Salter Conference," Pybus stated that the government intended to introduce early legislation to implement those recommendations "to provide for the licensing and the better regulation of the transport of goods by road."[190] On 14 February, at the invitation of the Conservative Transport Committee, and before an audience of 200 MPs, Salter defended the report on road and rail transport.[191] One economic issue about which Salter continued to campaign actively was the expansion of public expenditure, such as on public works, as a means to increase demand and thereby raise prices. He had spoken on this issue at the Manchester Reform Club on 10 February.[192] He continued with a letter to editor in The Times, suggesting that it would be wrong to "entertain extravagant expectations" as to the volume of public work that could be undertaken, or its immediate effects on the economy. However, taken together with his own advocacy of "reflation," action at least would have been taken. In both these respects he later wrote in The Spectator, he stood in total agreement with Keynes who was also actively promoting such policies. Salter took his own analysis further by suggesting that subsidized work might also find a place in the private competitive sectors as well.[193] Such were among the issues he discussed, when at the invitation of MacDonald, he spent the weekend of 1-2 April at Chequers. The prime minister wrote that he had "been wanting to see you [Salter] for a long time" and suggested "a short walk and talk about the outlook of things."[194]

Even as he prepared for his visit to Canada, Salter completed the page proofs for a forthcoming book, The United States of Europe, an article for Fortune on "the future of capitalism in a mechanized world," the subject of his Massey lecture, and two lengthy articles for The New York Times. The first of these was on the need to control the traffic in arms. Such a move, Salter argued, required a disarmament convention which would include qualitative prohibition of certain weapons. The next was an exhortation for the United States to provide leadership on the road to global recovery. He pointed out that the signs of recovery in the United States, based on its resources and internal market, would radiate abroad and increase confidence. He also noted that "Renewed hope in America will mean renewed hope everywhere."[195]

On the eve of his departure, Salter observed, "1933 hasn't started better than last year. On the contrary! But the pace of events has so quickened that there must be substantial change – good or bad. I've given up prophesying for the time." However, he also wrote that "all goes well with me personally, & I'm greatly enjoying life in London & the freedom which I now have to write & speak as I like."[196] On 7 April Salter sailed to Canada aboard the *Montclare*, disembarking in Quebec City and arriving by train in Montreal on 17 April, to be met by Vincent Massey and Sir Arthur Currie, Principal of McGill University. Salter's reputation as one of the world's leading economists had proceeded him and his views, already reported widely in the Canadian press, were eagerly sought in every city he visited. In his first such interview for the Montreal Gazette, he digressed on the forthcoming World Economic Conference, analyzing the nature of the monetary, credit and trade issues that had to be resolved. Another interview in the Montreal Star saw him unwilling to offer advice on the Canadian economy, but eager to promote "'freer trade' areas." Mid-day on 18 April, at a special convocation in McGill's Moyse Hall, Salter was awarded the Degree of Doctor of Laws, *honoris causa*. Salter was praised "for his broad vision, his keen insight, his judicial fairness and his sound sense." In the evening, he gave his Massey lecture on "Modern Mechanization and Its Effects on the Structure of Society." His speech, delivered at the Windsor Hotel Hall because of the massive demand for tickets, was before a distinguished and overflowing audience drawn from Montreal's professional and business communities, and was broadcast on 33 radio stations across Canada.[197]

He suggested that new forms of power (oil, coal and electricity) mechanization and communication meant that the resources required for global prosperity were available. Furthermore these complex developments necessitated wide-ranging changes. The older economic model, based on supply and demand, or "the competitive automatic process," he continued, was no longer effective, but must be replaced by "deliberate planning and direction." Salter pointed out that he did not advocate "a system of centralized State control." Rather his solution envisaged "developing appropriate institutions throughout the main spheres of financial and economic institutions activities," something he termed "a system of collective self-government." This would provide regulation and direction, while leaving "a free field for individual or group enterprise." Salter concluded by suggesting that his vision of the future was one that combined "order with liberty." The following day, Massey hosted a well-attended luncheon for Salter at the Ritz Carlton Hotel.[198]

From Montreal Salter travelled to Kingston on 20 April for a dinner with the CIIA. Here he surveyed international and economic affairs, and advocated again for a global policy of "controlled reflation." From there he continued by train to be the weekend guest of the Masseys at their home, Batterwood House, near Port Hope, and then to Toronto on 24 April where he addressed one of the largest audiences ever to attend the annual meeting of the Canadian Club in Toronto. "With engaging modesty and restraint," according to the Toronto Star, Salter spoke on "How Recovery May Come." He urged greater international effort on the three crucial spheres of monetary policy, the credit and debt problem and commercial policy. Salter "himself seemed pleased with the results" and followed that appearance with a dinner with CIIA members.[199] Lunch the next day was with the Centurions' Club and an *ex tempore* speech on current American economic policy. The following morning Salter left to meet with the CIIA's Hamilton branch to discuss US gold policy. An overnight train brought him to Ottawa on 26 April where he lodged at Government House, the home of the Governor-General. His first engagement that evening was a dinner with the CIIA, after which he answered questions and digressed for the first time on his views regarding economic and political planning. The following day it was lunch with the Canadian Club at the Chateau Laurier in Ottawa, on the subject, "Some Questions for the World Economic Conference." After reviewing his usual agenda of monetary policy, prices, debts and the credit system and tariffs, he concluded, to "loud and prolonged applause" that he was an "unashamed internationalist" and with an exhortation that instead of being "slaves of events we must be their masters."[200] On 28 April Mackenzie King hosted a luncheon and dinner for him attended by prominent politicians and civil servants. King noted in his diary: "I had a most enjoyable talk with Salter who is a very solid Liberal, with views essentially sound on National and

International, Industrial & Financial affairs. Does not believe in inflation – but only 'reflation' [to] get level of currency back to where it was. Thinks highly of Roosevelt." As well, they exchanged books they had authored and "had a few pleasant words as well of Violet Markham." On 29 April Salter returned to Montreal for another CIIA dinner at the University Club. He emphasized that "he took a middle course – he was neither an inflationist nor a deflationist, nor was he in favour of complete capitalism or socialism." Rather, he attempted "to combine the best in each extreme."[201] On 2 May he had his first meeting with the Prime Minister R.B. Bennett in Ottawa for what was a frank but inconclusive discussion. Afterwards, they moved on to a luncheon for some 300 individuals given by Bennett in Salter's honour. Despite describing himself as a "political mugwump," Salter repeated his pleas for "controlled reflation." He also suggested the formation of an economic national advisory council with economists, the business community and politicians working together. He concluded by saying "he would treasure the memories of his two weeks' stay in Canada as among the happiest of his life."[202]

On the eve of his departure for New York, Salter wrote to Violet Markham. "I have had a very interesting fortnight & am now going on to the U.S.A. for another. I have seen a good deal here of your friend Mackenzie King. He seems very well, but I think a bit desorienté." He added, "I've got a pretty good picture of people & things here I think, for I've been meeting & talking to representative people almost continuously all day & every day."[203] Salter spent the next fortnight in the New York and Washington areas, meeting with numerous American acquaintances and taking soundings regarding the new Roosevelt administration. He welcomed the new administration's friendlier attitude to the League, including its interest in the forthcoming World Economic Conference.[204] While in New York, he took on a new assignment, engaged by the North American Newspaper Alliance of which <u>The New York Times</u> was a member, to provide exclusive coverage of the conference.[205] As he prepared to return to England, Salter wrote to Massey, thanking him for the arrangements which had "provided for my making a real contact with the leaders of Canadian thought and action." Salter added that he had had an interesting time, both in New York and Washington, having no public engagements but productive private conversations. He never managed to see Roosevelt but met with his "Brains Trust," and even more regretted the fall of the dollar for both its "material and psychological" impact.[206] Salter wrote similarly to Ka Cox on 12 May:

> A rather hectic but very enjoyable time draws near a close....This is a different America from any I've known.... A new situation, a new psychology, completely new people in all the places of power.... R[oosevelt] & the people

round him genuinely wanting international cooperation & a better world system, but not adequately equipped with personnel, still unconscious of the extent of the new complications caused by the fall of the dollar, with strong protectionist forces against him in Congress & elsewhere. But for the fall of the dollar I should have thought the chances of success at the Conference favourable – now I'm doubtful.

Salter added that in Canada he "had all the speaking to suffice for a few months."[207] He left New York on 17 May aboard the *Berengaria* for his return journey and arrived in London a week later.

The return to London offered no let up for Salter, indeed, for the following month his name was hardly ever out of the news. From 29 May to 2 June he attended the International Studies Conference at the London School of Economics and Political Science. This was the sixth of the previously titled Conference of Institutions for the Scientific Study of International Relations, initiated by the League of Nations Institute of Intellectual Co-operation. In his opening address as chairman, Salter lauded the gathering for trying to build bridges "between research on the one hand and practical knowledge on the other." He went on to say that the challenges to the capitalist system, or what he preferred to call "the competitive system," required transformation and the restoration of "a world structure of politics, law, finance and [the] credit and monetary system." For the entire week two committees, meeting in private, discussed the depression and related issues of external trade and finance and the question of state intervention in the domestic economy. Salter played a prominent role in both committees, weighing in on questions such as tariffs, most favoured nation clauses, the Ottawa agreements, and world capital movements, as well as presiding over the final plenary session. The conclusions were submitted as a League document to the secretariat of the forthcoming World Economic Conference.[208] On a lighter note, and at Beveridge's invitation, Salter took on the part of a defendant in a "Mock Trial of Economists" on 13 June at the London School of Economics. For several years Beveridge staged the event in aid of King Edward's Hospital Fund. Accused of spreading "mental fog," Salter pleaded that politicians, not economists, were the real culprits. He lost his case and was condemned, along with Beveridge, "to five years of unsolitary imprisonment in the House of Commons."[209]

It was the World Monetary and Economic Conference, scheduled for 12 June to 17 July that now focused Salter's attention. In his first article as the special correspondent for The New York Times, he argued that the conference must attempt to stem the tide of economic nationalism which had been sapping world trade, and revive "a properly functioning credit system" to restore foreign lending. He also pushed his own agenda of "controlled reflation" to reverse the fall in price levels, and proposed the creation of "a joint equalization fund" of the major powers to provide confidence to capital markets. He cautioned readers that prospects for the conference would be impacted by such external events as the ongoing Disarmament Conference, war debt negotiations and the recent depreciation of the dollar. On 9 June, the American Secretary of State Cordell Hull referred to Salter's prescriptions for currency stabilization, and agreed to the extent that it would have to be part of the larger recovery package. The following day, Salter targeted current financial concerns, such as the balance of payments and currency depreciation, as the major impediments to trade. He regarded his prescriptions as "the framework of a practicable programme" for the conference, but failure would lead to the postponement of recovery and continued economic nationalism.[210] An editorial in The Times on 13 June commended Salter's "luminous" articles for showing what could practically be done by the conference.[211]

The middle of June saw the publication of The Framework of an Ordered Society, reprinting three lectures Salter had delivered in February at Cambridge University. At the time, Salter described his choice as speaker as "very much like being recognized as a real 'economist'!" Describing himself as not in the strict sense an economist, but rather "a practitioner" engaged in administrative work and applied economics, he digressed as to why "planning is now necessary to supplement the working of the competitive price system." He suggested that prevailing controls had merely been improvised, and that "planned control" was essential and should partly be delegated to unofficial institutions. He also further elaborated on his views of "a self-governing and self-regulating economic structure, based upon specialized institutions and group organizations," and how he envisaged the consequent interaction between, for example, an Economic Advisory Council and government. "I believe," he stated, that we can both plan and preserve freedom." He concluded that his lectures were an attempt to "find this middle, or new, way" as an alternative to Communism and Fascism. In reviewing the book, The Economist expressed reservations about Salter's plans for "the elaborate dovetailing of State control and advisory organizations based on private enterprise." However, it praised his bold attempt to contribute to the search for a "third alternative to private Capitalism and Socialism." The New York Times likely went too far in its review by suggesting Salter was recommending "a sort of modified Soviet system of economic planning."[212] The end of the month saw another of Salter's publications, The United States of Europe and Other Essays. This reproduced 17 memoranda he had written while in the service of the League. He described them as documents intended both to clear his own mind so as to decide on action and also intended to possibly influence colleagues and their views. The volume, edited by his friend Will Arnold-Forster, was well reviewed. The Times described the contents as "of exceptional interest," while The Economist noted that Salter had dealt with certain topics, such as economic sanctions under article 16, years before they became "burning questions." Salter confessed that the reviews were better than he expected, even though the book sold poorly.[213]

On 11 June, the eve of the opening of the World Economic Conference, attended by 66 nations, Salter contributed another major article to The New York Times Magazine. He wrote that the conference was meeting at a time of "unprecedented crisis" and carried with it the fate of the world. He then highlighted three major issues that needed resolution – monetary policy, problems of trade and indebtedness, and tariffs. As for the first, he advocated his usual prescription of "controlled reflation" and currency stabilization, noting that there was already widespread agreement on this prescription. He foresaw some progress being made as a result of "the stimulus of cheap money and a prospective rise of prices." He also hoped the conference could agree on measures leading to a fall of both long and short term interest rates, and advocate some principles which could lead to tariff reduction. Finally, he added his usual denunciation of economic nationalism, praised the Roosevelt administration for its renewed interest in international affairs and advised his American readers that "The only way to avoid being the slave of events is to be their master."[214] Writing at the end of the first week of the conference in The New York Times, Salter noted the initial "the mood of deep anxiety" and the atmosphere of "skepticism and doubt." Tariffs, indebtedness and credit problems had complicated proceedings, along with divergences of views among the delegations, leading to talk of failure for the conference. However, he took some comfort from Neville Chamberlain's statement in favour of raising prices by both monetary and economic measures, a move Salter had long favoured, and led him to see the first week ending on a note of "cautious optimism."[215] Beside his public profile, Salter was also active behind the scenes. "I am plunged in the middle of this Conference," he wrote on 28 June. "I have no official position, but am seeing MacDonald each day & doing a good deal of liaison work between him & the different delegations."[216] This arrangement lasted but a short time. At the end of the second week, Salter wrote that the proceedings had "suffered a serious setback." He attributed this to an American reversal of policy on currency stabilization, now taking the new view that it was untimely.[217]

On 2 July, in the middle of the conference deliberations, Salter was invited to argue the case for "economic internationalism" in a front page article for The New York Times Magazine. He contended that there were practicable alternatives between the two extremes of complete free trade or complete isolation. In his view, this could be based on collective security, a credit system that ensured capital liquidity, monetary stabilization, whether based on gold or not, and a moderate system of tariffs.

Failure to achieve these objectives, he concluded, would delay recovery and lead to "an increased menace of war."[218] During the third week of the conference, Salter wrote that the proceedings were dominated by the fluctuations of the American dollar and hence finding any agreement on currency stabilization was difficult, with the added danger of "imminent disaster."[219] Indeed, on 9 July in Salter's words, the conference experienced "a definite setback." This followed Roosevelt's 3 July message to the conference that measures of temporary stabilization, that is, limiting exchange rate fluctuations, were untimely. Salter believed that "a new effort" was required.[220] However, he had been less optimistic on 8 July when he addressed the 23rd National Peace Congress at Oxford, attended by more than 500 members, and conceded that the World Economic Conference "has not been killed, but for the moment it has been crippled."[221] On 20 July he met privately in London with Stimson for a general discussion of the economic situation. Salter praised Roosevelt's steps to balance government expenditure, however, going off gold and the 3 July statement were "as bad as could be." Afterwards Stimson wrote in his diary that Salter had given him "the best statement of views" on economic matters that he had had in London.[222] In what was to be his final comment as special correspondent covering the World Economic Conference, Salter acknowledged on 23 July that it had achieved "virtually nothing." He foresaw no such similar gathering, a period of high protective tariffs and recovery being yet further delayed. He summed up the reasons for the failure as "due to a combination of misfortune, premature convocation and inadequate political preparation."[223] In the event, the conference was finally adjourned on 27 July.

In early August Salter returned to the public eye, albeit it in an unusual format. On 22 March he had dined with the socialist and historian G.D.H. Cole and the journalist, and pacifist, Beverley Nichols. Their discussion of the subject "Is Peace Possible Under Capitalism?" was transcribed in a chapter of Nichols book, <u>Cry Havoc!</u> published on 24 July. Salter spoke first, positing that "that peace can be maintained under capitalism on certain conditions," principally that no one part of the system, such as the armaments or oil industries, should ever be allowed to dictate public policy. Cole maintained that peace was "more likely under socialism." From there, he and Cole debated the role and usefulness of the League, with Salter arguing, "The League is what we make of it." The book became a bestseller and was extensively reviewed, with <u>The Times</u> regarding the Salter-Cole exchange as "a very instructive conversation."[224]

The disenchanted tone of Salter's observations in the summer of 1933 on international affairs likely spoke of his personal predicament. Since his resignation from the League, he had pursued what he termed a "freelance life without office or specific duties."[225] Much as he had enjoyed the experience, it was soon to come to an end.

It might have been partly financial but it was more likely that Salter's prescriptions for the worldwide economic crisis were being increasingly ignored. The collapse of the World Economic Conference presaged a very different world than the one he had championed for years and years. Indeed, in August and September his public pronouncements and contributions diminished and appeared somewhat desultory. On 9 August he spoke to the Liberal Summer School at Cambridge and urged that the demand for the prevailing policy of cheap money should be further stimulated by a programme of public works. The critical reaction of some readers to The Times' report of these views forced him to provide further clarification. On 18 August he conceded that public works would involve some additional costs that could be financed by loans. However, he added that he was not recommending "relief work," but rather expenditure on capital schemes, such as slum clearance, housing and infrastructure by local authorities.[226] On larger issues, Salter used The New York Times to observe that Roosevelt's first six months in office had seen an unprecedented programme of planning implemented "in time of peace and without revolution." Among the questions he addressed were several which would preoccupy him throughout the 1930s. "Is there a tolerable half-way stage between capitalism and communism? Are effective planning and control compatible with economic and political freedom? Will the system which so grows up be compatible with world trade and the development of economic life upon a world basis? Should planning ultimately be national or international?" In a changing world of adequate material resources, knowledge and skills, he argued that cooperation must replace competition. He emphasized that any planning and control should not be left entirely with government but must be supplemented by what he termed "institutional self-discipline." He then applied such a principle to a variety of sections of the economic and financial systems, including currency, international trade, the credit system and industry, also advocating the use of regulatory agencies such as a National Economic Council, the BIS and a new National Investment Board, with the equivalent structures at the international level. Salter suggested that he already saw signs of this "middle way" emerging.[227]

At the same time, however, Salter's reputation remained at its height and his advice sought at the highest level of governance. On 18 September, he joined Stamp and Layton to meet with MacDonald at 10 Downing Street to discuss the decline of the US dollar and the implications of a public works programme. News of the meeting leaked out and reporters dubbed the three economists as "Britain's Brain Trust," much to the prime minister's annoyance.[228] Stimson, who was at the time visiting Britain, then asked for a talk with MacDonald, as well as "Salter, Stamp and Layton as representative British economists." The group reconvened at Downing Street, without Layton who could not attend. Stimson was asked to enter No. 10 by the back door to avoid any of the publicity surrounding the first meeting. The group then discussed some ideas on commodity "price index developments and methods." Stimson found that both Salter and Layton favoured "controlled inflation," but not "bald inflation," that is by printing more money. Stimson afterwards wrote to Salter: "I came away with the impression that while the difficulties of remedial treatment of the present situation are immense and critical, there was a growing unanimity (or rather consensus) as to the diagnosis of the evil."[229]

"Every day brings its tale of disaster – it looks as if Vienna is losing its fight for its soul – it is a cruel tragedy," Salter wrote on 13 September.[230] His growing disillusion, however, was tempered by two future prospects. During the course of the World Economic Conference, Salter had been asked by T.V. Soong, the Chinese delegate, to consider a return visit to China. This tied in well with the fruits of his 1931 visit, with the Chinese following his recommendations to establish a National Economic Council. As well, the China Committee of the League of Nations, founded earlier in the month and dedicated to overseeing the technical cooperation in progress between it and the Chinese government at Nanking, had formally begun to function. Thus on 5 July Salter accepted an official invitation "to advise them in regard to their new plan of reconstruction." He was not hopeful, however, writing later that "I fear the prospects of really doing anything there are not bright."[231] Nonetheless, The Sunday Times, in praising his appointment, described him as "one of the few British economists with a world-wide reputation."[232]

The other development was to have a lifelong significance. During June, Lionel Curtis, himself a Fellow of All Souls College, Oxford, "strongly pressed" Salter to put his name forward for the position of Gladstone Professor of Political Theory and Institutions, established in 1912. The position had become vacant when its first appointee, W.G.S. Adams, took on the position as Warden of the College. On 21 June Adams had urged Salter to accept, downplaying the teaching requirements and emphasizing that it would leave him "very great freedom – especially for big things." Adams continued: "Think of this post not as it is but as what it can be. It is a great call, not only from Oxford but from men all over the world." On 5 July Salter declined, writing that while the position was attractive and offered good opportunities, he felt that he was "better fitted for other work." Salter recalled that "I felt that I was not really qualified by temperament or intellectual equipment for academic life." Personally, he could himself not say how or why he finally did accept. However, further persuasion from Lionel Curtis likely convinced him to change his mind. On 14 October he was officially informed of his election as Gladstone Professor, with the public announcement on 24 October, and the appointment beginning the first day of Trinity Term 1934. The appointment also carried with it a Fellowship of the College. He disclosed privately that he had "made all stipulations as to being able to resign."[233] After almost a year at the University, he observed, "I like my Oxford work, but I still regard myself as mainly a Londoner." Salter retained the chair until he resigned in 1944, but was replaced in wartime by Sir Robert Ensor who was then succeeded, in the renamed chair of Gladstone Professor of Government and Public Administration, by Professor K.C. Wheare.[234]

On the eve of his departure to China, Marian Henderson described Salter as "well, happy, enjoying himself." Salter himself wrote to Felkin about the future:

> I am just off to China again, & wish you were coming with me. I expect to be back in March. Things looked more promising when I agreed to go: with greater uncertainty there & things more critical here I should probably not have agreed to go if the proposal were being made at this moment. Geneva must, I fear, be a gloomy place at the moment, & likely to remain so.[235]

On this second visit to China Salter was accompanied by Guy Wint, a graduate of Oriel College, Oxford. W.D. Ross, the Provost, had asked Salter for letters of introduction for Wint who wished to go to China. Salter replied that he would take Wint along as his private secretary. Having focused his undergraduate studies on the Far East, Wint proved an invaluable assistant, and the trip, as Salter noted, was "the foundation of a long and valued friendship."[236] Since his first visit to China in March and April 1931, the League presence had grown both in terms of personnel and reconstruction. On his arrival in China, Salter was met by Dr. Ludwik Rajchman who had been appointed on 18 July 1933 as "technical agent" to oversee liaison between Nanking and Geneva. He was also joined by Jean Monnet who in a private capacity was there to help organize a Chinese banking consortium, a development bank to oversee bond issues in western markets.[237] All three were independently attached to the National Economic Council which was in charge of reconstruction. Salter defined his mission as firstly to examine economic and financial changes since his last visit, and secondly to recommend future direction for the National Economic Council.

Salter began with a visit to Hangchow in the province of Chekiang from 3-10 January. Although the smallest province in China, it was regarded as the most prosperous, the target of intensive economic reconstruction, and completely under the control of the Nanking government. Thereafter, it was a period of intense consultations which left little time for anything else. He did meet, however, with Chiang Kai-shek who insisted that, while he could not resist Japan in Manchuria, he hoped "some day he would be in a stronger position." In his final report, Salter's noted that since the winter of 1931-1932 China was in the throes of "a severe and deepening Depression," partly due to global economic conditions, but also because of domestic political and external developments. Hence, while China's silver standard had been spared for some time, the departure from the gold standard (the pound, rupee, yen and dollar) had put pressure on the Chinese currency, leading to falling prices and trade, and deflation. In addition, the loss of resource rich Manchuria, and the ongoing conflicts with Japan and the Communists had led to a flight of both silver and gold. At the exact time when capital was needed for reconstruction, China was instead being "decapitalised." Nonetheless, Salter pointed to the potential of reconstruction of the Chinese economy, which if "wisely directed and well administered" could succeed. Hence, he recommended increased exports and agricultural production, balanced budgets, and an expansion of the railways rather than road-building. While planning was essential, given the internal situation in China, he suggested that the National Economic Council intensify its research. Among his suggestions to receive the most attention abroad, was that there should be no "departure from the present silver basis of the Chinese dollar." In a postscript to the report, he professed that his recommendations were "modest and limited," and commented on the difficulties of his mission, including the problems of communication and eliciting vital information.[238] Even before the report was published, his general views were widely quoted in the press, with The Financial Times adding that the analysis would be considered carefully as it came from an "eminent economist."[239]

"It was an enjoyable & interesting time, & great fun to be working with Monnet again," Salter afterwards wrote to Felkin. He continued, "But of course it didn't amount to anything, as I knew it could not when T.V.S[oong] went out [resigning as Finance Minister]. I was already as far as Vancouver when that happened, & though I tried to cancel my arrangements then they pressed me to go & I had no real alternative." He also revealed that he had cracked his ankle jumping across a ditch and "had to hobble about in plaster for a few weeks."[240] Salter then travelled, via Honolulu aboard the *President Lincoln*, to the United States. While in Honolulu he spent some time in the company of Parker Gilbert with whom he had worked on reparations questions.[241] He arrived in New York on 14 March, staying as a guest of Lamont, who once again acted as host. That same evening Lamont arranged a "stag dinner" for Salter, with guests including Owen D. Young and other dignitaries.[242] Salter's only formal speaking engagement was on 21 March to the semi-annual meeting of the Academy of Political Science at the Hotel Astor. There he set a whole new tone, confessing that, while he remained "a believer in internationalism, unrepentant but modest, reasonable and realistic," he recognized the need for "compromise and adjustment." On the one hand, he expressed his interest in what he called "the great American experiment" of combining centralized control with the capitalist system. On the other hand, he called for a more modest agenda, advocating consistency and the avoidance of sectional interests in national policy with an increase in international trade. Turning to international relations, he feared that the prevailing "armed and anxious peace" might result in war. Thus, "not only as an internationalist but as a private citizen of the world," he renewed his plea for a "collective peace system" as the only way to avoid another war.[243] Afterwards, Salter circulated a draft of his report on China among financial circles in New York and Washington.[244] Among many others, he had a long conversation with Stimson, where the subject of China and silver was discussed. He expressed his disapproval of Roosevelt's economic policies, including the purchase of gold as "the wrong way to inflate," preferring instead "expenditures for public works paid for in government bonds." Salter returned to London, aboard the *Ille de France*, leaving New York on 24 March and arriving at Plymouth on 30 March. According to Ka Cox, Salter returned "in good form" and she looked forward to seeing him and Ethel Bullard who was back from Geneva.[245] Reflecting after his long absence abroad, Salter wrote that to many foreigners England appeared as "an oasis of stability, liberty, liberalism and comparative prosperity." Admittedly, "the National Everyman," the majority in Britain, genuinely believed this to be true. But Salter argued that prevailing political and economic institutions were more like "structures built by the instincts of beavers and ants than the deliberately designed creations of reason." The rate and quality of change over recent years, both in government and economics, he continued, required a "combination of self-discipline and public direction. To preserve we must reform, and reform both quickly and drastically. This is surely the lesson, not only of reason, but of the fate of other countries."[246]

Shortly after his return, Salter took up his position at All Souls College. "I am going into All Souls tomorrow and am looking forward to trying a new line of work," he wrote to Lamont on 20 April.[247] Thus began an association which Salter cherished all his life, though not always uncritically. He was given "a beautiful set of rooms" looking across the college lawn to the square of Radcliffe Camera and beyond to his old college, Brasenose. Initially, his instinct that he was not suitable for academic life seemed confirmed. He did not see himself as "a learned or studious person," he felt the age gap between himself, "a bachelor and unsocial official," and undergraduates, and he considered the standard lecture "an unsatisfactory medium." Later he was to find "the meticulous quibbling on trivia matters" of university committees "irritating and exhausting."[248] Much as he had anticipated, however, there was initially one drawback. "Life at Oxford is pleasant," he admitted, "though lecturing is the form of speaking I most dislike, & I can't understand a word of the jargon I find people talking about concepts of political philosophy!"[249] With the approval of university authorities, Salter hired a younger All Souls Fellow, A.L. Rowse, to offer an annual course of 30 lectures on Political Theory (including History & Theory), beginning each October. Rowse, elected a Fellow in 1927, recalled that "Salter knew no political theory and, a life-long civil servant, could not bear the thought of mugging up Aristotle. Hobbes, Locke, Rousseau and Co. So he fixed up a lectureship for me, as his deputy." Rowse also observed that Salter, a middle-aged bachelor, was "very much a fish out of water," in the sense that residential life at the College was dominated "by clever young men" such as Richard Pares and Isaiah Berlin. "At table they kept up a clever-clever 'in' conversation, which Salter was kept out of; he much resented this childish treatment." For his part, Rowse looked up to Salter's wide experience of public affairs and the two quickly formed a friendship that lasted almost for a lifetime.[250] This was a very intimate friendship, but one which Rowse later recalled was completely non-physical; as he wrote, Salter was "hopelessly heterosexual."[251] Salter preferred to describe himself as "not celibate, but not promiscuous."[252]

Given his phenomenal capacity for hard work, Salter threw himself into his new profession, both adapting and innovating at All Souls. Without the burden of lecturing, he instituted a debate-style seminar, with subjects varying according to international developments, for carefully selected undergraduates.[253] He also advised on select graduate research topics and supervised several graduate theses.[254] "Salter was most friendly and helpful to us young would-be economists and politicians," one Fellow recalled, "He was prepared to talk long hours into the evenings both on economics and his great practical experience."[255] Further, given his commitment to marrying the theoretical with the practical and the academic with the non-academic, he arranged meetings between Oxford dons and visitors from Whitehall and Westminster. He also established and chaired the Politics Research Committee and set as its research programme an analysis of advisory bodies, "their influence on government generally, and their place in the thinking of individual departments." Its secretary and co-editor of the book that resulted from the research, was Nicholas Mansergh, who recalled that the exercise enabled Salter to become more familiar with many Oxford dons.[256] An indication of his academic commitment was that his massive journalism output tapered off. Some brief exceptions were a contribution to The Canadian Forum, largely recounting the highlights of his visit to China, and an article in the Daily Herald which suggested that the Communist movement might be contained if economic conditions for the peasants could be improved.[257] This coincided with the official publication in May of China and the Depression, with most of it re-published as a supplement to The Economist. The Economic Forum in New York also published an edition in June under the title China and Silver, emphasizing the aspect of most interest in the United States.[258] The report was carefully read in the Foreign Office where it was described as both "excellent" and "too optimistic."[259]

Some time after his appointment, Salter had written to Mildred Bliss "I am now a don at Oxford, though it is only a part time occupation & I still spend most of my time in London. The two places, & types of work, make a pleasant mixture."[260] The first exercise, using All Souls as a base, soon led to the foundation of the group called "The Next Five Years." For some time Salter had been using such phrases as a "middle vision," a "middle course," and, as in his <u>The Framework of an Ordered Society</u>, a "middle, or new, way." In advocating that there should be a new path between right and left, he was not unique. Many engaged individuals, spanning much of the moderate political and intellectual spectrum, and colleagues or acquaintances of Salter, such as Harold Macmillan, Malcolm MacDonald, Barratt Brown, Norman Angell, Arnold-Forster, J.J. Mallon and, most importantly, Clifford Allen, were equally proactive. On 15 February a manifesto, "Liberty and Democratic Leadership" had been published, signed by 150 individuals prominent in politics, the churches, the universities, arts and sciences. It called for far reaching measures of international and economic reorganization. Another manifesto, with a similar number of signatures, soon followed.[261] Salter had not initially been associated with either, though its purposes would have appealed to him. However, it was Clifford Allen, who described himself as the "directing person" of a new movement, which at this point drew in Salter. Allen intended "keeping Salter's name private so as not to scare him off." The plan was to convene a meeting on 1 July at All Souls of some 50 people where Salter was expected to present a major written document. Allen expected that the result of the meeting with Salter would "make it a little easier for people in all the political parties to speak with one voice on certain subjects of immediate policy." The All Souls meeting proved to be very successful, and it was agreed to expand the two manifestos into a book and to solicit "support from distinguished people."[262] After dining with Allen on 23 July, Salter agreed "to draft two sections for the Oxford Group pamphlet dealing with domestic and world economics. This is great news," Allen wrote, "though he [Salter] wishes it to be kept private." Allen also was hoping that Salter would become the general editor of the undertaking, and foresaw the headquarters of the enterprise staying at All Souls. Indeed, it was initially named the "All Souls Group."[263]

This proved to be a quiet summer for Salter, "a lazy one" as he described it. This was partly due to the fact, which he admitted when lunching with Stimson at his flat in London on 22 July, that he "had been suffering from gall bladder trouble." As always their conversation ranged widely, and Salter confessed "that he had broken with his government on the issue of their non-cooperation with me [Stimson] as to Manchuria." Neither one was optimistic about Germany, especially after the "night of the long knives" on 30 June.[264] In the first week-end of August, as he done so often before, Salter attended the Liberal Summer School at Oxford. This time he weighed in during the debates about education, arguing that all university graduates should add to their academic specialization "a framework of elementary general knowledge."²⁶⁵ This was among the last times that Salter attended, as support continued to drop, and the school was increasingly seen as "a collection of elderly people."²⁶⁶ On the other hand, he set off a flurry of discussion when he first wrote to The Times on the question of a housing policy to meet demands for low-cost rental units for wage-earners. He contended that, given low-interest rates, the government should directly intervene with guarantees for capital, thereby stimulating a housing boom to meet the severe housing shortage and continue with economic recovery. "Housing is by general consent," he observed, "a key industry in the economic process."²⁶⁷ At the same time, on a closely related issue, Salter joined the National Housing Committee in its lobbying efforts for more exacting town planning, an issue which was to interest him for a lifetime.²⁶⁸ For the rest of the month, Salter cut himself off from all activities, writing afterwards, that "I am really in good health now after a summer holiday," spent mainly at Zennor, St Ives, Cornwall, with Ka Cox and Arnold-Forster.²⁶⁹

As for his now reduced output of public commentary, there was an apparent new realism and pragmatism in Salter's contributions, especially relating to the future of the League and the prospects for global economic recovery. On the former issue, he had already argued that, despite some recent setbacks, he still affirmed his belief in "the collective system" embodied by the League, albeit with some modification to Article 15, bringing it in line with Article 11 (namely, action to be taken by unanimous decision other than the disputants).²⁷⁰ Then, in a BBC broadcast on 5 September, he asked what should be the future strategy of the League, hampered as it was by "political isolation and economic nationalism?" He reminded listeners of the extensive work performed by the League in such areas as health, disease prevention, the relief and re-establishment of refugee populations and the success of the ILO, among much else. And until the great powers either returned or joined the organization, he hoped that every effort must be made "to develop the non-political work of the League."²⁷¹ On the latter issue, he acknowledged in The Times on 25 September, while the League Assembly was meeting, that Geneva could contribute little to world recovery, while "national policies" guided global economic policy. Nonetheless, he suggested that the key requirement was a restoration of world trade. Within this narrow focus, he continued, the League could provide the technical expertise and data to convince governments to move towards a real balance of trade. That same expertise, he argued, could also be applied to provide confidence, via indexes to world price levels, to help secure and foster more international lending. Salter considered the two proposals "immediately practicable." While it was reported from Geneva that there was interest but no agreement on the second, The New York Times reprinted the article, with an accompanying editorial on 14 October.²⁷² Despite his increasing reluctance at forecasting the economic future, Salter wrote in The Yale Review that the intensity of the Depression had diminished and the "general trend of economic activity has been upward for a full two years." At its current rate, he made, what he termed a "rash assumption," that by 1936 the world would have returned to the 1928 levels of industrial production and employment. He cautioned, however, that massive government spending could not forever replace the necessary revival of private investment. In his conclusion, Salter expressed his belief that a new economic system was emerging "in which the elements of socialization and private enterprise will be combined in different proportions from those we have witnessed in the past."²⁷³

It was this last assertion that Salter continued to elaborate in public. During a BBC broadcast on 10 December, he laid out his case for "increasing socialization." He wished to see increased redistribution of income through taxation, more public utilities, stabilization of employment and greater state direction over private enterprise. He did not regard this as "a mere compromise between two alternatives of State planning and price adjustment," but "a selective compromise designed to unite the best of both methods," through "a process of evolution rather than revolution."²⁷⁴ In The Spectator, he tackled the question of how far to extend planning? He did not envisage completely replacing the automatic adjustments though changing prices and competition. Total collectivism, in his view, was incompatible with political and economic freedom. Rather, he envisaged ongoing state intervention in the social services, with greater "planned socialization" in such areas as currency, capital issues, tariffs and protection, but short of complete collectivism which he termed a "disaster."²⁷⁵ Taking his mandate public was not just for effect, for Salter had been moving in a liberal-leftwards direction for some time and this was being monitored, especially by Beatrice Webb. She always followed his career, in the hope that one day he might see things her way. After listening to his BBC broadcast, she wrote that "he is about where we were some ten years ago," but given his new position at All Souls, she thought he might "feel free to adventure." She regarded Salter as "saner than Keynes and more open-minded than Beveridge; more public spirited than either of them; less indifferent to the common people."²⁷⁶

Also concentrating Salter's attention was the continuing involvement with the "All Souls Group." Since his last meeting with Allen on 23 July, Salter had thrown himself into the task of drafting the sections dealing with domestic and international economics. His growing concern was how "to get what is both desirable & likely to cover wide agreement." As the draft grew in length, and at Salter's suggestion that there be "someone who can handle the document as a whole," Allen enlisted Harold Macmillan to help with revisions and to add material on industrial reorganization. This also led Allen to suggest that the material would be more suitable as a book, supported by "the signatures of two or three hundred of the most distinguished thinkers of all parties." The drafting committee (Salter, Allen, Arnold-Forster, Barratt Brown, Macmillan and Geoffrey Crowther) and others met again at Oxford on 25 November for further discussion.[277]

It was the theme of recovery, which Salter had analysed a month earlier in The Yale Review, that he first returned to in the New Year. In The New York Times, he contended that there was indeed a general trend towards recovery. He singled out the reduction in debts, the activity in the building industry, cheap money, and the "repair of the American banking system." He regarded as significant that "the bulk of the improvement has come as the result of adjustments made by individuals and individual concerns, that is, by the operation of natural forces," and predicted that this recovery was well on the way. He also foresaw some small revival in levels of foreign trade, with domestic capitalist systems moving towards "a middle system between that of freedom and socialism."[278] Even as he looked to the future, Salter was still being called upon for his prior experience. On 28 September 1934 the League Council had instructed the secretary general to appoint a group of experts to study the prevailing committee structure. When invited to become a member, Salter at first demurred, citing his Oxford academic and London commitments and the writing he wished to get on with. Finally, on 4 March, he wrote to Avenol, agreeing to serve for only one week beginning on 25 March, and ruling out any following up work.[279] At the same time Salter found himself once more involved, albeit from a distance, with Chinese financial policy and the ongoing silver problem. As the American government continued its proactive policy of purchasing large amounts of silver, following on from its Silver Purchase Act of 19 June 1934, the Chinese economy continued to deteriorate, with increasing deflation, a rise in the price of silver and declining exports. On 12 January T.V. Soong enlisted Salter's help to lobby the British government and Treasury to secure a new loan for China for currency stabilisation, short of its abandoning the silver standard and linking its currency to gold or sterling. Salter followed up with discussions at the Treasury over the next few days and floated his idea that one option for China would simply be "to reduce the silver content of the Chinese dollar by about 30%" and perhaps ask the Americans for a silver loan.[280] The other, also not accepted, would be for "the establishment of [a] managed currency allied with sterling."[281]

Even as the consultations behind the scenes continued, the Chinese government was informed on 19 January of Britain's refusal to extend a loan of £20 million. The Foreign Office began to view the Chinese financial situation, and those lobbying on its government's behalf, with some skepticism.[282] As well, and inevitably, the political situation in China, the question of Japanese-Chinese relations, and hopes to reach agreement in ongoing naval negotiations began to complicate matters; and that included Salter's role as unofficial advisor. Earlier in February Salter had been reliably informed that the Chinese government expected to invite him "to proceed urgently by Siberia to Nanking." That invitation never materialized, and as he personally explained to Anthony Eden, the Foreign Secretary on 22 February, he feared that the Japanese government was "steadily squeezing" the Chinese authorities to accept help from Tokyo and on its terms. He pointed out his own dilemma, namely, that any financial advice that he offered the Chinese government would inevitably be conditioned by the state of Chinese-Japanese relations, about which he was not informed. As for financial assistance, he added, that "it was conceivable that Japan could perhaps at the price of stiff political conditions help China materially." Salter then digressed on the wider situation in the Far East, warning that Japan regarded the interest of other powers in the area with contempt, and added that Japanese policy "aimed at nothing less than the elimination of other Powers in the Western Pacific." When Eden asked about policy options, Salter advised joint British-American-Russian consultations, to be followed by a clear warning to Japan that any contravention of the open door would result in economic sanctions. Eden recorded, "Sir Arthur continued that he had always held the view that had greater firmness been shown in September 1931, the Manchukuo incident would not have developed as it did." Eden's response, if any, to this latter observation is not known, however, it evoked lengthy comments from Foreign Office officials. These were all highly critical of Salter's proposal for great power consultations and a trade blockade. "Sir A. Salter may be an able economist but his political judgment is poor," began the first of many minutes. He was accused of belonging to those "amateur political strategists" (including Lord Lothian) who were advocating for a return to balance of power politics in the Far East. The Chinese, for their part, were accused of "perverse ingenuity" by playing off one power against another. In addition, "the Chinese in the hope of loosening our purse strings have managed to persuade Salter, Lothian, Rajchman and Co. that China is about to fall into Japan's arms unless Japan was restrained." Sir Robert Vansittart ended the discussion, noting that "Sir A. Salter talks much dangerous nonsense. So does Lord Lothian. They will never learn that there is nothing real to be expected from the U.S.A., let alone Russia."[283] T.V. Soong, however, continued to keep Salter informed of developments in China. As Salter explained to the Foreign Office on 28 February, he was not an intermediary, nor did he personally have any financial interests in China. Rather, he had seen a good deal of Soong when in China, and "the latter was prone to write and telegraph to him for advice on financial matters."[284]

Despite Salter downplaying his role, the reality was otherwise and not always positive. He continued to receive requests from Soong to try and ferret out what might be British policy on the questions of a loan and the future of silver. On 5 and again on 9 March, for example, Salter conferred with Sir Warren Fisher on these questions, to determine what should be China's response, but none was forthcoming from the British side. Nonetheless, Salter got it right when he advised Soong that it was Britain's expectation that Chinese-Japanese "consultation would contribute to establish better relations in the East." When Rajchman also got involved along with Salter, the Foreign Office agreed with the Treasury view "not to have anything to do with these unofficial emissaries." Besides, it was the understanding in the Foreign Office that Salter might not be *persona grata* with the Japanese, "who seem to regard Salter with something of the disfavour that Rajchman has earned with them."[285] By mid-March the agenda appeared to alter when the discussion shifted towards China possibly adopting a managed currency, linked to sterling. Even so, the Foreign Office continued to advise non-involvement, noting that the Chinese government could enlist "any number of English economists, e.g., Sir Arthur Salter in to help them." Indeed, on 3 April Soong was still contemplating inviting Salter to China, to which the Foreign Office reply was to suggest the decision was entirely a Chinese one. In the following days, it was the Foreign Office understanding that the whole matter was "slowing down."[286] After it was acknowledged that the ongoing delay in appointing a financial expert was creating an embarrassing situation, on 5 June Sir Frederick Leith-Ross was appointed to work on financial reconstruction and currency reform in China.[287]

Far Eastern affairs, however, continued to attract Salter's attention. In a document he prepared on 2 March for the League of Nations Union, on whose Council he sat, he urged the organization to press the British government to formulate a new Far Eastern policy. He wanted this to be based on a reiteration of the principals of the Washington Naval Agreement – equality of security in the Pacific, the integrity of China and the open door principle. Failure of the Japanese to comply, he argued, should be followed by close Anglo-American consultation, with a possible trade boycott and sanctions. With the events of 1931 very much in mind, he cautioned against resorting to "ineffective initiatives later abandoned on Japanese pressure." Indeed, his views on economic sanctions were hardening. Short of dealing with a "lunatic government," he suggested, "Simultaneous exclusion of the imports from the aggressor is usually most likely to be the easiest politically to agree upon, the easiest to enforce (for we all have the machinery!), [and] the most decisive in stopping the aggressor if anything short of war can."[288] Another pressing matter on Salter's horizon was his return to Geneva, for a commitment not extending beyond a week. Indeed, he had cautioned Avenol that "I cannot possibly come for a second meeting," and wrote privately "that I accept no responsibility for any work beyond what we can get through in one week."[289] On 14 June, prior to his departure, he consulted with several officials at the Foreign Office. Then from 18 to 22 June he worked in Geneva with the Committee on League Committees, completing the draft report, and overseeing its publication on 5 August. It was soon recognized as "largely the work of Sir A. Salter."[290] The report recommended that League committees should "be in the hands of the Governments," and that committee membership be amended so as to guarantee expertise. The report and its conclusions were adopted by the Assembly on 28 September.[291]

The work of the "All Souls Group" had meanwhile continued, with its formal inauguration as "The Next Five Years" at the Oxford Union on 3 February. An executive committee then was approved, with Allen as chairman and Salter among the members.[292] There is abundant evidence that Salter played a pivotal role, not only in the drafting, Allen called him "the vital key," but also in bringing so many disparate minds into agreement.[293] After a crucial meeting of the principals involved on 27-28 April, Allen complimented Salter for "the genius you showed in helping us over our difficulties. I have rarely witnessed a more wonderful skilfulness during the whole of my political life." With a complete draft in hand in early June, Salter began to approach various individuals, in each case asking for "sympathetic attention" to the book, and pointing to the contributors as symbolizing the attempt "to find a broad basis of agreement for the progressives of all parties." He also emphasized that adding a signature merely signified "sympathy with the general policy," rather than "agreement with every detail."[294] The results of his approaches were mixed, and this led to some of the final signatories being flagged as agreeing with only parts of the book. Thus Cecil, who had at first refused Salter's invitation to sign, consented on condition it was noted that he agreed only with the international relations section.[295] On the other hand, Keynes wrote he was "in sympathy with nearly all of the practical proposals," but he could not add his signature. He explained that he was himself moving towards "a new underlying economic theory and philosophy of the state." Keynes was in fact referring to his current project, published the following year as the <u>General Theory of Employment, Interest, and Money</u>.[296] Among others, whom Salter personally approached but who refused to sign, were Hubert D. Henderson, W.G.S. Adams and Lord Astor.[297]

Though engaged in pragmatic action, Salter turned his attention in early July back to questions of finance and currency stabilization.[298] In two articles in <u>The Economist</u>, he acknowledged that since Britain went off the gold standard there had been economic recovery. However, with ongoing "exchange uncertainty" in France and the United States, he favoured "some form of limited and conditional stabilization," short of a fixed exchange rate but also offering some of its advantages. A limited form of stabilisation, he suggested, would reduce the risk of deflation." This could be achieved by establishing and maintaining by various methods "specified ratios" between such currencies as the pound, dollar and franc. Any currency under threat would be supported by either the government, the BIS or National Equalization Funds buying and holding it. The result, he concluded, would be a return to confidence, continued economic recovery, and even tariff reductions.[299] But this was overtaken on 26 July with the publication of <u>The Next Five Years: An Essay in Political Agreement</u>. The Foreword, signed by 152 notable men and women, "drawn from different parties and schools of thought," commended the program as attainable over the next five years, while not necessarily endorsing all the details. That such disparate support could be gathered, confirmed the main thrust of the book that the politics of progressive, centrist liberal opinion sufficiently overlapped for a middle road to be evident and achieved in the life of one parliament. The framers of the programme regarded the mid-1930s as offering:

> a new opportunity and a new challenge: a challenge to give leadership in organizing a world order free from the menace of war, a challenge to develop an economic system which is freed from poverty and makes full use of the growing material resources of the age for the general advantage, and a challenge to safeguard political liberty and to revitalize democratic government.

The first part of the book, largely drafted by Salter, posited the case that "the historic controversy between individualism and socialism – between the idea of a wholly competitive capitalist system and one of State ownership, regulation, and control – appears largely beside the mark." Instead, there should be a "mixed" system, comprising "direct State ownership and control," "management by public and semi-public concerns," and "private competitive enterprise." Further recommendations included purposive economic planning, limited tariffs, nationalization of transport, electricity and armaments, and some degree of public control of the Bank of England and joint-stock banks. A National Development Board would promote a program of public works, electrification and housing. The question of social justice was also targeted with a call "to get rid of extreme inequalities of wealth and of economic power" and to provide a range of social services. The second part of the book, devoted to international relations, argued that the threat of a major war within the next decade was "extremely grave." The only way to rebuild confidence was to strengthen Anglo-American co-operation and "the collective peace system." A series of suggestions followed, designed to restore confidence in the League, the Covenant and the Locarno treaty and to enable a system of control and supervision of the international arms traffic. The Epilogue noted that the signatories believed that theirs was a last call "for a coherently planned reconstruction of the nation's life, for readjustment of the social order, for preservation as well as imaginative development of the land we inherit, and for a vigorous effort to strengthen the collective peace system."[300]

A day after publication of The Next Five Years, and on Salter's suggestion, Allen issued a statement denying the book was in any way connected with Lloyd George's parallel Council of Action for Peace and Reconstruction launched on 2 July. Indeed, some feelers for cooperation between the two groups ended in failure.[301] In fact, the field for liberal progress, reconstruction and internationalism was getting crowded by the mid-1930s and Salter was to find several of his "homes" here. He had earlier joined another group, Political and Economic Planning [PEP], where he had been was an active member since January 1932, sitting on its Directorate and its Council of Management until 1966.[302] He was also on the General Council of Chatham House from November 1931 until resigning in May 1945.[303] As well, he was a member of the League of Nations Union and from 1937 on its executive committee, and on 7 February had been appointed to the newly reconstituted General Advisory Council of the BBC.[304] Abroad, he was a member of the Council of the Geneva School of International Relations. By the middle of the 1930s, therefore, he enjoyed a wide-range of networks outside of All Souls, and a schedule of work which eventually took its toll. For some years he had suffered from gall bladder problems. Although he had had a recurrence in the summer of 1934, this seemed to have eased by the fall.[305] On 23 July he wrote to Lady Astor from a Harley Street clinic, "This miserable thing – gall troubles – has been poisoning me for years & I have a good chance of getting much better general health." He reassured Ka Cox that otherwise "I'm in very good general health." His gall bladder was removed two days later.[306] Salter anticipated a month of recovery, leaving his temporary new secretary Aubrey Jones to manage his affairs. Jones later recalled that Salter proved to be a "hard taskmaster" but the epitome of kindness.[307] For some of the recovery period, Salter indulged his favourite pastime, a motoring trip that took him to Zennor in Cornwall, at Ka Cox's invitation and back to London.[308]

It did not take long, however, before Salter returned to the fray. And it was not surprising that an international crisis involving the League of Nations was to draw his attention. Italy's hostile intentions against Ethiopia were of great concern internationally at least since 1933. On 3 January 1935 Ethiopia had brought the situation to the attention of the League Council, and that ushered in what has been described as "the most decisive chapter in the history of the League." Addis Ababa, however, on 16 and 17 March, formally appealed to the League to take up the issue, under Article 15, for arbitration and settlement. The appeal was repeated again on 15 April and 20 May, when the arbitration process was postponed to 4 September. On 31 July the

Council agreed to put the Italo-Ethiopian question on the agenda, even while Italian military preparations for an invasion continued unchallenged.[309] Thus with prospects that the League would finally take up the dispute, Salter had sent Lord Robert Cecil some "notes" on the evolving Italo-Ethiopian situation and agreed to be associated with any action by the latter which accorded with the analysis. Cecil wrote to The Times on 7 August, under his own signature but in accord with Salter's views, urging the British government to make it clear, in advance, that it was prepared to participate in collective action, if necessary, to give effect to sanctions under article 16.[310] On 25 August Salter further shared his views on the evolving crisis with Cecil. He admitted that for the time being he had no criticism of behind the scenes diplomacy, because he realized the key was to secure French co-operation, without which Britain could justifiably decline to impose sanctions. However, he wished again to see the British government "publicly urging collective action at Geneva" with warnings against the consequences of aggression. Such a move, he admitted, "may not be effective now and sanctions may therefore have to be applied; and in the mood of Italy this may mean war." However, he believed that it was dangerous was to let the situation drift and only later "to embark upon some half-hearted sanctions which will lead to a humiliating withdrawal." The only safeguard against war, he concluded, "was the strength of the collective force and the known determination to use it if necessary."[311] Salter was also concerned about the prevailing misapprehensions regarding sanctions. In The Spectator, he wrote that sanctions were an alternative neither to conciliation nor to the possession of collective military force. Their place in the Covenant was to apply some form of physical pressure to reinforce moral persuasion. For sanctions to be effective, there had to be "a collective determination to impose them," without room for doubt, even while military and diplomatic activity continued. As to the sanctions themselves – the exclusion of imports or the prohibition of exports – Salter preferred the former, regarding the latter as ineffective, even with a blockade. Finally, he explained that "'Pinprick' sanctions are not only useless but dangerous."[312]

Salter's continued interest in the Abyssinian crisis was also matched by his ongoing advocacy in financial matters. Earlier in the summer he had contributed to the debate between stabilisation or a managed currency. He returned to the subject later in August in The Manchester Guardian. This time he focused on how contracts, both long and short term, were adversely affected by ongoing uncertainty regarding currency fluctuations. To secure that confidence, and as a supplement to the currency system, he proposed "a series of indices of commodity prices." These would then be used as a "suitable basis" to revitalize contracts and hence return some semblance of stability. Finally, he looked forward to the upcoming League Assembly. Seeing no other prospect of success for it in the area of financial and economic problems, he suggested his proposal would be a suitable area for action. "I'm afraid there will again be the customary general & empty discussions of economic & financial things at Geneva this September," he wrote Layton on 22 August, "with nothing done at the end." Taking up the idea of world price indices, he suggested, would give the Assembly "some limited, modest but useful job."[313] Salter's article proved to be of immediate interest at Geneva and he was asked to expand on his notion of price indices. This he did and his proposals were discussed by the Finance Committee which met in early September. It then requested further amplification from Salter, but the matter was later dropped from its agenda.[314] Nonetheless, the debate about how to achieve currency stabilization continued both in London and New York, and Salter's ideas were debated there and found favour. There was further widespread agreement that a return to the gold standard to achieve this monetary goal was out of the question.[315] Given the debates' continuing relevance, Salter amplified his views in Foreign Affairs. He pointed out that Britain had so far successfully managed its currency and this had led to considerable recovery. Further improvement, he argued, lay in the direction of stabilization and not a return to the gold standard. He suggested that the British and American Treasuries, with French participation, should confer with the object of securing "agreement upon a policy to maintain specified ratios between the main currencies." Such a step would increase confidence, spur recovery, lower tariffs, lower the risks of deflation and possibly reduce the intensification of economic nationalism. The New York Times gave the proposals partial approval, but stipulated that the programme needed elaboration in cases of disagreement between the contracting parties.[316]

It was usually the case that Salter was busy at All Souls once the Michaelmas term had started. He certainly took his academic and administrative duties seriously, and he continued to invite to Oxford "eminent personalities in Whitehall" to meet with colleagues in his rooms. "In spite of my limitations," Salter recalled, "I gained much, and even perhaps gave something, in my Oxford years."[317] The wider domestic and international world, however, continued to draw his attention. The Next Five Years proved a publishing success, requiring a second impression and selling almost 8,000 copies. Allen had first raised the question with Salter as early as 17 July as to where to go next.[318] For Salter, one aspect of the road map was quite clear, "We are not trying to form a new political party." Later he recalled, "We hoped to formulate an outline of policy corresponding with the views of many in every party, and of the increasing number of those who had no party allegiance, and so to 'permeate' each party, and narrow the difference between the rivals."[319] Meeting at Toynbee Hall on 15 September, with Allen in the chair and Salter and 16 others of the core group attending, it was resolved to promote the policies advanced in The Next Five Years through organizational means. For this purpose the original drafting committee was given the task of writing a constitution, for the new "The Next Five Years" group which dedicated itself only to advancing "educational and propaganda purposes," but not to engage in electoral activity. The following day, a letter to Lloyd George, co-signed by Salter and five others, finally indicated that there would be no merger of any kind between the two organizations.[320] Another meeting on 29 September approved the draft constitution and formally appointed the drafting committee as the executive committee. Its task was to promote "The Next Five Years" group as an "association to promote economic reconstruction, social justice, and international peace." Some of the activities envisaged included future publications, research, lobbying, public meetings and the formation of local branches. Salter volunteered to serve on several sub-committees and was given the task of making contact with PEP.[321] Work advanced quickly in the following weeks, with vice-presidents successfully recruited (including Cecil whom Salter recruited), the executive committee enlarged, finance raised, office space offered by Macmillan, and liaison with PEP confirmed. The draft constitution was published and plans went ahead to launch a paper, The New Outlook.[322] Salter strongly believed, as he wrote when congratulating Mackenzie King on his 14 October election victory, "Liberalism is politically weak except in Canada." In Britain, "the Liberal Party has been almost annihilated," but that liberalism was "more nearly the real general desire of the country" and therefore, he argued, "the middle way is obscured by party developments." The range of support given the group was "a novel phenomenon in English political life."[323]

The ongoing Italo-Ethiopian crisis continued to absorb Salter. He had already joined with others in "The Next Five Years" group in signing a letter to the editor of The Times on 17 September. This urged the British government to affirm in advance its support for the League Covenant and its sanctions provisions.[324] Salter shared with so many others the fear that the crisis was to be the ultimate test for the League, an institution to which his name, and a decade of work, was so intimately involved. [325] After Italy invaded Ethiopia on 3 October, the League set in motion its laborious procedure, with a Sanctions Committee which first met on 12 October and agreed on a complex array of sanctions against Italy and a timetable for their implementation. Responding to a letter that Stimson had written and sent him, Salter praised his efforts "to bring the U.S.A. into closer association with the collective system, & to make an effective reality of the Kellogg Pact."[326] For his part, Salter had watched the activity at Geneva from a distance. However, as the sanctions issue unfolded, and given his previous analyses of the issue, it is not surprising he weighed in. On 29 October he was among the speakers at a conference organized by the National Peace Council on "Peace and the Colonial Problem." Introducing the topic,

Salter tried to rebut Italian (and to an extent German and Japanese) claims that they needed colonies as an outlet for surplus population and for access to raw materials. With regard to the former, he argued their population growth would always outstrip the number of voluntary settlers. And as for the later, he suggested that, given the "open door" policy and the surplus of raw materials, the real problem was lack of foreign exchange to make such purchases. Thus non-self-governing colonies should be held under a "double trusteeship – 1) to the inhabitants of the country and 2) to the world in general," and that trust would be executed "under a mandate to an international authority." Such a system would remove any economic disabilities suffered by non-colonial powers and guarantee equal access to raw materials. Salter's proposals received the support of other speakers.[327] Some time later, at the Liberal Summer School at Oxford, he went on record as opposed to the transfer of any of Germany's former colonies. To do so, he stated, "we should not only not buy peace, but should buy additional trouble." He saw no point in a process which he regarded as trying to "buy off" Nazi Germany.[328]

It was on the series of sanctions imposed by the League during October, including economic sanctions agreed on 19 October, which continued to preoccupy Salter. On 1 November he had written to Layton arguing that all the League sanctions so far endorsed "can have no material effect on the present campaign which extends to May."[329] On 4 November the Foreign Office learned of these observations and the further argument that "The only sanction which in his view would have a more rapid effect would be the cutting off of Italy's supplies of oil." While there was agreement with Salter's views, it was further noted that any oil embargo required the effective co-operation of Germany, Japan and the USA, all not members of the League.[330] Salter publicly returned to the charge with a letter to the editor of The Times on 27 November, which had been approved by the executive committee of "The Next Five Years" group. He began by reminding readers that for 10 years while at the League he had been the person especially concerned with economic sanctions. Those already in force, in his view, would prove to be ineffective. He concluded that:

> No purely economic sanctions offer so good a prospect of inducing a willingness to stop the war quickly and on satisfactory terms as the general and immediate stoppage of oil supplies; and nothing could contribute to securing this result so effectively as a decisive British lead at the moment.

The leading article in The Times that day affirmed that Salter's "long experience of the practical working of the League entitles him to a hearing." However, it went on to point to the problems of maintaining collective action with non-members of the League, and with the USA in particular. Others also wrote to support Salter, most notably Cecil, and the former's views were also brought up in the House of Commons on 5 December.[331] Salter's lobbying for Britain to provide a lead, unfortunately, found no support when sanctions were discussed at year's end in the cabinet.[332] The issue of foreign policy was also on the agenda when "The Next Five Years" group met on 22 December. The question of a possible political affiliation continued to concern members of the group.[333] Salter himself was convinced "that we cannot hope in any foreseeable future that the Liberal Party will attain power." Hence, he reaffirmed his belief "in the middle way" and the need "to work at 'uncovering' the latent agreement between reasonable men of good will in all the parties."[334]

The year ended on a note of sadness for Salter. He later wrote in <u>Memoirs of a Public Servant</u>, "This was, moreover, for other reasons a time in which a greyer sky was replacing the sunshine of the preceding years." He referred to his surgery in July and confessed that he felt "weakened for some months." Mostly, he lamented that "death took some of my best friends."[335] Earlier, he had contributed a moving introduction to a post-humous book by William Martin, <u>Understanding the Chinese</u>. Salter was well acquainted with Martin, foreign editor for more than a decade of the <u>Journal de Genève</u>, and praised Martin for having been "a great publicist; a great liberal; a great internationalist."[336] At the same time, on reading of the death of Jeremiah Smith Jr, Salter wrote, "He was a great character. I hope it was not Hungary that killed him. It probably gave him the best of his days."[337] On 16 August he had heard of the death of his former roommate in London, and colleague from early post-war years, Sir Basil Blackett. In a tribute in <u>The Times</u>, Salter gave Blackett full credit for the success of the financial aspects of the 1922 Austrian reconstruction plan. He also lauded Blackett for "his eclectic and individual opinions."[338] On 2 December Marian Henderson died after a long illness and unsuccessful surgery.[339] Salter took her death badly, calling her "an intimate friend" whose passing was "an irreparable personal bereavement." Ethel Bullard, then permanently resident in London at the Connaught Hotel in Carlos Place, wrote to Felkin, "Arthur sounds pretty cut-up about it all," and he has "taken it very hard." She also revealed some of her own plans which were to bring her into more constant contact with Salter. She no longer intended to share the Geneva flat at 43 Quai Wilson with her sister Louise, but only to use it when visiting. "My role in Geneva has not been a very happy one in some ways recently," she wrote. Besides, her own health, looked after by a London physician, entailed less travel and absence from the constant activity of Geneva.[340] Later in the New Year Salter lamented, "I have in the last few days three funeral wreaths to send, a serious operation with the result uncertain to another friend, an accident to yet another who was to have stayed with me – a grim record."[341]

The beginning of the 1936 Hilary term meant Salter was once again fully involved in academic and administrative life at Oxford, often refusing London or other commitments, because of college responsibilities. For example, early in the New Year, he refused an offer to take on the post of League High Commissioner for Refugees from Germany.[342] Further rumours suggested that he would replace Beveridge as Director of the London School of Economics.[343] On the other hand, he accepted a position as honourary treasurer of the campaign to raise funds for an extension to Ruskin College, where his friend A. Barratt Brown was principal.[344] And he also continued his involvement with the National Housing Committee, being one of the signatories of its third report in February 1936. This urged that house building must be tied in closely "with an efficient system of town and country planning."[345] It was "The Next Five Years" group, however, that captured much of his ongoing attention. The group was soon established on a sound financial basis, membership was vastly enlarged and an office opened in Mowbray House in the Strand. Salter undertook to participate in several sub-committees, including, foreign policy and economic and social services. The most ambitious project, in which he lent a hand, was the production of a weekly, <u>The New Outlook</u>.[346] And although he willingly added his signature to the group's letters to the editor, such as on the need for a national food policy to include free milk for children,[347] it was international affairs that still drew his attention. On 29 February he restated his position on the question of an oil embargo, suggesting this could no longer be solved by an American initiative, but must be acted upon by Britain taking the lead. Only if League members "do their plain duty unconditionally," he suggested, would the USA also cooperate.[348]

The conciliatory tone might have been conditioned by several engagements that lay ahead for Salter. On 3 May 1935 he had accepted a renewed invitation from the President of Swarthmore College, the educationalist Frank Ayedelotte, to deliver five lectures the next Spring. Ayedelotte noted that Salter had "a very large following among thoughtful people in the United States."[349] On 19 February he excitedly wrote of his forthcoming engagements and his eagerness "to take the opportunity of course of seeing my friends both in New York & Washington." He noted, "I am greatly looking forward to getting across again. I have come to regard one visit a year as part of a good life."[350] On the eve of his departure, in the wake of the 7 March German re-occupation of the Rhineland, he confessed that "this is not a week I should have chosen to be leaving Europe."[351] On 11 March he left from Southampton aboard the *Berengaria* and arrived in New York on 17 March for a busy series of engagements. On 19 and 26 March and 9, 12 and 16 April he delivered the five lectures at Swarthmore College. During that time he was a guest of the Ayedelottes and also made himself available for informal discussion with students and faculty.[352] The lectures, published later as World Trade and Its Future, first surveyed the system of international trade prior to 1914 and noted that its success was due to automatic adjustments "through competition and changing prices, private enterprise and profit, within governmental policies of laissez-faire." The 1914-1918 World War was followed by a period of recovery to 1928 and then the "devastating collapse" of 1929, an event which he largely attributed to the misguided efforts after 1919 to rebuild "the old system on insecure foundations." Future international trade, however, would be influenced by such factors as greater government intervention, large-scale industrial production requiring overseas markets, problems adjusting the balance of payments and trade, low levels of foreign investment, and the existence of tariffs, quotas and exchange restrictions. In order to expand world trade, he offered several recommendations. These included currency stability, through the use of "joint equalization funds," and co-operation between central banks "to maintain a reasonable stability in the general level of gold prices." He further suggested tariffs be established on a unified national level and then, through bilateral and multi-lateral trade negotiations, expand most-favoured nation clauses and create thereby "low tariff clubs." In conclusion, he stated that his proposals required progress "in collective government, in the collective regulation of investment, in the collective control of currency as well as in commercial policy."[353] World Trade and Its Future received significant attention, with reviewers ranging from those who regarded the proposals as "the most realistic programme yet devised for the freeing of trade," to "requiring the national leadership and international cooperation which in the present dark hour do not exist."[354] The New Statesman noted that "as a populariser of economic common sense Sir Arthur Salter has few rivals."[355]

Between his two separate visits to Swarthmore, which Salter found "a pleasant & peaceful place," he travelled first to Washington on 27 March where he stayed with the Stimsons as an overnight guest. In wide-ranging discussion, Stimson found Salter "rather gloomy," thinking war was "likely or even probable in five years." Salter lamented that with the coming of the Depression, "one after another the props which had been laboriously built up crashed to the ground and dashed all his hopes." In particular, he recalled all his efforts at the League in post-war economic and financial reconstruction. He admitted that "there must have been fatal errors in the foundations which they had laid so carefully" to explain the emergence of dictatorships, exchange and currency collapse, tariff barriers and economic nationalism. Among the many topics the two surveyed was Stimson's forthcoming book on the Far Eastern crisis of 1931. He showed Salter several documents which confirmed the latter in the position he had adopted at that time, with the result, Stimson noted, "the Foreign Office was closed to Salter after that."[356]

Salter then travelled to New York where he stayed with the Lamonts. On 1 April Lamont hosted "a small men's dinner" for Salter, where the guests included Jean Monnet, Lewis Douglas and Governor Alfred E. Smith, and on the following day he accompanied Salter to a dinner of the American Academy of Political Science.[357] On 3 April The League for Political Education hosted a luncheon at Hotel Astor where Salter, the guest of honour, told an audience of 800 that in the modern world a policy of isolation was futile, arguing that "isolation is not the opposite of entanglement; it is often the precursor."[358] On 7 April, and again under the aegis of The League for Political Education, Salter delivered the second annual Jonathan Peterson Foundation lecture, established in 1934 to promote better understanding among English-speaking peoples. He chose as his topic "The English Speaking Peoples and World Peace" and began by cautioning his audience that he was not going to offer "an evening's entertainment." Instead, he intended to discuss the deteriorating international situation "as courteously as is consistent with candour, and as candidly as is consistent with courtesy." From the point of view of government, he defined the English speaking peoples as the British Commonwealth of Nations and the United States, whose combined resources were overwhelming. He denied advocating any special form of Anglo-American association, which he regarded as "impractical and undesirable." Rather, he posited that the English speaking peoples, acting together, could play a special role in advancing towards a world system to maintain peace and the rule of law. He was convinced that ultimately this would lead to "a form of federal world government." Meanwhile, in the prevailing "inter-national" system as embodied in the League of Nations and the Kellogg Pact, Britain was trying to diffuse various European crises and rejected any form of isolation. In contrast, refusing to engage in the question of whether or not a United States policy of isolation was practicable, he suggested that American support for the Kellogg Pact should be restated and consultations with other signatories made a regular practice. He told his audience that the United States would one day take an international role commensurate with its power. "The only question is whether she will do so before the catastrophe – which she can prevent – or afterwards, when she can only help to gather up the fragments of a ruined civilization."[359]

The contentious nature of Salter's remarks, despite his protestations that they were personal, evoked various comments. Support came from Lamont who moved the vote of thanks.[360] A critical account of the event was sent by the British Library of Information in New York to the News Department of the Foreign Office. It stated that Salter spoke too long and caused the audience to get restless. "Sir Arthur Salter's political judgment," wrote Roger Makins of the Foreign Office, "has never been equal to his abilities as an economist."[361] Salter would not have been surprised by that comment, however, he have been taken aback had he read a private observation by Lamont, "Some people think that Salter is no longer selling at his 1929 high, nevertheless, he is an interesting fellow."[362] Be that as it may, Salter had for years enjoyed the attention of the American media and elite opinion and an extensive circle of American friends and colleagues. Indeed, on 6 April he met with the editorial council of The New York Times which gave his views extensive coverage.[363] Indeed, after completing his last lecture at Swarthmore on 16 April, Salter travelled back to Washington where in a letter to Lady Astor he shared some of his impressions. "Recovery is not only unmistakeable but it has transformed the general psychology," he wrote, "I've again been enjoying the extraordinary welcome that is given to a visitor." He commented on the increased friendliness towards England which he thought was "very largely allowed to run to waste through the continued ignorance of English governing classes of America. The general growth of isolationist feeling is of course disastrous – but it is inevitable with a European situation like the present – & its significance is some times exaggerated." Salter envisaged that after the forthcoming presidential elections there would be opportunities for resuming Anglo-American co-operation which had been interrupted by the Depression." He most feared that "peace societies will put their efforts into keeping USA out of wars instead of helping to prevent them from occurring."[364] Salter returned to New York on 22 April and sailed the following day aboard the *Bremen*, returning to London on 19 April.[365]

Two principal concerns, besides his academic duties, occupied Salter in the following weeks. The first was the ongoing development of activities of "The Next Five Years" group, especially centered on The New Outlook. After considerable discussion the first issue appeared on 10 June, containing a symposium on sanctions, and a group photograph of Macmillan, Angell, King-Hall, Salter, Barratt Brown, Allen and the editor, Henry Brinton. Salter's contributed an article on "The League and the Problem of Change" where he addressed the question of how to alter article 19 to allow for territorial revision.[366] The second of Salter's major concerns was the League, particularly because on 9 May, four days after Italian troops entered Addis Ababa, Italy proclaimed the annexation of Abyssinia. The event called into question both the future of the League and the remaining sanctions. On 14 May in a letter to The Times Salter argued that the experience of the League was grounds neither "to abolish nor to emasculate" the institution but to recreate the conditions under which a "collective system of security" could work. This required a "collective preponderance of strength" to act as a deterrent, and for that reason article 16 should be retained. Economic sanctions, likewise, could only succeed if they were backed by the same resolve. "The mechanism of the League has not failed," he concluded. "Rather it was the delays and limitations regarding sanctions – limits set by Britain and France – which caused the failure.

Therefore, every effort must be made to re-establish the "collective system", not only to restrain war but to secure change in the status quo by peaceful means.[367]

The issues raised by Salter evoked considerable discussion in The Times and he returned to the charge on 16 June. He wrote that reform of the League, as commonly advocated, "really means euthanasia," for a League without coercive power meant the abandonment of collective security.[368] During this time, from 29 May to 7 July, Salter also participated in a series of meetings, under the auspices of Chatham House, on the future of the League. Opinion naturally divided between those who contended that the League could not fulfil the promise of a world order, and others were inclined to put force behind the concept of collective security. On 15 June Salter opened his session on "Practical Suggestions for Reform" by emphasizing that his remarks were not a result of the League experience of "the Abyssinian tragedy" where "resolution and consistency" might have produced a different effect on Italy. Rather he specifically turned to Article 11, the conciliation clause, and Article 19, the territorial change clause and termed both of these "inoperative." The need for unanimity was certainly a defect in Article 11, but Salter argued that it could be creatively bypassed by proceeding to co-co-ordinated action, and discounting the vote of the disputant. As for Article 19 he regarded it as "the greatest weakness" of the Covenant and the League. He wanted the principle adopted that, where the League recommended some reasonable change in the status quo which was refused, that power would be denied protection under the Covenant in case war resulted. As for its implementation, he suggested that a request for change should be approved by a two-thirds majority vote in the Council and Assembly, leading then to an enquiry by a League commission, whose recommendations would need a majority vote for passage. Any state rejecting the League recommendation would not be entitled to collective protection if war ensued. Salter's remarks provoked a lively discussion, during which he added that he thought the time was past "when concessions would have been effective as an appeasement of Germany."[369] In an article which he contributed later in the year to The Political Quarterly, he argued that the task was "not to tinker with details of the League machinery," but to concentrate on the political conditions to rebuild the collective system, for which there was no alternative.[370]

Salter was growing increasingly pessimistic with European developments. "The prospect here is indeed obscure & gloomy," he wrote to Stimson on 28 May, "& few of us feel that we can recommend any course with complete confidence that we are right."[371] The question of sanctions was a matter of national and international interest, and Salter felt himself in the thick of these discussions. On 17 June, after the British cabinet agreed to the lifting of sanctions against Italy, he participated in a hastily convened meeting of "sanctionists" in the outer lobby of the House of Commons, including representatives from all parties, various societies and the press. His expressed the view that "we must fight very strongly for the continuation of the sanctions system, and demonstrate that it has been ineffective because it was too slow and too little." The final resolution which appeared in the press the next day urged that sanctions against Italy "should be maintained, and if necessary strengthened, until she is ready to agree to a settlement of the Abyssinian problem acceptable to the League and in conformity with the principles of the Covenant."[372] At a follow-up meeting on 1 July to debate the next step, Salter agreed with most others that there was little to be done about Abyssinia. To many it was clear that Czechoslovakia would be the next target for Germany and the meeting ended without agreement.[373] Several of the participants in these meetings, including Salter, Angell and Eleanor Rathbone, Independent MP for the Combined English Universities, were among the 28 signatories of a new letter to The Times from "The Next Five Years" group. The letter, drafted by Salter, Allen and Angell, rejected the popular view that the Covenant was defective, and urged British representatives at the League to propose that the Assembly adopt its "Map of Peace." This included the return of Germany to the League, detaching the Covenant from the Treaty of Versailles, treating both east and west Europe as one, and arranging a process for peaceful changes in the status quo. Any nation rejecting this "new settlement" would then face a combined multi-state alliance designed "to secure preponderance of collective strength over any aggressor against the system." The plan, described by The Times as "ambitious" but not endorsed, sparked a lively debate.[374] For example, Sir John Fischer Williams targeted the proposal to strengthen the provisions of Article 16, suggesting that this was impossible, given the absence of several major powers from Geneva, and that its application should be "permissive." Salter responded by arguing that such permissiveness would only encourage an aggressor to gamble and take action nonetheless. In his view this strengthened the need for a "collective system," including Russia, to rebuild the League into a credible deterrent. Lytton later put it more succinctly, writing that the plan needed "greater definition and better preparation for the next crisis."[375]

If all this activity was not enough to interest Salter, on 1 July he accepted a position, offered him by the Minister of Labour, as the independent chairman of the Railway Staff National Tribunal. The tribunal was part of new conciliation machinery, agreed to by the railway companies and related unions on 26 February 1935, as the court of appeal to adjudicate between the railway companies and railway trade unions when the Railway Staff National Council could not reach agreement.[376] It met for the first time on 15 July 1936 to examine the claims of the National Union of Railwaymen and the Railway Clerks' Association to restore the 2.5% cut in wages made in March 1931 and also to return to former rates of overtime pay. At the opening of the enquiry

Salter expressed the hope that any conclusions would "promote industrial peace and strengthen the new machinery of negotiations." The tribunal held four hearings between 15 and 20 July, with Salter rendering his decision on the 27 July. The complex settlement included the decision to reduce the rate of deduction in wages from 2.5% to 1.25%, restore the standard rate of time and a quarter for overtime, but with no change for night or Sunday duties. The decision was quickly approved by all parties.[377] Salter was successfully to preside over six of these tribunals, with decisions that satisfied most claimants, until the fall of 1939 when he resigned because of his appointment as parliamentary under-secretary to the Ministry of Shipping.[378] He later wrote that "in every dispute the tribunal was unanimous, the four railway companies and the three railway unions accepted its recommendations, and strikes, whether official or unofficial, were averted."[379]

In the summer of 1936 the BBC broadcast a series of programmes titled "Auto-Obituary." Salter opened his talk by noting that he was in recent years "a publicist and a professor," however, this was "only an appendix to his career as an official." Since resigning from the League, he had filled his time "with dispersed and varied activities," but confessed that he had shown "less aptitude for creative work outside the sphere of official action. His 'floruit' was therefore between the years of 1912 and 1932 – in his thirties and forties."[380] The admission gave an important clue to his state of mind at the time. In <u>Memoirs of a Public Servant</u> he wrote:

> I continued, however, to suffer from a nostalgia for London and the world that pivots round Westminster and Whitehall, and has so many affiliations with other countries; and an itch for executive action, or some contact with it, was aggravated by the growing menace of war.[381]

An opportunity to enter active political life soon occurred, and in a form calculated to fit Salter's political inclinations and wider views. Oxford University was represented in the House of Commons by two Burgesses. The impending resignation of Lord Hugh Cecil (later Lord Quickswood), the Senior Burgess and a Conservative, would require a by-election.[382] Salter was approached by a small committee, consisting of three former parliamentary candidates, representing all three major parties, Professor Gilbert Murray, the last Liberal candidate, the historian and principal of Hertford College, C.R.M. F. Cruttwell, official Conservative candidate at the last election, and G.D.H. Cole, chairman of the University Labour Committee. At the meeting on 5 August Salter agreed to contest the election as an Independent and on the basis of the policies advocated by "The Next Five Years" group. In an aide-mémoire of that conversation, he wrote that he agreed to support a policy "for such armaments as are necessary as a counterpart of collective policy, in order to secure <u>collective</u> preponderance of strength of loyal members of the <u>collective</u> system over those threatening it." Cole reassured Salter that the Labour Party would run no candidate at the by-election and would support him. As well, Cole, Murray and Crutwell were to invite members to form the election committee whose task was to gather the support of individuals of influence. Following this "a general communication for all electors" was to be prepared after which Salter would distribute his election address. It was agreed that this address would "include criticism of Government (e.g., for its vacillations in foreign policy). It will, at the same time, make clear that A.S. is standing as an Independent, taking the whip of no party. It will not include <u>general</u> anti-Government declaration, the position of 'independent' being maintained and opposition being on merits of each question. It will re-state main principles of policy, e.g., economic as in N.F.Y. strong support of collective system, etc."[383] Salter's first choice of electoral agent, Roy Harrod, declined, citing friendship with Professor F.A. Lindemann, head of the department of Experimental Philosophy, who had declared on 15 July his intention to stand as an Independent Conservative. However, Harrrod added, "I think it would be a most magnificent thing if you got in and do much to justify university representation." Salter then fell back on the second choice for agent, James Edward Meade, a Fellow, lecturer in economics and bursar at Hertford College. Announcing the news on 12 August, <u>The Times</u> noted that there were now two local professors after the seat.[384]

Work speeded ahead to organize the election committee, which included, besides, Murray, Crutwell and Cole, Julian Huxley, Macmillan, Rathbone, Sir Richard Livingston, Rowse and Professor J.L. Stocks (last Labour candidate), and also to draft a nomination statement. This emphasized that it was in the public interest for the House of Commons to include some members who were independent of party, but enjoyed the confidence of all parties and that it was "especially suitable for such members to find their seats through University representation." Among Salter's greatest supporters was Rathbone, who wrote on 10 August, to both Murray and Salter, "that a strong Independent candidate, who ran the election almost entirely on the International issue of a strong League ought to have a good chance." Salter later became a great admirer and when she died on 2 January 1946, he wrote of her as "a selfless humanitarian" and "a true independent."[385] From another supporter, Macmillan, came further encouraging words. On 13 August he wrote to Salter: "First, about the University seat. Splendid! It is really great & I feel sure you will get in. Then I will hand over to you the leadership of the Independent Progressive Party, & become your single best loyal follower!"[386] For his part, Salter wrote to Felkin, "I've got a reasonable chance," given the support of Cole, Murray and Crutwell, which was "without precedent. But there's a pretty solid orthodox Conservative vote against me. I've never been very keen on being in the H. of C."[387]

Whatever Salter's reservations, the following weeks proved busy ones. Besides working on numerous organizational matters, and keeping up his Oxford academic commitments, he still maintained an interest in wider issues. One of these was the continuing fallout from the 1931 Manchurian crisis. Salter had always retained his view that an opportunity for British co-operation with the United States had been squandered at the time. This was a subject he had several times discussed with Stimson, including at their last meeting in October 1935, during which Stimson contemplated offering Salter the chance to read a copy of his forthcoming book, <u>The Far Eastern Crisis</u>. That offer never materialized, but Salter received an advance review copy and wrote to Stimson on 13 September that he "read it through, on the day I received it, with the greatest interest & admiration." In his review for <u>The Spectator</u>, Salter suggested that September 1931 "has a strong claim to be regarded as the principal 'turning point' in recent history." He contended that Stimson was deeply disappointed at the limited British communiqué of 11 January in response to his earlier note of 8 January 1932 on non-recognition. This response, Salter argued, was another failed opportunity to strengthen Anglo-American cooperation, which had to be the basis on which to rebuild a "collective system."[388] At the same time, he privately expressed his reservations regarding rumours of a new Anglo-Japanese rapprochement. While desirable in some ways, he feared that its outcome "would mean a set-back in our relations with America."[389]

Economic and financial issues, as always continued to concern Salter, though his published output diminished. With recovery becoming more widespread, he acknowledged that the prevailing parity between the dollar and the pound was contributing to relative stability, but the continuous crises affecting the franc, still tied to gold, concerned him. He had argued as early as July 1935 in <u>The Economist</u>, and again in July in <u>The Rotarian</u>, that the only recourse was a "conditional stabilisation" between the pound, dollar and franc.[390] It was hardly surprising, therefore, that he applauded the French decision on 29 September to devalue the franc. This he described as "the most important economic event" since the devaluation of the dollar in 1933. He looked forward to greater cooperation between France, Britain and the United States, leading to recovery in international trade, the reduction of tariffs, quotas and other restrictive measures. He also expressed the hope that economic stability would lessen the chances for world war.[391]

While leisure time was a rarity for Salter, he continued to enjoy occasional weekend visits to the Astors at Cliveden, where he could both keep in touch with and try to influence establishment opinion.[392] He carried on a reduced schedule of lectures, speaking to the Fabian Society on 12 November on the familiar subject of "Economic Nationalism: Can it Continue?"[393] Similar themes returned in his 1936 Merttens lecture delivered to the Society of Friends on 3 December. He emphasized the current inter-connectedness of economics and politics as providing the conditions for the outbreak of "the next great war which is threatening us." He contended that, with the fate of the League uncertain, only a return to a collective system could avoid war. With regard to economic issues, he argued that "Economic appeasement is not sufficient. It is no substitute for political appeasement or for a system of international government." Thus he wished to see the traditional "open door" colonial policy replaced by one of "equality of opportunity," and a way found to conquer economic nationalism in order to avert war.[394] Salter's concentration on economic nationalism, the need to reduce it and the close association between diplomacy, politics and economics, led him to take his concerns to the highest levels of government. "Some time ago you kindly invited me to make any suggestions as to policy which might occur to me," Salter wrote to Eden on 16 December. The reasons for his silence, Salter explained, were that some times the government's foreign policy accorded with his own views, and comment was unnecessary. At other times, "frankly, the line that was being in fact pursued by the Government was so different from what I would have wished that I thought no suggestion of mine could be of any use." Nonetheless, a recent speech by Eden, wrote Salter, prompted him to forward a memorandum he had written regarding the inter-connectedness between international economic co-operation and the reduction of political tensions. With the trade cycle in an upward movement and a possible danger of inflation, he suggested, the time was right to implement a series of measures, among which he included reduction of tariffs and the extension of currency co-operation. Salter's submission was discussed at all levels of the Foreign Office. While it was noted that some of his recommendations accorded with prevailing Foreign Office views, "the practical difficulties appear to be greater than he imagines." In his eventual response, Eden thanked Salter for the memorandum and promised to study the document.[395]

Salter's growing sense of urgency regarding the prospects for another war was increasingly on his mind. In a BBC broadcast on 23 October, for which he drew extensively on his wartime experience as Director of Ship Requisitioning, he had pointed out that victory in 1918 was achieved "as much on sea as on land." Then he asked, "What of our preparations in case of another?" In his view, the government must implement, from the outset of the war, control over supplies and shipping and revive the convoy system for merchant ships. More immediately, however, he urged, a start be made on the peace-time storage of wheat, food-stuffs and oil. "This, in my opinion, ought to be one of our principal measures of defence." He finally added that immediate plans should be made to study the impact of and response to, air war, especially with regard to the security of British ports and distribution routes.[396] He followed this up with a letter to the editor of The Times, advocating "serious and urgent consideration" for the immediate storage of "grain, feeding stuffs and oil." Storage, while costly, he added, increased security, reduced the need for naval convoys, and was entirely defensive in character. Although he acknowledged that the issue was not a popular one, it led to a flurry of letters to the editor, including a generally supportive editorial.[397] Equally important, it was to provide Salter with one of the central issues on which he was to lobby as a future member of parliament.

The unfolding of the Oxford by-election was proving to be of interest beyond the confines of the university, and ultimately to Salter's advantage. On 7 September a statement published in The Times from some of Lindemann's Conservative parliamentary supporters urged his adoption as official candidate, although with apologies that many were not in fact "Oxford men." On 24 October the Oxford University Conservative Association concluded that Lindemann would not have official party support.[398] At this point Salter confessed that the election was "full of uncertainties." Although he did not have the substantial press support enjoyed by Lindemann, he observed, his real chances rested on a Conservative split vote.[399] On 30 October Lindemann's supporters brought Winston Churchill to Oxford where, on the one hand he praised Salter as "a most able gentleman and a great authority on economic subjects," but condemned his judgment for having "highly eulogized" Ivar Kreuger in Recovery. Churchill also derided the "confused popular front doctrine" offered by Salter, criticised Cruttwell for losing his deposit in the last election, derided Cole whom he could not take seriously, and sang the praises of Lindemann.[400] Churchill's intervention likely proved counter-productive and most certainly helped Salter. On 9 December it was Sir Farquhar Buzzard, the elderly Regius Professor of Medicine and one of the Royal physicians, who was chosen as the Conservative candidate, while Lindemann insisted on running as an Independent Conservative. With the Conservative vote thus likely split, Salter's chances to win the seat were, in his own words, "certain."[401] At year's end he was already rethinking his commitments, offering to resign from the Council of Chatham House.[402] On the other hand, he allowed his name to be placed on the advisory council of a new organization spearheaded by de Madariaga, The World Foundation, dedicated to the development of "a world consciousness," to prepare the way for "a system of world management."[403]

Oxford electors, Salter later recalled, "are jealous of two traditions, that there should be no speeches by or on behalf of Oxford candidates, and that no one who is not himself an Oxford man should take any hand in the election."[404] Consequently, he could only bide his time while keeping otherwise busy. At the suggestion of the historian, E.L. Woodward, he examined the widespread accusation that the Allies deliberately starved Germany by maintaining the blockade after the armistice. He consulted Cecil, who conceded that "when the subject is fully investigated the Allies will not cut a very good figure." However, Cecil attributed the main cause of German suffering to the general dislocation of the war. In his article for The Spectator, Salter contended that starvation was due to the shortage of supplies and shipping, the delay caused by discussions about future reparation claimants and administrative confusion – "but not the blockade, and not deliberate malice."[405] He also contributed another article to The Rotarian, praising the Rotary International movement, and similar organizations, for their efforts to advance peace by uniting people with common interests and occupations. Building on this, Salter advocated further development of what he termed "a horizontal as well as a vertical organization" of human interests and pursuits.[406] By this time, as well, he had given up any prospects of writing another book, or even revising and updating Recovery, as suggested by his publisher. "I fear I am an unsatisfactory author," he replied. "I've written nothing beyond articles or lectures – & see no particular prospect of doing so – having too many dispersed interests & activities."[407] In his familiar vein, however, he returned to the charge again on the issue which he had raised with Eden on 16 December 1936, and in very similar words. The opportunity to restore world trade, he wrote in The Times on 20 January 1937, was pressing. Again he emphasized the inter-relatedness of economics and international affairs, and called for "a strong and determined initiative" on the part of the British government.[408]

On 29 January Lord Hugh Cecil finally resigned to take up his position as Provost of Eton and the Oxford by-election became a focus of enormous attention. On the same day, Salter published his list of supporters which included heads and former heads of Oxford Colleges, the Archbishop of York and several bishops and members of both the Lords and Commons. The Times wrote of the "contest between three Professors … [as] a novel experience for the electors of Oxford." Salter and Buzzard had the support of Oxford residents and academics. Lindemann had limited academic following, but in an unusual move had published the names of members of parliament, not graduates of the university, as supporters.[409] Salter foresaw that his chief opponent would be Buzzard, "distinguished" and "personally popular," but someone who "has never been known to express any personal views in public on either domestic or foreign policy." He thought his own chances depended on Lindemann taking a considerable proportion of the Conservative votes.[410] On 10 February, Salter's nomination was officially handed in to the returning officer, and he followed this with the issue of a 15-page pamphlet, Letter to the Electors of Oxford. Such a step had been initiated by A.P. Herbert, the essayist, humourist and divorce law reformer who had won the Oxford seat in the 1935 election, and who was also running as an Independent. "Mine is longer and rather more comprehensive," Salter noted, "also duller."[411] "I stand as an Independent in the fullest sense, not Independent Conservative, or Labour, or Liberal, but Independent pure and simple." With these words Salter began his Letter, adding that he had been nominated with all party support as a non-party candidate. He then detailed his policies on a range of issues, noting that he stood on his record of his previous public advocacy, including raising the school leaving age and for universities to move away from "unco-ordinated specialization." He rejected nationalization in favour of "an extension of the 'public utility' principle" and state aid to foster new industries and revive foreign trade. He made a final plea that only an effective League could ensure a lasting peace; though he did acknowledge that "we must supplement action through the League by other measures outside it."[412] In the following days, the issues and personalities involved in the by-election attracted national attention and some controversy. Salter was forced to defend his decision to support the Labour candidate Noel-Baker in the 9 July 1936 by-election in Derby, a seat which the latter won. He had to explain yet again that if elected as an Independent, his loyalty was "not to a party but to the principles of policy" which he had adopted in his address.[413] And once again he had to reiterate his view that reform of the League was not the issue. Rather he favoured prior consultation and agreement on common action by loyal League members, to recreate the political conditions under which the League could function.[414]

When the Oxford University by-election results were announced on 27 February, Salter was declared the winner. Even with the split in the Conservative ranks, he won the seat with a clear majority (7,580) over both Buzzard (3,917) and Lindemann (3,608). The results drew trans-Atlantic attention, with The New York Times describing them as "a tribute to a man of unusual abilities and long devotion to the public service." The Times declared that his victory showed "how attractive the necessary ambiguities of Independence can be." The historian, J.A.R. Marriott, speculated that Salter had captured the vast majority of the 3,190 eligible women electors on the strength of his League reputation.[415] For his part, among the many he thanked was the editor of The Manchester Guardian, noting that his newspaper's support was "a very great factor" in the result.[416] In his first post-election interview, Salter declared that "The electors had voted not for me, but for the principles and policy for which I stand. They strongly desire that a middle policy, selected from both the Right and the Left, should be given full expression in Parliament."[417] On the same day as the results were announced, Salter made his first public speech as an MP. At the annual dinner of the Oxford University China Society, at Rhodes House, he light-heartedly noted that he was unsure "what particular measure of wisdom or folly" he would bring to his new job.⁴¹⁸ Personal letters of congratulations poured in, including one from Lloyd George. In his responses Salter modestly declared that the majority was certainly "a surprising result."⁴¹⁹ However, writing to Allen, he went further: "It is a real NFY [Next Five Years] victory, for I fought upon it, & there can be no doubt that what the electors meant is just what we stand for."⁴²⁰ On 5 March Salter took the same line in The Spectator, noting that the significance of the Oxford result was "political and not personal." He was convinced that the Oxford electors, scattered across the country, represented the majority of people in England who preferred the "middle policy" enunciated by the "Next Five Years" group, "a policy not of mere compromise but of creative selection." As further evidence of his victory, Salter wrote that it was achieved despite the fact that the principal Conservative newspapers, except The Times, endorsed Lindemann, while only The Manchester Guardian, the News Chronicle and The Spectator supported him.⁴²¹ To Elisina Tyler, he wrote more candidly. "I had the good fortune however to have one competitor who was gentlemanly to the point of being completely inactive while the other was active to the point of being completely ungentlemanly – & each attitude lost votes."⁴²² On 3 March, "marching in perfect step and bowing in perfect union" with his Independent colleagues and sponsors, Rathbone and Herbert, Salter was introduced into the House of Commons.⁴²³ Now represented by two Independent MPs, Salter's co-parliamentarian Herbert recalled that "Oxford University to-day is represented by a boat-builder and a buffoon."⁴²⁴ Certainly, the Conservative stranglehold on the Oxford University seats was fully broken and it was now up to Salter and Herbert to prove the ongoing validity of the university franchise and the benefits of non-party affiliation.

The election campaign appeared to have exhausted Salter. On 15 March, on the eve of his departure for an extended Hellenic cruise with the Laytons, he wrote to Felkin: "I shall find the H. of C. interesting, unless & until I find that I can't do anything in it, which is highly probable, for the elderly novice is rarely a success. Anyhow I find it difficult to go into it with quite the same spirit as I might have a few years ago – or even a year & a half ago."⁴²⁵ On 31 March, after stops at several Greek islands, he wrote to Elisina Tyler from aboard the Donaldson liner *Letitia* that he was having "a most enjoyable & successful holiday."⁴²⁶ That same day Salter's father, James Edward Salter, died after suffering from heart trouble for some time. Both The Oxford Mail and The Oxford Times gave extended coverage to the life and career of James Edward Salter. Returning quickly to Oxford, Salter wrote a tribute to his father which The Oxford Mail carried on 5 April. He detailed the many contributions his father had made to Oxford's civic and public life. More personally, he wrote of how his father "combined a personal humility, a gentle courtesy and a charity of judgment with great tenacity of purpose." While "reticent and reserved where his deeper experiences were involved," he could also reveal "depth and delicacy of feeling." The funeral held the same day at the Wesley Memorial Church was crowded with representatives from all walks of Oxford life. The service was followed by interment at Wolvercote Cemetery where the driveway was lined by employees of Salter Bros. Among those who sent flowers was Ethel Bullard, at the time in London, in better health, and in the eyes of Ka Cox eager "to move on to the next stage."[427] This was a sad period in Salter's life, for his father's death was followed a day later by that of Sir J. Reeve Brooke, a colleague and later friend since the World War. On 27 April Ka Cox wrote that Salter "is well – though the shock of his Father's death & Reeve Brookes' just as he got back from a holiday – made very heavy days for him."[428]

There was more weighing on Salter's mind. Earlier on 20 February Helen St. George Saunders, a member of the League secretariat and as Felkin described her, his "beloved mistress," had suddenly died after surgery.[429] The news reverberated around Salter's own group of friends, including Ethel Bullard and her sister Marchesa Louise de Rosales. In fact, the former telephoned the news on 22 February to Salter who immediately wrote to comfort Felkin. Beginning with references to his own personal experiences of loss, Salter wrote that "I have learnt much about myself, & what bereavement means, from what was by far the worst thing that ever happened to me. But I know that for you as for me there must be a hard time ahead. You are perhaps at first numbed & it is necessary to be prepared for perhaps what is worse later, as the realization of the finality comes clearer & the sense of emptiness. During this time by far the best thing is I believe to dope yourself by work." He conceded that it was not possible to avoid all recourse to memories, however, "if you don't reduce the time by some form of doping, I'm afraid you may crack – at least that was my experience. I am thinking much of you."[430] So too was another member of the intimate circle, Ethel Bullard. She herself had a bout of surgery on 7 February, which left her, in the words of her sister "horribly ill," and with the "question of whether she wd. pull through or not for some days after the operation." From her sick bed at the London Clinic, she wrote to Felkin, "I know perhaps better than anyone how you loved her." She added, "I have always felt no personal fear of death," noted that she had had "a narrow squeak," and concluded, "If only I could have gone on & Helen stayed as I told my surgeon. She was needed so much more."[431] As for Felkin, his diaries provide ample evidence of how devastated he felt by the loss but also comforted by friends, noting that "Arthur is quite right about its being worse later."[432]

When the "Next Five Years" group held a celebration lunch on 13 April, at the Trocadero Restaurant in London, Salter spoke of his victory as proof there was "a vast body of people politically homeless" who supported a "progressive, constructive realistic policy similar to that outlined in the N.F.Y. publications."⁴³³ Ka Cox, who was informed of the speech, was told that Salter "was so anxious to make an impersonal statement of policy," that he forgot to offer thanks for the lunch.⁴³⁴ Indeed, the activities of the group had continued apace, with Salter making occasional contributions. To keep the momentum generated by the publication of its book in July 1936, a shorter pamphlet, A Programme of Priorities, had been published on 16 February. Its first section proposed some new reforms, such as a National Public Medical Service and a national minimum wage. The second, dealing with the economy, advanced proposals for massive state planning, including the nationalization of coal and electricity. The final section, drafted by Salter the previous fall, urged the re-establishment of a system of collective security to resist aggression against such states as Czechoslovakia. As well, it proposed fact-finding commissions to examine such outstanding problems as colonies, tariffs and currency questions. Allen summarized the initiative as "not political manoeuvring but social engineering."⁴³⁵ The launching by the group of The New Outlook in June 1936, never really attracted Salter's attention, other than the two articles he contributed, one on reform of the League and the other his address to his Oxford constituents. In fact, the journal ceased publication after 12 numbers, because of financial loss, with its last issue on 8 May 1937.⁴³⁶

Concurrently, Salter accepted an invitation to sit on the executive committee of the League of Nations Union [LNU] and on 8 April attended his first meeting. He had in 1928 and 1929 occasionally been present at the Economic Committee of the LNU to advise on issues being discussed at the League of Nations.⁴³⁷ During April, he initially threw himself into his new responsibilities, trying to use the organization to further his own agenda. Thus, at this first meeting and subsequently, he urged the LNU to play a more proactive role with regard to the Spanish civil war, given the ineptitude of the Non-Intervention Committee. A week later he completed a memorandum on "A New Opportunity for Foreign Trade," stressing the urgency of closer Anglo-American economic co-operation, especially in light of Cordell Hull's public appeal on 5 April for nations to rebuild international political and economic relationships. The Economic Committee agreed, on the basis of Salter's memorandum, that the moment was right to pursue "economic appeasement."⁴³⁸ While he was committed to the organization, his Salter's attendance was often erratic, so much so that he soon wished to resign. It was only the persuasive powers of Cecil that convinced him to carry on, with the understanding that he would only attend for subjects of interest.⁴³⁹

In anticipation of taking his seat in the Commons, Salter had written, "I don't know what I shall make of it – most elderly novices make a hash of it. Anyhow I'm going to study the place with some care for a little time before I open my lips."⁴⁴⁰ After two brief interventions on 14 and 21 April, Salter made his maiden speech on 22 April, two days after the government tabled its budget. He modestly admitted to "diffidence" in rising to speak on such a complex matter, but added he was no stranger to budgets and public finance in many other countries. He began, however, by describing what he conceived to be the proper position of an Independent Member – "a rare, though I am glad to say not an entire solitary, animal in this House. My own view is that it is at once his privilege and his duty to express his views on specific proposals without regard to what may be his views on other matters." Salter then proceeded, in a 22-minute speech, to welcome the provisions for an increase in direct taxation, as being of principal benefit to the lower income classes, and suspended judgment on the proposed new graduated tax on excess profits. In closing, he made an earnest plea for the government to turn away from its strict protectionist policies and join with other countries, particularly France and the United States, to restore international trade. According to The Manchester Guardian, Salter's speech "fully came up to expectations, was short, clear, weighty, and a master of phrases" and was greeted with loud applause.[441] Salter's reservations regarding the National Defence Contribution led to widespread criticism and to an extended debate later in May in the columns of The Times, when he was able to further amplify his reservations. In the end, the government backed down and settled on a flat rate on profits.[442]

With the opening in London on 14 May of what was to be the last Imperial Conference, Salter surveyed the prospects in The New York Times, singling out foreign affairs and defence as the most important topics on the agenda. He did not disguise his own wish that, given the "vulnerable and dispersed" nature of the empire, a new world order, including the League and the Kellogg Pact, must be established to act as an effective deterrent against war. For the rest, he examined the factors which made for the enduring survival of the empire and suggested the formation of an "imperial secretariat" or a "permanent Commonwealth Foreign Office," which would plan agendas for future conferences. His conclusion returned to his plea for "a real and effective system of collective security." This he reinforced the next day in a letter to The Times, again pointing to the vulnerability of the Empire and urging a change of view toward seeing the League as an integral part of Britain's defence – "a mutual insurance club, not a charitable society."[443] He also continued to focus on what he discerned as the issue of greatest concern, the need to increase world trade and remove various obstacles such as industrial quotas, exchange controls and even Imperial preference. These were subjects he examined during his second major contribution to the House of Commons on 25 May, when he forcefully singled out Britain as among the major protectionist states. In particular, he proposed a new Anglo-American commercial agreement, modifications to the 1932 system of Imperial preferences, an extension of the low tariff movement, and a return to the policy of the open colonial door. The Times noted that his speech "attracted and held a good audience."[444]

Salter was indeed working both publicly and behind the scenes on an array of questions. On 9 June he joined with other leading Oxford economists in writing to The Times about "the danger of a recession in trade activity leading to a severe Depression within the next few years." The group advocated the state, local authorities and other public bodies respond immediately with "expenditure on works of capital development as the slump begins."[445] On 11 June Lamont wrote to him about an array of American concerns regarding British protectionist policies and praised the latter's public efforts to encourage Anglo-American economic co-operation. Salter responded that he had been working on the issues both with the government and members of the Commons, but added, "I confess that the result has so far not been very encouraging."[446] On 18 June he added his name to a letter to The Times from the "Next Five Years" group endorsing a restoration of international trade and the reduction of tariff barriers.[447] The next day, he also took up the question of the massive influx of gold into the United States in a letter to the editor of The Times. He suggested that the British empire was the primary producer and the only way to deal with the problem was to increase Anglo-American trade.[448] In the Commons on 28 June he entered the debate about the Exchange Equalisation Account. Responding to the Chancellor's proposals to increase its capitalization, he asked for greater cooperation in this area with the United States and France, and further clarity about its practices.[449]

Not all of Salter's concerns during this period were narrowly economic. He continued to take a close interest in the Spanish Civil War and, after the bombing of Guernica on 27 April, lobbied for the evacuation of women and children from Bilbao. Internal show trials in Nazi Germany also began to capture his attention.[450] In May 1934 Salter had been among the founding members of the newly formed Association for Education in Citizenship. Its mandate was to prepare young people, through a liberal education, to deal with "the problems of citizenship in a democratic state" and thus strengthen democracy against the threat of totalitarianism. It was expected that the addition of such subjects as "civics, economics, and politics" would produce character, vision, a global perspective and a democratic citizen.[451] The association organized its first major conference from 8-14 July 1937, with representatives of all three major political parties, to hear speeches from several statesmen, economists, philosophers and politicians. Salter spoke last and used the occasion to push his own perceptions of democracy, which encompassed a society where there was less income disparity and where social inequality were diminished. It would also need leadership, competence and planning, and not merely improvisation. He concluded with his credo, namely, his test for any religion, political or social system "was whether or not on the whole it contributes towards the free and full and rich development of varied human personality."[452] At this same time, and as a member of the Social Studies Research Committee at Oxford, Salter assisted in setting up a new summer school on Colonial Administration.[453] As well, it was announced on 24 July that he had accepted an invitation to serve as President of Morley College for Working Men and Women, a position he held until his resignation on 17 December 1951.[454] The announcement in the college magazine, written by Principal Eva M. Hubback, who was also the honourary secretary of the Association for Education in Citizenship, welcomed Salter as "a man of high political integrity and ideals."[455] Although the presidency was intended to be largely honorific, Salter took a more hands-on approach, visiting the college and making suggested improvements to the college calendar. Speaking for the first time at the college's annual dinner, his only officially required duty, Salter praised the college's mission, for "While it gave an enlargement to the mind and character it was non-vocational, non-examinational, non-misogynistic, but sociable and self-governing."[456] Then on 20 July he began a new series of hearings, which extended over eight days, in his capacity as chairman of the Railway Staff National Tribunal. The decision was rendered on 11 August with Salter approving the complete restoration of cuts dating back to 1931.[457] The pace of such activity led him to ruefully comment that he had "made no plans myself" for a summer vacation, although he did visit the Tylers at Antigny-le-Chateau and from there went to Salzburg later in August.[458]

Salter finally found his voice in the House of Commons when he emerged during July as the leading proponent for the peacetime storage of food and strategic raw materials. Here he was able to speak from his personal experience as Director of Ship Requisitioning at the Ministry of Shipping during the First World War. That experience convinced him that the storage issue had to be implemented well in advance of hostilities to avoid what he termed as "panic" decisions that conflicted with military policy. He could now do so, however, as a member of parliament rather than a lobbyist. On 16 July he had met with Sir Thomas Inskip, the Minister for Coordination of Defence, to press his views, initially on acquiring and storing a year's supply of grain. Salter returned to the subject on 27 July in the Commons, determined to find a place for it in the debate about national defence. His experience during the World War, which he described as "terrible," and the fact that his name was being associated with the proposals, he stated, prompted him to emphasize the subject. Initially, he focused his remarks on the need to implement a "scheme for dispersed inland storage of essential foodstuffs." The advantages were that it would be convenient for transport, less vulnerable to destruction, and obviated the need to increase domestic production or imports. He went on to criticise the "negative and discouraging" attitude exhibited by Inskip, in his 18 February reference to the Food (Defence Plans) Department, created on 16 December 1937, but whose mandate was only to plan for the supply, control and movement of food in wartime. Given that it was the youngest and thus the "Cinderella of Departments," he exhorted Inskip to "fulfil the role of fairy godmother" and take strong measures to give it teeth. Salter explained that dispersed inland storage covered a wide range of foodstuffs, not necessarily a balanced one, but the equivalent to a year's consumption of wheat. Such a scheme would enable Britain to fight for several years undisturbed by the prospect of starvation, and it would relieve the burden on shipping. In his reply, Inskip noted that the issues were complex and planning was ongoing.[459] The Times noted that Salter had argued his case "impressively" and referred to his "great experience" on the subject.[460]

Salter followed up with a lengthy memorandum he sent to Inskip on 5 August further supporting the case for food storage and its dispersal as "an essential part of our war preparations." He noted the fact that even with command of the seas in the first war, Britain was "for some time in grave danger of defeat through starvation." With the new danger of aircraft attacks against merchant shipping, the situation was even more serious. What followed was a detailed analysis of prevailing stocks of wheat, fats, meat, and other foodstuffs such as sugar and eggs, intended to buttress his contention that increased domestic production was "impracticable." The only strategy, therefore, was dispersed storage, with immediate steps taken to choose sites, construct storage facilities and stock such necessities as wheat and sugar.[461] While faulted on some technical matters, Salter's views were treated seriously by the government, and it was suggested that if circumstances worsened, "the Government would be well advised to examine these proposals more closely than they have done to the present time."[462] For his part, Salter agreed that food supplies in war needed to encompass what The Times endorsed as a combination of "home production, food storage and imports." However, his advocacy of the second measure, he wrote in response, was not as an alternative but because it would provide exceptional security and was "entirely unprovocative in character."[463] Another attempt at publicity was a lengthy article he contributed The Economist on 2 October, covering familiar ground which he had conveyed to Inskip and in the Commons. However, he was also critical of the government's indecision on the subject, and emphasized that the situation was more serious than in 1914: there were millions more to feed; gross merchant tonnage was down; and to the submarine menace was now added the threat of the bomber. Salter concluded with a six-step programme designed to give immediate effect to his plans. He further stepped up his campaign when he had his article reprinted, at his own expense and with some revisions. It was widely distributed and attracted considerable attention.[464]

Even as he grappled with the food storage issue, Salter was involved in other ongoing concerns. An incident on 7 July between Chinese and Japanese soldiers at the Marco Polo Bridge near Peking had soon escalated into an undeclared war between the two Far Eastern powers. On 21 September he met with Stimson and Layton in London, and suggested that the League should "go through the process of collecting the facts" as a starting point, knowing full well that any punitive action was out of the question and would in any case require the participation of the United States. At the same time, he circulated a memorandum written by Guy Wint which examined the effect of possible future economic sanctions against Japan. Salter's covering letter conceded that, given the European situation and isolationist opinion in the United States, there was little possibility of implementation.[465] He was equally very sensitive to the fact that nothing should be done to encourage American isolationists who feared that Britain, "in the name of collective security, is trying to get America to pull its chestnuts out of the fire."[466] Nonetheless, he felt heartened by a letter which Keynes wrote to The Times on 29 September, supporting economic sanctions against Japan. Writing to Keynes the following day, Salter emphasized the importance he attached to bringing about a change in American opinion, but expressed his fears that any proactive move would provoke suspicions among the "'neutralists' – as to the hidden hand of British policy in America." Given that he was a personal target of a best-selling book of the day, England Expects Every American to Do His Duty by Quincy Howe, Salter confessed that he would refrain from any public comments on American politics. Nonetheless, he confided to Keynes that he had in fact written to Hull, to which Keynes responded that the letter "could not be bettered."[467] At this time, too, and after a long period of absence, Salter re-engaged with the League of Nations Union. Here he spoke in favour of reviving "League principles," but cautioned against any rash actions, particularly if these would alienate the United States. In reality, Salter confided to Cecil, he was losing his faith in the organization.[468]

Ironically, October saw the publication of an article by Salter, presumably written before his "vow of silence" on the subject, "Europe Looks to America." He began with a sympathetic survey of the place of the USA in the global context – inherently isolationist but with world-wide influence. However, he went on to make the case that a determined President, acting on the basis of American adherence to the Kellogg Pact, could regain the freedom of manoeuvre to confront aggression. For the near future, while avenues for diplomatic cooperation were "practically annihilated," Salter considered both Roosevelt and Cordell Hull as amenable to any movement to revive world trade and help reduce international tension.[469] On 1 November, and in the same spirit, Salter headed a delegation to meet with the new Prime Minister Neville Chamberlain at 10 Downing Street, to discuss an array of subjects, including tariffs and the international economic situation. On the following day in the House of Commons he looked ahead to a period of large scale unemployment or a Depression following completion of the rearmament programmes. Echoing the views voiced by a group of leading economists in The Times on 9 June, he suggested that a Depression could come "at no very distant date" and government must take immediate steps to prepare, at both the national and local levels, programmes for public works. In conclusion, he returned to the food storage question, criticising the government for its procrastination, and avoiding any decisions on principal or policy.[470] When Chamberlain publically complained about the undue economic pessimism espoused by some, Salter responded in The Times that he and other economists were not making predictions, but merely asking for government preparedness. Keynes then followed with another letter strongly supportive of Salter's views. The need for long range preparations, including questions of food storage and civil defence, may have been rejected by the government at the time. But it gained support from The Economist and The Times, and led to a period of collaboration between Salter and Keynes on these issues.[471]

Given the consensus that had been achieved with the "Next Five Years" group, Salter began to consider whether a similar agreed programme of action on foreign policy was possible. The group had last met on 19 June at Balliol College, Oxford, to consider its "Programme of Priorities," but its activities were winding down. Its last foray was to be in February 1938 when it published its only "Occasional Communications No. 1," an examination of the question of public works. This document, clearly drafted by Salter, was discussed at the 19 June conference, but without any resulting action.[472] In foreign affairs, on which Salter increasingly focused, his concerns were the Spanish Civil War, the continuing Japanese sweep through China and the increasingly hostile international environment. He concluded that it would be worthwhile to form what he termed the All Souls Foreign Affairs Group. He explained to prospective members that a number of people, "most of us starting as believers from the beginning in League principles, have been feeling the need for a fuller & more informed exchange of views as to the best practicable line of foreign policy."[473] He later explained:

> I found myself in grave doubt as to the course of policy to support and advocate, a doubt extending to some of the gravest issues presenting themselves; and in consulting others who started with a similar general outlook I found they were all experiencing equal, though not identical, anxieties. I hoped that we might help each other in clearing our minds and in solving the individual problem presenting itself to each of us as to his own line of conduct.[474]

The first meeting of the All Souls Foreign Affairs Group, convened by Salter and Sir Harold Nicolson, was held on 18 and 19 December. Among those attending, beside Salter, were several of the original members of the "Next Five Years" group, Allen, Arnold-Forster, Barratt Brown and Macmillan, as well as Curtis, Layton, Liddell Hart, Gilbert Murray, Rowse, Arnold Toynbee and Guy Wint, among others.[475] Three initial questions were addressed: "What is our power? Where is the first challenge likely to occur? And what steps should be taken to meet the challenge?" Agreement was initially reached on a few points: the world could be divided between League and anti-League powers; British policy could not be based on American assistance; and while Japan and Italy were dangerous, "Germany was the centre of the whole problem," further concessions to Germany were "futile," and playing for time was "too negative." The consensus was that "British policy towards Germany should be one of firmness followed by conciliation," and to this end work was begun to draft the terms of a general settlement.[476] Shortly thereafter, Salter made his first speech in the Commons on foreign affairs. His comments on 21 December were characteristically sympathetic to the government, which faced the task of "attempting something between conciliation or concession on the one hand and resistance on the other." He then turned to the situation in the Far East and suggested, on the basis of his two visits to China, that reconstruction might have succeeded except for Japan's military campaigns to dominate the country. This he called "one of the greatest historic tragedies of the world." He further accused Japan of aiming at complete hegemony in the Far East and the exclusion of western powers. However, given Japan's dependence on imports from both Britain and the USA, and if effective and combined economic pressure could be applied, Salter believed the risks were worthwhile.[477]

Salter's reputation in the United States as a commentator, while perhaps diminished, still retained some clout. Writing by invitation in The Yale Review for December, he returned to what he regarded as "the perils of recovery." He focused on the autumn business recession in the United States and the poor performance of the stock exchange, with its widespread fall in prices. In his view, the underlying economic and financial factors were sound and he did not envisage a return to 1929. However, he then focused on the decline in investment and a general lack of confidence which he attributed in part to what he termed a "strike of capital," and a "distrust of Washington by the leaders of capital." He concluded by suggesting that other factors were responsible for the economic downturn and that a change of attitude and action was required by all concerned.[478] On 29 December American Assistant Attorney General Robert H. Jackson addressed the American Political Science Association. After describing Salter as "one of the most informed and disinterested observers of our business life," he quoted from the article and leapt on the phrase "strike of capital" to defend the Roosevelt administration's economic policies. Salter did not respond, having already stated in his article that it would be "impertinent for a foreigner" to assess the weight of responsibility. In the subsequent controversy in Washington between Democrats and Republicans, Salter's views were finally and fairly represented.[479] The year ended with Salter and Violet Markham taking a continental vacation which included a meeting with Elisina Tyler at Hyères on the south-east coast of France.[480]

The All Souls Foreign Affairs Group next met on 15 January 1938, and now included, for the first time, Layton, Adams and Rowse. With the knowledge that an "affirmation of strength" in the Far East was impossible without American support, the group realized that any boycott of Japanese goods or League of Nations intervention raised the spectre of war. The only feasible policy, therefore, was to hasten the shipment of supplies to China, institute a boycott against oil and abandon Hong Kong if it were attacked. On the question of Anglo-German relations, one participant supported the Foreign Office view that any "head-on collision" with the Axis should be avoided, while playing for time, while others argued for the improvement of relations with the USSR. The discussion then turned to the possibility of organizing "a positive peace-group," based on "a constructive economic policy" and the building of a new economic order, associated with the League of Nations, and strong enough to attract Germany and Italy. On Sunday morning, 16 January, the agenda turned from resistance to conciliation. Could Germany be trusted with the organization of a British-style commonwealth in south-eastern Europe? Did Britain still have the power to enforce its traditional balance of power policy in Europe? It was agreed that any direct overtures to Germany would be taken as a sign of weakness, but there was disagreement on ways to discover what concessions would be "neither dishonourable nor disastrous."[480] Afterwards Liddell Hart noted with approval "the way in which so many individual viewpoints converged towards a common view," while Salter stressed what he called the "real value" of the meetings.[482] However, he was not generally sanguine about the future, writing, "I look forward to the next few months with great apprehension."[483]

While some meagre progress was evident at the All Souls Foreign Affairs Group, Salter's parallel campaign on food storage for defence was moving forward. He believed the time was ripe for what he called "a really effective push." On 10 January he sent a letter to several MPs, inviting them to a meeting in one of the committee rooms in the House of Commons. The objective would be a briefing on the issue of food storage, followed by a deputation to the prime minister, and ending with the creation of an "All Party Movement" on the issue.[484] While this initiative floundered, support continued to grow, at least as evidenced by letters to the editor in The Times. As a result, on 19 January the paper devoted a lengthy and supportive editorial on the issue. Salter followed up two days later with a letter to The Times, in which he pointed out that six months after his parliamentary speech on food storage, no decision had yet been announced by the government. "Surely it is of vital importance that there should be no further delay," he concluded.[485] The good fortune of Labour MP John Parker in securing a private member's motion supporting food storage forced a parliamentary debate on 9 February. Salter spent the previous day working at home and inclined "to nurse my throat for tomorrow." He also confided that "The general air of the H. of C. is not very favourable."[486] Speaking in advance of a statement from Inskip, Salter explained that he advocated "storage of food of different kinds equivalent in total to the food value of a year's wheat," at a cost of 1-2% of the country's annual defence expenditure. He then attacked the "casual, light-hearted" attitude adopted by Inskip towards the work of the Food (Defence Plans) Department, describing it as a "late-born, unwillingly conceived, miserable child," and the minister as "the greatest Parliamentary stone-waller of all time." The question of food storage, the "fourth branch" of defence, Salter continued, required a dedicated minister. He concluded, "This is a job which wants pre-eminently a Minister who will say, 'What the situation needs, I will get on with.' With great respect, I suggest that if we were choosing from this House a Minister with that particular quality, it is not the right hon. Gentleman that we would choose." Inskip's responded by indicating that the question was complex, not open to a simple decision in principle, and required yet further study. When a vote was taken, the Labour motion was defeated.[487] The Manchester Guardian regarded Inskip's contribution as "a great disappointed to members of all parties."[488]

One of the consequences of Salter's efforts was that he was becoming increasingly gloomy over international and domestic affairs. Writing on 19 February he suggested that, from an economic point of view, the country was "in a period which is more like one of war than one of normal peace." Hence, preparations for war required "an extensive alteration of our economic system," including the establishment of a Ministry of Supply, and the diversion of some of the unemployed towards the building of air raid shelters.[489] In a wider context he was also moving even more left of centre. He observed that the British state was expanding its interventionism into such areas as agriculture, electricity and coal, thus "building up a completely new economic system." However, he pleaded for a balance between the public and private spheres. "There are very many who, like myself," he wrote, "if forced to choose between an obviously unjust semi-state system imposed by a State which has been captured by sectional interests, and a more complete State system, from which private enterprise has been eliminated, would, reluctantly but without hesitation, choose the latter."[490]

The All Souls Foreign Affairs Group, meanwhile, continued its efforts to reach a consensus, with Salter anticipating the next date, 6 February, as perhaps the final meeting.[491] The discussion centred on a paper, written by Allen, the most persistent advocate of Anglo-German reconciliation, which advocated "a display of strength with an outline of proposals to meet legitimate grievances and claims." Thus he proposed that Austria and Germany should be permitted to unite and that Czechoslovakia should adopt a cantonal system to deal with minority problems and become a neutral state.[492] Participants were then invited to make revisions, but unfortunately the next meeting at All Souls on 26 February made little progress. The group debated the questions of whether their final document would be for private or public circulation, and would it propose amendments or alternatives to government policy? It was agreed that one of the members would prepare a new draft document to be considered at the next meeting. The resignation of Eden as Foreign Secretary on 20 February also led to a discussion first of Anglo-Italian relations and then issues of collective security and policy towards Germany. On the former, it was agreed that in a deal with Mussolini "he could offer words and we must give deeds." On the latter issues, some argued for a clear understanding in advance between Britain, France, and the USSR to act as a "possibly decisive deterrent" to German. Others regarded Germany and Italy as unstable regimes which would collapse if war could be avoided. "The policy therefore suggested was one of minimum commitment east of the Rhine," the minutes recorded. A basis for a settlement, which garnered some approval, rested on encouraging a cantonal system in Czechoslovakia, and recognizing that German economic hegemony in eastern and central Europe was inevitable. The group finally endorsed a concerted effort to improving air-raid protection and home defence.[493]

Salter did not participate in the 7 March Commons' debate on the government's Defence White Paper. Rather he aired his views on the subject that day in The Times, writing that its "most notable feature is the extent to which 'Home Defence' preparations are lagging behind the rest." He surveyed the wide range of people and interests who supported his campaign. As to why such widespread opinion was being ignored, he suggested that Inskip was merely "a coordinator," food storage was represented by "a 'Defence Plans' Department," and there was no executive minister to make the issue a priority.[494] The same day, as well, he addressed the London Chamber of Commerce on the subject of "Storing Food for Wartime." The weakest links in Britain's defence plans, he argued, were civil defence against air attacks and adequate food storage. Given the decline in Britain's mercantile marine, another 4 million mouths to feed and the air menace, he considered Britain's position worse than in 1914. If his scheme were adopted, he concluded, "it would reduce our danger of war; and if war should come it would reduce our danger in war." As a result of his remarks, the Council of the London Chamber of Commerce adopted a resolution endorsing Salter's views and sent it to the prime minister.[495]

The objective of the next meeting on 16 March of the All Souls Foreign Affairs Group, if consensus emerged, had been to discuss the publication of a statement. Prior to that, however, on 8 March, Curtis, Murray, Nicolson, Salter, and Allen met with Toynbee at Chatham House. The latter was concerned that one of the consequences to Britain if she gave up the League, might be that the country would sink to the position of a second-rate power like Holland. Salter proposed the notion that without Russian assistance "we must play for time" and opposed, therefore, any commitments to the Czechs. Nicolson stated that the real issue was "between the traditions of our policy (namely to oppose the strong and to protect the weak) and an experiment in a new policy of trying to conciliate the strong."[496] Salter's followed up his remarks with a memorandum, "Notes on Foreign Policy," which he completed just prior to departing for New York. The case he advocated, which he admitted was "a very painful one, but one personally I feel unable to escape," was for "surrender east of the Holland-France line but not everywhere." He could not escape the conclusion that "We have not, and cannot in the near future, secure such a combination of strength as will enable us to prevent without war (or probably even to defeat in war) the realization of the central core of Hitler's (and now Germany's) ambition – the association in some form of the Germans in Czechoslovakia and German Austria with the *Reich*." Salter may have later regretted not settling for the "cooler reflection" he admitted the situation required.[497]

On 7 December 1937 Salter had accepted an invitation from University of California President, Robert Gordon Sproul, to be the Charter Day speaker on both the Los Angeles and Berkeley campuses. The occasion, on which he was also to receive an honourary degree, was to mark the founding of the university in 1868. He also agreed to become the Hitchcock Professor and stay on at Berkeley for further lectures and consultations with faculty and staff. Likely for the first time, he asked a series of questions to assuage his anxieties, as he put it, "when I lecture away and in circumstances little known to me." He requested a microphone, writing that "I have a reasonably strong voice, but the character of the location, somewhat affects the treatment and the pace of delivery." He also wished to know whether his lectures would be published, in which case he would provide a text and read it, although this, he wrote, "cramps my delivery." Otherwise, he confided, "I think I can make rather a better thing of a free delivery from ample notes." He was reassured on the first query and advised to provide a written text on the latter for possible publication.[498] On 9 March Salter embarked on the *Ille de France* for New York and while still on board, he heard news of the German invasion of Austria on 12 March. Writing to Elisina Tyler on

15 March, as was his habit on their shared birth date, he commented, "It is indeed a dreary prospect that opens before us as we each start a new year of life. I left England last Wednesday, with much anxiety but no expectation that this blow at Austria would fall, at least so soon. What a collapse there has been in everything that you & Peter & I have cared & worked for these last twenty years." Salter had intended to stay in the United States for about six weeks, half in California and half on the east coast: "Now I don't know quite what my plans will be," he confided.[499] The following day, despite the impulse to return at once, and after consulting with the British ambassador, Sir Ronald Lindsay, he decided to fulfil only his Charter Week speaking obligations and return early to London. "There are black days to come," he wrote to Mildred Bliss on 16 March and added, "how much blacker, God alone knows."[500]

When questioned by the press on his arrival by a Union Pacific train in Los Angeles on 20 March, Salter, described as "one of the world's leading economists and educators," stated that the survival of the democracies depended on a show of "strength, determination and efficiency." The next morning, at the Josiah Royce Hall auditorium of the Los Angeles campus, before a capacity audience of 2,400 students and faculty, Salter gave his Charter Day address on the subject of "The Threat to Democracy." He declared, speaking from notes, that "Civilization as we know it is being destroyed before our very eyes." After outlining his vision of the merits of democracy over totalitarianism, he argued that the former's future rested on finding a lasting cure to unemployment and the business cycle.[501] On 23 March, he lectured at the Berkeley campus, Gymnasium for Men, before an audience of over 8,000. In an address titled "The Adventure of the 20th Century," he spoke of the significance of a 19th century laissez-faire environment, an age of "adventurous individualism," giving way to the current need for "adventurous corporate effort."[502] Then reviewing recent international events, in light of the Austrian Anschluss, he declared, "Once more the lights of Europe are going out one by one – the lights of culture, learning and of human kindliness. We lost those lights last, but not least, in Austria a few days ago. The days ahead are dark. The prospects are uncertain." Finally, and "without impertinence" as he put it, he asserted that the invulnerability of the United States gave it a special responsibility in case of war to help preserve civilization. He was then presented with his honourary Doctor of Laws. In the evening, Salter addressed the annual Charter Day banquet at the Palace Hotel in San Francisco.[503] The following day he spoke to the Commonwealth Club of California on the subject of "Why Democracy?" He stressed that the democracies must respond to the appeal of dictatorships by enlarging the role of government "to remove causes of discontent and economic pressure." He concluded, quoting the British historian Thomas Macaulay, "Reform that you may preserve."[504]

In view of the crisis atmosphere following the Austrian Anschluss, Salter had on 17 March negotiated a release from his commitment to remain for a further month as the University's annual Hitchcock lecturer.[505] At midnight on 23 March he left by rail to return first to Washington, for informal consultations arranged by the British ambassador.[506] On 29 March, with the prior arrangement of Royall Tyler, and in the company of Stimson, he then visited Mildred and Robert Bliss at Dumbarton Oaks. According to Stimson's diary, Salter "was very gloomy over the outlook," predicting that Hitler would turn his attention by June towards Czechoslovakia which was, in his view, "quite indefensible from a military standpoint." He predicted that Hitler would not incorporate the purely Czech portion of the country, but an occupation would "very likely inspire demands from Hungary and Poland which would strip Czechoslovakia to insignificance." Salter worried too about the vulnerability of London to air attack and the vast civilian casualties which would ensue. On the subject of Spain, he explained his support of the Loyalists, arguing that they represented the majority. His choice, he added, was partly the result of the future threat posed by Franco with the support of Germany and Italy. Finally, reviewing the events of the last few years, he "reiterated his faith that the debacle had not been inevitable but the product of avoidable circumstances." He singled out in particular French domestic and foreign policy decisions made in the late 1920s. "Altogether there was no sugar in his cup at all," Stimson noted in his diary. The visit ended with a tour of the gardens, and the diary continued: "Salter said he had never seen anything like it and I certainly hadn't."[507] Thanking Mildred Bliss for the visit, Salter wrote:

> I take back a vivid picture of what are the human values of this civilization that it is now menaced in Europe. They may have to be brought back from the invulnerable continent to one that has been devastated. I cannot believe that this madness will last many years, but it's extraordinarily difficult to see how we shall get through the next few without a war in which even victory will be more barren than before. I greatly hope, & in spite of all obvious anxieties, I still have an instinctive belief, that we shall meet again under happier conditions.[508]

He also wrote to Rowse on 30 March, "New York is, as usual, a great stimulus to me & I feel infinitely fitter than when I left England. I well remember the effect it had on me when I came over in 1917, & I never fail to feel new energy when I come here." He sailed from New York aboard the *Normandie* on 31 March, and in his haste left behind a pair of spectacles.[509]

Stimson observed that Salter had made "a helter skelter trip across the ocean and the continent, from London to California and back again, travelling 18 nights of the 26 that he was going to be away from London."[510] Indeed, Salter was hurrying back to take his place in the House of Commons. Later he recalled that he was greeted at Westminster "with expressions of surprise that I had come back for a 'crisis that had already passed'!"[511] In his absence, the All Souls Foreign Affairs Group had met on 16 March in the aftermath of the Anschluss. The strategic consequences for France and Britain of an imminent collapse of the Spanish government were first examined. This problem had formed part of Salter's reasoning in favour of "surrender east of the Holland-France line." For the meanwhile, it was decided to make no statement about Czechoslovakia.[512] What received final approval was an aide-mémoire, designed for private for distribution, which argued that a Franco victory was a strategic threat to both Britain and France. However, the eastern Mediterranean was described as an area where "geography and sea-power still tell heavily in our favour" and some form of effective action was possible. What this might be was not articulated.[513] Then, acting on the mandate derived from the meeting of 26 February, a member of the group had drawn up a 28 page memorandum, "Foreign Policy Now." The Introduction emphasized that the paper was the outcome of six weekend discussions by individuals "from different political parties not including the extreme political Right or Left." As a result, "certain conclusions emerged so clearly from our non-partisan discussions that we finally decided to prepare and publish this paper." "Foreign Policy Now" posed the question: "Somewhere, somehow, some day, a stand will be made. Where? In what conditions? For what cause, and in what company, would British power be used, if it has to be used, in war?" The answer it suggested was unequivocal: "It is in Spain, rather than in Czechoslovakia, that British power – which is still in the main naval power – can be brought to bear most effectively." As for the on-going Czech-German crisis, the memorandum suggested that "The lesson of the Austrian *Putsch* is that we must hang together or we shall be hanged separately." Finally, the British government was again urged to rearm, improve London's air defences, and hasten the storage of food and other essential commodities.[514] When the group next met on 23 March it concurred that if France were involved in war because of Czechoslovakia, Britain could not stand by. Finally, the *raison d'etre* of the group itself was raised, with some wishing to continue with a publication, while others held that the group's function was to act as a "Brains Trust."[515] During the meeting on 31 March, that inconclusive tone and divisiveness resurfaced, although it was decided to continue work on a statement. Afterwards, Nicolson wrote in his diary that "our main line is that a purely negative policy gets us nowhere and that there must be some more constructive drive."[516]

With his return to London and Oxford, Salter renewed his lobbying efforts on a wide range of issues. The conclusion of the Anglo-Italian agreement on 16 April 1938, which envisaged trading British recognition of Italy's conquest of Abyssinia for the withdrawal of Italian volunteers from Spain, and the upcoming parliamentary debate on the budget on 26 April, prompted the next meeting of the group at All Souls on 24 April. The minutes detail a new urgency for diplomacy to be directed towards "appeasement and the finding of a modus vivendi with the aggressor states." It was more difficult to translate this into "a middle policy between resistance and retreat." The preconditions to avoiding a war were "the incorporation of all important irredentist communities within the *Reich*," the acquisition by Germany of colonies, the likely disappearance of Czechoslovakia, and a League stripped of any coercive functions. Salter insisted that in conversations with Hitler, British emissaries should emphasize that if the Germans cooperated "they could probably attain all their main ambitions in East Europe and in the colonies, but that their present methods are likely to cause an explosion." Salter was considered as one such possible emissary, "peculiarly fitted" for such a task. Indeed, Guy Wint thought that Salter "has a sufficiently pugnacious manner to impress the Germans; and is sufficiently near the centre to be taken as representative." Salter, however, was "not enthusiastic" about such a personal mission, citing his long experience of international negotiations which convinced him of the necessity of meticulous advance preparations. Before concluding, the group decided to press on with a draft statement for publication.[517]

Another concern Salter targeted on his return was the issue of air raid defence. Almost from the outset of the All Souls meetings, he had expressed concern about Britain's vulnerability to air attack. On 21 April he spoke with Curtis to whom he gave, in the latter's words, "an appalling account of our general unpreparedness against air raids." Salter enlisted Curtis to invite Lord Nuffield, the industrialist and philanthropist, Sir John Anderson, and Robert Brand, the banker and economist, to a meeting at All Souls on 8 May. When extending the invitations, Curtis wrote he considered Salter as someone "who knows what he is talking about" and "better informed than anyone else outside Government circles." Curtis proposed that the exercise should lead to the formation of an Air Defence League, which if non-party, would attract members and act as a national lobby group.[518] The meeting, which also included General Swinton and the MP Sir Leo Amery, laid the groundwork regarding "the serious nature of the situation" of air defence. No progress was made on establishing, as yet, an Air Defence League, however, with Curtis bowing out due to other commitments, the role of spear-heading an all party organization was left to Salter who then carried his campaign to the House of Commons.[519] Speaking on 28 April lauded the first efforts from the government, after having "procrastinated and prevaricated," to buy wheat, whale oil and sugar, even if it was "only an instalment of what is to be done." From here he turned to what he termed "mingled condolence and condemnation" of the government's foreign policy since 1931, years which he described as ones of "lost opportunities." He continued: "I believe that the fate of our Empire and of the heritage of civilisation of which it is the trustee will be won or lost, not at the periphery, but at the centre." The situation required, in his view, "something much nearer to a war economy," and a reduction of "our vulnerability to air attack." Only this united effort would "immensely reduce not only our dangers during war but the danger of war."[520] Later, he put his view more bluntly to Layton, writing that given Britain's vulnerability to air attack, extra funding for re-armament should go to air defence. "The whole perspective of our defence preparations is, I think, fundamentally wrong," he wrote. In his view, "It is more vital to remedy a deficiency than (as in battleships) to increase an existing superiority."[521] To these major concerns, Salter added yet another focus for his growing fear of war. During a House of Commons' debate on the estimates for the Air Ministry on 12 May, he urged the government to establish a Ministry of Supply. Only such a co-ordinating ministry, in his view, could deal with the problem, before and not after war broke out. He added, "It can be done, but I am not sure that it will be done." In conclusion, citing London's vulnerability, he stated: "It may be that strangers from distant lands and alien races will stand upon the desolate site of Westminster, and, whether in exultation or sorrow, will chant the words of the Apocalypse: 'Alas, Alas! That great City, Babylon, that mighty City. In one hour is thy judgement come'." Returning to the subject in The Times several days later, Salter detailed the powers and duties to be invested in a Ministry of Supply, convinced as he was that the prevailing system was insufficient.[522]

Even after eight meetings of the All Souls Foreign Affairs Group, and a mounting body of paperwork, unanimity was as elusive as ever. However, Allen agreed to produce some sort of policy statement, despite the fact, he noted, that it "suffers from my attempt to meet points of view which are not entirely my own."[523] By 10 May he completed a 29 page document, titled "A Peace Policy for the Immediate Present." Allen argued that the state of European affairs demanded "an effort towards appeasement," to include recognition of Italian sovereignty in Abyssinia, and the negotiation of "a new peace settlement" with Germany. He concluded with a scenario for his "transitional policy" which, he wrote, combined rearmament, further military co-operation with France, economic co-operation with the United States and "vigorous efforts towards appeasement."[524] The paper was discussed at All Souls on 15 May, but again without agreement and possibly worse. Nicolson afterwards observed, "There is really a split between the realists and the moralists."[525] Murray likewise noted Allen's preference "that the way to peace is to satisfy Germany; most of us thinking that resistance, and the maintenance of international law, more important." Allen himself began to doubt whether an agreed document would ever emerge and the divisions within the group widened.[526] As a result, after conferring with Salter, Allen turned for assistance to J.A. Spender. He and Salter paid the latter a visit on 27 May, and explained the group's inability to agree on an interim statement. They provided Spender with relevant documents, including Salter's memorandum of 8 March, and asked him to attempt an acceptable synthesis. This Spender had completed by 8 June and his memorandum was circulated to the group by the end of the month. In essence, this argued that, given the limits of British power world-wide, Britain should pursue peace with any co-operative government, irrespective of its ideology.[527]

For some brief time Salter's unrelenting pace of activities was slowed, yet again, by the death of a very close friend, Ka Cox. Ever since they had first befriended each other in the later period of the World War, they had maintained a very close relationship. After her marriage to Will Arnold-Forster in 1918, Salter had numerous professional dealings and associations with Will Arnold-Forster, and had also been a frequent visitor to Eagle's Nest, the house on the moors close to Zennor, Cornwall after it was purchased by the Arnold-Forsters in 1920. For many years afterwards and particularly in the 1930s Salter had found a safe haven there, some times in moments of distress or ill-health. Ka Cox's untimely and mysterious death on 23 May at Eagle's Nest left Salter stunned. In an obituary tribute in The Times, he paid tribute not onlyto her record of public activity, but to "her genius of friendship." He dwelt on her capacity to cultivate "a catholicity of friends," while at the same time she "kept her own self intact and unimpressionable. There are many who live through their friends; her friends lived through her." He added that she possessed "an Elizabethan quality of spaciousness and depth."[528] Writing later to Felkin who also knew her very well, Salter revealed that he had telephoned the Eagle's Nest on 22 May only to be told that she had had a stroke the night before and died the following day. Salter described how, despite her fatigue, she had convinced herself to spend the night with "a half-crazy couple" in a hut above Eagle's Nest who claimed to be seeing "ghosts & spirits at night." He continued that in her effort to help the couple, she had climbed the hill and had the stroke in the hut. "The end was tragic & characteristic," Salter wrote. Will Arnold-Forster, at the time in Canada, attended neither the funeral nor the memorial service held on 1 June in London.[529]

The lobbying Salter had done on questions of storage seemed finally to show results. On 31 May an all-party Food Storage Committee met for the first time, with Salter in the chair. Discussion centred on a government proposed Essential Commodities Reserves Bill, that is, to empower the Board of Trade to gather information about stocks and storage space, and finance the purchase of commodities essential in wartime.[530] Moving the second reading of the bill on 2 June, the President of the Board of Trade, Sir Oliver Stanley, acknowledged that Salter had spoken on the subject "with very great authority" and with "cheerful geniality." He then went on to explain why "certain foodstuffs, forage, fertilisers and petroleum" were chosen as essential commodities and why inland storage was not "practicable." In his response, Salter welcomed the bill, but criticised its vagueness, suggesting, "We have powers, but neither promises nor policies nor plans." He then pressed for inland storage and the equivalent of various foodstuffs to "a year's supply of wheat." Finally, he exhorted the government to pursue food storage with "a great deal more drive," given that public opinion supported measures of "passive defence" and that action in this sphere might act as a deterrent to war and the results invaluable should war come.[531] As the bill made its way through parliament, Salter kept in close touch with Keynes on some aspects of the legislation. Keynes wanted the bill to provide "aggregate figures" for stocks and to include non-food materials. Salter thought the bill did give the Board of Trade powers to publish the former, but doubted it would. He also wished the powers to be extended to "non-food commodities," though he confessed that Stanley was quite opposed. In conversation later with Stanley, Salter was confirmed in his initial estimate, and was unable to effect any change in government policy, but not for want of trying.[532] On 15 June, in the House of Commons, he digressed on the wider issues of "economic appeasement," suggesting that this should be placed in the larger context of a political settlement at some future, more propitious time. He concluded that "there is certainly no way of salvation in the mere competition of power in which we are now engaged."[533] He then tried to further his campaign both privately and in the press. Responding to a speech made by Chamberlain on 2 July, Salter argued that the reserves set aside by the government, mainly wheat, sugar and whale oil, for a "'first emergency period'" were too limited. In his view, this was only sufficient for the brief dislocation after the outbreak of war, and inadequate for a longer conflict with its inevitable decline in imports. He pointed to 1916 and 1917 when loses of ships and thereby imports "endangered our whole war effort," and urged that funding be provided for storage on a recurring annual basis. Amery, a fellow campaigner on the issue, joined Salter and others, on 6 July, in a deputation to Inskip to explore, without success, the issues of food storage. Amery also wrote to <u>The Times</u>, suggesting that "elementary common sense" supported Salter's arguments. In the event, the Essential Commodities Reserve Bill, unamended, received Royal Assent on 29 July.[534]

"The situation remains intensely irritating in Parliament," Salter wrote to Rowse on 16 July, and continued, "if there is a debate – or even questions – on foreign affairs, the actual result is almost always to make things worse from every point of view."[535] Salter was similarly downcast when he met with Stimson on 27 July for their annual summer get-together. Stimson afterwards wrote in his diary that Salter "exhaled an atmosphere of profound gloom and it was a shock to me to find that this man whom I regard as having one of the best economic brains in Europe – an expert in political economy and government finance – had for over a year been devoting himself to the purely military problem of the air defence of London."[536] Perhaps also weighing on Salter's mind was the collapse of the All Souls Foreign Affairs Group. A meeting scheduled for 16 July had been cancelled, and instead Salter spent the weekend of 16-17 July conferring with Allen and drafting a letter to the editor of The Times, proposing third-party mediation in the German-Czech dispute. Many of those invited to sign refused, the Foreign Secretary Lord Halifax thought the time inopportune, and the group never reconvened.[537] It had served precisely the purpose designed by Salter as a Brains Trust, helping some of the best elite minds of the time clarify their positions on foreign and domestic policy. Although the group had quickly focused on a dual policy of firmness and conciliation, an agreed statement evaded it, as did the attempt to find a middle policy between resistance and retreat.

After concluding another session as chair of the Railway Staff National Tribunal on 4 August, Salter slipped away from London. "I'm a fraud in that I concealed what I was doing at the beginning of this month," he confessed later to Rowse. He began with a secret medical check-up, having been "a good deal dissatisfied" with his general health. A "thorough overhaul revealed that there was nothing organically wrong anywhere," but that "almost everything is functionally slow through fatigue." Nonetheless, he had decided that he would have to take a lengthy holiday. Writing to Rowse on 10 August, he outlined plans which included a week with the Laytons, another taking Margaret Brooke for a now customary summer motoring tour, and a few days with John Buchan. For the final week, he offered Rowse "a little car-holiday with me – anywhere you like." Rowse had undergone surgery for a duodenal ulcer in late May and Salter had promised to assist in his recovery. He arranged to meet with Rowse at Bristol and tour Wales, an experience Rowse recalled as "a slow, stopping tour," with the two ending up finally at Criccieth for a visit with Lloyd George.[538]

Salter returned briefly to London, mainly to catch up on correspondence. Among the most important was his response to a public proposal by Keynes to increase government incentives to individual enterprises to store stocks of materials. Salter replied that he was doubtful about the specifics of financing storage in the manner which Keynes was promoting, and he preferred staying with his more limited "security measures." The Economist likewise had reservations about Keynes' proposals, while complimenting Salter for "forcing into public prominence" his more limited and targeted scheme for storage of food and raw materials as a defensive measure.[539] In an unusual gesture, he let several correspondents know that he was leaving London on 2 September and would be staying with Ethel Bullard at the Chateau Garengo in Céligny, near Geneva.[540] Over the last years she and Salter had often been in touch on both sides of the Atlantic. Her health had also been of on-going concern to him as she underwent several bouts of surgery and lengthy periods of recovery. On 4 April 1932, because of multiple fibroids, she had had a hysterectomy, and while recovering had been visited by Salter.[541] Further complications required surgery in September 1936 and again in January 1938.[542] Their relationship no doubt was growing much closer, especially given Salter's greater openness about it. In fact, in March 1939 he gave up his flat at 66 Cornwall Gardens and moved into the Royal Automobile Club where he stayed Mondays to Thursdays before returning to his rooms at All Souls. With Ethel Bullard having taken up residence at the Connaught Hotel, they were now both in temporary accommodations.

Salter had planned to stay in Switzerland until 24 September.[543] However, his vacation was cut short because of the worsening situation in Europe. On 10 September, on the eve of his hasty return to London, he wrote to Elisina Tyler:

> The news from England yesterday & today makes me feel that, member of Parliament, I must fly back direct to London to-morrow. No one can tell what will be brought back on Saturday morning, or how quick or upon exactly what issues all groups concerned in any way with foreign policy will have to consult & take their line. How happy the years when we worked together were – happy indeed they were & seemed at the time: but in retrospect they are like a Paradise Lost – may there be a paradise Regained! There is still of course hope of a settlement: but it seems only too likely that we shall have to steel ourselves once more at least for a period of anxiety. May we meet again soon, dear Elisina, & under happier conditions.[544]

In the same disheartened vein he wrote to Stimson, "Geneva is in some respects rather a painful place for me to revisit. I have found pleasure in seeing some old friends – but for me the place is too full of ghosts – both of persons & of causes."[545] Salter flew back to London on 11 September to be present in the House of Commons as the Anglo-German negotiations regarding Czechoslovakia unfolded. He did not contribute at all during September, but preferred the role of witness. He attended an emergency meeting of the executive committee of the LNU on 26 September when a resolution was passed endorsing Churchill's statement that a "solemn warning" against an invasion of Czechoslovakia should be sent to Germany. As well, following up an idea discussed but not endorsed by the meeting, Salter wrote to The Times suggesting the immediate formation of a parliamentary Foreign Affairs Committee "of the most trusted members of the different parties and sections." He wished this committee to be given secret information in order to advise "on the vital issues of the time."[546] For himself, Salter privately wrote that he was "expecting bombardment as a possibility any night."[547] On 29 September he was in the Commons to hear Chamberlain's announcement of his meeting with Hitler and Mussolini at Munich. The next day Salter attended a small all-party meeting of MPs at the Savoy Hotel in the Strand. One of those present, Nicolson, noted that Salter stated "that he was all for fighting the Germans, but he would like to know whether we are likely to win."[548] During the subsequent debate on the Munich settlement in the Commons from 2-6 October, Salter only rose once, on 5 October on a point of order. He enquired whether the motion was asking for approval of the foreign policy of the government generally, or only during the recent crisis. Chamberlain responded that it was the latter which the motion addressed. Salter abstained on the crucial vote for approval of the government's foreign policy, although the motion was passed. His abstention was only partly due to the fact that he thought defeat would trigger an election.[549] But his abstention was solidly rooted in his unrelenting absorption with questions of foreign policy throughout the 1930s and the failure of the All Souls Foreign Affairs Group to reach a consensus. Equally, when later challenged on his voting record as an Independent MP, he explained: "When my views on a situation could not be properly expressed by a mere 'Yes' or 'No' to a motion as drafted (as in the case of the Government's motion on October 6), I have abstained."[550]

Clearly never one to jump to any conclusion that was not carefully considered, and following his lifelong habit of clearing his mind on paper, Salter therefore took time off to think and write. By 14 October he had completed a 16 page pamphlet entitled, <u>Is It Peace? The Nettle and the Flower</u>," published by <u>The Spectator</u> for three pence. His approach was to bypass what he termed the "Grand Inquest of the Nation" into recent events. Instead, he suggested that the crisis signaled "the victory of the threat of force over the processes of reason and peaceful negotiation." While critical of the rationale offered by the Chamberlain government for the Munich agreement, he conceded that "the prospects of defending or even restoring Czechoslovakia were not sufficiently good to justify a war on that issue." Looking to the future, he argued that a sound foreign policy required "adequate defensive strength" to deflate the illusion that Britain was vulnerable to "a knockout blow from the air." A national effort was required to strengthen the Air Force and all civilian defence measures. After further detailing the failures of what he described as "a procrastinating and incompetent administration," he then made a passionate plea for a complete reorganization to include a minister of civilian defence, a manpower requirements department, and a ministry of supply. "Munich cannot be reversed," he continued, "We must face the consequences," which he wrote were not all bleak and outlined some of the probable conditions of a settlement. Given that Britain's ability to exert influence in Central Europe was severely limited, the country must face the "unpalatable fact" that it would have to make concessions to a resurgent Germany. He suggested, therefore, that the British government should consider fully "what it is prepared to contribute and where it must cost." He was above all anxious that a policy of "appeasement leading to a general settlement" should be realistic and practical. He then reiterated his belief in the necessity to establish a parliamentary "Committee of Foreign Policy and Defence." As well, he emphasized his view that "a substantial margin of collective preponderance of strength," rooted in League of Nations principles was required "not merely to defeat, but to deter, aggression."[551]

In a follow-up contribution to The Spectator, and in a somewhat more subdued tone, he urged that "the first thing now necessary is to adjust our policy to the limits of our strength, national and collective; and to concentrate on a national effort to increase that strength, especially where we are now weakest." He also cautioned that "we must not expect that Germany's demands have reached their limits."[552] Salter distributed dozens of copies of his pamphlet and the response was generally positive, with some even complimenting him on reviving the format. Writing from his sick bed, Allen noted that Salter was "one of the few living people who can now lead progressive people." From H.G. Wells came a card addressed "My dear Member for Sanity." Geoffrey Faber, always the publisher, proposed that Salter expand the pamphlet into a book. In fact, Salter had started to write what would prove to be his next book. The difficulty, as he responded to Faber, was that he had "to work in snatched times between railway journeys, etc., and that is not a good method for literary composition."[553] Violet Markham, wrote to Salter that she thought him "happier and in better form than you have been for years! You can't live without a crisis!"[554] To another close friend, Joyce Newton Thompson, he wrote:

> I have been rather less upset than most people by this recent crisis, because I have thought for years that the danger was greater than most people realized & now I think the situation less desperate than they do. I do not think the danger of war is now greater, though it is nearer than it has been for years. We may accommodate ourselves to a great, but still not dominant Germany. Or of course we may not.

Salter continued, "I love to think that you are one of those with whom friendship does not lapse or even weaken with absence." He concluded, "I am working as hard as I can, but through external organizations & pressure, not within the Govt."[555]

Salter was indeed busily following up on various aspects of the September crisis. On 12 October he visited the Foreign Office to suggest that a proactive policy of "economic and financial interest" in Hungary might help the country resist complete German domination, even at the cost of turning a blind eye towards Hungary's irredentist claims against Slovakia and Ruthenia. He added that Hungary was a subject "about which he might claim to speak with some knowledge."[556] The Munich crisis had also highlighted the inadequacy of Britain's air raid protection measures. Beginning on 16 and 23 October and, working now with the former chief general manager of the London and North Eastern Railway Company, Sir Ralph Wedgewood as co-initiator, Salter convened the first of a new series of conferences at All Souls. These were designed "to bring more effective pressure" on the question of civilian defence against air attack, leading to the formation of an Air Raid Defence League. He envisaged a bottom-up effort, mobilizing key individuals from such areas as finance, industry, transport, food and utilities, to prepare policy initiatives. In his view, only thorough preparation and implementation could Britain survive an early "knock-out" blow. Chatham House and PEP were also engaged for their input, and a new institute was planned for the "scientific study" of the issues. A further meeting on 30 October led to the foundation of the League and another on 6 November formulated a statement of aims and set up an executive.[557] One auspicious sign was the appointment on 1 November of Sir John Anderson as Lord Privy Seal, with overall responsibility of co-ordinating civil defence. Salter welcomed this appointment when he spoke in the Commons on 17 November. He also addressed the main issue of the sitting, the establishment of a Ministry of Supply, admitting he was prepared to accept a peacetime ministry with restricted powers that would be enlarged in wartime. Despite government resistance, Salter predicted that in due course the country would get it Ministry of Supply, and he explained why:

> I have for two years watched the way in which, in one after another of the defensive preparations, the Government have first shown what the House has realized to be inexcusable inertia; then there has been a growing movement of indignation and the Government in answer to the demand have said, 'Never, never;' then the protest has continued and a few months later the Government have said, 'Not yet.' In yet another few months they have admitted in principle the demand of the critics and then have acted, but even then done much too little and done it much too late.[558]

Another subject, one on which Salter could claim much experience from his time at the League in the 1920s, was the growing number of European refugees fleeing

Germany, Spain and eastern European countries. The problem had been yet further worsened by the Czech crisis, which involved the redrawing of its boundaries, and the anti-Jewish *Kristallnacht* of 9-10 November. Following Chamberlain's comments in the House of Commons on 21 November, about the possibility of resettling Jews in British Guiana, Salter asked the prime minister on 13 December, whether the government would consider making a practical reality of the offer. At the invitation of the prime minister, Salter agreed to draw up a detailed scheme, including costing. Two days later he submitted a lengthy covering letter and a 10-page attachment, written with the assistance of Sir John Hope Simpson with whom he had collaborated in the work of Greek resettlement. Salter's letter pointed out that the refugee problem, which he estimated at between 3-5 million people, was on such a scale that previous methods of "absorption into other communities by infiltration, or colonial migration of the ordinary type, will be entirely inadequate." However, "group settlement," in areas allotted to "homogeneous communities and developed intensively," was feasible if it was comprehensive and backed by government financing. If Britain would implement such a plan, and encourage other colonial powers to follow, Salter was convinced that that the Jews, "with their industry and organizing ability, with Jewish capital and the Jewish Associations behind them," were quite capable of establishing "modern and prosperous communities." The memorandum pointed to the success of Jewish settlement in Palestine, as evidence of "the qualities of the Jewish emigrant and the power of Jewish organizations," but also indicated that "Palestine can obviously not by itself meet the need." It concluded with the view that such resettlement would serve to reduce racial tensions and growing anti-Semitism. After reading the submission, Halifax wrote, "it is difficult to avoid Salter's conclusion that Government action is essential," and regarded the long term strategy as on the right lines.[559] In a further attempt to stimulate public discussion, Salter wrote in an article in The Times on 27 December that the refugee question was "a formidable world problem." He restated some of the proposals he had sent to the government, with the cautionary note that "The sentiment associated with the Jews' historic home would have brought a concentration of effort that cannot be expected elsewhere." Hence government assistance would be required for any alternative settlements, accompanied by similar French support.[560]

Year's end saw Salter unburdening himself to Joyce Newton Thompson in a somewhat more sober mood. After reading some good news of her family, Salter noted he was almost persuaded "to regret being a bachelor!" Turning to the international situation he wrote:

> I don't think the danger has become greater but only more imminent. We have a respite for the moment. The sense of the overhanging cloud is rarely

absent here. But there is a kind of consolation. Perhaps one enjoys some things more dearly. And to work at the overwhelming tasks – air raid defence, refugees, etc. – brings a kind of vitality even if – time drains it. I confess I felt fitter in the months during & after the crisis than I had done before. Violet laughed at me & said I looked ten years younger through feeding like a vulture on human misfortunes.

There is no doubt, however, as he wrote to Allen on 11 January 1939, that he looked "forward to the next few months with great apprehension. If Hitler tries ultimata the situation will I think blow up."[561] This was to be Salter's last contact with Allen who died on 3 March. He wrote to Lady Allen on 5 March, offering his sympathy and noting "how great a privilege I feel it has been to have worked with him these last five years. He was one of the great men of our time." In an obituary tribute in The Times, Salter emphasized that Allen "combined moral with physical courage, a lofty idealism with a knowledge of the technique of organization, and a strong will with sympathetic responsiveness to others."[562]

The various lobbying efforts Salter was engaged in prompted a Treasury official on 4 January 1939 to note that "Salter has so many irons in the fire that he is perhaps rather apt to offer his good advice without making quite sure of the actual position before he writes."[563] This slighting comment was in reference to Salter's 15 December 1938 letter to Chamberlain on the question of the settlement of refugees. Salter's follow-up article in The Times on 27 December prompted both an editorial and a spate of letters, mainly supportive of his contention regarding the role of government and the need for appointed experts to formulate long-term policy.[564] The proposal itself was examined by the Treasury, the Home Office and the Colonial Office. It was finally the Secretary of State for Colonial Affairs, Malcolm MacDonald, who provided the draft on which Chamberlain based his reply to Salter. Writing on 1 February, Chamberlain acknowledged Salter's arguments that large-scale settlement required government intervention. However, he considered it "premature to consider any steps of this kind" until further investigation of various possibilities.[565] On the other hand, Salter's campaign for an Air Raid Defence League proved much more successful. Having laid the groundwork in late 1938, he had stepped up efforts to get the organization off the ground. By 21 November he could write that the project was "now well advanced," and that he had the support of "personalities of distinction in different spheres of national life, in advance of a more general public appeal."[566] On 7 February 1939, the same day the Air Raid Defence League was publicly launched, he noted that "No one can hate more than I do being forced into what is, for me, the hateful & disgusting work of shelters & evacuation, etc., to the abandonment of all I've worked for many years." Reporting on its formation, The Times welcomed "an organization which will be wholly independent of the Government, yet ready to cooperate in every effort of the Government which its own expert opinion considers salutary and to suggest other useful efforts for the Government to make." The Manchester Guardian noted that it had "an extremely strong" list of members, drawn from all parties. The New Statesman also congratulated the League for its determination "to put some sense into our civilian defence."[567] The League declared that its objectives were to secure protection for the civilian population against air attack and concentrate public interest on the issue through meetings, speakers, and relevant publications. Salter was at pains to emphasize that, given Britain's strategic weakness in the air, it was vital to make Britain "at least immune from the risk that a quick blow would knock us out."[568] Lord Hailey, formerly of the Indian Civil Service, was appointed chairman of the League, but the driving forces remained Salter and Wedgewood. A high profile was maintained throughout the following months, with advertisements headlined "Some bombers must get through," and encouraging public membership.[569] The League issued its first "Bulletin" on 31 March and maintained that the protection of civilians required a combination of both deep and shallow (nicknamed the Anderson) shelters. This was followed by five further bulletins over the coming months providing information and advice on all aspects of the subject, and still highly critical of the slow pace of government preparations.[570]

Both in parliament and elsewhere, Salter kept up the pressure. On 2 March in the House of Commons, he first turned to the subject of private food supplies as a supplementary reserve to government storage. He even suggested a slogan: "To buy more than you need in war-time is hoarding and a civic crime; but to buy more than you need in peace-time is storing and a civic crime." For the rest he continued to exhort the government to make long-term purchases, rather than merely provide food for dislocation in the early stages of war. The reluctance to thus act, he attributed to the fact that there was no one minister with executive responsibility. Instead, the issue was being left to three separate ministers, the Lord Privy Seal, the Minister for the Co-Ordination of Defence and the President of the Board of Trade. Passing then to the question of air-raid protection, he pressed the case for the expansion of "deep shelter protection."[571] Salter also kept up his focus on Spain, writing to Halifax on 7 March to express his concern about the fate of political and trade union leaders in Madrid, threatened by its imminent capture and their likely execution by Franco. This letter was mentioned the following day in the cabinet during a discussion about republican refugees. It was agreed that mass evacuation was impossible, while Chamberlain ruled out what he regarded as any action amounting to intervention. The reply to Salter, when it came on 22 March from Halifax, preferred to rely on Franco's reassurances that he would "not resort to wholesale executions."[572] At a later date Salter again returned to the subject, urging Halifax to assist in transporting Spanish refugees from French internment camps to Mexico.[573] He did the same for refugees from Czechoslovakia who had escaped after the occupation of Prague to Poland, asking for further assistance to help bring them to Britain."[574] In other areas, however, Salter's campaign was beginning to show progress, not least because of his sheer persistence. On 9 March he wrote to Chamberlain, notifying the prime minister of his intention to raise in the Commons both the subject of food reserves and storage, and the question of ministerial responsibility. Salter drew on his and others' experiences in the World War to argue that war would inevitably reduce imports, and that the answer was not increased domestic production, dependent as this was on imported fertilisers. Rather, he repeated his "comparatively modest proposal" for the importation and storage of various commodities "equivalent in total food value to a year's consumption of wheat." On the question of responsibility, he urged the prime minister appoint a minister solely charged with the issues of food reserves and storage.[575]

Salter's initiative in writing to Chamberlain and giving notice of questions had an effect. Chamberlain's No. 10 staff provided immediate feedback and a draft reply, while Salter's memorandum was circulated to four ministers for whom food defence was of concern.[576] On 14 March Chamberlain replied to Salter, stating that his questions, including that of ministerial responsibility, would receive "careful consideration." He added that the issues of maintaining food supplies in a long war and supplementing the purchase and storage of essential commodities were under consideration. In his response, Salter expressed his gratitude on the issue of ministerial responsibility but added that its consideration had been "handicapped" precisely by the question of accountability. Chamberlain also instructed Cabinet Secretary Sir Edward Bridges to assemble those officials involved and examine the administrative issues, on which he thought "there was some case for a change in the existing arrangements." He personally thought the Board of Trade should have the final responsibility.[577] The meeting of departmental representatives, specifically called to discuss Salter ideas, assembled on 16 March. The main concern was that the Minister for Co-ordination of Defence was responsible for policy, but its execution lay with the Board of Trade, while the Lord Privy Seal ensured that food arrangements were co-ordinated with other civil defence plans. The conclusion was reached that "the primary responsibility for questions of policy in regard to food reserves and storage, as well as for the execution of that policy, should rest with a single Minister." This would still leave the Lord Privy Seal responsible for co-ordinating food storage and purchase with other civil defence plans. The

President of the Board of Trade, Sir Oliver Stanley, however, was reluctant to take on any additional duties.[578]

Under the shadow of the German invasion of Czechoslovakia on 14 March, and without any government consensus on Salter's concerns, it was not surprising that his on-going questions in parliament elicited nothing new. To the issue which he again posed on 23 March, regarding the appointment of a departmental minister responsible for food reserves policy, Chamberlain responded that he had reached no final decision. This brief exchange, highlighted in <u>The Times</u> the following day, noted that the issue was one Salter had "consistently argued" and that the prevailing arrangements were unsatisfactory.[579] The prime minister's office, in fact, was quite aware that Salter was "likely to press for a definite reply before the Easter recess." As a result, Bridges reminded Chamberlain's personal advisor Sir Horace Wilson of the matter on 4 April and the latter recommended the appointment of the Chancellor of the Duchy of Lancaster, William Morrison, as most suitable, a decision in which Chamberlain concurred just in time. For that evening, supported by 22 all-party members of the Commons, Salter tabled a motion that it was "expedient" for the government to commit to adequate storage in case of a protracted war. However, the motion was withdrawn because on 6 April, in response to a question from Salter, Chamberlain announced that the Chancellor of the Duchy of Lancaster had agreed to take on the responsibility for the Food (Defence Plans) Department, previously under the Board of Trade. While this did not entail a new cabinet position, Salter was evidently mollified on this result.[580] Shortly afterwards, he wrote to Morrison: "I do entreat you to give your personal & urgent attention to the question of bringing in large supplies at once." Pointing to the prevailing focus on supplies only for "the early period of dislocation," and to the likelihood of a long war, Salter detailed "the fact that <u>everyone</u> with relevant experience outside the Govt. service is unanimous about the need for providing for the second danger." Morrison responded, stating "I greatly value your views," and that the concerns were among those "to which I am giving urgent attention."[581]

Salter took no satisfaction from his proactive campaigns – so clearly rooted in an increasing fear of war. This was evident in what he wrote to Elisina Tyler on 16 March:

> And for myself my world is the one in which everything I've worked & cared for over a quarter of a century is in ruins, and most – though happily not all – of the people I've cared for are gone. I jog along, getting perhaps hope [?] rather than satisfaction, on such jobs as I seem to have any experience that's at all relevant – food reserves, or refugee schemes or air raid defence; not idle indeed but occupied with a dispersed & usually rather futile activity. For

myself, I am well, but older & much too normally tired. I have given up my flat at 66 Cornwall Gardens, which was useless to me as I am three days a week at Oxford and for the rest usually here or hereabouts from 10 in the morning till 11 at night. So for the time at least I sleep at the R.A.C. in Pall Mall, where incidentally I get my only form of exercise in a swim before breakfast each morning.[582]

Nonetheless, Salter continued his lobbying on several fronts. On 5 April he contributed to the Commons' debate on the second reading of a civil defence bill and air raid shelter requirements. While praising the work done by Anderson in rolling out the "Anderson steel shelter," he urged further precautions, such as deep shelters, referencing the advocacy on this issue already done by the Air Raid Defence League. He also wanted more attention to be paid to such issues as evacuation, publicity and the training of air raid wardens. He concluded by entreating the government to hasten decisions so that there "should then be a much more powerful impulse from the centre in order to make this great, cumbersome and intricate machine work more rapidly than we can rely upon it working as it is at present."[583] His final public plea on the issue of food storage was an address to a conference on nutrition and public health, on 27 April, sponsored by the British Medical Association.[584]

On 18 April Salter wrote that he had for some time "been fiddling with fragments of a possible book," intended largely "to clear something out of my system & satisfy an uneasy conscience I must finish the book." He chose Macmillan and Co., partly because he had often discussed with Harold Macmillan many of the issues in the manuscript, and partly because the latter was "extremely keen & interested." However, what dictated the choice was the rapidly changing international situation, and Macmillan promised speedy publication.[585] The manuscript was in Macmillan's hands on 20 April and published on 16 May. In the preface to <u>Security: Can we retrieve it</u>? Salter wrote that he wished to deal with such questions as to the inevitability of war, what policies could avert war, the future of the League, and the feasibility of a dual policy "which combines both strength to resist and a discriminating willingness to concede?" He admitted that given the pace of recent events, "political geography will soon have to be taught with a cinematograph rather than an atlas." Nonetheless, he wished to show that all the various measures and policies he had been advocating publicly and privately were an integral part of a coherent policy. The first part of the book, "The Peril and the Prospect," set the context by examining the passing of Britain's island immunity, the advantages of the Nazi economic system in its reliance on a rearmament industry to stimulate growth and demand, and the significance of "the new grouping" of European powers. Salter then went on to analyse the possibility of framing "a constructive peace policy," to unite the democracies and appeal to the Axis powers. On the question of collective security, he looked into the future when a new system would have to be reconstructed, based on a balance between "idealism and realism," between revisionist and status quo powers. In the third and highly controversial part, "National Strength," he reviewed the on-going "deficiencies of our defensive preparations," and specifically targeted what he termed "The Personal Equation." Here he singled out a series of individuals, whose personalities were subjected to a critical, colourful and epigrammatic analysis which Salter displayed for the first and not the last time in his writing. Among the outstanding vignettes were his observations of Chamberlain, to whom he devoted a 30 page chapter. "Spare, even ascetic, in figure, dark-haired and dark-eyed; with a profile rather corvine than aquiline …. In debate and exposition his speech is lucid, competent, cogent, never rising to oratory, unadorned with fancy, and rarely touched by perceptible emotion. In manner he is glacial rather than genial and what he does not feel he never professes to feel." He continued, "Mr. Chamberlain is compact, cold, correct, concentrated, with both the limitations and the strength which these qualities involve." In the event Chamberlain resigned and a national government was formed, Salter advocated a small inner cabinet, without departmental duties, to focus on planning for the next "total," "mechanised," and "totalitarian" war, with an all-party parliamentary "Committee of Foreign Policy and Defence (or Public Safety)." The latter he regarded as the forerunner of the National government that would inevitably emerge in the event of war.

Salter then laid out what he called "The Foundations of a New Peace," broadly conceived and clearly announced. He was aware that such an exercise would be misconstrued as the "academic futilities" of a liberal internationalist. Therefore, he emphasized that he was under "no illusions about the acceptability" of his ideas to Nazi Germany, and negotiations would only begin if and when the conditions for discussion were suitable. Salter envisaged the cancellation of the war guilt clause of the treaty of Versailles, assuaging German fears of encirclement by agreement on spheres of economic influence, a return to colonial free trade, access to raw materials and arms limitation. Finally, he formalized all these proposals into "A Draft Manifesto of British Policy," pointedly adding that "changes demanded under menace can bring no such results."[586] British reviews of Security were generally favourable with some reservations. The Economist noted, "It is not possible to make concessions to aggressor states without guarantees of good will, and no such guarantees are forthcoming." The Times regarded the Draft Manifesto as "the most important of his constructive passages," but took issue with the character sketches – "not always quite kind; perhaps a taste for epigram, even when restrained, is not altogether compatible with balanced characterization." In a similar vein, The Times Literary Supplement regarded the book as "rich in constructive ideas," even if readers might not agree with its criticisms of policies and people. The New Statesman praised Salter's career accomplishments, and observed that his analysis was "lucid and valuable, if not particularly original."[587] Reviews in the USA, where the book was published on 2 June and adopted as a Book-of-the Month choice, were very mixed. The New York Times thought Security, was "poorly organized," noted that "a good deal of dirty linen is washed in public" with Salter's pen portraits, and regarded the Draft Manifesto as "vague." The Washington Post denigrated Salter's "calling only for the recreation of an age already dead," and questioned whether the Manifesto was "even remotely touched with the breath of reality." As similar critical reviews followed, The New York Times on 29 June returned to Security and observed that its "cocksure critics" were treating the book "as though it were the product of an enthusiastic but slow-witted schoolboy." It emphasized that Salter's interest in finding a *via media* was "the sort upon which any kind of permanent international understanding must ultimately be based."[588] The most comprehensive review, however, was written by Lamont for The Saturday Review of Literature. Lamont had met with Salter in mid-July on his return from Europe, when Lamont cautioned his friend that he would be "taking his name in vain." That became clear in his review where he generally praised the Draft Manifesto, but also considered it "as savouring far too much of the policy of appeasement." For the rest Lamont went on to argue against any fresh proposals to Germany until it returned to peaceful methods of negotiation.[589]

There was nothing particularly surprising to Salter in the critical reaction, some of which he had anticipated. On 24 June he wrote to Tyler comparing Security to Recovery, and noting that "it's not so good a book, as a book. It was written more hurriedly, & with its purpose more directed to certain immediate objectives of policy & action here, & it's consequently less of a unity." Parts were taken from previous papers, and it was completed "after three weeks of the most intense work I've ever had." Other parts, he noted, he would have written differently, "if I had had time to read & ponder in cold blood & to go over each chapter with the meticulous care which I did in fact devote to the Chapter on the P.M. & the scene in the H of C of Sept. 28 [1938]." Salter concluded, "I feel sure this summer will see either war or a protracted crisis."[590] He also discovered indirectly that Chamberlain "was not too pleased" with the book or the "politely phrased condemnation of his policy of appeasement."[591] What surprised Salter, however, was that the note of caution he had included, writing that any negotiations with Germany would only take place when prospects were favourable, were ignored Thus some critics took Security as endorsing an early return and/or continuation of appeasement. In The Times, several letters were published endorsing Salter's Draft Manifesto as the basis for a new offer to Germany at a new peace conference.⁵⁹² The issue gathered momentum, when on 29 June, Halifax made a major foreign policy speech that echoed passages from Security. For Halifax also addressed the "dual policy" of resistance to aggression and pursuing a constructive peace process.⁵⁹³ Salter later noted of the book, "I have been able to trace a number of changes or developments in policy to it. For example, Lord Halifax had read it & instructed his principal officers to do so, shortly before his speech of June 29th which reflects it in a number of passages. This kind of thing is what I most wanted from writing the book."⁵⁹⁴

Even as Security continued to reverberate, there had been no let-up in Salter's lobbying efforts. On 12 May he had written to Felkin: "I have been mainly occupied in prodding the Govt. about civil defence, Ministry of Supply, air raid defence & food reserves. It's a hateful business, & the Govt.s' been lethargic, but we are getting some results."⁵⁹⁵ Indeed, on 20 April Chamberlain had announced in the Commons that a Ministry of Supply, agreed to by the cabinet the previous day, would finally be established. Salter found that the proposed ministry, to be headed by Leslie Burgin, had only limited scope, no compulsory powers, and was confined to army supplies: "Once more action is too late and too little."⁵⁹⁶ When the bill finally came to its second reading in the Commons on 8 June, Salter stated the bill was "narrowly drawn" and "inadequate for its purpose," and that "while we shall have a Ministry of Supply Act, we shall not have a Ministry of Supply but only a Ministry of Army Supply." He wished to see the bill's powers extended to cover other departments and have the powers of the 1915 Ministry of Munitions, including the ability to set priorities, such as for raw materials.⁵⁹⁷ During the debate, Burgin had passed a note to Salter asking for a talk, to which Salter first replied on 12 June with a letter summarizing his views about a range of proactive initiatives the new ministry should undertake. On 19 June in the Commons he insisted the government should be setting up "a real Ministry of Supply." With only three appointments to the new ministry, he commented, "Here, indeed, are generals without an Army." Even so, at the conclusion, Salter voted in favour of the bill.⁵⁹⁸ At their meeting on 22June, and drawing on his experience as Director of Shipping Requisitioning in the 1914-1918 war, Salter explained both to Burgin and Sir Arthur Robinson, the new parliamentary secretary for the ministry, that his concern was not so much with the "actual acquisition of necessary commodities as with the reduction of importing capacity in an emergency." He was convinced that air warfare against the British merchant fleet would worsen the situation. Thus, the more commodities imported in peace-time for storage, the less would have to be imported in wartime. Burgin explained that his intent in the meeting was to convince Salter that more had been done than was generally known.⁵⁹⁹ Still unsatisfied, Salter wrote to Robinson the following day, to explain that he was not concerned, as was the ministry, with acquiring specific stocks of particular commodities, rather, "I am solely concerned with provision against the total reduction of our importing capacity." And on balance, he maintained, "we should, in a protracted war, be able to import substantially less than in the last war." He then reiterated his appeal for an immediate and urgent increase in food reserves and other raw materials, because "We may have only a few weeks or months before war comes." He concluded, firstly, with an assurance that he was not turning the question into a political one but only trying to reduce a series of dangers. Secondly, he requested secret information, subject to confidentially rules, a request Robinson accepted.[600]

In the interim, Salter pressed ahead with his other lobbying efforts. On 14 June, during a Commons' debate on deep shelters, he approved some of the measures advanced by Anderson. However, he repeated the Air Raid Defence League's advocacy of deep shelters for especially vulnerable zones, such as the docks areas of the Thames, and most of all in the early stages of a *blitzkrieg*.[601] But it was the issues of reserves and raw materials that most concerned him, intensified by his increasing fear of an inevitable war. On 24 June he informed Felkin he would not be visiting on the continent, partly because the Commons would not rise for several more weeks. He continued, "Even if we don't have war, we shall I think certainly have a period of prolonged & acute crisis."[602] On 29 June he completed a comprehensive 10-page memorandum about food and raw materials. Subtitled "The Case for Immediate and Drastic Action," it began with a reminder that "We were in 1917-1918 brought near starvation and the loss of the war through a reduction of imports and the absence of sufficient reserves of food and raw materials. The prospect in this respect is now on balance much worse than it was in the last war." For the rest, the memorandum served as a consolidation and restatement of those arguments Salter had advocated for more than a year. His final exhortation was to "Buy and ship at once every possible ton of imported raw materials" which could be stored, including timber, ores and minerals.[603]

For some time Salter had been discussing these issues with Amery who wrote to Chamberlain on 1 July, enclosing the former's memorandum.[604] Amery endorsed the document, noting that it stated the case conclusively, that it came from a person who "probably knows more about it than anyone else," and agreed the situation was urgent. That was not the view of Chamberlain who thanked Amery for "Salter's interesting memorandum," and passed the material on to the Minister of Supply for comment.[605] It was this increasing sense of urgency which then prompted Salter and Amery to write a joint letter to the editor of <u>The Times</u>. They urged immediate action to purchase "to the utmost capacity of all available ships and ports, reserves of essential imports."[606] Keynes, too, publicly endorsed their "plea," writing that it was "unanswerable" and suggested that Salter and Amery should be hired to attend to the matter.[607] Behind the scenes Salter was still busy. On 3 July he had forewarned Robinson about the forthcoming letter to The Times, and pointed out that the concern was not about particular commodities, but about the importation of extra raw materials "to ease the general shipping (& financial) position under war conditions." The following day Salter met with Robinson, leaving a copy of his memorandum on food and raw materials. Writing to Burgin about their conversation, Robinson noted what Salter was now advocating was "an entirely new policy in regard to reserves."[608] Salter kept up the pressure with an article on ensuring adequate food reserves in The Observer and by widely circulating a bulletin published by the Air Raid Defence League, "Food in War Time," in which his views were endorsed.[609] As for the Air Raid Defence League itself, it discontinued active operations after the outbreak of the war and was wound down by May 1940.[610]

Action on the part of the government seemed clearly required. It began on 18 July with a survey of government stocks of food and raw materials, conducted specifically in response to the representations from Salter, Amery and the Air Raid Defence League. The three ministers concerned, Burgin (Ministry of Supply) Morrison (Chancellor of the Duchy of Lancaster) and Lord Chatfield (Minister for the Co-ordination of Defence) agreed that, for the short term, additional stocks of selected items of raw materials and food, above and beyond those already authorised, should be purchased and delivered by 15 October. Long term storage, it was suggested, should be reviewed by the Committee of Imperial Defence during the fall. These recommendations became the subject of a cabinet paper drawn up by Chatfield, discussed at the meeting of the cabinet on 26 July, and approved with the condition that total purchases should not exceed 20 million pounds.[611] In the last report of the Committee on Economic Information, the primary recommendation was to build up reserves of essential commodities.[612] It was not until 4 August that Salter and Amery were personally informed of the cabinet decision. "Broadly speaking," the record of the meeting noted, "the two gentlemen concurred in the steps which the Government were taking so far as they understood them in general terms, but thought that these steps were halting and inadequate, and pressed for a bolder and more resolute series of purchases." The note concluded, "The interview was extremely cordial."[613] It was only on 21 August, however, that Chamberlain replied to Amery regarding his letter of 1 July and the attached Salter memorandum. The prime minister dwelt, almost entirely, on the "practical issue," namely the problems associated with acquiring large scale reserves "in the neighbourhood of £100 million capital," and the fact that stores were already larger than previously estimated. He did hint that "the process of expansion [of reserves] has been hastened recently."[614]

While partial success in the lobbying sphere might have proved somewhat satisfying, a more public trial soon faced Salter. The mixed reception given to Security, and the "A Draft Manifesto of British Policy" it contained, continued to reverberate. Perhaps Lloyd George had some presentiment when he thanked Salter for a copy of the book and wrote that it "appears at an opportune moment."[615] During June ongoing discussion of Security continued and the notion took hold of what The Times termed Salter's "dual policy of resistance to aggression and of settlement by negotiation." More extreme interpretations concluded, "What! More Appeasement?" or praised Salter for his realism in advocating further negotiations with Hitler.[616] In response, Salter took the initiative and quickly wrote a pamphlet The Dual Policy, published on 3 August. Here he argued that the "dual policy" differed from appeasement as pursued prior to the Nazi occupation of Prague on 15 March, namely, "*First* stop aggression; *then* a magnanimous general settlement." While some of what followed was derived from Security, Salter spelled out what was now different from the prior experience of appeasement. "It offers immediate resistance to further aggression. It attempts to increase the collective resources available for opposition to the Axis Powers. It proposes at once to define and offer a constructive peace settlement on condition that aggression is abandoned." To render such a policy viable, Salter advocated continued rearmament, an alliance with Russia, if possible, a "peace policy which is boldly conceived and clearly stated," and never "to yield under menace." The details of a "constructive peace settlement" followed those he had advocated in Security.[617] Salter further developed the crucial question of timing when he addressed, for the first time since 1936, the Liberal Summer School at Cambridge on 6 August. There he reiterated his thoughts on the dual policy and added that immediately after an alliance with the Soviet Union, if the ongoing negotiations were successful, the British government should propose a White Paper to form the basis of a "constructive peace policy."[618] The New Statesman endorsed Salter's efforts at "ending the international anarchy," while The Spectator suggested that Salter had fashioned a useful "middle line."[619] However, as cautious and emphatic as Salter had been on the question of the timing and the details of a dual policy, some misinterpretation prevailed. A United Press dispatch, carried in American papers, declared that the plan was gaining favour in the ranks of all three major British parties. The New York Times declared that "An apparent paradox is the emergence of what is coming to be called 'appeasement on the left' among sections of the Liberal and Labour parties." Leadership of the movement was attributed to "independent thinkers like Sir Arthur Salter."[620] The Times struck a more balanced approach in a leading article on 16 August. This suggested that when the "peace front" was strengthened by the successful conclusion of the Anglo-French negotiations with the USSR, the time would be right for a new initiative along the lines promoted by Salter.[621]

With the future so uncertain, Salter made no vacations plans other than to join Ethel Bullard on 17 August for a few days. She was still recovering from surgery and had since 6 August stayed at Taymouth Castle in Perthshire, at the time operating as a hotel. "Arthur is coming up," she wrote on 15 August. "I hope he will like it & not be too bored. He is bringing up his own car & so I hope we can do some driving about." Her sister Louise also soon joined them.[622] However, earlier in the month, on 1 August, Salter had written to Stimson that "we shall I imagine be very near war all this month & perhaps next even if we don't go over the line."[623] That line was drawn, in fact, with the signature of the Nazi-Soviet pact on 24 August. Salter at once returned to London, devastated and hardly able to complete a letter he wrote on 28 August to Joyce Newton Thompson. The letter began: "I write as we are on the brink & apparently to go over."[624]

Endnotes

1. Entry of 11 June 1930, Felkin Diary, AEF/1/1/7. Entry of 21 June 1931, Felkin Diary, AEF/1/1/8 has details of Salter's income, investments and losses during the Depression. Afterwards Salter engaged Sir Eric Drummond's son, John Drummond who worked in the City, as his financial advisor. Author's interview with John Drummond, 17th Earl of Perth, 30 May 1980.
2. Salter to Ethel Bullard, 24 Dec. 1930, Salter Papers, File 8, Salter-Ethel Bullard Correspondence, 1929-1931.
3. T.V. Soong and Chiang Kai-shek to Drummond, 7 Jan. 1931, LNA, Box R2667, 1928-31, 10A/24177/24177, Minutes, 1st Meeting of the 62nd Session of the Council, 19 Jan. 1931, League of Nations, Official Journal, no. 2744. In fact, it was Robert Haas, Director of the Transit and Communications Section, who was invited in China.
4. The Times, 14 Jan. 1931, The New York Times, 14 Jan. 1931.
5. Keynes to Salter, 21 Jan. 1931, Keynes Papers.
6. See NA-UK, FO371/15485, F304/304/10.
7. The Times of India, 10, 21, 22, 26, Jan. 1931, entries of 8, 9, 10 Jan. 1931, Felkin Diary, AEF/1/1/8.
8. Felkin's 1931 diary provides a detailed, lengthy and often intimate description of the visits to India and later to China in Salter's company. See Felkin Diary, entries of 1 Jan.-13 May 1931, AEF/1/1/8.
9. The Times of India, 29 Jan. 1931.
10. Entry of 28 Dec. 1930, Felkin Diary, AEF/1/1/7, Sir Arthur Salter, A Scheme for an Economic Advisory Organization in India (Calcutta, 1931), 1-2, Salter, Memoirs, 208-210, Salter, Slave of the Lamp, 108-109.

11. Salter to Ethel Bullard, 18 Jan. 1931, Salter Papers, File 8, Salter-Ethel Bullard Correspondence, 1929-1931.
12. Salter to Violet Markham, 22 Jan. 1931, Markham Papers, 25/73.
13. Salter to Ethel Bullard, 10 Feb. 1931, Salter Papers, File 8, Salter-Ethel Bullard Correspondence, 1929-1931.
14. Entry of 26 Jan. 1932, Felkin Diary, AEF/1/1/8.
15. The Times of India, 16 Feb. 1931, entries of 15, 16, 17, 18, 19 Feb. 1931, Felkin Diary, AEF/1/1/8.
16. Salter, A Scheme for an Economic Advisory Organization in India, 2-36, Salter, Memoirs, 209. The Times of India, 10, 11 June, The Times, 10 June, The New York Times, 28 June and The Economist, 112(13 June 1931), 1268 gave the report extensive coverage.
17. Salter to Violet Markham, 20 Feb. 1931, Markham Papers, 25/73, Salter to Elisina Tyler, 14 Feb. 1931, Tyler Papers, Salter to Lamont, 8 Feb. 1931, Lamont Papers, 129-11,1922-1931.
18. See "Penang and the Dinner Jackets," "An Incident at Shanghai," and "An Afternoon at Nanking," Salter Papers, File 1, Anecdotes and Incidents.
19. Pearl S. Buck to the author, 6 Sept. 1972, author's archive, "An Afternoon at Nanking," Salter Papers, File 1, Anecdotes and Incidents.
20. Salter to Elisina Tyler, 15 Mar. 1931, Tyler Papers.
21. Salter to Ka Cox, 11 Apr. 1931, Salter Papers, File 7, Salter – Mrs. W.E. Arnold-Forster (Ka Cox) Correspondence, 1920s-1933.
22. T.V. Soong to Salter, 16 Apr. 1931, Drummond to Soong, 4 June 1931, LNA, 1928-32: 10A/29179/29179. For further details on the new Economic Council, see NA-UK, FO371/15485, F3618/304/10.
23. Minutes by Cecil and Noel-Baker, 16 May 1931, NA-UK, FO371/15485, FO371/15485, F2809/304/10.
24. Minute by Cadogan, 16 Feb. 1931, Drummond to Salter, 5 Feb. 1931, NA-UK, FO371/15485, F990/304/10.
25. See minutes in NA-UK, FO371/15485, F1190/304/10, and Susan Howson and Donald Winch, The Economic Advisory Council, 1930-1939: A Study of Economic Advice During Depression and Recovery, 1930-1939 (1977), 75. For the Foreign Office response to the Committee's report, see NA-UK, FO371/15479, F160/160/10.
26. See e.g., minute by Pratt, 25 Mar. 1931, NA-UK, FO371/15485, F1918/304/10.
27. Minute by [?], 5 May 1930, Lampson to Foreign Office, 30 Apr. 1931, NA-UK, FO371/15485, F2427/304/10, Moss to Lampson, 29 Apr. 1931, NA-UK, FO371/15485, F3618/304/10.

28. Lampson to Henderson, 30 Apr. 1931, minute by Pratt, n.d., NA-UK, FO371/15479, F2871/160/10.
29. "Supplementary Note on China," NA-UK, FO371/15479, F3962/160/10.
30. Salter to Felkin, 10, 15 June 1931, Felkin Papers, AEF/3/1/114, Minutes, 2nd Meeting of the 63rd Session of the Council, 19 May 1931, League of Nations, Official Journal, no. 2806.
31. Salter to Felkin, 12 Apr. 1931, Felkin Papers, AEF/3/1/111, "Some Reflections on the World Economic Depression," 4 May 1931, The Manchester Guardian, 7 May 1931. For Salter's further views on the relation between the supply and demand for gold and its impact on prices, see RIIA, The International Gold Problem: Collected Papers (1931), 126-127.
32. The New York Times, 10 May 1931, The Economist, 112(16 May 1931), 1035.
33. Salter to Ethel Bullard, 30 Apr. 1931, Salter Papers, File 8, Salter-Ethel Bullard Correspondence, 1929-1931.
34. Salter to Ethel Bullard, 3 May 1931, Salter Papers, File 8, Salter-Ethel Bullard Correspondence, 1929-1931.
35. Report on Sir Arthur Salter's Visit to Japan, 1 June 1931, LNA, R2668, 10A/31161/24177.
36. Salter to Ethel Bullard, 3 May 1931, Salter Papers, File 8, Salter-Ethel Bullard Correspondence, 1929-1931, Salter to Ka Cox, 6 May 1931, Salter Papers, File 7, Salter-Mrs. W.E. Arnold-Forster (Ka Cox) Correspondence, 1920s-1933.
37. Salter to Violet Markham, 20 Feb. 1931, Markham Papers, 25/73.
38. Salter to Ka Cox, 8 Feb. 1931, Salter Papers, File 7, Salter-Mrs. W.E. Arnold-Forster (Ka Cox) Correspondence, 1920s-1933.
39. Salter to Ethel Bullard, 15 Mar. 1931, Salter Papers, File 8, Salter-Ethel Bullard Correspondence, 1929-1931
40. Ethel Bullard to Salter, 8 Apr. 1931, Salter Papers, File 8, Salter-Ethel Bullard Correspondence, 1929-1931.
41. Salter to Ka Cox, 6 May 1931, Salter Papers, File 7, Salter-Mrs. W.E. Arnold-Forster (Ka Cox) Correspondence, 1920s-1933.
42. Salter to Violet Markham, 12 May 1931, Markham Papers, 25/73.
43. Howland to Salter, 16 May 1931 and the enclosed Schedule, Salter Papers, File 2, Miscellaneous Political Correspondence, 1916-1950, The Los Angeles Times, 22 May 1931.
44. Salter to Elisina Tyler, 21 May 1931, Tyler Papers, Salter to Ethel Bullard, 30 Apr. 1931, Salter Papers, File 8, Salter-Ethel Bullard Correspondence, 1929-1931, The New York Times, 26 May 1931.
45. Frederick W. Allen to Lamont, 14 May 1931, Lamont Papers, 129-11, 1922-1931.

46. "Note for Radio Broadcast," 31 May 1931, Salter Papers, File 10, Mission to China, Jan.-Apr. 1931.
47. "The Silver Problem," <u>Political Science Quarterly</u>, 45(Sept. 1931), 321-334. For Lamont's opening comments see Lamont Papers, 140-6, 1 June 1931. Salter also gave Lamont a copy of his note on silver, first prepared for T.V. Soong, which emphasized the "dangers" of a conference. Salter to Lamont, 28 May 1931, Lamont Papers, 129-11, 1922-1931. <u>The New York Times</u>, 2 June 1931, gave extensive coverage to the speech, as did <u>The Economist</u>, 113(4 July 1931), 16, <u>The Wall Street Journal</u>, 2 June 1931, and <u>The Washington Post</u>, 3 June 1931.
48. Salter to Felkin, 10, 15 June 1931, Felkin Papers, AEF/3/1/114.
49. See Butler to Salter, 2 Mar. 1931, Howland to Salter, 16 May 1931, Boyden to Salter, 4 June 1931, Salter Papers, File 2, Miscellaneous Political Correspondence, 1916-1950, Lamont to Salter, 2 June 1931, Lamont Papers, 129-11, 1922-1931.
50. Morrow to Salter, [?] June 1931, Morrow Papers, Box 41/ Folder 5/Salter, J.A., <u>News Chronicle</u>, 7 Oct. 1931, letter to the editor, <u>The Times</u>, 7 Oct. 1931.
51. <u>The New York Times</u>, 3, 4 June 1931.
52. Entry of 13 May 1931, Felkin Diary, AEF/1/1/8.
53. Herbert Hoover Presidential Library, Appointments Calendar, 4 June 1931, entry of 6 June 1931, Stimson Diary, vol. 16, 134, Stimson Papers, Yale University Library, New Haven, CT, Lindsay to Henderson, 8 June 1931, NA-UK, FO371/15487, F3566/672/10.
54. <u>The New York Times</u>, 16, 17 June 1931, <u>The Wall Street Journal</u>, 17 June 1931.
55. <u>The New York Times</u>, 19 June 1931.
56. Salter to Ka Cox, 12 June 1931, Salter Papers, File 7, Salter-Mrs. W.E. Arnold-Forster (Ka Cox) Correspondence, 1920s-1933.
57. Salter to Felkin, 10, 15 June 1931, Felkin Papers, AEF/3/1/114.
58. Ethel Bullard to Salter, 8 July 1931, Salter Papers, File 8, Salter-Ethel Bullard Correspondence, 1929-1931.
59. Felkin to Jennifer Hart, 12 July 1932, Jennifer Hart Papers, MS.Eng.c.7511, fol. 66, Bodleian Library, Oxford.
60. Salter to Joyce Felkin, 9 July 1931, Felkin Papers, AEF/3/1/114. In later years Salter readily acknowledged that Felkin had been of "great help" to him. Transcript of Interview between Lord Salter and M. Jean Siotis, 22 Jan. 1969, 2-3, author's archive.
61. "Geneva in Retrospect," <u>Index</u>, 7(1932), 287.
62. Entry of 8 July 1931, Felkin Diary, AEF/1/1/8, "Conference Held at New College, Oxford, 11-12 July 1931," Lloyd Papers, Section 7/26.
63. Chatham House Speech, 15 July 1931, RIIA Papers, reprinted in <u>International Affairs</u>, 10(Sept. 1931), 592-596. Salter was a founding member of the RIIA and

on 3 Nov. 1931 was elected to its Council. See Salter to Sir Neill Malcolm, 30 July 1931, MacAdam to Salter, 4 Nov. 1931, RIIA Papers, Salter, Memoirs, 230.

64. Salter to Felkin, 23 July 1931, Felkin Papers, AEF/3/1/114, The Observer, 26 July 1931.
65. Salter to Ka Cox, 12 June 1931, Salter Papers, File 7, Salter-Mrs. W.E. Arnold-Forster (Ka Cox) Correspondence, 1920s-1933.
66. Stanley Unwin to Salter, 20 July 1931, Salter to Unwin, 24 July 1931, Stanley Unwin Papers, Stanley Unwin Publishers, London.
67. Salter to Wellesley, 31 July 1931, minute by Pratt, 8 Sept. 1931, NA-UK, FO371/15480, F4260/160/10. See also Roberta Allbert Dayer, Finance and Empire: Sir Charles Addis, 1861-1945 (1988), 274ff.
68. Salter to Felkin, 6, 11 Aug. 1931, Felkin Papers, AEF/3/1/114, Marian Henderson to Felkin, 21 Aug. 1931, Felkin Papers, AEF/3/1/115, Curtis to Macadam, 14 Aug. 1931, RIIA Papers.
69. Cadogan to Salter, 6 Sept. 1931, LNA, Box R3357, 1928-1931, 15/29963/28548, Ka Cox to Felkin, 17 Sept. 1931, Felkin Papers, AEF/3/1/115.
70. League of Nations, Official Journal, Records of the 12th Ordinary Session of the Assembly, Minutes of the Second Committee, 6th Meeting, 18 Sept. 1931 (Geneva, 1931), 30-32.
71. "The Financial Crisis of 1931," Salter Papers, File 1, Anecdotes and Incidents, Salter, Memoirs, 228-229, A.C. Temperley, The Whispering Gallery of Europe (1938), 157.
72. Cecil to Simon, 21 Sept. 1931, minute by Sargent, 23 Sept. 1931, NA-UK, FO371/15733, W10884/10884/98, minute by N.B. Ronald and attachment, 21 Sept. 1931, NA-UK, FO371/15733, W10999/10884/98. See entry of 20 Sept. 1931, Felkin Diary, AEF/1/1/8 for details of his conversation with Salter on the events of the day.
73. League of Nations, Official Journal, Records of the 12th Ordinary Session of the Assembly, Minutes of the Second Committee, 9th Meeting, 21 Sept. 1931 (Geneva, 1931), 48-49
74. See Cecil to Reading, 28 Sept. 1931, NA-UK, FO371/15733, W11526/10884/98.
75. League of Nations, Official Journal, Records of the 12th Ordinary Session of the Assembly, Minutes of the Second Committee, 12th Meeting, 23 Sept. 1931 (Geneva, 1931), 62-64. The Economist, 113(26 Sept. 1931), 557-558, 560-561 endorsed his analysis.
76. The New York Times, 22 Sept. 1931.
77. The Times, 2 Oct. 1931. Salter's performance was also praised during a post-address meeting at Chatham House on 13 October. See The Earl of Lytton,

"The Twelfth Assembly of the League of Nations," <u>International Affairs</u> 10(Nov. 1931), 754-755.
78. Salter to Hilda Matheson, 31 July, 6 Aug., 22 Sept. 1931, BBC WAC, R Cont. 1, Salter Talks, File 1, 1926-1948.
79. "What I Would Do with the World – I," <u>The Listener</u>, 6(7 Oct.1931) 567-570, 599-600.
80. Salter to Layton, and encl., 3, 6 Oct. 1931, Layton Papers, $10^{73-74(1-13)}$.
81. Memorandum by Stephen King Hall, 12 Oct. 1931, RIIA Papers, <u>The Times</u>, 17 Oct. 1931.
82. <u>The Spectator</u>, 147(12 Dec. 1931), 800-801.
83. "The World Financial Crisis," <u>The Yale Review</u>, 21(Dec. 1931), 217-232, <u>The New York Times</u>, 19 Sept. 1932.
84. Unwin to Salter, 13 Oct., 21 Nov. 1931, Unwin Papers, Salter to Curtice Hitchcock, 13 Nov. 1931, MS1640/6058, George Bell and Sons Papers, Special Collections, University of Reading, Reading.
85. Minute by Sargent, 4 Nov., Leith-Ross to Sargent, 6 Nov. 1931, NA-UK, FO371/15198, C8317/172/62, C8318/172/62.
86. Ka Cox to Felkin, 8 Dec. 1931, Felkin Papers, AEF/3/1/117.
87. See Dormer to Simon, 25 Nov. 1931, NA-UK, FO371/15531, F7750/9/40, Dormer to Simon, 11 Dec. 1931, NA-UK, FO371/16259, F249/200/40.
88. Tyrrell to Simon, 3 Dec. 1931, NA-UK, FO371/15503, F7204/1391/10.
89. Salter to Garvin, 13 Nov. 1931, J.L. Garvin Papers, University of Texas Library, Houston, TX.
90. Salter to MacAdam, 5 Nov. 1931, MacAdam to Salter, 12 Nov. 1931, Salter to Cleeve, 10 Dec. 1931, Cleeve to Salter, 12 Dec. 1931, RIIA Papers.
91. <u>The Observer</u>, 27 Dec. 1931. <u>The New York Times</u>, 27, 31 Dec. 1931 reiterated Salter's views, as did an editorial in <u>The Times</u>, 31 Dec. 1931.
92. Salter to Elisina Tyler, 31 Dec. 1931, Tyler Papers.
93. Salter to Lamont, 14 Jan. 1932, Lamont Papers, 129-12, 1931-1934.
94. <u>The Listener</u>, 7(13 Jan. 1932), 37-8, 72. <u>The Observer</u>, 3 Jan. 1932 and <u>The Manchester Guardian</u>, 4 Jan. 1932 carried summaries of his broadcast.
95. "An Outline of World Policy," in Sir Arthur Salter, et al., <u>Halley Stewart Lecture, 1931, The World's Economic Crisis and the Way of Escape</u> (1932), 17-39. Other contributors were Stamp, Keynes, Blackett, Clay and Beveridge. When Salter and Layton met with Ramsay MacDonald on 8 Jan. 1932, they also argued against the cancellation of debts. Minute by MacDonald, 8 Jan. 1932, NA-UK, FO800/286.
96. <u>The Economist</u>, 114(11 June 1932), 1297. Salter's relations with <u>The Economist</u> were very close; on occasion he even attended the Monday morning editorial meetings. Author's interview with Graham Hutton, 3 June 1980.

97. The Times, 19 Jan., 6 Feb. 1932.
98. "England's Dilemma: Free Trade or Protection?" Foreign Affairs, 10(1932), 188-200.
99. Matheson to Salter, 11 Feb. 1932, BBC WAC, R Cont. 1, Salter Talks, File 1, 1926-1948.
100. The Listener, 24 Feb., 2, 9,16, 23, 30 Mar. 1932, 291, 298-299, 329-330, 361, 376-377, 436-437, 466-467. The talks, arranged under the auspices of the Central Council for Broadcast Adult Education, via the BBC, were published in The Modern State, Mary Adams, ed., (1933), 253-316. The others contributors were Leonard Woolf, Lord Eustace Percy, Beatrice Webb, and W.G.S. Adams.
101. H.G. Wells, The Work, Wealth and Happiness of Mankind, 2 vols. (1931), 30, Salter to Wells, 21 Mar. 1932, Wells Papers, Folder S-021.
102. Salter to Wells, 31 July 1939, Wells Papers, Folder S-021.
103. Cox to Felkin, 20 Jan. 1932, Felkin Papers, AEF/3/1/117, Cox to Felkin, 5 July 1932, Felkin Papers, AEF/3/1/121.
104. Memorandum by Salter, 2 Feb. 1932, minute by Eden, 9 Feb. 1932, NA-UK, FO371/16146, F950/1/10.
105. "The Shanghai Crisis," International Affairs, 11(1932), 171-173.
106. The Times, 18 Feb. 1932. Other signatories were Cecil, Charles Addis, Arthur Haworth, A.D. Linday and Gilbert Murray.
107. The Times, 8 Mar. 1932. Other speakers included Lord Grey, Lord Cecil and Sir Frederick Whyte.
108. Salter to Felkin, 3 Feb. 1932, Felkin Papers, AEF/3/1/118.
109. "China, Japan and the League of Nations," Contemporary Review,141(1932), 288. On Salter's further views on the Kellogg Pact, see The Manchester Guardian, 15 Jan. 1935.
110. Salter to Stanhope, 9 Apr., 3 May, 13 June 1935, NA-UK, FO371/19324, F2631, F2944, F3898/1307/10. These files also contain considerable related documents. See also Stimson to Salter, 6 Apr., Salter to Stimson, 26 Apr. 1935, Stimson Papers.
111. The Morning Post, 3 Mar. 1933, "Past, Present and Future," Lloyd's Bank Review, 3(1932), 54-73. Salter's views were discussed in the Foreign Office, where the merits of cancellation versus reduction were debated. See NA-UK, FO371/15908, C1808, 1809/29/62, C2694/29/62.
112. The Times, 1, 5 Apr. 1932, The Manchester Guardian, 5 Apr. 1932.
113. The Times, 2 Apr. 1932.
114. Salter, Memoirs, 232, House of Commons Debates, 5th Series, [H.C. Debs.] vol. 265, 6 May 1932, col. 1443.

115. Pybus to MacDonald, 24 Mar. 1932, NA-UK, MT33/130, Part II, File 1931-1934, Hurcomb to Salter, 7 Dec. 1967 Salter Papers, File 30, Author's London Draft of Salter Biography, Ministry of Transport, <u>Report of the Conference on Rail and Road Transport, 29 July 1932</u> (1932), 4-12. Minutes of the conference are in NA-UK, MT33/130, Part I, 689/2
116. Salter to Violet Markham, 11 Apr. 1932, Markham Papers, 25/73.
117. Salter to Bickers, 14 Jan. 1932, George Bell and Sons Papers, MS1640/6059.
118. <u>Recovery: The Second Effort</u> (1932), vii-xvi, 1-306.
119. Salter to Joyce Newton Thompson, 3 June 1932, Newton Thompson Papers, BC 643 B22.9, <u>The New York Times</u>, 18 Apr. 1932, Note by Salter, 30 Apr. 1932, Salter to Bickers, 16 July 1931, Bickers to Salter, 18 July 1932, George Bell &Sons Papers, MS1640/6059.
120. <u>The Times</u>, 7 Apr. 1932. See also <u>The Manchester Guardian</u>, 7 Apr. 1932, <u>The Financial Times</u>, 7 Apr. 1932 and <u>The Economist</u>, 114(16 Apr. 1932), 836-837.
121. <u>New York Herald-Tribune</u>, 7 Apr. 1932, <u>The New York Times Book Review</u>, 10 Apr. 1932.
122. <u>The Times Literary Supplement</u>, 28 Apr. 1932, 300, Sir Basil Blackett, "'Recovery'," <u>Nineteenth Century and After</u>, 140(1932), 525-532, Sir Ernest Benn, "'Recovery' According to Salter," <u>The English Review</u>, 54 (June 1932), 633-642.
123. Sidney Webb to Salter, 1 Apr. 1932, Salter Papers, File 12, <u>Recovery</u> (London, 1932), Correspondence, 1932-34, Entries of 1 Feb, 9 Apr. 1932, Beatrice Webb Diary, vol. 46, 5257, 5293-5297.
124. See Salter Papers, File 12, <u>Recovery</u> (1932), Correspondence, 1932-34. An embarrassing episode resulted from Salter's reference in <u>Recovery</u> to the Swedish "Match King," Ivar Kreuger, as a person "of creative vision." The latter's suicide in Paris on 12 March and the discovery of his fraudulent financial practices forced Salter to delete the reference from the US edition. See Salter Papers, File 1, "Ivar Kreuger" <u>Anecdotes and Incidents</u>, H.V. Hodson to the author, 31 Aug. 1979, and Sir Noel Hall to the author, 28 Apr.1981, author's archive. Privately, Salter wrote of the "terrible tragedy" of Kreuger's death. Salter to Lady Aberdeen, 30 Mar. 1932, Lady Aberdeen Papers, courtesy of Lady Aberdeen. The issue was shortly afterwards raised in the Commons. See <u>H.C. Debs</u>, vol. 267, 23 June 1932, col. 1283.
125. Salter to Violet Markham, 11 Apr. 1932, Markham Papers, 25/73, Salter to Joyce Newton Thompson, 3 June 1932, Newton Thompson Papers, BC 643 B22.9, Salter to Lippmann, 11 Apr. 1932, Lippmann Papers.
126. Salter to Joyce Newton Thompson, 16 Apr., 3 June 1932, Newton Thompson Papers, BC643 B22.8-9.

127. Salter to Felkin, 3 Feb. 1933, Felkin Papers, AEF/3/1/118, Salter, Memoirs, 232-233, Joyce Newton Thompson to Violet Markham, 26 Mar. 1933, Newton Thompson Papers, BC 643 B18.50.
128. See NA-UK, FO371/15790, A2796/1043/51, Salter to Leith-Ross, 21 May 1932, Leith-Ross Papers, NA-UK, T188/273.
129. Lippmann to Salter, 28 Apr. 1932, Salter Papers, File 12, Recovery (London, 1932), Correspondence, 1932-34.
130. See minutes in NA-UK, FO371/16450, A4986/1992/45. For the same view regarding Salter's influence, see Gary B. Ostrower, Collective Insecurity: The United States and the League of Nations during the Early Thirties (1979), 140-143.
131. "The Guide Post," The Living Age, 342(June 1932), 2.
132. See CEI, Second Report, 8 March 1932, NA-UK, CAB58/30, Howson and Winch, The Economic Advisory Council, 1930-1939, 100, 106-110, The Times, 19 July 1932.
133. Salter, Memoirs, 230.
134. Author's interview with Lord Salter, 6 Oct. 1970.
135. The Manchester Guardian, 23 Feb., 9, 12 13, May 1932, The Times, 12 May 1932.
136. The Times, 23 June 1932, The Oxford Mail, 22 June 1932, The Oxford Times, 24 June 1932.
137. See The Times, 4, 7, 8, 9 June 1932.
138. The Times, 14, 17 June 1932, The Financial Times, 14 June 1932, Salter to Tyler, 29 June 1932, LNA, Tyler Papers.
139. The Times, 30 June 1932, The Financial Times, 8 July 1932. On 2 July, 16 economists signed a letter to the editor in support of Salter's views on "reflation." The Times, 2 July 1932.
140. Political Aspects of the World Depression, Being the Burge Memorial Lecture for the Year 1932 (Oxford, 1932), 5-21.
141. The Financial Times, 11 July 1932.
142. Salter to MacDonald, 15 July, MacDonald to Salter, 19 July 1932, MacDonald Papers, NA-UK, PRO30/69/678/3, Salter to M.M. Butler, 20 July 1932, Layton Papers, 67[52(1)].
143. Speech by Salter, Chatham House, 15 July 1932, RIIA Papers. Cf., "Chatham House Annual Dinner, July 14th, 1932," International Affairs, 11(1932), 849-851.
144. "The Conferences of this Year: Geneva – Lausanne – Ottawa – London," Political Quarterly, 3(1932), 467-488. See also his "The Forthcoming Conferences," The News-Letter: The National Labour Fortnightly, 1(11 June 1932), 7-10.
145. "Ottawa and the World," The Spectator, 148(1932), 821-822.

146. The New York Times, 17 July 1932, "The Conferences of this Year," Political Quarterly, 3(1932), 475-480.
147. Pybus to Salter, 9 Aug. 1932, NA-UK, MT33/130 Part II, File 1931-1934.
148. Ministry of Transport, Report of the Conference on Rail and Road Transport, 29th July 1932 (1932).
149. MacDonald to Salter, 16 Aug. 1932, MacDonald Papers, NA-UK, PRO30/69/678/3,
150. The Times, 17, 18 26, Aug., 21 Oct. 1932, The Financial Times, 17 Aug. 1932, The New York Times, 18 Aug. 1932, Salter Memoirs, 233. For the next two months, the letters to the editor column of The Times continued to debate the report. Finally, on 6 Oct. 1932, an editorial in The Times defended the report of the "Salter Conference."
151. "Introduction" to Sir H. Osborne Mance, The Road and Rail Transport Problem (1940), viii.
152. "The Economic Causes of War," in The Causes of War: Economic, Industrial, Racial, Religious, Scientific and Political, Arthur Porritt, ed., (New York, 1932), 1-25.
153. "The Future of Economic Nationalism," Foreign Affairs, 11(1932), 8-20. His article received much publicity in the US. See The Wall Street Journal, 26 Sept. 1932 and The Washington Post, 26 Sept. 1932.
154. The New York Times, 2 Oct. 1932. The editorial endorsed Salter's criticism, stating it put him in line with Roosevelt.
155. The Times, 27 Sept. 1932.
156. "Ottawa and the World," The Spectator, 149(8 Oct. 1932), 438-439.
157. Entry of 6 Oct. 1932, Beatrice Webb Diary, vol. 46, 5357-59.
158. Salter to Violet Markham, 10 Oct. 1932, Markham Papers, 25/73.
159. Tyler to Elisina Tyler, 14 Oct. 1932, Tyler Papers.
160. Salter to Violet Markham, 10 Oct. 1932, Markham Papers, 25/73.
161. "Disarmament," Round Table, 22(1932), 532-551.
162. Salter to Murray, 28 Sept. 1932, Murray Papers, vol. 214, The Times, 12 Oct. 1932.
163. C.A. Siepmann to Salter, 15 Sept. 1932, BBC WAC, R Cont 1, Salter Talks, File 1, 1926-1948, "Disarmament – the Prospects," The Listener, 8(26 Oct. 1932), 577-578. Salter had similarly spoken on 15 Sept. 1932 to a National Peace Council luncheon. The Times, 16 Sept. 1932.
164. The Times, 17, 21 Oct. 1932. Other signatories were D.H. MacGregor, A.C. Pigou, Keynes, Layton and Stamp. The New York Times, 17 Oct. 1932 described the signatories as "known throughout the world but seldom in agreement."
165. The New York Times, 2 Oct. 1932.

166. Salter to W.H. Mallory, 13 Oct. 1932, RIIA Papers.
167. Chamberlain to MacDonald, 2 Nov. 1932, MacDonald Papers, NA-UK, PRO30/69/1442, Salter to Chamberlain and MacDonald, 3 Nov. 1932, NA-UK, FO371/15913, C9194/29/62, Salter to MacDonald, 4 Nov. 1932, MacDonald to Salter, 14 Nov. 1932, MacDonald Papers, NA-UK, PRO30/69/678/3.
168. See The Wall Street Journal, 4 Nov. 1932.
169. "Digest of the Remarks by Sir Arthur Salter, November 9, 1932, Council on Foreign Relations," RIIA Papers.
170. Salter to Felkin, 11 Nov. 1932, Felkin Papers, AEF/3/1/123, entry of 11 Nov. 1932, Stimson Diary, vol. 24, 79-80.
171. "A New Framework for the Economic System," in The Obligation of Universities to the Social Order, H.P. Fairchild, ed., (New York, 1933),146-168, The Wall Street Journal, 17 Nov. 1932.
172. "Steps Toward Recovery," Academy of Political Science, Proceedings, 15(1933), 126-135.
173. Salter to Elisina Tyler, 31 Dec. 1932, Tyler Papers.
174. The New York Times, 19 Nov. 1932.
175. James R. Angell to Salter, 26 Nov. 1932, Salter to Angell, 9 Dec. 1932, Yale University Library, Manuscripts and Archives, University President Record Unit 24, Box 170, Folder 1793.
176. Salter to MacDonald, encl., 6 Dec. 1932, MacDonald Papers, NA-UK, PRO 30/69/1442.
177. The Times, 10 Dec. 1932, The Manchester Guardian, 10 Dec. 1932, The New York Times, 10 Dec. 1932, "What America Thinks of the War Debt Settlement," The Listener, 8(28 Dec. 1932), 928.
178. "War Debts," International Affairs, 12(Mar.-Apr. 1933), 147-167.
179. Salter to Beatrice Webb, 22 Dec. 1932, Passfield Papers, Section II, 412.
180. "Preface," to H.V. Hodson, Economics of a Changing World (1933), v-xvi, and Salter to Geoffrey Faber, 14 Dec. 1932, Faber and Faber Papers.
181. W.L. Cross to Salter, 13 Sept. 1932, Salter Papers, File 2, Miscellaneous Political Correspondence, 1916-1950, "A Year and a Half of Crisis," The Yale Review, 22(1932), 217-233.
182. Salter to Hurcomb, 24 Oct. 1932, minute by Hurcomb, 31 Oct. 1932, Salter to Pybus, 14 Dec. 1932, NA-UK, MT33/130, Part II, 1932-1934, The Times, 19 Dec. 1932, The Financial Times, 19 Dec. 1932.
183. The Economist, 115(24 Dec. 1932), 1189.
184. Salter to Elisina Tyler, 31 Dec. 1932, Tyler Papers.
185. The New York Times, 9 Jan. 1933, The Times, 10 Jan. 1933.

186. The Times, 9 Jan. 1933. The Salter lecture was discussed by Liberal Party leader, William Mackenzie King and the Masseys on 11 January 1933. Massey arranged for Salter to visit with King. Entries of 11 Jan., 2 Feb. 1933, Mackenzie King Diary, (J13) p. 39.
187. Massey to Salter, 26 Oct., 3 Nov. 1933, 6 Jan. 1933, Salter to Massey, 5, 14 Nov. 1933, B87-0082, 085#10, Vincent Massey Papers, University of Toronto Archives, Toronto, ON.
188. "The Week Abroad," The Listener, 9(15, 22, 29 Mar. 1933), 402-403, 461, 480-481.
189. The Times, 1 Feb., 16 May 1933, The Financial Times, 16 May 1933.
190. H.C. Debs., vol. 274, 7 Feb. 1933, cols. 38-39.
191. "Summary of Points Raised by Sir Arthur Salter," 14 Feb. 1933, NA-UK, MT33/130, Part II, The Financial Times, 15 Feb. 1933
192. The Manchester Guardian, 11 Feb. 1933.
193. Letter to the editor, The Times, 21 Mar. 1933, "Why Mr. Keynes is Right," The Spectator, 150(24 Mar. 1933), 417-418.
194. MacDonald to Salter, 29 Mar. 1933, MacDonald Papers, NA-UK, PRO30/69/1443 PT 2.
195. Salter to Unwin, 6 Apr. 1933, Unwin Papers, "Obsolete Jobs Not Obsolete Men," Fortune, 3(Apr. 1933), 60-63, The New York Times, 2 Apr. 1933, The New York Times Magazine, 16 Apr. 1933.
196. Salter to Joyce Newton Thompson, 8 Apr. 1933, Newton Thompson Papers, BC 643 B22.10.
197. General Sir Arthur Currie to Massey, 5 Jan. 1933, Massey Papers, B87-0082, 085#10, Montreal Gazette, 18 Apr., Montreal Star, 18 Apr. 1933. See the large collection of press cuttings on Salter in the R.B. Bennett Papers, University of New Brunswick, Harriet Irving Library, MG H96 Box 1035.
198. Modern Mechanization and Its Effects on the Structure of Society (1933), 1-42, Montreal Star, 19 Apr. 1933, The New York Times, 19 Apr. 1933, The Times, 19 Apr. 1933, and guest lists in Massey Papers, B87-0082, 085#09.
199. "Diary of Sir Arthur Salter's Visit," in Massey Papers, B87-0082, 085#10, guest lists in B87-0082,085#08, press cuttings in Bennett Papers, MG H96 Box 1035, "How Recovery May Come," The Canadian Club, 24 Apr. 1933, http://www.canadianclub.org/SearchResults.aspx?IndexCatalogue =SearchIndex&SearchQuery=Salter
200. "Diary of Sir Arthur Salter's Visit," in Massey Papers, B87-0082, 085#10.
201. Entries of 28 Apr., 2, 9, May 1933, Mackenzie King Diary, "Diary of Sir Arthur Salter's Visit," in Massey Papers, B87-0082, 085#10.
202. Bennett to Salter, 1 May 1933.

203. Salter to Violet Markham, 1 May 1933, Markham Papers, 25/73.
204. See Arthur Sweetser to Salter, 4 Apr. 1933, Fosdick Papers, Box 2.
205. The New York Times, 7 May 1933.
206. Salter to Massey, 17 May 1933, Massey Papers, B87-0082, 085#10.
207. Salter to Ka Cox, 12 May 1933, Salter Papers, File 7, Salter-Mrs. W.E. Arnold-Forster (Ka Cox) Correspondence, 1920s-1933.
208. League of Nations, Sixth International Studies Conference, A Record of a Second Study Conference on The State and Economic Life (1934), 13-18. Salter's comments were reprinted in International Affairs, 12(1933), 540-546. The first study conference took place in Milan, 23-27 May 1932.
209. Beveridge to Salter, 25 May 1933, Beveridge Papers, BEV5/13, BLPES, London, The Sunday Times, 18 June 1933, Lord Beveridge, Power and Influence (1953), 228-230.
210. The New York Times, 4, 11, June 1933.
211. The Times, 9, 10, 13 June 1933.
212. Salter to G.H. Bickers, 15 Jan. 1933, George Bell & Sons Papers, MS1640/6631, The Framework of an Ordered Society (1933), 1-57, The Economist, 122(8 July 1933). 77, The New York Times, 11 June 1933.
213. The United States of Europe and Other Papers, edited with notes by W. Arnold-Forster (1933), Unwin to Salter, 20 July, Salter to Unwin, 24 July 1933, Unwin Papers, The Times, 30 June 1933, The Economist, 117(15 July 1933), 132.
214. The New York Times Magazine, 11 June 1933. Salter's articles were based on memoranda he first wrote, copies of which are in the Tyler Papers, LNA.
215. The New York Times, 18 June 1933.
216. Salter to Massey, 28 June 1933, Massey Papers, B87-0082, 085#10, Salter, Memoirs, p. 234.
217. The New York Times, 25 June 1933.
218. The New York Times Magazine, 2 July 1933. See also Salter, "The Economic Conference: Progress Up-to-Date," The Listener, 10(5 July 1933), 10.
219. The New York Times, 2 July 1933.
220. The New York Times, 9 July 1933.
221. "The Economic Factor," in In Pursuit of Peace: Ten Addresses Delivered at Oxford, July 1933, G.P. Gooch, ed., (1933), 64-73.
222. "Diary of Trip to Great Britain," entry of 20 July 1933, Stimson Diary, vol. 26, 195-197.
223. The New York Times, 23 July 1933.
224. Entry of 22 Mar. 1933, Beverley Nichols Papers, Box 2, 1933, Appointment Book. Box 5, Clippings Book, 1933-35, University of Delaware Library, Beverley Nichols, Cry Havoc! (1933), 90-205, The Times, 4 Aug. 1933. On the origins and impact of Cry Havoc!, see Beverley Nichols, The Unforgiving Minute (1978), 164-172.

225. Salter, Memoirs, 237.
226. The Times, 10, 18 Aug. 1933, The Manchester Guardian, 10 Aug. 1933.
227. The New York Times, 10 Sept. 1933.
228. The Times, 19 Sept. 1933, The New York Times, 19 Sept. 1933.
229. "Diary of Trip to Great Britain," entry of 21 Sept. 1933, Stimson Diary, vol. 26, 200-204, Stimson to Salter, 22 Sept. 1933, Salter Papers, File 2. Miscellaneous Political Correspondence, 1916-1950.
230. Salter to Violet Markham, 13 Sept. 1933, Markham Papers, 25/73.
231. The Times, 21 July 1933, Salter to Adams, 5 July 1933, Salter Papers, File 2, Miscellaneous Political Correspondence, 1916-1950, Salter, Memoirs, 234.
232. The Sunday Times, 10 Sept. 1933.
233. Salter, Memoirs, 238-241, Adams to Salter, 21 June 1933, Salter to Adams, 5 June 1933, The Registrar to Salter, 14 Oct. 1933, Salter Papers, File 2, Miscellaneous Political Correspondence, 1916-1950, Salter to Tyler, 19 Oct. 1933, Tyler Papers, LNA.
234. Salter to Siepmann, 19 July 1934, BBC WAC, R Cont. 1, Salter Talks, File 1, 1926-1948, The Study of Politics: A Collection of Inaugural Lectures, Preston King, ed., (1977), ix-x, K.C. Wheare, "The Machinery of Government, An Inaugural Lecture, 16 Nov. 1945," Public Administration, 24(1946), 75-76.
235. Cox to Felkin, 11 Jan. 1934, Felkin Papers, AEF/3/1/132, Salter to Felkin, 20 Oct. 1933, Felkin Papers, AEF/3/1/130.
236. Author's interview with Lord Salter, 4 Aug. 1970, Salter, Memoirs, 234. Wint, who continued to serve in the 1930s as Salter private secretary, except for a two-year absence in the Far East from 1934-36, went on to be a noted journalist, author and expert on Far Eastern affairs. See Guy Wlnt, The Third Killer: Meditations on a Stroke (1965), 159-160.
237. League of Nations, Council Committee on Technical Co-operation between the League of Nations and China, Report of the Technical Agent [Rajchman] of the Council on his Mission in China, from the date of his appointment until April 1st, 1934 (Geneva, 1934), Monnet, Memoirs, 110-112, François Duchêne, Jean Monnet (1994), 52-54.
238. Entry of 22 Mar. 1934, Stimson Diary, vol. 17, 22, The National Economic Council, China and the Depression: Impressions of a Three Months Visit (National Government of the Republic of China, May, 1934), 5-149.
239. The Financial Times, 19 Apr. 1934.
240. Salter to Felkin, 30 Apr. 1934, Felkin Papers, AEF/3/1/135.
241. Salter to Lamont, 28 Feb. 1938, Lamont Papers, 129-14, 1937-1947.
242. See Lamont Papers, 129-12, 1931-1934, 129-15, 1934.

243. "International Aspects of Recovery," <u>Academy of Political Science, Proceedings</u>, 16(Apr. 1934), 117-124.
244. See Salter, "Note as to Chinese Report," Lamont Papers, 129-13, 1934-1936.
245. <u>The New York Times</u>, 24 Mar. 1934, <u>The Times</u>, 31 Mar. 1934, Ka Cox to Felkin, 5 Apr. 1934, Felkin Papers, AEF/3/1/135.
246. "England Revisited," <u>The Observer</u>, 27 May 1934.
247. Salter to Lamont, 20 Apr. 1934, Lamont Papers, 129-13, 1934-1936.
248. Salter, <u>Memoirs</u>, 239-240.
249. Salter to Felkin, 30 Apr. 1934, Felkin Papers, AEF/3/1/135.
250. Salter to Rowse, 20 June n.d., A.L. Rowse Papers, Box 162, University of Exeter Library, Exeter, "Arthur Salter," in "Lives of Fellows of All Souls College," Rowse Papers, MS113/1/2/4 (vol. 4).
251. A.L. Rowse, <u>A Cornishman Abroad</u> (1976), 236.
252. Author's interview with Lord Salter, 8 Sept. 1970.
253. Arthur J. Brown to the author, 9 Sept. 1979, author's archive, enclosing lecture notes taken during one of Salter's seminars.
254. See Lincoln Gordon, <u>The Public Corporation in Great Britain</u> (1938), viii.
255. Douglas Jay to the author, 26 July 1979, author's archive.
256. Notes on "All Souls, 1934-1939," Salter Papers, File 23, "Preface," to <u>Advisory Bodies: A Study of their Uses in Relations to Central Government, 1919-1939</u>, R.V. Vernon and N. Mansergh, eds., (1940), 7-9, Mansergh to the author, 12 Jan. 1980, author's archive.
257. "China in 1934," <u>The Canadian Forum</u>, 14(May 1934), 293-294, <u>The Daily Herald</u>, 4 May 1934.
258. "China and the Depression," supplement to <u>The Economist</u>, 118(19 May 1934), <u>China and Silver</u> (New York, 1934), 3-117. See also Salter, "China and the World Depression," <u>Round Table</u>, 24(1934), 531-547.
259. See minutes in NA-UK FO371/18047, F3112/3/10, and Salter to Sir J. Pratt, 23 Aug. 1934, NA-UK, FO371/F5258/3/10.
260. Salter to Mildred Bliss, 26 Apr. n.d., Bliss Papers, HUGFP 76.8, Box 36, Series I: "Salter, Arthur 1927-1941."
261. Both manifestos were reprinted in <u>The Next Five Years: An Essay in Political Agreement</u> (1935), 312-320.
262. <u>The Times</u>, 15 Feb. 1934, Allen to Angell, 16 May 1934, Allen to Arnold-Forster, 17 May 1934, Allen to Gerald Barry, 25 May 1934, Allen to Macmillan, 18 Oct. 1934, Lord Allen of Hurtwood Papers, Box XII, University of South Carolina Library, Columbia, SC, Arthur Marwick, <u>Clifford Allen: The Open Conspirator</u> (1964), 127-129.

263. Allen to Arnold-Forster, 24 July 1934, Allen to Macmillan, 18 Mar. 1935, Allen Papers, Box XII. Macmillan recalled that Salter, who could "write and synthesize," did most of the work, while the others "would jaw, jaw, jaw." Author's interview with Harold Macmillan, 2 July 1981.
264. Salter to Bickers, 10 Oct. 1934, George Bell & Sons Papers, MS1640/6627, entry of 29 Sept. 1934, Stimson Diary, vol. 27, 57-59.
265. The Times, 6 Aug. 1934.
266. A.J. Sylvester to Lloyd George, 6 Aug. 1934, Lloyd George Papers, G/21/3/58, Michael Freeden, Liberalism Divided: A Study in British Political Thought, 1914-1939 (1986), 340-342.
267. The Times, 26 July, 3 Aug. 1934.
268. See letters to the editor, The Times, 9 Jan. 1935. The letter was also sent to MacDonald, whose response was printed in The Times, 15 Feb. 1935.
269. Salter to Stimson, 21 Sept. 1934, Stimson Papers, BBC Internal Memo, 24 Aug. 1934, BBC WAC, R Cont 1, Salter Talks, File 1, 1926-1948.
270. "Back to the League," The Spectator, 153(3 Aug. 1934), 156-157.
271. Salter to Siepmann, 10 Aug. 1934, BBC WAC, R Cont 1, Salter Talks, File 1, 1926-1948, "The Social Work of the League," The Listener, 12(12 Sept. 1934), 434-436.
272. The Times, 25, 27 Sept. 1934.
273. "Recovery: The Present Stage," The Yale Review, 24(Dec. 1934), 217-236.
274. "Planned Socialisation and World Trade," The Listener, 12(12 Dec. 1934), 978-979, reprinted in The Burden of Plenty, Graham Hutton, ed., (1935), 118-131. This was the same message he had delivered in an address to the Industrial Co-Partnership Association on 6 Dec. 1934. See "National and World Recovery," Co-Partnership, 43(Dec. 1934), 10-11.
275. "A Progressive Policy: II, Planned Socialization," The Spectator, 154(11 Jan. 1935), 39-40.
276. Entry of 12 Jan. 1935, Beatrice Webb Diary, vol. 49, 5897-5898.
277. Salter to Allen, 7 Sept., Allen to Salter, 8 Sept. 1934, Allen to Macmillan, 8 Oct. 1934, Allen to Canon F.R. Barry, Allen Papers, Box XII.
278. The New York Times, 13 Jan. 1935.
279. Salter to Avenol, 2, 13 Feb., 4 Mar. 1935, LNA, 1933-40, Box 5739, 50/16759/13801, Salter to Felkin, 13 Feb., 5 Mar. 1935, Felkin Papers, AEF/3/1/140, pp. 1931a, 1931, minute by Strang, 8 Jan. 1935, NA-UK, FO371/19672, W255/164/98, Walters to Strang, 9 Mar. 1935, NA-UK, FO371/19672, W2164/164/98.
280. Soong to Salter, 12 Jan. 1935, S.D. Waley to Sir F. Phillips, 16 Jan. 1935, NA-UK, FO371/19238, F342/6/10.
281. V.M. Grayburn to O.J. Barnes, 19 Jan. 1935, NA-UK, FO317/19238, F487/6/10.
282. See Pratt, "The Silver Situation in China," 25 Mar. 1935, NA-UK, FO371/2006/6/16.

283. Minutes by Eden, 22 Feb., Pratt, 25 Feb., and Vansittart, 27 Feb. 1935, NA-UK, FO371/19312, F1242/553/10. For Lothian's views on the Far East, similar to Salter's, see The Times, 18 Feb. 1935.
284. Minute by R.L. Craigie, 27 Feb. 1935, NA-UK, FO371/19239, F1376/6/10.
285. Waley to Orde, 7, 11, 13 Mar. 1935, NA-UK, FO371/F1590, 1655/1683/6/10, minute by Orde, 9 Apr. 1935, NA-UK, FO371/19240, F1988/6/10.
286. See minutes in NA-UK, FO371/19240, F1834, F2383/1888 /6/10.
287. Leith-Ross, Money Talks, 195-226, minute by A.W.G. Randall, 4 June 1935, NA-UK, FO371/19241, F3562/6/10. On 4 November 1935 the Chinese silver dollar was replaced by banknotes. On the broader issues involved, see Tomoko Shiroyama, China During the Great Depression: Market, State, and the World Economy, 1929-1937 (2008), 177-178.
288. Letter from Salter, 25 Feb. 1935, Murray Papers, vol. 221, Salter to Murray, 23 Mar. 1935, Murray Papers, vol. 223.
289. Salter to Avenol, 4 Mar. 1935, LNA, 1933-1940: Box 5739, 50/16759/13801, Salter to Felkin, 5 Mar. 1935, Felkin Papers, AEF/3/1/140, p. 1931.
290. Minute by Makins, 14 June, minute by Strang, 28 June 1935 NA-UK, FO371/19672, W5208/164/98, Salter to Attolico, 15 July 1935, LNA, 1933-40, Box 5739, 50/17623/13801.
291. Minute by Ralph Stevenson, 19 Aug. 1935, NA-UK, FO371/19673, W7334/164/98, Report of the Committee Appointed to Study the Constitution, Procedure and Practice of Committees of the League of Nations, 5 Aug. 1935, LNA, 1933-40: Box 5739, 50/17623/13801.
292. Salter, Memoirs, 241.
293. See Allen to Macmillan, 18 Mar., 10 Apr., Allen to Arnold-Forster, 12 Apr., Allen to Salter, 4 May 1935, Allen Papers, Box X11.
294. Salter to Keynes, 28 June 1935, Keynes Papers.
295. Cecil to Salter, 3 June, Salter to Cecil, 4 June 1935, Cecil Papers, ADD MSS 51113, vol. 43, ff. 65-67, Salter to Allen, 13 June, Allen to Salter, 18 June 1935, Allen Papers, Box XII.
296. Keynes to Salter, 10 July 1935, Keynes Papers.
297. Salter to Allen, 13 June, 9 July, Allen to Salter, 1, 9 July 1935, Allen Papers, Box XII.
298. See The Times, 12 July 1935.
299. "Conditional Stablilisation," The Economist, 121(6, 13 July 1935), 3-4, 57-58.
300. The Next Five Years: An Essay in Political Agreement (1935), i-xvi, 1-320. Salter's role is also discussed in Freeden, Liberalism Divided, 356-363, and Thomas C. Kennedy, "The Next Five Years Group and the Failure of the Politics of Agreement in Britain," Canadian Journal of History, 9(1974), 45-68.

301. Allen to Arnold-Forster, 27 July 1935, Allen Papers, Box XII, The Times, 27 July 1935, Marwick, Clifford Allen, 130-132, Martin Gilbert, Plough My Own Furrow: The Story of Lord Allen of Hurtwood as Told Through His Writings and Correspondence (1965), 304-307.
302. Fifty Years of Political and Economic Planning, 1931-1981 John Pinder, ed., (1981), 17, 19, 27, 33-34, 217.
303. Dorothy Hamerton to the author, 8 Aug. 1979, author's archive.
304. The Times, 7 Feb. 1937, Asa Briggs, The History of Broadcasting in the United Kingdom, vol. 2, The Golden Age of Wireless (1965), 267-268, 467-472, correspondence in General Advisory Council, BBC WAC, R6/25.
305. Ethel Bullard to Felkin, 8 Nov. 1933, Felkin Papers, AEF3/1/130, Salter to Tyler, 6 Nov. 1934, Tyler Papers.
306. Salter to Lady Astor, 23 July 1935, Lady Astor Papers, MS1416/1/2/163, Special Collections, University of Reading, Reading, Salter to Ka Cox, 11 July 1935, Salter Papers, File 7, Salter – Mrs. W.E. Arnold-Forster (Ka Cox) Correspondence, 1920s-1933.
307. Author's interview with Aubrey Jones, 5 June 1980.
308. Jones to Lord Davies, 15 Aug. 1935, Lord Davies Papers, National Library of Wales, Aberrystwyth.
309. Walters, History of the League, 623, 627-635
310. Salter to Cecil, 23, 24 July 1935, Cecil Papers, ADD MSS 51113, vol. 43, ff.86-87, The Times, 7 Aug. 1935. The editorial that day regarded the suggestion as "ill-advised."
311. "Notes on Some Features of the Abyssinian Position," in Salter to Cecil, 28 Aug. 1935, Cecil Papers, ADD MSS 51113, vol. 43, ff. 88-93.
312. "Real Sanctions or None," The Spectator, 155(6 Sept. 1935), 347-347.
313. The Manchester Guardian, 22 Aug. 1935, Salter to Layton, 22 Aug. 1935, Layton Papers, 107[5(1)].
314. See Salter-de Bordes, 28 Aug.-11 Dec. 1935 in LNA, 1933-40: R4566, 10C/19612/342.
315. The New York Times, 8, 16, 23 Sept. 1935, The Economist, 121 (7 Sept. 1935), 464-465.
316. "Stabilization and Recovery," Foreign Affairs, 14(Oct. 1935), 12-25, The New York Times, 23 Sept. 1935.
317. Salter, Memoirs, 242.
318. Allen to Salter, 17 July 1935, Allen Papers, Box XII.
319. Gilbert, Plow My Own Furrow, 307, Salter to Cecil, 10 Oct. 1938, Cecil Papers, ADD MSS 51113, vol. 43, ff. 98-99, Salter, Memoirs, 244.
320. The "Next Five Years" Group, Minutes of Meeting, 15 Sept. 1935, Salter, et al. to Lloyd George, 16 Sept. 1935, Allen Papers, Box XIII.

321. "Proposals for Future Work Arising Out of the Publication of the Book Entitled "The Next Five Years," n.d., Cecil Papers, ADD MSS 51113, vol. 43, ff. 100-102, The "Next Five Years" Group, Minutes of Meeting, 29 Sept. 1935, Allen Papers, Box XIII.
322. The "Next Five Years" Group, Minutes of Executive Committee Meetings, 3, 16 Oct., 22 Nov., 22 Dec. 1935, Constitution of the "Next Five Years" Group (1935), Allen Papers, Box XIII.
323. Salter to Mackenzie King, 19 Oct. 1935, Mackenzie King Papers, ff. 194641-194642.
324. Letter to the editor, 17 Sept. 1935. There were 19 other signatures, including, Allen, Angell, Layton, Macmillan and Hugh Molson.
325. MacDonald to Salter, 17 Sept. 1935, MacDonald Papers, NA-UK, PRO30/69/682.
326. Salter to Stimson, 22 Oct. 1935, Stimson Papers. For Stimson's letter, see The New York Times, 11 Oct. 1935.
327. National Peace Council, Peace and the Colonial Problem (1935), 5-10, The Manchester Guardian, 30 Oct. 1935, Kenneth Ingram, Fifty Years of the National Peace Council, 1908-1958 (1958), 14-15.
328. The Times, 5 Aug. 1936, The Manchester Guardian, 6 Aug. 1936.
329. Salter to Layton, 1 Nov. 1935, Layton Papers, 10^{83}.
330. Minutes by Roger Makins, 4 Nov., and Lord Stanhope, 5 Nov. 1935, NA-UK, FO371/19212, J7518/5499/1.
331. Letters to the editor, The Times, 27, 28 Nov. 1935, H.C. Debs., vol. 307, 4 Dec. 1935, col. 252. Salter also provided The New York Times with an advance copy. See The New York Times, 27 Nov. 1935.
332. See e.g., Cabinet Minutes 50(35), 2 Dec. 1935, NA-UK, CAB23/82.
333. Salter to Lothian, 11 Dec. 1935, Lothian Papers, GD40/17/305.
334. Salter to Massey, 19 Oct. 1935, Massey Papers, B87-0082, 171, file 17.
335. Salter, Memoirs, 241.
336. "Introduction," to William Martin, Understand the Chinese (1934), v-ix.
337. Salter to Elisina Tyler, 11 Apr. 1935, Tyler Papers, The New York Times, 13 Mar. 1935.
338. The Times, 16, 19 Aug. 1935.
339. The Times, 3 Dec. 1935.
340. Salter to Macadam, 5 Dec. 1935, RIIA Papers, Salter to Lamont, 19 Feb. 1936, Lamont Papers, 129-13, 1934-36, Salter to Felkin, 9 Dec. 1935, Felkin Papers, AEF/3/1/146, Bullard to Felkin, 4 Dec. 1935, Felkin Papers, AEF/3/1/146.
341. Salter to Lady Astor, 3 July 1936, Lady Astor Papers, MS1416/1/2/163.
342. See NA-UK, FO371/19918, C47/16/18, C300/16/18.
343. Entries of 14-15 Feb, 1936, Beatrice Webb Diary, vol. 50, ff. 6122, 6125.
344. The Manchester Guardian, 19 Feb. 1936, The Times, 22 Feb. 1936.

345. Housing and Planning Policy: Interim Report of the National Housing Committee (Feb. 1936), 1.
346. Allen to Salter, 15 Jan., 18 Feb. 1936, Minutes of the Executive Committee, 5, 28 Feb. 1936, Allen Papers, Box XIII.
347. See The Times, 21 Feb. 1936.
348. Salter to de Bordes, 15 Feb. 1936, Allen Papers, Box X, The Times, 29 Feb. 1936.
349. Ayedelotte to Salter, 15 Apr. 1936, Salter to Aydelotte, 3 May 1935, Frank Aydelotte Presidential Papers, RG6./Ser.D07-A, Box 20, Friends Historical Library, Swarthmore, PA.
350. Salter to Lamont, 19 Feb. 1936, Lamont Papers, 129-13, 1934-36.
351. Salter to Lamont, 10 March 1936, Lamont Papers, 129-13, 1934-36. Salter and Arnold-Forster drafted a press release in the name of "The Next Five Years" group condemning the reoccupation but endorsing negotiations with Germany for her return to "the collective peace system of the League." It was not approved. Letter by Allan Young, 10 Mar. 1936, Allen Papers, Box XIII.
352. Salter to Ayedelotte, 10 June, 5 July 1935, Ayedelotte to Salter, 19 June, 15 July 1935, Ayedelotte Presidential Papers, RG6./Ser.D07-A, Box 20.
353. World Trade and Its Future (Philadelphia, 1936), 1-101. The book was reprinted three times but Salter, who was paid $2000 for the lectures, refused any royalty payments.
354. The Economist, 126(6 Feb. 1936), 304, The American Political Science Review, 31(Apr. 1937), 369.
355. New Statesman, 13(27 Mar.1937), 528.
356. Salter to Lamont, 22 Mar. 1936, Lamont Papers, 129-13, 1934-36, entry of 27-28 Mar. 1936, Stimson Diary, vol. 37, 23-28. They also discussed a warning about the Rhineland coup which Von Fritsch had delivered to Brüning.
357. See correspondence in Lamont Papers, 129-16, 1936.
358. Salter to Robert E. Ely, 15 Jan. 1936, Ayedelotte Presidential Papers, RG6./Ser.D07-A, Box 20, The New York Times, 4 Apr. 1936, The Wall Street Journal, 4 Apr. 1936.
359. The English Speaking Peoples and World Peace: Second Jonathan Petersen Lecture (New York, 1936), 3-36.
360. Vote of Thanks by Lamont, 7 Apr. 1936, Lamont Papers, 158-40, The New York Times, 8 Apr. 1936.
361. Fletcher to News Department, 13 Apr., minute by Roger Makins, 30 Apr. 1936, NA-UK, FO371/19829, A3398/180/45.

362. Lamont to Eliot Wadsworth, 24 Mar. 1936, Lamont Papers, 129-16, 1936.
363. The New York Times, 8 Apr. 1936, and see correspondence in Lamont Papers, 129-13, 1934-36.
364. Salter to Lady Astor, 19 Apr. 1936, Lady Astor Papers, MS1416/1/2/163.
365. Salter to Royall Tyler, 11 Apr. 1936, Tyler Papers.
366. "The New Outlook – Prospectus," Allen to Salter, 6 June 1936, Minutes of the Executive Committee, 9 June 1936, Allen Papers, Box XIII, Gilbert, Plough My Own Furrow, 312-321, The Times, 19 June 1936.
367. The Times, 14 May 1936.
368. The Times, 16 June 1936.
369. "Practical Suggestions for Reform," in Royal Institute of International Affairs, The Future of the League of Nations (1936), 64-94.
370. "Reform of the League," The Political Quarterly, 7(Oct. 1936), 465-480.
371. Salter to Stimson, 28 May 1936, Stimson Papers. In his reply, Stimson mentioned that he had decided against burdening Salter with the task of reading the proofs of his forthcoming book. Stimson to Salter, 8 June 1936, Stimson Papers.
372. Conference on the Abyssinian Situation, House of Commons, 17 June 1936, Layton Papers, $1^{9(1-17)}$, The Times, 18 June 1936.
373. Second Conference on the Abyssinian Situation and Its Results, House of Commons, 1 July 1936, Layton Papers, $1^{10(1-8)}$.
374. Note by Allan Young, 1 July, Allen to Salter, 10, 14 July, Allen to Angell, 23 July 1936, Allen Papers, Box XIII, The Times, 1 Aug. 1936.
375. Allen to Angell and Salter, 21 Aug. 1936, Allen Papers, Box XIII, The Times, 19, 25 Aug., 3 Sept. 1936.
376. The Manchester Guardian, 2 July 1936, The Financial Times, 2 July 1936.
377. Minutes of Proceedings and Documents, Submitted to the Tribunal, July 1936 and Decision No. 1, 27 July 1936, NA-UK, RAIL1025/66, The Financial Times, 16, 17, 24 July, 12 Aug. 1936.
378. For Salter's further Decisions, 2-6, see NA-UK, RAIL1025/67-71, 110, 112.
379. The Times, 27 Feb. 1951.
380. "Auto-Obituary – VI: A Civil Servant's Career," The Listener, 16(19 Aug. 1936), 346.
381. Salter, Memoirs, 242. Author's interview with Lord Salter, 21 Sept. 1970 confirmed this desire to abandon academia and return to public life
382. The Manchester Guardian, 12 Aug. 1936.
383. Salter Papers, File 30, Author's London Draft of Salter Biography.
384. Harrod to Salter, 9 Aug. 1936, The Collected Interwar Papers and Correspondence of Roy Harrod, vol. 2, Correspondence, 1936-1939, Daniele Besomo, ed., (2004),

579, The Times, 12 Aug. 1936, R.F. Harrod, The Prof: A Personal Memoir of Lord Cherwell (1959), 164.
385. Salter Papers, File 30, Author's London Draft of Salter Biography. Salter gave the address at a memorial service for Rathbone on 23 January 1946. See copy in Eleanor Rathbone Papers, RPXIV.5.84, Liverpool University Library, Liverpool, and The Times, 24 Jan. 1946.
386. Salter Papers, File 30, Author's London Draft of Salter Biography.
387. Salter to Felkin, 17 Aug. 1936, Felkin Papers, AEF/3.1.152.
388. Salter to Stimson, 13 Sept. 1936, Stimson Papers, The Spectator, 157(18 Sept. 1936), 462. Salter also reviewed the book for Pacific Affairs, 10(1937), 84-86.
389. Salter to Lothian, 25 Sept. 1936, Lothian Papers, GD40/17/332.
390. See his "World Trade Awaits Stable Money," The Rotarian, 49(July, 1936), 9-11, 60-62.
391. The New York Times, 1 Oct. 1936, "British Monetary Policy, A Symposium," The Economist, 125(14 Nov. 1936), 297-298.
392. See Salter to Lady Astor, 24 Oct. 1936, Lady Astor Papers, MS1416/1/2/163, entry of 3 May 1936, Tom Jones, A Diary with Letters, vol. 3, 1931-1950 (1954), 192-194, entry of 28 June 1936, Harold Nicolson, Diaries and Letters, 1930-1939, Nigel Nicolson, ed., (1966), 266.
393. "Economic Nationalism: Can It Continue?" in G.D.H. Cole, Sir Arthur Salter, et al., What is Ahead of Us? (1937), 48-75.
394. Economic Policies and Peace, Merttens Lecture, 1936 (1936), 7-38. He recommended to his audience G. Lowes Dickinson, The International Anarchy, 1904-1914 (1937). When Lowes Dickinson died on 3 Aug. 1932, Salter had written, "There are few men for whom I have so real a respect & admiration as I had for him." Salter to Felkin, 4 Aug. 1932, Felkin Papers, AEF/3/1/122.
395. Salter to Eden, 16 Dec. 1936, minute by Leith-Ross, 1 Jan., Eden to Salter, 15 Jan. 1937, NA-UK, FO371/20462, W18458/542/50.
396. "The Direction of Shipping in Time of War," The Listener, 14(28 Oct. 1936), 794-797. The BBC submitted the draft of the talk to the Admiralty for comment and several corrections were suggested. G.R. Barnes to Salter, 14, 16 Oct. 1936, BBC WAC, R Cont 1, Salter Talks, File 1, 1926-1948.
397. The Times, 20, 23 Nov. 1936.
398. The Times, 7 Sept., 26 Oct. 1936, The Observer, 25 Oct. 1936.
399. Salter to Layton, 26, 27 Oct. 1936, Layton Papers, 10^{79}, $10^{80(1-2)}$.
400. The Oxford Mail, 31 Oct. 1936.
401. Earl of Birkenhead, The Prof. in Two Worlds: The Official Life of Professor F.A. Lindemann, Viscount Cherwell (1961), 150-156, Salter, Memoirs, 245-247, Harrod, The Prof.,164-165.

402. Salter to Macadam, 8, 31 Dec. 1936, RIIA Papers.
403. The World Foundation: A Proposal for Immediate Action on a World Basis (Oxford, 1936), Salvador de Madariaga, Morning Without Noon, Memoirs (1973), 396-397, 412.
404. Salter, Memoirs, 247.
405. Salter to Cecil, 5 Jan., Cecil to Salter, 9 Jan. 1937, Cecil Papers, ADD MSS 51113, vol. 43, ff. 91-92, "Did We Starve Germany?" The Spectator, 157(22 Jan. 1937), 117-118.
406. "Broadening Foundations of Peace," The Rotarian, 50(Feb. 1937), 8-11, 64-65.
407. Salter to Bickers, 10 Jan., Bickers to Salter, 21 Jan. 1937, George Bell Papers, MS1640/6997.
408. The Times, 20 Jan. 1937.
409. The Times, 29 Jan., 1 Feb. 1937, The Manchester Guardian, 29 Jan. 1937, Adrian Fort, Prof: The Life of Frederick Lindemann (2003),152-158.
410. Salter to Layton, 7 Feb. 1937, Layton Papers, $10^{76(1-2)}$.
411. Salter to Layton, 7 Feb. 1937, Layton Papers, $10^{76(1-2)}$.
412. The Manchester Guardian, 5 Feb. 1937, Letter to the Electors of Oxford University: Oxford University By-Election 1937, (Oxford, 1937), "Oxford By-Election, Sir Arthur Salter on His Candidature," The New Outlook,1(Nov. 1936), 3-5, The Times, 12 Feb. 1937. The Manchester Guardian, 12 Feb. 1937 carried a long interview with Salter on the election issues. For a summary of Lindemann's and Buzzard's addresses, see The Times, 15 Feb. 1937, and The Oxford Times, 19 Feb. 1937.
413. Salter, letters to the editor, The Times, 18, 22 Feb. 1937.
414. The Times, 20 Feb. 1937.
415. The Times, 1, 5 Mar. 1937, The New York Times, 3 Mar. 1937.
416. Salter to W.P. Crozier, 2 Mar. 1937, The Guardian Archive, A/57/1-2, Manchester University Library, Manchester.
417. Oxford Mail, 1 Mar. 1937, The Oxford Mail, 5 Mar. 1937.
418. The Oxford Mail, 1 Mar. 1937.
419. Salter to Lloyd George, 3 Mar. 1937, Lloyd George Papers, G/17/8/1, Salter to Felkin, 6 Mar. 1937 Felkin Papers, AEF/3/1/156.
420. Salter to Allen, 28 Feb. 1937, Allen Papers, Box XIII.
421. "The Oxford Election," The Spectator, 158(5 Mar. 1937), 397-398.
422. Salter to Elisina Tyler, 6 Mar. 1937, Tyler Papers.
423. The Manchester Guardian, 4 Mar. 1937.
424. Quoted in A.P. Herbert, Independent Member (1950), 114.
425. Salter to Felkin, 15 Mar. 1937, Felkin Papers, AEF/3/1/156.
426. Salter to Elisina Tyler, 31 Mar. 1937, Tyler Papers.

427. Oxford Mail, 5 Apr. 1937, The Oxford Times, 9 Apr. 1937, Cox to Felkin, 27 Apr. 1937, Felkin Papers, AEF/3/1/158.
428. Cox to Felkin, 27 Apr. 1937, Felkin Papers, AEF/3/1/158.
429. Entry of 4 Apr. 1937, Felkin Diary, AEF/1/1/12. Felkin went on to edit a collection of Helen St George Saunders' poems, using her maiden name, Helen Foley, Poems (1938).
430. The Times, 22 Feb. 1939, de Rosales to Felkin, 21 Feb. 1937, Felkin Papers, AEF/3/1/155, Salter to Felkin, 22 Feb. 1937, AEF/3/1/155.
431. de Rosales to Felkin, 16 Feb, 1937, Ethel Bullard to Felkin, [Feb. 1937], Felkin Papers, AEF/3/1/155.
432. Entry of 21 Mar. 1937, Felkin Diary, AEF1/1/12.
433. The Times, 14 Apr. 1937, The Manchester Guardian, 14 Apr. 1937, A. Barratt Brown to Harold Macmillan, 12 May 1937, Sir Harold Macmillan Papers, MS. Macmillan, dep. C. 375, document 30, Bodleian Library, Oxford.
434. Cox to Felkin, 27 Apr. 1937, Felkin Papers, AEF/3/1/158.
435. Allen to Salter, 30 Nov. 1936, Allen Papers, Box XIII, The Times, 17, 18 Feb. 1937, The "Next Five Years" Group, "A Programme of Priorities" (1937).
436. "The League and the Problem of Change: A Suggestion," The New Outlook, 10 June 1936, 22-25, "Oxford University By-Election: Sir Arthur Salter on His Candidature," The New Outlook, 12 Nov. 1936, 3-5.
437. See League of Nations Union, Minutes of the Economic Committee, 8 Feb. 1928, 22 Oct. 1929, League of Nations Union Papers, III.19.
438. League of Nations Union, Minutes of the Economic Committee, 8, 15, 20, 29 Apr., 6 May 1937, LNU Papers II.15, "Peace and Economic Policy," Peace, 5(July-Aug. 1937), 62-64.
439. Cecil to Salter 6 July, Salter to Cecil, 8 July 1937, Cecil Papers ADD MSS 51113, vol. 43, ff. 94-95.
440. Salter to Elisina Tyler, 6 Mar. 1937, Tyler Papers.
441. The Manchester Guardian, 23 Apr. 1937.
442. H.C. Debs., vol. 322, 22 Apr. 1938, cols.1974-80, letters to the editor, The Times, 26 May, 1 June 1937.
443. The New York Times Magazine, 16 May 1937, The Times, 17 May 1937.
444. H.C. Debs., vol. 324, 25 May 1937, cols. 143-151, The Times, 26 May 1937.
445. Salter to J.E. Meade, 17 May 1937, Meade Papers, 2/6, BLPES, London, The Times, 9 June 1937. The New York Times, 27 June 1937, reported on this with the headline, "Group in England Fears New Slump."
446. Lamont to Salter, 11 June, Salter to Lamont, 22 June 1937, Lamont Papers, 1229-14, 1937-1947.

447. The Times, 18 June 1937.
448. The Times, 19 June 1937.
449. H.C. Debs., vol. 325, 28 June 1937, cols. 1692-96.
450. H.C. Debs., vol. 323, 28 Apr. 1937, col. 318, The Times, 29 Apr., 10 June 1937.
451. See The Times, 17 May 1934, 25 Apr. 1935, The Manchester Guardian, 17 May 1934.
452. The Challenge to Democracy," in Sir Ernest Simon, et al., Constructive Democracy (1938), 199-214. See also Salter, "Foreword," to Moral Foundations of Leadership, M. Alexander Pink, ed., (1952), 5-7.
453. The Times, 24 June, 6, July 1937.
454. The Times, 24 July 1937, Morley College Council Minutes, 21 June, 20 Sept. 1937, 17 Dec. 1951, Morley College Archives, London.
455. Morley Magazine, Sept./Oct. 1937, 9, Eva M. Hubback to Salter, 1, 15 Oct., Salter to Huback, 15 Nov. 1937, Morley College Archives.
456. Morley College Council Minutes, 17 Jan. 1938, Morley College Archives, The Times, 7 Feb. 1938.
457. The Times, 12 Aug. 1937.
458. Salter to Felkin, 14 July 1937, Felkin Papers, AEF/3/1/160, Salter to Rowse, Rowse Papers, EUL MS113/3/1/Corr.S.
459. "Note of Interview between Sir Arthur Salter and Sir Thomas Inskip," 16 July 1937, NA-UK, MAF72/678, H.C.Debs., vol. 326, 27 July 1937, cols. 2930-2940.
460. The Times, 28 July, 6 Aug. 1937.
461. "Food Storage," enclosed in Salter to Inskip, 5 Aug. 1937, NA-UK, MAF72/678.
462. See LNU Minutes in NA-UK, MAF72/678.
463. The Times, 6, 10 Aug. 1937.
464. "Food Storage for Defence," The Economist, 129(2 Oct. 1937), 12-16. Salter covered the same ground in a speech he gave at the Manchester Reform Club. See The Manchester Guardian, 3 Dec. 1937.
465. Entry of 29 Sept. 1937, Stimson Diary, vol. 28, 75, circular letter by Salter, and attached memorandum by Guy Wint, 20 Sept. 1937, Stimson Papers.
466. Salter to N.B. Foot (The New Commonwealth), 9 Oct. 1937, Lord Davies Papers.
467. The Times, 29 Sept. 1937, Salter to Keynes, 29 Sept., Keynes to Salter, 30 Sept. 1937 in The Collected Writings of John Maynard Keynes, vol. 28, Donald Moggridge, ed., (1982), 84-86. Quincy Howe, England Expects Every American to Do His Duty (New York, 1937), 52, 74-75, 182, 187, 198, pilloried Salter, among others, for advocating an Anglo-American alliance against the dictatorships.
468. Minutes of the League of Nations Union, Executive Committee, 9 Sept., 7, 14, 21 Oct., 4 Nov. 1937, LNU Papers, II.16, Salter to Cecil, 15 Dec. 1937, Cecil Papers, ADD MSS 51113, vol. 43, fol. 96.

469. "Europe Looks Towards America," The Political Quarterly, 8(Oct. 1937), 467-481.
470. The Times, 2 Nov. 1937, H.C. Debs., vol. 328, 2 Nov. 1937, cols. 851-860.
471. The Times, 16, 18 Dec. 1937, 6 Jan., 31 Jan. 1938, The Economist, 130(1 Jan. 1938), 1-2.
472. The Next Five Years Group, "Occasional Communications No. 1, Public Works and Slump Control," (Oxford, 1938).
473. Salter to Cecil, 7 Dec. 1937, Cecil Papers, ADD MSS 51113, vol. 43, fol.95.
474. Salter, "Notes on Foreign Policy," 8 Mar. 1938, Liddell Hart Papers, LH5/1, Liddell Hart Centre for Military Archives, King's College, London.
475. For a detailed history of the group, see Appeasement and All Souls: A Portrait with Documents, 1937-1939, Sidney Aster, ed., (Cambridge, 2004).
476. Conference on Foreign Affairs, 18-19 Dec. 1937, Documents 'A' and 'B', Liddell Hart Papers, LH5/1.
477. H.C. Debs., vol. 330, 21 Dec. 1937, cols. 1850-1857.
478. "The Perils of Recovery," The Yale Review, 37(Dec.1937), 217-234.
479. The New York Times, 30, 31 Dec. 1937, 1, 2 Jan. 1938.
480. Salter to Elisina Tyler, 15 Mar. 1938, Tyler Papers.
481. Conference on Foreign Affairs, All Souls, 15-16 Jan. 1938, Liddell Hart Papers, LH5/1, notes, 6 pp., attached to entry of 15-16 Jan. 1938, Nicolson Diary, Balliol College Library, Oxford.
482. Liddell Hart to Salter, 17 Jan. 1938, Salter to Liddell Hart, 18 Jan. 1938, Liddell Hart Papers, LH5/1.
483. Salter to Allen, 11 Jan. 1938, Allen Papers, Box XV.
484. Salter Papers, File 30, Author's London Draft of Salter Biography.
485. The Times, 19, 21 Jan. 1938. The Manchester Guardian, 20 Jan. 1938 was equally supportive.
486. Salter to Felkin, 8 Feb. 1938, Felkin Papers, AEF/3/1/164.
487. H.C. Debs., vol. 331, 9 Feb. 1938, cols. 1108-1128. Salter further clarified his views in a letter to the editor, The Times, 11 Feb. 1938.
488. The Manchester Guardian, 10 Feb. 1938.
489. The Observer, 19 Feb. 1938.
490. The Times, 9 Feb. 1938. The Economist, 130(12 Feb. 1938), 329 endorsed Salter's views.
491. Salter to Liddell Hart, 18 Jan. 1938, Liddell Hart Papers, LH5/1.
492. "Document C," encl. in Wint to Nicolson, 12 Feb. 1938, Liddell Hart Papers, LH5/1.
493. Entry of 26 Feb. 1938, Nicolson Diary, Foreign Affairs Group, Meeting of 26 Feb. 1938, Liddell Hart Papers, LH 5/1.
494. The Times, 7 Mar. 1938.

495. The Times, 8, 10 Mar. 1938.
496. Curtis to Ivison Macadam, 2 Mar. 1938, MSS Curtis 12, fol. 39, Bodleian Library, Oxford, Murray to Cecil, 4 Mar. 1938, MSS Murray 232, entry of 8 March 1938, Nicolson Diary.
497. Salter, "Notes on Foreign Policy," 8 Mar. 1938, and pencilled note by Salter attached and dated 8 Mar.1938, Liddell Hart Papers, LH5/1. See also, Salter to Curtis, 9 March 1938, RIIA Papers.
498. Salter to Sproul, 7 Dec. 1937, 24 Jan., 28 Feb.,1938, Sproul to Salter, 5 Jan. 1938, Office of the President's Record, 1914-1958, 1937, 1938, Folder 185, University of California, Bancroft Library, Berkeley, CA.
499. Salter to Elisina Tyler, 15 Mar. 1938, Tyler Papers.
500. Salter to Mildred Bliss, 16 Mar. 1938, Bliss Papers, HUGFP 76.8, Box 36, Series I, Folder, "Salter, Arthur 1927-1941."
501. The Los Angeles Times, 20, 21, 22 Mar. 1938.
502. "The Adventure of the Twentieth Century," CA Monthly (May 1938), 6-7, 42, 44. The original text is in University of California, Office of the President's Records, 1914-1958, 1938, Folder 194.
503. Oakland Tribune, 22, 23, 24, 25 Mar. 1938, "Program, Annual Charter Day Banquet, 23 Mar. 1939," California Historical Society, MS3863, "Charter Day," The Southern Alumnus, Mar. 1938, 5, 18, The New York Times, 16, 20 Mar. 1938.
504. "Why Democracy?" The Commonwealth: Official Journal of the Commonwealth Club of California, 14(29 Mar. 1938), 75-76.
505. Salter to Sproul, 17 Mar. 1938, University of California, Office of the President's Records, 1914-1958, 1937, 1938, Folder 194, The Los Angeles Times, 17 Mar. 1938.
506. Salter to A.R. Robb, 24 Mar. 1938, University of California, Office of the President's Records, 1914-1958, Lindsay to Morgenthau, 19 Mar. 1938, Henry Morgenthau Papers, 1938, Folder 194, Franklin D. Roosevelt Library, Hyde Park, NY.
507. Entry of 29 March 1938, Stimson Diary, vol. 28, 127-131, Royall Tyler to Mildred Bliss, 15 Feb. 1938, Tyler Papers.
508. Salter to Mildred Bliss, 31 Mar. 1938, Bliss Papers, HUGFP 76.8, Box 36, Series I, Folder, "Salter, Arthur 1927-1941."
509. Salter to Rowse, 30 Mar. 1938, Rowse Papers, Box 162.
510. Entry of 29 March 1938, Stimson Diary, vol. 28, 127.
511. Salter to Rowse, 30 Apr. 1951, Rowse Papers, EUL MS113/3/1/Corr.S.
512. Foreign Affairs Group, Meeting of 16 March 1938, Liddell Hart Papers, LH5/1, entry of 16 Mar. 1938, Nicolson Diary.

513. Hodson to Liddell Hart, 16, 18 Mar. 1938, Liddell Hart to Hodson, 17 Mar. 1938, Liddell Hart Papers, LH5/1.
514. "Foreign Policy Now," n.d. [19 Mar. 1938], Liddell Hart Papers, LH5/1.
515. Foreign Affairs Group, Meeting of 23 Mar. 1938, Liddell Hart Papers, LH5/1.
516. Foreign Affairs Group, Meeting of 31 Mar. 1938, Liddell Hart Papers, LH5/1, entry of 31 Mar. 1938, Nicolson Diary.
517. Foreign Affairs Group, Meeting of 24 April 1938, Liddell Hart Papers, LH5/1, Wint to Allen, 4 May 1938, Allen Papers, Box 15, Correspondence 1937-1938, Aster, Appeasement and All Souls, 214-215.
518. Curtis to Nuffield, 21 Apr., Curtis to Ivison Macadam, 22 Apr., Curtis to Brand, 25 Apr., 1938, MSS Curtis 12, ff. 89-90.
519. Curtis to Allen, 11 May, Curtis to Macadam, 18 May 1938, MSS Curtis 12, ff. 120, 126-128.
520. H.C. Debs., 28 Apr. 1938, vol. 335, cols. 372-383, 443-444.
521. Salter to Layton, 4 May 1938 and attached memorandum, n.d., Layton Papers, $10^{78(1)}$.
522. H.C. Debs., vol. 335, 12 May 1938, cols. 1836-1841, The Times, 16 May 1938.
523. Note by Allen to Members of the Foreign Affairs Group, n.d., Liddell Hart Papers, LH5/1, Allen to Curtis, 10 May 1938, MSS Curtis 12, fol. 113b.
524. Allen, "A Peace Policy for the Immediate Present," 10 May 1938, Liddell Hart Papers, LH5/1. Salter also attempted something similar in Salter to Allen, 4 May 1938, Allen Papers, Box 15.
525. Entry of 15 May 1938, Nicolson Diary.
526. Murray to Edwyn Robert Bevan, 1 June 1938, MSS Murray 233, Allen to Toynbee, 17 May 1938, quoted in Gilbert, Plough My Own Furrow, 400-401.
527. Allen to Spender, 20 May 1938, ADD MSS Spender 46394, vol. IX, ff. 103-106, Spender to Allen, 8 June 1938, with attached "Memorandum," Allen Papers, Box 15, Correspondence, 1937-1938, Christina Hole to All Souls Group, 29 June 1938, Liddell Hart Papers, LH5/1.
528. The Times, 28 May, 2 June 1938.
529. Salter to Felkin, 11 June 1938, AEF/3/1/166, Felkin Papers. Another intimate friend, Virginia Wolfe, recorded a very different and somewhat jaundiced view on hearing of the death of Ka Cox. See The Diary of Virginia Wolfe, vol. 5, 1936-1941, Anne Olivier Bell, ed., (1984), 142-144.
530. Salter to Layton, Sunday [sic, 29 May 1939], Layton Papers, 10^{77}, The Times, 1 June 1938.
531. H.C. Debs., vol. 336, 2 June 1938, cols. 2281-2282, 2301-2311.

532. Keynes to Salter, 6 June, Salter to Keynes, 8, 16 June 1938, Keynes Papers. Also in Collected Writings of J.M. Keynes, vol. 21, Elizabeth Johnson, ed., (1983), 454-456.
533. H.C. Debs. vol. 337, 15 June 1938, cols. 255-263.
534. The Times, 9, 12, 30 July 1938, entry of 6 July 1938, in The Empire at Bay: The Leo Amery Diaries, 1929-1945, vol. 2, John Barnes and David Nicholson, eds., (1988), 506-507.
535. Salter to Rowse, 16 July 1938, Rowse Papers, EUL MS113/3/1/Corr.S.
536. "Visit to Europe," Stimson Diary, vol.18, 154-158.
537. See Aster, Appeasement and All Souls, 215-221.
538. Salter to Rowse, 16 July, 10, 19, Aug. 1938, Rowse Papers, EUL MS113/3/1/Corr.S, A.L. Rowse, All Souls in My Time (1993), 115, author's interview with A.L. Rowse, 31 May 1980.
539. Salter to Keynes, 31 Aug. 1938, Keynes Papers, The Collected Writings of John Maynard Keynes, vol. 21, 456-475, The Economist, 132(20 Aug. 1938), 353-354.
540. Salter to Stimson, 1 Sept. 1938, Stimson Papers, Salter to Royall Tyler, 7 Sept. 1938, Tyler Papers, Salter to Bickers, 13 Jan. 1939, George Bell Papers, MS1640/125/4.
541. Http://masscases.com/cases/sjc/313/313mass72.html, Salter to Davis, 13 Apr. 1932,Norman H. Davis Papers, Library of Congress, Washington, DC.
542. Ethel Bullard to Felkin, 20 Sept. 1936, Felkin Papers, AEF/3/1/158, de Rosales to Felkin 16 Jan., 16 Feb. 1938, Felkin Papers, AEF/3/1/164, Salter to Sir Richard Hopkins, 1 Feb. 1940, NA-UK, MT62/102.
543. Salter to Will Arnold-Forster, 9 Sept. 1938, Will Arnold-Forster Papers, courtesy of Jake Arnold-Forster.
544. Salter to Elisina Tyler, 10 Sept. 1938, Tyler Papers.
545. Salter to Stimson, 10 Sept. 1938, Stimson Papers.
546. Minutes, Executive Committee, LNU, 26 Sept. 1938, LNU Papers, II.16, The Times, 29 Sept. 1938.
547. Salter to Felkin, 1 Oct. 1938, Felkin Papers, AEF/3/1/169.
548. Diary entry, 29 Sept. 1938, Harold Nicolson, Diaries and Letters, 1930-1939, 172.
549. H.C. Debs., vol. 337, 5 Oct. 1938, cols. 350, 554-562, Is It Peace? The Nettle and the Flower (1938), 1. Of the 615 MPs in the Commons, the vote was 366 to 144, with 105 abstentions or absences.
550. The Times, 1 Nov. 1938. The letter was in response to a challenge from the historian J.A.R. Marriott to disclose his voting record in the Commons. The Times, 27 Oct. 1938.

551. Is It Peace? The Nettle and the Flower, 1-16. The title was derived from the words Chamberlain quoted before leaving for Munich on 29 September, from Act II, Scene II, Henry IV, Part I: "Out of this nettle, danger, we pluck the flower, safety."
552. "British Policy Now – II," The Spectator, 161(21 Oct. 1938), 643-644. Other contributors were J.L. Hammond, Sir Arnold Wilson, Lord Lytton, Angell and Spender. See The Spectator, 161(14, 28 Oct., 4, 11, 18 Nov. 1938). Salter expressed similar views when he participated in a discussion of a paper prepared by Toynbee at Chatham House on 27 Oct. 1938. See RIIA, "After Munich: The World Outlook," Chatham House, 1 Nov. 1939.
553. Allen to Salter, 15 Oct., H.G. Wells to Salter, 24 Oct., Geoffrey Faber to Salter, 26 Oct. 1938, Salter Papers, File 13, Is It Peace? The Nettle and the Flower. (1938), (letters to Salter from recipients of pamphlet), Salter to Faber, 27 Oct. 1938, Faber and Faber Papers.
554. Violet Markham to Salter, 21 Oct. 1938, Salter Papers, File 13, Is It Peace? The Nettle and the Flower (1938), (letters to Salter from recipients of pamphlet).
555. Salter to Joyce Newton Thompson, 24 Oct. [1938], Newton Thompson Papers, BC 643 B22.13.
556. Minute by Mallett, 12 Oct. 1938, NA-UK, FO371/21571, C12627/2319/12.
557. Salter to H.G. Wells, 9 Nov. 1938, with encls., "Civilian Defence Against Air Attack," "Purpose of Conferences at All Souls, Beginning October 16th, 1938," and "Air Raid Defence League," Wells Papers, Folder S-021.
558. H.C. Debs., vol. 341, 17 Nov. 1938, cols. 1163-1170.
559. Salter to Chamberlain, 15 Dec. 1938, and memorandum, "The Refugee Problem & Group Settlement," Halifax to MacDonald, 4 Jan. 1939, NA-UK, FO371/22540, W16725/104/98.
560. The Times, 27 Dec. 1938. Salter's interest in the subject continued into the New Year, when he joined a delegation to the Colonial Secretary to lobby for the development of the Negev as a place for Jewish settlement. See The Times, 5 July 1939.
561. Salter to Joyce Newton-Thompson, 20 Dec. [1938], Newton Thompson Papers, BC 643 B22.12, Salter to Allen, 11 Jan. 1939, Allen Papers, "Extracts from Important Correspondence 1938-1939."
562. Salter to Lady Allen, 5 Mar. 1939, courtesy of Lady Allen, The Times, 11 Mar. 1939.
563. S.D. Waley to D.P. Reilly, 4 Jan. 1939, NA-UK, FO371/24073, W256/45/48.
564. See The Times, 4, 7, 11, 17 Jan. 1939.

565. Halifax to MacDonald, 4 Jan. 1939, NA-UK, FO371/22540, W16725/104/98, MacDonald to Halifax, 18 Jan. 1939, NA-UK, FO371/24074, W1066/45/48, Chamberlain to Salter, 1 Feb. 1939, NA-UK, FO371/24087, W2234/1369/48.
566. Salter to Liddell Hart, 21 Nov. 1938, Liddell Hart Papers, LH5/1.
567. The Times, 7 Feb. 1939, The Manchester Guardian, 7 Feb. 1939, New Statesman, 17 (11 Feb. 1939), 198. See also Salter, "The Public and the Air Menace," New Statesman, 17 (18 Feb. 1939), 238–239, and the interviews he gave on the subject in The Manchester Guardian, 9 Feb. 1939, and in The Observer, 12 Feb. 1939.
568. The Times, 8 Feb.1939.
569. Curtis to MacAdam, 20 Jan. 1939, RIIA Papers, Salter to Curtis, 7 Feb. 1939, MSS Curtis 13, ff. 94-96, The Times, 11 Feb., 29 Mar. 1939.
570. See The Times, 31 Mar., 28 Apr., 14 June, 10, 30 July 1939.
571. H.C. Debs., vol. 344, 2 Mar. 1939, cols. 1557-1614.
572. Salter to Halifax, 7 Mar., Halifax to Salter, 22 Mar. 1939, NA-UK, FO371/24153, W4756/2082/41, Cabinet Minutes, 10(39), 8 Mar. 1939, CAB23/97.
573. Salter to Halifax, 16 May 1939, NA-UK, FO371/24156, W7975/2694/41.
574. "Notes by Salter on the Case for Further Government Assistance for Refugees from Czechoslovakia," encl. in Balfour to Halifax, 3 Aug. 1939, NA-UK, FO371/24100, W11762/1873/48.
575. Salter to Chamberlain, 9 Mar. 1939, NA-UK, PREM1/370, Salter to Chatfield, 9 Mar. 1939, NA-UK, CAB21/743.
576. B [?] to O.S. Cleverly, 13 Mar. 1939, and attached memorandum, NA-UK, PREM1/370.
577. Chamberlain to Salter, 14 Mar. 1939, Salter to Chamberlain, 15 Mar. 1939, minute by Cleverly, 14 Mar. 1939, NA-UK, PREM1/370.
578. "Notes of a Meeting, 16 Mar. 1939," NA-UK, CAB21/743, memorandum by Bridges, "Responsibility for Food Reserves and Storage," 17 Mar. 1939, Bridges to Sir Horace Wilson, 22 Mar. 1939, NA-UK, PREM 1/370.
579. See H.C. Debs, vol. 345, 14, 15, 23 Mar., vol. 345, cols. 199, 397-399, 1446-1447, The Times, 24 Mar. 1939.
580. Bridges to Wilson, 3 Apr. 1939, minute by Wilson, 4 Apr. 1939, NA-UK, PREM1/370, The Times, 8 Apr. 1939, H.C. Debs., vol. 345, 6 Apr. 1939, cols. 2980-2981.
581. Salter to Morrison, 10 Apr. 1939, Morrison to Salter, 12 Apr. 1939, NA-UK, MAF72/696.
582. Salter to Elisina Tyler, 16 Mar. 1939, Tyler Papers.
583. H.C.Debs., vol. 345, 5 Apr.1939, cols. 2835-2841.
584. "Inaugural Address," in Nutrition and Public Health, Proceedings of a National Conference on the Wider Aspects of Nutrition, April 27-29, 1939 (1939), 7-16.

585. Salter to Faber, 18 Apr. 1939, Faber and Faber Papers.
586. Security: Can We Retrieve It? (1939), vii-xv, 3-390. There is no doubt Salter's criticism of government ministers, in the words of Kingsley Wood, "ticked us all off." See Dalton Diary, 5 July 1940, Dalton Papers, I 23 4, British Library of Political and Economic Science, London. Salter expanded on his views of the League in "Use the League Now for World Peace," Headway, 1(July 1939), 1-3.
587. The Economist, 125(20 May 1939), 417-418, The Times, 16 May 1939, The Times Literary Supplement, 20 May 1939, New Statesman, 17(27 May 1939), 828.
588. The New York Times, 29 June, 2 July 1939, The Washington Post, 21 May, 11 June 1939.
589. Lamont to Charlton Ogburn, 4 Aug. 1939, Lamont Papers, 159-8, The Saturday Review of Literature, 30(29 July 1939), 3-4, 13-15.
590. Salter to Tyler, 24 June 1939, LNA, Tyler Papers P32. Salter's views on the imminent prospects for war derived partly from conversations with G.F. Hudson. See Salter to Halifax, 24 May 1939, NA-UK, FO371/22971, C6405/15/18.
591. Entry of 2 June 1939, Beatrice Webb Dairy, vol. 53, 6662-3.
592. See The Times, 20, 23 June 1939.
593. Lord Halifax, Speeches on Foreign Policy, H.H.E. Craster, ed., (1940), 287-297.
594. Salter to Stimson, 1 Aug. 1939, Stimson Papers.
595. Salter to Felkin 12 May 1939, Felkin Papers, AEF/3/1/172.
596. Ministry of Supply Bill, NA-UK, CAB24/287, The Times, 24 Apr. 1939.
597. H.C. Debs., 8 June 1939, vol. 348, cols. 653-709.
598. H.C. Debs., 19 June 1939, vol. 348, cols. 1873-1875.
599. Salter to Burgin, 12 June 1939, Memorandum of Interview with Sir Arthur Salter, 22 June 1939, NA-UK, AVIA22/2563.
600. Salter to Robinson, 23 June 1939, Robinson to Salter, 27 June 1939, NA-UK, AVIA22/2563.
601. H.C. Debs., vol. 348, 14 June 1939, cols. 1388-1390.
602. Salter to Felkin, 24 June 1939, Felkin Papers, AEF/3/1/174.
603. "Reserves of Food and Raw Materials," 29 June 1939, NA-UK, PREM1/375.
604. Salter to Amery, 30 June 1939, L.S. Amery Papers, AMEL1/5/42, Churchill Archives Centre, Cambridge.
605. Amery to Chamberlain, 1 July 1939, enclosing memorandum by Salter, "Reserves of Food and Raw Materials," 29 June 1939, minutes by Chamberlain and Sir Horace Wilson, 3 July 1939, Chamberlain to Amery, 4 July 1939, NA-UK, PREM1/375. Amery wrote similarly, attaching the Salter memorandum, to Chatfield. See Amery to Chatfield, 3 July 1939, NA-UK, MAF72/696.

606. The Times, 5 July 1939. The Economist, 136(8 July 1939), 60-61, wrote that Amery and Salter had put their case "trenchantly." See also L.S. Amery, My Political Life, vol. 3, The Unforgiving Years, 1929-1940 (1955), 316.
607. The Times, 7 July 1939.
608. Salter to Robinson, 3 July, Robinson to Burgin, 4 July 1939, NA-UK, AVIA22/2563.
609. Minute, H.L. French to Morrison, 10 July 1939, NA-UK MAF72/696, The Times, 10 July 1939, The Observer, 9 July 1039. On the Air Raid Defence League, see also Salter, Security, 90-192, 245-257.
610. See Wedgewood to Salter, 22 May 1940, NA-UK, MT62/108.
611. Draft Memorandum by Chatfield, [?] July 1939, NA-UK, MAF72/696, Robinson to R.D. Fennelly, 18 July 1939, NA-UK, SUPP14/634, "Reserves of Food and Raw Materials," NA-UK, CAB24/228, Cabinet Minutes, 39(39), 26 July 1939, C.P.165(39), NA-UK, CAB23/100.
612. "Twenty-Seventh Report of Committee on Economic Information," 25 July 1939, C.P.167(39), NA-UK, CAB24/288.
613. "Memorandum of Interview with Mr. Leo Amery and Sir Arthur Salter," 4 Aug. 1939, NA-UK, AVIA22/2563,
614. Chamberlain to Amery, 21 Aug. 1939, NA-UK, PREM1/375.
615. Lloyd George to Salter, 25 May 1939, Lloyd George Papers, G/17/8/2.
616. The Times, 30 June 1939, The New York Times, 6, 23 July 1939.
617. The Dual Policy, Oxford Pamphlets on World Affairs, No. 11, (1939), 1-32.
618. The News Chronicle, 7 Aug. 1939. Richard S. Grayson, Liberals, International Relations and Appeasement: The Liberal Party, 1919-1939 (2001), 73-74, described Salter's speech as "a clear strategy for action," but too late to offer an alternative to Chamberlain's policy.
619. "Peace Terms," New Statesman, 18(5 Aug. 1939), 203-204, "Peace Front Terms," The Spectator, 163(11 Aug.1939), 204-205.
620. The Washington Post, 8 Aug. 1939, The New York Times, 13 Aug. 1939.
621. The Times, 16 Aug. 1939.
622. Ethel Bullard to Felkin, 15 Aug., de Rosales to Felkin, 12 Aug. 1939, Felkin Papers, AEF/3/3/174.
623. Salter to Stimson, 1 Aug. 1939, Stimson Papers.
624. Salter to Joyce Newton Thompson, 28 Aug. 1939, Newton Thompson Papers, BC 643 B22.14.

CHAPTER 6

"I AM GLAD ON THE WHOLE TO BE INSIDE AGAIN," AT WAR ONCE MORE, 1939-1945

The outbreak of war on 3 September 1939 was accompanied in Britain with the formation of a War Cabinet. Winston Churchill received the summons and returned to his position of First Lord of the Admiralty, one he had held in the First World War. Other veterans of the 1914-1918 period, including Salter, Beveridge and Keynes, were left on the sidelines. Given his pre-war lobbying efforts on food storage and air raid defence, and his continued criticism of the Chamberlain government's foreign policy, Salter had no expectation he would be recalled to office. Nonetheless, he was determined to continue to pursue a proactive role, despite his exclusion from any war-related duties. The day following the outbreak of the war, he played an active part in the formation of an All-Party Parliamentary Action Group, designed to lobby ministers and government departments on war-related issues. Beside Salter, 19 members of parliament, including Quinton Hogg, Harold Nicolson, Eleanor Rathbone, Dingle Foot and Robert Boothby, first met on 13 September and regularly thereafter. Among the subjects discussed, and one which bore Salter's imprint, was the advisability of asking either for secret sessions of parliament or the formation of a small group of "high standing" MPs for briefings with the government. Rathbone and Boothby were given the task of approaching Lloyd George's Council of Action for research assistance.[1]

Behind the scenes Salter remained vigorous and continued to pursue his deep interest in the evolving conduct of the war. Already on 7 September he became a member of what was styled the "Old Dogs," a group of First World War officials, hosted by Keynes and including Salter, Beveridge, Layton and H.D. Henderson, although the latter had found a post at the Treasury. The group first met on 20 September, and subsequently weekly for several months, to discuss such issues war aims and blockade policy.[2] Among the first initiatives was a paper in which Salter proposed offering Germany "a reciprocal arrangement for the exemption of certain essential food-stuffs, especially wheat, from the blockade and counter-blockade." He argued this would "bring immense political advantages" both in neutral countries and the USA. In his response to Salter, Keynes agreed on the grounds such a move would help use up Germany's foreign exchange.[3] On 24 September Salter had also sent these proposals to Leith-Ross at the Ministry of Economic Warfare. His response, a month later, was to suggest they were full of difficulties and impracticable.[4] Nonetheless, during the next few months the group continued to produce memoranda on subjects including war aims, post-war credits, the blockade and contraband.[5]

Salter's initial interventions in the House of Commons during this time were few. Perhaps to project an image of loyal support, his brief comments or questions related to details on evacuation, the blackout, petrol rationing and profiteering.[6] Finally, on 18 October he contributed to a Commons' debate on the co-ordination and control of wartime economic policy. This move had been partly occasioned by the government announcement on 9 October that Lord Stamp had been appointed as a part-time adviser on economic co-ordination to a ministerial committee reporting to the Chancellor of the Exchequer, Sir John Simon. Just prior to Salter's rising, another speaker, the Labour MP, Emanuel Shinwell, had asked why the government was not making use of the skills and experience of such economists as Salter, Layton, Beveridge and Keynes. For his part Salter joined the critics to assert that the current, multi-layer system was not working. The issue was not only a question of departmental organization, but also co-ordination and economic strategy. He declared the "profound anxiety" in the country suggested a lack of executive drive, ability and energy and the "sound economic strategy" required in a long war that would turn on economic resources. While avoiding naming any current cabinet ministers, Salter drew comparisons with Lloyd George, Lord Maclay and Lord Rhondda who exhibited the "executive drive and ability" that achieved success in the 1914-1918 war. As for the question of economic co-ordination, he singled out 15 separate government departments with responsibility for economic policy but which no cohesive strategy. This "departmentalism," he argued, was at the core of the problem – the absence of a sound economic strategy.[7] These ideas were further developed in an article Salter wrote for Contemporary Review. Analysing what economic strategy to pursue in wartime, he predicted this would require "an effective, if temporary, form of State Socialism, as the experience of twenty years ago proved." He also contended that what was required, as in the last war, was a "War Cabinet" consisting "only of Ministers without portfolio as its permanent members," with one minister to oversee all economic strategy.[8] The same urgency imbued his analysis of the related question of war aims. In The Spectator and Picture Post, he rejected the term "war aims," preferring to distinguish between "war purposes" and "peace aims." With regard to the former, these must include an end to "Hitlerism," that is, "the recurrent aggression and forcible domination" of one country after another, and the liberation of Czechoslovakia and Poland within renegotiated boundaries. As for "peace aims" to be pursued after hostilities, he included some forum for interstate cooperation, an admission of the failures of the Versailles Treaty, and disarmament, among much else.[9]

In private, Salter was far more outspoken, noting on 23 October, "I am much disturbed at the incompetence of our administration on the economic side." He continued:

> The contrast between Simon, Burgin, Cross, O. Stanley, Gilmour & W.S. Morrison in our six vital Ministries & Lloyd George, W. Churchill, Cecil, Lord Ashfield, Maclay & Rhondda in the corresponding Ministries in the last war is shocking. Not one in the first list has shown any sign of drive & executive ability; everyone in the second had it. I think Chamberlain's choice of personnel is perhaps the most serious danger confronting the British Empire. I suppose a change will come as the pressure of the war increases. For the time I would prefer myself to be outside the machine & free to plan & criticise rather than accept the only kind of job they would be likely to offer me, one in which I should be both impotent & muzzled.[10]

All the more surprising, therefore, was the news on 13 November that Salter had accepted the position of parliamentary secretary to the Ministry of Shipping. A Ministry of Shipping, headed by Sir John Gilmour, had been announced on 13 October, with the appointment meeting considerable press and public criticism. To this was transferred the Mercantile Marine Department of the Board of Trade.[11] "Such an invitation would never have been given," Salter wrote, "nor could I have accepted it, except in war. But I could obviously not now refuse to accept office, in effect as a technician."[12] Among the first people he wrote to on that day was G.D.H. Cole who in 1937 had supported his candidacy at the Oxford by-election. Noting he had accepted "with a heavy heart," Salter explained that any other under-secretaryship he would have refused, "but when I was asked back into my old Dept., I felt that I could not." His acceptance, he explained, was accompanied by two stipulations:

> First that, as an under secretaryship gives no power but only an opportunity for influence, I should want to resign, even apart from principles of policy, if I found that I was not doing enough to make it worth while for me to give up what I can do outside; second, that I must be able to refrain from voting with the Government on matters on which I differ from them in my own judgement – this being required by the pledge I gave when I was elected & any practice since. It is most certainly true that I did not aim at or want office, that I should

have refused office if offered before the war – & also that I should have preferred that the present offer should not have been made now & in present circumstances. But as it is, I feel I've got to try my best at it."[13]

Violet Markham observed that "It was a hard struggle for him to accept office in a Government against whose incompetence, he has struggled for years. But he made the right decision in the nation's interest."[14] Letters of congratulation and encouragement followed the news, echoing the view of The Times that the appointment "will be widely approved," and The Manchester Guardian that it was "almost an insupportable sight" to see Salter "sitting unemployed" in the Commons.[15] Amery wrote that he was delighted, to which Salter replied, "what a minor Minister can do depends on the top. I wish to heaven you were there."[16] Harold Butler commented he would have preferred Salter to be "No. 1 instead of No. 2," and added that he and others agreed "that it is the best appointment the government have made for a long time."[17] Keynes wrote, "A line to say how extraordinarily glad I am that even Neville has seen the light at last – and just in time. I had practically given up hope. Of course you ought to be the Minister, but in the actual circumstances of the case I expect you will be it in all but name."[18] Responding to a letter of congratulations from Lloyd George, Salter noted, "I simply cannot express how much I value it. There is no one on earth from whom appreciation means so much."[19] E.D. Simon wrote to Salter, "Thank God the Government has at last made one really good appointment!" To which Salter replied, "Yes, I am glad on the whole to be inside again, though I can't tell what power I shall have and it has meant giving up a great number of things that I much value."[20] Similarly, he wrote to General Sir Ernest Swinton, "It was a hard decision for I am now, of course, imprisoned and muzzled. Whether the opportunities of inside work are sufficient to compensate for this I can't yet tell, but I shall enjoy having a try."[21] Finally, Royall Tyler wrote of Salter's appointment, "I'm really delighted that he should have made the sacrifice of his prejudices, and stopped just sitting in his tent and sulking." After dining with Salter some days later, he observed that his friend "is well and very happy to be in it up to the neck once more."[22]

On 14 November Salter took his seat for the first time on the Treasury Bench of the House of Commons. His presence was welcomed by numerous members, including Churchill who greeted him with "a warm handshake."[23] Shinwell reminded the House that he had previously urged such an appointment and now suggested that the government would benefit from Salter's "well-equipped and well-informed mind." Another member, Benjamin Smith, noted that Salter had "the ability to do the work" and would "hold the scales evenly in all that he does, whether for shipowners or for the men who go to the sea in ships." Ellen Wilkinson added that Salter would now have the benefit of knowing the answers to questions he had been raising in parliament.[24] During the debate the Minister of Shipping faced a withering array of criticisms on wartime shipping issues. However, he first commented that "I re-echo those expressions of good will towards my hon. Friend who has undertaken to work with me. I welcome his assistance, and I trust that with the valuable experience he gained in the last war we may be able to meet the difficulties which lie ahead of us." For the rest, his limited comments led one member to conclude "that he has not given one specific answer to any one specific question that has been put?"[25]

The same day Salter moved into his sixth floor office at the Ministry of Shipping in Berkeley Square House. In retrospect, he noted that the office of parliamentary secretary "is a curious one. It gives opportunity but not authority. He is dependent for what he can do upon his personal influence with the Minister and the chief permanent official of his Department." In this respect he considered himself fortunate that the director general was Sir Cyril Hurcomb, his friend from school days and colleague at the Ministry of Shipping in the First World War.[26] Among Salter's first steps was to resign as chair of the Railway Staff National Tribunal. Its final report was for the first time not unanimous, but the majority opinion which included Salter had recommended wage increases for various categories of railway workers. Privately, Salter denied this would encourage a movement to increase wartime wages. Indeed, he pointed out that he had for some been considering the problem of a wartime "wage inflation spiral." In a memorandum, Salter conceded that government efforts to keep prices down could not possibly succeed across the board. Instead, government "should distinguish from these the basic necessities and concentrate their efforts specially upon holding those down so as to form a sure foundation for a relatively stable wage policy."[27] Such ideas were occupying the "Gordon Square meetings" hosted by Keynes and which Salter continued to attend.[28] In two articles on the subject, "Paying for the War," which Keynes contributed to The Times on 14 and 15 November, he argued that rationing and anti-profiteering measures were not sufficient. What was required was to balance inevitable price increases with a scheme for "compulsory savings" or deferred earnings and direct taxation. On 21 November Salter gave Keynes a copy of his own memorandum, "Stabilization of Cost of Living and Wages." Given the dangers of wartime inflation, due to the increase in the cost of living and the resulting pressure to increase wages, he argued this would have to be controlled and accompanied by a reduction in real wage rates. Hence, he agreed with Keynes' proposals in The Times, but insisted the scheme, whether adopted or not, required "as an essential complement," namely, the stabilisation of those commodities measured in the cost of living index, such as food (bread, milk, butter, margarine, sugar and tea), rent, fuel and light and clothing." He also envisioned a scheme for cheap standardized clothing rations and a new "Central Wages Authority" to oversee specialized wage negotiations and act as a court of appeal. He was confident that such a policy would be acceptable to the trade union movement.[29] Keynes wrote to Salter that there was "a great deal in the idea" of standardized rations. Keynes' thinking on the subject went through several iterations before he finally published his How to Pay for the War on 27 February 1940. The acknowledgements mentioned that "The proposal for the maintenance of an 'iron ration, at a low price was first made to me by Sir Arthur Salter."[30]

Peacetime preparations for shipping control in war, in Salter's view, had been "very inadequate." The work of the new ministry, as revealed in parliament, was to cover a vast array of subjects, including convoy, allocation of tonnage, control of freight rates and supervision of civil shipbuilding. Barely a week after taking up his position, Salter noted that he was "watching the weak tonnage position with care," urged that reserves of food had to be built up and "measures of economy," such as the use of potato flour in bread, should be implemented as soon as possible. Indeed, the shortage of shipping was the only immediate consequence of the outbreak of war not foreseen.[31] And as a direct consequence, he quickly took under his wing the question of ship requisitioning. He had previously raised the subject in the Commons on 31 October, asking the minister whether remuneration for requisitioned ships was to be at "a normal rate of net profit on peacetime standards and no more?" A firm answer was not forthcoming but became Salter's primary concern for many weeks ahead. He was determined to pursue requisitioning, however unpopular it proved to be to shipowners. When it was finally implemented, he wrote, it "saved us from anything comparable with the scandal of excessive profits and prices of 1915 and 1916."[32]

As early as 24 November Salter chaired a meeting in his room with departmental officials, including Hurcomb and Sir Vernon Thomson, principal shipping advisor. The discussion centred on a memorandum prepared by Salter on "Policy as to Rates of Hire, Controlled Freight Rates and Insurance Values." Thomson took aim at Salter's views, arguing that nothing should be done which would decrease the competitiveness of the British mercantile marine after war's end. He also aimed a personal criticism at Salter, noting that "war conditions should not be used to advance political theories such as nationalization of shipping." In response Salter denied advocating any political theory, or having any ulterior motives, and certainly not the nationalization of shipping. Nonetheless, in a series of memoranda he continued to advocate for the replacement of the prevailing licensing scheme. In operation since the outbreak of the war, licensing or "direction" which the shipowners preferred, required that no owner could send a ship to sea without obtaining a license, which laid out the conditions for any trade the ship could engage in, the goods to be carried and the freight rates. Salter regarded this as "a foolish scheme," and lobbied for immediate comprehensive requisitioning. On 13 December, with the ground well prepared, he wrote to Gilmour, "I think the case for proceeding by rapid stages to a complete requisitioning of all British tonnage, both tramp and liner, overseas and coastal, is overwhelmingly strong." He urged the minister to make an immediate "decision of principle" and issue a general policy statement.[33] In the following days, Salter played a vigorous role in the crucial discussions regarding compensation, monetary or in kind, for lost ships, suitable rates of hire and insurance premiums.[34] He also contributed on 28 December, on the basis of his First World War experience, to the drafting of the official letter announcing the introduction of ship requisitioning. Despite the alarm expressed by the shipowners at the anticipated move, and their claims of not being adequately consulted, the news of the decision to requisition "all ships on the United Kingdom and Colonial Registers" was announced by Gilmour on 4 January 1940. He added that "the same reasons which had been found to have compelling force in favour of this policy in the last War actuated him now."[35] In the BBC series, "The Empire at War," it was Salter who explained on 8 January the decision to overseas audiences.[36]

Some weeks before, Salter had privately shared some of his fears with Violet Markham. As regards the shipping situation, and the inevitable shortage of tonnage, he wrote, "the worst is yet to come," particularly losses from "air attacks at sea or in port." He also feared there was insufficient reduction of domestic demand for imports, particularly food. "We know what we did in 1917 (when we had fewer ships & active warfare all over the world) & we can do it again. But it is time we began." Finally, he wrote: "It's evident that I'm what Aristotle calls the 'slave in the soul', for I revel in the shackles of an office after the impotent freedom of an MP."[37] The general shipping situation was indeed very worrying to Salter, and inevitably gave rise to criticism. In response, he always patiently explained that the "shipping men" and "the Civil Servant element of the Ministry" were working together extremely well. However, there were numerous wartime variables which included trying to match loss of shipping with new building, providing for increased imports of oil, raw materials and troop transfers, and the complications of the convoy system. There was also the ongoing problem of competition between British and French shipowners. It was only by 1917, Salter explained, that the Allies had been able to impose joint control over both imports and shipping. He expected this issue to be resolved this time earlier rather than later.[38]

Salter later recalled that at this time, with requisitioning in place, he had offered advice on a whole range of issues, many outside his departmental duties. For example, he urged Stamp to increase arms purchases in the United States and not worry about exhausting Britain's dollar reserves. Sir John Simon was the target of another of Salter's initiatives which suggested that the British economy could support "a larger expansion of the Army than was at first thought possible."[39] It is certainly the case that he rarely hesitated to offer information or opinions on which he felt he had some particular expertise. Such was the question of Anglo-French co-ordination and co-operation on the complex issues of shipping in relation to "the supply and purchase of munitions, food, coal and other commodities." The driving force for a formal Anglo-French organization throughout the fall was Jean Monnet. On 6 December agreement was reached in London to set up the Anglo-French Co-ordinating Committee. The First World War Allied Maritime Transport Council was the model for such co-operation. Jean Monnet, instrumental in its establishment in the fall of 1917, was appointed as the chairman of the new Anglo-French Co-ordinating Committee. Salter recalled that from its initial meeting on 11 December "I worked with him privately from the first in building up the new system." The problems at first were enormous and included a "lack of adequate statistics, and adequate machinery for determining priorities," the decline of British gross tonnage since 1914 and the urgent need to co-ordinate Anglo-French purchases, particularly arms, from the United States.[40] Progress was slow, however, and on 15 January 1940 Salter was again urging that "British and French supply and shipping programmes must be run as one."[41] Finally, on at least one occasion Salter offered his views on the vital issue of arranging a Balkan bloc prepared to resist aggression, otherwise he foresaw disaster in the Balkans. He made a case for a series of territorial exchanges, initiated by Britain ceding Cypress to Greece, to satisfy the revisionist claims of various Balkan powers, thus encouraging regional opposition to Germany.[42]

Salter's activities suggest he was under-employed in his official position as parliamentary secretary, a fact which was publicly noticed.[43] In the coming weeks, he frequently answered, often perfunctorily, the numerous questions directed towards the Ministry of Shipping. Issues included the replacement of loss tonnage, delays in announcing agreement on rates for requisitioned ships, the provision of "wireless telegraph or telephone apparatus" for coastal ships, "the supply of comforts" for seamen in the Merchant Navy, providing casualty figures, and promising wider provision of lifeboats on newly built shipping.[44] Matters came to a head on 20 March when the opposition launched a vote of censure which regretted "the absence of efficiency and foresight in the administration of the Ministry of Shipping," and called "for speedy expansion" in the shipbuilding programme. References were also made to the fact that shipowning circles were "seething with discontent" and "wildly indignant" with the Ministry. Finally, there was criticism that although ships were being requisitioned, management remained in the hands of the owners, even if under the direction of the Ministry. Gilmour first rose to counter such criticisms, which he found difficult, as he put it, because "I am continually interrupted." It was only after listening to the debate for more than six hours that Salter rose at 10:21 p.m. to wind up for the government. "This evening," Salter noted, "I start on my maiden voyage under this flag. I start with rather a considerable cargo of criticism." As a consequence he explained that he would focus on some core issues, and only on the period since the establishment of the Ministry of Shipping. He firstly digressed on the complexity of management, direction, assembly and convoy arrangements required in wartime conditions, when the system of demand and supply was no longer operative. Shipping in wartime, he cautioned, "is a tremendous task, and it is a novel task." He then turned to rebutting some areas of criticism. He defended the requisitioning system, which allowed the government to examine the entire range of imports, shipping capacity and thus plan ahead. He also defended the system which saw genuine co-operation between shipowners and civil servants, and concluded with an exhortation for the public to reduce its imports. When the question was put, the motion was defeated. The next day, The Times complimented Salter on his "fluent final reply for the Government." The Economist thought his closing speech "was as convincing as the Minister's own speech was undistinguished." For his part, Salter later noted that the Commons was "not unjustly critical" and "the combined Civil Service and business world machinery of control" eventually worked very efficiently.[45]

Following the sudden death of Sir John Gilmour on 30 March, it might have been presumed that Salter would step into that portfolio. Indeed, Gilmour's obituaries noted that his original appointment had "aroused a storm of criticism that increased rather than abated," and some even mentioned Salter as a possible successor.[46] However, that was not the case when Chamberlain announced a cabinet reshuffle on 3 April with Sir Robert Hudson becoming the Minister of Shipping. Sir Samuel Hoare, the new Secretary of State for Air, thought Salter was bypassed because he "had got across the shipowners."[47] This was echoed by The Economist which noted that Salter's "claims have been overlooked, presumably on political grounds." The Spectator regarded Hudson's appointment "over the head of Sir Arthur Salter, whose brilliant record in the control of shipping in the last war qualifies him better than any other man in the country is worse than incomprehensible."[48] Salter left no trace of his own reaction, although he never mentioned Gilmour by name in any of his subsequent memoirs. Another vivid memory that soon followed, however, stayed with Salter for a lifetime. He was at the ministry, working late into the evening, as telegrams of the German invasion of Denmark and its almost immediate surrender on 9 April continued to arrive at the Ministry of Shipping. His mind immediately turned to the hundreds of thousands of tons of Danish shipping at sea, much of it in British service and all of great value. He also anticipated that "Obviously Danish wireless stations would be in German hands, and it was to be expected that orders, purporting to come from the owners, would at once be wirelessed to all these ships to proceed to an area where they would come under German control."[49] Acting at once and on his own initiative, Salter immediately telephoned the BBC which agreed to broadcast for 24 hours, both in Danish and English, the following note he had written:

> Message to Danish ships telling them to proceed to Italy, Spain or other neutral ports was made under German dictation and should be disregarded. In view of forcible occupation of Denmark, the Masters and crews of Danish vessels which proceed to Allied ports will be treated as friends, not enemies. Every protection will be afforded by British Admiralty to such vessels and they will receive welcome and compensation for their services.[50]

In view of the German "invasion and annexation" of Denmark, Salter pointed out, its "ships have legally become enemy tonnage and as such subject to seizure in Prize, like German ships, and as such liable to seizure without compensation." However, he advised that ships that had voluntarily entered British or Allied ports should receive adequate compensation. Half the Danish tonnage that had escaped the Germans was thereby saved for British wartime purposes.

A similar result followed as Germany continued its next attack against Norway. Salter again drafted and had the BBC broadcast his message to Norwegian shipmasters.[51] On 18 April he turned to the wider picture of the war at sea when he spoke to the Merchant Navy Officers' Federation. Germany "had tried every known form of attack against our ships restrained neither by rules of law nor considerations of humanity," he observed. Yet its mercantile marine "had been swept from the oceans of the world" and was sheltered in neutral ports or shut within the Baltic. British losses of 3% of its marine fleet, had almost all been replaced by building, capture and purchase. As for recent events in Denmark and Norway, he informed his audience that the bulk of Danish vessels and almost all the Norwegian were out of German hands. In answer to a question, he noted that "The German Navy, was weak in relation to ours last September; it is now much weaker still." Similar information and reassurances were also made by Hudson in a speech in Southampton later that month. Then on 7 May Salter addressed the annual meeting of the Mercantile Marine Service Association in Liverpool. Here he tried to assuage concerns regarding higher rates paid for neutral tonnage, that remuneration rates being paid were insufficient to provide reserves for post-war replacement of tonnage, and the need for speedier construction of new tonnage.[52]

Such comforting public performances, however, did not match Salter's private concerns. "We are considerably embarrassed, in dealing with criticisms of our shipping policy," he wrote to Geoffrey Crowther, Layton's successor as editor of The Economist, "by the fact that so few people, either in the shipping world or outside, understand the fundamental fact in the problem of the direction of ships in wartime." The issue, Salter continued was "that a war economy is replacing a peace economy over the general field of supply." Thus decisions as to what ships should carry could no longer be left to changing freight rates but had to be made "on the basis of a deliberate judgement of relative importance of different commodities, up to certain quantities, and within the limits of our importing capacity." He added, "We find great difficulty in getting this essential difference, and its inevitable consequences, understood." He enclosed a copy of a memorandum he had written on 2 April, "The Control of Merchant Shipping: Licensing or Requisitioning." This was originally intended, Salter wrote, "primarily for the purpose of getting people in this office to understand the position." He suggested, therefore, that some articles about the problems of shipping policy would be a useful public service. "We doubtless make mistakes," he concluded, but "in our broad policy we are right."[53] Crowther followed up by publishing two articles on the subject of "Shipping in War," seen in draft beforehand by Salter and drawing heavily on the latter's memorandum. The first instalment made the case that "full requisitioning is the only rational policy," the second countered the criticism from the community of shipowners.[54] In a similar vein, Salter provided extensive materials and assistance to the anonymous author who wrote on the subject of "Shipping Control" in Round Table, which tried yet again to explain the necessity for requisitioning.[55]

The collapse of the Neville Chamberlain government, under the impact of the German onslaught against Scandinavia and the invasion of Holland and Belgium on 10 May, led to Winston Churchill's appointment as prime minister. This entailed a coalition government and a cabinet reconstruction which took the next few days. When the exercise was completed and the appointments published by 15 May, Salter had retained his previous position as parliamentary secretary. However, he now had a new minister, Ronald Cross, replacing Hudson.[56] Whatever his personal feelings, he continued to immerse himself in the work, which in the following days was to place him at the centre of events. In conversation with an old colleague, Huntingdon Gilchrist, he noted generally that "I did not disguise my view of the gravity of the situation, but was certainly not defeatist." What worried him most was that "the greatest cause of weakness now is that for so long people have not realized the nature of the effort needed to attain success."[57] Indeed, as the battle for France intensified, with the Germans advancing daily towards the French coast, the decision was taken to evacuate the remnants of the British expeditionary force. From 24 May to 3 June more than 335,000 troops had been evacuated from France.[58] In the midst of this crisis, Salter addressed the Royal National Lifeboat Institution at Central Hall, Westminster. He described the evacuation as "a heroic drama unsurpassed and in its kind unequalled in the history of the world." He concluded with words of caution, namely, that "civilians might soon have to face trials and dangers in which they would need to summon in themselves the same qualities of courage that had been daily shown by those at sea."[59] At the end he also expressed himself as satisfied that "Not a man, French or British, who could get to the coast was left behind. When the operation was ended the ships were coming back half empty because there were no more to bring."[60]

As the fall of France appeared imminent, Salter emerged as a central figure in a historic sequence of events. Jean Monnet, as chairman of the Anglo-French Co-ordinating Committee, had worked tirelessly for closer Anglo-French economic relations. His constant companion and fellow advocate in these efforts was Salter. Later in June Salter noted, "I've been working desperately with Monnet these last few weeks on things that we hoped would contribute to avert this awful disaster. We have failed, but I have never (except once or twice in my life) been so conscious of being with a great man as I have with Monnet in these days."[61] He was referring to the historic and unique offer of Anglo-French union, announced by Churchill on 16 June in the House of Commons. Already in late May Salter and Monnet had begun an even closer collaboration. On 28 May Monnet requested, because of the French situation and his need to spend more time in Paris, that Salter be appointed as vice-chairman of the Anglo-French Coordinating Committee. It was explained that they had worked together in the First World War "and they get on very well together." The appointment was approved on 31 May and this brought Salter and Monnet once again together.[62] On 4 June Salter was responsible for drafting a memoranda and a covering letter, sent to Churchill that same day, over Monnet's signature. Monnet proposed that immediate preparations be undertaken for the future return of the British Expeditionary Force to the continent. This depended, it was argued, on the effective mobilization of all existing "stocks and resources" both in the United Kingdom and France. Salter spelled out all the organizational details required to construct such a "common pool for use wherever the need is most urgent."[63] However, with the Germans advancing quickly in France, this proposal was soon outdated replaced by broader proposals for Anglo-French collaboration. On 13 June Amery wrote in his diary:

> Salter came in very anxious about the possibility of France going out of the war unless we showed ourselves more completely at one with her. He naturally sees a great deal of Monnet, who so ably represents the French economic side over here, and suggested we might lunch together. Lunched with Salter and Monnet at Monnet's flat in South Street. Monnet put to me two main

points. If France is to sustain the terrible ordeal of continued struggle in her own country and then carry on outside if necessary we must make it clear that we stand in with her making good her losses afterwards and in fact that we are for the war and afterwards in effect one country. A clear promise to do this coupled with some dramatic gesture emphasizing our unity would help a lot.

Afterwards Amery set about lobbying in favour of the idea.[64] The following day, 14 June, Monnet and Salter "put the finishing touches to a paper," titled "Anglo-French Unity." This proposed a total union – "real unity of Great Britain and France dramatically expressed and fully realized by the two peoples" – as the only safeguard of ultimate victory over Germany.[65] The same day, Salter, Monnet and Amery consulted with Lloyd George, but without effect. However, after the War Cabinet meeting Amery wrote Churchill a note, enclosing "Salter's memorandum based on our talk." In reply to his follow-up enquiry, Churchill was informed that the "memorandum was drafted by Sir Arthur Salter on the basis of a conversation between Salter, Mr. Amery and M. Monnet (of the Cabinet Office.)"[66] Throughout 15-16 June "the Monnet-Salter-Amery memorandum was further amended and discussed with several French and British officials, including Vansittart, who drafted the final "Declaration of Union." The text proposed that "at this fateful moment in the history of the modern world," there be an "indissoluble union," reciprocal rights of citizenship, "joint organs of defence, foreign, financial and economic policies," a single War Cabinet and joint financing of post-war reconstruction. "And thus we shall conquer." The document, with some amendments, was approved the next day by the War Cabinet and communicated to the French government, but it failed to halt a French capitulation. "The Declaration of Union was no longer a factor in the fate of France."[67] It was, however, as witnessed by one of Churchill's private secretaries "a stupendous idea" and a "revolutionary project – on which, of course, Monnet, Amery, Salter, etc., had been working behind the scenes." Afterwards in his <u>Memoirs of a Public Servant</u>, modestly noted, "I was used to help in drafting the famous offer of joint citizenship."[68] However, privately he later wrote:

The idea was Jean Monnet's.... In the desperate situation of June 1940 he conceived the idea. I had no conviction myself as to its probable success. But it seemed to me just conceivable it would have the same effect on other French Ministers as, in fact, it had on Reynaud; the prospect of the surrender of France seemed to me the end of all things; and in the circumstances I accepted Monnet's view that it gave just a chance, and I think I wrote a good deal of the actual draft.[69]

"Amid these anxieties," Salter recalled, "I reached an oasis of personal happiness." On 11 June he became engaged to Ethel Bullard who shared the news with "Molly" Hamilton. The latter recorded in her diary:

Lunch with Ethel who has become engaged, at last, to A.S. I was hoping for this, she is so amazingly much better. She was in great form and evidently very happy. This is the one piece of good news for many weeks. It has to be a secret as he thinks it would look bad their marrying in such a crisis: but I hope he'll get over that. Anyhow he is living at the Connaught now.[70]

Among the very few people with whom Salter shared this news was A.L. Rowse. On 13 June he wrote, in a letter marked "Personal & Secret":

You know I have long been an intimate friend of an American – Ethel Bullard – who is a widow of a late colleague of mine at Geneva. She was very ill in the winter, but has now made a very remarkable, though not quite complete, recovery. Well, we should in fact probably have contemplated marriage before the war but for her state of health. Now the war has necessitated some urgent decisions, e.g., whether she should return to the U.S.A., on which she (like her sister, who is in London) decided in the negative. I felt myself that it would be better to do nothing at present; because I didn't see why an American citizen should, if the worst happens, be involved in whatever may be my fate. She has however reacted strongly against such a consideration, & if she's going anyhow to become a British subject there are advantages to its being soon, in view of the general position about aliens.

    Well, the net result is that we're going to be married soon; I don't yet know the exact date. I shall simply walk out, go through the ceremony, & come back to the office, with no interruption of work except for the hour or so; & there will be a bare notice in The Times the day after. Till then we're keeping everything absolutely secret, as I am anxious for obvious reasons to avoid any publicity, & I'm not asking anyone to the ceremony which will be of the quietist & quickest kind. I can't expect that you will do anything but disapprove, or even deride, an elderly marriage like this. But an elderly marriage, though a quite different thing from a young one, has its own advantages in companionship, especially if, as in this case, there is both a large measure of common interests with at the same time complementary qualities & experience.

Salter went on to write of Ethel Bullard's qualities as a linguist, her ear for music, her extensive network of international acquaintances and connections, and her "quality of gay courage which is something of an antidote to the sombre outlook which you know is mine." He concluded, "Well, don't let me lose your friendship, which is among the things I value most of recent years."[71]

On 15 June, Ethel Bullard and Salter were married, by special license, in a ceremony at St Sepulchre's Church, Holborn Viaduct. Salter's brother, Reverend George Herbert Salter, the Rector, officiated and the witnesses were Marchesa Louise de Rosales and a friend of the bride, the American journalist, novelist and winner of the first Pulitzer Prize in fiction for 1918, Ernest Poole. The notice in <u>The Times</u> mentioned that the wedding "took place very quietly."[72] Salter himself afterwards wrote:

> Well, I can at least feel a clear conscience about not being diverted from public affairs by personal duties. My wedding day was characteristic. I did not know two hours beforehand whether it would take place that day. I went into the church at 12, was back in the office at 12.43 & went on with my work till after midnight.[73]

Commenting on the event in his memoirs, Salter observed that his wife was "cosmopolitan in education and experience. She had a combination of zest for life, genius for friendship and practical efficiency of which I had not known the equal."[74] The impact of the marriage at All Souls Oxford might be gauged by a comment made by his college scout, "What next? First the fall of France – and now this!" Salter was aware, and hence the lengthy letter, that Rowse would disapprove of the marriage. Indeed, Rowse himself confessed that "Much as I disliked my friends marrying I gave Salter my moral support."[75] In fact, on 17 June Salter thanked Rowse for his "generous letter."[76]

With regard to Salter's work at this point, he confessed to Rowse that "I've done little lately at Shipping." On the other hand, he continued, "Recently I've been doubling my work at the M. of Shipping with work at the Anglo-French Supply organization at Richmond Terrace (with my old friend Monnet), which I find intensely interesting & useful." This work found Salter at one or another of his desks from early morning to very late evenings, even complaining that he had been unable to get to Oxford since March.[77] With the fall of France imminent, an event which Salter described on 21 June as "about the worst moment of the war we have had to date," he was already pondering the lessons for Britain.[78] In a memorandum completed on 24 June, he argued that the collapse of France, after the original German breakthrough "was mainly a matter, not of military defeat, but of disorganization and demoralisation." This was the result of the breakdown of government, administration and communications. In order to avoid a similar situation in Britain, for an invasion which he foresaw "in the immediate future," Salter recommended drastic measures to control the movement of civilians, including martial law, and ensuring the continuous functions of government, partly through dispersal of non-essential personnel. His final suggestion was to provide all civilians with "ear stoppers." Of all his suggestions, he was told that the last measure was something the government had already put in train.[79]

One consequence that immediately impacted on Salter after the fall of France was the resignation on 2 July of Monnet as chairman of the Anglo-French Co-ordinating Committee. As a result that committee and its several Permanent Executive Committees and the Anglo-French Purchasing Board in New York were also dissolved.[80] However, the same day saw Salter plunge into the fray. He pointed out that the British war effort "will depend increasingly and perhaps decisively upon supplies, especially of war material, from the U.S.A." Close cooperation and skill, therefore, were vital in order to co-ordinate British needs with unfolding American defence programs. As a result, he went on to praise the "technical and diplomatic skills" of Arthur Purvis, head of the British Purchasing Commission in New York, and the "unique knowledge" Monnet had of American personalities and industries. Their combined expertise had made it possible for Britain to draw so largely upon American supplies. Salter then suggested replacing the Anglo-French Committee by a British office for American supplies, and urged the retention of Purvis and the recruitment of Monnet.[81] He gave the memorandum to Bridges who then sent it to the prime minister's office, where it was endorsed by Sir Horace Wilson. On 4 July Wilson advised adopting a "central organization" to co-ordinate demands made on the British Purchasing Mission in the United States. He also recommended the appointment of Salter "to exercise a general oversight" over the new organization.[82] As a result the North American Supply Committee was immediately set up "to exercise a general oversight" and to "co-ordinate the demands" made on the British Purchasing Mission in the United States. Salter was appointed its chairman with the mandate to "consider all major questions of policy arising in relation to the co-ordination of supplies from both the United States of America and Canada." He was also given oversight of the newly created Central Office for North American Supplies, directed by T.H. Brand.[83] In the event, Purvis became the director general of the British Purchasing Commission in New York, while Churchill accepted Monnet's offer to serve, and on 16 July appointed him to assist Purvis. The new arrangements, which included Salter now having another office in the Offices of the War Cabinet in Richmond Terrace, were disclosed to parliament on 11 July.[84]

These were new and onerous responsibilities which Salter accepted with relish and vigour, all the more so because the position carried with it considerable executive authority. Almost at once, he called an inter-departmental meeting which he chaired on 8 July. He proposed what he described as a strategy "to obtain the fullest advantages from North American productive capacity," replacing the prevailing practice of ordering supplies only for current requirements. Instead, he proposed drawing up "a large, long term programme" of requirements from the United States, with the British Purchasing Mission given authority to proceed without constant reference back to London. In this initiative, Salter had the support of Purvis and Brand and it was shortly to become official policy.[85] On 10 July he chaired the first meeting of the North America Supply Committee [NAS], where agreement was quickly reached on numerous questions of procedure and terms of reference. As well, a memorandum written by Salter on the functions and organization of the Central Office for North American Supplies was approved. Among the changes was the provision that supplies from Canada, previously handled by the British Supply Board in Ottawa, would in future be handled by the two new organizations.[86]

With the organizational side in place, Salter turned his attention to what he described as "the principles on which our programmes of armaments purchases from America should be drawn up." After consulting with the Supply Departments and Greenwood, and a late evening conversation with Churchill on 14 July,[87] he went to work on a strategic document. When the North American Supply Committee met on 20 July, he hinted that "the vast increase in the Defence Programme of the United States" required urgency in drawing up British priority for purchases, including raw materials.[88] His final memorandum was discussed on 31 July by the North America Supply Committee. He began with the premise, based on comprehensive information from Purvis, that the American administration was embarking on a massive defence programme "to mobilize the industrial capacity of the country for war preparation." In his view, British military requirements would best be filled if these were standardized, even to the extent of accepting American types for the main classes of armaments, and purchases to be made of "complete munitions" rather that requesting raw materials and machine tools. In addition, "if we can now give in broad outline a comprehensive picture of what we should like to obtain from the U.S.A in 1941 and 1942, we can in effect get our own supplies as part of the U.S. programme." Explicitly stating requirements and placing large orders, he added, would also facilitate negotiations about types. Salter went on to review existing armament programmes in light of his strategy. The situation with regard to aircraft production he found satisfactory and exemplary due to Lord Beaverbrook's decision to buy up to 3,000 aircraft a month from the USA as of January 1941. With regard to both army and navy requirements, he emphasized the urgency to "talk big and at once," and suggested that an offensive campaign might be possible by 1942. He concluded, "A bold comprehensive, imaginative statement of the whole of what we think we may wish to obtain [would] be an urgent and imperative necessity."[89]

As Salter had written to Beaverbrook, the best way to deal with the American administration was "to talk big at the moment when their plans for increasing capacity are being made." He had in fact already asked other departments to provide estimates of their needs for deliveries to the end of 1941.[90] Greenwood recommended Salter's memorandum to Churchill, writing on 1 August that there was a "tendency on the part of departments to be too modest in their demands." Getting rid of this modesty, he continued, would be the best way "of getting our fair share of American supplies."[91] However, when the North American Supply Committee met on 5 August to discuss Salter's memorandum, there were strong reservations. Fears were expressed that rising demands would prejudice rapid delivery of orders already placed and interfere with deliveries of other requirements, such as machine tools and raw materials.[92] What were termed "the Salter-Purvis arguments,"[93] however, made some headway, even if the more far-reaching implications encountered considerable opposition.

Salter was indeed making an impact as the summer progressed. When Churchill asked General Hastings Ismay, his chief military assistant, to report on munitions imports, the query was forwarded to Salter who replied to Churchill on 14 August. Salter provided an update on the increases in orders from the United States for all branches of the military. He then observed that the USA "is becoming an arsenal for us which, in a long war, might be of comparable importance with the UK itself, in view of its special advantage of being invulnerable to air attack." Again, he urged that agreement on "types" would require concessions to the Americans. And finally, in order that they be given a comprehensive picture of Britain's requirements "of what we are likely to need for a long war, extending to 1942 or later," he alerted Churchill to his efforts to find someone "with the necessary width of experience and knowledge" to go on such an extended mission to the United States.[94] In fact, for some time Salter had been lobbying for such a mission and on 19 August he took the initiative and asked that Walter Layton, Director of Programmes at the Ministry of Supply, be sent on a mission to the United States.[95] On 28 August the North America Supply Committee approved Salter's initiative as well as instructions he had drafted for Layton. Also approved was a memorandum by Salter which provided a complete picture of British requirements from North America, based on an army of 55 divisions, to the end of 1941. He recommended Layton should be given "full power and authority to negotiate, in consultation with Mr. Purvis, concerning types, quantities and expenditure within certain broad limits."[96]

On 30 August, the War Cabinet met, with Salter attending, to discuss the Layton mission and another memorandum on its scope prepared by Salter. Here he argued that it was imperative that the United Kingdom have a "closely co-ordinated, and indeed, integrated" programme of purchases in the United States, with full agreement on common types. Success, he contended, depended on taking the US administration "into our confidence and put before them a complete picture of our position and our requirements." Salter's draft instructions for Layton included three requirements: to brief the US Administration and its Defence Advisory Committee of Britain's supply of munitions and requirements, to make recommendations on future policy and procedure with regards to supplies, and to speed up decisions regarding ongoing negotiations. However, while the mission and the instructions were approved by the War Cabinet, Salter's request for giving Layton almost plenary powers was circumscribed by the War Office, chary of giving such unlimited powers to a civilian.[97]

Nonetheless, Salter was pleased with the success of his initiative and the considerable functions and powers entrusted to Layton. In fact, it was the issue of North American supply that had been, and continued to be, among his primary concerns. It was true that, while occasionally he attended and contributed to War Cabinet discussions of shipping and supply issues, he rarely addressed the Commons.[98] However, with Layton's eventual arrival in Washington on 20 September the pace of Salter's activity on supply and related issues accelerated. Among his earliest initiatives, after being appointed chairman of the North America Supply Committee, was to instruct that telegraphic communications between himself and Purvis were to have their own "serial numbers and will bear the prefix 'PURSA'." It was his intention that these exchanges would be reserved for "only general matters and questions of policy and large-scale programmes." As it turned out, the massive number of PURSA telegraphic exchanges, more than 500 from 11 July to 30 December 1940 alone, indicate that Salter treated minute and technical questions of supplies and materials as seriously as he dealt with the larger ones of policy.[99]

One immediate question Salter faced concerned French war contracts in the United States which had been closely co-ordinated with British supply requirements. With the fall of France, the British government had committed itself to taking over all these previous Anglo-French contracts. This so called "French Assignment Agreement" of 16 June meant an enormous financial commitment, but also provided proof of British determination to keep on fighting, besides ensuring supplies not being diverted to other countries' use. With over 2,000 separate French contracts to review, Salter and Purvis carried an enormous burden during the summer. From the outset, however, and given the many policy questions involved as well as separate ministries, it was Salter who provided the guidance regarding cancellations of contracts.[100] On the other hand, Purvis led the way in advising swift responses to any American requests for information.[101] Both he and Salter equally lobbied successfully, and as early as

20 July, on the vexed question of types for the adoption of American designed field guns and tanks.[102] On 12 August Purvis advised Salter that if the British co-operated on such questions tanks could be coming to the UK as early as April 1941.[103] In early August, however, Salter cautioned Purvis, with regard to French contracts, that the "Dollar drain is now such that it is imperative to secure every possible saving." In response, Purvis provided assurances that he would seek approval "where large capital outlays are involved."[104] Salter kept pushing on the issue of tanks, writing on 19 August, that Britain must accept "the basic design of the American M.3 tank for production for us in the U.S.A." and that it was "of absolutely vital importance" that a decision be made within the week.[105]

That decision was made and just in time, as other issues, such as British orders for American machine tools, came under scrutiny. Purvis cautioned Salter on 28 August, after attending a meeting with representatives of the American military and relevant manufacturers, that the interested individuals were finding it difficult to deal with several missions concerned with the same subject, such as tanks, which made co-operation difficult. What was advised for the future was joint discussion for joint production. Salter replied, urging Purvis "to hold position" until the arrival of Layton, and promised to do something "to arrange for unified control of our own purchases."[106] It was thus for good reason that Salter noted on 28 August that "the whole future of our supply arrangements may largely depend upon the success of Layton's visit."[107] On 6 September, Salter wrote to Layton, who was just leaving London, to emphasize the importance of expressing every confidence to Purvis in the work he was doing. As well, he advised Layton "that your real job is the programme and that you are in no way going as an inspector for the organization."[108] The same day he reminded Eden of the crucial nature of the Layton mission. The US War Department, Salter noted, was annoyed at the overlapping missions the British were sending to Washington. Therefore, he urged the British government to accept the American built M. 3 tank and get on with it. Salter added that in future all such negotiations be carried on only by Purvis and Layton, and directly with the Defence Advisory Committee. The heart of the Layton mission, he wrote, was "ending the previous trouble of piecemeal and imperfectly co-ordinated negotiations." It was this mandate, he reminded Eden, that was at the heart of his taking on the chairmanship of the North American Supply Committee and now too at the centre of Layton's mission.[109]

In the following days Salter took his first leave since the outbreak of the war. He was exhausted not only because of the immense responsibilities he carried, but also because he had to travel between separate offices for his duties both at the Ministry of Shipping, in Berkeley Square, and the North American Supply Committee, in

Richmond Terrace. Complaining that he "performs two functions and sits in two places two miles apart," a solution was found that had him put his own car at the disposal of the state in return for a chauffeur and the cost of petrol.[110] All too soon back at work, several matters of pressing concern emerged. These included an accelerated programme of merchant shipbuilding, for which Salter oversaw the despatch of a mission.[111] As well, there was the need to procure American machine tools urgently required for the production of munitions in Britain.[112] As a result of Salter's urgings and Purvis' persuasion, a larger release of American machine tools for export to Britain was finally approved. This was followed, after Churchill explained that the situation was urgent, with the secret release through Purvis of 250,000 rifles. "Congratulations on the result of your efforts," Salter cabled to Purvis on 24 September.[113]

Among Salter's many tasks at this time was to monitor and assist the Layton mission which had begun its work on 22 September. However, the temporary nature of that mission, as well as several others still ongoing, had come to Churchill's attention, and he urged Salter to outline "proposals for a considerable tidying."[114] On 1 October Salter responded and offered some guidelines both as to the authorization of the despatch of special missions and the authority under which they should work. He explained that the American government controlled all stocks and productive capacity through a single body, the US Defence Advisory Committee, acting under the authority of Roosevelt and Henry Morgenthau Jr, the Secretary of the Treasury. Given the fact that Purvis had established himself firmly as head of the British Purchasing Mission and that he enjoyed good personal relations with Morgenthau, Salter argued that "the channel for negotiations" must be through Purvis. He also suggested yet further centralization though the use of his own North American Supply Committee. For the meantime, he pointed out that the Minister of Aircraft Production, Lord Beaverbrook, preferred to bypass Purvis.[115] Furthermore, as a result of exhortations from Layton and Purvis, and strong lobbying support provided by Salter, the latter proposed in a cabinet paper that a "consistent policy as to the disclosure of secret information (both operational and tactical)" was essential to the success of supply arrangements in the United States. If precautions were taken to avoid leakage, he advised, then "we must take the risk" and give the British ambassador in Washington, Lord Lothian, permission to offer Roosevelt and Morgenthau "full disclosure."[116] The matter was eventually discussed at length by the War Cabinet on 21 November with Salter in attendance. He again made the case for full disclosure to avoid delays in supply negotiations, and with appropriate safeguards for different classes of information. Churchill preferred to "proceed cautiously," agreeing with Salter regarding supply programmes but with reservations regarding details of "technical devices," and "operational information." This was agreed to by the War Cabinet and a consequence was the formation of the Committee on Disclosure of Secrets to USA, answerable to Churchill. Salter later confessed that "the Cabinet did not go quite so far in some respects as I should have liked."[117]

On 9 October Layton had sent Salter an interim report of his activities in New York and Washington, beginning with his meeting with Roosevelt on 27 September. One consequence of that meeting was an attempt to reach a "general settlement of Ordnance orders" previously placed in the United States.[118] Another was his request to provide Roosevelt, Hull, Morgenthau and Stimson with a comprehensive list of British war requirements. Although Layton regarded the American administration as "not yet organized on a war basis," he expected "we shall get our programme launched."[119] To expedite this process, Salter pressed the view that Purvis should visit London for consultations, a move that was supported by the Cabinet Office.[120] Another opportunity to review the situation was at the meeting of the North American Supply Committee on 24 October, which was attended by Lothian, then on a visit to London. Lothian observed that American opinion had come round to the belief that the defence of the United States lay overseas, in particular by assisting British rearmament. The next stage, however, was the difficult one of finance, or as he phrased it, "sooner or later America would have to find money for us." Lothian finally praised both Purvis for "his genius for establishing personal relations," and Layton for having set out "for the first time a full picture of our supply position."[121] Indeed, the latter's efforts led two days later to the news that the US administration had agreed to provide Britain with all the American produced equipment needed for a ten-division force by the end of 1941. Layton immediately informed Salter that Churchill had accepted the ten-division plan.[122]

Although this was welcome news, Salter also pushed ahead to finalize once and for all a consolidated statement of British supplies as soon as possible after the American election of 5 November. With similar urgency, he was concerned to find the means to accommodate the future increase in aircraft production in the US and the means to bring them to Britain, either in the air, aboard newly designed ships, or to utilize the Greenland flying route for medium bombers. By the end of the following month, he was able to report that an order of 60 new ships in the United States would enable the transport of airplanes across the Atlantic.[123] Finally, as Lothian prepared to return to Washington, Salter sent him an aide-mémoire on 9 November. This reaffirmed some of the results of the visit, namely, "coming clean" with the US administration on sharing secret information, and the centralisation of British supply requirements and missions through Purvis.[124] The fact of the matter, however, was that the whole Anglo-American supply relationship was to undergo major changes. On 15 November

Layton recommended to Salter that a single Council be established and that Monnet's unofficial status be rectified by making him its deputy chairman. Only such a reorganization, which involved the incorporation of the British Purchasing Committee, could achieve the administrative efficiency necessary to co-ordinate the increasing complexity of British supplies. Besides, it was also what the American administration insisted upon.[125] That same day, Monnet too wrote Salter to reinforce Layton's recommendations. Monnet confirmed that much had been achieved with regard to the air programme, army supplies and credit facilities. However, he contended that the process had been too slow and on too small a scale. For the rest, he argued that the British leadership must be persuaded that the outcome of the war depended on treating the United States "as a partner willing to provide England with all that she needs to finish the job. It is for England to speak, to state clearly what she wants from this country, and state it in big terms."[126] With Purvis' arrival in London on 25 November, and with Churchill taking an interest in the issue of coordinating the various supply missions in the United States, Salter went into action. On 26 November he chaired a meeting of the North American Supply Committee to discuss the co-ordination of supply missions in the United States by the establishment of a North American Supply Council. Later that day he informed Churchill that no agreement had been reached, other than to have the relevant ministers consult further. "The root problem," a clearly frustrated Salter wrote, was that Beaverbrook, the Minister of Aircraft Production, insisted that the Air Mission in Washington retain its autonomy.[127]

It was Beaverbrook, in fact, who now made the running, proposing another variation of a British-North American Supply Council, chaired by Purvis. Under this proposal, the three Supply Ministries (Army, Navy and Air Force) retained their separate organizations, but with representatives on the new council. However, a new Supply Committee, attended *inter alia* by Beaverbrook and the First Lord of the Admiralty, A.V. Alexander, and chaired by the Minister of Supply, Sir Andrew Duncan, was established in London at the Ministry of Supply. The proposal was discussed by the War Cabinet on 4 December, gained final approval on 12 December and emerged under the name of the British Supply Council in North America.[128] These new arrangements were to take effect formally with Purvis' return to the United States. However, the following day, Salter advised Duncan that in light of the War Cabinet decision, "it is clearly impossible for me to continue to exercise any authority within this sphere." The final paper circulated to the North American Supply Committee on 24 December advised of these changes and noted that it had been superseded by the Supply Committee, to be chaired by Sir Andrew Duncan.[129]

Salter once again found himself under-employed, but only temporarily. In the coming weeks, he returned to a more active role in the House of Commons, answering questions for the Minister of Shipping.[130] Additionally, he turned his attention to the general shipping situation which had been deteriorating. In a memorandum on 2 January, he warned that British shipping losses were running at an annual rate of 5 million gross tons and building at the rate of 1¼ million. While "we can squeeze through 1941, in 1942 and afterwards only one thing can pull us through, namely, American building." In a follow-up memorandum of 10 January, prepared for Halifax, Salter analysed the causes for "the shipping crisis," including the vast diversion of tonnage needed for military purposes, and the growing decline of imports, both raw materials and food, into Britain as a consequence. He concluded that "North American building is the only possible compensating influence. There is no long-term solution except in the mass building of ships."[131]

Salter's renewed interest in the shipping issue, and his brief for Halifax, arose in part from an unrelated matter. After the death of Lothian on 12 December 1940, Churchill had on 21 December appointed Halifax as the new ambassador in Washington. Salter was among those whom the latter consulted before leaving to the United States. Following their meeting on New Year's Day, Salter wrote two long letters to Halifax on 6 January. The first answered Halifax's request for the names of those with whom he might "establish personal relations of some intimacy" and whom Salter described as the "inner ring of Americans." Noting that they were all personal friends and could be relied upon for advice, he mentioned Norman Davis, Thomas Lamont, Frank L. Polk and Felix Frankfurter. Salter added, "My wife who knows most of these as well as myself, and some better, agrees with this note." He also noted that the group in general was "rather elderly" and outside of the administration. As for members of the government, he pointed out that Stimson was "absolutely reliable" and "profoundly in sympathy with us," while Morgenthau, though a "prima donna," was "indispensable" in relation to the supply programme. The second letter dealt with Halifax's enquiry as to whether he should bring to Washington a special economic advisor and would Salter go if invited. In response to the former query, Salter expressed his belief that "the issue of war is likely to turn upon what America does – how much, how soon, and in what form." In the expectation that the war was prolonged, he expected that "North America must be our main arsenal if we are to have any hope of outmatching the enemy's resources." The existing supply organization, headed by Purvis, was in Salter's view adequate for the meantime. However, there remained the necessity of lobbying the American administration on questions of long-term economic policy, and emphasizing the views and requirements of the UK. It was in this area, of garnering the support of finance, industry, public opinion, especially in the isolationist west and midwest of the United States, that Salter endorsed the appointment of an economic advisor. "He would need to be an economist, with some reputation as such in the U.S.A., to know how Americans work and to have an aptitude for speaking, not so much to general public audiences as to groups of people with specialised knowledge of economic and industrial questions." Concerning his own suitability for the position, Salter pointed out that with the Ministry of Shipping now well organized, and with requisitioning policy determined, there was little scope left for creative work. He observed that he could be far more effective in Washington than in London in securing the vast building programme for merchant ships that was urgently required. Salter concluded, "If the Government wish me to go, I am entirely ready to do so and to throw myself whole-heartedly into my new work."[132]

Salter himself provided little evidence about his life during the Battle of Britain. He admitted that "in these days it is only too easy to let letters slip." However, writing to Joyce Newton Thompson from the Connaught Hotel on 3 January 1941, in response to her congratulations on his wedding, he noted:

> Well, I've now had six months of marriage & so far as public affairs allow any of us happiness, am very happy. It has certainly been a great personal help in these hard days. Now as 1941 opens we are at least in an immensely better position than we could reasonably have hoped six months ago that should be. But it will, at best, be a hard & dangerous year. It's an anxious life under air bombardment. We had two months in London in which the raids came every night but one, usually lasted all night, with many day raids as well: and some were undoubtedly very unpleasant. On two successive nights I found myself wandering the streets for shelter because about 2 am unexploded bombs or adjacent fires [rattled?] our hotel. But in the morning the hotel was still standing – though one bomb blew out 274 windows; but one gets used to it, & recently raids here have been much less frequent, though greatly intensified in certain other areas. How I should like a period for resting, writing, travelling & renewing friendships.[133]

While a response to his offer to go to Washington was not immediately forthcoming, Salter kept himself busy. In an interview with American newspaper correspondents on 19 January, he observed that "America is becoming an arsenal which, with our own resources, will enable us to outmatch the enemy." He added, "We are building, buying and chartering all we can," but there was still a shortfall of between 5-6 million tons a year. In addition, while Britain still retained 97% of the total sea-going tonnage under the British flag in 1939, losses were mounting with the Germans using French ports as bases for attack. He looked to the United States, therefore, as the world's largest producer of steel and with its vast pool of engineering skills, to match or even surpass its 1918 record of building and launching over three million gross tons.[134] Speaking later at Newcastle-on-Tyne, when opening two Danish clubs for seamen and officers, Salter exhorted all involved in the shipping industry to redouble their efforts in order to achieve an early Allied victory.[135] In a letter to Stimson on 20 January, Salter confessed that "we have many anxieties" at the Ministry of Shipping. He also shared something of his private life:

> My wife and I have been here continuously, staying in a hotel [the Connaught Hotel] within a few yards of the office. We have had some trying experiences from time to time in the 'blitz' but on the whole I think our American friends would be surprised at how nearly life proceeds normally, at least during the hours of daylight. The tales of how the ordinary man and woman are taking it are incredible.[136]

Still unsure of his future, on 27 January Salter accepted two additional positions; as vice-chairman of the Committee for the Co-ordination of Allied Supplies and chairman of its Sub-committee on Civil Supplies.[137] However, on 6 March Halifax telegraphed that, after consulting with various British officials in Washington, he had concluded that merchant shipping was the most pressing question. This required the presence of someone with the expert knowledge and sufficient standing to deal with the American administration. The duties would be to explain the general import situation, emphasize the need for making better use of foreign ships laid up in American ports, and to supervise the purely technical questions arising from the building programme. Halifax agreed that the individual "selected for this task should be someone already possessing good American contacts," and Salter "would fill the post admirably."[138] Churchill, in fact, acted at once to this proposal. Lady Salter recorded in her diary how the news was received and what followed:

> (Friday, March 7th) We were going to Coombe this P.M. but Arthur got invitation from Prime Minister to lunch with him tomorrow. There is talk of his being asked to go to U.S. Very exciting. I think Gil Winant may have a hand in it. Anyhow Halifax has cabled. Louise and I lunched with Arthur at Berkeley – very noisy. We dined alone and talked over possible future.
>
> (Saturday, March 8th) Arthur went to lunch with Mr. Churchill at Chequers today. He phoned me from Oxford. The P.M. talked to him about going to U.S. for some time and apparently would not mind my going. He was very nice to Arthur and I gathered Arthur was really cheered up by his visit and long talk with him. Arthur went on to All Souls for annual party.

(Sunday, March 9th) Arthur returned about 6.45. Had a very nice talk with Churchill yesterday. I think it is practically assured he will be asked to go to U.S. P.M. also suggested he was to get an honor – P.C. or something. Gil Winant told me on phone visit had gone very well, I am thrilled – hate also leaving England and rather terrified at all it involves. Very happy for Arthur – afraid I won't help him enough. Hope nothing happens to me.

(Monday, March 10th) Arthur heard he was to be appointed to Washington. He seems very pleased. Louise came back to town today so I could tell her. It's hard telling everyone and I am proud for Arthur but sad at going.

Lady Salter was in fact a long-time friend of Winant and had welcomed him on the day of his arrival in London as US ambassador. On 1 March she had written to him, "It is so wonderful to know you are here and to represent the U.S.A. I cannot tell you how thrilled we are."[139] On 9 March Churchill had approved Salter's appointment, writing, "Am much in favour of this. He is very keen, and undoubtedly has most valuable contacts in the United States. Winant spoke to me most earnestly about importance of sending him." Churchill observed that "we cannot get through 1942 without several million tons of United States new construction of merchant ships. Salter will be excellent in keeping all this alive." He noted, as well, that Salter's mission to the United States would be "to expedite and animate the whole business of merchant shipbuilding."[140] Halifax responded, "I entirely agree about Salter, and the sooner he comes the better."[141] On 10 March Churchill notified several key ministers of his decision to send Salter to Washington, writing, "Nothing is more important than the shipping problem, and the key to its solution lies largely in America."[142]

After Salter agreed to undertake the mission, Churchill on 10 March drafted a letter to him setting out the mission's terms of reference. Addressed to "My dear Salter," it read:

As you know we hope that, now the Lend-Lease Bill is through, the United States Administration will be prepared to give us assistance on a scale far surpassing anything which they have hitherto done. Of all our needs none is more pressing than that of obtaining from the United States the assistance which is required in the matter of merchant shipping. In order to convince the United States Administration of our needs it will be necessary for the general shipping problem in its widest aspects to be explained to and constantly kept before them. This can best be done by someone who, like yourself, can speak with authority and first-hand knowledge of the problems confronting us. I therefore invite you to undertake this supremely important task and I ask you to proceed to the United States as soon as this can be arranged.

It will be your task, under the general direction of His Majesty's Ambassador in Washington, to explain to the United States Administration our general import situation, to inform them of the measures we have taken and are taking to ensure that the fullest use is made of all the tonnage in the allied service, and to emphasize the various ways in which the United States Government can and should both add to the tonnage at our disposal, and help us to use that tonnage to the maximum advantage.

At the same time it will be your duty to supervise the handling of the technical questions arising from the programme of merchant shipbuilding on our behalf in the United States of America, which must be pressed forward with the utmost vigour. You will therefore be the head of our Mission which deals with these matters, and as such you will be a member of the British Supply Council in North America.

The battle of the Atlantic has begun. The issue may well depend on the speed with which our resources to combat the menace to our communication with the Western Hemisphere are supplemented by those of the United States of America. I look to you to bring this fact home to the United States Administration and to convince them that they must act accordingly.[143]

When shown the draft, Salter asked, given his lack of expertise "to deal with technical question," that the first sentence of third paragraph be changed to: "At the same time you will also be concerned with questions of policy arising from the programme of merchant shipbuilding." The amended terms of reference and Salter's release were approved by the Minister of Shipping, Ronald Cross, on 11 March in a letter to Churchill.[144] On 12 March Salter received the official letter from Churchill, one that remained the terms of reference for his upcoming mission.[145] This was accompanied by another, in which the prime minister proposed that he retain his ministerial office. As well, Churchill wrote that he was submitting Salter's name as a Privy Councillor, "in view of your past distinguished services as well as of the importance of the part you will now play."[146] The following day, Churchill approved the terms of the public announcement of the Shipping Mission, and an accompanying Food Mission led by the banker and economist Robert Brand, while at the same time Halifax gave Morgenthau advance notice of the Salter Shipping Mission. The press release on 14 March stated, "In no sphere of our war effort is the help which the United States can give us under the Lend-Lease Legislation more urgent than that of shipping." The same day Salter was received by King George VI and was sworn a member of the Privy Council.[147]

The announcement of the Shipping Mission was widely approved in the press on both sides of the Atlantic. Salter was praised as "one of our foremost shipping experts," "well qualified for the mission," and familiar with, and known in the United States. Noting the passage of the Lend-Lease Act on 11 March, the arrival in London on 1 March of the new American ambassador Gil Winant, and Averell Harriman, as Roosevelt's personal representative to co-ordinate the delivery of American supplies, besides the appointment of Salter and Brand, The Observer wrote that "A great week in the history of the world has been launched."[148] These events were noted by Lady Salter, who wrote in her diary, "I am really very pleased. There was a secret debate on shipping in Parliament today (Thursday, 13 March and 14 March). Arthur's appointment was announced secretly and people seemed very nice. I went to the Pope- Hennessys and told them my news. They seemed very sad. Heavy raids over England last night and tiresome alerts on and off."[149] Three days later Salter wrote in long-hand to Churchill: "May I say in two lines how grateful I am to you for giving me this opportunity of work in the U.S.A. & for the honour of a P.C. I will do my best."[150]

The following week proved to be a hectic one for both Lady Salter and Salter. Salter had to be fully briefed and also helped to prepare a statement of the shipping and import position so as to inform the United States administration "of the measures we are taking to meet the critical situation and to enumerate the various ways in which the Americans could assist."[151] In addition, he immediately recruited Cyril Thompson as a shipbuilding expert, an area where he could claim no special expertise, among several others.[152] He also arranged that while abroad he would be kept thoroughly informed, through Cross' Private Office, of both official and "less tangible" developments, or as Hurcomb put it, "'chatty letters' as well as the important departmental details."[153] On his last full day in London, 20 March, he lunched with Churchill at 10 Downing Street, in the company of W.P. Crozier, correspondent for The Manchester Guardian. In the course of the conversation recorded by Crozier, Churchill digressed over numerous subjects. The first topic of discussion turned on the allegations made that very morning in the Commons by Geoffrey Mander regarding a new breach of privilege committed by Robert Boothby. Salter at once sprung to Boothby's defence, saying that "he has been punished enough" and Churchill generally agreed. The latter and Salter disagreed about what would bring the United States into the war – Salter thinking it would be a German attack against an American warship, Churchill arguing that the American "crusading spirit" would be the catalyst. It was during this meeting that Churchill showed Salter some lines of poetry by Arthur Clough.

And not by Eastern windows only,
When daylight comes, comes in the light.
In front the sun climbs slow, how slowly!
But westward, look, the land is bright.

Finally, Churchill instructed Salter to confer with Beaverbrook and reassure him that the Shipping Mission would never encroach on the latter's area of responsibility.[154] Salter acted on Churchill's wish and reported back that he had had a "friendly and cordial" talk with Beaverbrook.[155]

"I am eager for this new work," Salter wrote Rowse on 18 March, "but there's much I hate leaving – & among the chief All Souls – & you, my dear. Your friendship has meant more than I can express these last five years."[156] Lady Salter's diary provided further evidence of their hectic last days in London.

(Friday, March 14) Admiral Moore lunched with us – a charming man in charge of convoys. Had a thrilling suggestion for our getting to U.S.A. I with Tommy and Drummond left for Coombe this p.m. Very pleasant there. Endless planes overhead.

(Saturday, March 15) Went to All Souls to lunch with Arthur. Professor Goodhart there.

(Sunday March 16) Returned to Connaught from Coombe this evening. Gorgeous weather there and spring flowers coming out. Archie and Jack Balfour lunched with us and Arthur discussed America with latter. Tom Brand and his wife came to dinner, also Louise. I am terribly upset about our leaving. Arthur appears to have passage on "Clipper" leaving here on Wednesday 19th but without me. I feel he ought not to go without me but that I should not press for me. Am very miserable.

(Monday, March 17) Our passage finally decided after many vicissitudes. Averell Harriman and Admiral Phillips came to dinner. The latter is a dear. Former very competent and pleasant.

(Tuesday, March 18) Phone from Brand tonight asking whether we wanted to go by "Clipper" tomorrow. Impossible now to change at such late date. Violet Markham for breakfast. Walter and Dorothy Layton for dinner. I was dead to the world.

(Wednesday, March 19) Terrible rush packing. Arthur lunched with Herschell Johnson. Margaret Brooke came to breakfast. Molly Hamilton lunched with me – very forlorn. Louise very pathetic. It is very hard. I hate leaving. Arthur thrilled. Compliments on all sides. The guns are booming away. It quite overcomes me when I think we are absorbed in our little chores and those men are out there protecting us in such horrible circumstances – the planes are zooming overhead.

At last on 21 March the Salters began their journey to the United Stated. That day Lady Salter wrote in her diary:

(Friday, March 21) Arthur and I left Euston at 10.30 a.m. seen off by Louise, Drummond and Tommy. The station was packed with troops. Such a muddle of men – some very good looking, some funny. We were beautifully looked after. A carriage labelled "Not for Public Use" which Arthur says someone in Parliament said meant for convicts, lunatics, corpses and Cabinet Ministers. Arrived in Liverpool nearly on time. After leaving London the only sign of war were a few camouflaged factories – otherwise all perfectly peaceful. Received at station by Captain Boase, many medals. A fat marine took our luggage in a camouflaged army truck. A Mrs. Ashcroft who drives the Captain as her war job took us to the "Georgic," passed endless wrecked docks. Fires had caused much damage. But on the whole everything looked much better than even London does. Very officious customs man in Liverpool, full of importance and gold braid, insisted on calling Arthur "My Lord" every sentence.

(Saturday, March 22) Still at Liverpool. Very foggy. This ship is certainly a queer medley. We had our life boat drill this a.m. and were told how to wear life belts, not smoke, show lights, etc. Masses of aviators, some training in Canada, some of the best for flying bombers back, every kind of officer and soldier and service and rank. About 14 woman. We have a nice sitting room, stateroom and bath. Some of the convoy got out this a.m., but then the fog settled down and we are all held up.

(Sunday, March 23) We were supposed to leave today. Moved out about 5 but no motion of going. Such a motley crowd of Americans, English aviators, gunners, everything. A wearying day up and down, around the deck – restlessness. No news – in sight of dear old England and yet so far away. Out of touch with people one cares for – what is happening?

(Monday, March 24) A very difficult day. Arthur very restless and tense – back and forth. Every effort to distract him – not very successful. Very disappointing to find the ship anchored near Anglesey. Finally, got off at 7.30 – destroyers, merchant ships – a pretty sight. I am too miserable to really enjoy it. Worried anxious in many directions. What will happen? I realize more than ever the separation from England at war. I just have to hold up my end till it's finished.

(Tuesday, March 25) We're really under way. Two battleships – several destroyers escorting us. Gorgeous sight. Waves breaking over destroyers. Felt as though I were in a dream movie. We go around looking ridiculous with life belts slung on arms – I forgot the blasted things all the time. It's incredible – what good would they be in the ocean? Anyhow we're steaming on and away. What problems face us in U.S.A.?

(Wednesday, March 26) It grew more swelly by evening. So quite a few including Arthur felt weak. He asked about 18 merchant captains for drinks in the smoking room. Almost all had been torpedoed, bombed or mined. A good tough fine English crowd – all so full of grit and fundamentally nice.

(Thursday, March 27) Calmer today and gorgeous sun. The convoy a lovely sight. "Rodney" and "Revenge" always in sight. A few destroyers, I think 4 gone back. There's also 1 or 2 cruisers. I see about 26 ships all the time. 2 ships bombed north of us yesterday. It seems so tragic – just out of the air – and so futile.

(Friday, March 28) The convoy left us this a.m. and the Rodney etc. and proceeded on their way around the Cape. Arthur asked the ferry pilots to cocktails before dinner, about 20 of them.

The next three days proved uneventful and on Tuesday, 1 April the Salters landed in Halifax. "The battleship went in first. It was a glorious day. Various people and press came on board to meet us," Lady Salter wrote in her diary. Salter stated that his purpose was to accelerate cooperation with the United States in shipping matters. American aid, he noted, was needed "'badly and quickly'." The next stop was Montreal where the Salters spent just over two hours and left again by train to Washington where they arrived at one o'clock in the afternoon of 3 April. Lady Salter recorded their return to Washington in her diary:

Lord Halifax's private secretary met us with his car – also Frances Perkins and Jean Monnet and several others. Frances took us up to California Street and lunched with us. Lovely flowers in the house. We dined with Jean Monnet. I was terribly tired – very emotional at coming back to this house.

The Salters were fortunate with respect to accommodation which was at the time scarce in Washington. Lady Salter had leased her house at 2326 California Street to her friend, Frances Perkins, who was then serving as Secretary of Labour. It was a spacious, three-storey, 10 rooms, brick townhouse built in 1915 with several bedrooms and bathrooms. A letter to Perkins prior to their departure had ensured that the house was vacant and ready on arrival. It was fully furnished and with adequate staff prepared to see to the needs of the new occupants.[157] Shortly afterwards, Lady Salter also arranged to reoccupy the 265-acre estate, Hickory Farm, Tyringham, which she had purchased in May 1936 from the Tiffany family and usually leased thereafter. That summer she added to the estate by purchasing an adjacent dairy property, Hop Brook Farm, and began renovations which included enlarging a natural swimming pond for Salter to enjoy.[158]

Salter's arrival in Washington was greeted by the media with much good will and considerable comment. Time thought him "particularly fitted" for the mission and noted his recent marriage to an American and a Washingtonian. It described him as the "worst-dressed man in Geneva," a "sparrow in large round glasses," and anticipated that with his arrival "the fur will fly."[159] It was also noted that as a first gesture Salter would accept the transfer of 50 reconditioned American merchant ships suitable for convoy work. The Washington Post noted that he would already find a structure for Anglo-American shipping co-operation in the Maritime Commission and its exercise of voluntary controls with shipowners.[160] The New York Times, in two comprehensive articles, anticipated that Salter's arrival would accelerate what it called "the battle of the shipyards," and lead to a building program "unprecedented in world history." Given what it described as Britain's "almost limitless" need for shipping, and the fact that in 1941 sinkings would outstrip building, the articles concluded, correctly in the event, that the outcome of Salter's mission would be the centralized control of all American shipping, "and eventually, perhaps, the pooling of Anglo-American shipping."[161]

The task that lay before Salter was to secure: a large allocation of existing US tonnage for British services; an increase in US shipbuilding; help with repair facilities and defensive equipment from US yards; administrative cooperation in general shipping problems; and by a presentation of the seriousness of the shipping position, to hasten US naval protection.[162] "The difficulties ahead were great and at first appeared insuperable," he later noted.[163] In essence, he wrote, "Against the grave U.K. dangers of starvation, the closing of munitions factories for want of raw materials, and the crippling and immobilization of the British war effort, there was only one conceivable source of substantial relief – the U.S.A."[164] It was generally agreed that Britain's potential to wage war successfully was dependent upon merchant shipping. Since the outbreak of the war Britain's net loss of shipping was 5 million deadweight tons. By the spring of 1941 losses were at an annual rate of 7.7 million deadweight tons, while new building amounted only to 1.4 million deadweight tons.[165]

The environment that Salter faced in the United States, however, was mixed. On the one hand the American merchant marine was relatively small and the shipbuilding industry had been run down since 1921. In addition, the Neutrality Act strictly limited the diversion of any American ship into a war zone, although the passage of the Lend-Lease Act held out better prospects for assistance. On the other hand, as Salter later reported to Churchill:

> I was fortunate in arriving at the psychological moment, when events in the Battle of the Atlantic, your messages, and the reports of Harriman, [Wendell] Willkie, Winant, had given merchant shipping a foremost place in the mind

of the President and his colleagues. I was, therefore, welcomed cordially and given opportunities of presenting our case in intimate talks and written notes which received immediate attention. The President, with H. Hopkins as his constant adviser, talked frankly and listened sympathetically, and I was able to establish quickly intimate relationship with the Ministers and departmental chiefs mainly concerned. In this I was helped by the fact that a number of them, like Stimson, were already close friends of mine while most of the others were intimate friends of my wife, whose presence with me has been of great value.[166]

As he wrote similarly to Hurcomb, "I was fortunate in arriving when the tide was favourable, merchant ships being foremost in the President's mind. I found myself cordially welcomed and given every chance of putting my case."[167]

The best welcome that Salter received on his arrival in Washington was Roosevelt's announcement on 4 April that $629,000,000 had been appropriated under the Lend-Lease authority for shipping, with most of it going for construction of ships and shipways, and repairing damaged British ships. That evening, Salter, dubbed the "trouble shooter for Britain," held his first press conference in Washington. He declared that "The Battle of the Atlantic is now engaged," and that it could "be won in the shipyards of America." He made no specific suggestions as to how the US might assist Britain, but laid out the gravity of the shipping situation. He reported that Britain was annually losing about one million tons of shipping, with both American and British building amounting only to two million tons. He pointed out that at the end of the last war the combined total was more than 5.5 million tons, with 233 shipyards at work then compared to the current 40 in use. "Plan your building on the largest possible scale," he stated. "The important thing from our point of view is for America to make her potential capacity her actual capacity."[168] This was in fact to be the strategy that Salter employed throughout his mission in Washington. In its implementation he was assisted by an extremely talented and able group. These included Jack Maclay (later Secretary of State for Scotland), Richard Powell (later permanent secretary of the Board of Trade), Donald Anderson (later chairman of the Peninsular and Oriental Ship Company), and William "Tony" Keswick (governor of the Hudson's Bay Corporation and director at the Bank of England). Salter later wrote "they were as good a team as I have ever worked with." While Salter maintained overall responsibility for policy, each member was expected to take the initiative.[169] Powell later recalled that, in his dealings with the US administration, on occasion Salter was "apt to be carried away." As a result, he and others had "to exercise a restraining influence on him lest he should risk undoing the good that he had already achieved."[170]

Something of what the Americans could expect from Salter surfaced almost immediately. On 4 April, a day after his arrival, he was asked to secure six high speed 16-knot cargo vessels required to sail on 20 April to meet a convoy date. Six such ships had just been built, but they were not physically in position to load and sail by the prescribed date. They also were, as Salter termed them, "the pride of the American mercantile marine."[171] Although he initially regarded the request as extremely difficult, he at once went into action on this and related issues, negotiating both with the Maritime Commission and working to secure the intervention of Roosevelt. On 6 April he dined with, among others, Stimson, Morgenthau, Brand and Purvis. According to Stimson, Salter emphasized the shortages in shipping, "a somber picture but not out of line with what we have already learned from other sources."[172] For his part, Morgenthau left, "tremendously impressed with the need that we move on these Danish ships." He immediately urged Hopkins (de facto Lend-Lease administrator, until the Office of Lend-Lease Administration was set up in October 1941 under Edward Stettinius) to take the issue of the 60 Danish ships directly to Roosevelt for a final decision.[173] On 10 April Salter attended his first meeting of the British Supply Council in North America. As chairman, Purvis welcomed him and stated that his presence "will be a source of strength and encouragement to all."[174] On 11 April Salter met with Rear Admiral Emory Scott Land, chairman of the United States Maritime Commission and his assistant, Vice-Admiral Howard L. Vickery. Afterwards Land wrote to Roosevelt, "If we do not watch our step, we shall find the White House on route to England with the Washington Monument as a steering oar."[175]

In the press it was noted that Salter had "arrived like a medium tank through underbrush."[176] Salter observed, "I have been pressing hard," and the "negotiations have been very difficult." On 12 April he had his first meeting, a lunch appointment, with Roosevelt and Hopkins to discuss the broad outlines of his mission and the 16-knot cargo ships. Afterwards Salter wrote that the ultimate allocation of four, not the six, ships was a result "produced only by direct Presidential intervention" arranged through Hopkins. Salter regarded the latter's support as "magnificent," and added, "It has been my best piece of good fortune to establish intimate relations with him. I talk to him almost daily and he always responds at once."[177] He paid special tribute to the "most effective co-operation and great energy" of the Maritime Commission and as a consequence the ships sailed on time under a British flag and with British crews. Writing to Land to thank him, Salter noted that "we all realize what it meant to divert exceedingly valuable ships of this kind at such short notice."[178] His colleague, Ashley Sparks, later wrote that what Salter and Maclay had accomplished "already speaks volumes for the necessity of having them over here."[179] This early success by Salter, which he later described as "the result of courage born out of desperation," was to shape his approach on how to do business in Washington.[180] He candidly admitted afterwards, "From the moment of my talk with the President [on 12 April] I was convinced that, to get big results, a general order by him was essential."[181] Maclay confirmed that as a result of this initial episode "during 1941/1942 Arthur could be sure of getting anything of importance through to the President at very short notice."[182]

This was not the only success Salter enjoyed in the weeks following his arrival. On 11 April Roosevelt announced that he was removing the combat zone at the entrance to the Red Sea, enabling American shipping to carry supplies right to the mouth of the Suez Canal at Ismailia. On the way to pay his first visit to Secretary of State Cordell Hull, Salter stated that the move "would give very valuable aid to Great Britain." Indeed, it enabled Britain to free up shipping from that area to serve in the North Atlantic lanes, and by the end of April the Americans had allocated 15 ships, with up to 100 promised, to carry American supplies to the Middle East. As well, Salter had his eyes on the 69 Danish, German and Italian ships in American ports under detention, and which Roosevelt had been given the power to requisition on 31 March.[183] In the meantime Salter worked at a fever pitch on what proved to be a decisive document in this, the early stages of his mission. He had taken with him from London a massive quantity of documents and materials. These he collated with information gleaned during his stay in Washington, resulting in an eight-page memorandum, titled "The Shipping Problem," which he discussed with Hopkins on 22 April. "Two things are necessary:" Salter began, "(a) to out-build losses as early as possible in 1942; (b) to bridge the interval." Since the collapse of Western Europe the previous summer, he continued, Britain was losing British an average rate of five million gross tons a year, with building at a rate of up to 1.5 million gross tons. Only US building, he argued, could make up the deficiency and that must reach four million gross tons as early as possible in 1942. "The most energetic action is, therefore, needed at once." He pointed out that, given the current rate of loss, imports both of food and raw materials had been seriously reduced by almost 50%. He suggested the tonnage shortfall could be made up partly by pressing into service the foreign ships in US ports (some 3.4 million gross tons), but largely by "American 'flag tonnage'," both existing ships and the new ships produced until June 1942. He estimated the existing American mercantile marine to be about 7½ million gross tons. Hence, he argued, "The problem, therefore, though urgent and difficult, is not insoluble." He then pointed out that for the coming year: "a ship supplied tomorrow is worth two ships in six months;" the rate of losses was hard to know; that it was clearly "better to save a ship than to build one in replacement;" and that to secure results in 1942 "action is required now." Finally, he unabashedly suggested that effective cooperation between the British supply organization and the Maritime Commission depended totally on the latter body having "sufficient authority and sufficient time to carry though the work involved, in daily collaboration with the members of the British shipping Mission, by the decisions of policy taken from time to time by the President."[184]

In a follow-up letter, also on 22 April, Salter sent Hopkins three separate memoranda. The first digressed on the oil and tanker situation, and stressed the serious shortfall of oil imports. He thus also asked for additional American assistance with tankers from every available source, even including those being built for private owners. The second gave details of Britain's most urgent needs over the next four months, and this included oil tankers, ships for Middle East service and dry cargo ships. The third suggested that if the United States ship production reached four million gross tons by the end of 1942, this plus British output would match losses.[185] Salter's final letter to Hopkins that day, attaching a note, "entirely unofficial," titled "Suggested 'Directives'." This advised the immediate acquisition, repair and deployment of all foreign tonnage in US ports and that all new tonnage coming off slipways be put directly to war service.[186] The several memoranda which Salter submitted on 22 April were the fulfillment of the first objective of his mission – to provide the Roosevelt administration with a comprehensive review of the shipping and import situation. The strategy that he had employed was deliberate and in the end effective. In framing the shipbuilding programme, "He drew the picture as a world picture, not a British picture." Ships, he argued, were needed to meet the world shortage; allocation would be left to a later date. He was confident that they would then be properly deployed. "The President and his advisers accepted the case as stated in determining the scale of the effort to be made."[187] On 24 April Salter informed a meeting of the British Supply Council in North America of the satisfactory progress being made by the Merchant Shipping Mission and the excellent support being received from the Maritime Commission.[188]

The end of the month brought the good news, proving that Salter's strategy was decisive. His 22 April memorandum had also been sent on to the White House which then sent a copy to Morgenthau on 28 April. Attached was the first draft of a "directive" from Roosevelt to Land.[189] In fact, on his own initiative, Salter had already sent his memorandum to Morgenthau, acknowledging the latter's "friendly interest and active help" on issues of American assistance to Britain.[190] Its contents became public on 1 May when Roosevelt, in a letter to Land dated 30 April, directed the Maritime Commission at once "to secure the service of at least two million tons of merchant shipping which now exists" and "make their cargo space immediately effective in accomplishing our objective of all out aid to the democracies." Instructions were also included to speed up the shipbuilding programme by keeping all existing shipyards in continuous operation. Reporting this news directly to Churchill and Cross, Salter noted that "this general direction goes as far as could possibly be hoped now and marks definite stage which should greatly assist our negotiations on particular needs." He concluded, "In sum, we now have good strategical position for future merchant ship negotiations. The tactical utilization of this position will be long and difficult but with favourable prospects." Indeed, this was the best-case scenario that Salter had lobbied for during his first month in Washington. As he explained a few days later, with "broad policy laid down by the President," ongoing special interventions from London would no longer be necessary.[191] As for his personal assessment, he noted that "Shipping is the crucial point of the war, & immensely more depends on what is done here than upon anything in our control from London."[192] He privately admitted that he was simply "overwhelmed with current work."[193] Another Fellow of All Souls, Isaiah Berlin, attached to the British embassy in Washington and never sympathetic to Salter, noted that "he is a definite success."[194]

On 9 May Salter wrote directly to Churchill to report on the progress of his mission. He pointed out that the Roosevelt had taken two major decisions since his arrival. The first was the commitment to build ships at a rate to outmatch losses before the end of 1942 with a goal of four million gross tons, and to transfer existing ships to bridge the interval. The second was the "Two Million Ton Directive," about which Salter noted that he was consulted throughout, and that it was deliberately left vague as to whether these were gross or deadweight. Already, Salter continued, 24 ships had been assigned to carry British stores to the Middle East and 23 tankers were bringing oil from the Dutch West Indies and the US Gulf to North Atlantic American ports for transfer to British controlled ships. "All is, therefore, going well for the time." Digressing then to offer some impressions, Salter estimated American public opinion as "prepared for action which is likely to lead to war, while still disliking the conclusion." He described Roosevelt as "frank, exuberant and realistically sanguine," and quoted the President as stating: "'If the battle of the Mediterranean is lost, that of the Atlantic can and will be won'."[195] That day Salter also wrote to Land, thanking him for the tankers, especially given the serious tanker loses sustained by Britain in recent months.[196] Privately, Salter observed that he intended, even before the two million ton target was reached, to "be watching every chance of either getting it more broadly interpreted or supplemented by the addition of new ships coming of the stocks."[197]

Salter was later to write that "The harvest is still to be gathered, however, and the administrative, as distinct from the diplomatic, side of my work is constantly increasing. There are as many problems as ships."[198] This was indeed to be the case following his first report to Churchill. On 2 May it had been announced that the separate Ministries of Shipping and Transport were to be amalgamated into a newly titled

Ministry of War Transport, headed by F.J. Leathers, with Hurcomb as its new director general. Salter cabled his congratulations and received in return a reassurance from Leathers that he wished Salter to continue with his mission.[199] When Leathers was made a peer on 19 May, it left Salter and Colonel J.J. Llewellin, newly appointed, as joint parliamentary secretaries to the new ministry. Among the first instructions from Leathers was to prepare weekly summaries of Salter's activities which were sent to 10 Downing Street. These reports provide the detailed evidence supporting Salter's contention that there were "as many problems as ships."[200] Thus in the following two weeks, from 11 to 25 May Salter reported that deliveries of new ships from American shipyards were expected to increased dramatically, with Britain getting its share depending on losses. The Maritime Commission was releasing more tugs for British use, providing a further 25 tankers, and allocating 100 ships for service to the Middle East over the next nine months. As well, he affirmed that the Maritime Commission was working with "ardour, rapidity and ruthlessness" to remedy Britain's estimated seven million ton import deficiency during the next 12 months, that being the difference between the essential requirement of 35 million tons as against imports of only 28 million tons.[201] On 27 May Leathers wrote to Salter, "I am most impressed with the progress you have been able to achieve in so short a time with your small staff and I am very pleased that Maclay is proving helpful and energetic." In his response, Salter cautioned that "We are, of course, reaching what is in some respects our most difficult stage as the squeeze becomes more severe."[202]

In his submissions for the first three weeks of June, Salter reported further progress on the allocation of American tankers for service. In addition, given the shortage of passenger accommodation on the North Atlantic, the Maritime Commission was prepared to use American liners and some Danish ships to transport, provided they were in mufti, service men across the North Atlantic. He also reported further progress on the question of Britain acquiring a substantial number of the Danish ships for direct service. The issue of cross trades, whereby ships traded between two ports in neither country of which the ship was registered, was tackled with increased attention. Although fraught with complex legal implications for post-war shipping, Salter was able to report that the Maritime Commission was willing to supply alternative ships under what was termed the "No Prejudice Either Way" formula – designed to level the shipping playing field after the war. In other words, "while there will be no automatic return to pre-war status quo there will equally be no stabilization of position as it happens to be at the end of the war." Salter's exact wording was left open for subsequent discussion with Land.[203] In the event, Salter made very little progress on the question, concluding on 5 October 1942 that at war's end, with a larger American mercantile marine than a British one, there would be no return to the pre-war status quo.[204]

If progress could be recorded on various fronts during June, the same could not be said about the ratio between shipbuilding and losses. On 27 May Roosevelt had revealed that the US and Britain together were only replacing one ton of shipping for every two tons sunk. Plans for the closing of the gap between losses and replacement, an essential component of Salter's mission, had envisaged a target date of the spring of 1942. However, the press in Britain was calling for greater American military intervention with naval deployment and long range aircraft surveillance.[205] Such an outcome was beyond Salter's mandate. However, he continued his efforts by directly lobbying both Hopkins and Morgenthau and demanding from the Ministry of War Transport even more detailed statistics about British shipping losses to illustrate the seriousness of the shipping situation. These he received and was instructed to share them with the American administration.[206] On 17 June he told Morgenthau that in light of the sinkings, the five million tons of Anglo-American building he had advocated was no longer adequate. "He seemed very discouraged," Morgenthau noted, and added that Salter seemed to be pushing for a real convoy system. As a follow up, Salter provided Morgenthau with detailed figures for British shipping losses between 28 April and 1 June, amounting to 689,000 gross tons.[207]

Writing to Walter Lippmann on 17 June, Salter noted," I have been very much submerged lately," and added he was leaving Washington for Boston and Canada.[208] On 19 June at the Harvard University graduation ceremony, Salter was one of four Oxford University delegates when Lord Halifax, Chancellor of the University, presided over a special convocation. This was to confer on Roosevelt, in absentia, an honourary Doctor of Civil Law.[209] From there Salter travelled to Ottawa where on 23 and 24 June he conferred with Canadian ministers and officials on shipping related questions. His visit originated with the Hyde Park economic agreement signed between Roosevelt and Mackenzie King on 20 April 1941. Under its terms, in so far as it related to shipping, the Maritime Commission would place orders in Canada for ships which would then be "lease-lent" to Britain. It was hoped to produce by the end of 1942 over 70 ships of various kinds and capacities.[210] Prior to his visit, Salter had written to Mackenzie King, requesting a meeting, adding, "I have always had the pleasant feeling of having a closer personal relationship with you than the comparative infrequency of our actual meetings would perhaps warrant, a feeling which was happily confirmed by the very kind cable you sent me last year at the time of my marriage." Salter met with Mackenzie King on 23 June, where the conversation centred on the breaking news of Germany's attack against the USSR.[211] Most of his time, however, was spent conferring with C.D. Howe, who was to play a central wartime role as Minister of Munitions and Supply. From there Salter travelled to Montreal and Halifax to confer with various local shipping contacts. That entire collaboration in shipbuilding, cemented by his visit to Canada, had the result that by 1943 Canada was building merchant shipping at a rate of one million gross tons a year, just 15% less than Britain.[212] Salter afterwards noted that his week's visit to Canada was mainly "a visit of courtesy" and had been very useful.[213]

A return to Washington meant Salter was once again immersed in the details of the shipping mission. He could report by 29 June that additional Italian and Danish ships were soon to be ready to load for the North Atlantic route and that 25 tug boats for which he had been negotiating would be arriving in Britain by the end of September. And he noted that before 25 August a total of 55 ships would have loaded cargoes and sailed for the Middle East.[214] On the serious issue of the shortage of tankers, which he had first raised on 22 April, he commended on 28 June "the promptitude and generous scale" of American assistance. However, he cautioned that by the end of the year, at the current rate of loss, there would be a deficit of 65 tankers with stocks of fuel nearly exhausted. Even with new construction and the possible transfer of ships in shuttle to combat zone service, among other possible remedies, he concluded that there was an "imminent danger" of a slowdown in British industrial output and a reduction in the activities of the armed forces.[215] This memorandum became the basis of the second large-scale request by Salter for tanker assistance from the American government. His April 22 request had been for 75 tankers of which 43 had been placed in shuttle service. The number for the second request was raised to more than 90 ships to meet UK consumption and to rebuild stocks. Once again, the response by the United States was to fulfill almost all of Britain's tanker needs.[216]

Even with so much achieved, there were yet bigger plans in the offing. Salter had already been given advance notice of Roosevelt's request to Congress on 11 July to authorise vast new military expenditures. This included funding to the Maritime Commission, and doubling the shipbuilding programme for 1942 to 556 ships of more than 5.5 million deadweight tons, with an equivalent programme for 1943.[217] This had enormous implications for Britain and Salter was quick to act. Responding to a request from Hopkins, on 8 August Salter wrote a lengthy memorandum on the shipping situation over the next three years, with reference to the transport of Lend-Lease materials. After analyzing imports and shipbuilding since the start of the war, he then observed that 1942 would begin "with a seriously stringent shipping situation, but not one which will entail disaster if the situation improves." He foresaw that the combined shipping output of Britain, the United States and Canada would continue to exceed losses well into 1943. At the same time, the demands on shipping, particularly for the transportation of raw materials, now including the USSR, would increase. Hence the outcome of the war "may well turn upon the ability of shipping to transport the men and supplies for campaigns not yet planned." At this point Salter argued that the war effort could be maintained as already planned, however, he suggested several measures by way of "insurance against unexpected disaster." These included better protection for Atlantic shipping, meeting scheduled shipbuilding programmes rather than increasing output, and reducing civilian consumption of certain food products.[218]

After four months in Washington, Salter felt that his mission had reached a benchmark. On 8 August he wrote to Churchill stating that "A definite stage has now been reached in the work of my Mission." American policy, he continued, "if fully carried out, looks like giving a real solution of the shipping difficulties – if losses do not again increase. The harvest is still to be gathered, however, and the administrative, as distinct from the diplomatic, side of my work is constantly increasing. There are as many problems as ships." Salter praised the quality of his staff, singling out Maclay, even as had earlier asked for additional staff for his mission. Finally, he added, "So much has happened in Whitehall and the world during these last four months that I think it would be a good thing for me to come over for a fortnight or so next month to renew contacts and exchange ideas." Enclosed with his letter was a "Progress Report" covering the period April to July 1941. With regard to the allocation of ships, he observed that the request for 100 ships to carry US supplies to the Middle East was being met; half of the 200 ships requested to carry imports to the UK were already in service; while sufficient tankers, both in the shuttle service and transferred for combat zone work, had solved the spring oil crisis. As for new building, he wrote that it would "perhaps be prudent to put the combined building output figure, for the UK, the USA and Canada, at about 5.5 million gross tons per year for 1942 and 1943." As for repairs, there were at any time nearly 100 British ships under repair in American yards, while administrative cooperation was working well.[219] Salter wrote similarly to Leathers the same day, noting that, "so far as main policy decisions are concerned, we have pretty well got what we aimed at," and he enclosed a copy of the "Progress Report."[220] Churchill circulated Salter's report to Cherwell, personal assistant to the prime minister, who observed that Salter's estimates for future shipbuilding were "reasonable." Leathers, who responded to Churchill's request for feedback and approval for a visit from Salter, noted that he was "satisfied with the Mission's work," and approved Salter's request to briefly return home.[221] In the following days, the Salters seized some time for a vacation at Hickory Farm. This included, as it was always going to in the future, entertaining guests at their box at the Tanglewood Festival. The guests this time included Elliot Felkin and his daughter Penelope.[222]

In the meantime, the work achieved by the Merchant Shipbuilding Mission to the US, which had negotiated the construction of additional tonnage in the fall of 1940, with contracts signed on 20 December 1940, had finally come to fruition. On 16 August 1941 the first of these 60 mass-produced cargo steamers, ordered by Britain before

Lend-Lease, was ready for launching, ahead of schedule. Thirty were being built by Henry J. Kaiser's Todd-California Shipbuilding Corporation shipyard at Richmond, California, a site which had been mud flats just seven months earlier. Thirty others were scheduled for construction at the Todd-Bath Iron Shipbuilding Corporation in Portland, Maine, with another 26 similar vessels to be built in Canada.[223] Salter had specifically invited Admiral Land's wife to perform the naming ceremony for the first completed ship, the *Ocean Vanguard*. However, even as Salter spoke and just as Mrs. Land was able to swing the bottle of champagne across its bow, the 10,000 tons deadweight freighter left the slipway six minutes early.[224] The launching, according to the Oakland Tribune, left Lady Salter in tears. In his remarks Salter called the *Ocean Vanguard* a portent of victory. The outcome of the war, he stated, "turns on the contest at sea, and this ship symbolizes the decisive factor in that contest – the entry into it of America as a great shipbuilder." He added, "The Battle of the Atlantic is not yet won, but this ship shows how the battle can be won. Since America can produce as much steel as the rest of the world together the key to victory to this war of steel is here." Land added that two ships a day would be built in the USA over the next two year: "Two ships a day will keep the Germans away."[225]

"We hurried back sadly to Washington," Salter recalled, referring to the tragic news that he had received before his departure. On 14 August Purvis, along with all the other passengers and crew, was killed when his plane on the way to Newfoundland crashed shortly after take-off from Prestwick airport in Scotland.[226] The loss of someone, whom Salter described as "my friend and colleague," was to have an impact on him. On 19 August Churchill wrote Leathers that "I am not thinking of inviting him [Salter] to fill the Purvis vacancy."[227] Shortly thereafter, on 29 August, Leathers telegrammed to Salter approving his visit to London to renew contacts.[228] However, Salter was already mulling over the implications of Purvis' death. On 21 August he wrote to Lionel Curtis of his hopes to get to England for three weeks in September, "but now Purvis' tragic death has made it doubtful whether I can manage this." Salter used the letter also to reflect on his American mission to date:

> For the first few months here the pace was very hot & everything except the daily task got pushed out of mind. This has for me been one of the most satisfying periods of my life, for I have had the whole of my plan adopted by the American government, stage by stage, & unless the rate of losses rises seriously again the really vital danger of being starved of food or supplies by the sinkings will be past. It may of course rise again – & there are many other perils but this is something. Ethel is extremely well – miraculously indeed after her illness of a year & a half ago & has plunged with great zest into Washington,

where her intimate friendship with almost everyone in authority has been of great value to my work, as well as otherwise adding to the amenities of life.[229]

Salter had planned to leave Washington for London on 14 September. However, as he notified Hopkins on 8 September, he had developed a very serious eye infection. Leaving Maclay in charge, he and Lady Salter first travelled to New York for specialist treatment and then retreated to Hickory Farm for a period of recovery. Frances Perkins, who had discovered Salter's illness, wrote that "I know it must be a great nuisance to him." For a brief period, in fact, Salter feared that he would lose the sight in his right eye.[230] By 27 September he was back in Washington and well enough to broadcast on the eve of the first anniversary of "Victory Fleet Day," and to celebrate the mass launching of 14 Liberty Ships in one day. He was also able to return to attendance at the North American Supply Council, where on 1 October he reported that the Maritime Commission had met British needs both for oil and tankers. However, this was causing some domestic criticism due to resulting oil shortage on the east coast.[231] Salter's return to shipping work, however, coincided with an unexpected diversion from his primary mission. In February 1941 the British government had begun examining questions of post-war reconstruction with the State Department. Among the earliest and most contentious issue discussed during subsequent Anglo-American trade discussions was the question of free trade versus protectionism. Against this background, the International Wheat Advisory Committee, representing experts from Britain, the United States, Argentina, Canada and Australia, met in Washington from 10 July to 3 August to draft a new comprehensive wheat agreement. Following the meeting, an American draft was circulated, designed *inter alia* to end imperial preference, and stipulating that Britain and the USA would not discriminate "against the importation of any produce originating in the other country."[232] The proposal, not unnaturally, was roundly criticised in London. Writing to Eden in support of the draft agreement on 17 September, Winant argued that the purpose was to expand world trade in wheat by reducing import barriers, to stabilize wheat prices, adjust production away from excess to market requirements, maintain adequate reserves and provide supplies for post-war relief. An early solution, Winant suggested, would impress all nations with evidence that the democracies could collaborate effectively on both wartime and post-war problems.[233]

Into this extremely complex and sensitive web of negotiations, Salter was invited in late September to lead the British delegation to the next round of the Wheat Conference.[234] He responded that while he appreciated the invitation, it was hard to accept without knowing the particulars. Among the difficulties that he could foresee was that he had no technical knowledge of agriculture and wheat problems as such, his well-known opposition to protectionism might conflict with the British government's brief, and his concerns about how long the talks would take and thus further postpone his visit to London. Greenwood replied that the points Salter raised posed no obstacles. After this reassurance and after having read the relevant documentation, the latter agreed on 12 October to head the delegation.[235] In the days prior to the opening of the conference on 14 October, in the United States Department of Agriculture, the War Cabinet had discussed the American position which was regarded as "unacceptable," while work went ahead to complete new detailed instructions for Salter.[236] While it was agreed that stable prices after the war were desirable, this should not be achieved at the expense of restricting output of wheat production in European countries and the exclusion of the USSR, a major wheat producing nation and now an ally. Churchill, in particular, appeared moved by the non-economic implications and even suggested the subject of wheat should be subsumed into the larger questions of post-war, Anglo-American economic collaboration.[237] The War Cabinet mulled over these questions, tentatively concluding on 6 October that further consultations were required, including a personal letter from Churchill to Roosevelt to further explore the issues.[238] Thus Churchill wrote to Roosevelt on 8 October, reiterating British reservations regarding any action which could be construed as "implying Anglo-American interference in European agricultural policy," and also that Russia, now an ally, should also be consulted. But he also noted that the proposal to establish a wheat pool for post-war relief was welcomed and that Britain still favoured a larger Anglo-American discussion of post-war economic collaboration.[239] Roosevelt's reply, which did not arrive until 17 October, continued to maintain the American position and looked forward to an agreement emerging from the conference.[240]

Despite such misgivings, the conference convened on 14 October at the US Department of Agriculture.[241] In his opening statement, Salter praised the efforts and methods adopted by the experts who, in the summer, had explored the issues and prepared a Provisional Draft Agreement for the current conference. He then reviewed the British government's position, especially in light of two important developments. He pointed out that the Atlantic Charter – agreed upon between Churchill and Roosevelt at Placentia Bay on 14 August – emphasized equal access to trade and raw materials for all nations, as well as the emergence of the USSR as an ally. The draft agreement, he continued, might be construed as imposing on European nations external forms of control. He looked forward to "some really useful work" being achieved at the conference, and concluded by suggesting something of the positive proposals Britain would advance, including an immediate post-war "relief pool," and greater price stability for wheat.[242] During the following meetings, Salter doggedly argued the merits of the British approach, maintaining that an agreement on wheat should only be part of "a general scheme for the better ordering of international commerce" and the "wider organizations dealing with the relief problem as a whole." To exclude European wheat producing nations, such as the USSR, would be disastrous. Nothing would move the American delegates from their position that importing countries abandon protection and subsidies.[243]

Reporting to London on 7 November, Salter noted that all the delegations had made statements of their positions, that committees had been formed to examine "prices relief and export quotas" and that some agreement had been reached on "relief pool proposals." However, the State Department continued to stand firm on the need to conclude a wheat agreement prior to any other economic and financial agreements. Thus, Salter observed, "I do not think it will be possible to reach agreement within limits of the present instructions but I am not yet in a position to report what change in these instructions will make agreement possible."[244] On 12 November he added that the United States was not letting up on its demand for an immediate wheat agreement and that the real drawback was not the wheat negotiations but more general questions governing Anglo-American relations. He pointed out that much American public opinion was "embittered" by the fact that such generous gestures as Lend-Lease were countered by the British tendency to bargain on the wheat question. "Whether we think this attitude reasonable or not it exists and is serious," Salter concluded. His observations, it was noted in the Foreign Office, "deserve to be treated with great respect."[245]

Privately, however, Salter was more outspoken. Writing on 20 November to Rowse, he referred to the "tiresome wheat negotiations." He also shared with Rowse some musings on life in Washington:

> It's a queer life here, especially in Washington, with a country half at war, an eager administration & a very self-awakened nation, the luxury, prosperity, & patchy realization of what all this is about. The general movement & direction is clear, but with every kind of conflicting & retarding forces – anti-British sentiment, now latent, now flaring up, pacifism, anti-communism, an isolationism equally based on Lindbergh's 'the British are already defeated' & Hoover's 'The British will win without more intervention by us.' But it moves forward, by next year the war output will be impressive. In my own particular field of shipping, things have gone more fortunately & more rapidly. Last Spring we had had no shipping at all from the American Government & the building programme for 1942 was only 2 mill. tons. We have since had a hundred

tankers & some hundreds of ships turned over to us, have had other hundreds repaired in U.S. yards & the building output next year should be about 5 mill. tons (about the rate at which the Germans are destroying shipping, without counting our own building). So that, in shipping, we have practically all we could get if the country were at war: but without war the full industrial capacity will never be developed, to say nothing of expeditionary forces.

Personally, I have had great luck. I arrived just at the psychological moment, knew almost everyone concerned personally – while Ethel was an intimate friend of all the rest. It is very pleasant to be here in Ethel's house, with her own servants; and we have a simply enchanting small farm in the country, though of course I can only rarely get to it for a week-end. During the summer the work was intense & the heat very trying. I expect that the consequent fatigue was largely responsible for my eye trouble.

Ethel is on the whole extremely well, & much in her element here, though she has recurrent bouts of fatigue. Well, I won't make any prophecies for 1942 - it's bound to be a grim year at best for all of us.[246]

Even as the wheat negotiations continued, on 28 November Salter consulted with Halifax and they agreed that a breakdown would have "consequences certainly grave, and possibly very grave," with regard to the wider issue of Anglo-American wartime cooperation. Salter's growing frustration was shared with Eden to whom he wrote on 5 December regarding "this unhappy wheat problem." The bottom line, in Salter's view, was that ultimately the considerations involved were essentially political, and that the State Department and the Department of Agriculture had conflicting agendas.[247] That same day, too, Salter completed two pages of what he termed "Notes" on the wheat negotiations. His assessment was that no agreement was possible within the terms of his current instructions. However, he cautioned against a breakdown which would have adverse political effects. It would alienate farmers, the Department of Agriculture, the State Department, critics of British policy, and complicate future Lend-Lease appropriations. He continued, "Briefly, we want <u>agreement</u>; the State Department, <u>an</u> agreement; the Department of Agriculture, <u>the</u> agreement (or at least one with a binding and specific price formula); the other exporting countries want either no agreement or one with a binding price engagement." The crux he pointed out was price determination and control, and "if we can swallow this," then the negotiations could proceed to Britain's advantage.[248]

The entry of the USA into the war on 8 December, after the Japanese attack against Pearl Harbour, also had its impact on the wheat negotiations. While Salter continued to support the Foreign Office view of trying to reach some sort of accommodation, Britain's Treasury officials preferred to take a harder line, refusing to accept any form of price control.[249] Writing on 21 December, Salter could report little progress, although he suggested that there was some American recognition that agreeing on "a precise price formula and mechanism for enforcement," would be difficult without Russian participation. He also cautioned that "Any indication that, because America is a belligerent we feel we need not now be so anxious to meet her wishes, would be resented and would probably have unfortunate consequences." He went on to suggest some possible modifications of his original instructions and several suggestions regarding the question of prices.[250] Indeed, the impression in London near the end of December was that Salter had made considerable progress in narrowing divergences on the subjects of "wheat acreage, restrictions on wheat imports, policing of non-signatories, [and] Relief Pool."[251] On this basis it was decided to continue the discussions in Washington into the New Year. Salter now took a somewhat different approach, tending to rely more on what he termed "private discussions." As a consequence he reported on 19 January that the State Department had come round to the view that it would be important to bring the USSR into the negotiations before any final agreement was concluded. He further advised that the best course would be to reach a provisional agreement, without any agreed price formula, and then seek to secure an adjournment. In the event, this advice was accepted in London. Finally, Salter asked for "someone to replace me as it is essential that I should now be able to concentrate entirely on my own task of shipping which under the new circumstances has become both more capricious and more difficult." [252]

On 29 January, at the 43rd meeting of the Wheat Conference, Salter proposed just such "a record of points of agreement," or as he also termed it, "a provisional agreement," before adjournment as more acceptable to non-represented nations. In due course, a Draft Convention was finally agreed on 22 April 1942, the final session of the wheat meetings. Although the Draft Convention was never implemented, Salter's proposal to establish an International Wheat Council was incorporated as Article 7 in the agreement and was set up the following August.[253] However, that was also the last meeting Salter attended. In conversation that day with Halifax, he insisted that he be relieved of these duties. "His shipping work is so pressing and important that I cannot contest his views," Halifax noted after agreeing to this request and adding that the embassy would take on the responsibility. Soon afterwards, the Foreign Office cabled to Salter its "warm appreciation of the time and leadership" he had given to the wheat discussions.[254]

Salter's insistence on leaving the wheat negotiations was linked both to the American entry into the war and the establishment of a new Combined Shipping

Adjustment Board. It was publicly noted that the general shipping situation for the United Kingdom, after two years of war, had remarkably improved, with the British Mercantile Marine meeting "heavy and incessant demands."[255] In early December, Salter noted that "the April task may be considered to have been accomplished." For example, shipbuilding was outstripping losses, imports of food exceeded consumption, and replenished oil stocks in Britain enabled the return of 40 tankers, previously on loan to the United States. However, with the growing need to find shipping to supply the USSR, and after the Japanese attack against Pearl Harbour and the declaration by Italy and Germany of war against the United States, suddenly "the whole shipping outlook had undergone a violent and drastic change."[256] Salter had already, on 2 December, written to Hopkins about "the urgent need of the additional machinery for planning ships and supplies."[257] On 8 December Roosevelt took such a step with the establishment of a Strategic Shipping Board to determine "policies for and plan the allocation of merchant shipping." In the event, that agency quickly proved unsuitable, without the requisite executive power.[258] Then in response to Churchill's personal request on 3 January 1942, Salter wrote a note on "Merchant Shipping – Arrangements for Allocation." He pointed out that "the strain on shipping, at least in 1942 and perhaps also in 1943, will be much greater than any yet experienced." This was largely due to Soviet needs, Pacific war demands, and the transportation of American troops and supplies. "The real problem now is one of allocation," he pointed out. As a consequence, he recommended the Strategic Shipping Board should also meet as a "Joint Consultative Board" with himself attending and his staff collaborating with American officials to prepare submissions to the Board. Salter followed up with another note on 9 January, showing that the American army and navy were bypassing the Maritime Commission and appropriating ships directly and at the expense of British needs. Therefore, he urged Churchill to ensure that his Merchant Shipping Mission be central to any emergent allocation system. When forwarding the note to Hopkins, Churchill endorsed Salter's suggestion for the Consultative Board, adding, "There surely should be a joint Consultative Board so that your people can hear what we have to say before taking decisions on allocations."[259]

At the time Churchill was on a three-week visit, code-named "Arkadia," having arrived in Washington on 22 December. Among the numerous decisions taken by the new Allies were several relating to the future of Anglo-American shipping collaboration. The one affecting Salter, who along with Land, Vickery, Beaverbrook, Hopkins and Churchill had met with Roosevelt on 2 January,[260] was the establishment of Combined Shipping Adjustment Boards, one in Washington, the other in London. Salter played a major role in its formulation. On 13 January he again wrote Churchill with a redraft "of the proposed instrument for the establishment of an 'Adjustment

Board for the Use of Merchant Ships'." Its success, he continued, depended on the choice of the American member. He continued: "I will, of course, do my best to make this a success." Looking ahead to 1942 he cautioned that "Total transporting capacity in 1942 cannot exceed that of 1941" and some form of reduction would be required. He concluded "In my view the actual shortage this year is more serious than any experiences in the worst period of the last war."[261] In the short term, Salter was in fact instrumental, after speaking to Douglas and approaching Hopkins, in getting Douglas to take on the position of advisor on the Combined Shipping Adjustment Board and later deputy administrator at the War Shipping Administration.[262] The details of this new machinery to co-ordinate the Anglo-American war effort, including Salter's role, were leaked to the press.[263] After advising the War Cabinet on 17 January of this development, one of the "most important results" of his Washington visit, Churchill circulated to the War Cabinet on 19 January a note detailing the establishment of three Combined Boards; an "Anglo-American Shipping Adjustment Board," with two others dealing with raw materials and munitions assignments. The note on the Shipping Board first stated that "In principle, the shipping resources of the two countries will be deemed to be pooled. The fullest information will be interchanged." However, the movement of shipping around the British Isles, and the movements and allocations of United States shipping remained under separate London and Washington control. Salter was chosen for the Washington Board, "representing, and acting under the instructions of the British Minister of War Transport [Leathers]." The War Cabinet approved all three documents that same day.[264]

Churchill informed Roosevelt that the proposals had received "warm approval" from the War Cabinet and proposed announcing these new organizations in a White Paper presented to Parliament on 27 January, in fact, the same day Roosevelt made his own announcement from the White House.[265] American approval was telegraphed to Churchill by Roosevelt on 26 January. After naming Land to be the American representative working together with Salter, but also continuing as chairman of the Maritime Commission, the President requested that a new name be used – "Combined Shipping Adjustment Board" [CSAB].[266] On 28 January these developments were welcomed and analysed on both sides of the Atlantic. The more optimistic saw the boards as "the nucleus of a supreme supply command of the United Nations."[267] Others cautioned that the last paragraph of the public announcement emphasized that "executive power will still be centred in the appropriate shipping agencies of the two countries."[268] It was The New York Times which noted that the combined boards implemented one of Salter's lessons gleaned from his experience of the First World War, namely, "that the responsible authorities in the several national administrations should be brought into direct contact with each other."[269] This development was followed on 9 February with a Presidential Executive Order creating the War Shipping Administration (WSA), a body separate from the US Maritime Commission. While the two entities remained linked, the former took over all operational and allocation responsibilities and the latter concentrated on shipbuilding. Land, who still remained chairman of the Maritime Commission, was also appointed the Shipping Administrator of the new agency. His extended responsibilities included not only dealing with the British Ministry of War Transport, but also the overseas maritime requirements of the American army, navy, Federal civilian departments and shipping agencies of the United Nations.[270] Vickery, with whom Salter intimately worked, was to direct new shipping construction. Salter found him "constructive and creative," a person who "thought, and preferred to act, on the largest scale."[271]

In the interim, however, Salter had been busy behind the scenes. He later asserted that it was the result of his lobbying with Vickery, Land and Hopkins that Lewis W. Douglas, whom he described as an administrator of "genius" with "demonic energy," was recalled from London, and appointed as advisor, then as deputy administrator to Land, dealing with allocations.[272] As well, after consulting with Land and Averell Harriman, Roosevelt's Lend-Lease representative in London and soon to be the US representative on the London counterpart, Salter wrote to Hopkins on 10 February. In his covering letter he asserted that the physical proximity of personnel was an important key to integrating two national administrations and successful collaboration. Hence he requested that he and the 70 members of his mission should be under the same roof as Land "qua shipping administrator." He also signaled that shipping allocation would be both difficult and important in 1942, given the rate of losses so far that year and the fact new building only gradually came into service. Losses for the first four weeks of 1942, he continued, would lead to an annual rate of 6¼ million gross tons, compared to 4½ million gross tons in 1941. The first attachment was a summary of points agreed upon by Salter and Hopkins. The most important was the suggestion that the CSABs in Washington and London should "be thought of neither as executively controlling any ships, nor of even recommending a programme of allocation for all ships. They will recommend allocations from one pool to the other country's service." Because the balance of transfers would be from the US to the UK, it was agreed that the main channel of negotiation would be via Salter to Land, not Harriman to Leathers. The second attachment by Salter about the CSABs' organization followed the lines of his consultations with Harriman and others. He took the White House announcement of the Boards to mean that "there will in effect be two pools of shipping and two centres of control." British and US needs, respectively, would be met by ships under their respective control. "The function of the two Boards will be to secure such interchange and combined use as will result in economy and the allocation of shipping to different services of either country in proportion to their relative importance." Such a view did not accord with American perspectives which envisioned "an agency which would carry on combined planning and programming of a joint shipping pool." Nonetheless, the organization which eventually emerged embraced the British view and "was the work primarily of Sir Arthur Salter."[273]

The first meeting of the CSAB on 16 February discussed a proposed memorandum of organization drafted by Salter. This was further fine-tuned by Land and Salter, approved by them on 20 February, and publicly announced the next day. This declared that the tasks of the CSABs "will be to prepare and maintain currently a full survey of the employment of all tonnage in both the American and British pools, to make possible economies in the use of shipping by interchange and combined use of resources, and to prepare and maintain currently a full survey of all shipping requirements."[274] During all these developments, Salter was sensitive to his own future role, as well as the executive role that Leathers exercised over British ships and the tonnage acquired by arrangement with exiled governments in London. As a consequence, he wrote to reassure Leathers that the new arrangements reaffirmed that "the main centre, not of shipping control generally, but of negotiation for allocation from one country to another, should be in Washington." He conceded that "This is, however, a paper scheme. It will only gradually become a reality." He was optimistic that with the US as a co-belligerent the future guiding principle would be the "best allocation of tonnage for a common war effort on the assumption of equal sacrifice." Salter cautioned that "the stringency of shipping is more serious in 1942 that it was in even the worst year of the last war." Finally, he praised the dedication and hard work of leading members of his organization, Maclay and Anderson, among many others. He added:

> As to myself, I had as you know some temporarily serious eye trouble last September, but have not had to have any break for the last six months. I am hard pressed now to keep the innumerable contacts necessary with U.S. authorities, our Mission and the Allies, but by this time have established personal relations with all concerned which at least make this much easier that it would otherwise be.

Salter concluded by expressing his understanding of the strain being experienced by Leathers and his Ministry. "These anxieties are not felt less acutely by us temporary exiles – especially when we feel our ability to secure relief from here reduced by the increased difficulties."[275] In his response, Leathers expressed pleasure at how well Salter's staff were performing and promised additional help if necessary. He concurred that a visit to London by Salter for "consultation and renewal of contacts" was possible at the time.[276]

By all accounts what amounted to a new Anglo-American shipping alliance and organization proved to be as Salter expected, "a slow and difficult process."[277] The reality was that American interdepartmental rivalry hindered the effective functioning of the CSAB. The WSA never clearly established administrative boundaries between civilian and military shipping management responsibilities. As a result, the army in particular was constantly at loggerheads with the WSA over shipping control questions. In addition, there remained a lingering resentment in some Washington circles that individuals such as Land, Douglas and Hopkins were too deferential to Salter and British wartime needs. The relationship between the CSAB in London and Washington was also never clearly delineated.[278] Finally, Salter's single-minded determination, regarded by some American colleagues as "manipulation," began to arouse resentment.[279] Despite such issues, Salter charged ahead, as before.

The shipping situation, in fact, had drastically deteriorated since the start of the year. To begin, as Salter wrote, "The competition too was no longer between British war needs and American peace needs but between two sets of war needs. The terrain of negotiations thus largely changed."[280] British shipping needs had to be met not at the expense of commercial and civilians requirements but out of the operations and plans of the navy and army, with each service demanding its own pool of shipping. When united, the services demands could hardly be resisted. Even more telling was the sudden rise in shipping loses in the early part of the year. According to Salter, the losses from early January to 27 March 1942 of 1,739,000 gross tons were equivalent to an annual rate of 7½ million gross tons. He further pointed out that since September 1939 shipping losses amounted to 12 million gross tons, compared with less than five million tons in the first 2½ years of the last war. He feared that there was no way to make up such losses in 1943 because of new demands from Russia, the Far East and the transport of American troops. He was also worried about UK imports, which had amounted to 44 million tons in the first year of the war, but loadings for the first quarter of 1942 were at an annual rate of 21 million tons. There was no doubt that Salter's figures, while real, were also alarmist and he shared these statistics in a letter to Hopkins on 27 March. Salter wrote, "The plain fact is that this year shipping losses are taking us rapidly along the road to perdition – and somehow a brake must be put on." He added that a high percentage of these losses were within a short distance of the shore between Canada and the Caribbean and went on to suggest various preventive measures. Salter acknowledged to Hopkins that his approach was unorthodox but it was the only "possible way of getting more 'heat' turned on. So I turn to you, as everyone does." Hopkins thought Salter was "getting a little out of his bailiwick," but advised Roosevelt to read the letter.[284]

Salter's urgency was further reflected at the highest levels, with Churchill writing to Roosevelt on 5 March: "Everything however turns upon shipping." Later Churchill reflected that at this point in the war, "Shipping was at once the stranglehold and sole foundation of our war strategy."[282] On 13 March the Maritime Commission announced an increase in its 1942-1943 "Victory" ship construction programme from 18 million to 20 million deadweight tons, thereby adding another 200 ships.[283] In the meantime, however, losses continued to exceed the US building programme. For Salter this meant greater attention had to be paid to questions of allocation. This became the focus of attention as the CSABs developed, because they raised a challenge to the American decentralized system of procurement, building and allocation. Further questions of organization and personnel formed the agenda of the CSABs early meetings and not unexpectedly Salter was a leading contributor. In fact, he successfully argued against an early suggestion to include representatives of the army and navy.[284] From the outset he had always argued that the CSABs would only work if each side knew "everything relevant about all requirements and all the ships of both groups of countries."[285] For such reasons Salter supported the early formation of a Cargo Clearance Committee when it was discussed at the CSAB meeting on 27 February. He approved of the formation of such a committee for relating import and export requirements to the availability of shipping and that it be attached to the CSAB. At the same meeting, Salter laid out a lengthy agenda on policy issues, including the clearance of high priority cargoes and the need to prepare statistical returns on the shipping position at any time.[286] Although the Cargo Clearance Committee was approved at the CSAB meeting on 4 March, significantly its responsibilities excluded establishing priorities between projected military operations and other claims on shipping. Finally, Salter pressed for closer liaison with the USSR on shipping matters, and the forms for statistical returns both for "operation" and "information" were approved.[287]

On occasion the work of the CSAB was interrupted by wartime events. On the eve of the surrender of the Netherlands East Indies to Japan, for example, the CSAB met on 6 March to discuss the disposition of some 40 Dutch ships overseas or at Allied ports. Salter, naturally, argued that these Dutch ships should be chartered in London and become part of the British pool. He contended this would reduce the need for allocations to Britain from the American pool, but finally agreed to a compromise allocation.[288] In the following meetings, however, the CSAB returned to its more usual tasks of allocations of tonnage from one pool to the other and finding shipping efficiencies, such as combining cargoes. Salter focused on what had emerged as a major problem. The issue of allocation, by definition, was closely linked to questions of priorities.²⁸⁹ The practical problems, notably the threat to UK imports declining in importance in relation to Soviet demands for war materials, continued to be discussed at the CSAB meetings of 11 and 25 March. Salter almost demanded of the Board that shipping for imports into the UK and for military supplies to the Middle East, the so-called Red Sea service, should be regarded as having a priority as high as that accorded to any other service." In response, Lewis Douglas stated that "the basic question was how priorities could be established in an orderly manner. That was the most serious question underlying the whole shipping situation," and neither the Board nor the WSA could decide such strategic questions. Salter agreed that "it would be some time before the most difficult organizational problem of the war would be settled." He preferred, however, not to press the point at this time.²⁹⁰

Despite this, Salter returned to the charge at the CSAB meeting on 1 April and, as usual, spoke his mind. He asserted that decisions were being made which pushed other services down in the priority scale and without consideration of their possible adverse effects. For example, he pointed out, for UK imports there was a point below, if the service fell, the British could not continue their war effort. He also urged that priority should be given to maintaining the volume of ships in the Red Sea service. Thus he insisted that "machinery should be brought into operation to secure the appropriate priority rating," with such decisions being made after due consideration of all effects and then make recommendations to the president and prime minister. Salter then visualized how such a procedure would operate, beginning with a comprehensive balance sheet of available and required shipping which was the "foundation for all fully informed action." He continued, in a very frank manner, to look at the organizational problems, beside the tonnage ones. He stated that it had been his hope that by this time, 1 April 1942, the CSAB and other boards "would have attained a position where allocations of tonnage would be made in relation to a reasonable determination of the relative importance of requirements." He concluded, "The system did not, however, yet work as had been hoped." Both he and Land agreed that the WSA was not yet in control of American shipping, and in particular allocations to the army. In the interim, Salter suggested that the deficit in each national pool should be approximately equal, and hence any ships becoming available, including Dutch shipping, be placed in the British pool. Both Land and Douglas promised to follow up on Salter's recommendations.²⁹¹ Those regarding allocation and priority machinery were ultimately aborted, and his vision of the board system was never fully materialized.²⁹²

The blunt views Salter aired at this CSAB meeting were indicative of his mood at this time. On 30 March he had dined, along with Douglas, at Stimson's home. Here he pressed again the issue of British priority shipping needs for the Middle East, suggesting that a lack of assistance might lead to a withdrawal from the area. Stimson was unmoved but thought the discussion was "carried on in the best of spirit."[293] On 6 April, a year after his arrival in Washington, Salter wrote a long letter to Leathers, in which he tried to rise above daily events and intended as he put it, to "painting the general background of our work here." It also appeared to be an effort to counter criticism that his mission might have been prone to "half-hearted support of the British view by British representatives here." Reminding Leathers that he had been working and negotiating with Americans for a quarter of a century, he wrote that he "found them generally good to work with, on very certain definite conditions, and subject to certain very real dangers." They were "capable of generosity on a large scale, and very hard bargainers if they feel that it is a bargain that is being made. There is a particular combination of the generous idealist and the horse-trader, with a mood that switches quickly from the first to the second." As for his colleagues, he described Land as an "executive person" who improvised, found planning of shipping policy irksome and difficult, but possessed "shrewdness and common sense." As for Douglas, Salter thought of him as having "a first rate intellectual, as well as practical, ability. He thinks ahead and around his problems; is subtle, industrious and, with a quiet and persuasive manner, strong-willed." Like Roosevelt and Hopkins, Salter wrote, Douglas "wants to win the war as they do, and will subordinate everything to that end." Thus he was devoting himself to expanding the WSA which in time, Salter went on, along with the CSAB would be improved. He then pointed out that American shipping personalities inevitably looked at the post-war situation and saw American mercantile shipping as replacing pre-war British maritime hegemony. Given this new attitude, Britain had "to adjust our methods of negotiation." The Americans had to be convinced "to take on a job, which we should otherwise have to do, as a job of their own," and "to make the 'partnership' conception, which is now supposed to determine the way in which we allocate the tonnage under our respective controls, a reality."

Salter continued to review his mission's first year. His strategy, which he regarded as successful, consisted of placing all the facts of the shipping situation before the relevant authorities, putting it "as a world picture, and not as a British picture," with shipbuilding needed to meet future world shortages and not mere British requirements. As for the current shipping situation, he emphasized that "the most important general objective to aim at is that of making the 'partnership' idea, implicit in the Combined Board System, a reality." He continued:

> To put this another way, this means doing everything to encourage the 'generous' not the 'horse-trading' mood. This is obviously the more important because when it comes to 'trading' the Americans have almost all the cards

almost all the time, since it is we and not they who have existing and inescapable commitments beyond our own shipping resources.

Salter held out hope that the "partnership" idea would eventually prevail, however, the struggle for control of resources would continue, with the US War Department overriding the WSA. He concluded with the expectation that the previous nine months of increased imports over consumption would provide "some consolation to you in the dangerous days ahead."[294] The next day he shared some thoughts regarding his first year in Washington, writing to Nancy Nettlefold:

Ethel and I have been here for a year. It has been anxious, difficult, exacting but hitherto, as far as my own work is concerned, successful. On the basis of the war as it was before December 7, we should have had the shipping problem solved. Now it is more anxious than at any time even in the worst of the last war. We have both been well. Ethel is quite astonishingly stronger than two years ago. She still has recurrent pain but has extraordinary vitality and recuperative power.[295]

Informed by Salter's update, Leathers provided the War Cabinet on 9 April with an assessment of the shipping situation. It began with a caution that "The uncertainties of the shipping situation are probably now greater than at any previous time," partly due to the uncertainty about how much of new US merchant shipping would accrue to Britain, and partly to the military situation in the Far East. Leathers reminded the War Cabinet that at the beginning of 1942 Salter had warned that the future position of American shipping assistance to the United Kingdom was worsening and could not meet "all the new demands and projects." The only option was to estimate carrying capacity on the basis of existing British resources and what was in construction for Britain in the United States. He also mentioned a recent telegram from Salter that estimated shipbuilding in the United States for 1942 might slip back by 300,000 gross tons, although the prospect for 1943 was somewhat improved, with a projected net gain of five million gross tons.[296] In a further assessment which Salter compiled on 11 April, he noted it would be possible to meet 1942 shipping demands only if losses could be kept down to six million tons deadweight. Nonetheless, he cautioned that whatever the rate of attrition and building, vital decisions with regards to priorities would have to be taken; one such issue was whether to allow food stocks to fall in the UK to the point of starvation.[297]

In the following weeks Salter's main preoccupation became the meetings of the CSAB and its resultant issues. He continuously pressed for improvements in the statistical data, particularly requirements and available tonnage, thereby avoiding "the danger of 'bunching' of ships in excess of port capacity." And even before priorities had been established, Salter pressed for adequate shipping to be maintained between the United State and Australia, South Africa and India. The latter was an issue which had a successful outcome thanks to his influence.[298] Questions relating to the support capacity of Russian ports and railroads also concerned him and he pressed that this issue be handled by the CSAB in Washington rather than in London. In fact, he was equally forthright in expressing his concerns at the Council on North American Supplies. However, his proposal there to set up a special organization to deal with supplies and shipping to the USSR was defeated.[299] On 5 May, after much delay, the Priorities and Allocations Committee held its first meeting. Although it had been strongly championed by Salter, and he worked hard to get it properly organized, the committee held few meetings and then lapsed. This was to some extent "a reflection upon the limitations and uncertainties which surrounded the whole combined board undertaking from the very beginning."[300] As for the CSAB it continued to deal with issues as disparate as negotiating with members of the United Nations for representation on the Board, desertions of shipping crew members, congestion at the port of Halifax, new convoy arrangements, and compensation for Danish shipping taken over by the United States. In addition, on 14 May Salter informed Leathers that the US had agreed to place 70 tankers at the disposal of the UK because of severe tankers losses, despite the fact that this might lead to changes in the shipbuilding programme. When thanking Roosevelt for these tankers, Churchill wrote that without them stocks in the UK "would have fallen to a dangerous level by the end of the year."[301] The high losses led to a brief moment when the CSAB debated whether to start building wooden ships, but Salter was among those expressing strong reservations to this desperate ploy.[302]

On 20 May Salter's appeal, initially made to Hopkins on 10 February, finally succeeded. On that day he and his staff, by then 80 strong, moved into the Department of Commerce Building which already housed Land's WSA, the Maritime Commission and where Salter's new office was adjacent to Land and Douglas.[303] In fact, that same day the announcement was made that Douglas had been elevated from Land's "chief advisor" to his deputy director with executive powers over the contentious issue of allocation. Salter had advance notice of this appointment and wrote that it confirmed his original judgment: "He is extremely able; a man of great strength of character who desires to subordinate every other interest to the most effective prosecution of the war." Salter then proposed that he return on a visit to London, accompanied by Douglas, to confer with Churchill and review questions of organization and outlook, a request which this time was granted.[304] After 14 months in Washington, Salter observed that the reality of separate missions in London and Washington meant that there were "always two alternative centres, and two channels of communication." However, he reaffirmed his view regarding "the imperative necessity of having one centre of negotiation, and one channel of communication, for each particular problem." He recommended that where a proposal needed "executive action by the U.S. Government the centre must be Washington (and the channel Leathers-A.S.-Land)" with Harriman in a secondary role. And where a proposal needed "executive action by the British Government the centre must be London (and the channel Land-Harriman-Leathers)" with his own intervention again being merely supportive. Reasons for such an approach, he concluded, were overwhelming because it was "essential that the real argument should be where the Executive power resides." Salter finally noted that he and Harriman had agreed to these principles of negotiations.[305]

By early June it was evident at the CSAB meetings in Washington that closer integration of joint Anglo-American production programmes was required. In Salter's view "the problem was partly one of assignment of material and partly one of production."[306] Added to the complication was the emergence of the "Bolero Programme," designed to build up the forces needed to open a future "second front" in Europe. This was discussed for the first time in the CSAB on 10 June, when both Douglas and Salter agreed that the needs of Bolero, along with an increasing rate of shipping loses and rising demands for supplies to the USSR, made it necessary to determine priorities. The same meeting also heard from Harriman, then on a visit to Washington, who confessed that the London Combined Board "had done little so far on concerting general plans for the combined usage of tonnage," but had dealt with problems as they arose. He also advised that the Ministry of War Transport had little idea of what American shipping assistance was available in the short term and the long range effects of new building."[307]

In the context of this complex and dangerous situation, and with a mission to more closely integrate British and American production programmes, the British Minister of Production, Sir Oliver Lyttleton, had arrived in Washington on 3 June.[308] In a brief he prepared for the minister, Salter projected that the total transporting capacity in 1942 would only be equal to that of 1941. However, given extra demands, such as shipments to the USSR, the Pacific war, the need to transport US forces and supplies to Britain, increased naval use of merchant ships and Bolero plans, reductions and economies would have to be made. He recommended that the US army would have to scale back its supply programmes and implement a policy of "direct, instead of indirect, shipment." This meant that any supplies produced and shipped from the US were to go directly to the theatre of war, rather than shipped via the UK. He also foresaw that total available tonnage by the end of 1943 would exceed anything since the outbreak of the war, naturally depending on annual losses. He cautioned that, in the final analysis, "shipping will continue to set the limit to military effort."[309] On his arrival Lyttleton discovered that the US army authorities were proposing to take over the entire war production of the United States, with very little assigned to Britain. As a result, consultations led to the announcement on 10 June to set up the British conceived Combined Production and Resources Board, an effort to combine Anglo-American production into a single integrated programme. In effect, all future production was to be related to the requirements of "the defensive and offensive theatres of war by the 1st April 1943." This new effort at establishing strategic benchmarks had important implications for the Salter Shipping Mission. At its first meeting on 17 June the Combined Production and Resources Board was given instructions to prioritize materials and facilities for merchant ships and other naval shipbuilding, and "to submit a survey of shipping available for strategic production and import plans for 1943." The meeting also endorsed the important proposal, "direct, instead of indirect, shipment." Salter had urged this on Lyttleton, then aired by Salter at the CSAB on 3 June, and then reframed as a joint letter by him and Land to the new Combined Production and Resources Board.[310]

The arrival of Churchill in Washington on 18 June also kept Salter busy. He joined the prime minister on 23 June for a lunch meeting with Roosevelt at the White House, officially described as "one of the most important conferences" of the visit. The others included Hopkins, Harriman, King, Land, Douglas and naval advisers.[311] The discussion centred on the question of adjusting the production of escort vessels and merchant ships. There was a need for extra escort vessels to protect coastwise shipping and the newly instituted American convoy system. After much discussion this was agreed with the proviso that this programme would not cut into the output of merchant ships coming into service during the "vitally important period between the Autumn of 1942 and the Summer of 1943."[312] Immediately following this meeting, and at Churchill's request, Salter provided several notes, including a copy of the brief he had prepared for Lyttleton, and another on the risks and benefits of increasing the troop capacity of the two "Queens."[313]

It was now almost a year that Salter had been forced to delay his visit to London. Since then the shipping situation had become both more precarious because of losses off the coast of North America and more complicated because of Japanese triumphs in the Far East and the needs of Bolero. His absence from the House of Commons had occasionally been noted by the leader of the Independent Labour Party, James Maxton. On 25 June, for example, Maxton asked whether, when in Washington, Lyttleton had met Salter "who has been roaming about there for over a year?" Lyttleton responded in the affirmative but it rested with Lady Astor to rise to

Salter's defence, stating that he "is doing very good and useful work." The Manchester Guardian, reporting on Maxton's remark, noted that Salter was "the most successful British representative" in Washington.[314] At last on 4 July, aboard the same flight as Lord and Lady Halifax, Salter returned to London and took up residence once again at the Connaught Hotel. The following days proved to be busy ones. He consulted with colleagues at the Ministry of War Transport, conferred with members of the London CSAB and attended several War Cabinet meetings. He returned to take his seat in the House of Commons and, most importantly, continued to consult and plan for the pooling and production of shipping needed to implement the strategic decisions made by Churchill and Roosevelt in Washington. As Salter later observed, his visit coincided with a shipping situation in which "we were again in an extremely grave crisis."[315] Indeed, the War Cabinet had been informed on 25 June that the shipping situation over the next 12 months would become critical unless the German U-boat campaign could be contained.[316]

On 8 July, and in the following days, Salter mainly answered questions in the House of Commons. These largely concerned issues such as how to restrict unnecessary rail travel by the public and to facilitate quicker railway travel for the armed forces, sanitation aboard troop ships, the possible post-war nationalization of the railways, why extra summer holiday trains were being permitted, and whether sufficient steps were being taken to recycle the many iron signposts on country roads.[317] However, among the main purposes of his leave was to brief fellow members of the House. On the morning of 8 July he had attended a meeting of the War Cabinet at 10 Downing Street. The discussion centred on the forthcoming Commons' debate on the shipping situation. When Churchill suggested that Salter open the debate, he demurred, noting that the House "Wd. resent opening speech by person known to have bn. out of the House for 15 months." It was finally agreed that the debate would be held on 16 July in secret and with the reply made by Salter. His instructions were to not disclose exact figures for shipping losses or new naval construction, and that the balance between losses and new building was to be stated in general terms.[318] Despite some considerable opposition to a secret session, both in public and even within the House, the debate went ahead. Salter later recounted that "The Government, Parliament and the country realized that the fate of this war might turn on the position of our merchant shipping. We had a Debate which was in secret and had to be in secret."[319]

Doubtless, Salter's contribution to the secret session, besides the update on the American shipbuilding effort and Anglo-American pooling arrangements, would have included some alarming information brought to the attention of the War Cabinet. The first report from a special Shipping Committee, appointed in May, examined requirements for the period from January 1942 to June 1943. Without additional and substantial American assistance the prospects were regarded as "grave."[320] This was accompanied by increasing loses, with the news from the WSA that during the week of 12 July sinkings had reached the highest level since the beginning of the war, in fact exceeding new construction.[321] Indeed, Salter's tasks for his return to Washington were affirmed both at cabinet meetings, after the secret sessions debate, and in numerous other meetings and consultations in early August. On 20 July and again on 28 July Churchill told the War Cabinet that, before agreeing to reduce imports, Britain had to have assurances about the tonnage that would be available in 1943 from the United States. He urged that the approach to Washington should now be based on the need to provide shipping to import 25 million tons of dry cargo in 1942 and 27 million tons in 1943 as the "irreducible minima." Further, he stated that shipping for the Bolero operation should rank as a second priority to the imports programme.[322] The following day the first, and most important, of four joint sessions of the London and Washington CSABs was held at Berkeley Square House. Salter, Douglas, recently arrived in London, along with Leathers and Harriman attended. The meeting approved a statement which forecast the amount of shipping available until 31 March 1943 to meet the requirements of Bolero and similar operations. The situation was further discussed at 10 Downing Street, at a special meeting on 31 July, chaired by Churchill, with Harriman, Douglas, Leathers, Cherwell and Salter. It was agreed that the prime minister would write to Roosevelt to emphasize that there "would be a deficiency of 1.55 million gross tons between the amount of shipping available for supplementing the British war effort and for meeting Bolero requirements and the amount which was required for these two purposes."[323]

Even as his future tasks were being formulated at the War Cabinet, London provided Salter with some additional opportunities to advance his future work in Washington. On 6 August he attended a meeting of the North American Supply Committee, which had not met in some time. Under its newly agreed terms of reference, a revived North American Supply Committee was "to consider questions of Anglo-American economic and supply policy which affect more than one Department or are not covered by existing Committees." As well, it was to consider any issues of policy arising out of the work of the various Combined Boards or Committees. The terms of reference of the British Supply Council in North America were then also modified and now clearly reflected Salter's contention "that it should be clearly recognized that the centre where the activities of the British representatives on the Combined Boards would be fused into a single policy was the North American Supply Committee in London, rather than the Supply Council."[324] Douglas' presence in London at this time along with Salter's also allowed for a series of discussions on improving the work of the Washington and London CSAB. As well, in order to secure better collaboration between the WSA and the Ministry of War Transport, agreement was reached to give "each National Agency the responsibility for shipping programmes to particular areas."[325]

London provided other diversions for Salter. On 24 July he had assisted in the opening ceremony of a Merchant Navy Club, housed in a former restaurant in Rupert Street, London.[326] In his little spare time, he corresponded with colleagues on war-related questions, including Lionel Curtis with whom he discussed post-war ideas about federal union. On that subject Salter took a very cautious view, referring Curtis to the passage in <u>Security</u>, "union where possible, 'compacts' where they're not."[327] The Reform Club provided a retreat where he could meet with various acquaintances. For example, after a conversation with Salter on 22 July A.G. Gardiner wrote: "I found him remarkably cheerful (you know how cautious & restrained he is naturally) & most enthusiastic about America. This is comforting to me for there is no one on whose judgment in this war (as in the last) I rely on more than Salter's. It was a mercy he was sent out to Washington which is the key to the Atlantic situation."[328] Finally, on 14 July, "Molly" Hamilton had dined with Lady Sybil Colefax at the Connaught Hotel. After Salter briefly joined them, "Molly" Hamilton wrote, "A. Salter joined us for a half hour, looking very fit & gay."[329]

As he prepared to leave London on 13 August, after a period which he described as "a terrible rush," Salter could look back at three important developments, among others, during his stay. The 27 million ton UK import programme for 1943 was agreed to and taken into the calculation of shipping required to move American troops to Britain. Secondly, it was agreed that the thorny question of the permanent transfer of flag and title with respect to "net tonnage lost (i.e., losses in excess of gains)" would be dealt with as part of the post-war settlement. Finally, agreed was the notion "to divide the world geographically on the basis of Import Programmes" with separate responsibilities for the WSA and the Ministry of War Transport.[330] On his return to Washington, Salter soon faced a very different shipping picture. At a meeting on 19 August of the CSAB, and then the British Supply Council in North America, he suggested that in order to merge the requirements of the US army and the UK import programmes "it was necessary to treat the ships, cargoes, and ports on a combined basis."[331] He again pressed the same point at a meeting of the CSAB on 26 August, suggesting that the time had arrived to prepare a "written picture of the shipping situation" for presentation to all the other combined boards and to the Combined Chiefs of Staff.[332] At this point, Salter took his first week of holiday since arriving in Washington. He joined Lady Salter at Hickory Farm where she had spent the summer.[333]

In the following weeks statistics began to show that total buildings were beginning to exceed total losses, even as British shipping requirements were becoming very serious.[334] A paper prepared by the CSAB on 31 August indicated that to date the United Nations had a net loss of 2.8 million deadweight tons. This situation meant that greater military requirements had to be met from reduced tonnage capacity. As a result, among many recommendations, was the exhortation to increase shipbuilding in the United States, decided when the two Boards had met in London in late July and early August.[335] As a consequence, the Merchant Shipping Mission engaged in intensive negotiations with the WSA. As usual Salter worked behind the scenes, writing to Hopkins on 12 September, firstly to congratulate him on his marriage. Then Salter continued:

> This is a very crucial stage of the shipping problem. For, at last, we may reasonably hope that more ships will be coming out of the yards each month than are being sunk, while at the same time this surplus will be much less than what are needed for a developing military effort; and the existing mechanism and procedures for deciding up to what point each of many competing claims for tonnage shall be met at the expense of the rest is clearly not adequate, now that the issues are so vital.

The letter ended with an invitation for Hopkins to join Salter and Douglas with their wives for dinner at 2326 California Street.[336] Soon afterwards Salter contributed to the nationwide observance of Victory Fleet Day on the anniversary of the launching of the first Liberty cargo ship, the SS Patrick Henry, on 27 September 1941. In a radio broadcast, he revealed that the Allies were producing new cargo ships at a rate which offset sinkings by German submarines. He continued, "How soon victory comes will, therefore, depend upon how quickly we can carry America's strength across the seas." Equally encouraging was the announcement from the Maritime Commission that the shipbuilding goal of eight million deadweight tons for 1942 would be achieved.[337]

In the meanwhile Salter kept pondering how to allocate the prospective excess of building over losses, and especially "to increase monthly allocations to British services so as to meet British deficiency accruing each month."[338] In a memorandum completed on 26 September, he calculated that for the period 1 September to 31 December 1942, assuming a US building surplus over a British deficit, there would be a surplus of over two million deadweight tons of shipping. He proposed, therefore, "That there should be a normal increase in allocations of U.S. tonnage in aid of services within the British sphere of responsibility corresponding to monthly British net tonnage losses," subject to changing circumstances. In future, he concluded, "it should be regarded as normal to add to the monthly standard allocation to British services as much tonnage as to correspond approximately to the net deficiency in the last month for which records were available," namely beginning with August.

He concluded by suggesting that what he was proposing was "only a directive to make what was already understood as to the character of the United Nations surplus effective."[339] In effect, Salter was advising, subject to revision and circumstances, the principle of replacing losses. Its primary advantage was "that the basis of monthly allocations would be a simple arithmetical fact, namely, gains and losses, not an argument as to need extending over the whole range of requirements."[340]

Salter's relentless pursuit of this objective, besides its merits in the eyes of some and opposition from others, was successful. On 6 October the WSA, with the approval of the CSAB, announced that:

> an appropriate portion of the net gain in the merchant tonnage of the U.S. shall be used to relieve the burden of the war services of each of the United Nations. The monthly amount of any net gain should be measured by their respective needs to maintain as nearly as possible their unimpaired war activities, their remaining net gain to be employed for the expanding war effort in any such directions as appropriate authority may decide.[341]

Here indeed was a new and revised shipping agenda for the Salter Shipping Mission to pursue. However, as early as 6 October Douglas cautioned that "the full application of these principles must be expected to take effect only over a period of time."[342] His note was informed by the growing realization in Washington that the entire combined board system was not functioning effectively. In the view of the Bureau of the Budget, this was partly because of "a reluctance to submerge national programs in the greater combined needs."[343] On 3 November Salter had warned Leathers that the shipping situation in Washington was dominated by the demands of the American army and navy, leaving British needs in a dangerous situation. "This situation brings out clearly fundamental defeat of combined system viz. absence of effective combined strategy. In other words C.S.A.B. can function efficiently within framework of combined strategy but not otherwise."[344] Nonetheless, the first of the new monthly allocations meetings was held on 6 November. It was agreed that the calculation of losses should begin as of 1 August when the United Nations surplus had begun to emerge.[345] This decision, still needing to be finalized, coincided with the arrival in Washington on 4 November of Lyttleton for a month long visit. Lyttleton brought a letter from Churchill to Roosevelt, dated 31 October, that focused attention away from Salter's preference for replacement of losses with the prime minister's personal appeal for maintaining a minimum programme of 27 million tons of imports for 1943.[346]

Salter and his mission had been forewarned on 31 October of this change and feared that "there was a danger that the negotiations on the more advantageous basis of replacement of ship losses would be frustrated," and that the authority of the CSAB would be endangered. During the succeeding days it appears that the Salter's expertise was somewhat ignored. On 12 November he wrote to Leathers and provided several memoranda which reflected the lines upon which he had been negotiating with the WSA. "I have been deeply conscious that we should be fighting a losing battle if we had to struggle day by day, and month by month, for extra ships without the aid of any general 'directive' or understanding, or accepted principle." As a result he advocated that "Much the best principle to cling to was that of compensation for net lose." The advantage was "that it had, at its base, incontestable facts (viz. the sinkings and buildings) and not estimates." Salter respected the fact that Lyttleton was "trying the '2½ million related to the 27 million import'," but sensed that such a guarantee would likely be broken in 1943 under the pressure of war.[347] The final American reply, in a letter on 30 November from Roosevelt to Churchill, was drafted by Hopkins and later shown to Salter. It confirmed that the 27 million tons of imports was substantially correct, that "this pipeline of food and material" would be maintained, and promised to increase merchant shipbuilding to 18 million deadweight tons. Roosevelt added that his reply was by way of a statement of policy and that monthly allocations, subject to change, would still be the responsibility of the CSAB.[348]

Whatever Salter's views on this matter, he generally preferred not to speak out at the time. After the war, however, he observed that "It is true that the method of approach and the form of the aid requested was somewhat different from what we had been adopting in the Mission. But the total aid sought was almost as identical." He added, however, that the discussions between Lyttelton, Hopkins and Roosevelt "were carried on with too little participation of either Land or myself, and that Land and his office were naturally a little froissés." Salter was inclined to dismiss the episode as a minor procedural difference, but he understood that the situation was more difficult with the US as a co-belligerent requiring shipping for itself.[349] Indeed, he had confided to Leathers on 7 November that the increased demands of the US army and navy, without a combined Anglo-American strategy, were endangering the future of the CSAB.[350] Further, at a meeting of the North American Supply Committee on 11 November, Salter noted that there were still defects and lapses which hindered negotiations with American wartime agencies.[351] At a meeting of the CSAB on 1 December, Salter referred to the previous discussions between Roosevelt and Lyttleton, and expected that the results would be reported to the Board.[352] This proved not to be the case for some time. When providing a written report for the War Cabinet on 9 December, after his return to London on 5 December, Lyttleton noted *inter alia* that he and Salter had had discussions with Land and Vickery "who were both emphatic that they could build 20 million tons of merchant ships in 1943 without encroaching on other programmes, if they were given the materials." After examining future supplies of bulk steel, however, a programme of 18 million deadweight tons was agreed. Lyttleton also noted, "I tried, at the instigation of Sir Arthur Salter and Mr. Lew Douglas, to get the White House to accept a formula by which British nett [sic] shipping losses – as from the 1st August 1942 – would be made up from the nett [sic] gain in American shipping. This was refused." He observed finally that "I would not like my colleagues to think that the task of Sir Arthur Salter and Mr. Lew Douglas will be an easy one. The monthly adjustments of tonnage necessary to fulfill the programmes will always be a matter of difficulty. Both men are first-rate at their job" and Douglas was committed to "the principle of carrying on the war as an alliance and as a combined struggle."[353]

While Lyttleton was in Washington, it had been announced in London on 23 November that Colonel J.J. Llewellin had been appointed to the new position of Minister Resident in Washington for Supply. His responsibilities, as explained to the War Cabinet, were to co-ordinate the work of the British civilian missions and members of various Combined Boards. Specifically excluded from his duties was any intervention, for example, in the work of the Salter Shipping Mission, except if requested by Salter.[354] Reassurance on this point came directly from Leathers who wrote to Salter on 17 December: "I think that the upshot of all this is that you will be left undisturbed to carry on your work, the very high value of which is recognized by everyone on this side."[355] Such reassurances were well received. At the start of the New Year, having heard rumours of such an appointment, Salter had written to Leathers, noting his very strong misgivings about such a move and its possible negative impact both on the minister and Salter himself.[356]

Even as he received these assurances from London, Salter's work in Washington grew more difficult. On 4 December Salter noted that he was still awaiting details from the WSA with regard to implementation and procedure.[357] With the approval of Hopkins, Douglas wrote to Salter on 11 December reminding him of the 6 October declaration by the WSA and the 30 November letter from Roosevelt to Churchill. Both documents, Douglas cautioned, contained a series of restrictions and limitations which enabled the President to retain freedom of action to modify any tonnage allocations.[358] On 15 December, at a meeting of the CSAB, Salter urged Land to confirm the addition of 2.8 million tons of shipping to the building programme for 1943. This Land did, but offered no information about how demands would be divided between different types of vessels.[359] On 22 December Salter advised Douglas of the seriousness of the UK's position with regards to declining imports. "What we need to draw up," Salter urged Douglas, "is a 'standard allocation' month by month, which takes into account the already known factors which will necessitate a lower allocation in the earlier months and adjusts in later months so as to give, as nearly as can now be calculated, the total result required." Salter added that his mission had already begun the preliminary research and statistical work for such a schedule of available shipping and projected allocations.[360] At the meeting of the CSAB on 31 December he again took the initiative to press the Board to be more proactive on the question of allocations. He pointed out that a month had elapsed since the undertaking was given. While his discussions with Douglas were continuing, Salter noted that the undertaking "was obviously an integral factor hence-forth in the CSAB work." He followed this with a series of no less than six proposals, all but one approved, to implement the future central role to be played by the CSAB for a schedule of monthly allocations from January to November 1943. Salter's initial strategy thus appeared to have been generally effective.[361]

On the first day of the New Year Salter informed Leathers that "the principal factor in the whole situation" was the renewed and strong attempt by both the American army and navy to control their own pools of shipping.[362] The next day he advised Leathers that Roosevelt's letter of 30 November had created considerable difficulties for all British missions in Washington. It had still not been officially communicated to the relevant American departments, had created further anti-British resentment in army and navy circles, and aggravated relations between the WSA and the War Department. Salter could only reassure Leathers that he was "pressing as urgently as possible for schedule of implementation."[363] When Salter next raised the subject at the CSAB meeting on 5 January 1943, he met sharper opposition than previously. Douglas insisted that his priority was to have Salter provide the fullest possible information on available British shipping before projecting monthly allocations of American shipping for the British.[364] Thus Salter completed another memorandum, "The Record of 1942 and the Prospects for 1943." In his view August 1942 was the turning point in the balance of losses and gains, largely because of the increase in US building. However, the prospects for 1943 would require implementing Roosevelt's promise to Churchill of 30 November. Indeed, Salter even argued that an additional half million deadweight tons of dry cargo vessels would be required monthly, largely for the transportation of troops and materials. In essence, he argued that the shipping problem for 1943 would be "increased demand, not reduced tonnage."[365] As a follow up, he presented Douglas with a draft target schedule for allocations which he suggested be used by the WSA, as well as estimates of available British tonnage for 1943.[366] In addition, Salter received permission from Leathers to share virtually every detail of British wartime shipping resources and requirements.[367]

As if to add further pressure, in a radio broadcast Salter warned that U-boats were being built faster than they were being destroyed. "The battle of the sea lanes is still anxious and critical," he stated.[368] Further meetings of the CSAB on 13 and 18 January, however, revealed that the American members were not going to allow Salter to use the Board to affect allocations to Britain. Indeed, at the special meeting of 18 January, Land and Douglas communicated to the CSAB instructions received by the WSA from Roosevelt implementing his 30 November letter to Churchill, regarding allocations of American controlled tonnage to British service in 1943. Salter immediately voiced his concern that the projected WSA assistance would leave a deficiency in 1943 of at least seven million tons in the UK import program. The WSA inferred that the tonnage assistance was only an estimate and not a commitment. Indeed, if it was found that projected UK imports for 1943 of 27 million tons could be further reduced, then allocated tonnage would be correspondingly reduced.[369] Writing to Leathers and Hurcomb the following day, Salter explained that he understood the proposed allocation would only give additional imports for the first half of the year of a little over one million tons, whereas the deficit for 1943 stood at over seven million tons. He added that the WSA would in future be doing its own statistical calculations for allocations to the UK. However, he was hopeful of getting increased allocations from March onwards.[370] Salter's estimates were reported to the War Cabinet with suggestions about possible future economies in food consumption and raw material stocks.[371] The impact of the discussion, and its immediate fallout, indicated that the issue of allocation was now largely outside the purview of the CSAB.

It was clear that Salter both appreciated and reluctantly accepted the new roadmap in Washington. Speaking at the North American Supply Council on 20 January, he was already looking ahead when he emphasized the importance of making sure to fill the additional shipping space which was to be provided.[372] In the following days he was continuously in touch with Leathers, trying to put the best face on the turn of affairs. On 1 February he cabled that he was indeed hopeful of increased allocations from March onwards. However, he cautioned against any protest over the head of the WSA by an immediate message from Churchill to Roosevelt on the issues. He suggested waiting until the decisions at the Casablanca Conference, which had just ended on 24 January, were brought into the picture. He was aware that several of these were taken without properly calculating what British and American shipping was available for the import programme. Indeed, he hinted that his main preoccupation was calculation of tonnage for military operations.[373] The minutes of the CSAB meeting of 4 February record that Salter strongly defended the expertise of the civilian shipping authorities with regard to the rate of new building, though he conceded that the naval authorities were the experts with regard to estimating shipping loses. Nonetheless, he pointedly informed the board that future allocations would be largely negotiated directly between the Ministry of War Transport in London and the WSA in Washington.[374] In a conversation with Douglas on 5 February, Salter made one last effort to secure additional allocations, noting, "great immediate assistance was essential without regard to longer term reviews." Salter's record of the conversation suggested that Douglas held out some hope with respect to additional allocations.[375]

On 11 February the schedule of assistance proposed by the WSA for the first five months of 1943 was communicated by Douglas to Salter and then discussed that day at the CSAB. The proposal was to increase the deadweight available for dry cargo to 1,665,000 tons in the first five months of 1943, amounting to a net improvement in the British import position of about three quarters of a million tons. Salter graciously offered his appreciation for the work done and its generosity.[376] As he worked through the implications of the WSA's communication, he was careful to caution Leathers that the proposed allocations were subject to the risk of new military demands, but were drawn up after thorough enquiries. Leathers informed the War Cabinet on 10 February of the allocations and of Salter's advice to await new figures from the WSA. On 18 February Leathers cabled his agreement with Salter's approach.[377] Not surprisingly, however, by the end of February Salter was already advising Leathers that other military needs, including Bolero as previously but now also Anakim (the plan to retake Burma), posed serious threats to the allocation schedule.[378]

Looking back at these developments, Salter observed that while "the actual bulk of the Shipping Mission's work is still increasing, it will consist henceforth mainly of detailed adjustments, not of major negotiations." Among the tasks, for example, he had to undertake during February was to lobby to protect the allocations against other emerging military needs, even as he realized that Roosevelt could override the schedule any time.[379] On 22 February, he had written to Lady Astor:

Washington, as you may imagine, is more than ever a buzzing hive – not many drones in it, I think, but certainly hornets as well as bees – & stings as well as honey. My own shipping work becomes continuously more exacting, as the proportion of U.S. ships needed in British services goes up & general demands made by the military services of both countries increase. Lew Douglas is the man I deal most directly with, & I am very fortunate that that is so. He is certainly one of the most remarkable men in the country & with the right point of view.[380]

Specifically with regard to the CSAB Salter admitted that its powers were quite diminished. Though it continued to have a vested interest in the balance of shipping and requirements, future decisions lay with the WSA, the Maritime Commission and with Land and Vickery.[381] Indeed, after the first week of March the CSAB no longer met weekly. The agendas included such items as cargo movements, finding an agreed loss rate and civilian supplies for North Africa.[382] The larger issue of the "shipping aspects of military requirements," as Leathers put it to Salter on 6 March was the crux and the minister proposed that Salter's Shipping Mission should be enlarged to include a small sea transport section. Noting that the work in relation to military projects was growing, Salter welcomed any additional help. He insisted, however, that the complications between military and civilian authorities in the US necessitated him staying in Washington. Hence, he welcomed a return to London for consultation but no permanent alterations.[383]

The fast changing shipbuilding picture, and the fallout from the Casablanca Conference, where shipping commitments were made but not fully discussed, convinced Salter to give one of his rare press conferences.[384] Described in The Washington Post on 4 March as "the gray, bald and stockily-built British official," Salter admitted that the shipping situation was serious and full of anxiety. He stated that shipbuilding was not outpacing losses, that demand for shipping space was constantly increasing, and therefore the shipping shortage would continue for the rest of the year. This placed limitations on what the United Nations could do militarily. Nonetheless, he paid tribute "for the manner in which the American and British merchant fleets were now being used as if they were one," and complimented American shipbuilding efforts which were projected to reach 19 million tons in 1943.[385] The increasing marginalization of the Salter Shipping Mission was apparent during the 12 March arrival of Churchill for the Second Washington Conference. Shipping was of course closely intertwined with strategic planning which in 1943 focused on the Mediterranean and the invasion of Europe. On this occasion, however, Salter was absent from any of the White House meetings, although Leathers accompanied Churchill. Salter did meet on 15 March with Eden who was then also on a visit to Washington and afterwards provided Eden with a briefing on shipping. Salter indicated that while the United Nations shipping position was improving, the British import situation was worsening. British imports from November 1942 to February 1843, he warned, had dropped to a record low of 1¼ million tons a month, a quarter of the total in a good pre-war year, due to the scarcity of ships for this purpose. He concluded by reminding Eden that adequate imports were "an indispensable condition" of the security of the United Kingdom and were as vital to the war effort as supplies to the front lines.[386]

As the second anniversary of the Shipping Mission approached, hints emerged that Salter was thinking not only about his future but the mission's as well. On 20 March he wrote to Leathers appealing against the recall of Donald Anderson to his work at P & O. He complimented Anderson's "first rate general ability, his shipping experience [and] his sound and reliable judgment." He admitted that in due course other mission members would be able to do the negotiating side of Anderson's job, particularly with the WSA. Salter went on:

> The central and main task of this Mission in regard to W.S.A. allocations is increasing and becoming more complex with the increased allocations, the greater shipping stringency and the fact that all allocation policy now revolves round strategic plans. This semi-military work is now at the centre of all our main work. In general the efficiency of this mission in all its work depends upon personal quality of a very small number and their standing with Americans. It would be regrettable if at this stage when the allocation of U.S. ships is becoming determining factor in main military plans and operations the level of efficiency were impaired.

He further argued that the establishment of a separate sea transport section was not the solution, and hoped to discuss this personally with Leathers when a return to London was finally confirmed.[387] On 31 March the CSAB reported on its first year of activity, with Salter broadcasting publicly on the subject. He admitted that by the end of 1943 the US would have surpassed Britain as the world's leading merchant marine power.[388] He returned to the subject of shipping when he spoke on 7 April at a meeting of the American Academy of Political Science, and stated: "Progress in our fight for freedom thus depends upon shipping. How do we stand?" He cautioned that, although the United Nations were building more tonnage than they were losing, shipping continued to be the most precarious of the links binding the Allies. Nonetheless, he also looked into the future to a post-war world where concerted policy and action would be needed to restrain aggression. Drawing on his own experience of two world wars, he stated that "power expressing itself, where necessary, in physical force" was vital to guarantee peace. His speech was certainly blunt and straightforward. Afterwards, explaining his tone to an American friend, he wrote, "We are, thank heaven, now Allies not deserving mendicants – and some of my compatriots do not always seem to realize that by parading our deserts they imply mendacity." His attendance was also the occasion to accept a scroll naming Churchill an honourary member of the academy.[389]

Salter returned to the subject of the post-war world when he later addressed the American Society of International Law. The central issue of the current war, he contended, was the need to establish "an adequate and effective international law, unless we are to fall again into international anarchy and into war." He did not have in mind a "World State." Rather he preferred that, if there was a threat of war, there must be in place a system which could impose a preponderant majority of force upon those who threaten the peace. "At that point there must be something like a world legislature and a world court and a world force to impose their will." As for less threatening situations, he foresaw international law developing a set of sanctions to deal with the separate issues of treaty breaking. Finally, drawing on the inter-war faith in the power of public opinion to uphold international law, he concluded that "while public opinion is of the utmost importance in the world, the acid test of its strength, of its sincerity, of its value, is that it shall be able to enlist and direct the use of adequate physical power and force, if need be." The inability to do so was the reason, in his opinion, the League of Nations failed. In the final analysis, the future depended on establishing "effective law to govern and control the relations of States, buttress the law with sufficient power, [and] make it the instrument of truly united nations."[390]

Salter then turned to what was emerging as his main task, insuring and protecting allocations. By 27 March he believed, for a time, he had the WSA committed to allocations "on basis of 60 April 80 May 100 June and 100 each subsequent month."[391] At the meeting of the CSAB on 30 March, Douglas indicated that he was working on allocations for the UK import programme for 1 June to 30 November 1943. Afterwards Salter cautioned Leathers that his own prior figures were likely too optimistic. Military planning, he noted, made it difficult to secure a schedule both reasonable and satisfactory.[392] The next week Salter informed Leathers that he now had the allocation figures ending on 30 November, but that he was pressing to extend these to the end of the year. He felt somewhat optimistic that this could be achieved, given that both Roosevelt and the WSA were working sympathetically to satisfy Britain's import needs. He did admit, however, that the original prospect of an assured 27 million tons of imports was not going to be fulfilled, and cautioned against any criticisms from London.[393] The ensuing weeks provided more of the same for Salter and his increasingly marginalized mission. When Anderson's return to P & O was confirmed, Salter wrote on 8 April, "we may be able to carry on though Anderson's loss will be severely felt."[394] As for the CSAB, it met once more on 20 April and thereafter not until 8 June.[395] In reality, the issue of allocations was slowly passing out of Salter's purview. Besides, having negotiated the 1943 allocations, he was forced in late April and May to concern himself with the question of guaranteeing that there was sufficient dry cargo, in the right place, to fill the ships. His own hands were somewhat tied as the solutions were, as he put it, "in London's hands." There adjustments were made between the "allocation of British ships as a supplement to the known W.S.A. schedule" and steps taken to increase cargo. He was particularly worried should any difficulty in filling ships become known in American circles and rebound negatively on ongoing shipping negotiations. For his part, Salter conferred with the various British supply missions to increase procurements and informed the 5 May meeting of the North America Supply Council of his efforts.[396]

From 11 May to 26 May Churchill was in Washington for the Trident conference on Anglo-American strategy. Among the large group who accompanied him on the visit was Leathers. While he consulted with Salter on a range of shipping issues, the latter again took no active role at the White House, though he dined at the British embassy on 23 May. On his return to London, Leathers reported to the War Cabinet that he had worked with Salter in successfully lobbying Land, Douglas and Vickery against the unilateral American decision to replace all the slower Liberty ships with the faster 15-knot "Victory" ship. A more measured conversion was promised, along with another increase in US shipbuilding of 2.4 million tons deadweight.[397] However, Salter's own future had also been discussed in Washington. On 22 May, in a letter marked "Secret & Personal" Halifax wrote to Eden:

> I have been talking to Leathers a good deal about Arthur Salter, and it looks as if, for one reason or another, Leathers will be bringing him home in the not too distant future. Salter has done invaluable work here and we all owe him a great debt. I do not think, if and when he gets home, that he will wish to continue in the shipping Ministry on your side, nor do I know in the least whether any other work is likely to turn up for which he might be considered. I am afraid Winston is not likely to feel greatly disposed to fit him in! It had, however, occurred to me that you might possibly be able to use him in the field of Post War Thinking and if and when he gets home I would be glad if you could have a talk with him and explore any possibilities that may suggest themselves. He is not everybody's cup of tea but he really has served well of the republic. Have a word with Leathers too.

Eden later minuted, "I hardly think that Salter could help us much," and a reply in this sense was returned to Halifax.[398]

In the near term Salter continued to oversee the now familiar aspects of his mission. At the last substantive meeting of the CSAB on 8 June, Douglas reported on his conversations with Salter on the board's future. He pointed out that until recently the board had been primarily concerned with questions of major policy. These had now largely been settled and future work would focus on operational decisions.[399] In fact, the CSAB was not to meet again until 5 November, having clearly outlived its usefulness. The main forum for Salter's reports now became the North American Supply Council. Here he was able to report on 16 June that the shipping situation continued to improve, sinkings had declined and allocations for the period of January to May were above expected levels. In fact, losses of Allied and neutral merchant ships from submarines in June were the lowest since the US had entered the war.[400] With such generally improving news, Salter decided he could return London. He later recalled that "The time of acute danger was past."[401]

Salter took his place among the ministers sitting on the Treasury Bench at question time on 30 June in the House of Commons. <u>The Times</u> reported that he was impressed by the improvement in the shipping situation and by the magnitude of America's shipping achievements.[402] During this visit issues of post-war reconstruction were already beginning to emerge on various agenda. Thus on 1 July the War Cabinet discussed its approach to a forthcoming debate, demanded by the Labour Party, on post-war shipping policy. As recorded in the cabinet secretary's notes, it was agreed that while there would be no nationalization of shipping, there was "much to be said for state control of railways, gas, some mines, etc." It was further agreed that Salter would wind up the debate for the government.[403] Thinking ahead to that session, Salter wrote to Lady Astor, after having spent the week-end at Cliveden: "I am rather hoping to get the chance of telling the tale of America's contribution to the shipping crisis in tomorrow's debate, but can't tell whether the course of the debate will make this possible. Somewhere & somehow, it must be told."[404] In that regard he was successful.

On 14 July the debate in the Commons began with a request for the government to state its post-war shipping plans. After several members complemented Salter "on the very magnificent job of work he has done in America," he rose to reply. He emphasized the contrast with the previous year when he addressed the House in secret session and at a time of grave anxiety. On this occasion, he pointed out, the improvement in the shipping situation, and with the minds of MPs turning to the post-war period, a public debate was possible. He considered it premature to expect a statement of post-war shipping policy from the government, or to project anything about the post-war size of the British mercantile marine. He preferred to see two debates, the first to raise questions and the second to provide answers. He then digressed to talk about the American contribution. As someone "who has been at every stage in intimate and close contact with those who took the decisions to increase the American shipbuilding programme," he stated, these had been undertaken with no motive other than to win the war. There were two periods, Salter continued, when the shipping issue threatened the outcome of the war. In the spring of 1941, the country was "in fairly imminent danger either of famine conditions here or of closing our factories through lack of raw materials." Soon afterwards, however, the American shipbuilding programme which had amounted to only one million tons for all of 1941 was raised for 1942 to eight million tons. The second period, after the entry of Japan into the war, proved even more serious, with losses far exceeding building. By the summer of 1942, he continued, "we were again in an extremely grave crisis." In response, the US further increased its building from eight million to 14 million tons, and with continuing losses the figure was revised upwards to 20 million tons. With the co-operation Douglas, Land and Roosevelt, the new building was made available to the United Nations and schedules worked out. Such a successful example of daily co-operation, he concluded, was cause for hope in dealing with a range of post-war problems. Salter's speech was widely reported in the press with <u>The Times</u> describing it as "a striking account." <u>The New York Times</u> observed that it was "the frankest admission made publicly yet of how close Britain came to defeat" in 1940.[405]

Salter later observed that "My speech on that occasion, in July 1943, was my swan song as Head of the Mission. My personal task accomplished."[406] In the short term, his future included both familiar and unfamiliar activities. On 15 July he represented the Ministry of War Transport at an exhibition on post-war redevelopment sponsored by the London County Council. He spoke of the amazement felt by many Americans at the intellectual leadership Britain was showing in already tackling various post-war problems.[407] He was kept briefed by the Foreign Office and his own ministry on events in Washington. On Churchill's initiative, the War Cabinet agreed on 4 August to appoint a Demobilisation Committee, on which Salter served as a member. Its mandate was "to carry out a general survey of our demobilisation plans, on the basis of a two-stage ending of the war." The committee's report was completed on 16 November and presented to the War Cabinet on 22 November. It proposed that the rate of demobilisation be governed by military needs and not by the availability of civilian employment, that it was to be fair and reasonable, and accepted by both the men and women concerned.[408] On 9 August Salter attended a meeting of the War Cabinet where the question of shipping and the supply of nitrates to Egypt to increase the production of cereals were discussed. The following week he again was present for a discussion about relaxing the blackout in industrial establishments.[409] As well, there was the usual round of official engagements, including the attendance at a Privy Council on 10 August.[410]

As Leathers was accompanying the prime minister to the Quebec Conference which began on 17 August, Salter agreed to Churchill's request to delay his return to Washington. On 27 August, in a speech at Hull, Salter stated, "For years we had had to think of our ships as a life-line; now we thought of them as a conduit pipe for victory, through which flowed the vast strength of American and British production. The faster it flowed the sooner would come the day of victory."[411] Most weekends he stayed at All Souls in the company of Fellows with whom he always enjoyed stimulating conversations. On 5 September he gave Liddell Hart an interview at All Souls.

The conversation consisted of a dramatic retelling by Salter of his shipping mission to Washington from its inception in 1941 to August 1943. He confided to Liddell Hart that in the third week of August not a single allied ship had been lost.[412] And as usual there was time to catch up with colleagues and friends. Salter dined with "Molly" Hamilton who found him "in very good form."[413] Violet Markham also thought he was "looking very well." She continued, "His marriage is a great success & has done him a power of good. Ethel bustles [?] him & contradicts him & has cleaned him up to an astonishing degree. He is no longer the untidiest man with the worst brushed clothes in London."[414]

Although Salter had refused on 14 July to share with the House of Commons any post-war plans, this did not mean that he was not already thinking in that direction. On 3 September he completed a memorandum, marked "Secret" and titled "Shipping 'Expansion' Policy," intended to examine a policy appropriate to a rapid expansion of shipping. What motivated the exercise was his observation that from 1 January to 29 August 1943, there had been a net shipping gain of 8,875,000 tons deadweight, of which 8,015,000 was dry cargo. Taking into account such variables as the submarine threat and the competing demands of the US military, Salter went ahead and made several suggestions. He encouraged an increase in the production of landing craft and passenger-carrying ships for the repatriation of prisoners and demobilisation, and increasing stores of food, such as sugar and grain, and raw materials to help liberated countries. Leathers thought that Salter's suggestions were somewhat premature.[415] In the event, this memorandum turned out to be among the last that Salter was to write as head of the Shipping Mission.

On 20 September after having spent far too long in London, Salter wrote to Churchill stating that he was about to return to Washington and requested a personal meeting, albeit at short notice. Salter added that "After clearing up in Washington and elsewhere and a farewell visit to Canada, I should as arranged be returning permanently to London later in the year." Churchill responded the same day, advising Salter to return to the United States as planned and wind up his affairs. Because a speech due in the House the next day was preoccupying him, Churchill suggested they meet on Salter's return to London when "I shall be quite ready then to discuss your future plans with you."[416] On 28 September Salter finally returned to Washington, with little more to do than tender his resignation, a move he had clearly decided upon.[417] He later recalled:

> By the autumn of 1943 it seemed certain that, whatever the issue of the war, it would not turn on a shortage of shipping. The dovetailing of the complicated

supply arrangements would still require a great deal of Anglo-American work in Washington. But I felt I was myself no longer required, and was indeed temperamentally not so well adapted as my colleagues for the patient, exacting work of detailed administration. And I wanted badly to get back to Whitehall and Westminster.[418]

Salter resigned from his position as joint parliamentary secretary to the Ministry of War Transport on 6 October. The official "British Merchant Shipping Mission in the United States" concluded that "The original task of the Mission had been completed by the end of 1943." The following had all been secured: assistance for the United Kingdom imports programme; a vast increase in American shipbuilding; assistance with repairs and naval protection; and administrative cooperation in more general shipping problems.[419]

In the following weeks, Salter made his farewell rounds in Washington. On 2 November he wrote to Roosevelt requesting to pay his respects in a personal meeting. He continued, "I would like to express my deep gratitude for the cooperation, under your directions, of all the American authorities concerned." Both in the spring of 1941 and in mid-1942, "the whole war effort seemed in danger of disaster through the shortage of ships. In both cases the situation was saved by the unprecedented American shipbuilding effort." Salter concluded that "the danger that for so long seemed the greatest seems to have ended." Roosevelt granted Salter's request and the two met at the White House on 8 November at noon.[420] Salter left with an abiding admiration for the President and his nation's gratitude for the American war effort.[421] On 3 November Salter had reported to the British Supply Council in Washington, with evident pleasure, that the shipping situation continued to improve. The United Nations were building more than five ships for each one lost. The meeting concluded with the announcement from the chairman, Llewellin, that Salter was relinquishing his position as head of the Shipping Mission. He was praised for the fact that "American production had been stepped up and allocation of shipping to the British [had been] obtained by his strenuous efforts. Not only the Council but the United Kingdom as a whole were deeply indebted to him for the work he had done."[422] On 5 November Salter attended his final meeting of the CSAB. Douglas announced Salter's retirement and expressed his "warm appreciation of Sir Arthur's work as a member of the Board and keen regret that he would no longer be present to take part in its deliberations."[423] The same day, Harold Ickes, the War Petroleum Administrator, wrote to Churchill that "At a crucial period Sir Arthur Salter has contributed to the common cause in a critically important way, and I should like you to know of our appreciation of this fact."[424]

Freed of routine responsibilities Salter, accompanied by Lady Salter, undertook a final tour of west coast shipyards. After leaving Washington, they first visited the Los Angeles facilities of California Shipbuilding Corporation on Terminal Island and the Consolidated Steel Corporation in Wilmington. Here he exhorted, "More ships are the answer to the needs for a quicker victory."[425] From there they traveled north to Vancouver, where Salter revealed that Canada was building almost as many ships as Britain. He then cut his trip short, cancelling a speaking engagement in Toronto, and returned quickly to Washington.[426] His future now hung in the balance. The London Evening News on 9 November reported that the Salters were returning to London. Salter was to take up new duties, as Minister of Reconstruction, while Lady Salter's return would be an adventure in setting up home in England for the first time.[427] However, that was not yet to be. On 9 November, with 44 nations signing the document in Washington, the United Nations Relief and Rehabilitation Administration (UNRRA) had been established. It was to be administered by a director general with executive power, a Council, made up of one representative from each of the member from each of the member states, as a policy formulating body, and a Central Committee (China, the USSR, the UK and the US) for urgent policy decisions. The first session of its Council was held at Atlantic City from 10 November to 1 December where agreement was reached about the broad lines of policy to guide the work of the new agency.[428]

Former New York Governor Herbert H. Lehman, who had been elected on 11 November to serve as UNRRA's first director general, requested Salter's assistance. On 4 December Salter replied, in a letter marked "Personal," that he was consulting Churchill on the matter, and noting "that I am ready either, at the Prime Minister's wish to undertake work in London if he wishes to assign me to anything equally important and suitable, or alternatively to accept your offer." That offer was for Salter to take up the position of deputy director general, the executive arm of UNRRA responsible for operations. The position was to run for six months, renewable with the agreement of both individuals.[429] Salter wrote to Churchill about the offer on 5 December, and the response was for him to accept. Attlee, at the time in Washington, also wrote to Churchill, noting that Salter was the best person for the position, particularly in light of his experience of reparations and the League of Nations. Churchill later wrote Salter that "It is most important U.N.R.R.A. should be successfully launched and in this your experience will be invaluable."[430] Salter accepted Lehman's invitation and stated that he would start work on 9 December "privately and without prejudice to the ultimate decision," and would immerse himself "'con amore' in this very interesting work."[431]

Salter had hoped to prevent this news from leaking out. However, his appointment as "no. 2 to Lehman in Relief" was already a topic of discussion on 1 December when "Molly" Hamilton dined with Elliot Felkin and Marchesa Louise de Rosales. On 20 December The Manchester Guardian broke the story.[432] The War Cabinet was informed of Salter's appointment on 23 December.[433] In fact, Salter had fully discussed the situation with Halifax who agreed with him that the appointment should be announced as a provisional one. It was Salter's view that this approach made it easier for him to return to London at short notice should the opportunity emerge.[434] Finally, on 29 December Lehman sent Halifax a cable, written by Salter to be forwarded to London, which contained the formal announcement to be carried in the press on 31 December. This stated that in view of Salter's "experience in earlier international administrations," he had consented to assist in the organizational period of UNRRA. He had also agreed to stay in Washington for the time being before returning to England, but still retain his seat in the House of Commons. As a result he had resigned his position as head of the Shipping Mission and as joint parliamentary secretary to the Ministry of War Transport.[435] The press carried the news on 31 December and noted that the position was temporary.[436] News of the appointment was covered in The Washington Post which commented that "Friends of Sir Arthur and Lady Salter are delighted to know that they are not returning to England, after all."[437] On 31 December Churchill cabled Salter to inform him that his name had been submitted to King George VI for the Knight Grand Cross of the Order of the British Empire (GBE). He added that this was "in recognition of your most excellent work in the United States."[438] The public announcement came in the annual New Year Honours List on 1 January 1940, which singled out individuals for their contributions to the prosecution of the war.[439]

Salter's brief service as deputy director general of UNRRA was eventually to prove a disappointment to him. He later wrote that "It was a frustrating experience, for an attempt to plan relief for an unknown date and unknown circumstances is likely rather to hamper the actual work, when it comes, through unsuitable plans and rules, than to help it."[440] For his part, Lehman recalled "I don't think he was entirely sympathetic with this work, and he and I didn't see eye to eye on it."[441] Nevertheless, with his usual sense of duty, responsibility and diligence, Salter threw himself into his new position. The Atlantic City resolutions made no attempt to define the detailed administrative structure of UNRRA or determine such issues as personnel, regional offices, field missions and the powers each was to deploy. In effect, as early appointees, Lehman and Salter faced the prospect of developing "a workable organization on a global scale."[442] Compounding the tasks were the pressures of the ongoing global war and with priority still to be given to military demands for supplies and personnel. As deputy director general, Salter acted as adviser to, and the channel of authority from the director general to the other sections of the UNNRA.[443] After settling into UNRRA's new headquarters in the Walker-Johnson Building on Connecticut Avenue at Dupont Circle, one of Salter earliest concerns, on 31 December, was to persuade Lehman to tackle the thorny question of UNRRA's future relationship with the military. Lehman followed up with a letter to the chiefs of staff, defining the problems and raising questions. At the same time, Salter personally met with representatives of the Combined Boards to assess their relationship with UNRRA and discuss issues of supplies for relief and rehabilitation. "In short," Halifax observed on 12 January 1944, "Salter is taking first things first."[444]

Salter was in contact with the Foreign Office and others in Washington in the following weeks to secure personnel and to plan for the detailed organization of UNRRA. Despite his eagerness on the former question, it was noted on 29 January both in London and Washington that until "agreement [was] reached on organizational structure and allocation of duties," not to speak of salary, progress on the personnel issue would be slow. Nonetheless, considerable progress was soon reported from Washington on the growing number of appointments at senior levels, including several deputy directors.[445] Among the most difficult organizational issues for Salter was the question of UNRRA having a London office and defining its relation with Washington. Both he and the British embassy in Washington added their pressure, at the end of December, to the ultimate decision to open a European Regional Office in London.[446] On 19 January Leith-Ross, chairman of the Inter-Allied Committee on Post-War Requirements since September 1941, was appointed as its deputy director general, to be sited in London, and the office was officially established on 1 February.[447]

During the course of January and February Salter was working his way towards both theoretical and practical structures for postwar United Nations organizations. On 23 January he spoke to a meeting of the American Society for Public Administration. Although his remarks were off the record, he used his address as the basis of an article, "From Combined War Agencies to International Administration," which appeared soon afterwards in the Society's journal. The international machinery which worked in wartime, the combined war agencies, "built up piecemeal and adjusted to operating needs," he wrote, would have to be rethought in a post-war world. The primary requirement was "some central body of higher authority," dominated by the three or four countries who at war's end would have "a vast preponderance of power to assure the framework within which the world can be reconstructed or reconstruct itself."[448] On 25 January the future of UNRRA was the subject of an extensive debate in the House of Common. Salter's appointment was praised for bringing "great qualities and much relevant experience to the task." Afterwards Leith-Ross wrote to him, "The general tone was extremely helpful; the main points being the need to get on with the organization as quickly as possible."[449]

On a daily basis, in fact, Salter was working at a breakneck pace. There persisted the ongoing issues of hiring personnel, planning for "uniform budget control and accounting," convincing the military on both sides of the Atlantic that UNRRA was alone "responsible for formulating relief and rehabilitation requirements for the post-military period," and even arranging for free transport for UNRRA officials.[450] Among the most pressing and complex of issues, however, was the organization of the London Regional Office and its relation to headquarters in Washington. On 15 February Salter produced a first draft of his own vision, "Relations with London Regional Office." He wrote that the London office should operate on the basis of authority specifically delegated to it by the Director General. However, "The problem of deciding the extent to which authority should be delegated to London, and of making the consequent administrative and personnel arrangements, is one of the most difficult which has to be faced in UNRRA's organization." He was emphatic that headquarters in Washington would remain responsible for "the initial determination of principles of policy" and the centre for all aspects of supply and finance. However, subject to such limitations, delegation and decentralization was to proceed as far and as fast as possible. He therefore recommended that the London office be organized under three deputy directors general, together constituting an Administrative Council with each having responsibility respectively for Administration, Services and Areas, and Supply. Some of the areas of responsibility which he specified were liaison with European member governments and development of plans and provision of staff for relief and rehabilitation services in Europe. Salter's memorandum "supplied the basis on which subsequent developments rested."[451]

Flexibility was a guiding principle for Salter as he continued to plan the detailed organization of UNRRA. It was impossible, as yet, to foresee the course of the war and when and how UNRRA would eventually operate. As a consequence, in the first draft of his plan dated 1 February, Salter wrote that "No set of rules drafted beforehand can determine precisely, and in detail, the part which each of the principal officers will take in discharging the different tasks of UNRRA." To a great extent this would have to be resolved by officials as they went about their tasks. As a consequence, he continued, "The team spirit is essential, and the 'jurisdictional' mind is its greatest danger. Administrative orders may be practicable later, but these will aim at consolidating arrangements which have already been worked out by those concerned." Thus he wished instead to focus on the main principles to encourage cooperation among the Deputy Directors General and their main areas of responsibility.[452] Salter circulated his draft for comments and these largely recognized the difficulties of planning for an unknown future.[453] He signed the final revised draft on

9 March as promising "the most authoritative general description of UNRRA's organization available." It was intended to assist the various deputy directors general in working both with each other and in organizing their departments. There followed an extensive document which detailed the main functions, beside his own position as deputy director general, of such officers as the Diplomatic Adviser, the Financial Adviser, the Public Relations Officer, the General Counsel, and the several Deputy Directors General for Secretariat, Finance and Administration, Supply, Areas, Regional Liaison, Health, Displaced Persons, Industrial relations and Welfare. While there were subsequently various additions and rearrangements to the Salter memorandum, there were no major changes for the next 18 months.[454]

There was little about the evolution of UNRRA in March and April that gave cause for satisfaction. Lehman's reluctance to consult, for example, with the British embassy prior to meetings of UNRRA committees, was a cause of major concern to Halifax. The latter was advised to discuss the matter informally with Salter.[455] In addition, UNRRA's responsibility for rehabilitation was too narrowly defined, in Salter's view, to distinguish it from reconstruction, thereby limiting the organization's freedom of manoeuvre.[456] In addition, Salter's proposal to set up the first of four projected Health Planning Commissions in London, responsible initially for the western theatre of war, namely, France, Belgium, Holland and Norway, was overruled in London.[457] On 30 March it fell to Salter, who was then acting director general with Lehman abroad, to announce that the second session of the Council of UNRRA would convene in Montreal on 23 June. He envisaged this as a brief business session and to last about ten days.[458] On 19 April he invited Mackenzie King to address the opening plenary meeting of the Council.[459] As for himself, he let it be known that he was planning to visit London in the middle of May, return for the June Council meeting, and then, adhering to his original intention to stay with UNRRA for only six months, resign his position. British officials both in Washington and London regarded Lehman as having so far provided "somewhat feeble leadership." The accepted view was that "It is of course Salter who is now at the helm." As a result the prospect of finding a successor to him was regarded as so daunting that another effort was to be made, during his upcoming visit to London, to convince him to remain.[460]

Salter's then redoubled his efforts to prepare the massive documentation needed for circulation prior to the 23 June Council session. By 21 April he was able to distribute the provisional agenda and detailed information regarding arrangements for the session.[461] One problem that continued to preoccupy him was the respective responsibilities of the Washington and London Offices "as we draw to the end of the planning and enter the operational period."[462] The central issue still left in abeyance was Salter's 21 February recommendation on decentralization. On 10 May Lehman convened a staff meeting to prepare the ground on this issue, prior to Salter's departure to London. He opened the meeting with a statement regarding "the organizational problem involved in developing the London office by way of either delegation of authority or transfer of personnel and the consequences of either course upon the Headquarters Office." Salter followed with a clear re-affirmation that Washington must continue to be the headquarters of UNRRA, with the permanent retention there, for example, of the Bureau of Finance and Administration and the Bureau of Supply. However, the time had come to begin the detailed planning of operations in relation to Europe. "In his view, this was work best done in London; in fact, he doubted whether it could be effectively done elsewhere." He wished, therefore, to see the London office developed so that "in planning, full advantage might be taken of its proximity to the military authorities, to the Allied Governments, the European Advisory Commission (through which European policy was co-ordinated between the US, the UK and Russia in London) and the Civil Affairs authorities." In essence, what Salter foresaw was "a transfer of functional services planning in respect of European region to London" where this could be done more effectively. In response to these proposals Lehman stated that they had merit and agreed that the London office needed to be strengthened. But he was still not clear whether this should be accompanied by a delegation of authority. In the absence of any consensus, he scheduled another meeting the following day. By that time Salter had prepared a memorandum which detailed his conception of the division of functions and personnel between Washington and London. Some concern was expressed that his proposals would "reveal a duality in authority." Salter responded that his proposals were not necessarily the final word on reorganization, but his primary concern was "to transfer authority and work to the most effective working points now available." Lehman again expressed his concern about a lack of clarity in Salter's proposals but accepted them if they were interpreted not as a major reorganization of UNRRA but rather as a change of procedures. A compromise was finally agreed upon, which included: giving greater authority to the Functional Directors in London; appointment of a resident senior deputy director general; changing the authority of the Administrative Council to one of consultation only, and moving to London the Directors of Functional Divisions (Health, Displaced Persons and Welfare). As the deputy director general, Salter was given the mandate to implement these changes in London as he saw fit.[463]

Salter, accompanied by Lady Salter, left for London on 13 May, with his primary concern being the reorganization of the London office of UNRRA. While his 21 February memorandum on "Relations with London Regional Office" largely accorded with the views held by some in charge in London, it was the indeterminate results of the 10-11 May meetings that had yet to be further developed and acted upon.[464] Although he expected to return within a month, this was not to be. With the announcement on 16 May that the session of the UNRRA Council scheduled for 23 June was postponed because of the emergency ban on travel and communication from Britain,[465] Salter extended his stay and even took his place occasionally in the House of Commons. It was understood in Whitehall that his visit was to devise ways to make the London office of UNRRA the effective centre of operations for Europe.[466] However, even as Salter went about UNRRA business, he was also occupied with his own situation. On 26 May Minister of State Richard Law informed Eden that despite Salter's wish to relinquish his position, it was in Britain's best interest to support the growth of UNRRA as an efficient international organization and that Salter was the best person to achieve this objective. Law urged Eden to speak to Churchill to ensure that the prime minister emphasized "the importance we attach to U.N.R.R.A. and to Sir Arthur Salter's continued association with it as Senior Director General." Salter's departure, he concluded, "will place us in a very embarrassing position." Eden followed up on this suggestion and wrote to Churchill that pressure might have to be brought to bear on Salter, and hinted that the prime minister might be the person to do this. "It will not be possible for me to see Sir Arthur Salter in the near future," Churchill replied and added, "It would be very nice if you were to see him and explain to him exactly how things stand. Pray also deal with U.N.R.R.A."[467]

After a few weeks in London, involving extensive consultations and meetings, Salter wrote to Richard Law on 15 June in continuation of their conversation that day. He confirmed that Lehman wished to move the effective UNRRA planning and eventual focus of operations for Europe to London. However, Salter confided that he found a "pervasive adverse atmosphere" in Whitehall which would hinder it. Only firm British government and ministerial support would make it effective. Salter expressed his wish to further follow up directly with Eden, which he did and the latter promised to elicit from Churchill a declaration of British support for UNRRA.[468] Eden then informed Churchill that he personally favoured the proposal to transfer the main responsibility for Europe to London. He thought the move to be politically advantageous to the UK, giving it influence in the post-war period and encouraging the military and supply departments to cooperate with UNRRA, even before the end of hostilities. "If the European side of U.N.R.R.A.'s work continues to be centred in Washington, it will be badly done and that is to nobody's advantage." Eden further reported that a condition of the transfer of responsibility was that the move should be known to have the full backing of the government. He also urged Churchill, who appeared agreeable at this point, to issue a directive stating that the British government favoured the transfer and was determined to ensure the success of UNRRA.[469]

Even as Salter worked to further the transfer to London, he equally busied himself with finding his successor at UNRRA, a task the Foreign Office had also been pursuing. The first candidate, Sir Andrew McFadyean, had experience of international administration but was too involved in his business interests.[470] Salter himself approached several possible candidates such as Malcolm MacDonald and Lord Harlech. At one point he considered that Lord Dudley would make a suitable successor. One candidate he did not favor, Oliver Franks, nonetheless was warmly endorsed by the Foreign Office and Lehman.[471] However, finding someone of Salter's stature and expertise was sufficiently daunting that Richard Law, responsible for the search, concluded that "Salter should be induced to stay."[472] It was only much later, on 24 August that Law admitted "that it is no use asking him to go on." Two weeks later the War Cabinet decided that Franks could not be spared but every effort would be made to find a British replacement for Salter.[473]

Salter's first report back to Washington dwelt on the variety of organizational difficulties he was having, as well as the "political suspicion" he had encountered.[474] In fact, a similar pessimism about the future of UNRRA also prevailed in Washington. On 15 June a member of the British embassy there reported that doubts were being expressed about UNRRA's "lack of purpose and inefficiency." A particular concern was that Lehman "has not proved a first-class pilot," and hence the urgency of finding the best possible replacement for Salter.[475] Lehman himself called on Halifax on 19 June to discuss Salter's successor. He doubted that Salter would return to his post, despite pleas to reconsider his decision to retire. Lehman impressed on Halifax that any replacement must be an individual "of broad reputation and real administrative ability." Halifax admitted that such individuals were already fully engaged. In a follow-up, Lehman wrote to Salter on 21 June, enclosing the memorandum of his talk with Halifax. He complimented Salter on his work, stated that he would welcome his return, strongly urged him to reconsider and proposed he could even divide his time between Washington and London.[476]

On 28 June Salter provided Lehman with a further update on the UNNRA position in London. He conceded that "UNRRA is now, beyond question in a serious condition." Its personnel were inadequate in numbers and quality, its prestige poor, and cooperation with both military and civilian authorities in contributing countries was lacking. The main cause, in Salter's view, was the uncertainty as to UNRRA's tasks and this had led to "frustration, demoralization, unrealistic plans, and loss of prestige." In order to overcome these obstacles, he recommended that UNRRA should make no further plans or acquire supplies or personnel until a better relationship with the military was established. He then suggested, for immediate action, "a bold counter-attack" in order to "meet the insidious undermining of UNRRA's position."

This included an ultimatum to the US and the UK governments that UNRRA would be unable to implement its mandate unless cooperation was immediately forthcoming in the military or pre-UNRRA period. He then admitted, in a somewhat self-critical tone, that UNRRA's own organization was unnecessarily complicated, with two headquarters, London and Washington, and thus co-ordination was difficult. The "pervasive atmosphere of hostility, indifference or depreciation," he concluded, was the result of a "big power attitude towards a composite international authority," and that "a future national authority" must be founded, unlike the League, "upon a 'hard core' of the countries with the most power."[477] Salter was in fact already considering a return to Washington, but the decisive factor affecting his future came on 2 July in a letter from Churchill. The prime minister now wrote that Eden would be the contact person for all UNRRA matters and continued:

> With regard to more personal affairs, I have not, at the present time, any ministerial post which I could offer you, and the difficulties between the Parties and of fitting people in at a particular moment are so complex that I could not make any plans for the immediate future. You know how much I value the good work you have done.[478]

Salter at once informed Lehman of his willingness to return to Washington and remain with UNRRA until after the Council meeting. Lehman was delighted with the news and requested Salter stay on until early August to finalize some administrative changes for the London office.[479]

The problems Salter had to address in London concerned both the internal organization of UNRRA and its external relations, mainly with the military. In order to start up the machinery of UNRRA as effectively as possible, he advanced several ideas. With regard to the London office, he initially suggested that: the Administrative Council be used only for consultative purposes; the Deputy Director General for Areas and Services would co-ordinate the work of the functional divisions; and the executive secretary would serve the entire European Regional Office and not just the Administrative Council. He reported generally that the Council was working effectively and that the office had settled down.[480] In reality, that was hardly the case. Salter had advocated fine-tuning the UNRRA administration before committing to procuring supplies for liberated areas. Indeed, addressing a public concern that UNRRA was being sidelined, he explained that the military would be responsible for purchasing and distributing supplies during the military period presumed to be about six months. The Manchester Guardian commented, "Though the field of U.N.R.R.A. has shrunk, its organization is still large."[481] On the other hand, on 6 July Leith-Ross wrote to Lehman that Salter's proposals were unnecessarily complicating the administrative functions, and criticised his methods as "disturbing to the morale of the office here." Leith-Ross contended that UNRRA was giving an impression of "building up an enormous machinery and engaging in much theoretical study," while being unprepared to offer effective assistance for future problems. He advocated therefore a clear statement from both the British and Americans governments that the tasks of relief and rehabilitation were genuinely to be entrusted to UNRRA.[482]

By mid-July the problems hindering the development of UNRRA were, firstly, that Britain and the United States were not sufficiently supportive of UNRRA, and secondly, that the military in both countries was keeping UNRRA at arm's length and not allowing it to play an immediate role in supply questions affecting liberated countries.[483] Harold E. Caustin, first Salter's and then Lehman's principal assistant, later observed that the situation in London was getting "embarrassing."[484] It was this subject that Lithgow Osborne, deputy director general in the European Regional Office, expanded upon when he returned from London to meet on 12 July with UNRRA's Washington staff. He thought the difficulty was due to the fact that the Allied governments regarded UNRRA "merely as a standby in case things were worse than they expected." He also revealed that morale in the London office was not particularly good. Finally, Osborne mentioned that Salter was working to rectify this situation with the British government.[485] While the ostensible reason for Osborne's visit was to vacation, he in fact had returned to resign his position. His distressing observations, along with others reaching Lehman, prompted the latter to write to Salter on 21 July, stating the problems were urgent and instructing Salter on how to proceed. Lehman insisted, on Osborne's advice, that the functional divisions, health, welfare and displaced persons, should have independent technical responsibilities but these should be integrated into other UNRRA activities. He also made it clear that the London office must have a single executive head, that the Administrative Council would take overall responsibility for co-ordination, and ultimate authority still rested with him as director general.[486] The issues identified by Salter in the relations between Washington and London were not in fact resolved before his departure from UNRRA.

Salter had arranged to return by ship to Washington, leaving on 5 August and accompanied by Lady Salter.[487] His remaining time, and chief concern, was to convince Churchill to issue a directive in support of UNRRA. Salter had returned to the charge and he now drafted the directive. Eden proved receptive and was eager "to get this old coach moving." Then on 15 July he forwarded Salter's draft, now further revised, to Churchill with another request for it to be issued. Eden added, "In short, unless we make U.N.N.R.A. work to our advantage, it will work to our grave disadvantage and we shall be more and more at the mercy of political winds in

America."[488] For some time Churchill failed to act. When reminded on 3 August that Salter was returning to the United States and wished to take the directive with him, Churchill wrote to Eden the following day: "I should not like to issue such a directive. The first thing is to win the great battles on which we are engaged all over the world. I do not wish to crucify Britain on U.N.R.R.A."[489] Undaunted and convinced that the directive was required and in British interests, Eden again exhorted Churchill on 11 August to go ahead. "The peoples of liberated Europe have to be fed and clothed," he wrote, and "I would press you most earnestly to approve the directive." Salter was informed on 14 August that the directive was still under consideration. Finally, Churchill relented on 18 August, replying to Eden, "I have reluctantly initialed your draft directive. I am very apprehensive of Britain being overburdened after the war, but still I recognize the force of your argument that as we have got into this we had better have as large a share of the personnel controlling it as is possible."[490] Churchill's directive, dated 26 August, affirmed it was in Britain's interest to make UNRRA a success. He continued that failure would prejudice "our attempts to secure orderly international collaboration" after the war. Therefore, he exhorted all British military and civilian departments to provide UNRRA with "the fullest possible assistance" in carrying out civilian relief and to release experienced personnel to assist the new organization.[491]

Churchill's directive of 26 August was the single most effective result of Salter's visit to London, and largely due to his efforts. It was intended for internal circulation and as a cabinet paper. However, Salter was given permission to "spread the news unofficially" and hinting that that the prime minister had shown his personal interest in the work of UNRRA. He immediately notified Lehman, writing that the document was an important step "to disperse the impalpable influences adverse to U.N.R.R.A."[492] This proved of enormous benefit, as on Salter's return to Washington Caustin updated him about a large number of unresolved policy issues. These included questions such as whether UNRRA should undertake relief work in Italy, a former Axis country, and whether it was possible to supply relief to Poland and Yugoslavia if UNRRA were asked. As well, among other issues were the preparations for the cancelled Montreal meeting of the Council, now re-scheduled for 15 September.[493] On 21 August Salter held a press conference in Washington where he reviewed developments regarding UNRRA and proposed that more policy revelations would be forthcoming in Montreal.[494] On the same day, and over the course of several subsequent staff meetings convened by Lehman, preparations for the Council meeting proceeded.[495] The meeting in Montreal was in fact held at a critical time for UNRRA. While the first meeting at Atlantic City was concerned with plans and procedures, the September meeting was being held when large areas were already liberated from enemy occupation.

Clearly, the credibility of UNRRA and its ability to fulfill its mandate was on the line and would have to be reinforced in Montreal. Otherwise, it was feared UNRRA would collapse and a scramble for relief supplies would ensue with no orderly process for dealing with displaced people. In addition, there were some who regarded Lehman as adopting "almost a defeatist attitude with regard to the future of UNRRA."[496]

Arrangements and the agenda for the second session of the UNRRA Council were given final approval at meetings of the Central Committee of the Council on 5 and 8 September.[497] Due to inclement weather, which delayed the departure of the majority of delegates travelling by train from Washington, the UNRRA Council opened on 16 September when more than 400 delegates from 44 nations gathered at the Windsor Hotel in Montreal. Lehman delivered his keynote address on 18 September, emphasizing that "the fight against the privation, disease and destruction" wrought by the war was just beginning, and outlining some of the plans already in place for relief and rehabilitation. The leaders of the British and American delegations, Richard Law and Dean Acheson, deputy director general in the European Regional Office of UNRRA, respectively, drew attention to the fact that public approval for UNRRA was receding. It was all the more urgent, therefore, to move UNRRA forward and to substitute action for planning.[498] This was the subject of many subsequent Council plenary sessions and committee meetings. The decision was also made to provide Italy assistance with medical services and supplies and enable the return of displaced persons. Progress was sufficient for Lehman to announce during the final plenary on 26 September that, in committee, agreement had been reached on all issues. This was followed by the unanimous adoption of reports and resolutions before the Council. It was now abundantly clear, especially with the rapid military advances by the Allies that UNRRA would be moving onto its next phase, relief and rehabilitation in the liberated areas of Europe. As the second session of the UNRRA Council drew to a close Lehman announced Salter's immediate retirement and his early return to London.[499]

Even as he was leaving UNRRA Salter shared his experiences in a letter on 2 September to Cecil. He regarded it as vital that UNRRA should be given all the resources it required, with first class personnel, to become an efficient organization. However, he admitted that he was "a good deal distressed" with the prevailing view that UNRRA was in any way a model for future international administration. This should not be, he suggested, because it was an improvised organization constructed while hostilities prevailed, deprived of the best available personnel, and with an effective working relationship with the USSR not yet established. In addition, he pointed to other difficulties which could have been remedied by better support from London and Washington. While he praised the assistance received from the Foreign Office, he had found widespread "skepticism and depreciation" which had impeded progress. The most serious difficulty, he emphasized, was the "fending off" attitude by both the US and UK military towards UNRRA. This had "resulted in a frustrating and demoralizing experience of trying to plan for an uncertain task, at an unknown date under unknown conditions." Salter concluded that the first genuinely international organization, unlike UNRRA, should be comparable to the League of Nations secretariat in 1919 which had a clear mandate, the prospect of permanence and a vast field from which to select the best personnel.[500] Nonetheless, he could take credit for being instrumental in initiating a tenable organization on a global scale in a short time.

On his return from Montreal Salter retreated to Hickory Farm where he was met by Lady Salter who had not gone to Montreal. On 4 October Lady Salter wrote, with evident pleasure, "Arthur is through with U.N.N.R.A." From there they travelled to the River Club in New York where they spent 9 to16 October on a hectic round of official and social meetings.[501] Among the last pieces of UNRRA related business to occupy Salter at this point was the question of his successor. Despite his disapproval of Oliver Franks, that name remained at the top of the list.[502] Finally, on 5 September the War Cabinet decided that Franks could not be spared and Salter was so informed the following day.[503] The seriousness of the situation was sufficient for Churchill to note on 16 September that "We have a large investment in U.N.N.R.A. and it is important to secure a really good man."[504] Writing from Montreal on 22 September, Law had mentioned that he had made one last, but futile, effort to convince Salter to stay on until the end of November. He added that, if Britain wished to exert influence and control, then "we will have to provide a good man." Meanwhile a replacement had come forward – Sir Ernest Gowers, an experienced public servant, at the time responsible for the civil defence of London.[505] On 14 October, while visiting in the United States, he met both with Salter and Lehman at the River Club to discuss the position.[506] However, it was not until 3 February 1945 that Commander Robert G.A. Jackson, assistant to the British Minister of State in the Middle East, was released by the government to become Salter's successor.[507]

By 5 November the Salters had returned to London and taken up residence at the Connaught Hotel. Recognition of Salter's work in Washington came on 15 November when he had an audience with King George V who invested him with the Insignia of a Knight Grand Cross of the Most Excellent Order of the British Empire.[508] He had also received an invitation from George Bell, the publisher of his 1931 book <u>Recovery</u>, to replicate it in the context of the war's looming end. Salter politely declined the proposal and revealed something of his future plans. "After a long period of absence (& incidentally very exacting work)," he wrote, "I must devote myself in the first instance to re-establishing contact with current affairs here in the House of Commons."⁵⁰⁹ He returned to broadcasting for the BBC, with a talk on 18 December which examined the vast work of reconstruction the nation faced at war's end.⁵¹⁰ He did accept an invitation from Chatham House to serve on its council, and on 19 December delivered a lecture on the results of the Dumbarton Oaks Conference, held from 21 August to 7 October, to discuss the framework of the future United Nations. He took as his starting point the notion adopted at Dumbarton Oaks that the new, post-war international organization should be based on the principles of the "sovereign equality of all peace loving states." He argued instead that there must be some "dilution" of national sovereignty, that equality in power and influence was untenable between the great and lesser powers, and that states such as Germany, Italy, Spain and Portugal might not necessarily qualify as peace loving. As to the main framework of the future organization, he found it like the Covenant of the League, despite the emphasis on differences. When he turned to the post-war environment, he suggested that success depended not on a new organization but on the future ability of the great powers to cooperate. In this context, he turned finally to the problem of Germany. He had never before publicly commented on this issue, nor were his private conversations at all revealing.⁵¹¹ He then added, "I may be going to say some things which will shock my friends." After the First World War, he observed, he favoured "the most generous kind of peace for Germany, I was all for conciliation. But I am sure that nearly all of us went on too long and failed to see the point at which a laudable conciliatory policy became appeasement in the worst sense." He then raised the question whether this was the time, while the power and will existed, "to perform such a *surgical* operation on the war potentiality of Germany" so that she would never again attempt domination. He continued, "I do not want revenge, apart from war criminals, on the German public as public, except that which will be incidental to prevent another attempt at war. Now is the time to try and reduce that strain. What that means in practice I do not quite know, but it must mean careful military, scientific and economic consideration." Salter concluded that on balance the chances of future success were greater than in 1920.⁵¹²

As a London-based New Year opened, it was a time for the Salters to renew their social and political connections after their long absence abroad. For Lady Salter this meant a round of social engagements which included such friends as the Winants and "Molly" Hamilton among so many others.⁵¹³ Late in 1944 "Molly" Hamilton had published Remembering My Good Friends. The memoir contained numerous revelatory passages about Lady Salter, including her background. Salter later claimed that his wife was annoyed by the revelations. Lady Salter actually sent copies to numerous friends, including Frances Perkin, who replied that the book "made me feel very close to you."[514] In truth, Lady Salter had traditionally, at least in the English public eye, played the politician's wife in the background. However, an article in The Economist on 30 December compelled her to write to its editor, Geoffrey Crowther. She noted that, while the writer's intent was to put America in its place, she was still "profoundly disturbed" by the article's anti-American tenor. She added, by way of establishing her *bona fides*, that:

> I first came to England at the age of five – then I lived here intermittently till I went to Cambridge at 18 for three years. After that I returned frequently till I lived here from '12-'16, and then again frequently till '32 and after that every year from '32 up to my marriage in '40. I think that I may therefore claim from residence, as well as inheritance, to have an English point of view as well as an American one. [The article] has aroused deep resentment in one Anglo-American who loves her adopted country as her own and perhaps in some ways more.[515]

The New Year actually saw Salter off to a slow start. He agreed to serve on the Reconstruction Committee of the RIIA and spoke at a League of Nations Union meeting on 9 January on the subject of UNRRA and relief in Europe. On the other hand, he refused to contribute an article to The Manchester Guardian on UNRRA, stating he was not yet ready to comment.[516] He did host a large dinner for Lehman when he visited London. In his note of thanks, Lehman commented that "The office is running reasonably well, although we have the usual number of serious problems."[517] Salter's first contribution in the House of Commons after his return was on 17 January during a debate to abolish plural voting. The issue was that electors of the University seats enjoyed both a university vote and a residential vote. He argued that abolition would produce uncertain results because electors would choose to vote in the universities rather than in their home constituencies if they felt their votes would be wasted in the former. The bill on second reading was defeated.[518] He also intervened on 20 February during a debate on various aspects of education. He weighed in with a proposal, not adopted, to increase teachers' salaries and so attract more university trained educators.[519]

As important as such issues might have been, they indicate that Salter was still feeling his way. Indeed, he had written earlier in the year that he was not yet ready to retire "to the contemplation of obituaries." He admitted that "I suffer myself from the recurrent desire to retire, but it alternates (I think happily) with an equally recurrent urge to have another whack at things."[520] Such an opportunity was not long in coming, but in the meantime, he busied himself as best he could. On 1 March, on more familiar ground, he contributed to the ongoing debate on the declaration of policy agreed to by the USSR, the US and the UK at the recently concluded Crimea (Yalta) Conference. His primary concern was that, regarding Germany, there should be adequate safeguards for the future security of Europe. The best approach, in his view, was not partition or "perpetual garrisoning," but a settlement which would inevitably "be more severe by comparison with the wrongly-abused Treaty of Versailles." He approved the fact that, unlike in 1919, reparation would this time be in kind and not cash and that the presence now of the US and the USSR signaled a more hopeful future for international cooperation. As to the nature of a future international organization, however, he expressed his concerns that the veto could be misused, for example, by the USSR. He concluded by praising Churchill as "the most active architect of Allied unity" and signaled that he would vote in favour of the motion approving the Yalta accords. The motion was passed unanimously with a vote of 410 to 0 in the House of Commons.[521]

Salter returned to familiar ground when he contributed to a debate on 28 March regarding supplies to liberated areas of Europe. He addressed, for the first time, those who had expressed disappointment as to why UNRRA was not yet operational. The governments who created UNRRA, he stated, "started it too early, organized it too cumbrously, circumscribed it too narrowly and advertised it too enthusiastically." Planning had so far operated in a vacuum, and as a result it was difficult to recruit good people, maintain morale and acquire power. He urged that the military bring UNRRA into play as soon as possible, but that UNRRA should not be regarded as a real test of the future of international administration: "The first real test of an international organization will be the first organization that is created after the war has finished, and not one that is created now." Turning to the question of relief, he suggested that unlike 1918, the current devastation in Europe was continent wide, of unprecedented proportions, and Germany would also need some relief. Finally, with regard to reconstruction, a task not assigned to UNRRA, he proposed the establishment of "a superior authority." This would be comparable to the Supreme Economic Council, of which he was general secretary in 1919-1920, and might be named the "Supreme Reconstruction Council." With such a body there would there be "some hope of meeting the greatest challenge to the constructive effort of man that has ever been witnessed in the history of the world." Several MPs voiced their support for Salter's suggestion, as well as The Manchester Guardian which described his as "the most important speech."[522]

Salter had once again found his voice and the issues which mattered most to him. He followed his Commons' speech with an article in The Times, elaborating his proposal for a Supreme Economic Council. A liberated Europe, he wrote:

Would find large regions of scorched earth; arable land that had lost its seasonal sowing; movements of displaced and destitute persons to be numbered by tens of millions; transport denuded of locomotives, wagons and road lorries, and impeded by demolished bridges; many towns a mere rubble of dust, and industrial plant destroyed; an absence of all stocks of either food or raw materials; and, with leaders killed and national institutions dissolved, the whole framework of political and economic organization often shattered.

Such a situation demanded the creation of a Supreme Economic Council with adequate authority to co-ordinate Allied reconstruction in a liberated Europe. <u>The Times</u> endorsed Salter's suggestion and itself called for such "a central authority endowed with full executive powers."[523] In a follow-up article in <u>The Spectator</u>, informed by considerable research, Salter focused on the "grim picture" of a liberated Europe, with a scarcity of food and medical supplies and destroyed infrastructure. He noted that the productive capacity previously devoted to the instruments of war would be sufficient to repair the resulting devastation. To achieve this required not only a Supreme Reconstruction Council, but also assigning overall responsibility for the British contribution to a minister in the War Cabinet.[524] As an initial small step, Salter set up a House of Commons all party European Reconstruction Committee with himself as chairman.[525]

On 17 April Salter was again on his feet in the Commons, contributing to the debate about the San Francisco Conference, scheduled to open on 25 April and designed to finalize the charter, drafted at Dumbarton Oaks, of the future United Nations. He expressed concern that the Conference might be premature, in as much as the war had not ended and that full agreement might prove difficult. To this end he advised the government to let it be known that the new organization "will have as its task that of preserving the peace, but not that of making the peace settlement." Of further concern to him, as well as many others in the Commons, was to restrict the projected and extensive use of the veto on the Security Council. In time it was agreed at San Francisco that there should be no veto in the Security Council on placing items on the agenda or on discussion.[526]

The nature of the issues Salter was addressing, as well as his relevant experience in both world wars, appeared to make him a candidate for an emerging official position. Under the Protocol agreed at the Crimea Conference, an Allied Reparation Commission was to be set up in Moscow, consisting of representatives from the USSR, the UK and the USA. Its task, as defined by Eden, was to determine "Germany's capacity to make reparation and the forms in which it should be made." Churchill first suggested searching for a representative, but on 23 March he minuted, "I propose Sir A. Salter."[527] Opinion in the Foreign Office welcomed the suggestion, with a note that Salter was fully familiar with the issue of extracting reparations from Germany and had experience of international negotiations. Eden agreed, writing, "Yes, quite all right; so long as I don't have to listen to him often."[528] Churchill who still regarded Salter as "incomparably our best representative" met with him on 14 April and offered him the post. The prime minister afterwards wrote: "Sir Arthur Salter earnestly hoped he would not be pressed to take the post. He had been General Secretary of the old Reparations Commission. He had no special aptitude for getting on with the Russians. He had many interests here. He had been about a great deal. We must look elsewhere." The position, to Salter's relief, was finally accepted on 29 May by Sir Walter Monckton.[529]

Salter's reference to his many interests was certainly beginning to take shape. He was enjoying the return to London and the opportunities that lay ahead, writing on 26 April:

Ethel and I have been back now for nearly six months. It has been very pleasant to renew contacts here. On the whole I have been very cheered by what I have found here. There has I think been a great deal too much talk about Britain being tired. The standard of plays and acting, for example, is higher than I've ever known it and it corresponds to a real public demand. The demand for books is the same. And there is the most eager interest in all public affairs. The debates in our Parliament have been lively and good – and their influence on policy very real and, I think, beneficial. Ethel and I are in excellent health and much enjoying the combination of the most glorious spring weather in living memory, victory, and – for a month now – immunity from V2's which were very unpleasant and deadly while they lasted. We see Sybil Colefax frequently. She continues her extremely interesting and I think useful dinners, in which you find that you meet almost everybody you most want to see in London.[530]

On the same day he also wrote to Lippmann, "I find it extremely pleasant to renew contact here, & am pleasantly surprised at the vitality & reality of many, though not all, of the discussions in parliament. There's really quite an extraordinary amount of good & hard thinking about public affairs, & a very eager & widespread public interest."[531]

Salter himself was actually in the thick of this widening debate about public and foreign policy. Between 18 March and 9 June the BBC Overseas Services broadcast 12 talks which he had recorded earlier in the year.[532] Under the general theme, "Facing the Future," he examined an array of post-war problems facing Britain. Among these questions was foreign trade, international security, the future of the Commonwealth, the transition from a wartime to a peacetime economy and the degree of control that would govern this development. "We have great difficulties," he concluded his first talk, "but we also have great assets, and we shall face our future determined to succeed." In subsequent broadcasts he created a framework and prescription which echoed his 1931 book Recovery, but for a post-war world. Because the war had changed Britain from a creditor to a debtor nation, he envisaged an initial period of controls and rationing, but followed by a system of multilateral as opposed to bilateral trade. As for security and future peace, he was hopeful of the Allied powers' ongoing efforts to construct a new United Nations. Success, he anticipated, would depend *inter alia* on the ongoing unity of purpose of the wartime grand alliance. As for Commonwealth and colonial policy, he advocated "development and progressive emancipation" rather than outright "liquidation and dissolution." He foresaw the need to modernise and re-equip some of the older exporting industries (coal and textiles) but also to develop newer industries (plastics and nylon). This would necessitate continuing conscription, tax remissions to replace obsolete industrial plant, and economic controls such as food rationing, the allocation of essential materials, and investment and expenditure abroad. In this transition period, he was clear that there would have to remain "comprehensive State control of private enterprise." He further believed that unemployment could be reduced, that relations between government and industry required an extension of government control but not the abandonment of private enterprise, and that a million new houses had to be built by the government. While supporting the Beveridge plan for "cradle to grave" social security, he questioned whether the country could afford the cost. The final broadcast, "The New Democracy," suggested that parliamentary democracy was constantly evolving in Britain and it now faced the challenge of adding a social and economic democracy to the political democracy.[533] By this time, too, Salter had widened his involvement with the BBC. He had long been acknowledged as an experienced broadcaster and therefore required no rehearsals.[534] On 7 February he readily accepted an invitation to take part for the first time in the popular BBC programme the "Brains Trust," first aired on 1 January 1941. The Question Master chaired the discussion, by a panel of distinguished public intellectuals, of questions submitted by the public. Salter's first broadcast was recorded on 12 March 1945 in the 4th series, and he remained a popular and well-regarded panel member, although not a regular one, until his final contribution on 19 June 1951.[535]

Salter appeared to be fulfilling his wish "to be a comfortable private member and do some much needed thinking and writing."[536] However, he had also since the summer of 1943 hoped to fill a cabinet position and that opportunity finally came his way. With the dissolution of the wartime coalition on 23 May, Churchill reconstituted a caretaker government three days later, with election results scheduled to be announced on 26 July. Salter declared his candidacy once again as an Independent for Oxford University.[537] On 26 May the press carried the news that Salter had been appointed the previous day as Chancellor of the Duchy of Lancaster, with cabinet rank, and with special responsibility for European reconstruction. The appointment was favourably received, with <u>The Manchester Guardian</u> reminding its readers that Salter had himself argued that such a position be created, while both <u>The Observer</u> and <u>The Economist</u> called it a "wise" move. <u>The Times</u> noted that he was "particularly well equipped" for the position.[538] On 28 May Salter attended a Privy Council meeting and afterwards had an audience with the King and received his Seals of Office.[539] The following day Churchill, with input from Richard Law and the Foreign Office, wrote to him explaining his new responsibilities with regard to European reconstruction, "in order to avoid the possibility of any misunderstanding." The prime minister cautioned that the Foreign Secretary and the Minister of Defence retained their respective responsibilities with regard to restoring peacetime conditions in Europe. In view of Salter's experience and interests, however, Churchill wished him to provide advice on various problems, particularly economic ones where these concerned several ministers or the cabinet as a whole. Consequently, he assigned specific tasks to Salter, including acting as chairman of the newly constituted Emergency Economic Committee for Europe, and membership on the Ministerial Committees on Reparations and Supplies to Liberated Areas, Armistices and Post-War Problems, and the Industrial Disarmament of European Enemy Countries. Law, who helped draft the letter to Salter, noted that chairing the European Economic Committee, whose first meeting had been on 28 May, with Law as chairman, "is right up his street & he should do most useful work."[540]

Even as the country focused on the upcoming election, Salter set vigorously to work. However, despite how burdensome his workload might have appeared, this was not to be the case in most instances. The Emergency Economic Committee for Europe had held its inaugural meetings on 28 May, with its mandate limited to the promotion of co-operation in resolving Europe's economic problems. Its next meeting on 30 May, which Salter first chaired as a "supernumerary member" and not as a British national, dealt with procedure as did several subsequent business meetings. At a later meeting on 19 June, Salter proposed the establishment of "a semi-technical secretariat" to assist with policy regarding economic problems.[541] In contrast to the slow evolution of this committee, work proceeded quickly on the Ministerial Committee on Reparations, responsible for preparing the draft instructions for the British delegation to the upcoming Moscow Conference on reparations. The issue was a complicated one, as shown by the discussion in the cabinet on 11 June, to which Salter made several contributions. His suggestion that reparation deliveries "should be limited to a specified list consisting mainly of raw materials and semi-manufactured goods" was accepted. The meeting also established another committee, including Salter, to monitor the Moscow proceedings.[542] The next day the Reparations Committee settled on a final directive for Monkton as he departed for Moscow. It contained the injunction to give the Russians "the benefit of the experience which we gained in these matters after the last war. Security is more important than reparation."[543] Progress in Moscow was rapid and when the Reparations Committee met for the third and last time on 9 July it approved the "Statement of Principles" agreed upon in Moscow.[544]

During this time too Salter paid some attention to his election campaign. On 13 June "The Letter from Nominators" was published. This praised Salter for "having played an essential part in maintaining our supplies across the seas, and so making victory possible." It also endorsed the idea that universities should be represented by Independents, but should not be debarred from accepting government office. In his "Address to the Electors," Salter declared that he "was a Churchillian in all that concerned national defence" prior to 1939. In foreign policy he restated his belief "in a strong collective system," his opposition to converting Germany to an agricultural country and his support for the United Nations. In domestic affairs he reiterated his belief that the economy "should combine private enterprise with safeguards of the public interest, neither naked individual competition nor its replacement by a bureaucratised system; no wholesale nationalization; the 'public utility principle' in some cases, and the more purposive direction of state action where it is taken in the larger sphere in which private enterprise remains." He then explained his support for the election platform of the caretaker government, and for the prime minister personally and the reasons he had accepted office. He recalled his praising Churchill, on 1 March in the House, as the – "architect of Allied unity" – and added that the international situation demanded Churchill's return to office. His decision to accept office, he continued, was reinforced by loyalty and gratitude to Churchill. Finally, he added, a comment which he would later regret: "I remain an Independent; I shall not become a Conservative or a member of any Party, great or small."[545]

To Salter's existing committee work, accompanied by attendance where necessary at cabinet meetings, Churchill added yet more.[546] On 16 June the prime minister wrote to Eden, Salter and Sir James Grigg, the Secretary of State for War, that he wished to set up a committee to deal with the control or administration of ex-enemy territories in Europe. He envisaged this European Control Committee to be the conduit whereby he would be "kept in constant touch with these matters."[547] The terms of reference, composition and responsibilities took some time to complete. These were finally approved at the first meeting of the European Control Committee on 10 July, with Grigg as chairman and Salter, Jacob and William Mabane, Minister of State, in attendance. Salter was given the task of answering parliamentary questions of an economic nature.[548] The following day he attended the first meeting of the Overseas Reconstruction Committee, which replaced the Armistice and Post-War Committee (set up on 26 November 1943), chaired by Eden, and with Grigg, Lyttleton, Cherwell and Anderson in attendance. Its terms of reference, which had been approved by Churchill on 5 July, were to advise the cabinet on policy questions relating to liberated and ex-enemy countries. The committee's discussions ranged over an array of issues, from the nature of the control machinery for, and zones of occupation in, Austria, to the control and ownership of German industries and the need to separate the German and Austrian economies.[549] On 16 July Salter chaired the second, and his last, meeting of the European Control Committee. The main item was a progress report on the establishment of a centre in Germany to receive, edit and disseminate news to the Germans. Salter wholeheartedly endorsed the idea, approved by the committee, that control of this work should be retained by the Propaganda and Information Office and not the military. The committee also reaffirmed the policy that German research and development establishments were to be preserved intact for possible future Allied use.[550]

To his range of committee responsibilities, Salter added yet another. He was to become a Minister of Reconstruction with input across the whole range of issues. On 16 July he accepted the position as chairman of the London Co-ordinating Committee, originally set up in August 1944 to co-ordinate allied supplies to liberated or conquered areas. Given his considerable involvement in reconstruction work and his role as chairman of the Supplies to Liberated Areas, this was a natural step and Salter accepted the position.[551] He chaired the next meeting on 19 July where he was welcomed by the outgoing chairman, Sir Robert Sinclair, as "a member of the British Cabinet with special responsibility for the co-ordination of economic affairs affecting the liberated countries of Europe." Various issues were then discussed, such as prices for Danish food exports and the allocation of German exports.[552] This proved, in fact, to be the only meeting of the committee Salter chaired. When it next met on 17 August Salter was on the Opposition benches. Indeed, among the last meetings he attended in Churchill's interim administration was the Overseas Reconstruction Committee on 24 July. A variety of Far Eastern issues was discussed, including the future recognition of Siam. Salter was among those arguing against demanding compensation for the use of prisoner of war labour and for increased shipments of rice – a point of view which prevailed.[553] The final meeting he chaired was the Emergency Economic Committee on 1 August, where he raised the issue of publicizing some of its deliberations, a suggestion that was later turned down.[554]

In his two months as Chancellor of the Duchy of Lancaster, Salter's activity had centred largely upon his membership in several committees. As he was exempt from the departmental duties of other ministers, he had also studied a vast number of reports on conditions in liberated Europe. Indeed, as soon as he had accepted office, he confided to Churchill that his first objective was to write a comprehensive paper "reviewing the whole problem of European economic reconstruction."[555] His memorandum which he completed on 25 July suggested some material factors, such as shipping, port facilities and raw materials, were better than anticipated, yet "the prospect is grave. Millions, and it may be many millions, will suffer seriously in the next year from cold and underfeeding. 'First aid' in a few but crucial supplies, if quickly given, might be decisive in its effects for many years." The major obstacles to European recovery, in his view, were the need for trucks, while rail and barge traffic were being restored, and a shortage of coal, oils, fats, sugar and meat. The memorandum recognized that responsibility for relief differed from country to country as did the shortages, and as such the memorandum made various recommendations in each region. With regard to "reconversion and reconstruction," Salter argued that his "first-aid" measures would initially help but that financial assistance, by way of inter-governmental loan schemes, would be required in the longer term. He concluded:

> Fatigue and embitterment are widespread, revolution often threatened. Political chaos and economic disorganization are therefore probable. But if the situation is exceptionally chaotic it is also exceptionally influenceable and malleable. Prompt and generous 'first-aid' from the West may have an effect on Europe's future altogether out of proportion to its amount or its duration.

Salter sent the memorandum to Eden for circulation as a cabinet paper. However, the resignation of the Churchill government the following day prevented it from going forward. He followed up, however, by offering the document to the Labour Foreign Minister, Ernest Bevin, for information and circulation as appropriate.[556]

The election, with results announced on 26 July, returned a majority Labour government. Salter confessed he thought the outcome was "unexpected." It also saw him and A.P. Herbert, in results announced on 30 July, retain their seats as Independent MPs for Oxford University. One of the two defeated candidates was G.D.H. Cole who had supported Salter in the 1937 campaign and had run as a Labour candidate. Given Salter's position in the Churchill government, no Conservative candidate ran against him. The victory was also accompanied by his re-election as a Fellow of All Souls and inclusion in the category of Distinguished Persons Fellows.[557] Some time later he wrote that he regarded his service under Churchill in the wartime government "as the greatest privilege in my life in public affairs."[558]

Endnotes

1. Minutes, All-Party Parliamentary Action Group, 13 Sept. 1939, Rathbone to Lloyd George, 18 Sept. 1939, Lloyd George Papers, G/16/7/1-4, Boothby to Lloyd George, 2 Nov. 1939, Lloyd George Papers, G/3/13/15-18, Robert Boothby, I Fight to Live (1947), 195.
2. Layton to Salter, 7 Sept., Salter to Miss McLeary, 11 Sept. 1939, Layton Papers, 6[38, 40], "Draft Memoirs," chapter 17, p. 8. Layton Papers, Box 38, The Collected Writings of John Maynard Keynes, vol. 22, Donald Moggridge, ed., (1978), 15-16, David Hubback, No Ordinary Press Baron: A Life of Walter Layton (1985), 167-168, Robert Skidelsky, John Maynard Keynes, 1883-1946 (2003), 584-585.
3. Salter's memorandum, "Food Blockade" and Keynes' "The Financial Principles of the Blockade," enclosed in Keynes to Salter, 9 Oct. 1939, Keynes Papers.
4. Leith-Ross to Salter, 26 Oct. 1939, NA-UK, MT62/104.
5. The Collected Writings of John Maynard Keynes, vol. 22, 22, Hubback, No Ordinary Press Baron, 168-169.
6. H.C. Debs., vol. 351, 7 Sept., cols. 563-564, 14 Sept., cols. 799-780, vol. 352, 17 Oct., col. 653, 19 Oct., col. 1111, vol. 353, 8 Nov. 1939, col. 280. See also Salter to Layton, 28 Oct. 1939, Layton Papers, 10[81(1-2)].
7. H.C. Debs., vol. 352, 18 Oct. 1939, cols. 916-917, 942, 957-964. A.C. Pigou, president of the Royal Economic Society, also called for the government to enlist the services of Salter, Keynes, Beveridge and Layton, as did others. See The Times, 23 Oct., 2 Nov. 1939.
8. "The Economic Strategy of the War," Contemporary Review, 156(Dec. 1939), 641-651.
9. "War Purposes and Peace Aims – I," The Spectator, 163(27 Oct. 1939), 575-576, "What Are Our War Aims," Picture Post, 28 Oct. 1939, 47.
10. Salter to Sir Michael Sadler, 23 Oct. 1939, Sir Michael Sadler Papers, MSS Eng. misc.c549, Bodleian Library, Oxford.
11. Entry of 15 Oct. 1939, Euan Wallace Diary, Box 1, Euan Wallace Papers, Bodleian Library, Oxford, The Times, 14 Oct., 14 Nov. 1939.
12. Salter, Memoirs, 264.
13. Salter to Cole, 13 Nov. 1939, D.G.H Cole Papers, GDHC/C/6/1/1, Nuffield College Library, Oxford.
14. Violet Markham to Joyce Newton Thompson, 2 Dec. 1939, Newton Thompson Papers, BC 643 BI8.58.
15. The Times, 14 Nov. 1939, The Manchester Guardian, 14 Nov. 1939.

16. Amery to Salter, 13 Nov. 1939, Salter to Amery, 16 Nov. 1939, NA-UK, MT62/97.
17. Butler to Salter, 14 Nov. 1939, NA-UK, MT62/98.
18. Keynes to Salter, 15 Nov. 1939, NA-UK, MT62/103.
19. Salter to Lloyd George, 16 Nov. 1939, Lloyd George Papers, G/17/8/3.
20. E.D. Simon to Salter, 14 Nov., Salter to Simon, 16 Nov. 1939, NA-UK, MT62/107.
21. Salter to Swinton, 16 Nov. 1939, NA-UK, MT62/107.
22. Royall Tyler to Robert Woods Bliss, 17 Nov., Royall Tyler to Elisina Tyler, 24 Nov. 1939, Tyler Papers.
23. The Manchester Guardian, 15 Nov. 1939.
24. H.C.Debs., vol. 353, 14 Nov. 1939, cols. 608, 628, 643-644.
25. H.C. Debs., vol. 353, 14 Nov. 1939, cols. 674-682.
26. Salter to Chiozza Money, 18 Jan. 1940, NA-UK, MT62/105, Salter, Memoirs, 264-265.
27. The Times, 21 Oct. 1935, Salter to Ernest Brown, 17 Nov. 1939, Brown to Salter, 23 Nov. 1939, NA-UK, MT62/98.
28. Keynes to Salter, 19 Nov. 1939, Keynes Papers.
29. The Times, 14, 15 Nov. 1939, memorandum by Salter, "Stabilization of Cost of Living and Wages," encl. in Salter to Keynes, 21 Nov. 1939, Keynes Papers.
30. Keynes to Salter, 4 Dec. 1939, Salter to Keynes, 6 Dec. 1939, NA-UK, MT62/103, John Maynard Keynes, How to Pay for the War (1940), 88. Salter continued to support Keynes on this subject. See Keynes to Dawson, 11 Mar. 1940, in The Collected Writings of John Maynard Keynes, vol. 22, 101-104, Keynes to Salter, 16 Apr. 1940, MT62/103.
31. Salter to Sir Alan G. Anderson, 23 Nov. 1939, NA-UK, MT62/97, C.B.A. Behrens, Merchant Shipping and the Demands of War (rev. ed., 1978), 39.
32. H.C. Debs., vol. 352, 31 Oct. 1939, cols. 1752-1753, Salter, Memoirs, 265-266.
33. "Note of Meeting Held in the Minister's Room on 24th November 1939," memorandum by Salter, "General Policy as to Requisitioning and Licensing," 28 Nov. 1939, "Policy of Requisitioning," n.d., Salter to Gilmour, 13 Dec. 1939, NA-UK, MT62/123, Salter, Memoirs, 265.
34. See memoranda in "Compensation for Losses by War Risk, 4 Dec. 1939 to 31 Jan. 1940," NA-UK, MT62/122.
35. "Liner Requisitioning Scheme," 28 Dec. 1939, NA-UK, MT62/123, The Times, 18, 20 Dec. 1939, 5 Jan. 1940.
36. R. Boswell to Salter, 8, 11 Jan. 1940, NA-UK, MT62/98, "The Empire at War," 8 Jan. 1940, BBC WAC, Salter Scripts.
37. Salter to Violet Markham, 1 Dec. 1939, Markham Papers, 25/73.
38. Salter to F.W. Pethick-Lawrence, 10 Jan. 1940, NA-UK, MT62/106.
39. Salter, Memoirs, 266.

40. "Anglo-French Co-ordinating Committee, Note by the Secretary," NA-UK, CAB85/8, "Co-ordination of Anglo-French Economic War Effort," NA-UK CAB21/1271, Salter, Memoirs, 266, Behrens, Merchant Shipping, 72-77.
41. "Calendar of Papers on Shipping by Sir Arthur Salter," 15 Jan. 1940, NA-UK, CAB102/421. The file is a summary of Salter's major papers on aspects of shipping, compiled by the official historian C.B.A. Behrens.
42. Salter to Halifax, 4 Mar. 1940, NA-UK, MT62/102.
43. See The Times, 1 Apr. 1940, citing the Nineteenth Century.
44. See e.g., H.C. Debs., vol. 356, 18, 23, 30 Jan. 1940, cols. 272, 396-399, 433-434, 965-967, vol. 357, 8, 14, 26 Feb. 1940, cols. 431-432, 745-746, 1725.
45. H.C. Debs., vol. 358, 18 Mar. 1940, cols. 1659-1773, The Times, 19 Mar. 1940, The Economist, 138(23 Mar. 1940), 511, Salter, Memoirs, 266.
46. The New York Times, 31 Mar., 4 Apr. 1940, The Times, 1, 4 Apr. 1940.
47. Crozier Interview with Hoare, 3 Apr. 1940, Crozier Papers. Reprinted in W.P. Crozier: Off the Record, Political Interviews, 1933-1943, A.J.P. Taylor, ed., (1973), 160.
48. "Notes of the Week," The Economist, 138(6 Apr. 1940), 610, The Spectator, 164(5 Apr. 1940), 465.
49. "The Danish Ships," Salter Papers, File 1, Anecdotes and Incidents. Salter recounted this incident in both his Memoirs, 266-267, and Slave of the Lamp, 202-203.
50. "Message Addressed to Masters of All Danish Ships by British Government," NA-UK, MT62/121, The Times, 11 Apr. 1940.
51. Memorandum by Salter, 15 Apr. 1940, "Message to be Broadcast in Norwegian and English," 19 Apr. 1940, NA-UK, MT62/121, Behrens, Merchant Shipping, 97.
52. The Times, 19 Apr., 7 May, 1940, Behrens, Merchant Shipping, 92.
53. Salter to Crowther, 22 Apr. 1940, Crowther to Salter, 8, 22 May 1940, NA-UK, MT62/99.
54. Memorandum by Salter, "The Control of Merchant Shipping: Licensing or Requisition," 2 Apr. 1940, NA-UK, CAB102/41, "Shipping in War," The Economist, 138(25 May, 1 June 1940), 937-938, 978-979.
55. R. Coupland to Salter, 31 Mar. 28 Apr. 1940, NA-UK, MT62/99, "Shipping Control," Round Table, 30(1940), 603-619.
56. The Times, 16 May 1940. Hudson became Minister of Agriculture and Fisheries.
57. Salter to Cecil, 24, 25 May 1940, Cecil Papers, ADD MSS, vol. 43, ff. 106-107.
58. Martin Gilbert, Finest Hour: Winston Churchill, 1939-1941 (1983), 455, 463-464.
59. The Times, 1 June 1940.
60. "Calendar of Papers on Shipping by Sir Arthur Salter," [early June], NA-UK, CAB102/421.

61. Salter to Rowse, 17 June 1940, Rowse Papers, EUL MS113/3/1/Corr.S.
62. E.E. Bridges to Sir Horace Wilson, 28 May, Wilson to Greenwood, 31 May 1940, NA-UK, CAB21/1271.
63. Monnet to Churchill, June 1940 (sic), memoranda by Salter, "Equipment of the French and British Armies," and "General Note," 4 June 1940, NA-UK, MT62/116.
64. Entry of 13 June 1940, <u>The Empire at Bay: The Leo Amery Diaries, 1929-1945</u>, vol. 2, 622.
65. "Anglo-French Unity," Jean Monnet Papers, AME 8/2/2, Jean Monnet Foundation, Lausanne, Monnet, <u>Memoirs</u>, 21-30. Copy also in Amery Papers, AMEL2/3/8.
66. Entry of 14 June 1940, <u>The Empire at Bay: The Leo Amery Diaries, 1929-1945</u>, vol. 2, 622-623, Amery to Churchill, 14 June 1940, including memorandum "Anglo-French Unity, 14 June 1940," minutes, by Churchill and J.R. Colville, 16 June 1940, NA-UK, PREM3/176.
67. Minute by Vansittart, 16 June 1940, PREM3/176. This file contains the original draft of the declaration and the amended version agreed to by the War Cabinet. See also Minutes, Cabinet Meeting, 169(40), 16 June 1940, NA-UK, CAB65/7/64, Gilbert, <u>Finest Hour: Winston Churchill, 1939-1941</u>, 556-561, and entry of 15, 16 June 1940, <u>The Empire at Bay: The Leo Amery Diaries, 1929-1945</u>, vol. 2, 624.
68. Entry of 16 June 1940, John Colville, <u>The Fringes of Power: 10 Downing Street Diaries, 1939-1955</u> (1985), 159-160, Salter, <u>Memoirs</u>, 267. Halifax afterwards confirmed that the proposal was only binding for the duration of the war. See Halifax to Hankey, 23 June 1940, NA-UK, FO800/312.
69. Salter to Amery, 19 May 1955, Amery Papers, AMEL 8/83.
70. Entry of 11 June 1940, M.A. "Molly" Hamilton Diary, vol. 5, author's archive.
71. Salter to Rowse, 13 June 1940, Rowse Papers, EUL MS113/3/1/Corr.S.
72. Salter Papers, File 28, Marriage Certificate of Sir Arthur Salter to Ethel Bullard, 14 June 1940, <u>The Times</u>, 17 June 1940. The marriage was also noted in <u>The New York Times</u>, 17 June 1940, and <u>The Washington Post</u>, 17 June 1940. The latter wrote the bride wore "a tailored blue and brown gingham frock with hat of blue and white, and blue and white accessories."
73. Salter to Rowse, 17 June 1940, Rowse Papers, EUL MS113/3/1/Corr.S. In 1946 G.H. Salter revived the Festival of St Cecilia, the patron saint of music and musicians, with a special service, followed by a luncheon and an evening music concert at the Albert Hall. In November 1949 Salter was the guest speaker. See G.H. Salter, <u>St. Sepulchre's Church, Over Against Newgate in the City of London: A Watcher at the City Gate for Thirty-Eight Reigns, A.D. 1137-1956</u> (1956), 102-112, <u>The Times</u>, 8 Nov. 1949.
74. Salter, <u>Memoirs</u>, 267-268.

75. "Lives of Fellows of All Souls College, vol. 4, Arthur Lord Salter, Rowse Papers, EUL MS113/1/2/4, A.L. Rowse, All Souls in My Time (1993), 123.
76. Salter to Rowse, 17 June 1940, Rowse Papers, EUL MS113/3/1/Corr.S. The remarks about Salter's marriage are also in Richard Ollard, A Man of Contradictions: A Life of A.L. Rowse (1999), 125.
77. Salter to Rowse, 13, 17 June 1940, Rowse Papers, EUL MS113/3/1/Corr.S.
78. Salter to Stimson, 21 June 1940, Stimson Papers.
79. Memorandum by Salter, "Immediate Defence Measures," 24 June 1940, NA-UK, MT62/108, Anderson to Salter, 10 July 1940, NA-UK, MT62/97.
80. Anglo-French Co-ordinating Committee, Note by Monnet, 3 July 1940, NA-UK, CAB21/1271.
81. Memorandum by Salter, 2 July 1940, NA-UK, MT62/115, minute by Bridges, 8 July 1940, NA-UK, CAB21/1271.
82. Wilson to Sir Arthur Greenwood, 4 July 1940, NA-UK, MT62/108.
83. North American Supply Committee, Composition and Terms of Reference, 9 July 1940, NAS(40) 1, NA-UK, CAB92/27, Halifax to Lothian, 10 July 1040, NA-UK, FO372/25145, W8702/79/49.
84. Éric Roussel, Jean Monnet, 1888-1979 (Paris, 1996), 247-256, H.C. Debs, vol. 362, 11 July 1940, cols. 1341-1343.
85. Record of an Inter-Departmental Meeting, 8 July 1940, Annex 1, to NAS (40)2, 9 July 1940, NA-UK, CAB92/27.
86. NAS (40)1st Meeting, 10 July 1940, NAS(40)1, 9 July 1940, N.A.S(40)2, 9 July 1940, NA-UK, CAB92/27, T.H. Brand to Salter, 7 July 1940, MT62/98.
87. Greenwood to Churchill, 13 July 1940, NA-UK, PREM3/3483/3.
88. NAS (40)2nd Meeting, 20 July 1940, NA-UK, CAB92/27.
89. "Armament Programmes," Note by Salter, 31 July 1940, NAS(40)11, NA-UK, CAB92/27.
90. H. Duncan Hall, North American Supply (1955), 218, Salter to Beaverbrook, 24 July 1940, NA-UK, MT62/98.
91. Greenwood to Churchill, 1 Aug. 1940, Lord Cherwell Papers, H159/1-2, Nuffield College Library, Oxford.
92. NAS (40)3rd Meeting, 5 Aug. 1940, NA-UK, CAB92/27.
93. Hall, North American Supply, 175.
94. Minute, Salter to Churchill, 14 Aug. 1940, and attached "Munitions Imports: New Programmes." Both Bridges and Beaverbrook endorsed Salter's conclusions, including the issue of types. Minutes by Bridges and Beaverbrook, 22 Aug. 1940. NA-UK, PREM3/483/3.
95. Hubback, No Ordinary Press Baron, 173.

96. NAS (40)4th Meeting, 28 Aug. 1940, "Armaments Programmes," memorandum by Salter, 26 Aug. 1940, NAS (40)18, NA-UK CAB92/27.
97. W.P. (40) 337, 28 Aug. 1940, Proposed Mission to US, NA-UK, CAB66/11/17, Minutes, Cabinet Meeting 238(40) 30 Aug. 1940, NA-UK, CAB65/8/50, Hall, North American Supply, 184. On 21 July Salter had been advised by Purvis that virtually all purchases of military supplies would have to be approved by the Defence Advisory Committee. See Purvis to Salter, PURSA No. 20, 21 July 1940, NA-UK, AVIA38/105.
98. See e.g., his "Sale of Vessels Ordered by the Government to Shipowners Who Have Lost Vessels During the War," W.P. (G)(40) 216, 15 Aug. 1940, NA-UK, CAB67/8/16, Minutes, Cabinet Meeting 238(40), 30 Aug. 1940, NA-UK, CAB65/8/50, and H.C. Debs., vol. 364, 22 Aug. 1940, cols. 1504-1505.
99. Salter to Purvis, 11 July 1940, NA-UK, FO371/25145, W8702/79/49, Purvis to Salter, PURSA No. 2, 13 July 1940, NA-UK, AVIA38/105. For the PURSA telegrams, see NA-UK, AVIA38/105-106.
100. Hall, North American Supply, 146-155, 498-504, Purvis to Halifax, PURSA No. 1, 13 July 1940, Purvis to Salter, PURSA No. 4, 14 July 1940, NA-UK, AVIA38/105.
101. Purvis to Salter, PURSA Nos. 9, 13, 16, 19 July 1940 NA-UK, AVIA38/105.
102. Purvis to Salter, PURSA Nos. 16, 27, 20 July 1940, PURSA Nos. 47, 48, 4 Aug. 1940, NA-UK, AVIA38/105, Salter to Purvis, PURSA No. 5, 21 July 1940 NA-UK, AVIA38/106.
103. Purvis to Salter, PURSA No. 55, 12 Aug. 1940, NA-UK, AVIA38/105.
104. Salter to Purvis, PURSA No. 21, 9 Aug. 1940, NA-UK, AVIA38/106, Purvis to Salter, PURSA No. 60, 15 Aug. 1940, NA-UK, AVIA38/105.
105. Salter to Eden, 19 Aug. 1940, NA-UK, MT62/100.
106. Purvis to Salter, PURSA No. 78, 28 Aug. 1940, NA-UK, AVIA38/105, Salter to Purvis, PURSA No. 52, 29 Aug., No. 54, 31 Aug. 1940, NA-UK, AVIA38/106.
107. Salter to Eden, 28 Aug. 1940, NA-UK, MT62/100.
108. Salter to Layton, 6 Sept. 1940, NA-UK, MT62/104.
109. Salter to Eden, 5, 6 Sept, 1940, NA-UK, MT62/100. In fact a somewhat similar situation had already been rectified in Washington. On 19 June 1940 Stimson, a friend of Salter, Layton and Purvis, had been appointed Secretary of State for War. One of his early tasks, "a matter of the utmost importance," had been to ensure that all British supply requests, "complicated and chaotic," were to be handled by Purvis and "systematized" in his department. Stimson described Salter and Layton, as the "two men, who are perhaps the men I know best of all Englishmen." See entry of 10 Sept. 1940, Stimson Diary, vol. 30, 147-148, Purvis to Salter, PURSA No. 90, 10 Sept. 1940, NA-UK, AVIA38/105.

110. Bridges to Harold Parker, 18 Sept. 1940, Parker to Bridges, 19 Sept. 1940, NA-UK, MT62/98.
111. Salter to Purvis, PURSA Nos. 69, 11 Sept., No. 76, 15 Sept. 1940, NA-UK, AVIA38/106.
112. Salter to Purvis, PURSA No. 75, 14 Sept. 1940, NA-UK, AVIA38/106.
113. Purvis to Salter, PURSA Nos. 102 107, 108, 20, 22, 23 Sept. 1940, NA-UK, AVIA38/105, Salter to Purvis, PURSA Nos. 86, 90, 92, 24, 25, 26 Sept. 1940, NA-UK, AVIA38/106, Salter to Churchill, 23 Sept. 1940, NA-UK, MT62/99. For further details on the machine tools negotiations, see Purvis and Layton to Salter, PURSA Nos. 119, 135, 153, 27 Sept., 5, 12 Oct. 1940, NA-UK, AVIA38/105.
114. Churchill to Bridges, 29 Sept. 1940, quoted in The Churchill War Papers, vol. 2, May 1940 - December 1940, Martin Gilbert, ed., (1994), 881-882.
115. Memorandum by Salter, 1 Oct. 1940, NA-UK, MT62/115.
116. Purvis to Salter, PURSA No. 128, 2 Oct. 1940, NA-UK, AVIA38/105, Sinclair to Churchill, 22 Oct. 1940, NA-UK, MT62/107, memorandum by Salter, 12 Nov. 1940, W.P.(40)441, NA-UK, CAB66/13/21.
117. Minutes, Cabinet Meeting 293(40), 21 Nov. 1940, NA-UK, CAB65/10/13, Salter to Lord Hankey, 28 Nov. 1940, NA-UK, MT62/102. On 27 January 1941 this committee was amalgamated with the North American Supply Committee. See Minutes, Cabinet Meeting 10(41), 27 Jan. 1941, NA-UK, CAB65/17/10.
118. Layton to Salter, PURSA No. 131, 3 Oct. 1940, NA-UK, AVIA38/105.
119. Layton to Salter, 9 Oct. 1940, NA-UK, MT62/104.
120. Salter to Sir Andrew Duncan, 16 Oct. 1940, NA-UK, MT62/100, Bridges to Salter, 18 Oct. 1940, NA-UK, MT62/98.
121. NAS (40) 5th Meeting, 24 Oct. 1940, NA-UK, CAB92/27.
122. Salter to Churchill, 26 Oct. 1940, NA-UK, MT62/99, Layton to Salter, 28 Oct. 1940, NA-UK, MT62/115.
123. Salter to Butler, 29 Oct. 1940, NA-UK, MT62/98, Note of Meeting at Ministry of Shipping, 5 Nov. 1940, NA-UK, MT62/98, Salter to Col. J.J. Llewellin, 27 Dec. 1940, NA-UK, MT62/104.
124. Salter to Lothian, 9 Nov. 1940 and attached aide-mémoire, NA-UK, MT62/104.
125. Layton to Salter, 15 Nov. 1940, NA-UK. MT62/104.
126. Monnet to Salter, 15 Nov. 1940, NA-UK, MT62/115.
127. Bridges to Salter, 19 Nov. 1940, NA-UK, MT62/98, 6th Meeting, 26 Nov. 1940, NAS (40)38, Note by Salter, 25 Nov. 1940, NAS (40) 39, NA-UK, CAB92/27, Salter to Churchill, 26 Nov. 1940, NA-UK, MT62/99.
128. Minutes, Cabinet Meeting 300(40), 4 Dec. 1940, NA-UK, CAB65/10/20, memorandum by Beaverbrook, W.P. (G)(40) 318, Revise, 11 Dec. 1040, NA-UK,

CAB67/8/118, Minutes, Cabinet Meeting 304(40), 12 Dec. 1940, NA-UK, CAB65/10/24.

129. Salter to Duncan, 13 Dec. 1940, NA-UK, MT62/100, Note by the Secretary, NAS (40) 48, 24 Dec. 1940, NA-UK, CAB92/27. Jean Monnet was retained as an ex-officio member of the new Council. See Purvis to Duncan, PURSA No. 32, 15 Jan. 1940, NA-UK, AVIA38/140.
130. See H.C. Debs., vol. 367, 11, 12, 18 Dec. 1940, cols. 901-902, 918, 1071-1072.
131. Memoranda, 2, 10 Jan. 1941, in Calendar of Papers on Shipping, Sir Arthur Salter, NA-UK, CAB102/421.
132. Salter to Halifax, 6 Jan. 1941, NA-UK, MT62/102.
133. Salter to Joyce Newton Thompson, 3 Jan. 1941, Newton Thompson Papers, BC 643 B22.15.
134. Britain's Need for Ships, Ministry of Shipping, Statement by Salter, 18 Jan. 1941, copy in Stimson Papers, The Times, 20 Jan. 1941, The New York Times, 19 Jan. 1941, The Manchester Guardian, 20 Jan. 1941.
135. Salter to Rathbone, 4 Feb. 1941, NA-UK, MT67/106, The Times, 6 Feb. 1941.
136. Salter to Stimson, 20 Jan. 1941, Stimson Papers.
137. See Minutes, C.A.S. (41) 32, 27 Jan. 1941, NA-UK, CAB92/23.
138. Halifax to Eden, 5 Mar. 1941, NA-UK, FO371/28960, W2858/2211/49. Further details of Salter's appointment are in NA-UK, PREM3/487/1.
139. Lady Salter to Winant, 1 Mar. 1941, John Gilbert Winant Papers, Container 219, File Sa 1941-1946, Franklin D. Roosevelt Library, Hyde Park, NY.
140. Churchill to Halifax, 9 Mar. 1941, NA-UK, PREM3/487/1, Churchill to Woolton, 10 Mar. 1941, quoted in The Churchill War Papers, vol. 3, The Ever-Widening War, 1941, Martin Gilbert, ed., (2000), 340. John Gilbert (Gil) Winant, who arrived in London on 1 March as the new American ambassador, was a friend of Lady Salter. Winant confirmed that he had suggested Salter's name to Churchill. See John G. Winant, A Letter from Grosvenor Square (1947), 181.
141. Halifax to Churchill, 9 Mar. 1941, NA-UK, PREM3/487/1.
142. Churchill to Alexander, Duncan and Cross, 10 Mar. 1941, Winston Churchill Papers, CHAR 20/21B/134-138, Churchill Archives Centre, Cambridge.
143. Draft letter from Prime Minister to Sir Arthur Salter, 10 Mar. 1941, NA-UK, PREM3/487/1.
144. Churchill to Cross, 10 Mar. 1941, Cross to Churchill, 11 Mar. 1941, Bridges to Seal, 12 Mar. 1941, NA-UK, PREM3/487/1.
145. Churchill to Salter, 12 Mar. 1941, Churchill Papers, CHAR 20/21B/141. See Leslie Chance to E.F. Cliff (U.K. Treasury Delegation, Washington), 9 Mar. 1944, NA-UK, MT59/2206.

146. Churchill to Salter, 12 Mar. 1941, Churchill Papers, CHAR 20/21B/143-145.
147. Churchill to Salter, 12 Mar. 1941, Press Notice, 10 Downing Street, 14 Mar. 1941, NA-UK, PREM3/487/1, Halifax to Morgenthau, 13 Mar. 1941, Morgenthau Papers, vol. 382, pp. 89-92.
148. The Times, 15 Mar. 1941, The Washington Post, 15 Mar. 1941, The New York Times, 15 Mar. 1941, The Observer, 16 Mar. 1941.
149. Salter Papers, File 30, Author's London Draft of Salter Biography.
150. Salter to Churchill, 17 Mar. 1941, NA-UK, PREM3/487/1.
151. Eden to Halifax, 13 Mar. 1941, NA-UK, FO371/28960, W2858/1163/9.
152. Halifax to Eden, 17 Mar. 1941, NA-UK, FO371/28960, W3038/2211/49, Salter to Churchill, 20 Mar. 1941, NA-UK, MT62/99, Leathers Papers, Shipping Mission, NA-UK, MT62/4.
153. Salter to Hurcomb, 20 Mar. 1941, Hurcomb to F.H. Keenlyside, 24 Mar. 1941, NA-UK, MT62/4.
154. Crozier Interview with Churchill, 20 Mar. 1941, Crozier Papers, reprinted in W.P. Crozier: Off the Record, 208-214. These lines, quoted in Salter, Slave of the Lamp, 155, were used by Churchill in his broadcast on 27 April 1941. Salter and Boothby remained lifelong friends. See Lord Boothby, Recollections of a Rebel (1978), 243-244. Boothby recalled that Salter "gave me valuable support in my political life when I most needed it." Boothby to the author, 13 Dec. 1979, author's archive.
155. Salter to Churchill, 20 Mar. 1941, NA-UK, MT62/99.
156. Salter to Rowse, 18 Mar. 1941, Rowse Papers, EUL MS113/3/1/Corr.S.
157. Salter Papers, File 30, Author's London Draft of Salter Biography, The New York Times, 2 Apr. 1941, The Times, 3 Apr. 1941, The Washington Post, 4 Apr. 1941, Salter, Memoirs, 271, Salter, Slave of the Lamp, 162.
158. The New York Times, 4 May 1936, 22 June 1941, The Washington Post, 22 Apr. 1941, Daily Boston Globe, 21 Mar. 1941.
159. Time, 24 Mar., 14 Apr. 1941.
160. The Times, 22 Mar. 1941, The Washington Post, 27 Mar. 1941.
161. The New York Times, 30-31 Mar. 1941.
162. "The British Shipping Mission in the United States: A Brief Historical Sketch," 1, NA-UK, CAB102/121. This had been prepared in 1947 by Leslie Chance, a Canadian civil servant, previously seconded to the British Supply Council in North America.
163. Salter, Slave of the Lamp, 156.
164. Salter, "The American Merchant Shipping Achievement: Two Years Record," 2 June 1943, NA-UK, CAB102/421.

165. "The British Shipping Mission in the United States: A Brief Historical Sketch," 2-3, NA-UK, CAB102/121.
166. Salter to Churchill, 9 May 1941, NA-UK, PREM3/487/9.
167. Salter to Hurcomb, 5 May 1941, NA-UK, MT59/2213.
168. The New York Times, 5 Apr. 1941, The Washington Post, 5 Apr. 1941, The Observer, 6 Apr. 1941.
169. Salter, Slave of the Lamp, 161-162.
170. Sir Richard Powell to the author, 26 June 1979, author's archive. Keswick recalled that he would "go in support of little Arthur" to Hopkins' bedroom in the White House: "It was Lend Lease fishing." Sir William Keswick to the author, 1 May 1979, author's archive.
171. Halifax (from Salter) to Ministry of Shipping, 7, 17 Apr. 1941, NA-UK, MT62/5.
172. Entry of 6 Apr. 1941, Stimson Diary, vol. 33, 21, 141-142.
173. Transcript of Telephone Conversation, 8 Apr. 1941, Morgenthau Papers, vol. 382, 33-36.
174. Minutes, British Supply Council in North America, 10 Apr. 1941, NA-UK, CAB92/29.
175. Land to Roosevelt, 11 Apr. 1941, Hopkins Papers. Salter, Slave of the Lamp, 164, reproduced this memorandum which was published in Robert E. Sherwood, The While House Papers of Harry L. Hopkins, vol. 1, September 1939-January 1942 (1948), 284, and Emory Scott Land, Winning the War with Ships (New York, 1958), 30.
176. Time, 14 Apr. 1941.
177. Salter to Ministry of Shipping, 8, 11, Apr. 1941, NA-UK, MT62/5, Roosevelt Press Conferences, 11 Apr. 1941 Roosevelt Papers, p. 249, "FDR: Day by Day – The Pare Lorentz Chronology," Roosevelt Papers, Salter to Hurcomb, 5 May 1941, NA-UK, MT59/2213. The latter letter contains a detailed description of this episode.
178. Salter, "Battle of the Atlantic," n.d., encl. in Salter to Keenlyside, 5 May 1941, Halifax (from Salter) to Ministry of Shipping, 17 Apr. 1941, NA-UK, MT62/5, Salter to Land, 23 Apr. 1941, Hopkins Papers.
179. Sparks to Ministry of Shipping, 29 Apr. 1941, NA-UK, MT62/5.
180. Author's interview with Lord Salter, 22 Feb. 1972.
181. Salter to Hurcomb, 5 May 1941, NA-UK, MT59/2213.
182. Lord Muirshiel (Jack Maclay) to the author, 14 Aug. 1979, author's archive.
183. The Times, 12, 15 Apr. 1941, The New York Times, 12, 13 Apr. 1941, Salter, "Battle of the Atlantic," n.d., encl. in Salter to Keenlyside, 5 May 1941, NA-UK, MT62/5, Salter, "British Merchant Shipping Mission in U.S.A., Progress Report April to July 1941," NA-UK, PREM3/487/2.

184. Salter, "The Shipping Problem," 22 Apr. 1942, encl. in Salter to Hopkins, 22 Apr. 1941, NA-UK, MT62/5
185. Salter, "Oil and Tankers," "A Very Tentative Balance Sheet," "Immediate Needs," 22 Apr. 1942, encl. in Salter to Hopkins, 22 Apr. 1941, Hopkins Papers.
186. Salter, "Suggested 'Directives'," encl. in Salter to Hopkins, 22 Apr. 1941, Hopkins Papers.
187. "The British Shipping Mission in the United States," p. 4, NA-UK, CAB102/121.
188. Minute of Meeting, 24 Apr. 1941, B.S.C. No. 19, NA-UK, CAB92/29.
189. Oscar Cox to Morgenthau, 28 Apr. 1941 and encl., Morgenthau Papers, vol. 382, pp. 109-123.
190. Salter to Morgenthau, 24 Apr. 1941, Morgenthau Diaries, vol. 391, 197-208.
191. Supply Council (from Salter) to Churchill and Cross, 1 May 1941, Salter to Keenlyside, 5 May 1941, NA-UK, MT62/5, Salter to Churchill and Cross, 2 May 1941, Churchill Papers, CHAR 20/38/53-54, The New York Times, 1 May 1941.
192. Salter to Mildred Bliss, 28 Apr. 1941, Bliss Papers, HUGFP 76.8 Box 36.
193. Salter to M.K. Keenlyside, 1 May 1941, NA-UK, MT59/2213.
194. Isaiah Berlin, Flourishing: Letters, 1928-1946, Henry Hardy, ed., (2004), 371. Sir Edward Wilder Playfair to the author, 30 Sept. 1979 provided several anecdotes illustrating Berlin's negative views of Salter. Author's archive.
195. Salter to Churchill, 9 May 1941, NA-UK, PREM3/487/9.
196. Salter to Land, 9 May 1941, Land Papers, NA-USA, Official File 1705, Box 3.
197. Salter to Hurcomb, 5 May 1941, NA-UK, MT59/2213.
198. Salter to Churchill, 8 Aug. 1941, NA-UK, PREM3/487/2.
199. The Times, 2, 10 May, 1941, Salter to Leathers, 2 May, Leathers to Salter, 5 May 1941, NA-UK, MT59/2210.
200. The weekly summaries, covering the period from 1 May to 24 August 1941, were prepared by F.H. Keenlyside. See NA-UK, PREM3/487/3.
201. "Work of Sir Arthur Salter's Mission, 11-18 May, 19-25 May," NA-UK, PREM3/487/3, minute by Keenlyside, 27 May 1941, NA-UK, MT62/6, Salter to Hurcomb, 24 May 1941, NA-UK, MT59/2213.
202. Leathers to Salter, 27 May, Salter to Leathers, 30 June 1941, NA-UK, MT59/2219.
203. "Work of Sir Arthur Salter's Mission, 2-8 June, 9-15 June, 16-22 June 1941," NA-UK, PREM3/487/3, "No Prejudice Either Way" Formula, NA-UK, MT59/421, Salter to Land, 23 July 1941, Land to Salter, 21 Aug. 1941, W.O. Hart to F.A. Griffits, 20 Sept. 1941, Hurcomb to Salter, 24 Dec. 1941, NA-UK, MT59/421.
204. Salter to Hurcomb, 5 Oct. 1942, NA-UK, MT59/421.
205. See e.g., The Times, 2 June 1941, The Economist, 140(7 June 1941), 751.

206. Minute to Hurcomb, 18 June 1941, NA-UK, MT62/15, J.H. Peck to Keenlyside, 25 June 1941, NA-UK, MT62/15, minute by Hopkins, 25 June 1941, Hopkins Papers.
207. Salter to Morgenthau, 3 June 1941, Morgenthau Papers, vol. 382, pp. 374-376, Note by Morgenthau, 17 June 1941, Morgenthau Papers, vol. 382, pp. 203-204, R.R. Powell to Morgenthau, 25 June 1941, Morgenthau Papers, vol. 382, pp. 226-228.
208. Salter to Lippmann, 17 June 1941, Lippmann Papers, Series III, Box 100.
209. The Times, 20 June 1941, The New York Times, 21 June 1941.
210. "Work of Sir Arthur Salter's Mission, 1-10 May 1941," NA-UK, PREM3/487/3.
211. Salter to Mackenzie King, 6 June 1941, Mackenzie King Papers, MG26, 54, vol. 331, entry of 23 June 1941, Mackenzie King Diary, (J13) p. 521.
212. Hall, North American Supply, 223, The Montreal Gazette, 27 June 1941.
213. Salter to Leathers, 30 June 1941, NA-UK, MT59/2219.
214. "Work of Sir Arthur Salter's Mission, 23-29 June 1941," NA-UK, PREM3/487/3.
215. Salter, "British and Allied Oil and Tanker Position as at 1 June," 28 June 1941, NA-UK, MT59/1897.
216. Patrick Hill, "Memorandum on Requests to the United States Government for Tanker Assistance, April/July 1941," 25 Aug. 1941, NA-UK, MT59/1897.
217. "Work of Sir Arthur Salter's Mission, 30 June-6 July 1941," NA-UK, PREM3/487/3, The New York Times, 12 July 1941. Churchill had raised the question as to whether Roosevelt's shipbuilding figures were for gross or deadweight tons. Salter indicated that the President's figures were deadweight tons. See correspondence in NA-UK, PREM3/487/3.
218. Salter to Hopkins, 8 Aug. 1941, Hopkins Papers, Sherwood Collection, Shipping (1) Box 130.
219. "British Merchant Shipping Mission in U.S.A., Progress Report April to July 1941," in Salter to Churchill, 8 Aug. 1941, NA-UK, PREM3/487/2, MT62/58, minute by F.H. Keenlyside, 4 Aug. 1941, NA-UK, MT62/4.
220. "British Merchant Shipping Mission in U.S.A., Progress Report April to July 1941," in Salter to Leathers, 8 Aug. 1941, NA-UK, MT62/58.
221. Minute, Cherwell to Churchill, n.d., Churchill to Leathers, 19 Aug. 1941, Leathers to Churchill, 21 Aug. 1941, NA-UK, PREM3/487/2, Leathers to Salter, 29 Aug. 1941, NA-UK, MT62/58.
222. The Washington Post, 12 Aug. 1941.
223. See "Merchant Shipbuilding Mission to the USA, 1940-1941," NA-UK, AVIA38/117, "The British Merchant Shipping Mission in the United States," 8, NA-UK, CAB102/121.
224. Land, Winning the War with Ships, 24.

225. Salter to Mrs. Land, 31 July 1941, Land Papers, NA-USA, Box 1, Los Angeles Times, 16, 17 Aug. 1941, Oakland Tribune, 16, 17 Aug. 1941, New York Times, 17 Aug. 1941, Salter, Slave of the Lamp, 166.
226. The Times, 16 Aug. 1941, Winston S. Churchill, The Second World War, vol. 3, The Grand Alliance (1950), 396.
227. Churchill to Leathers, 19 Aug. 1941, NA-UK, MT62/58.
228. Leathers to Salter, 29 Aug. 1941, NA-UK, MT62/58.
229. Salter to Curtis, 21 Aug. 1941, MSS Curtis, ff. 206-207.
230. Salter to Hopkins, 8 Sept. 1941, Hopkins Papers, Sherwood Collection, Shipping (1) Box 130, Perkins to Lady Salter, 26 Sept. 1941, Perkins Papers, Personal "S", Salter to Rowse, 20 Nov. 1941, Rowse Papers, EUL MS113/3/1/Corr.S.
231. Minutes, British Supply Council in North America, 1 Oct. 1941, NA-UK, CAB92/30.
232. Notes communicated to Reuters, Washington Wheat Meetings, NA-UK, FO371/28880, W12964/283/49, encl. in Sir Kingsley Wood to Eden, 8 Aug. 1941, NA-UK, FO371/9748/37/49.
233. Winant to Eden, 17 Sept. 1941 in W.P. (G)(41), 24 Sept. 1941, NA-UK, CAB67/9/100.
234. Minute by Sir Horace Wilson, 29 Sept. 1941, NA-UK, FO371/28879, W11735/282/19.
235. Salter to Greenwood, 3 Oct. 1941, Greenwood to Salter, 10 Oct. 1941, NA-UK, FO371/28880, W12110/283/49, Halifax to Eden, 12 Oct. 1941, NA-UK, FO371/28880, W12144/283/49.
236. Minutes, Cabinet Meeeting 97(41), 25 Sept. 1941, NA-UK, CAB65/19/33, memorandum by Anderson, "Draft International Wheat Agreement," 3 Oct. 1941, W.P. (G)(41) 107, NA-UK, CAB67/9/107.
237. See memorandum by Cherwell, "Draft International Agreement," 24 Sept. 1941, W.P. (G)(41) 99, NA-UK, CAB67/9/99, Churchill, The Second World War, vol. 3, 739-740.
238. See memorandum by Sir John Anderson, "Draft International Wheat Agreement," Oct. 3, 1941, W.P. (G) (41) 107, NA-UK, CAB67/9/107, Minutes, Cabinet Meeting 100(41), 6 Oct. 1941, NA-UK, CAB65/19/36.
239. Churchill to Roosevelt, 8 Oct. 1941, in Minutes, Cabinet Meeting 101(41), 9 Oct. 1941, NA-UK, CAB65/19/37.
240. Alan P. Dobson, "'A Mess of Potage for Your Economic Birthright?' The 1941-1942 Wheat Negotiations and Anglo-American Economic Diplomacy," The Historical Journal, 28(Sept. 1985), 742.
241. Beside Salter, who headed the delegation, the others included H.F. Carlill, chairman of the International Wheat Advisory Committee, E.M.H. Lloyd, R.A. Furness

of the Ministry of Food, Enfield with the Ministry of Agriculture and Fisheries, and W. Godfrey, 3rd secretary at the British Embassy.

242. Washington Wheat Meeting, Amendments, 1/41, NA-UK, FO371/28880, W13104/283/49.
243. Minute by T. North Whitehead, 10 Feb. 1942, commenting on some of the October meetings of the Washington wheat meetings, and Minutes, Washington Wheat Meetings, 27th Session, 20 Oct. 1941, 31st Session, 27 Oct. 1941, NA-UK, FO371/32410, W19/19/49.
244. Salter to Eden, 7 Nov. 1941, NA-UK, FO371/28880, W13290/283/49.
245. Salter to Greenwood, 12 Nov. 1941, minute by C. Scott, 15 Nov. 1941, NA-UK, FO371/28881, W13504/283/49.
246. Salter to Rowse, 30 Nov. 1941, Rowse Papers, EUL MS113/3/1/Corr.S.
247. Halifax to Eden, 28 Nov. 1041, NA-UK, FO371/28881, W14226/283/49, Salter to Eden, 5 Dec. 1941, (emphasis in original) NA-UK, FO371/28881, W15115/283/49.
248. "Notes by Sir Arthur Salter on Wheat Conference," 5 Dec. 1941, NA-UK, FO371/32410, W302/19/49. These were "hastily dictated" by Salter and brought to London by Enfield and Lloyd for a briefing. Leith-Ross, "Wheat Negotiations," 24 Dec. 1941, NA-UK, FO371/32410, W302/19/49.
249. Dobson, "'A Mess of Potage for Your Economic Birthright?'," 744-746.
250. Salter to Halifax, 21 Dec. 1941, NA-UK, FO371/28881, W15271/282/49.
251. F.W. Leith-Ross, "Wheat Negotiations," 24 Dec. 1941, NA-UK, FO371/32410, W302/19/49. This was an extended commentary on Salter's note of 5 December, brought to London by Enfield and Lloyd.
252. Salter to Eden, 19 Jan. 1942, Greenwood to Salter, 23 Jan. 1942, NA-UK, FO371/32410, W1004/19/49.
253. Minutes, Washington Wheat Meetings, 43rd Session, 29 Jan. 1942, NA-UK, FO371/32412, W3805/19/49, "International Trade in Wheat: Memorandum of Agreement," in The American Journal of International Law, Supplement: Official Documents, 37(Jan. 1943), 24-41.
254. Halifax to Eden, 31 Jan., Eden to Halifax, 6 Feb. 1942, NA-UK, FO371/32410, W1579/19/49.
255. The Times, 15 Nov. 1941.
256. Chance, "The British Shipping Mission in the United States: A Brief Historical Sketch," 9, NA-UK, CAB102/121 In his comments on Chance's script, Salter wrote that he regarded the tanker negotiations as "perhaps our most dramatic success" in 1941. See The New York Times, 24 Oct. 1941 for the exchange of statements between Salter and Harold Ickes on the return of the tankers.

257. Salter to Hopkins, 2 Dec. 1941, Hopkins Papers, Special Assistant to the President, 1941-45, "Shipping," Box 219.
258. See S. McKee Rosen, The Combined Boards of the Second World War: An Experiment in International Administration (New York, 1951), 89-90.
259. Note by Salter, "Merchant Shipping – Arrangements and Allocation," 4 Jan. 1942, encl. in Churchill to Hopkins, 10 Jan. 1942, NA-UK, PREM3/487/9, Salter to Churchill, 9 Jan. 1942, NA-UK, MT59/2206.
260. "FDR: Day by Day – The Pare Lorentz Chronology," Roosevelt Library.
261. Salter to Churchill, 13, 14 Jan. 1942, NA-UK, MT59/2206. Salter updated his estimate in "Merchant Shipping in 1942," 5 Feb. 1942, encl. in Salter to Land, et al., 5 Feb. 1942, NA-UK, MT59/2203.
262. "Mr. Lewis Douglas and the Shipping Administration," Salter Papers, File 1, Anecdotes and Incidents, Robert Paul Browder and Thomas G. Smith, Independent: A Biography of Lewis W. Douglas (New York, 1986), 166-167.
263. The New York Times, 16 Jan. 1942.
264. Minutes, Cabinet Meeting 8(42), 17 Jan. 1942, NA-UK, CAB65/25/8, "Co-ordination of the Allied War Effort," W.P. (42) 27, 19 Jan. 1942, NA-UK, CAB66/21/7, Minutes, Cabinet Meeting 9(42), 19 Jan. 1942, NA-UK, CAB65/25/9.
265. Churchill to Roosevelt, 23 Jan. 1942, encl. in R.I. Campbell to Roosevelt, 23 Jan. 1942, Roosevelt Papers, Secretary's File, Confidential File, "Lend-Lease: Jan.-Feb. 1942," Box 12.
266. Memorandum, Hopkins to Roosevelt, 26 Jan. 1942, with attached draft telegram, Roosevelt to Churchill, 26 Jan. 1942, Roosevelt Papers, Secretary's File, Confidential File, "Lend-Lease: Jan.-Feb. 1942," Box 12.
267. The Washington Post, 28 Jan.1942.
268. The Wall Street Journal, 28 Jan. 1942.
269. The New York Times, 8 Feb. 1942.
270. The New York Times, 10 Feb. 1942, Salter, Memoirs, 271.
271. Salter, Slave of the Lamp, 160. See also Salter's obituary tribute to Vickery, The Times, 28 Mar. 1946.
272. Salter, Slave of the Lamp, 174-175, Salter, "Lew Douglas," The Spectator, 185(17 Nov. 1950), 505.
273. McKee Rosen, The Combined Boards of the Second World War, 98-99, Salter to Hopkins, 10 Feb. 1942, with encls., "Some Reflections on the Roles of A.H. [Harriman] and A.S. [Salter]," n.d., "Combined Shipping Adjustment Board – Organization," 10 Feb. 1942, Hopkins Papers, Sherwood Collection, Folder: Book 5: Organization of WSA, Box 312. Salter's request was granted and he

and his staff moved from the Willard Hotel on Pennsylvania Avenue NW to 1139 Connecticut Avenue.

274. CSAB Minutes, Meeting I, 16 Feb. 1942, RG 248, Records of the War Shipping Administration, Box 6, National Archives, Washington, DC [NA-USA], Land to Hopkins, 20 Feb. 1942, Hopkins Papers, Sherwood Collection, Folder: Book 5: Organization of WSA, Box 312, Hopkins to Stephen Early, The White House, Roosevelt Papers, Official File 4754, "Combined Shipping Adjustment Board, 1942-1944."
275. Salter to Leathers, 23 Feb. 1942, NA-UK, MT59/2210. Also in NA-UK, MT59/2219.
276. Leathers to Salter, 16 Mar. 1942, NA-UK, MT59/2210.
277. Salter, "The American Merchant Shipping Achievement: Two Years Record," 2 June 1843, NA-UK, CAB102/421.
278. See Kevin Smith, Conflict Over Convoys: Anglo-American Logistics Diplomacy in the Second World War (Cambridge, 1996), 81-83, which also contains a detailed analysis of the "Salter Shipping Mission," and McKee Rosen, The Combined Boards of the Second World War, 107.
279. McKee Rosen, The Combined Boards of the Second World War, 110.
280. Salter, "The American Merchant Shipping Achievement: Two Years Record," 2 June 1943, NA-UK, CAB102/421.
281. Salter to Hopkins, 27 Mar. 1942, encl. "Note on Shipping Losses – 1942," Hopkins to Miss Tully, 3 Apr. 1942, Hopkins Papers, Special Assistant to the President, 1941-1945, "Shipping," Box 219. The letter was addressed to "My dear Harry."
282. Churchill to Roosevelt, 5 Mar. 1942, NA-UK, PREM3/487/5, Winston S. Churchill, The Second World War, vol. 4, The Hinge of Fate (1951), 176.
283. The New York Times, 14 March 1942.
284. CSAB Minutes, Meetings I-II, 16, 27 Feb. 1942, NA-USA, RG248 [Records of the War Shipping Administration], Box 6. Salter appointed Maclay and Anderson as advisers, and W. Hart, G. Thorold, Mr. Scott, and A. Hogarth to other CSAB duties
285. "Some Reflections on the Roles of A.H. [Harriman] and A.S. [Salter]," n.d., "Combined Shipping Adjustment Board – Organization," 10 Feb. 1942, Hopkins Papers, Sherwood Collection, Folder: Book 5: Organization of WSA, Box 312.
286. CSAB Minutes, Meeting II, 27 Feb. 1942, NA-USA, RG248, Box 6.
287. CSAB Minutes, Meeting III, 4 Mar. 1942, NA-USA, RG248, Box 6.
288. CSAB, Minutes, Special Meetings, No. 1, 6, 25 Mar. 1942, NA-USA, RG248, Box 6.
289. McKee Rosen, The Combined Boards of the Second World War, 121.
290. CSAB Minutes, Meetings IV, VI, 11, 25 Mar. 1942, NA-USA, RG248, Box 6.
291. CSAB Minutes, Meeting VII, 1 Apr. 1942, NA-USA, RG248, Box 6. On the Red Sea service see also "Notes on Conferences," NA-USA, RG248, Box 12.

292. See McKee Rosen, The Combined Boards of the Second World War, 122.
293. Entry of 30 Mar. 1942, Stimson Diary, vol. 38, 72-73.
294. Salter to Leathers, 6 Apr. 1942, NA-UK, MT62/58. It is of interest that Salter made no reference to Leathers in either his Memoirs of a Public Servant (1961) or Slave of the Lamp (1967). Salter always maintained that he "ran his own show in Washington."
295. Salter to Nancy Nettlefold, 7 Apr. 1942, Newton Thompson Papers, BC 643 B22.16.
296. "The Shipping Situation," W.P. (42)157, 9 Apr. 1942, NA-UK, CAB66/23/37.
297. "Note of Merchant Shipping, April 1942," encl. in Salter to Field Marshall Sir John Dill, 11 Apr. 1942, NA-UK, MT59/2203.
298. CSAB Minutes, Meetings VIII, X, 8, 22 Apr. 1942, NA-USA, RG248, Box 6.
299. CSAB Minutes, Meeting IX, 15 Apr. 1942, NA-USA, RG248, Box 6, Minutes, Council on North American Supplies, NAS(42) 26, 15 Apr. 1942, NAS(42)24, 29 Apr. 1942, NA-UK, CAB92/31.
300. CSAB Minutes, Meeting XII, 6 May 1942, NA-USA, RG248, Box 6, McKee Rosen, The Combined Boards of the Second World War, 116. On Salter's administrative input, see CSAB Minutes, Meeting XVIII, 17 June 1942, NA-USA, RG248, Box 6.
301. CSAB Minutes, Meetings XIII, XIV, XV, 13, 20, 27 May 1942, NA-USA, RG248, Box 6, Leathers to Churchill, 14 May 1942, NA-UK, PREM3/487/9, Churchill, The Second World War, vol. 4, The Hinge of Fate, 303.
302. CSAB Minutes, Meeting XVI, 3 June 1942, NA-USA, RG248, Box 6.
303. Salter to Douglas, 2 Mar. 1942, NA-USA, RG248, Box 2, The Washington Post, 20 May 1942, Minutes, Council on North American Supplies, NAS(42) 30, 2 June 1942, NA-UK, CAB92/31. By the end of the year Salter oversaw a staff of 97 individuals, among the largest of the British missions in Washington. See, Statistical Table, 15 Dec. 1942, NA-UK, CAB92/32.
304. Salter to Leathers, 18 May, 22 May, NA-UK, MT59/2210.
305. Salter to Geoffrey Lloyd, 26 May 1942, NA-UK, MT59/2219.
306. CSAB Minutes, Meeting XVI, 3 June 1942, NA-USA, RG248, Box 6.
307. CSAB Minutes, Meeting XVII, 10 June 1942, NA-USA, RG248, Box 6.
308. See Minutes, Council on North American Supplies, NAS(42) 30, 2 June 1942, NA-UK, CAB92/31.
309. "The Shipping Position – June 1st, 1942," encl. in Salter to Churchill, 23 June 1942, NA-UK, PREM3/487/9.
310. "Report by the Minister of Production on a Visit to the United States, June 3 to 19 June 1942," W.P. (42) 268, 26 June 1942, NA-UK, CAB66/25/48, CSAB Minutes, Meeting XVI, 3 June 1942, NA-USA, RG248, Box 6, Land and Salter to Hopkins, 10 June 1942, CSAB (W) (42) 88, RG248, Box 1.

311. "FDR: Day by Day – The Pare Lorentz Chronology," Roosevelt Papers, Financial Times, 24 June 1942, The Washington Post, 24 June 1942, The Times, 24 June 1942.
312. Minutes of a Meeting Held at the White House, 23 June 1942, NA-UK, CAB99/20. Salter was strongly opposed to the diversion of building to the escort programme and accepted the change very reluctantly. See CSAB Minutes, Meetings XVIII, XX, 17 June, 1 July 1942, NA-USA, RG248, Box 6.
313. Salter to Churchill, 23 June 1942, NA-UK, PREM3/487/9.
314. H.C. Debs., vol. 380, 24 June 1942, col. 1986, The Manchester Guardian, 7 July 1942.
315. The Manchester Guardian, 7 July 1942, H.C.Debs., vol. 391, 14 July 1943, col. 311.
316. Minutes, Cabinet Meeting 81(42), Confidential Annex, 25 June 1942, NA-UK, CAB65/30/25.
317. H.C. Debs., vol. 381, 8, 14, 15, July 1942, cols. 750-753, 776, 1083-1084, cols. 1211-1218, 1239.
318. Minutes, Cabinet Meeting 89(42), 8 July 1942, NA-UK, CAB65/27/5, Sir Norman Brook Notebook: Minutes, Cabinet Meeting 89(42), 8 July 1942, NA-UK, CAB195/1.
319. H.C.Debs., vol. 391, 14 July 1943, col. 304, The Times, 13, 14, 16, 17 July 1942.
320. "The Shipping Situation," W.P. (42) 294, 14 July 1942, NA-UK, CAB66/26/24.
321. The New York Times, 22 July 1942.
322. Minutes, Cabinet Meeting 92(42), 20 July 1942, NA-UK, CAB65/27/8, Minutes, Cabinet Meeting 98(42), 28 July 1942, NA-UK, CAB65/27/14.
323. Record of a Meeting at No. 10 Downing Street, 31 July 1942, MISC.32 (42) 2nd Meeting, NA-USA, RG248, Box 10, File: Misc London Papers, July –Aug. 1942.
324. Minutes, North American Supply Committee (42), 1st Meeting, 6 Aug. 1942, NA-UK, CAB92/31. For the revised terms of reference, see memorandum by Lyttleton, W.P. (42) 353, 11 Aug. 1942, NA-UK, CAB66/27/33, Minutes, Cabinet Meeting 113(42), 17 Aug. 1942, NA-UK, CAB65/27/29
325. Progress Report, North American Supply Committee (42)65, 18 Sept. 1942, NA-UK, CAB92/31. Douglas' London diary indicates he met with Salter almost every day from 27 July to 8 August. See NA-USA, RG248, Box 10, File: Misc. London Papers July-Aug. 1942.
326. The Times, 24 July 1942.
327. See e.g., Hubert D. Henderson to Salter, 22 July 1942, Hubert D. Henderson Papers, 14/3, Nuffield College Library, Oxford, Salter to Curtis, 31 July 1942, NA-UK, MT62/99.
328. A.G. Gardiner to Frank Swinnerton, 26 July 1942, Frank Swinnerton Papers, fol. 174, University of Arkansas Library, Fayetteville, AR.

329. Entry of 14 July 1942, "Molly" Hamilton Diary, vol. 1942, ii, Feb.-Nov., author's archive.
330. Salter to Rowse, 28 July 1942, Rowse Papers, EUL MS113/3/1/Corr.S, "The British Merchant Shipping Mission in the United States," p. 15, NA-UK, CAB102/121, memorandum by Douglas, 3 Nov. 1942, NA-USA, RG248, Box 19, Reading File.
331. Minutes, Combined Shipping Adjustment Board, Meeting XXVII, 19 Aug. 1942, NA-USA, RG248, Box 6, Minutes, British Supply Council in North America (42)35, 19 Aug. 1942, NA-UK, CAB92/31.
332. Minutes, Combined Shipping Adjustment Board, Meeting XXVIII, 26 Aug. 1942, NA-USA, RG248, Box 6.
333. Salter to Sweetser, 29 Aug. 1942, Arthur Sweetser Papers, Library of Congress, Washington, DC.
334. "The British Merchant Shipping Mission in the United States," 15, NA-UK, CAB102/121, Salter, "The American Merchant Shipping Achievement, Two Years Record, 2 June 1943," 6, NA-UK, CAB102/421.
335. "The United Nations Shipping Position as at August 31st 1942," CSAB (W) (42) 144-Final, NA-USA, RG248, Box 5, File – CSAB General.
336. Salter to Hopkins, 12 Sept. 1942, Hopkins Papers, Special Assistant to the President, 1941-1945, "Shipping," Box 219.
337. The New York Times, 26, 28 Sept. 1942.
338. Salter to Leathers and Hurcomb, 26 Sept. 1942, NA-UK, MT59/2210.
339. Salter to Douglas, 28 Sept. 1942, memorandum, 26 Sept. 1942, NA-USA, RG248, File: Construction, Box 6, Minutes, Combined Shipping Adjustment Board, Meeting XXXIII, 29 Sept. 1942, NA-USA, RG248, Box 6.
340. "The British Merchant Shipping Mission in the United States," p. 16, NA-UK, CAB102/121.
341. "The British Merchant Shipping Mission in the United States," p. 17, NA-UK, CAB102/121, memorandum, Roosevelt to Land, 30 Nov. 1942, encl. in W.P. (42) 568, NA-UK, CAB66/31/48.
342. Minutes, Combined Shipping Adjustment Board, Meeting XXXIV, 6 Oct. 1942, NA-USA, RG248, Box 6.
343. Quoted in McKee Rosen, The Combined Boards of the Second World War, 122.
344. Salter to Leathers and Hurcomb, 3 Nov. 1942, NA-UK, MT59/2210.
345. "The British Merchant Shipping Mission in the United States," p. 17, NA-UK, CAB102/121. Salter regarded these meetings as "the central operative part" of the collaboration. Salter, Slave of the Lamp, 195-196.
346. Churchill to Roosevelt, 21 Oct. 1941, in Roosevelt and Churchill: Their Secret Wartime Correspondence, Francis L. Loewenheim, et al., eds., (New York, 1975), 262-264.

347. Salter to Leathers, 12 Nov. 1942, NA-UK, MT59/2210.
348. "The British Merchant Shipping Mission in the United States," pp. 17-20, NA-UK, CAB102/121, Roosevelt to Churchill, 30 Nov. 1942 in <u>Roosevelt and Churchill</u>, 287-290.
349. Salter to Hancock, 21 Sept. 1947, encl., "Notes and Suggestions on Chance's Script," NA-UK, CAB102/121.
350. "Shipping Assistance from the U.S.A.," Note by Leathers, W.P. (42) 513, 7 Nov. 1942, NA-UK, CAB66/30/43.
351. Minutes, Council on North American Supplies, NAS(42) 77, 11 Nov. 1942, NA-UK, CAB92/31.
352. Minutes, CSAB, Meeting XLI, 1 Dec. 1942, NA-USA, RG248, Box 6.
353. <u>The Times</u>, 7 Dec. 1942, "Report by Lyttelton on His Visit to America," 9 Dec. 1942, W.P. (42) 568, NA-UK, CAB66/31/48.
354. See "The Minister Resident in Washington for Supply," W.P. (42) 574, 11 Dec. 1942, NA-UK, CAB66/32/4, Minutes, Cabinet Meeting 169(42), 15 Dec., 1942, NA-UK, CAB65/28/39. Llewellin was to chair the British Supply Council and report to the North American Supply Committee. Philip Noel-Baker took his place as Joint Parliamentary Secretary to the Ministry of War Transport.
355. Leathers to Salter, 17 Dec. 1942, NA-UK, MT59/2210.
356. Salter to Leathers, n.d., and minute by Leathers, 2 Jan. 1942. NA-UK, MT59/2210.
357. Salter to Leathers, 4 Dec. 1942, NA-UK, MT59/2210.
358. Douglas to Hopkins, 11 Dec., Douglas to Salter, 11, 13, 21 Dec. 1942, NA-USA, RG248, Box 19, Reading File.
359. Minutes, CSAB, Meeting XLIII, 15 Dec. 1942, NA-USA, RG248, Box 6.
360. Salter to Douglas, 22, 26 Dec. 1942, NA-USA, Lewis Douglas Papers, RG248, Box 16, Salter Memoranda, University Libraries, University of Arizona, Tucson, AZ.
361. Minutes, CSAB, Meeting XLV, 31 Dec. 1942, NA-USA, RG248, Box 6.
362. Salter to Leathers and Hurcomb, 1 Jan. 1943, NA-UK, MT59/2210.
363. Salter to Leathers, 2, 4 Jan. 1943, NA-UK, MT59/2210.
364. Minutes, CSAB, Meeting XLVI, 5 Jan. 1943, NA-USA, RG248, Box 6.
365. Salter, "Merchant Shipping, The Record of 1942 and the Prospects for 1943," 7 Jan. 1943, Salter to Dill, 8 Jan. 1943, NA-UK, MT59/2203.
366. Salter to Douglas, 8, 11 Jan. 1943, NA-USA, Douglas Papers, RG248, Box 16, Salter Memoranda.
367. Leathers to Salter, 14 Jan. 1943, NA-UK, MT59/2210.
368. <u>The Wall Street Journal</u>, 18 Jan. 1943.
369. Minutes, CSAB, Meetings XLVIII, XLVIX, 13, 18 Jan. 1942, NA-USA, RG248, Box 6, "The British Merchant Shipping Mission in the United States," pp. 24-25, NA-UK, CAB102/121.

370. Salter to Leathers and Hurcomb, 19 Jan. 1943, NA-UK, MT59/2210.
371. "The Shipping Situation," 29 Jan. 1943, W.P. (43) 46, NA-UK, CAB66/33/46.
372. Minutes, 20 Jan. 1943, NAS (43)19, NA-UK, CAB92/32.
373. Salter to Leathers, 1 Feb. 1943, NA-UK, MT59/2210, Behrens, Merchant Shipping, 330-331, Richard M. Leighton and Robert W. Coakley, The United States Army in World War II, vol. 4, Global Logistics and Strategy, 1940-1943, (Washington, DC, 1955), 677-682. Salter repeated the same advice to not approach Roosevelt as yet, in Salter to Leathers, 13 Feb. 1943, NA-UK, MT59/2210.
374. Minutes, CSAB, Meeting LI, 4 Feb. 1943, NA-USA, RG248, Box 6.
375. Memorandum, Salter to Douglas, 8 Feb. 1943, Douglas Papers, RG248, Box 16, Salter memoranda.
376. Memorandum, Douglas to Salter, 11 Feb. 1943, Douglas Papers, RG248, Box 19, Reading File, Minutes, CSAB, Meeting LII, 11 Feb. 1943, NA-USA, RG248, Box 6, "The British Merchant Shipping Mission in the United States," p. 25, NA-UK, CAB102/121.
377. Salter to Leathers and Hurcomb, 17 Feb. 1943, Leathers to Salter, 18 Feb. 1943, NA-UK, MT59/2210.
378. Salter to Leathers and Hurcomb, 27 Feb., 3 Mar. 1943, NA-UK, MT59/2210.
379. See e.g., Salter to Leathers and Hurcomb, 22, 25 Feb. 1943, NA-UK, MT59/2210.
380. Salter to Lady Astor, 22 Feb. 1943, Lady Astor Papers, MS 1066/1/227.
381. Salter to Leathers, 25 Feb. 1943, NA-UK, MT59/2210.
382. See, Minutes, CSAB, Meetings LIV, LV, LVI, 23 Feb., 2, 9 Mar. 1939, NA-US, RG248, Box 6.
383. Leathers to Salter, 6 Mar., Salter to Leathers, 8 Mar. 1943, NA-UK, MT59/2210.
384. See e.g., memoranda, Salter to Douglas, 25 Feb., 3 Mar. 1943, RG248, Box 1, File: Allocations General, Salter to Leathers, 12 Mar. 1943, Salter to Douglas, 16 Mar. 1943, NA-UK, MT59/2210.
385. The Times, 4 Mar. 1943, The Washington Post, 4 Mar. 1943, The New York Times, 4 Mar. 1943.
386. The Washington Post, 16 Mar. 1943, Salter "The Shipping Situation," 22 Mar. 1943, NA-UK, MT59/2203.
387. Salter to Leathers, 20 Mar., 8 Apr. 1943, NA-UK, MT59/2210.
388. The Washington Post, 1 Apr. 1943.
389. "Pressing the Fight for Freedom," Proceedings of the Academy of Political Science, 20(May, 1943), 74-84, Salter to Lamont, 10 Apr. 1943, Lamont Papers, 129-14, 1937-1947, Salter to Churchill, 9 Apr. 1943, NA-UK, MT59/2206.
390. "Address," Proceedings of the American Society of International Law, April 30-May1, 1943, (Washington, DC, 1943), 19-25.
391. Salter to Leathers and Hurcomb, 27 Mar. 1943, NA-UK, MT59/2210.

392. Minutes, CSAB, Meeting LVIII, 30 Mar. 1943, NA-USA, RG248, Box 6, Salter to Leathers, 30 Mar. 1943, NA-UK, MT59/2210.
393. Salter to Leathers and Hurcomb, 6 Apr. 1943, NA-UK, MT59/2210.
394. Salter to Leathers and Hurcomb, 8 Apr. 1943, NA-UK, MT59/2210.
395. See Minutes, CSAB, Meeting LIX, 20 Apr. 1943, NA-USA, RG248, Box 6.
396. Salter to Leathers, 28, 30 Apr. 1943, NA-UK, MT59/2210, Minutes, NAS, 5 May 1943, NA-UK, CAB92/32.
397. "Shipping Discussions at the 'Trident' Conference," 21 June 1943, W.P. (43) 258, NA-UK, CAB66/38/8.
398. Halifax to Eden, 22 May 1943, minute by Eden, 6 June 1943, NA-UK, FO954/30.
399. Minutes, CSAB, Meetings, LXI, LXII, 8, 18 June 1943, NA-USA, RG248, Box 6.
400. Minutes, meeting of 16 June 1943, NAS(43)40, NA-UK, CAB92/32, Churchill to Roosevelt, 8 July 1943, NA-UK, MT59/2206. The 16 June meeting also accepted the resignation of Monnet who was going to serve on General Giraud's new French Executive Committee.
401. Salter, Slave of the Lamp, 196.
402. The Times, 1 July 1943.
403. Sir Norman Brook Notebook: Minutes, Cabinet Meeting 91(43), 1 July 1943, NA-UK, CAB195/2, Minutes, Cabinet Meeting 91(43), 1 July 1943, NA-UK, CAB65/35/1.
404. Salter to Lady Astor, 13 July 1943, Lady Astor Papers, MS 1416/1/2/237.
405. H.C. Debs., vol. 391, 14 July 1943, cols. 303, 304-313, The Times, 15 July 1943, The New York Times, 15 July 1943.
406. Salter, Slave of the Lamp, 196.
407. The Times, 16 July 1943.
408. Minutes, Cabinet Meeting 111(43), 4 Aug. 1943, War Cabinet, W.P. (43) 494, 22 Nov. 1943, NA-UK, CAB66/42/44.
409. Minutes, Cabinet Meeting 113(43), 9 Aug. 1943, Cabinet Meeting 115(43), 16 Aug. 1943, NA-UK, CAB65/35/23.
410. The Times, 11 Aug. 1943.
411. The Times, 28 Aug. 1943, The New York Times, 28 Aug. 1943. The New York Times noted that Salter had dropped a hint that the invasion of the continent was near when he mentioned that Britain's inland transport resources would be strained "in the historic months ahead."
412. "Notes for History, Talk with Sir Arthur Salter at All Souls, 5 Sept. 1943," Liddell Hart Papers, LH11/1943/51.
413. Entry of 6 July 1943, "Molly" Hamilton Diary, vol. 10, 28 Mar.-31 Dec. 1943, author's archive
414. Violet Markham to Joyce Newton Thompson, 6 Sept. 1942, Newton Thompson Papers, BC 643 B18.61

415. "Shipping 'Expansion' Policy," 3 Sept. 1943, minute by Leathers, 9 Oct. 1943, NA-UK, MT59/436.
416. Salter to Churchill, 20 Sept. 1943, Churchill Papers, CHAR 20/98A/90, Churchill to Salter, 20 Sept. 1943, Churchill Papers, CHAR 20/98A/89.
417. Salter to Lord Astor, 27 Sept. 1943, Lord Astor Papers, MS 1066/1/227.
418. Salter, Memoirs, 276.
419. "History of British Merchant Shipping Mission," chapter IV, 1.
420. Salter to Roosevelt, 2 Nov. 1943, Hopkins Papers, Official File 99, "American Merchant Marine, 1943-1945," Box 4, "FDR: Day by Day – The Pare Lorentz Chronology," Roosevelt Library.
421. See Salter's obituary tribute to Roosevelt, The Sunday Times, 15 Apr. 1945.
422. Minutes, British Supply Council in North America, 3 Nov. 1943, NAS(43)76, 27 Nov. 1943, NA-UK, CAB92/33. Maclay took Salter's place.
423. Minutes, CSAB, 5 Nov. 1943, Meeting LXIII, RG248, Box 6.
424. Harold Ickes to Churchill, 5 Nov. 1943, NA-UK, PREM3/487.
425. Los Angeles Times, 16 Nov. 1943.
426. Leader Post (Regina) 23 Nov. 1943, The Globe and Mail, 29 Nov. 1943.
427. The Evening News, 9 Nov. 1943.
428. See "Planning for the First UNRRA Council," UNRRA, S-0517-0018-0001, United Nations Archives and Record Management Section, New York, "Questions Arising Out of the Council Meeting of UNRRA," 21 Dec. 1943, W.P. (43)579, NA-UK, CAB66/44/29, and "Scope and Organization of UNRRA," 24 Mar. 1944, R.C. (44) 3, NA-UK, FO371/40530, U2480/41/73.
429. Salter to Lehman, 4 Dec. 1943, Box DG 11, 0812_0001, Herbert H. Lehman Papers, Special Correspondence Files, Rare Book and Manuscript Library, Columbia University Library, New York, Allan Nevins, Herbert H. Lehman and His Era (New York, 1963), 235-236.
430. Attlee to Churchill, n.d., NA-UK, BT25/70/SLA/9, Churchill to Salter, 31 Dec. 1943, Churchill Papers, CHAR 20/130/130.
431. Salter to Lehman, 4 Dec. 1943, Lehman Papers, Box DG 11, 0812_0001.
432. Entry of 1 Dec. 1943, "Molly" Hamilton Diary, vol. 10, author's archive, The Manchester Guardian, 20 Dec. 1943.
433. Minutes, Cabinet Meeting 175(43), 23 Dec. 1943, NA-UK, CAB65/36/43.
434. Halifax to Attlee, 27 Dec. 1943, NA-UK, FO371/35291, U6699/5/73.
435. Lehman to Halifax, 29 Dec. 1943, Halifax to Lehman, 29 Dec. 1943, UNRRA, S-0517-0037-0010.
436. The Times, 31 Dec. 1943, The New York Times, 31 Dec. 1943.
437. The Washington Post, 6 Jan. 1944.
438. Churchill to Salter, 31 Dec. 1943. Churchill Papers, CHAR 20/130/130.

439. The Times, 1 Jan. 1944.
440. Salter, Memoirs, 276.
441. Quoted in Nevins, Herbert H. Lehman and His Era, 236.
442. George Woodbridge, UNRRA: The History of the United Nations Relief and Rehabilitation Administration, vol. 1, (New York, 1950), 149.
443. Woodbridge, UNRRA, vol. 1, 150.
444. Halifax to Eden, 12 Jan. 1944, NA-UK, FO371/40520, U291/41/73.
445. Halifax to Eden, 25 Jan. 1944, Eden to Halifax, 29 Jan. 1944, NA-UK, FO371/40521, U593/41/73, Halifax to Eden, 19 Feb. 1944, NA-UK, FO371/40525, U1349/41/73.
446. Woodbridge, UNRRA, vol. 1, 166.
447. Lehman to Leith-Ross, 15 Dec. 1943, 19 Jan. 1944, A.D. Marris to Salter, 5 Jan. 1944, UNRRA, S-0517-0030-0009.
448. The Washington Post, 24 Jan. 1944, "From Combined War Agencies to International Administration," Public Administration Review, 4(Winter, 1944), 1-6.
449. H.C. Debs., vol. 496, 25 Jan. 1944, cols. 570, 593, Leith-Ross to Salter 1 Feb. 1944, UNRRA, S-0517-0030-0009. In sharp contrast was the debate in the House of Commons on 10 February where Salter's position with UNRRA was considered by some MPs ground for him resigning his parliamentary seat. See H.C. Debs., vol. 396, 10 Feb. 1944, cols. 1971-2002.
450. See Kenneth Dayton to Salter, 13, 18 Jan. 1944, UNRRA, S-1533-0000-0009, Hugh R. Jackson to Leith-Ross, 20 Jan. 1944, UNRRA, S-0517-0029-0013, Salter to Leith-Ross, 28 Jan., 3 Feb.1944, UNRRA, S-0517-0003-0009.
451. "Office for Europe, Draft," 15 Feb. 1944, UNRRA, S-0517-0029-0019, "Relations with London Regional Office," 21 Feb. 1944, UNRRA, S-1533-0000-0009, Woodbridge, UNRRA, vol.1, 167. Salter's note was reproduced in George Woodbridge, UNRRA: The History of the United Nation Relief and Rehabilitation Administration, vol. 3, (New York, 1950), 370-373.
452. "Note on UNRRA Organization," 1 Feb. 1944, UNRRA, S-1533-0000-0009, "Note on UNRRA Organization," 9 Mar.1944, quoted in Woodbridge, UNRRA, vol. 3, 363-364.
453. See e.g., Roy F. Hendrickson to Salter, 16 Feb., James A. Crabtree, 29 Feb. 1944, and others in UNRRA, S-1533-0000-0009, S-1533-0000-0008.
454. "UNRRA Organization," 9 Mar. 1944, UNRRA, S-1533-0000-0009, Woodbridge, UNRRA, vol. 1, 155. Other drafts are in UNRRA, S-1533-0000-0008. Excerpts are reproduced in Woodbridge, UNRRA, vol. 3, 363-366.

455. Halifax to Eden, 10 Mar. 1944, Eden to Halifax, 5 Apr. 1944, NA-UK, FO371/40528, U2158/41/73.
456. Salter to Antonin Fried, 20 Mar. 1944, UNRRA, S-1533-0000-0009.
457. Salter to Leith-Ross, 3 Apr. 1944, UNRRA, S-0517-0030-0009, "Proposed Health Commissions for Europe," Relief Policy Committee, 7 Apr. 1944, NA-UK, FO371/40534, U3034/41/73, Leith-Ross and Osborn to Salter, 14 Apr. 1944, NA-UK, FO371/40535, U3162/41/73.
458. Salter to Eden, 30 Mar. 1944, NA-UK, FO371/40536, U3439/41/73, The New York Times, 31 Mar. 1944.
459. Salter to Mackenzie King, 19 Apr. 1944, Mackenzie King Papers, MG-26, J1, p. 111737.
460. Minister Resident for Supply Sir Ben Smith to Minister of State Richard Law, 26 Mar., 1 Apr. 1944, Law to Anderson, 9 May 1944, NA-UK, FO371/40531, U2654/41/73.
461. "Provisional Agenda for the Second Session of the Council," in Salter to Eden, 21 Apr. 1944, NA-UK, FO371/40538, U3852/41/73.
462. Salter to Leith-Ross, 29 Apr. 1944, UNRRA, S-0517-0030-0009.
463. Hugh R. Jackson to Leith-Ross, 6 May 1944, UNRRA, S-0517-0029-0013, Minutes, Staff Meetings, 10, 11 May 1944, Annex – "Pre-operational Planning" and "Operational Directions for Europe," 11 May 1944, UNRRA, S-0517-0037-0010.
464. Hugh R. Jackson to Salter, 19 May 1944, UNRRA, S-0517-0029-0019.
465. Halifax to Eden, 16 May 1944, NA-UK, FO371/40539, U4380/41/73, The Times, 17 May 1944.
466. P.J.H. Stent [Foreign Office] to J. Wall [Ministry of Food], 24 May 1944, NA-UK, FO371/40540, U4756/41/73.
467. Minutes, Law to Eden, 26 May 1944, Eden to Churchill, 28 May 1944, Churchill to Eden, 29 May 1944, NA-UK, FO371/40541, U6001/41/73.
468. Salter to Law, 15 June 1944, encl. in Salter to Lehman, 28 June 1944, UNRRA S-0517-0029-0019.
469. Minutes, Eden to Churchill, 23 June 1944, Churchill to Eden, 29 June 1944, NA-UK, FO371/40541, U6001/41/73. Churchill to Eden, 29 June 1944, NA-UK, PREM4/29/4.
470. See minutes by E.L. Hall-Patch, 30 Mar., 14 Apr. 1944, Hall-Patch to Salter, 17 May 1944, NA-UK, FO371/40570, U5109/3740/73.
471. See Lehman to Sir Ronald I. Campbell, 29 July 1944, UNRRA, S-0517-0005-0003, minute by Richard Law, 24 Aug. 1944, NA-UK, FO371/41167, UR674/238/850.

472. Minutes by Hall-Patch, 1, 2 June 1944, NA-UK, FO371/40570, U5046/3740/73, minutes by Hall-Patch, 13, 21 June 1944, NA-UK, FO371/41140, UR187/40/850.
473. Law to Eden, 24 Aug. 1944, NA-UK, FO371/41167, UR674/238/850, Minutes, Cabinet Meeting 44(117), 5 Sept. 1944, NA-UK, CAB65/43/33.
474. Note, unsigned, 14 June 1944, UNRRA, S-0517-0005-0003.
475. Relief and Supplies Department to Relief Department, Foreign Office, 15 June 1944, NA-UK, FO371/40541, U5944/41/73.
476. Lehman, "Memorandum of Conversation," 19 June 1944, Lehman to Salter, 21 June 1944, UNRRA, S-0517-0037-0010.
477. "The Root of U.N.R.R.A.'s Difficulties – Uncertainty as to Its Task. A Plan of Action – (Europe)," in Salter to Lehman, 28 June 1944, UNRRA S-0517-0029-0019.
478. Churchill to Salter, 2 July 1944, Churchill Papers, CHAR 20/138A/2.
479. Lehman to Salter, 3 July 1944, UNRRA, S-0517-0037-0010.
480. Lehman to M. Menshikov et al., 4 July 1944, UNRRA, S-0517-0005-0003.
481. Sir David Waley, to Salter, 20 June 1944, NA-UK, FO371/40541, U5844/41/73, <u>The Manchester Guardian</u>, 14 July 1944.
482. Leith-Ross to Lehman, 6 July 1944, UNRRA, S-0517-0029-0019. See also Leith-Ross to Lehman, 1 July 1944, UNRRA, S-0517-0029-0019.
483. Foreign Office Minute, unsigned, 12 July 1944, NA-UK, FO371/41132, UR117/31/850.
484. H.E. Caustin, "Organization of UNRRA (2), Salter Plan and Salter Visit to European Regional Office," 30 Dec. 1946, UNRRA, S-1533-0000-0009, Caustin to the author, 5 Sept., 31 Oct. 1979, author's archive.
485. Note by Caustin of Staff Meeting, 12 July 1944, UNRRA, S-0517-0032-0002.
486. Memorandum for Telephone Conversation with Salter, 21 July 1944, UNRRA, S-0517-0029-0019, Lehman to Salter, 21 July 1944, 21 July 1944, UNRRA, S-0517-005-0003, "Memoir of Sir Arthur Salter," encl. in Osborne to author, 14 June 1970, 3 pp. MS, author's archive.
487. Lehman, "Memorandum of Telephone Conversation with Salter," 24 July 1944, UNRRA, S-0517-0037-0010.
488. Minute by Eden, 8 July 1944, NA-UK, FO371/41162, FO371/41162, UR165/165/850, minute by Eden, 15 July 1944, NA-UK, PREM4/29/4, Salter's Draft Directive, n.d., NA-UK, FO371/41162, UR165/165/850.
489. Minute by GCBD [Christopher Dodds], 3 Aug. 1944, NA-UK, PREM4/29/4, minute by Churchill, 4 Aug. 1944, NA-UK, FO371/41162, R165/165/850.
490. Minute by Eden, 11 Aug. 1944, minute by Churchill, 18 Aug. 1944, NA-UK, PREM4/29/4, Law to Salter, 14 Aug. 1944, NA-UK, FO371/41162, UR165/165/850.
491. Directive by Churchill, UNRRA, 26 Aug. 1944, W.P. (44)469, NA-UK, CAB66/54/19.

492. Minutes in FO371/41162, UR553/165/850, Minutes, Cabinet Meeting 117(44), 5 Sept. 1944, NA-UK, CAB65/43/33, Salter to Lehman, 25 Aug. 1944, Harold E. Caustin Papers, courtesy of Mr Caustin, author's archive, Lehman to Fred Hoehler, 4 Sept. 1944, UNRRA, S-0517-0005-0004.
493. Caustin to Salter, 11 Aug. 1944, UNRRA, S-0517-0037-0010.
494. The New York Times, 22 Aug. 1944.
495. Staff Meetings, 21, 29, Aug., 1 Sept. 1944, UNRRA, S-0517-0032-0002.
496. Richard Law, "Instructions to U.K. Delegation to Second Session of UNRRA. Council," 25 Aug. 1944, W.P. (44)466, CAB66/54/16.
497. Minutes of the 7th and 8th Meetings of the Central Committee of the Council, UNRRA, S-0517-0032-0002.
498. The Times, 16, Sept. 1944, UNRRA, Journal: Second Session of the Council and Related Documents of the First Session, Montreal, Canada, September 15-27 1944 (Washington, DC, 1944), 23-26, 46-48, 52-56.
499. UNRRA, Journal: Second Session of the Council and Related Documents of the First Session, Montreal, Canada, September 15-27 1944, 74-126.
500. Salter to Cecil, 2 Sept. 1944, Cecil Papers, ADD MSS 51113, vol. 63.
501. Lady Salter to Perkins, 5 Oct. 1944, Perkins Papers, Personal "S", Lady Salter to Winant, 4 Oct. 1944, Winant Papers, 219, Sa 1941-1946.
502. See Lehman to Sir Ronald I. Campbell, 31 July 1944, minute by Law, 24 Aug. 1944, NA-UK, FO371/41167, UR238/238/850.
503. Minutes, Cabinet Meeting 117(44), 5 Sept. 1944, NA-UK, CAB65/43/33, Law to Salter, 6 Sept. 1944, NA-UK, FO371/41140, UR187/40/850.
504. Churchill to Attlee, 16 Sept. 1944, Churchill Papers, CHAR 20/257/25.
505. Law to Eden, 22 Sept. 1944, NA-UK, FO371/41140, UR825/40/850, Law to Eden, 15 Sept. 1944, NA-UK, FO371/41167, UR747/238/850.
506. Caustin to Gowers, 12 Oct. 1944, Caustin to Salter, 13 Oct. 1944, UNRRA, S-0517-0005-0005.
507. Woodbridge, UNRRA, vol. 1, 155, H.E. Caustin, "Organization of UNRRA (4), Appointment of a Senior Deputy Director General," 30 Dec. 1946, UNRRA, S-1533-0000-0009, Jackson to the author, 4 Aug. 1979, author's archive.
508. The Times, 16 Nov. 1944.
509. C.A. Williamson to Salter, 17 Oct., Salter to Williamson, 7 Nov. 1944, George Bell Papers, MS1640/125/4.
510. "Getting Things Done," 18 Dec. 1944, BBC WAC, Salter Scripts.
511. See e.g., entries of 19 Apr., 27 Oct. 1944, Stimson Diary, vol. 46, 188-189, vol. 48, 188.

512. Salter to Macadam, 18 Dec. 1944, RIIA Papers, "Record of General Meeting Held at Chatham House, Dumbarton Oaks Conference, 19 Dec. 1944," RIIA Papers. When Salter accepted office on 25 May 1945, he resigned his position at Chatham House. Salter to Macadam, 31 May 1945, RIIA Papers.
513. See Winant to Lady Salter, Winant Papers, 219, Sa 1941-1946.
514. Perkins to Lady Salter, 2 Feb. 1945, Perkins Papers, Personal "S", Mary Agnes Hamilton, Remembering My Good Friends (1944).
515. Lady Salter to Geoffrey Crowther, 2 Jan. 1945, Layton Papers, $81^{37(2-3)}$. Lady Salter sent the letter with further comments to Layton. See Layton Papers, $81^{37(1)}$.
516. Macadam to Salter, 11 Jan. 1945, RIIA Papers, The Times, 9 Jan. 1945, Salter to A.P. Wadsworth, 15 Jan. 1945, The Guardian Archive, B/523/1-2.
517. Lehman to Salter, 18 Jan. 1945, Lehman Papers, Box DG11.
518. H.C. Debs., vol. 407, 17 Jan. 1945, cols. 307-308.
519. H.C. Debs., vol. 408, 20 Feb. 1945, cols. 677-679.
520. Salter to Gertrude Caton Thompson, 26 Jan. 1945, Caton Thompson Papers, author's archive.
521. H.C. Debs., vol. 408, 1 Mar. 1945, cols. 1579-1587.
522. H.C. Debs., vol. 409, 28 Mar. 1945, cols. 1442-1449, 1458, 1466, 1469, 1476, 1481, The Manchester Guardian, 31 Mar. 1945.
523. The Times, 16 Apr. 1945.
524. "The Task in Europe," The Spectator, 174(11 May 1945), 426-427.
525. The Times, 18 May 1945.
526. H.C. Debs., vol. 410, 17 Apr. 1945, cols. 132-137, 175-176.
527. Minutes, Eden to Churchill, 29 Mar. 1945, Churchill to Eden, 5 Mar. 1945, NA-UK, FO371/45775, UE774/624/77, minutes by Churchill, 22 Mar. 1945, Bridges, 29 Mar. 1945, NA-UK, PREM3/195A/2.
528. Minutes by Hall-Patch, 23 Mar. and Eden, 24 Mar. 1945, NA-UK, FO371/45776, UE1450/624/77.
529. Minutes by Churchill, 7, 14 Apr. 1945, NA-UK, PREM3/195A/2, minute by Eden, 24 May 1945, NA-UK, FO37145778, UE2232/624/77.
530. Salter to Lamont, 26 Apr. 1945, Lamont Papers, 129-14, 1937-1947. In their only ever joint obituary in The Times, Salter and Lady Salter paid tribute to Colefax who died on 22 Sept. 1950. The Times, 3 Oct. 1950.
531. Salter to Lippmann, 26 Apr. 1945, Lippmann Papers, Series III, Box 100.
532. See "Reconstruction Series," 22 Dec. 1944-2 Feb. 1945, BBC WAC, R Cont 1, Salter Talks, File 1, 1926-1948.
533. "Post-War Problems of Britain," London Calling: The Overseas Journal of the British Broadcasting Corporation, nos. 284-295, 25-31 Mar.-3-9 June 1945. The

broadcast series had the title, "Facing the Future, A British Point of View." BBC WAC, Salter Scripts.

534. Malcolm Brereton to Salter, 2 July 1937, BBC WAC, R Cont 1, Salter Talks, File 1, 1926-1948.
535. Peter Bax to Salter, 7 Feb., Salter to Bax, 8 Feb. 1945, BBC WAC, R Cont 1, Salter Talks, File 1, 1926-1948, BBC WAC, R41/22/2 P.C.S., Brains Trust, File 3 1944-1946, Wilshin to Salter, 13 June 1951, BBC WAC, R Cont 1, Salter Talks, File II, 1949-1962.
536. Perkins to Salter, 16 May 1945, Perkins Papers, Personal "S".
537. Salter to Cecil, 24 May 1945, Cecil Papers, ADD MSS 51113, vol. 43, fol. 113.
538. The Manchester Guardian, 26 May 1945, The Observer, 27 May 1945, The Times, 26 May 1945.
539. The Times, 29 May 1945.
540. Churchill to Salter, 29 May 1945, Churchill Papers, CHAR 20 194A 56-58, minute by Law, 28 May 1945, NA-UK, FO371/51269, UR1653/1600/53. Law concluded his minute by noting, "Under these proposals I really do think that Salter wd be useful & not too much of a nuisance."
541. Minutes, Emergency Economic Committee, 28, 30 May, 1945, NA-UK, FO371/51269, UR1600/1600/53, 8, 19 June 1945, NA-UK, FO371/51270, UR1937/1600/53.
542. Minutes, Cabinet Meeting 7(45), 11 June 1945, NA-UK, CAB65/53/7.
543. Minutes, Ministerial Committee on Reparations, (45)2, 12 June 1945, NA-UK, CAB98/59.
544. Minutes, Ministerial Committee on Reparations, (45)3, 9 July 1945, NA-UK, CAB98/59.
545. Letter from Nominators, Sir Arthur Salter's Address, 13 June 1945, copy in Beveridge Papers, BEV6/17.
546. See Minutes, Cabinet Meeting 7(45), 11 June 1945, NA-UK, CAB65/53/7, Cabinet Meeting 8(45), 15 June 1945, NA-UK, CAB65/53/8, Cabinet Meeting (10)45, 20 June 1945, NA-UK, CAB65/53/10, Cabinet Meeting 13(45), 10 July 1945, NA-UK, CAB65/53/13.
547. Minute, Churchill to Grigg, Eden and Salter, 15 June 1945, NA-UK, FO37150875, U5110/5081/70, Major General E.I.C. Jacob to T.E. Bromley, 21 June 1945, NA-UK, FO371/50875, U5081/5081/70.
548. ECC(45)1, 7 July 1945, Terms of Reference, NA-UK, FO371/50875, U5459/5081/70, Minutes, ECC, (45) 1st Meeting, 10 July 1945, NA.-UK, CAB98/58.
549. O.R.C. (45)1, Membership and Terms of Reference, 5 July 1945, NA-UK, FO371/50906, U5342/5342/70 (also in CAB21/2477), Minutes, O.R.C. (45)

1st Meeting, 11 July 1945, 2nd Meeting, 24 July 1945, NA-UK, FO371/50906, U5425/5342/70.
550. Minutes, E.C.C., (45) 2nd Meeting, 16 July 1945, Note by Mabane, E.C.C. (45)2, 14 July 1945, and Jacob, E.C.C. (45)3, 14 July 1945, NA-UK, CAB98/58.
551. Minute, Sir R. Sinclair, 4 July 1945, NA-UK, BT25/42/RG323/2, Note by Joint Secretariat, London Co-ordinating Committee, 16 July 1945, NA-UK, FO371/51463, 2400/1610/851.
552. Minutes, 21st Meeting, London Co-ordinating Committee, 19 July 1945, NA-UK, BT25/79/SLA/MISC20.
553. Minutes, O.R.C. (45) 2nd Meeting, 24 July 1945, NA-UK, FO371/50906, U5804/5342/70.
554. Minutes, E.C.C., (45) 3th Meeting, 1 Aug. 1945, NA-UK, FO371/51273, UR2824/1600/53, minutes in NA-UK, FO371/51272, UR2583/1600/53.
555. Cabinet Office Diaries of J.E. Meade, May 1945, Meade Papers, 47-49.
556. Memorandum, "Conditions in Liberated Europe," 25 July 1945, encl. in Salter to Ernest Bevin, 3 Aug. 1945, NA-UK, BT25/14/RG112. Drafts of the document are in Salter Papers, File 14, The Needs of Liberated Countries in Europe, July 1945.
557. F.P. Neill, Warden of All Souls College, to author, 3 Apr. 1980, author's archive, The Times, 28 June, 31 July 1945, Salter, Memoirs, 283-284. The results were Salter, 6,771, Herbert, 5,136, Cole, 3,414 votes.
558. Salter to Churchill, 24 June [?], Churchill Papers, CHAR 2/495.

CHAPTER 7

OUT OF AND IN OFFICE, 1945-1953

"A bouleversement indeed!" Salter wrote to Rowse on 2 August 1945. "I am very anxious about our position in international affair. I don't for a moment expect that the Labour Party will want me to do anything which would make it worthwhile for me to give up any freedom to speak & write." He added that he looked forward to "the prospect of a quite unexpected holiday," and continued, "It's extraordinary to see a packed House with only here & there a recognizable face. It may nevertheless be in the long run a good thing that the Labour Party, who would anyhow have had to face responsibility soon, should do so before the post-war pattern is set."[1] He wrote similarly to Cecil, noting, "It will be an interesting House to be in & I am glad to be there. But I confess I'm sorry to have to drop my work on European reconstruction, in which, after the two months of semi-suspension of the Government machine, I was just beginning to see some light. I confess too that I am in deep gloom about this atomic bomb. I have for long been hoping against hope that the scientists would run into some quite insuperable snag." Salter looked forward to the fact that a former colleague at the League, Philip Noel-Baker, was the new Minister of State responsible for reconstruction.[2] Although out of office, Salter continued to contribute to public and private life, and was some times even at the centre of pertinent debates. To his lifelong focus on finance and economics, for example, he now added European reconstruction and integration, and the future of atomic weapons. He also embarked on a multi-year journey which saw the independent university seats abolished and his move from liberalism into the ranks of the Conservative Party. The process was slow, and despite criticisms from friends, well planned and thought out.

In two leading articles in early August, <u>The Times</u> endorsed Salter's suggestion of a Supreme Economic Council and the necessity to supply food, essential goods and transport before winter in order "to avert disaster."[3] On 14 August Salter visited Buckingham Palace to take leave of the King and relinquish his Seals of Office. Within two days he was back in the pages of <u>The Times</u>, with a letter, "First Aid for Europe." What followed was drawn from his 25 July memorandum on European reconstruction, although somewhat updated. "Millions, perhaps many millions, may freeze and starve, with incalculable political consequences," he warned about the coming winter. He also suggested that with hostilities ending military authorities must relinquish their vast stores for civilian relief: "What has hitherto been military necessity has become at most military convenience." He urged US President Truman and the British government to instruct the military to provide every possible form of assistance.[4] Among these he pleaded for the immediate release of 100,000-150,000 trucks from military to civilian use. Salter's strictures were in fact echoed on 16 August by the newly elected Prime Minister, Clement Attlee, during the opening session of the House of Commons and in the press.[5]

Salter also began, at this time, to speak widely and write about the issue of atomic energy. He publicly expressed his "disquiet at the circumstances in which the bomb was first used." He admitted that the destruction of Hiroshima and Nagasaki was preferable to a long war with the loss of millions of lives. However, he would have preferred to see what was the effect of Soviet entry into the war against Japan, or a demonstration of the bomb's power outside an urban area, or waiting longer between the bombing of Hiroshima and Nagasaki.[6] On 22 August, in the context of the Commons' debates on the ratification of the Charter of the United Nations, signed in San Francisco on 26 June, Salter bought up the question of atomic energy control. "The world has supped on horror now for six years," he stated, and he wished to channel that revulsion against destruction. He regarded this as "the most important problem that now faces the world." He suggested some restriction on research but also more realistically some form of international control, even as he recognized its difficulty. He was concerned about the dangers of atomic proliferation during the years before the emergence of the peaceful applications of atomic energy. In conclusion, he declared atomic energy capable of "lifting humanity to a higher level of happiness and of civilisation than man has ever known."[7]

Salter was always unrelenting on those issues which he felt most strongly. As the debate in the Commons continued the next day, he was again on his feet urging the government to set up his Supreme Economic Council, but to no avail. The existing Emergency Economic Committee, of which Salter was reminded that he had been the chairman, and the newly created Economic and Social Council of the United Nations were regarded as sufficient.[8] On 26 August and 2 September, in The Observer, he made two further contributions under the title "The Rebuilding of Europe." The first article assessed the current needs for rebuilding. "The situation is still menacing," he wrote, "But it is manageable." If the worst-case scenario were to emerge, with millions freezing and starving during the coming winter, it would "be due to defects in organization, in and outside Europe, to psychological factors, in general to all that prevents the available man-power from making full use of the available factories, land and raw materials." Thereafter he outlined what was immediately required to avert famine and political chaos. In the second article he added that Attlee had reaffirmed in parliament the outstanding needs for coal and inland transport. With regard to the former, Salter urged the rapid expansion in production of the Ruhr coal mines. As for the latter, the release of more than 100,000 trucks from the military would meet the road transport requirements of the continent. For each deficiency – fertiliser, food, sugar, oils, fats and meats – Salter offered remedies, providing civilian necessity was given priority over military convenience. Finally, he conceded that the immediate winter crisis had priority over his aspiration for a Supreme Economic Council.[9]

On 18 September the Court Circular of The Times carried the announcement that Sir Arthur and Lady Salter had moved to West House, 35 Glebe Place, London S.W.3. "which will now be their permanent address."[10] Upon returning to London in December 1944 the Salters had begun house-hunting with their search focused on West House, where Lady Salter's mother had lived from 1913 to 1916.[11] On 26 April Salter had written to Lamont, "We are still living at the Connaught, but are hard on the track of a very pleasant house in Chelsea." On 4 May, responding to a letter from the Salters, Perkins wrote, "I was delighted to hear about your having found the house in which your mother used to live in Chelsea and being able to get it."[12] They acquired the lease, moved in August and it remained their home until 1975. West House had been designed by the architect Philip Webb as a "studio house" for George Price Boyce, the British landscape painter and watercolourist. It was built in 1868-69, renamed West House in 1871, enlarged in 1901 and is regarded as one of the earliest examples of the Queen Anne Revival style.[13] West House became the centre for the Salters' social and political life, a place where they entertained, housed guests and had intimate dinner parties for friends and colleagues from around the world. Their first reception at West House, of several annually, was on 25 January 1946. The Salters also allowed West House, "finely furnished, with every convenience and an excellent staff, and a tennis court in the heart of London," to be used by friends in their absence abroad.[14]

Once settled into West House, Salter returned to concentrate on the issues of atomic energy and reconstruction. Without the burden of office, he embarked on a vigorous schedule of lectures, articles and contributions to House of Commons' debates. On 8 October he spoke at Oxford to a rally under the joint auspices of the United Nations Association and Federal Union. He suggested that "if war recurs, civilization as we know it may perish; mankind may relapse into misery and savagery exceeding anything history records of the Dark Ages." He contended that it would be impossible for atomic energy to remain the secret monopoly of a few powers. He proposed, therefore, that the US, the UK and Canada immediately entrust the secret to the Security Council which would be given powers to institute an inspection system for member states and to destroy any future bomb-producing facility in a non-member state. He acknowledged the difficulties of his proposal, but he thought something must be done while there still was a period of secrecy. He also discussed the defects of the United Nations charter, noting that the new atomic age already made its military provisions outdated. With sanctions subject to a great power veto, he suggested that only a dilution of national sovereignty and revisions to the charter would ensure peace. In the meanwhile he urged both federalists and supporters of an inter-state system, such as that embodied in the Charter, should work together.[15]

With regard to the issue of reconstruction, Salter joined seven other MPs on 9 October to table a motion expressing their concern that millions of people on the continent might die from starvation and cold during the coming winter. The motion urged the government to help prevent the expulsion of Germans from Eastern Europe, to accelerate Ruhr coal production, to increase land and sea transport to distribute supplies, and to immediately form a Supreme Economic Council to co-ordinate European reconstruction. On 24 October Salter addressed the National Liberal Club on the subject of rebuilding Europe. The next day he was scheduled to join a delegation, which visited 10 Downing Street to lobby in favour of their motion, but had to withdraw at the last moment. Attlee expressed his sympathy for the delegation's objectives, but cautioned that Britain alone could not improve the situation. When the motion finally was debated on 26 October, 150 members of all parties had added their signatures.[16] While Salter opened the debate by recapping conditions on the continent, his focus was upon defects of policy and organization. He emphasized the ways to increase coal production in the Ruhr, and to release military trucks for distribution of wheat, sugar, clothing and raw materials. He also requested the government to make "urgent and renewed" pleas to halt the flow of expulsions. He conceded that a Supreme Economic Council, while required in the long run, provided no immediate solution. He concluded: "It is idle for the rest of the world to think that it can enjoy either prosperity of peace, if there is neither stability nor tolerable conditions of living for the ancient and populous Continent, Europe – the mother of civilization, the mother of strife." In the ensuing debate, Salter's contribution was praised, and after Bevin replied for the government, it was noted that there was much common ground between the two. Sir Ben Smith, the Minister of Food and final government speaker, however, took issue with almost all of Salter's information regarding foodstuffs and stated that there would be no immediate relief from rationing.[17] In a follow-up letter to The Times, Salter reaffirmed the accuracy of his position on world food supplies and urged the government to publish information about such resources worldwide.[18] In a similar exercise of clarification, he also wrote to The Spectator and urged the weekly to support his proposal to apply government pressure on the military in London, Washington and Ottawa to recycle its massive reserves for civilian purposes.[19]

In "The Relief of Europe" which Salter contributed to Contemporary Review, he wrote, "As we enter the winter, the prospects of starvation, disease and political chaos in a large part of Europe are black indeed. In mass and scale, the imminent human misery through cold and underfeeding will exceed anything previously known." In his view the tragedy was not the product of world shortages of necessities but a consequence of disorganization, and he added his familiar suggestions for effective remedies. However, he also now acknowledged that the growing division of the continent into two spheres, Eastern and Western, was making reconstruction more difficult. The Russians were more interested in "rendering Germany permanently incapable of aggression" than in humanitarian considerations. For long-term reconstruction, he returned to advocate for the establishment of his Supreme Economic Council. Suggesting that the proposal had been misunderstood, he explained that this was not intended to be a mere advisory council. What he envisaged was a council with executive power, whose members would have executive authority in their individual country. The familiar example he gave was of an American and British minister, each with executive control of shipping, who could agree as members of the council to allocate shipping.[20] The fact was Salter had emerged as one of the more prominent individuals echoing, both in public and the House of Commons, the concerns of the "Save Europe Now" movement in the fall of 1945. It is not surprising he was one of the prime movers of the notice of motion of 6 October which later gathered such large all-party support. In addition, he was also a speaker at an Albert Hall meeting on 26 November, attended by more than 7,000 people, to support an appeal for immediate food aid to Europe.[21]

On 30 October Salter was back in the House of Commons for another debate on the peacetime use of atomic energy, prior to Attlee's visit to Washington to discuss the issue. Again he turned to the inevitable period when the monopoly on atomic secrets would collapse and when there would emerge "a competitive race for this new weapon." He referred with approval to Albert Einstein's view that the American government "should commit the secret of the bomb to a World Government." As an alternative, Salter again offered the Commons his proposal to entrust the secret to the Security Council along with the right to enforce inspection for members and destruction of bomb-making facilities elsewhere.[22] Voicing skepticism about Salter's proposal, The Economist on 3 November suggested that it would be impossible to differentiate between the peaceful development of atomic energy and the manufacture of bombs, permitting the former and banning the latter. On the other hand, the weekly endorsed both his interpretation of the causes of impending starvation in Europe and his proposals to alleviate such a disaster.[23] The fact remained that Salter was focusing his efforts on what he regarded as his primary agenda. Thus on 5 November, during a Commons' debate on the expulsion of millions of Germans from Poland, Czechoslovakia and Hungary, he reminded the government of his previous requests for information. Only this, preferably as a White Paper, "could inform discussion, mobilise good will and remedy the problems of relief and reconstruction in Europe."[24]

Underlying many such discussions was a current of criticism of UNRRA. On 26 October, for example, Bevin had stated that UNRRA "came in with great trumpets. That is the misfortune of having a Press conference at the birth. You do not know how the infant will grow up."[25] Other than his comments in the Commons on 28 March, Salter had spoken little on the subject. On 16 November, however, and on his initiative, he opened a debate about UNRRA, noting with satisfaction that its responsibilities, work and presence on the ground had since that time vastly increased. For the rest he asked detailed questions to elicit further information about UNRRA's work both in Europe and the Far East, including its new responsibilities with regard to displaced people. Additionally, he queried the government on its financial contribution to UNRRA, and urged an even greater release of food for distribution. Once again he requested a White Paper on conditions in Europe and the resources available for distribution, a suggestion which received the support of several subsequent speakers. In his response, Noel-Baker dealt with the issues raised by Salter, admitting that he could not answer all of his questions, but reaffirming the government's determination that UNRRA would not fail.[26]

Even as the year drew to a close, Salter's commitment to the issues he felt so passionately about continued. In the House of Commons on 23 November, he praised the communiqué, issued jointly by the leaders of the American, British and Canadian governments on 15 November. This promised to share information about atomic science for peaceful purposes and ensure a system of effective safeguards against its use as a weapon. He particularly welcomed the implication that any inspection system implied a merging of national sovereignty. Finally, he wished to see the USSR associated with the establishment by the United Nations of a commission to implement these objectives. Following this, he added his name to a proposal, advanced by a distinguished group of British, French, Belgian and Norwegian politicians and scientists, to set up an international committee of scientists, attached to the United Nations, to promote research into the peaceful uses of atomic energy.[27] He also kept up his own personal campaign to convince the government to issue a White Paper providing information on Europe's needs for imported food and materials in the forthcoming winter. By 19 December he was informed that consultations on the question were in progress.[28]

Salter's primary concerns continued into the New Year. On 2 January 1946 he wrote to Noel-Baker ("My dear Phil") stating that his information indicated that Hungary's situation was desperate. Noel-Baker replied that the picture Salter painted was too gloomy and, in any case, there were no reserves to assist Hungary.[29] Salter was undeterred and arranged to meet with officials from several ministries on 21 January. He then further elaborated on his proposal for a White Paper suggesting that this should be the first of a series of official statements updating the situation. As the difficulties with such an exercise were explained, Salter "brushed them aside." "The meeting was not very fruitful," noted one official, while Salter warned that he would continue to pursue the matter in the House. This in fact he did, immediately giving notice of his intention to question Bevin as to when the White Paper would be expected. The draft reply stated on the one hand that information about coal and transportation was available, while also suggesting that publicity about the food situation was being considered. As well, while there was sympathy with Salter's wish to provide information about needs and resources, other governments had to be consulted.[30] The government's response in the Commons on 4 February followed these lines, and also indicated some sympathy with Salter's desire for making the facts about resources generally know.[31] However, when the government indicated the following day that the world food situation had deteriorated, Salter declared that the news came "as a great shock" to the House, and demanded detailed information. Meanwhile, his views garnered some public support. On 26 January The Economist had warned that "As the cold of mid-winter descends on Europe its peoples face the hardest, leanest, cruelest months the Continent has known for three hundred years." Much of the "mass misery" might have been avoided, it noted, if Salter's idea of a "General Staff for European Relief" had been pursued.[32] On 7 February The Times, in discussing the world food shortage and the shock it had engendered, endorsed Salter's views that one of the contributing causes was indeed administrative failure.[33]

Amid such concerns Salter diverted his attention to the debate on the second reading of the newly proposed National Insurance Bill, a comprehensive system of sickness, maternity, unemployment and pension benefits funded by employers, employees and the government. On 7 February he was critical of the fact that the Friendly Societies were to be excluded. He argued that this would disappoint its eight million members, create hardship for its officials and deprive the government of a store of experience. He then reminded members he was one of a half-dozen officials at the Treasury when the first Health Insurance Bill was going through the House in 1911. Further when the administration was being constructed he was head of the approved societies' branch. He urged that the Friendly Societies be used as "agents of the State for the administration of this scheme" for their own members. One option he suggested was for members to take their sickness benefit, whether voluntary or state, from the society, and other benefits such as old age pensions from the state. Failing all else, Salter asked that the suggestion he and Beveridge were making, for a trial period at the very least, should be adopted. Pleas to retain the services of the Friendly Societies also came from other MPs, but in the view of The Economist, it was best put by Salter. Beveridge also wrote to compliment Salter on his "excellent" speech. The second reading of the bill was carried without a division and then preceded to the committee stage.[34] When the bill was debated in the House some weeks later, Salter returned to the charge, this time explaining that his proposal was intended to be permissive rather than mandatory.[35] In another contribution to the public debate, he wrote a conclusion to a short booklet, which also carried a supporting introduction from Beveridge, The Way Ahead: The Strange Case of the Friendly Societies, asserting that exclusion would waste experience and human resources and would strike a "fatal blow" to the Friendly Societies.[36]

On 14 February Salter was again in the House of Commons when it debated the world food shortage. His focus was upon the admission, the previous week by the Minister of Food as to the severity of the situation. He challenged the government's ongoing contentions that information about this had in fact been forthcoming. Salter admitted that while the world food situation had been deteriorating for some time, the key factor was the withholding of information. For four months he had been pressing the government for a White Paper on the subject. He continued: "When I first asked for that I was told 'No.' Then I was told 'I will consider it.' Then, to cite only a few of the many procrastinations, I was told 'The possibility is not excluded.' Then I was told 'Preparations are being made for consultations with other Governments'." Transparency alone would not have solved the food crisis, he was forced to admit under vigorous cross-questioning, but it would have helped educate the public and would have led to earlier action.[37] Pressing the issue still further, Salter used The Observer to survey the serious deterioration in the world food supply. While Britain was "facing scarcity, many other countries are facing starvation." He proposed several remedies, including increasing the supply of locally caught fish and the importation of more vegetables and fruits. Salter's major recommendation for the long term, however, remained the need to increase "international planning, publicity and co-ordination of policy." Nor had he given up on his advocacy of a Supreme Economic Council.[38]

After two further interventions on the subject of a White Paper in the Commons on 20 February and 4 March, he was told on 25 March that it would be published as soon as possible.³⁹ At last, after cabinet approval on 1 April,⁴⁰ the White Paper, <u>The World Food Shortage</u>, was published the following day and debated in the House of Commons on 4 April. There Attlee admitted that "We are facing a world food shortage." He reviewed the reasons for this, including natural causes such as drought, and the many disruptions attributable to the war, and detailed remedial measures being taken both in Britain and world-wide. Many of the following speeches were critical of Attlee and the White Paper. Salter declared that after trying to get the White Paper for five months, he was disappointed. "I think that after such a long labour, we might have had a rather plumper mouse." He then launched into a critique of the document, citing such omissions as the lack of statistics and the reticence about Britain's domestic situation. It was a document, he continued, "which says hardly anything about what we need, what we have, and what it is possible we shall get." In its failure to foresee, as early as September, the current situation and act in time, he faulted in particular the Minister of Food, Sir Ben Smith. Winding up the debate, Smith made no reference to Salter's numerous criticisms other than to suggest that he would not reveal figures for individual commodities in Britain.⁴¹

During the course of his April 4 speech in parliament, Salter stated that the White Paper contained "a rather sinister suggestion" that daily caloric intake could reasonably fall to the 1,000 mark. He argued, however, that with the average food consumption in the UK in 1945 at 2,850 calories a day per head, the 1,000 calorie level meant starvation. Therefore, he believed that half the population in the British control zone in Germany, on 1,000 calorie rations, were on the verge of starvation. Indeed, he examined this further in a BBC broadcast and an article in <u>Picture Post</u>. He reviewed the familiar causes for the world food shortage, but admitted, contrary to his previous assertions, that there was a surprise shortage of cereals, such as wheat and rice, which emerged at the end of 1945. He warned that starvation for millions was inevitable, although "more production and more economy" would help make a difference in the long run. And he also urged greater co-ordination between such international organizations as UNRRA, the Combined Food Board (Canada, the United States and Great Britain) in Washington, the German Control Commissions, and the recently formed UN Food and Agricultural Organization. In a letter to <u>The Times</u> on 16 April, he wrote that 1,000 calories a day was "too much to let you die quickly, too little to let you live long." He suggested that a small caloric reduction in British consumption might be a possible solution.⁴² It was only on 9 May that the government did confirm that the current ration in the British control zone was indeed 1,000 calories.⁴³

A feature of Salter's concerns was the striking fact that he was so well-informed. Although he had always been a voracious reader and researcher, he also relied on his contacts and resources at All Souls College and Chatham House. With regard to the later, he was an active participant in several study groups. For example, the first such post-war effort in which he participated had led to the publication in January 1946 of British Security. This was an examination of the problems facing Britain in the search for national security in a post-war world, but the book did not identify individual contributions.[44] He specifically referred to this study, for example, when he later debated in the Commons the problem of defence and the Commonwealth. He argued the case, based on the Chatham House discussions, that Britain must enter a real partnership with the Commonwealth on all issues relating to defence policy, including costs and planning. Equally important, he suggested, only such a partnership would enable Britain to retain its status as one of the three great powers.[45] On 6 May he joined a group of scientists and non-professionals meeting at Chatham House to discuss the implications of atomic energy and its impact on international affairs. After it was agreed to set up a study group for this purpose, Salter worked together with Sir Charles Webster and Sir Oliver Franks. The three proposed that the need to erect an international system for the "inspection, control and development" of atomic energy would provide further impetus towards building collective security.[46] In a later discussion with a leading atomic scientist, Sir George Thomson, and broadcast on the BBC, Salter supported the so-called "Baruch proposals," to set up the Atomic Development Authority under the umbrella of the United Nations, to oversee the future development of atomic energy. During the course of the discussion, Salter confessed, "I wish you'd never discovered this thing."[47]

Given his ongoing interest regarding the British control zone in Germany, Salter was eager to acquire some first-hand knowledge. Both in Memoirs of a Public Servant and Slave of the Lamp, Salter wrote he made several visits to Germany after war's end.[48] The one he most documented himself, in letters and a diary, arose as a result of his request to the Foreign Office on 2 April to attend the Nuremburg Trials and then visit Berlin.[49] On 12 May Salter took off from Northolt airport aboard a Dakota airplane and landed at Nuremburg after a four-hour flight. He was immediately driven to the Grand Hotel, now repaired and under American management. After tea he paid a brief visit to the Stadium, its great gilt swastika removed and replaced by an American flag. He then went to see the old town, "unequalled as a scene of vast desolation," he noted in his diary and continued: "People apparently living in holes in rubble, or in gutted houses exposed to weather, or in hastily built wooden shacks built into ruins." The next morning, Salter paid his first visit through the impressive stone and marble corridors of the vast Court of Justice where the trial of former Nazis was taking place. From the first row of the visitors' gallery on the first floor overlooking the court he had a good view of the proceedings below. "The defendants are as clearly visible as the actors on a stage and every change of expression can be clearly seen," Salter wrote and continued:

> Nearest, & in the corner of the front row is Goering, with a grey, loose suit, obviously now too big for him; he looks clearly like a man who has been too fat but is so no longer, a pale, rather clean face, occasionally animated but for the most part resting his head on his right hand in a posture & with a look of boredom or dejection; on his left is Hess, looking even more mad than in the photographs; then Ribbentrop, a broken man, near now the edge of insanity, alternatively in a kind of bored stupor & then scribbling notes; then Keitel in uniform, by far the finest figure, upright, military and still apparently with respect for himself and his profession; then [Ernst] Kaltenbrunner, large with a sinister face; Rosenberg, an abstracted fanatic; Frank, small pale with black glasses; Frick, a big rustic figure in a tweed coat; Streicher, coarse, undistinguished, pallid; then as the last two in the row Funk & Schacht, each squirming away from each other, the one small and unnoteworthy, the second, tall, now aged & thin but immediately recognizable with his spectacled, pedantic & authoritarian face. In the second row there are first the two Admirals, Doenitz & Raeder, in mufti – impassive, grave, dignified. Von Schirach should have come next but he was absent, preparing his defence – for his case comes later this week; then Sauckel, pale, bald, paunchy and peaked; Jodl, also in uniform, a less distinguished & prepossessing Keitel; von Papen, looking just as in his photographs, but now greyer, looking both a diplomat and a crank; Seyss-Inquart, an interesting face, more academic & respectable bourgeois than the rest; Speer, dark haired, looking vigorous & competent; von Neurath, a fine figure of a statesman, rivalling Keitel as the best looking; & last Fritsche, young & second-rate looking.

After spending 13 and 14 May attending the trials, Salter observed that the "Court was admirably conducted; & all the arrangements very efficient." To Lady Salter he wrote that it was "an unforgettable experience." He continued, "The real difficulty will be to assess the crimes – how far should Hitler's associates be regarded as sharing in the crimes of starting an aggressive war; how far are breeches of the ordinary rules of war (sinking without warning, etc.) be regarded as crimes. The crimes against humanity – murder of prisoners etc. – are easier." On 15 May he set out by car to see the devastated countryside, reaching Frankfurt before proceeding via overnight train to Berlin. To his delight he discovered that he was to share accommodation with General Smuts. The following day, 16 May, he and Smuts set out to tour Berlin.

> Went round Berlin with him through Charlottenburg and Tiergarten (trees pulled for fuel & converted into small allotments). To Brandenburg Thor and along Unter den Linden (Russian zone) – all Berlin a scene of absolute devastation; everything either rubble or gutted. Adlon, Reichstag, embassies, Govt offices all in ruins. Alexanderplatz – black market – posters. S. E.D. (combined Communist –Socialist Party). Wilhelmstrasse all destroyed. Taken over Reichskanzlei by Russian commandant – vast building erected by Hitler 1939 – went over his underground bunker & saw rooms occupied by him & Eva Braun & Goebbels – place of death – elaborate underground constructions – air-conditioning etc. Then saw corner of British district of Berlin with Smuts.

"The effect on Smuts was tremendous," Salter wrote, "'this is the end – or the end for many years – of Germany, perhaps of Europe.'" During the next two days Salter attended a series of meeting and interviews to apprise himself of all aspects of the situation, social, financial, economic and political. He left Berlin by car on 18 May and, after staying overnight at Lubbecke for further briefings, returned the next day to England.[50] One of many results of his visit to a devastated Berlin was to be his suggestion, on 14 November in the House of Commons, that "it would be an easier task to build a new [capital] city in the wilderness, than to rebuild Berlin."[51]

On his return to London Salter wrote to thank the Foreign Office for the arrangements and anticipated that the visit would be "of the greatest possible value for a good deal of the work which I am doing."[52] Indeed, in the following weeks, some of the issues he wrote about or debated in the Commons arose directly from the information he had gathered abroad. These included the control of publications for the German public, the equalization of rations in the British and American control zones and the plight of displaced persons, such as he had witnessed, who refused to return home. In fact, in a debate about UNRRA on 7 June, he urged that displaced persons be appointed to administer its camps.[53] Nor did he give up on his ongoing concern with the world food situation. He had admitted earlier in the House that the winter had been an exceptionally mild one, and this had helped avoid catastrophe in Europe. However, he still focused on the famine which threatened world populations and on 22 May he asked for a follow-up to the White Paper on food.[54] He supported the announcement in Washington on 25 May of a new multi-state Emergency Food Council to replace the three member, wartime Combined Food Board, even as he repeated his call for a Supreme Economic or Reconstruction Council. Such a body, he reiterated, would have executive powers both to deal with the food issue as well as financial, industrial and commercial powers needed for reconstruction.[55] On 27 May the Minister of Food suddenly announced his resignation, noting that he had experienced "a very difficult and exhausting time."[56] Salter, a persistent critic of the minister, was quick to follow up on 31 May in the House of Commons. "After all, a resignation from office is not a funeral," he observed, "and we cannot be expected to preserve undue obituary reticence about the administration during the tenure of the former Minister." While he paid tribute to Smith's sincerity, he criticised the latter for not having foreseen nor forewarned the public about the world food shortage. Salter then spoke of his recent visit to the British zone in Germany, welcoming the news that the rations in the British zone were to be equivalent to those in the American zone, and praising the work done there by British military and political officials. Finally, he requested that the government produce an amended and updated version of the 2 April White Paper which he repeated was "not the lucid, candid and comprehensive document I had asked for." These comments were greeted by Opposition cheers.[57]

In the following weeks, Salter was unrelenting in his criticism of the government's food policy, its refusal to fully disclose information and failure to anticipate shortages.[58] The situation became even graver with the surprise announcement on 27 June by the new Minister of Food, John Strachey, that bread rationing would begin on 21 July. A motion tabled by several members of the Opposition, and including Salter, demanded the facts and figures about domestic and world supply of cereals which led to the unprecedented decision.[59] In the debate which followed on 3 July, Salter stated he had added his name "to the most modest Motion that had ever been put on an Order Paper," one requesting only facts. He registered his gratitude that the government, finally, was now far more forthcoming with respect to information. However, he still expressed his dissatisfaction with the inequality of rations in the different zones of Germany. Finally, he reminded the House that bread was never rationed in either of the world wars, and that it was difficult, expensive and fell unequally on the population.[60] When Salter rejoined the debate on 18 July, he questioned the logic of bringing in a rationing system within three days rather than waiting first for the results of the upcoming harvests. The 18 July motion to annul the implementation of rationing, introduced by Churchill, was defeated. However, the Second Review of the World Food Shortage was finally tabled on 31 July. Bread rationing lasted until 24 July 1948.[61]

On 19 July the Salters left aboard the *Queen Mary* for a summer vacation in the US until October. The liner called at Halifax to let off 2,254 brides and children of Canadian servicemen, and reached New York on 25 July. The Salters immediately went to the River Club, a summer routine which they followed for the next 23 years. A number of days were spent in New York to entertain and visit with their wide circle of American friends, both social and political. From there they journeyed by car to Hickory Farm, near Tyringham, Massachusetts. For the rest of the summer it was a leisurely round of country entertainment with friends and neighbours, visitors from England and frequent attendance at their box at the Tanglewood Music Festival. For Salter there was always some ongoing political matter. For example, in mid-August he continued a correspondence with Noel-Baker regarding the employment by UNRRA of displaced persons, an issue he had raised in the Commons on 3 June and 18 July. Salter remained unsatisfied by the explanation offered by Noel-Baker, responding that the situation illustrated the problems with UNRRA, "hopelessly enmeshed in its own red-tape."[62]

Returning to London on 22 October, Salter at once resumed his attendance at the House of Commons, even as the issues continued to change.[63] Increasingly, however, he offered his support to the Conservative critics of the Labour government. This movement to the right would eventually lead him to accept Churchill's request to run as a Conservative. On occasion, such as during a discussion which would have allowed the chancellor of the exchequer to make changes in the metal composition of currency by Royal Proclamation, he would rise to protect "the essential liberties and rights" of the House.[64] He still encouraged the government to find overseas countries willing to allow the immigration of displaced persons who could not return to their own countries.[65] Nor did he hesitate from contributing to debates on the larger international issues as they arose. For example, on 14 November he offered his thoughts on several issues related to Germany. He began by comparing the peace-making process in 1919 and 1946. "We shall be very lucky too if we get as good a treaty," he stated and then criticised the post-1919 "myth and legend" that Versailles "was a Carthaginian and a vindictive Treaty." The consequences were "due to the folly and weakness" of subsequent events and statesmen, rather than the treaty provisions. He continued, "It is about time that historic justice should be done to the framers of the Treaty of Versailles." Furthermore he urged the government to stop "pussyfooting around the periphery" and begin dealing with the many problems relating to Germany. Among the ones he focused on was a request for a third review of the food situation, establishing an equal calorie ration in the British and American zones in Germany and charges of "incompetence and maladministration" in the Allied zones. With regard to preventing any future German aggression, he favoured a campaign of education to discourage this, backed by a vigorous programme of disarmament. "It is politically more feasible, financially more economical, militarily more practical and humanly more tolerable," he argued, "to suppress an attempt when it is made, than to forestall that attempt by creating devastation and desolation." Finally, he alluded to Churchill's speech at Zurich on 19 September urging the formation "of a kind of United States of Europe." Salter believed the idea was premature until "suitable units" emerged and this depended largely on what happened in Germany and

France. Several days later the government promised another review of the world food situation early in 1947.⁶⁶

The attention of parliament soon turned to another issue of more than passing interest to Salter. On second reading of the Labour government's massive bill to nationalize British transport, a debate which lasted from 16 to 18 December, Salter was a prominent contributor. The first of his several interventions pointed out that as chairman of both the Road-Rail Conference in 1932 and the Railway Staff National Tribunal, which settled every dispute it considered, and as a contributor to <u>The Next Five Years</u> in 1935, he had always argued in favour of "'coordination' not of nationalization" of the country's transportation systems. His most telling argument, reported at length by <u>The Times</u> on 18 December, explained the reasons why he opposed the legislation:

> I do not approach this problem with any prejudice against socialisation. On the contrary, for 20 years, in speech, writing, and official conduct, I have been agitating for the socialisation of monopoly public utilities, and I have advocated an effective, and, if necessary, enforced coordination of road and railway. There is, of course, one criterion and one justification for a transport Bill. It is that it should secure a more convenient and economical transport system than either the present or any other practicable system.

The Transport Bill, he concluded, "is a vast monopolistic bureaucracy. It is an octopus with tentacles extending from tugs and port facilities to railways and road haulage, with even a tentative tentacle stretching out towards the coastwise shipping." He urged the government to take the bill back and rethink it. In the division on the second reading of the bill, he voted against it.⁶⁷

As the year drew to a close Salter wrote to an American friend that he and Lady Salter had "settled down to particular English brand of post-war annoyances, more drab & less dramatic than those on your side of the Atlantic. As far as we personally are concerned we are extremely comfortable, this being a very pleasant house and affairs here being very (& indeed much too) interesting. But I think as far as this new generation they are very different from those after the last war – if anything, a bit too serious, earnest & hardworking."⁶⁸ Ironically, the same might have been said about Salter himself as he worked intensively on a new book. As he wrote to Churchill on 7 December, the project was similar to one the latter had completed in 1937, <u>Great Contemporaries</u>, "but there is of course the difference that the angle of observation is for the most part that of an official." In response to Salter's request for any revisions to his sketch, Churchill replied, "I leave myself entirely in your truly friendly but also too complimentary hands."[69] Salter had already honed his considerable skill in writing pen portraits for the press, and most recently extended obituary appreciations of Lloyd George and Keynes in The Spectator.[70] On 16 January 1947, having read the manuscript which had been delivered a week earlier, Geoffrey Faber indicated that he wished to publish the book. After several weeks of negotiations regarding royalties, the extent of the print run, and a change of title from Master Spirits to Personality in Politics: Studies of Contemporary Statesmen, an autumn publication was agreed. The final manuscript was delivered to Geoffrey Faber on 27 February.[71] The book contained pen portraits of 22 public figures, from both sides of the Atlantic, as well as France, China and Italy. Each was designed "to give a general impression of character," illustrated by anecdotes of which Salter had first-hand knowledge, and also taking into account the role played by "incident and accident." His purpose, he explained, was to illustrate his belief that "History is the net result of the interaction of impersonal forces and the personalities of those who are in positions of authority." His hope was that such sketches and "anecdotage" would "claim a real, if minor, place among historical sources." The long-term reality proved Salter's point as the volume became a source of "anecdotage" for historians for generations to come.[72]

Even as the final details for publication of this new manuscript engaged him, Salter pursued a variety of other issues. When it was announced on 17 January that Churchill had assumed the chairmanship of a new all-party British Committee for a United Europe, and pointedly not the United States of Europe, Salter's name was not among the members.[73] His views were already on record in the Commons where on 18 November he had voiced concerns on the subject. But he was now persuaded by Lionel Curtis to write to The Times which had been critical of Churchill's project. This he did on 22 January and observed that despite the difficulties, with "necessity and great leadership," progress could be made in such preliminary areas as cultural and economic relations. He again reiterated his own particular slant, namely, that ultimate European Union would strengthen the United Nations. He continued: "'Federation' is only one of several forms of political association. Personally I believe it is the best when and where it is practicable; but in any case it cannot be all-comprehensive, and for relations with and between unfederated countries the 'inter-state' system is essential. Advocates of the U.N. and of federalism should therefore, I suggest, regard each other as complementary Allies not as rivals."[74]

Salter's public speeches also continued to focus on high policy. On 5 February, in the early afternoon, he addressed the Royal Empire Society on the role of the Dominions in imperial policy. Once more he here argued that if Britain was to carry its weight in the Anglo-American-Russian "trinity of power," it could only do so as a "British Commonwealth" and in an equal partnership with the Dominions. That partnership required not only a shared effort in war but also sharing the burden of policy making and defence spending in peace time.⁷⁵ In the evening he was again on his feet in the Commons during a debate on conditions in Germany. Firstly, he asked for a comprehensive report on the subject, including the extent of political devolution and the precise forms it would take down to the Länder level. "I think it is important," he stated, "however much we may still aim at a united Germany, to take steps to see that Western Germany can if necessary live, and live effectively, by itself." He further requested precise figures for the costs of the British Control Commission and Army of Occupation, made some suggestions on how to overcome the coal shortage, and finally made an eloquent plea for hastening the employment in Britain of displaced persons from the British zone of occupation.⁷⁶ Some obstacles to such a move were explained by government spokesmen, and these included trade union opposition. Nonetheless, speaking the next day at the News Review World Forum luncheon, Salter re-stated his view that the 269,000 displaced persons in the British zone provided a willing and skilled pool of labour for Britain.⁷⁷ He returned to the subject on 14 February when the House specifically debated the issue of displaced persons. Entry of such people to Britain, he noted, would offer hope to those "rotting in idleness," save the expense of keeping them in Germany and help with Britain's labour shortage. Referring to his visit the previous year to Germany, he stated that it was impossible not to admire "these men and women, who have had nothing but tragedy in the past and blank uncertainty in the future" and the way they maintained their morale. They were, in Salter's view, ideal emigrants and the sooner Britain acted the sooner would they get the most qualified.⁷⁸ On 21 February Salter led a deputation of the Refugee Defence Committee which was received by the Minister of Labour, George Isaacs, and tried to impress the minister with the urgency of getting a recruitment scheme into operation.⁷⁹ On occasion, as the British economy succumbed to a winter fuel shortage leading to cuts in electricity supply, Salter criticised the government for administrative incompetence and yet again requested "regular, sober, objective and illuminating statements as to the facts of the coal situation." Fellow MP Jennie Lee criticised his comments on a subject on which, she argued, he had little real expertise.⁸⁰

Ever since his intervention on 17 December 1946 on the second reading of the Labour government's Transport Bill, Salter had kept up a vigorous campaign of criticism. His membership on the Standing Committee examining the omnibus bill clause by clause allowed him further scope for criticism.⁸¹ In particular, he was very concerned about the powers proposed for the five Transport Commissioners, a point to which he returned when the issue was debated in the Commons on 3 March. He contended that these powers, including future policy regarding British ports, were so vast as to constitute "a grave assault upon Parliament's legislative function." He suggested that the government focus the proposed legislation only on the nationalization of the railroads and leave other means of transportation and communication to future legislation. He also wanted the bill to omit any oversight of the so-called "C" license holders, small road operators whose activities covered distances less than 40 miles. He concluded, "We are now governed by a tired bureaucracy directed by Ministers who are themselves tired bureaucrats, and it is a bureaucracy ineffectively criticised and controlled by an overburdened Parliament." The cabinet in fact gave way on 13 March and agreed that the Transport Bill should not restrict the operation of "C" license vehicles.[82]

In the course of that debate a member noted that Salter "was referred to the other night by the BBC as the Conservative Member for Oxford. I thought that was a pardonable mistake." In reality Salter was moving increasingly into opposition to Labour legislation not only domestically but also in imperial and foreign affairs. Thus on 6 March the Commons debated the Attlee government's proposal to set an arbitrary date for unilateral withdrawal from India, rather than continue to work towards a united India with or without Dominion status. Salter weighed in to support the Conservatives in their opposition to the proposal. He referred to his mission to India in 1931 and his hopes over the years that self-government would be possible without partition. He detailed what he regarded as the historic benefits of British rule, including a rising standard of living and relative freedom from external invasion and civil war. He expressed his fears that "the greatest possible disaster" might follow the withdrawal and India was to be "Balkanised." When the "obituary" of Britain's association with India will be written, he concluded, he hoped it would record "an honourable and peaceful passing."[83]

Domestic policy, particularly economic and financial affairs, also attracted his attention. On 19 March, he contributed to a debate on the British economy and manpower in the basic industries. Here he contended that the key to a rise in the standard of living was to increase production. That solution entailed attracting workers to industries where they were needed, with incentives produced by a policy designed to dampen wage increases until production increased. As for manpower, he pointed out that with massive demobilisation the issue was not a shortage but a lack of the necessary skills and experience for particular industries. Finally, he called on the cooperation of trade unions to spearhead a drive for increased output.[84] On 15 April, the Labour Chancellor of the Exchequer introduced his budget, the first after a full 12 months of peace, and one expected to provide some stimulus to British economic growth. Among its many stated purposes was to balance exports and imports. Salter mostly took a back seat during the initial debate, weighing in on 16 April with the observation that it was time to embark upon some counter-inflationary measures to offset the Labour government's policies of cheap money, nationalization and heavy expenditure.[85] On 22 April he spoke in favour of a provision in the budget for an increase in the tobacco tax. He argued that the dollar saving effect, resulting from reduced imports of American tobacco, would in fact be very small, however, the revenue result would be more significant. He projected that even with the additional revenue the currency deficit, when loans expired, would continue unless there was an improvement in British production and exports. To some reported "laughter and cheers" in the House, Salter mentioned that he had cut back his own consumption of cigarettes by 50 per cent.[86]

In the following days Salter was often in attendance at the House of Commons, usually to ask questions on such diverse subjects as miners' basic wage rates or the need for government to centralise the gathering of statistical information.[87] On 28 April the return of the Transport Bill to the Commons for a report stage debate once again galvanised Salter. In the Standing Committee examining the bill, he had often protested against the imposition of "guillotine" which limited discussion. In fact, more than a quarter of the bill was passed over without any discussion, allowing the government once again to determine policy by order instead of parliamentary authority.[88] During the Commons' debate, however, he weighed in on such aspects as adding part-time members to the Transport Commission, given the enormity of its responsibilities for railways, roads, canals, hotels, docks and harbours, and favouring a flexible date for implementation. At 9.30 on 30 April in a crowded Commons, the guillotine fell on the report stage of the Transport Bill, with 270 amendments yet to be discussed. [89] On 5 May Minister of Transport Alfred Barnes moved that the Transport Bill should get its third reading and come into effect on 1 July 1948. He acknowledged that "much disputation" surrounded the bill and criticism indeed continued with Salter playing an active role. Salter attacked the way the government had handled amendments, imposed guillotine, and ignored input from experienced parliamentarians. He affirmed his belief in the general principle of nationalization, for example, of the coal mines and electricity and even the railroads individually. However, he opposed the "vast bureaucratic system" created by the bill. In particular he targeted the Transport Commission, "with its vast monopoly, its single fund of finance," exempt from competition, criticism and effective financial control. During the debate Salter was challenged to defend his current position with the views he had advocated as a signatory of <u>The Next Five Years</u> (1935). This he did by reiterating his preference, there laid out, for the nationalization of the railroads but with co-ordination with the road haulage system. When the question was put, Salter voted against the bill which nonetheless passed with a substantial majority.[90] He also used a Liberal Party rally in London on 15 May to expand on his views regarding economic planning. He agreed that "certain parts of our economy were ripe for socialisation," but added, "we should attempt to limit the points of control to those most important, and leave the utmost freedom for enterprise and competition." When Britain's current difficulties were overcome, control should be "exercised in the form of Treasury measures rather than departmental regulations and restriction." Salter was clearly moving to the right in his advocacy of state control versus laissez-faire.[91]

After his prominent role in the contentious debates on the Transport Bill, Salter's parliamentary contributions returned to brief interventions. Some issues included the length of service for military conscription, and an update of the world food situation.[92] He was also beginning to take a greater interest in planning and environmental issues. He had already voiced his concerns about increased industrial development in Oxford in the Commons and on 23 May expressed his opposition to the proposed oil-fired Bankside generating station, unless it could be proven that the sulphur emissions posed no danger.[93] When he returned to the subject on 10 June all he could elicit was that the government had taken advice, would not publish this information and was going ahead.[94]

Salter was also soon engaged, however, on more familiar territory. On 5 June at Harvard University, US Secretary of State George Marshall announced the European Recovery Program, designed to provide massive American financial assistance to support the rebuilding of European economies, reduce tariff barriers, and modernize European industrial and business practices. In his first comment in the House of Commons, on what became known as the Marshall Plan, Salter urged the utmost speed in framing Britain's response.[95] In his mind the urgency resulted from Britain's massive trade deficit, with British exports running far behind its imports, and a resulting balance of payments problem. As Britain would soon exhaust existing American credits and Canadian loans, mainly in Canadian and US dollars, what was to be done, Salter had asked in a letter to <u>The Times</u> on 5 June. A reduction in American exports, he argued, could lead to a recession there, but American investment together with Britain in the sterling area might help increase imports over time.[96] In <u>The Sunday Times</u> on 15 June, he added that the plan provided a stimulus to aspirations for a United Europe. However, he cautioned that because it would take time to plan for a new European economy, he favoured trying to find agreement on the deficit required to be met by American capital and what investments would most speed production.[97] He returned to the subject on 19 June in the House and pleaded for urgency in setting up "the procedure, machinery and agenda" for the negotiations with regard to Marshall's proposals. Compounding the urgency was the fact that within a year British and European imports would no longer be financed by credits and loans. Then drawing on his experience with issues of relief and reconstruction after the First World War, he advocated machinery be set up independently from the United Nations, and that the dollar requirements should be set out in a "bold and comprehensive scheme." This should be based on a global estimate for the entire period of need rather than in a piecemeal fashion. The urgency of the situation and the necessity to succeed was, in his parting words, to avoid "the impoverishment" of Europe and a depression in the United States.[98] As a follow up, the editorial staff of The Observer published a statement, "The Rescue of Europe," after consulting with Salter, Beveridge and Sir George Schuster. This described Marshall's proposal as an "International New Deal" to avoid an economic collapse in Europe and pressed for its acceptance. It specifically echoed Salter's pleas for haste because of Europe's dollar needs and because any further delay into 1948, an American presidential election year, would result in Congress delaying any decisions into 1949.[99]

Salter returned to the subject in an address he delivered on 1 July to a large audience at Chatham House. He pointed out that the Marshall Plan was an invitation to Europe to plan, not for physical reconstruction but for rebuilding the economic future of Europe. The purpose of Marshall's initiative, he continued, was to foster democratic institutions, avoid piecemeal requests for loans and credits, and to ensure that Europe would eventually pay its own way. He stated that the background to the crisis was the clash between the "hard currency" countries, such as America exporting more than they were importing, and the "soft currency" countries, such as Britain where the converse was true. The gap between the two was being bridged by credits and loans of a non-renewable character. A reduction in British imports, such as that exemplified by the increase in tobacco tax, would not be sufficient nor could exports be adequately increased over the short term. Acceptance of Marshall Aid, framed by a "big, global constructive proposal," offered the best opportunity to "replace chaos and impoverishment by order and prosperity."[100] Salter firmly believed that the Marshall Plan was unprecedented "in its foresight, in its constructive political purpose and in its generosity in peacetime, as Lend-Lease was in wartime."[101]

In the final debates in the House of Commons before the summer recess, Salter turned his attention to several current economic issues. On 3 July, he argued, there was "no shortage of manpower" in Britain. He pointed out that this phrase was commonly used to cover three different issues at the root of the country's economic difficulties: misdistribution of manpower; poor output by the employed; and shortage or poor distribution of raw materials. He urged that this could be remedied by employing selected displaced persons with relevant experience. Besides the economic advantage, there would also be the humanitarian benefits. As for further measures, he suggested a system of incentives for smaller industries and a "wages policy" to combat inflation. He ended with an appeal to trade unions to curtail demands for wage increases until production had caught up with existing purchasing power.[102] Salter's proposal for a wages policy, quickly rejected by the Labour government, however, was endorsed by The Economist. The weekly anticipated an ongoing period of unofficial strikes, "a bitter harvest" of rising industrial costs, and the continued maldistribution of the labour force with prolonged effects upon the efficiency of British industry.[103] All this was left behind, however, when the Salters sailed on 10 July aboard the Queen Elizabeth, arriving in New York 16 July. After spending a week there, they retreated to Hickory Farm for the duration of the summer.[104]

The Board of Governors of the International Bank for Reconstruction and Development, conceived at the Bretton Woods Conference in July 1944, opened its second annual general meeting in London on 11 September 1947. On 16 September it announced Salter's appointment as chairman of its new Advisory Council, whose mandate was to brief the bank on questions of general policy.[105] In fact, the Council only met twice in Washington, from 19 to 23 July 1948 and 18 to 22 July 1949. At the conclusion of the former meeting, Salter circulated a note emphasizing his disappointment that the meeting, given limited latitude and with the widely different perspectives and experience of members, could not produce any formal and agreed report. He concluded that the only possible outcome was a record of the exchange of views.[106] On further reflection, and given his reservations, Salter convinced the Board of Governors of the need to have any future reports of the Advisory Council approved only by a majority vote.[107] After the second meeting, he recommended that under its mandate, it was unlikely that the Advisory Council "could render services commensurate in value to the time and expense involved."[108] The Council members and afterwards the Board of Governors agreed, suggested further study was required, but the Council never met again.[109] Reflecting on this experience, Salter observed that the whole idea was not only a waste of time and money, but also "naïve."[110]

During Salter's absence in the US, Personality in Politics: Studies of Contemporary Statesmen was published on 10 October to widespread acclaim. Extracts from the book had already appeared in The Manchester Guardian and, in the opinion of the editor, A.P. Wadsworth, were a great success."[111] "It was fun to write," Salter later noted, "& it's been extremely well received here, with good reviews."[112] Indeed, British reviewers uniformly complimented Salter for his "restrained and penetrating judgement," as "an excellent portrait painter," "a man of independent and penetrating mind with a terse and vivid style," with "the eye of the sympathetic and humane observer," who provided, with a sense of humour, "glimpses of the great as seen by one who has worked with them in a close advisory capacity," and for making "a real contribution to modern history."[113] A lengthy review in The Times Literary Supplement rightly predicted that the book would prove to be a "mine of rich and reliable output" for future biographers. This review also occasioned a large number of letters to the editor from, among others, Frances Lloyd George and Lucy Masterman.[114] The book prove to be a publishing success, going through its third impression in February 1948, recommended by The Book Society, and republished by Christina Foyle's The Right Book Club. American reviews were likewise fulsome, with a suggestion in the Saturday Review of Literature that Salter should write his autobiography, which he finally completed in 1961.[115] However, at the time his response to a friend's suggestion that he write his autobiography was that "I've many more interesting personalities to write about!"[116]

The return to London on 23 October meant a return to the House as the arena for Salter's attention. His interests and contributions continued to range widely, from questioning the vast expenses involved in administering the British zone in Germany to the controversy to end the basic petrol ration as one of the ongoing austerity measures. With regard to the latter, he asserted, both in the House and in the press, that the net dollar savings would be negligible and that the policy was a mistake.[117] This also led him to attack the motives of the Labour government, asking on 3 November whether it was its intention "to get out of a morass or to build a Socialist state?"[118] The next day came the disturbing news that Gil Winant, the former ambassador to the UK, had committed suicide at his home in Concord, New Hampshire. This was a terrible shock to the Salters. Lady Salter had known the Winants for many years, both in the United States and in Geneva. She and Gil Winant often exchanged greetings, gifts, books and flowers. A year before, Lady Salter had encouraged Winant, who had been replaced as the United States Ambassador on 10 April 1946, to use West House for the summer. She noted that "you will have enough servants to look after you," including the chauffer. Winant declined, thanked Lady Salter for her "kindness and great generosity," but continued to keep in very close touch.[119] In February 1947 Salter assisted Winant with the first of a projected two-volume memoir, partly because the latter was having trouble completing the project. Salter provided material about the shipping assistance given by Washington to Britain in the first 18 months of the war.[120] The book, A Letter from Grosvenor Square, was published post-humously on 18 November and Winant there revealed he had suggested Salter be sent to Washington in March 1941.[121]

A major issue which soon focused Salter's attention, following the resignation of Hugh Dalton on 13 November and his replacement by Sir Stafford Cripps as Chancellor of the Exchequer was the supplementary budget debate. Salter took a particular interest in the proposal to increase the "Profits Tax," both on distributed and undistributed profits, one of the measures taken by the government to fight inflation and narrow the gap in the overseas balance of payments. On 2 December he argued that the increase was not in the national interest, that it was actually inflationary, and placed unnecessary handicaps upon free enterprise. The following day he conceded that the increase in the tax on distributed profits would likely be only a temporary measure. However, he feared that the increased tax on undistributed profits might remain a permanent one and curtail the efficiency of the private enterprise system. The press was particularly taken by his statement that the increased tax would make people think twice before risking their capital. It was a question of "Heads I lose all that I lose; tails I gain only a fraction of what I gain little," he told the Commons.[122] The other major issue on which he contributed was the Parliament Bill introduced by the Labour government to reduce the delaying powers of the House of Lords from two years to one. This was designed to speed the passage of the nationalization of the iron and steel industry before the next election. In its early stages, the issue was to preoccupy parliament for the next two years. Salter contended that the bill was a breach of constitutional and parliamentary practice, mainly because it was introduced without adequate time for discussion and was to apply retrospectively. The Parliament Bill received its third reading on 10 December with Salter voting against it alongside the Conservatives.[123]

In the New Year Salter's interests focused on various issues. On 29 January, he spoke in support of the government success, in April 1947 at Geneva, in negotiating the General Agreement on Tariffs and Trade. Aimed at abolishing quotas and reducing tariff duties, the agreement had entered into effect on 1 January. Because he regarded it as "regulated and controlled multilateralism," he stated, "I am going to indulge this evening in the privilege which I do not often nowadays enjoy of supporting the Government." The Manchester Guardian afterwards thought that Salter's speech "had brought comfort to the Treasury bench."[124] As well, he continued to speak out on what he regarded as Great Britain's "dollar problem," particularly questioning Britain's ability to continue paying for overseas food and raw materials. During his BBC broadcast on 13 February, he pointed out that the country's gold and dollar reserves were nearly exhausted. The only remedy, in his view, was to curb inflation and to provide incentives to increase production, otherwise the outcome would be a reduction in the standard of living and rising unemployment due to a shortage of raw materials.[125]

The Labour government's move to abolish university representation in the House of Commons was another issue which absorbed Salter for months to come. On 30 January the text of its Representation of the People Bill was published, proposing to end plural voting by abolishing the university constituencies and franchise. This would remove from the House of Commons, at the end of the current parliament, the 12 members representing seven university constituencies.[126] Salter immediately circulated an aide mémoire intended to highlight some of the facts concerning the issue. He was not optimistic, writing that "We fight against odds but the circumstances on which the proposal is now being rushed are really so outrageous that I do not despair of the issue."[127] When the Commons was informed on 12 February that the second reading of the bill was scheduled as soon as 16 February, he immediately voiced his concern that it was a major departure from the agreed recommendations of the all-party Speaker's Conference of 1944 and that there was insufficient time for the required wide consultation. The 1944 conference had recommended the retention of the existing university representation and franchise. The government response, which rarely wavered over the next few months, was that sufficient time had been allowed and that a Speaker's Conference from a previous parliament did not bind any subsequent parliament.[128]

On 16 February the debate on the issue opened, with a speech from Churchill condemning the government for "bad faith." This was the approach Salter also adopted when he contributed to the three occasions, February, March and June, when the bill was debated. In first intervention on 16 February, which The Times regarded as one of "dignity and reason," he stated that it was not his intention to argue for the retention of university seats neither "as a refuge for the enfeebled" nor on the impact it had on his "personal fortunes." Rather he regarded the bill as a blow to the professional classes, learning, education, and most of all to the customs of the constitution. To ignore the consensus reached at the Speaker's Conference, in his view, was "a breach of a bargain."[129] The following day, he heard government speakers respond to his criticisms and he had to endure a taunt that he was "indistinguishable from a Conservative." To which Salter replied that as an Independent, he was "likely to be more often than not opposed to any Government, whether of the Right or the Left?" The bill passed on second reading with Salter among the eight who voted against it.[130] Prior to the committee stage of debate on the bill, Salter and five other university members tabled an amendment to retain university representation.[131] When the debate resumed on 16 March Salter conceded that there might be "perfectly respectable reasons" to abolish university representation. However, the real issue in his mind was the "breach of an honourable obligation" to which those government ministers involved should be held accountable. In his final remarks, besides asking for support for the amendment, he explained that it was the natural tendency of Independent representatives generally to oppose any government of the right or left. In consequence, they were inevitably disliked by any organized party. While Salter's remarks were commended by fellow MPs as "powerful and cogent," the amendment was defeated by 328 votes to 198.[132] A follow-up letter on the subject to The Times challenged the government to submit to an impartial enquiry the issue of whether there was indeed a "breach of faith." The challenge went unanswered, even as The Economist complimented Salter for pressing his case "with great vigour."[133] Indeed, when the committee stage resumed on 23 and 24 March, Salter took no part. Commenting on the disappearance of the university seats, and the absence of such dedicated parliamentarians as Sir John Anderson, Salter and Wilson Harris, The Observer noted that in future they would "have to wear the motley and dance the hustings boogie-woogie" to return to the House.[134] In retrospect, Salter suggested that on its merits there was much to be said "both for and against" the Bill. Indeed, in Memoirs of a Public Servant he dedicated an entire chapter to this episode.[135] Among the reasons he adduced for the retention of university representation was that it offered a genuine opportunity for non-party independent opinion. In his final word on the subject, fellow Oxford Burgess A.P. Herbert wrote: "A most stupid and spiteful act."[136]

Such issues focused Salter's attention, but he was not without other activities. On 10 February he spoke at the annual luncheon of the Ruskin Society. In his tribute he praised Ruskin as an artist, writer and critic, but also as "a pioneer and prophet" in economics, education, and sociology. Given the presence as well of another speaker, the Minister of Education George Tomlinson, Salter urged every effort be made to preserve the professional and middle classes, threatened potentially by inflation.[137] He also concluded a task he had undertaken, namely, to edit some issues of The BBC Quarterly. The journal, which had first appeared in April 1946, was aimed primarily at those who determined "the policy and character of broadcasting." Salter had been asked by the BBC's Director-General, Sir William Haley, on its 25th anniversary, to edit two issues of the journal devoted to the impact broadcasting had made "in the different spheres of our national life."[138] The choice for editor was not surprising, given Salter's popularity as a panel member of the Brains Trust and a frequent broadcaster on both the BBC's home and overseas services.[139] In addition, he was adept at being able, in his own words, "to strike the right balance between the technically difficult & the over-simplified."[140] Thus he successfully enlisted contributions from eight individuals, including Nicolson, E.L. Woodward, Lord Samuel and "Molly" Hamilton. Salter's first issue appeared in April and carried his introduction which addressed "the imprint" radio had developed so quickly. He pointed out that broadcasting had evolved from a medium of mainly light entertainment to one with cultural and educational possibilities. The increasing importance of politics in society, he continued, had made radio a tool of "political education and propaganda" as well as enhancing the appreciation of music, art and drama. In the July issue, he concluded that the BBC, as a public monopoly, was fulfilling its mandate but had to continue keeping its programming "imaginative, enterprising, and responsive to public taste." Equally, in its treatment of controversial subjects, the BBC had to ensure it always provided facilities for fair discussion. His final words were "Broadcasting is now of age."[141]

In the House of Commons Salter's varied contributions during March and April included "the war against crime." Given the fact that West House had been burgled on 21 December 1947, it was natural for him to encourage greater police recruitment to fight crime.[142] The budgetary and economic situation, as always, was a major concern. During a debate on the subject on 8 April, he returned to the inflationary pressures distorting the economy. He argued that at the root of the difficulties were wage increases, without a correspondent increase in production. Further, he opposed the increase in taxes on tobacco and alcohol, pointing out that the drinkers and smokers in Britain already provided one-third of the total revenue of the state. He also opposed another main budgetary proposal, the so-called "Special Contribution," suggesting that the new levy on investment income would have no impact as a counter-inflationary measure and would prove to be a disincentive. In essence, Salter condemned the budget, arguing that the best route would have been to reduce the countries' overseas deficit, or as he put it, "the extent to which we have been living on other people's money."[143] In a follow-up letter to The Times, he added that the "Special Contribution," designed to protect the budget surplus, would not reduce inflation, because it would be derived from new taxation, and not reduced state expenditure, and would discourage new investment. Under such criticism from Salter and others, the government soon conceded the case.[144]

Salter's thinking about a federated or united Europe also continued to unfold. On 19 January he had participated in the inaugural meeting of the Oxford University United Europe Movement. Its format was that of a brains trust, with Amery, Leslie Hore-Belisha and Lionel Curtis as the other panelists.[145] Another step was his signing an all-party motion tabled on 13 March in the House of Commons by 71 MPs. The motion, not associated with Churchill's United Europe Movement, called for the creation of a Council of Western Europe to prepare the way for "a democratic federation of Europe." It recommended the immediate convening of a constituent assembly, composed of representative from the 16 "Marshall" countries and Western Germany, to frame a constitution for the federation. The motion was duly tabled on 18 March but only came up for discussion as part of a foreign affairs debate on 5 May.[146] By that date 190 members had signed the motion. Salter initially defended American foreign policy and the Marshall Plan from criticism that it was exercising undue influence abroad. He regarded American generosity, from the time of lend-lease to the Marshall Plan, in scale and magnanimity, as "beyond precedent in the history of peace." Turning to the issue of Western Union, he insisted the movement was a "union of free people" – socialist or otherwise. He then conceded that the ultimate goal was Federal Union or "organic union." Thus it was necessary meanwhile to work towards that goal by dealing with the immediate problems, and constructing the relevant political and economic machinery. "Out of that," Salter stated, "I think we shall prepare the way for, and gradually construct, something like a closer union." Even if proceeding step by step, he concluded, he did not foresee federalism replacing either the inter-state system or the United Nations, nor could he conceive of a World Federal Union. In his view, two movements, Federal Union and the inter-state system, had to accept the reality of each other's approach and find their respective place in the relations between countries.[147]

It had been announced on 16 April that some 150 British delegates, including Salter, would be among the more than 800 individuals attending the Congress of Europe at The Hague from 7 to 10 May. The event brought together representatives of the main pro-European organizations. Much of the work of the Congress took place in the economic, political and cultural committees.[148] Salter spent most of his time in the economic committee, debating a draft resolution for economic union in Europe.[149] He had gone with a certain skepticism, unsure of what such a large gathering could achieve, in particular without adequate preparatory work by expert officials. In his view, "Nothing ever comes out of a large conference at the end that is not put into it at the beginning." Nonetheless, he admitted that the final agreed resolutions had "more substance in them than I should have thought possible in the circumstances." He also concurred that one of the purposes of the Congress, and a measure of its success, was to demonstrate the determination of the people of Western Europe to move towards closer political and economic union. As he later put it, "This is the gospel of the Congress of the Hague."[150] One of the major achievements of the Congress was the establishment of the Council of Europe on 5 May 1949. At the time Salter was uncertain whether this would remain a defensive organization or evolve into a United States of Europe.[151] His experience at The Hague prompted him to gather his thoughts for an article in the National Provincial Bank Review. Reviewing the scale of American assistance to Europe since 1940, he described it as without precedent in peace-time, and derived mainly from humanitarian and philanthropic motives. As well, it was in everyone's interest to preserve freedom on both sides of the Atlantic after the 25 February Communist coup d'état in Czechoslovakia and the threat of further communist expansion. Salter was convinced that a full European customs union could not be achieved in the short term. Instead, he argued in favour of "some intermediate system," beginning with a central organization focused on economic planning of the kind being constructed in Paris, the future Organization for European Economic Co-operation (OEEC), to implement Marshall Aid. As always, Salter's thoughts on such an important subject received widespread publicity, with The Manchester Guardian describing them as "brilliant."[152]

After the close of The Hague Congress, Salter and Lady Salter took a vacation on the continent, travelling to Switzerland, France and Italy, before returning to London in early June.[153] In the following weeks, some familiar issues remained Salter's main focus of attention in the House of Commons. On 3 June, during the committee stage of the Finance Bill, he returned to the subject of the Labour budget's "Special Contribution." He reiterated his opposition to it, and even quoted several government spokesmen since the measure was introduced on 6 April indicating some agreement with his point of view.[154] The anticipated return of the Representation of the People Bill to the Commons on 14 June for its report stage prompted another article from Salter, on 13 June, which he entitled "A Breach of Faith." For the most part he stuck to his previous critique and condemned "the Government's extraordinary breach of faith." The rejection by the Labour government of the recommendation of the 1944 all-party Speaker's Conference to retain the seats, he wrote, was "constitutionally irregular; the reasons given for it intellectually indefensible; and the conduct of individual Ministers personally discreditable."[155] When speaking in the Commons on the issue, he accused the government of acting "dishonourably." He suggested that those who had participated in the Speaker's Conference and now sat in the current parliament were guilty of "a breach of faith," and had struck "a wanton and unprovoked blow" against the "professional classes." Government speakers replied that the present government was not bound by the 1944 recommendations. Of further interest was Salter's aside regarding his allegiance in the House. Responding to criticisms that, although elected as an Independent, he usually voted against the government, he stated:

> [HON. MEMBERS: "Always."] Not always. Not more often than I voted against the Conservative Government at the time I was elected; and for the same reason. Whereas at the time of my first election the Government's proposals brought before the House were in my view too much to the Right, and I therefore voted against them, so proposals now brought before the House by a Government of the Left go, in my opinion, too much to the Left. It is not that I am not an Independent, or that I have shifted my ground.[156]

Salter could also not find much satisfaction on another issue which concerned him. As a follow-up to The Hague meetings, on 17 June he joined Churchill and an all-party deputation of 20 others who had attended the conference in a visit to 10 Downing Street. Copies of The Hague economic, political and cultural resolutions were given to Attlee who was also asked to support some form of a European

Assembly designed to work towards European Union. The prime minister agreed to examine the resolutions, including the one that national parliaments pass a motion in favour of establishing a European Assembly. Attlee further agreed to accept from Churchill a memorandum on the subject, a project in which Salter played the major role.[157] In a three-page note, Salter addressed the request from The Hague Conference for participating national parliaments to pass a resolution supporting a European Assembly. He accepted that a future European Assembly would derive its authority from parliaments, and that the implementation of its policies would still rest with national governments and parliaments. Even with these limitations, he argued, there were constitutional and political problems, the foremost being fears that a European Assembly would eventually lead to "a true federal system." Consequently, he suggested as a possible tactical procedure, compatible with "both governmental benevolence and governmental non-commitment," whereby the Speaker would take the initiative in proposing such a resolution. Salter's observations were sent on 27 June to Churchill and other members of the deputation for further discussion.[158]

The signature in Paris on 16 April of the Convention for European Economic Co-operation and the Anglo-American Economic Agreement of 26 June occasioned a two-day debate in the Commons. Under discussion was Britain's need to increase productivity, maintain its gold and dollar reserves and foster European economic co-operation. In his interventions, Salter defended American motives in providing its overseas economic assistance, which was unequal "in its generosity, constructive purpose and magnanimity." He signalled that he would vote in favour, stating, "It is obvious that I shall have the pleasure which I do not have too frequently nowadays, of finding myself one of a great majority in the Lobby when I vote tonight." He then expressed his concern that Britain would not be able to maintain its reserves, and would suffer a shortage of dollars making it impossible to import the raw materials to maintain full industrial production. He concluded with some critical comments on Labour's reservations regarding The Hague conference resolutions.[159] With regard to the latter issue, the procedural issues Salter had raised led to the abandonment of the idea regarding a role for the Speaker and, on 28 July, the temporary cessation of further pressure to convene a European Assembly.[160] By that time the Salters had already left to the United States where they arrived aboard the *Queen Elizabeth* on 14 July for another summer at Hickory Farm.[161] In early October the Salters visited with Stimson at his home on Long Island before sailing back to England on 16 October.[162]

On 1 November the Commons began a two-day debate on the Address in reply to the King's speech on 25 October. The latter had foreshadowed two areas of future legislation – the abolition of the university franchise and nationalization of the iron and steel industries. A surprise on the first day of debate was that no speaker from the

Opposition was on the Front Bench, but "the mantle of principal spokesman" fell on Salter.[163] Speaking immediately following Cripps and Churchill, Salter stated:

> Perhaps I might say, as this is the first time that I have appeared not, indeed, at this Table, but at this Box, that I have not joined the Conservative Party and that I remain an Independent. It is true that, nowadays, I usually vote and speak against the Government as, when I first entered this House, I usually voted and spoke against the Conservative Government of that time. It is also true that as I have watched the evolution of Conservative policy, and as I have watched the evolution of Socialism, in practice and as applied by the present Government, I have found myself in closer sympathy with a Liberalised Right than with an over-bureaucratised Left. It is for this and other reasons which will appear that I welcomed the invitation to appear at this Box today.

Salter moved on to a critique of the government's poor economic performance, the large trade deficit and the ongoing depletion of reserves. He felt vindicated that the capital levy, as he had predicted, was not reducing inflation. Turning to the proposal to extend nationalization, he stated, "I have watched their socialisation critically but not hostilely for the last three years." He preferred the nation's economy to be divided with a 20% public sector and an 80% private sector. And while much was understood about how capitalism worked and averting another depression, little was certain about the road to socialism, characterised by "sagging inefficiency and increasing costs." He contended that the "great public monopolies," such as created by the Transport Bill and the proposed Iron and Steel Bill, would only lead to higher costs to be passed on to the consumer.[164] When assessing his contribution the following day, The Financial Times observed that Salter clearly "found himself in sympathy with the Liberalist Right rather than a bureaucratic Left." The Manchester Guardian, commenting on Salter presence on the Opposition's Front Bench, noted, "An unusual thing happened to-day. One detects Mr Churchill's generosity in it."[165] Indeed, Salter later recalled his great pleasure when he was invited by Churchill to speak from the despatch box.[166]

Salter contributed little to the House debates on the nationalization of iron and steel. Having had his say there was little, indeed, that he could add. On 17 November, on the motion for the second reading of the bill, he voted against the government.[167] On 25 November the government outlined how it intended to proceed with the Committee and Report stages and the Third Reading of the Bill. Salter's only intervention was to explain, yet again, why in his opinion it was important for Britain "to earn so much by production and export as will enable us to import the raw materials, without which there would be unemployment, not in patches, but to the extent of one or two millions."[168] He pressed the same view when he spoke to the Industrial Co-partnership Association on 9 December, suggesting that the countries' economic performance in 1947 regained only the ground lost that year, putting the country back to the 1946 position. He strongly urged some adequate incentives be put in place to increase production.[169]

At the outset of the New Year, Salter wrote about Britain's long-term economic prospects for The Observer. His concern was how the country would maintain its standard of living, when external aid was no longer available, and the kind of effort needed for that purpose. Faced with such problems as an increase in population, and an increase in the price of imports over exports, he proposed, among other measures, individual incentives to increase productivity and ongoing efforts to curb inflation. The question of long-term objectives was one he also analysed in Foreign Affairs. His concern was how to overcome the "dollar deficit," so that "deficit countries" whose economies had suffered wartime damage must increase production and exports to pay their own way. On the basis of current trends and policies, he was not at all optimistic that this objective could be achieved. Part of the difficulty he foresaw was that American exports would not find suitable overseas markets, because of the lack of dollar resources, and this could lead to a possible recession. Turning to the issue of "Western Union," he wrote that while its advantages were indisputable, the obstacles, both political and economic, were formidable. As a result, he argued that Western Union would only grow gradually from intermediate stages, such as through the OEEC. His final words were to exhort American economists, leaders of finance and exporting industries to agree on a forecast of America's future balance of payments and the consequences.[170] Similarly, in the Commons Salter was among those arguing that Labour's long term economic forecasts were erroneous and too optimistic.[171] In public too, for example, when addressing the American Chamber of Commerce in London on 3 February, he referred to the gap between exports and imports which would prevail after the end of the Marshall Plan. He predicted that European countries would still not have achieved self-sufficiency. As well, he urged American investors to interest themselves in the underdeveloped parts of the world, including British colonies. Indeed, when addressing the Royal Empire Society on 9 February, he expressed his fears that after Marshall Aid ceased, unemployment could return because the money to buy raw materials would not be there.[172] This theme he referred to as "a new form of unemployment," avoidable only if prices were kept in check, and he returned to it during the coming months.[173]

All the while, however, Salter continued to focus on wider European political issues. On 23 March, during the course of a Commons' debate, he drew attention to the refugee issue, stating that one in four Germans in the British and American zones were refugees, including a large proportion of the elderly, orphans and invalids. In his experience, he continued, which included dealing with the resettlement of Greek refugees from Turkey, the scale and complexity of the problem was without precedent. He also drew attention to his most recent visit to the British zone where he witnessed first-hand the magnitude of the problem. He concluded that the political, economic and social recovery of Germany was almost impossible without some resolution of this issue. While he admitted that massive emigration was not feasible, he thought the clearing of displaced persons' camps would help the relocate of some of these refugees. Also helpful would be if the British government opened up immigration for domestic work in the United Kingdom with the dominions following suit.[174]

From time to time Salter also turned his attention to environmental issues in which he took a lively interest, often when it impacted on his beloved Oxford. Most recently, he had joined a group in a letter to the editor of The Times on the "imperative need" for the proper planning both of Oxford city and its university, including the relocation of the Oxford gasworks.[175] This was just part of larger concerns which he addressed when the Commons debated the National Parks and Access to the Countryside Bill. The bill was intended to preserve the beauty of the countryside and enable greater public access. Salter agreed with the overall imperative of "the preservation and enhancement of natural beauty." However, he differed from the government in one important respect. He believed that the real threat to the countryside derived not from private individuals or companies, but from "public authorities, local or central" intent on building roads and expanding power grids and gasworks. As a result, he recommended that a permanent cabinet committee be established to vet any project with an environmental impact on the countryside. His views received considerable support when the debate resumed the following day.[176]

As the Commons debated the budget proposals and the economic situation in early April, Salter only took a desultory part. From time to time he asked for clarification or offered a corrective.[177] This was partly because the economic situation was showing some improvement, due to ongoing Marshall Aid and an increase in British exports. In addition, on 10 May the last major item of Labour's nationalization program, the Iron and Steel bill, received its third reading, with Salter voting against the government, and was then sent to the Lords.[178] In some respects, however, the focus of his interests was changing. Thus to coincide with the publication by a Chatham House study group on the topic of Western European Union, Salter addressed a meeting there on 28 April with a title of "Western Union."[179] He acknowledged that recent progress on the political front was greater than economic progress towards western union. He went on to emphasize that he personally stood somewhere in between the federalist and the inter-state advocates, what he termed "the middle way." In his view Western Union would "be built up out of, from, and with" existing and projected institutions, such as the United Nations, the defensive alliances embodied in the Brussels and Atlantic Pacts, OEEC and the emerging plans for a European Council and Assembly. To this he also added the Churchill-led European Movement and upon all of these, with "extension and adaptation," he insisted would Western Union emerge. He then reflected on the difficulties that would arise in the process. A customs union would be problematic, given the loss of revenue from tariffs and the resulting unemployment. To be successful it, as well as a potential military union, would have to be given political authority. The difficulties standing in the way of complete federal union, such as the suppression of sovereignty and diversity in language, tradition and outlook, he regarded as insurmountable in the short term. He then pleaded for the advocates of both the inter-state and federal principles to abandon "fratricidal strife," and work together even as they promoted conflicting principles. Western Union, he concluded, would be a process of "organic growth" built on the basis of "functional, improvised and temporary institutions."[180] It is thus unsurprising that on 12 May Salter voted with the government to approve the North Atlantic Pact.[181]

Current foreign affairs issues continued to attract Salter's interest. He was critical of the United Nations, suggesting that some form of reform would be inevitable. He also had concluded that reconciliation with the USSR was unlikely for the foreseeable future. As a result of the experience of Nazi Germany, however, "the danger of provoking an intended aggressor by strength is much less than that of tempting him by weakness."[182] Thus, too, the question of recognising a new Communist Chinese government was one on which he expressed strong opinions. Speaking in the Commons on 5 May, he cautioned that a Communist victory in China would be a threat to the free world and urged that British commercial interests should not influence the question of recognition. He predicted, based on his two missions to China in the early 1930s – in the event incorrectly – that the Communist leaders would have difficulties in converting China to a centrally managed country. He urged the government to withdraw the British ambassador from Nanking, already in Communist hands, and not to drift into any form of diplomatic recognition under pressure.[183]

It was the question of European Union that inevitably continued to preoccupy Salter. On 8 June he addressed a lunch meeting at the Royal Empire Society on "The Best Route to Western Union." On this occasion he stated that one of the purposes of Western Union, given the ongoing ideological conflict with the Soviet Union, was to serve as a form of collective defence and deterrence. Only this would provide "the best possible chance of achieving a real and satisfactory settlement, which must be negotiated not from weakness but from strength." He then made his argument that the route to Western Europe would be built on the foundations of several existing and specialised institutions. These were the Brussels and North Atlantic Pacts, the OEEC, the European Council and, what he termed "the irregulars or partisans," such as Churchill's European movement. The emerging structure, he pointed was "untidy" and was merely a system of inter-state governance which preserved national sovereignty. Further progress, Salter suggested, required steering clear of "five fruitful fallacies" – fallacies because each could lead to deadlock, fruitful because each contained some element which had to be included in any satisfactory system. The five encompassed: the "blueprint complex" which was the notion that European Union could be achieved following a symmetrical structure; the "functional fallacy," suggested that a series of specialist organizations, such as the World Bank, could achieve supreme political authority; the "economic illusion," posited that increasing prosperity would itself destroy the roots of war; "Utopian federalism," was perhaps desirable in the long run but feasible only on a regional basis; and the "Socialist heresy," which posited that Western Union could only be a Union of Socialist States." Salter continued:

> First of all we must contemplate an amorphous structure. I contemplate units of especially close union, such as Benelux; then a wider but looser union of Western Europe; then a still wider union for united purposes such as the Atlantic Pact; and lastly a still wider and looser association in the United Nations. Secondly, we must be careful of our timing and priority. We must build on the actual institutions now in existence and functioning. But as soon as we possibly can we must go further towards a true form of super-government that can secure and ensure decisions. That does not mean universal and immediate federalism.

The ultimate objective, he concluded, was once and for all to replace the "international anarchy of uncontrolled sovereign states by a form of super-national government."[184]

There were some among Salter's colleagues and friends who were watching his career, his politics and his approach to European Union with more than casual interest. Following his participation at a United Europe Movement meeting at Oxford on 26 May, Gilbert Murray criticised some of his comments and Salter responded at length. There was no one in public life, he wrote, "for whom I have so sincere and profound respect as for you, Cecil and Churchill." However, he suggested that Murray had misunderstood his speech. In fact, he stated that, given the ongoing alienation between the USSR and the West, the United Nations could not fulfil its main purpose of providing security. In other respects, the United Nations, while overly expensive to run, was doing some work of modest usefulness. Thus he wished to see "a scaling down of the organization to the dimensions of its present – modest – work of real utility." One thing he emphasized was that he did not want any of his comments to be seen as expressing the jealousy of those associated with the League of Nations.[185] Lionel Curtis, also a Fellow of All Souls and a fervent champion of world federation, was following Salter's public utterances but with increasing disappointment. It would be tragic, he wrote of Salter, "if he relapses into the role of a political raconteur." Curtis continued:

> Between the wars he could not cross one of the continents without being summoned to consult with its leading statesmen, whether Roosevelt or Chiang-Kai-shek. He is in danger of forgetting the great position he had acquired with public opinion and Parliament where he is always heard with attention. The project of Western Union only needs a leader to put it over in a few years. Winston could do that if he were not preoccupied with his book. Salter has the full confidence of Winston, believes in Western Union and has all the knowledge to take the lead if he could rouse himself to the opportunity. He is embittered by the loss of his constituency which has driven him towards the right where he does not belong.

Towards this end, Curtis tried unsuccessfully to enlist the help of Violet Markham and Lady Salter whom he regarded as "rightly ambitious for her husband." On another occasion, however, he blamed Lady Salter, "the rich luxurious society wife," for Salter's making the mistake of virtually joining the Tory party.[186]

That was not to be for some time yet. Meanwhile, the Salters' summer routine continued with their disembarking from the *Queen Elizabeth* in New York on 13 July. Interviewed by The New York Times on his arrival, Salter briefly discussed his concerns regarding Britain's financial situation.[187] After presiding for the last time as chairman of the Advisory Committee of the International Bank for Reconstruction and Redevelopment, in Washington from 18 to 22 July, Salter joined Lady Salter for their annual vacation at Hickory Farm. August brought Violet Markham for a three day stay.[188] As well, each summer provided some distraction which led Salter to attend a dinner in his honour on 6 October, hosted by William M. Chadbourne, a prominent New York lawyer and member of the Council on Foreign Relations.[189]

The British economic and political landscape facing Salter on his return from the US on 20 October had also undergone important changes. On 18 September Cripps had announced the long-rumoured devaluation of the pound from $4.04 to $2.80. From Hickory Farm, and at Churchill's specific request for a briefing paper,

Salter had responded on 22 September with a lengthy note on the pros and cons of devaluation.[190] On 24 October Attlee reviewed the decision to devalue which was then followed by a lengthy parliamentary debate. Three days later Salter rose in the Commons to add his critique of the decision. He joined a chorus of those who argued that devaluation was not a solution but an admission of economic failure on the part of the government. He approved the act of devaluation as "a surrender to necessity," to preserve the reserves before they were exhausted. However, he went on, "All that I criticise is the previous policy, the defects of which were reflected in the devaluation, the timing, the method, the amount, and in particular the absence of any accompanying policy." In his view, even maintaining the devalued pound depended on "our new dollar export drive," namely, to increase exports to the American market and to continue fighting inflation. He was not optimistic on either account if not accompanied with continued cuts in government expenditure. Furthermore, the only way the country could maintain its standard of living was to increase the productivity of the docks, the mines and the building industry, by whatever inducements required. His final remarks, somewhat forward facing, were: "In the not distant past we had a leadership which meant that the country increased its efforts to the measure of its needs. We could have it again but we need both the appropriate policy and worthy leaders."[191]

Salter took his critique of the economic situation outside the Commons, when on 8 November he addressed the Institute of Bankers on the issue of the "dollar shortage." He pointed out that, despite such temporary measures as Lend-Lease and Marshall Aid, Britain has not been able to increase exports to the United States. This had forced the country to draw on its rapidly depleting reserves of gold and foreign exchange, leading eventually to devaluation. While devaluation would not be effective across the board, he stated, greater cuts in government expenditure were required. "We cannot maintain our standard of living unless we produce more, and more economically." In his final prescription aimed at "deficit countries," he argued, "what is needed first is sufficient budget economies and revenue surplus to eliminate inflation and then every possible incentive to increase production of exportable goods at low enough prices." Secondly, he urged the United States to encourage foreign investment abroad to increase "both dollar-saving and dollar-earning forms of production." Otherwise there would be no end to the disequilibrium in the balance of payments with America.[192] Salter covered much the same ground in an article he completed for Foreign Affairs, at the personal request of its editor, Hamilton Fish Armstrong. He suggested that Britain's devaluation was a reminder of the failure of allied belligerents in Europe to restore their economies after the war. Here he concluded on a positive note, writing that

Britain and Europe were in fact capable both of closing the dollar-gap and moving towards economic recovery.[193]

On 13 October Attlee had announced that, given the economic situation, there would be no general election in 1949. This decision had some further significance beyond the fact that Salter stood to retain his seat a little longer. During the course of the summer he had met twice with Winthrop W. Aldrich, president and chairman of the board of Chase National Bank, and a future ambassador to Britain. Since 17 June 1946 Aldrich had been serving as chairman of President Truman's Advisory Committee for Financing Foreign Trade, designed to provide advice on American investment abroad. It was originally agreed that Salter would act as a salaried consultant to Aldrich on such questions as convertibility of currencies, foreign investment and Britain's experience as a creditor nation. This plan was based on the assumption that he would soon lose his parliamentary seat. When this proved to be incorrect, he wrote to Aldrich on 21 October that he preferred his work to be on a voluntary basis and immediately began a study of Britain as a creditor country.[194] He then consulted with such individuals as the recently appointed governor of the Bank of England, Cameron Cobbold, and others in the Treasury and the financial and economic sectors.[195] Salter was soon able to advise Aldrich that there was little prospect for private American capital to invest in the sterling areas. At the same time he applied himself to an examination of a history of British investment over the past 75 years in relation to current problems.[196]

An unexpected political milestone for Salter was the Commons' debate of 1 December on the first annual report of the British Transport Commission, established with the nationalization of the railroads on 6 August 1947. Introducing the debate, the Minister of Transport referred to the Salter Committee of 1932 and the Road and Rail Traffic Act, 1933. Salter responded that indeed his experience as chairman of the Railway Staff National Tribunal, and the "unsatisfactory condition of our transport finances," convinced him that it would be impossible for the Transport Commission (chaired by Sir Cyril Hurcomb) to make ends meet in 1949. However, on the positive side he suggested that there might be considerable improvement if there were greater co-ordination between road and rail.[197]

Salter's performance in the Commons was occasionally criticised by fellow parliamentarians. On one occasion his contributions were described as "very scholastic and academic."[198] On 1 December, however, when he was criticised as too often sitting on the fence in debates, another member deplored the attack, describing Salter's speeches as "able," and added, "this House will be much the poorer if he does not find himself a constituency before the next Election."[199] Indeed, a day earlier Salter had guessed that it would be in the government's interest to call an election before introducing a budget which would be unpopular and would be accompanied by a further fall in reserves. "On the whole," he wrote to Aldrich, "I plump for February 23rd as the Election date."[200] His prediction regarding the date was to prove accurate, but not so his guess there would be a small Conservative majority. Parliament was in fact prorogued on 16 December, with the Royal assent given to over 30 acts. These included the Parliament Act, 1949, even though it had never been passed in the House of Lords. Such actions strengthened Salter's concerns that under the Labour government there had been a shift of power from parliament to the executive branch of government. This was leading to what he termed, "cabinet bureaucracy." He contended both in lectures and in print, that parliament was increasingly preoccupied with economic issues, beyond the expertise of most members. This resulted in debates which were "inexpert, uninformed and ineffective." He was also concerned about the "expansion of delegated legislation, enacted under the authority of widely drawn Acts of Parliament through Orders in Council" which took effect with little or no debate. Finally, he expressed his concern about the Labour government's frequent resort to closure and guillotine. Among his several proposals for change was the institution of unofficial committees of MPs for informal and expert discussions of major topics before debate in the Commons, thereby making for a more informed discussion.[201]

Parliament was dissolved on 3 February with elections scheduled for 23 February. This brought to an end Salter's career as an Independent MP, as well as university representation which dated back to 1603. The Manchester Guardian decried this development, asking "What does the House of Commons gain by silencing his authoritative and independent voice at this time of all others in our economic history?"[202] On 2 February The Times published a letter jointly signed by Salter and A.P. Herbert: "May we, through you, say 'Farewell' and 'Thank you' to the graduates of Oxford University who have supported, or suffered, us as their Burgesses in the House of Commons for 14 and 13 years respectively?" The letter went on to lament the loss of "civilized and inexpensive" elections, "electors who had passed an intellectual test, and a working example of proportional representation." The letter concluded that the loss of university seats was "a stupid and spiteful act."[203]

By this time Salter was thinking not only of the forthcoming election, but also his own political allegiance. His father and uncle, both mayors of Oxford, had been leading members of the Oxford Liberal Party. Of himself he wrote, "For the greater part of my adult life I have been more in sympathy with the Liberal Party than any other."[204] There must have been considerable surprise, therefore, to read in The Sunday Times on 12 February an article by Salter titled "Why I Shall Vote Conservative." He criticised the Labour cabinet for having been "wasteful and extravagant administrators," for applying their nationalization policies indiscriminately, and for causing inflation. "Bureaucratic centralization," "punitive financial policy," and the "decline of Parliament" were indications that the country faced a real threat to personal rights and freedoms. Only in the sphere of foreign policy did he find little to criticise. These were the negative reasons Salter gave to explain his disillusion with socialism in practice. The positive one, he then explained, was that "Conservatism has been liberalized," and he added, the "Liberal mantle has fallen on the Conservatives." In conclusion, he reminded his readers that he remained an Independent, although in the forthcoming election, the interests of the country would best be served by a victory for the Conservative Party.[205] A sympathetic colleague later noted that in truth "Salter was a Churchillian – not a Conservative."[206] In the following days, he further developed these ideas. He had already argued that in pursuing nationalization, Labour was "alone in this folly in the whole of the free world."[207] On 18 February, in The Manchester Guardian, he continued to develop his case against further nationalization. He admitted that for many years he had been a fervent believer that certain public utilities should be brought under national ownership and control. However, he found no logical principles followed by Labour in its pursuit of nationalization, nor had it provided answers to such questions as the best form of management, how collective bargaining was to be adapted to national monopolies, and how incentives were to be activated. As well, he stated the welfare state could only be supported if the great mass of competitive industries were left to generate the resources needed to finance it. An editorial that same day supported his arguments that there must be no further nationalization and that the practice in other countries had proven "disappointing."[208]

On 20 February, almost on the eve of the general election, Salter commented in The Times on three main election issues. In foreign affairs, he believed that Churchill, supported by Eden, had the necessary prestige to lead the country. Secondly, the Labour Party must call a halt to its nationalization programme. Finally, "restrictions and compulsions" must give way to the restoration of personal incentives.[209] The election results of 23 February, however, illustrated that the country was not yet prepared to turn its back on the Labour Party. It was returned to power, but with a loss of 78 seats, giving it a majority of just 17 over the Conservatives. In the aftermath, Salter observed that the country was in for a "period of uncertainty." He found it significant that the Communists had lost their two seats and had a reduced popular vote, and that the Liberals were again rejected, losing one of their ten previous seats. A determining factor in his opinion was the floating vote, in particular the 2.6 million who voted for the Liberals but were unlikely to do so again, given their continuing decline. He very briefly then expressed regret that he would not be in the House, but was quite resigned henceforth to be a private person.[210] In reality Salter was ambivalent about the loss of his parliamentary seat. Thus on 1 December he had written to Churchill on a variety of subjects, but included an expression of regret at his own absence from the House.[211] He followed this up with another letter to Churchill on 27 February 1950 stating that "I am of course entirely at your disposal if you think I can be of any use to you at any time." Although reminded on several occasions about Salter, Churchill still demurred offering him anything.[212] The call would not come for another year.

On Salter's 70th birthday on 15 March, no longer an MP, he completed what he called a "stock-taking and a plan for the future." In a seven page, hand-written note, he tried to map out the remaining active years of his life. As far as retirement, he was nominally attracted by the prospect of resting on his laurels and regarding the "public-work" phase of his life as ended. Such a decision would carry with it the pleasures of devoting himself to a personal life at home, the company of friends, and the pleasures of the arts and music. However, such a decision he regarded as being tantamount to "killing much that is best in me." He came to the conclusion, therefore, that he must do some work which would make use of his abundant talents and experience. He realized at his age he would not be offered work involving real executive responsibility. He continued:

> Advancing years do not necessarily impair intellectual quality, and they provide assets for some kinds of work in the greater experience and status they some times bring. Nor do they make it impossible to handle a special problem which may involve intense work, and difficult decisions, for a short period. But they do, inevitably and invariably, diminish the nervous strength required for sustained and continuous effort, especially where a daily conflict of wills is involved – and that is the essence of continuous executive work.

Therefore, the work he could do was, firstly, writing that crystallized his experience of international administration, including articles and shorter books. The rest of his time could be devoted to collaboration with Winthrop Aldrich, attractive both for income to replace his parliamentary salary, and to maintain links to the world of executive action. As well, there would still be time devoted to other claims, such as the family business of Salter Brothers and the Thames Catering Company. There were also ongoing associations with such public institutions as Chatham House, and of course academic life at All Souls. The final part of Salter's stocktaking was an intricate analysis of potential income and what he called "A Budget of Time."[213] The irony of these careful calculations was that the twilight phase of his career would nevertheless be very active. For a short time, initially, he indulged what he termed "some nostalgic regrets" at leaving Westminster. However, his first year without responsibility was a happy one. As he later recalled, "almost without exception each decade had been richer than the one before it, widening experience bringing a gain that outweighed any loss."[214]

On 7 April, accompanied by Lady Salter, he left London to undertake a series of lectures on behalf of the Foreign Office, first in Copenhagen and then in Oslo. In the former capital, from 11 to 14 April, his subjects included Western Union and the dollar shortage. In the latter, between 15 to18 April, his topic was "The New Pattern of the World."[215] Returning to London, leisure did not prevail, for a man of Salter's stature could hardly be cut off from the pressing problems of the day. Thus on 9 May French Foreign Minister Robert Schuman had made the surprising proposal to pool Franco-German production of coal and steel within the framework of an organization open to other European countries. Such a common foundation for economic development, he declared, would be the first step towards "the federation of Europe."[216] Salter immediately sensed, as he wrote in two articles for The Times, that the movement for Western European Union had reached a critical stage. The impact and implications of Schuman's declaration were bound to widen the gulf between those who believed European federalism was impractical or undesirable in the near future, and others who contended that economic integration, embodied in a customs union, was too high a price to pay for sacrificing Imperial preference. Yet, Salter was enough of a realist to contend that "closer union" was essential both for defensive strength and economic progress. To answer how these differences could be resolved, he offered several suggestions. He wished to see the existing Council of Europe, with its two constituent organs, the Committee of Ministers and the Consultative Assembly, given specific responsibilities by inheriting the mandate currently being entrusted to the OEEC, after Marshall Aid ended in 1952. The goal, he declared, should not be a customs union but a limitation of tariffs, the convertibility of currencies and the removal of other barriers such as quotas. "Britain need not choose between Imperial preference and European Union," he wrote, "She can choose both." As for the best form of constitution for a European Union, he agreed there would have to be some "'merger' of sovereignty." While there were too many obstacles to a European federal system, he suggested an "intermediate, or transitional, system" could be based on the Consultative Assembly of the Council of Europe. This had the great advantages of being non-party and could act "as a bridge between the present system of organized diplomacy and a true European Government." An editorial on 17 May in the The Times endorsed Salter's suggestions, describing them as "a constructive alternative" and not an apology for inaction.[217] Salter himself noted that "Though such reactions as I've had are favourable they've cut very little ice so far." However, he was asked by a member of the secretariat at Strasbourg to send copies of the articles to members of the Consultative Assembly.[218] His most enthusiastic supporter, however, was once again Lionel Curtis who thought the articles "monumental," and gave them the widest possible circulation at his own expense.[219] As well, Curtis had just finished his own book, The Open Road to Freedom, which he discussed extensively with Salter, while still in draft form. Curtis tried unsuccessfully to enlist Salter to lead the movement for his "international commonwealth." However, Salter demurred, suggesting that Curtis had over-simplified the complexity of a world-wide federation and criticised his generalisations as too sweeping.[220]

In mid-July the Salters left London to travel by car for a three week stay in St. Moritz and visits with friends.[221] On their return, Salter felt compelled to caution Curtis against any suggestion that he was going to lead the movement for world federation. "I hope to give some help," he wrote, "but shall not be able to take the more ambitious role which you seem to contemplate for me." Curtis replied:

> Realise that whether you like it or not, your life will be written by someone. Ask yourself what your biographer will say when he comes to 1950 and realizes that your friends are looking to you to lead them in a final movement to end the fear of war once for all. He will realize that nothing was wanted but a leader, if only because Churchill is too preoccupied in writing a book which ought to be written, to carry to its issue the movement he started in 1946. He will realize that your service on the League, during the war and in Parliament has given you an authority with the public second only to Winston's.

Curtis concluded with an admonition to Salter to not reply, and for some time the latter complied.[222] Instead, in a final flourish before departing to New York, and under the impact of the invasion on 25 June of South Korea by the North, Salter publicly urged the government, as part of its renewed defensive measures, to begin the strategic stockpiling of raw materials and foodstuffs. In an editorial, The Times urged that his proposals should get a more sympathetic examination than his similar campaign before 1939, and several letters to the editor likewise added support.[223] The Salters boarded the Queen Mary on 22 August for New York and then went on to Hickory Farm for an extended stay to the end of October.[224] Before his departure, and noting the interest his letter had publicly evoked, and the private letters of support he received, Salter kept up the campaign.[225] In The Financial Times he urged the "simple precautionary measure" be taken to store adequate stocks of food and raw materials, not as an alternative, but as a supplement to other defensive measures. While acknowledging that the dollar shortage made such purchases difficult, he suggested that stockpiling was a defence measure and therefore eligible under any military aid given to Britain.[226]

When Salter finally replied to Curtis from Hickory Farm, it was initially to refuse the latter's suggestion that he stand as a candidate for the Oxford City seat. "I have never been a Conservative," he wrote, "and should find it difficult (especially perhaps in Oxford) to stand as one." With typical modesty, he added that he had neither the experience nor the temperament to be an effective private member, unless it was from the Treasury Bench. He continued:

> I didn't cut much ice in the last Parliament and never really caught its ear; and I get more attention when I write than when I speak. At the same time the drain upon time and energy (when the limits of both become narrower with age) in a Parliament which is equally divided is such as to leave nothing over – even apart from constituency duties from which one was exempt in a University seat. All these considerations should doubtless be regarded as outweighed if one felt able to move opinion by speeches in the House and had a cause which one could thus promote. But those conditions are not satisfied in my case.

Curtis replied that he quite understood, but at the same time returned to the charge with regard to The Open Road to Freedom. He asked Salter to consider joint authorship especially given the latter's work on the early drafts.[227] Salter responded on 28 September, refusing to appear as one of several joint authors, adding that in his view such projects were ineffective. He referred back to the The Next Five Years (1935) and added that "it cut no ice."[228] Curtis reluctantly accepted but his continued lobbying finally forced Salter to respond with an expression of annoyance on two accounts. Firstly, Salter indicated that he was finding it embarrassing to discover that some supporters of federalism both in London and New York thought he was leading the movement. He reminded Curtis that, when the latter made the suggestion, he indicated at once that he would not take any such role. Salter continued, "my general approach and conception of the relation between federalism and the main and most urgent problems of today disqualify me from undertaking the role which you and others have suggested." Secondly, Salter again refused to be part of a jointly authored The Open Road to Freedom. On 29 November Curtis apologized for any difficulty he had caused and together with Salter drafted a letter to various individuals.[229] This explained their different approaches, namely, Curtis' view that an international state should be created in one operation with a draft constitution on which electorates would vote, while Salter preferred the "complementary method of step by step adaptation." Curtis concluded, "We must once for all abandon our dream that he [Salter] would be our leader."[230] Nonetheless, he continued to keep in touch with Salter and even seek his advice.[231]

Since the outset of the New Year, Salter had been preoccupied with his work as consultant for Aldrich and the task of producing a study of Britain's experience of foreign investing during its creditor period from 1880 to 1913. As early as 27 January he had completed a first draft which he confessed had involved more work than originally contemplated. However Aldrich found it "illuminating and helpful" and even suggested it be published.[232] A revised draft, based on further "informed and responsible London opinion," was sent on 6 April, with Salter adding that he would need to rewrite the study before publication.[233] On 13 June Aldrich had visited London and dined with the Salters, Lord Balfour of Burleigh, Halifax and Anderson at West House. The following day he and Salter agreed that the latter be retained as an official consultant to the Chase National Bank, with a fee of $11,000.[234] Later, on 11 September, Aldrich was advised that, because Salter's study gave a dim picture of the possibilities of private American investment overseas, he should not endorse it. As a result, during his three-week stay in New York in October, Salter agreed to have the study published by Princeton University in its series "Essays in International Finance."[235] The study analysed Britain's experience as a creditor nation, noting that British trade and investment overseas were complementary, largely exporting manufactured goods and importing raw materials. In contrast, the United States produced most domestic products and the returns from such investment outstripped any returns on investment abroad. In the post-1945 period, he concluded that there were simply too many impediments for any increase in private foreign investment. American capital export would continue mainly in the form of government loans, military aid and other such grants.[236] Salter carried on with his advisory role until July 1951 when the Committee for Financing Foreign Trade was dissolved. However, after his return to parliament on 9 April, he gave up his retaining fee.[237]

Early in the New Year Salter observed that there was increasing public discontent with rising food prices, excessive wage demands and growing dissatisfaction with the Labour government.[238] While he focused his attention on the political and economic arenas, it remained the case, as he had written to Curtis, that he lacked "a cause which one could promote" by holding a seat in the House of Commons. That opportunity suddenly came his way when on 2 February, while reading the morning papers and still in bed, he received a telephone call from Churchill. The following conversation ensued:

'Have you seen The Times?' 'No,' 'Well, when you do you will see that Ronald Cross is going to Tasmania. That vacates the Ormskirk seat. I want you to take it.' I gasped and stammered, 'I must have time to think. I've never thought of going back to Westminster.' 'Well, think it over now; what time – this morning – will you come and give me your answer?'[239]

The reality was that occasionally, and most recently on 6 December 1949, Salter had been providing Churchill with economic briefs on such subjects as the dollar gap, convertibility and devaluation. In turn, Churchill asked Salter to review notes he had written on a common dollar/sterling currency.[240]

Following their telephone conversation, Salter met later that morning with Churchill at Hyde Park Gate and after some brief conversation, he accepted. "No other man living could at that time have made me do it," Salter wrote, "But I had obeyed him too long to stop doing so now."[241] Curtis was among the few people with whom he shared this development, writing the following morning, "I wish – intensely – that I hadn't been asked; and it would be a great relief if the local people won't agree. If they take me I've got to go with it, though it's with a heavy heart." Salter concluded that he had "no reason to think that Winston wanted me – now, he evidently does – & I just can't refuse."[242] On 6 February he wrote to Churchill, "I confirm my promise of Friday [2 February] to do what you wish me to do." However, Salter expressed his concerns that, given his age and his prior career as an Independent, his candidacy might be regarded as the result of pressure from Conservative Headquarters. Indeed, after Churchill met six of the leading Ormskirk Conservatives, he replied to Salter on 11 February that there were some "local difficulties" which likely would be overcome and that he would make every effort, as Salter had urged, to prevent any premature publicity.[243] On the same day, Churchill wrote to Henry Lumby, chairman of the Ormskirk Constituency Conservative Association, stating he was "most anxious" to have Salter on the Opposition Front Bench. He noted that Salter:

> made a real and important contribution to our great business with the United States throughout the crisis of the war. His knowledge of finance and economics is of the highest order. In this time of crisis, when intricate debates on vital matters are so frequent, he would be an invaluable reinforcement to our able but hard-worked band of ex-Ministers; and I am sure that the representation of Ormskirk would gain in distinction by his presence at Westminster.[244]

On 19 February Salter received the invitation from Lumby to meet with the Association's executive committee which he did on 1 March.[245] Among those Salter briefed were Aldrich, writing to him on 3 March that Churchill "has been pressing me hard to help him in the House of Commons" by standing in the Ormskirk by-election. Salter continued, "The prospect is not one that fills me with joy. It will mean a great deal of very arduous, and largely frustrating, work. I have regarded him for many years as my leader, and have a deeper loyalty (with an almost idolatrous admiration) to him than to any other man living; and I simply could not refuse." And if elected, Salter added, he would have to terminate his role as advisor to Aldrich.[246]

The press carried the news on 3 March that the Ormskirk Conservative Association had selected Salter as the candidate to contest the by-election. It was The Manchester Guardian that reminded its readers of the article Salter had written a year ago for The Sunday Times explaining why he would vote Conservative. Salter was officially adopted as the Conservative candidate on 14 March, handed in his nomination papers on 17 March and began his first experience of electioneering a week later.[247] This quickly led him to apprise Churchill of his concern that, given the difficulties of drumming up enthusiasm during a by-election, he might not be able to match Cross' previous large majority [28,654 to Labour's 14,583]. As a result Salter appealed to Churchill to record a brief message of support for broadcast at the local cinema and on the travelling loud speakers. "Your voice will be worth many votes," he concluded. Privately, Salter shared his concern about the apathy he was encountering in the constituency.[248] Although he was getting support from Front Bench speakers, such as Walter Elliot, Sir David Maxwell-Fyfe, John Boyd Carpenter and Harold Macmillan, and several private members, he was fearful of a reduced majority.[249] After a renewed appeal from Salter, who described how he and supporters "have been holding three meetings a night, driving to little village halls through rain and canvassing with a devoted band of workers," Churchill relented. He contributed both a press statement of support as well as the broadcast. In both he attacked Labour, called for an early general election and praised Salter for his "distinguished record of public service."[250] Salter profusely thanked the prime minister, all the while still emphasizing the problem of fighting the campaign with a new-comer as candidate.[251] On 29 March Salter published his message to the Ormskirk electorate with a statement of his support for Labour's rearmament policy. However, he argued for greater incentives for increased production and savings, drastic economies, "an end to extravagance" and a halt to nationalization. Lady Salter added to the message: "Though I am a stranger I hope soon to make many friends among you."[252] Salter also recorded his message and this along with Churchill's speech was broadcast at the cinema on 31 March, apparently causing a "minor sensation."[253]

As Salter predicted, one of the main election issues was the size of his majority in a solid, rural Conservative seat. In speaking to the press, he indicated that an increased majority would help hasten a general election.[254] The answer came on polling day, 6 April, when the final results showed he held Ormskirk for the Conservatives and with an increased majority of 15,221 [24,190 to Labour's 8,969]. Afterwards he could not restrain his excitement, commenting, "It is amazing that I should have a majority that is actually greater with a poll under 65% as compared with 83% at the previous election, and that the Conservative ratio should have risen from two to one to almost three to one." As soon as the results were announced, Churchill cabled, "Warmest congratulations on your magnificent fight and victory."[255] Lady Salter observed that the election "went way above expectations and was very satisfactory in every way."[256] Salter afterwards noted that his new constituents were "A very likeable lot of people."[257] As for himself, he wrote somewhat later, "I found the novel experience of fighting a political campaign exciting & enjoyable – & I have of course been plunged straight into the fray."[258]

On 9 April Salter took the oath and his seat in the Commons, introduced by Churchill, ready to play his role in what he later described as the "last assaults on the Socialist Government."[259] He returned just in time for the debate on the first budget presented by the new Chancellor of the Exchequer, Hugh Gaitskell. The 10 April budget, unlike its predecessor, dealt with the need for a massive defence programme, an adverse balance of trade, and the shortage of materials to increase production. Among the measures proposed was an increase in income, petrol and purchase taxes. On 12 April Salter contributed to the debate, sitting now on the Opposition Front Bench. He opened with the comment, "An elderly and somewhat battered bride who, after a short interval, embarks upon another venture need, I believe, neither assume the modesty nor claim the indulgence that is appropriate to a maiden." He acknowledged that a budget debate was currently more difficult when its primary object was "not, as it used to be, to equate revenue and expenditure but to control inflationary pressure." He then launched into an extended critique of both the budget and the government's most recent Economic Survey. He admitted that some of the government's financial difficulties, such as the need for increased defence expenditure, lay outside its control. However, he still held it responsible for "the mismanagement of the nationalized monopolies." He asked for additional "administrative economies," admitted that the country had reached "the limit of tolerable taxation," and asserted that the inevitable inflation caused by war had continued into peacetime. He did not believe that the new income tax, the increase in profits tax and any other measures would be counter-inflationary. He concluded that it was time to replace an administration of "misguided, exhausted and incompetent ministers" with a Conservative government. Salter's return to the House was welcomed by some, while others took issue with his conversion to Toryism. However, despite being labeled "a prophet of doom" by a fellow MP, many of his comments were well received. The next day <u>The Times</u> noted that the speech was greeted with Conservative cheers, and observed that the Conservative case "gained much weighty reinforcement from the careful scrutiny to which Sir Arthur Salter subjected the national economy."[260]

During the 12 April meeting of the House, both Salter and others made reference to the issue of strategic stockpiling, one which he had campaigned for in the press in August and September. The Commons that day in fact heard that the government had already decided in July to embark on a strategic stockpiling programme.[261] However, on 20 April, G.R. Strauss, the Minister of Supply, suddenly announced that there was a serious shortage of strategic metals such as nickel and tungsten, necessary for the rearmament programme, and this required cutting back on their use by civilians. When Salter rose to speak, he agreed on the gravity of the situation and referred to his own public campaign. He could not refrain from adding that an earlier effort to stockpile such metals would have meant they could have been purchased more cheaply and been readily available.[262] The subject came up again on 27 April when Salter's letter of 18 August 1950 was the target of Labour criticism. Salter had to defend himself by pointing out that his advice then was to transfer "dollar reserve" into "dollar goods" and thus obtain raw materials at a cheaper price.[263] The fact was that Salter was quite content to return to parliament. As he wrote to Frances Perkins on 25 April, "I never expected to be back in the House again," and it was only Churchill who had convinced him. He continued, "I am finding it rather amusing now I am there."[264] In fact, he seemed quite buoyant by the prospect, as he wrote to Aldrich, that the election date was most likely 25 October, that the Conservatives would get a majority of about 80, and that he personally would be offered some position, though not as Chancellor of the Exchequer.[265]

It was the budget and the deteriorating economic and international situations which continued to capture parliament's attention. Salter played a role from the Opposition Front Bench in the discussions after the Finance Bill was read a second time on 8 May. It was the government's view that the period of budgets and finance bills aimed at freeing Britain from American dollar aid was over. Moreover, current policy was aimed at financing rearmament, avoiding inflation and maintaining the social services. The following day, at Churchill's request, Salter wrote a lengthy brief on Anglo-American relations in light of the Korean War. It urged Churchill to coordinate with the Americans, who were bearing the burden of the fighting in Korea, and embargo certain strategic materials to China. In response, Churchill thanked Salter for his "very valuable notes."[266] In anticipation of the committee stage of the Finance Bill, Salter along with R.A. Butler tabled an amendment to shield the shipbuilding industry from the negative effects of proposed new taxes on profits.[267] On 6 June Salter launched an attack against the Labour government's proposals to increase income taxes, arguing they posed hardship for low income earners, diminished incentives to work, discouraged enterprise and encouraged inflation. His bottom line, however, was to seek reassurances that the additional taxation revenue would be directed towards the rearmament programme. Gaitskell commended Salter for his "very moderate," but "rather gloomy" speech and then took issue with much that Salter had stated.[268] Salter continued to take an active role as the debate on the budget continued. His most successful intervention took place during an all-night debate on 7-8 June. Drawing fully on his experience with shipping in both world wars, he pleaded, ultimately successfully, that the shipbuilding industry should continue to receive allowances for expenditure on new building. It was not until 3 July that the Finance Bill was read for the third time and passed in the Commons.[269] Douglas Jay, the Financial Secretary to the Treasury, admitted in conclusion that the bill had been "improved by our long debates."[270] These in fact continued, and even intensified, when the Commons on 26 July opened a debate on the economy. Gaitskell conceded that, since the budget had been introduced on 10 April, uncontrolled inflation and rising costs and prices threatened the future economic stability of the country and thus demand must be limited. As one of the principal speakers from the Opposition Front Bench, Salter focused on the speed at which the economic situation had deteriorated, describing government explanations as a "tale of woe." He was critical of newly proposed measures, such as prohibitions on imports and new price controls, describing these as "petty patchwork palliatives." In the ensuing debate both Salter and the Opposition generally were criticised for failing to offer any realistic alternatives.[271] The Economist, normally supportive, also noted that neither of the two Opposition Front Bench spokesmen, Salter or Lyttleton, had "succeeded in saying anything striking" about what the Conservatives would do if returned to power.[272]

The House of Commons adjourned for the summer recess on 2 August with reassembly scheduled for 16 October. The Salters departed later than usual to New York and Hickory Farm, but returned earlier than planned. On 19 September Attlee announced that a general election would be held on 25 October. "Congratulations on good news," Salter at once cabled to Churchill and continued, "May we whom you command be an adequate majority in next Parliament here as elsewhere. There is ardent hope your resounding success."[273] The Salters hurried back by plane to London on 25 September and Salter began the campaign to retain the seat he had first won just six months earlier. Parliament was dissolved on 5 October with a state opening by King George VI scheduled for 6 November. On 13 October Salter accepted the nomination to stand again as the Conservative candidate for Ormskirk. His previous large majority buoyed his confidence and his meetings were better attended than at the by-election. Indeed, he even took the time to speak in support of candidates both in London and the counties. The Times described him as "making thoughtful speeches in which our economic anxieties are traced to their causes. He contrasts the attitude of the parties to incentives, controls and profits, and draws the moral that an increase in productivity is the real key to the reduction of the cost of living."[274] In his message to the electors of Ormskirk, he pointed out that the election was not about objectives, such as improving social services or standard of living, rather it hinged on proposals to achieve these ends and the persons to administer them. With regard to policies, he favoured greater productivity, curtailing rising prices, an end to further nationalization and a "Britain strong and free" under the leadership of Churchill and Eden. He cautioned that "the dangers and difficulties ahead are great," but with leadership and determination peace and prosperity could be achieved. In a brief contribution, Lady Salter stressed that her husband would continue assisting in cases of "individual hardship."[275]

When the election results were announced on 26 October, Salter retained his Ormskirk seat with a decreased but still decisive majority of 13,821 (26,729 to Labour's 12,908) and Churchill and the Conservatives returned to power. Writing on 30 October, Salter thought the small Conservative majority of 16 was unsatisfactory, and largely due to the "smear campaign" against Churchill – "Churchill means war." As for the future, he noted, "Apart from the general international situation, the danger of another financial crisis is obviously very serious. I do not know yet whether I shall myself be in the Government in any capacity. I think Butler a good appointment as Chancellor."[276] The next day it was announced Salter had been appointed Minister of State for Economic Affairs. As he later recalled, Churchill offered the "choice between an independent Economic Ministry of my own or the post of second Minister in the Treasury, where R.A. Butler was Chancellor of the Exchequer." Salter chose the latter, knowing he could not create a new ministry sandwiched between the Treasury and the Board of Trade. As a condition of his appointment, as a cabinet ranking minister but without a seat in the cabinet, Churchill agreed he could attend cabinet meetings when necessary.[277] According to Butler, when offered the Treasury position by Churchill, the latter added, "'It is no great matter that you are not an economist. I wasn't either. And in any case I am going to appoint the best economist since Jesus Christ to help you.' I asked who this might be and he replied 'Arthur Salter'." Butler noted, "Arthur, a nice man with a record of progressive thought but very many years my senior, was accordingly provided with a high-ranking ministerial title and for thirteen months wrote me numberless minutes in green ink, with which I did not always agree."[278] While <u>The Economist</u> foresaw the potential for conflict in the appointment, <u>The Manchester Guardian</u> noted that Salter had emerged as "one of the most convinced and earnest opponents" of Labour's economic policies and looked forward to the future application of "his disinterested intellectual approach to economic problems."[279] No doubt Churchill's choice was largely a testament to the genuine respect he had for Salter's knowledge of finance and economics. In part, it also looked good that Salter, a former Independent and liberal, would be part of the prime minister's search to form a "broad based Government."[280] And finally, Churchill later admitted, "I put him [Salter] in to strengthen the economic side."[281] As his parliamentary private secretary, Salter chose Aubrey Jones who later recalled, "I would not have done it for anyone else."[282]

Among the first items discussed by the new Churchill cabinet on 2 November was the future of university representation. It was decided, with input from Salter, to postpone any decision on the wider issue, although it was agreed there should be no return to plural voting.[283] The more relevant issue facing the new Conservative government, however, remained the deteriorating economic situation. On 7 November, during the Commons' debate on the King's Speech, Butler rose to make "a grave statement" about the economic crisis and then announced a series of counter-measures. After reviewing the worsening balance of payments deficit, affecting all sterling area countries, he proposed a series of measures. These included reductions in imports of some rationed foods, a slowdown in the strategic stockpiling programme, and raising the bank rate, which had been at 2% for 13 years, to 2.5%. Except for some brief interventions, usually answering questions in Butler's absence, Salter took no part in this or subsequent debates on economic affairs, although he had helped Butler to fashion the budget.[284]

As The Financial Times noted, the division of labour between Butler and Salter "has not yet been worked out in the light of experience." Initially both attended meetings with the Federation of British Industries, the Trades Union Congress and the British Employers' Confederation to review government economic policy.[285] Clarification finally came during a 21 November debate in the Commons on the subject of salaries for the new ministers, Salter included. Butler confirmed the value that he placed on Salter and continued:

> He will have the freest and most complete access to the Treasury staff and papers so that he can not only advise me on questions of general finance and economic policy, but also help me within the Treasury. In particular, his work will lie in the field of our financial relations with overseas countries, including trade and payment negotiations and our exchange control administration. I am sure that hon. Members who have questions to raise in this field will find his approach sympathetic and will value advice he will give.

Butler added that Salter would also attend meetings of international organizations when he was unavailable and be available on Thursdays in the House to answer questions.[286] Salter was also appointed to the Economic Policy Committee, set up on

21 November on Churchill's instructions, "To exercise a general oversight over financial and economic questions, both external and internal."[287] Nonetheless, Salter's appointment continued to raise questions, not least in The Times which commented that his role as Minister of State for Economic Affairs was "not very clear."[288]

The potential problems were soon clarified during a Commons' debate on 23 November on the subject of borrowing by local authorities from the Public Works Loans Board. In Butler's absence in Rome, Salter spoke for the first time from the despatch box in the Commons. His comments, as The Times noted, provoked a series of "taunts and challenges" from the Labour opposition. Referring to a statement made by Butler on 7 November on increased interest rates, Salter suggested that the government's policy of "disinflation" would involve "very great and grave economies in public expenditure" both at the central and local levels. Immediately, these remarks were taken as revealing government intentions to impose "very heavy cuts" to spending on housing and the social services. Salter repeatedly attempted to clarify this statement, arguing that his comments did not differ from Butler's, that he was not enunciating any new policies, and that "economies" did not necessarily mean "cuts." Completely unconvinced, several Labours members gleefully noted that Salter would be "in for a wigging on Butler's return to London," that he "has not had too good a morning," that his exact functions remained quite obscure and, despite "his innocuous personality," he too was "one of the sinister figures of the Government." Salter was again pressed on the issue on 27 November when he stated that the details of the "economies" had to await further consultation and examination.[289] The following day Butler rose in the Commons to Salter's defence. "I do not know why all this mystery and cloak of extraordinary characteristics should be cast round the very able and genial personality of my right hon. Friend the Minister of State for Economic Affairs." Butler then repeated that Salter would have "special duties" involved with "the exchange position and with overseas finance" as well as various aspects of the work of the Treasury.[290] When Salter was again the target of criticism on 30 November, the Financial Secretary to the Treasury, John Boyd-Carpenter, rose to his defence, stating that such comments "overlook the long years of devoted service that he [Salter] has given to the country, and his high character, integrity, and intellectual ability." This was followed by "Ministerial cheers."[291] Behind the scenes, however, Salter's performance in the Commons allegedly led Churchill to comment "that he had not meant S.[alter] to make any speeches, just to think."[292] Many years later Boyd-Carpenter observed that "The House of Commons is a difficult place to come to at Salter's age and he never felt at home there." Moreover, Boyd-Carpenter added, Salter "for all his great qualities lacked the warmth, humanity and easy humour which the House of Commons likes."[293]

Against this background, Salter must have welcomed the opportunity, announced on 26 November at the meeting of the Consultative Assembly of the Council of Europe, to represent the British government in its capacity as a member of the Committee of Ministers. His task in Strasbourg was to officially present to the Assembly a second report, drafted by the OEEC, which surveyed the financial situation in Europe and the dangers of further inflation.[294] It was anticipated, however, that Salter would also reveal something about where the new Churchill government stood on the question of European unity. Thus, prior to his departure, Salter was fully briefed both on how to present the report and Britain's future policy towards Europe. On 21 November his wish to publicly welcome the closer relationship developing between the OEEC and the Council of Europe, and thus the strengthening of the European community, were both denied by the Foreign Office.[295] Another meeting on 28 November discussed the draft of his speech to introduce the OEEC report. When Salter again insisted on adding something personal by way of encouraging recent European developments, he was cautioned that it would be "undesirable to trespass in this way into the political field." Although still pressed to keep as close as possible to prepared briefs, Salter was finally permitted to add something of his experience and career with international organizations.[296]

This Salter did on 4 December when he presented the OEEC report to the Council. At the outset he made it clear that he spoke not as a British representative and therefore would make no policy pronouncements. However, he reminded the Assembly of his many years of international work. "I have long thought of myself," he pointed out, "as not only an Englishman but a European." He then referred to his proposals, along with Aristide Briand, for a United States of Europe "attempting to give reality to the dreams of so many earlier European statesmen," and also to the successful work of financial reconstruction which he spearheaded at the League of Nations in the 1920s. Turning then to the essence of the OEEC report, he suggested that Western Europe must increase its production by 25% over the next five years in order to fight inflation and right the balance of payments. He also expressed regret that Britain's own worsening balance of payments had required emergency cuts in some European imports. He finally added that Churchill had just come to office and European policy would be developed as the facts emerged. Personally, he intended to report back on what was in the "minds and hearts" of continental colleagues. Winding up the discussion the following day, Salter spoke favourably of closer association between the sterling area and the European Payments Union, the mutual credit system, and admitted that greater productivity might require an exchange of labour between countries. Finally, he added that he personally was able to look back 30 years to when he had heard the issues being now discussed first "thrashed out in Geneva and he thought that the perspective of the years had brought collective action closer."[297] By all accounts the speech was well received and the Assembly was "obviously pleased" at the presence of a Minister "who had so long and distinguished a connexion with the work for European unity." The Manchester Guardian noted that Salter's visit "has done more good than any speeches made by the Ministers to the Assembly."[298]

On his return to London, and in the following weeks, Salter reverted to answering routine parliamentary questions on behalf of Butler. Looking back on this period of his career, he described himself as engaging in the "unrewarding duties of lobby tramping."[299] However, with the continuing difficulties experienced by the British economy, and in preparation for the forthcoming meeting of the Commonwealth Finance Ministers, Salter asked Brand to chair a Chatham House group to recommend policy on re-establishing "stability to the Sterling Area." Its report was ready by 5 January and contended that, in order to achieve a surplus in the balance of payments, necessary to maintain the solidarity of the sterling area, "an anti-inflationary monetary policy and a drastic reduction of public expenditure" were required both in Britain and throughout the sterling area. This should also be accompanied by restricting imports, expanding exports, reducing domestic subsidies, for example on food, and asking Commonwealth members to take similar measures. Finally, the report suggested that any attempt to abandon a fixed dollar rate of exchange would be "highly disagreeable to contemplate." This report, which also found its way to the Bank of England, was to be highly influential on Salter's thinking. He soon found himself at the centre of a historic conflict about sterling policy which, as he recalled, "dominated all my life and work."[300] The reality was that Britain was in the throes of its third post-war economic crisis, "wider than the 1947 convertibility crisis or the 1949 dollar crisis. It was not one of dollars only but of the overall balance of payments." The drain on the gold reserves, if continued, would result in a massive reduction of one third by 30 June 1952.[301]

During a sub-committee meeting of the Economic Policy Committee on 10 January 1952, Salter clashed with Butler, arguing that the latter's estimates for the 1952-53 budgets were not anti-inflationary, and would be vitiated by an increase in service estimates.[302] The disagreement was part of a larger and more serious crisis which had emerged. On 5 January Butler had alerted the cabinet that a balance of payments crisis had enveloped the sterling area, leading to a substantial drain on the central gold reserves. If the run continued, he warned, the sterling area "will dissolve into chaos."[303] When this was discussed at the cabinet on 10 January, it was decided, that "while no steps could be taken in present circumstances towards greater convertibility of sterling, the ultimate aim should be to achieve total convertibility based, not on fixed rates of exchange, but on flexible and variable exchanges."[304] That discussion was to have a considerable impact on Salter and lead to his involvement in one of the most contentious debates in post-World War Two British economic history. On 15 January Salter was among the British officials who attended the opening meeting of Commonwealth Finance Ministers. The plan was to convince members of the sterling area to take emergency action, such as that undertaken in Britain, to fight inflation, wipe out the deficits in their balance of payments, and reduce expenditure outside the sterling area by cutting back on imports. It was also anticipated that the meetings would serve as a stepping stone to some longer-term polices designed to secure the viability of the sterling area, such as convertibility.[305]

At the 18 January meeting of the Commonwealth Finance Ministers, Salter took a leading role. He invited representatives of the attending countries to study the options for a programme to implement convertibility which he stated "would be the glittering reward of present sacrifices." He indicated that the task would be to define "whether we meant convertibility at a fixed exchange ratio which we would try to keep stable, as in the years following the recent war, or at a freely fluctuating rate, as in September 1931 when sterling left gold." In suggesting that "a fluctuating currency with the support of an Exchange Equalisation Fund might be the best solution," he may have exceeded his instructions.[306] At a further meeting on 21 January, Salter was designated as the chairman of the "Working Party on Convertibility." The public statement issued that day, at the close of the conference, confirmed his role in studying "the steps which should be taken along the road to convertibility."[307] During this time, however, the country's economic situation continued to deteriorate. On 17 January Butler had told the cabinet that deflationary cuts had so far failed to remedy the deficit in the balance of payments.[308] In fact, the continuing rapid fall in the gold and sterling reserves led to a series of cabinet meetings in late January which were designed to work out an emergency plan to prevent, what Butler termed, "a major calamity for sterling."[309] This was followed by an important statement by Butler on 29 January in the Commons. He described the serious situation faced by Britain, "the largest debtor country in the world," and outlined the measures he would take to enable Britain to pay its own way, including proposals for cuts both to imports and external expenditure. He also referred to Salter's Working Party, examining "the steps to be taken towards the convertibility of sterling." Thereby, he declared, "we proclaimed our faith in the future."[310] This was followed on 30 and 31 January by a debate in which the government was accused of moving too quickly towards convertibility. Butler was forced to deny that he had ever stated that "convertibility was around the corner." He added that he was "deriving great benefit from the advice of the right hon. Gentleman [Salter] on these very difficult matters."[311]

As chairman of the Working Party, which met for the first time on 23 January, Salter offered a series of suggestions as to its agenda.[312] He then followed this with a memorandum, titled "General Notes on Convertibility," intended to guide future discussions. He held strongly to his view that "Whatever degree of convertibility is offered must be supported by at least a balance of trade and payments between the sterling area and the non-sterling world and by reserves adequate to provide for periods when that balance is not attained." A primary condition, he stressed, was "the maximum possible expansion of sterling area exports to the dollar area." It was also necessary to define precisely what distinctions, if any, were to be made between sterling held by residents of the sterling area and non-resident sterling holdings? Equally important, in his view, was the question of whether any given degree of convertibility should operate at fixed rates, flexible rates or floating rates of exchange between the pound and other currencies. Finally, he detailed the successive steps required to create the conditions necessary for convertibility. What Salter foresaw was the Working Party submitting an interim report, based on considerations in his memorandum, and the participating governments reconvening in a few months to discuss future action.[313] Following its first meeting, the Working Party met a further eight times until 9 February when Salter signed, on behalf of the group, its Interim Report. It largely followed and approved the original guidelines proposed by Salter, and detailed the various conditions which would have to be satisfied before convertibility could be introduced. Agreement on all the issues, however, proved to be impossible.[314] It was only on 19 February that Salter formally submitted the Interim Report to Butler, who minuted, "To read at more leisure – a good bit of work. Review in light of crisis."[315] The communiqué issued from the Treasury the same day only mentioned that the first series of meetings had been completed with resumption some months later. In fact, no further action was taken on the Interim Report and the Working Group, under Salter's chairmanship, never reconvened.[316]

The issue of convertibility, however, was raised in the Commons on 22 February. Salter was forced to defend the mandate of his Working Party as essential to long-term planning and indicative of the special relationship with the Commonwealth.[317] However, at the same time, officials in the Overseas Finance Division of the Treasury and Bank of England, in a high level and secretive process, were examining the merits of an "External Sterling Plan," later named Robot, containing three main themes: floating of the exchange rate; blocking of sterling balances; and convertibility of the pound.[318] The objectives, to be announced as part of the 4 March budget, were to take the strain off the reserves of gold and dollars and transfer it to the rate of exchange, restructure foreign exchange and economic policy, and find a solution to Britain's ongoing economic crises. The proposal, originally circulated on 25 January by Richard W.B. "Otto" Clarke of the Overseas Finance Division, and developed after several iterations with the Bank of England, was first presented to Butler on 13 February.[319] On 20 February Cobbold discussed the scheme with Churchill who dubbed the plan "the new financial super-crisis." This convinced the prime minister to delay the budget to 11 March so as to enable further consultation.[320]

Robot then led to an extensive and some times rancorous controversy at the highest levels of British governance. What emerged was an informal alliance of Cherwell, Salter, Sir Edwin Plowden, Head of the Central Economic Planning Staff of the Treasury, and Robert Hall, Director of the Economic Section of the Cabinet Office, deployed against what was then also known as "the Bank scheme." The former group believed that convertibility was too risky given Britain's declining reserves, that it would not correct the balance of payments position, and that more drastic cuts in imports and defence spending, and a higher bank rate were required. As well, they feared that it might alienate American opinion so committed to the post-war Bretton Woods monetary system of fixed rates of currency exchange.[321] Butler, an avid supporter of "the Bank scheme," admitted that a cornerstone of the plan was "to rehabilitate sterling as an international currency and absorb some of the external pressures on the exchange rate instead of on the reserves."[322] Salter was brought into the discussions on 20 February and again when he met privately on 26 and 28 February with Plowden and Hall. They had been providing Salter with various "Top Secret" documents they had written, and found him in sympathy with their views.[323] Indeed, both Plowden and Hall afterwards acknowledged the value of Salter's support.[324] In addition, on 27 February Salter had attended an informal meeting of cabinet ministers where he sided with those opposing Robot and urged instead a further round of import cuts, an increase in bank rate, and possible borrowing from the International Monetary Fund. He concluded, "If we have to take the step proposed by the Chancellor, we should only do so later as a result of *force majeure.*"[325]

On the basis of such discussions, on 28 February Salter provided Butler with a nine-page memorandum expanding his own views and casting further doubt that Robot was a viable solution. Part of the issue, he contended, was timing. He wished to see any external action delayed in order to gauge the impact of the budget and, if taken in due course, for this step to be seen as "acting under *force majeure.*" Moreover, he thought the consequences, particularly political ones from Europe to Australia, would be "quite devastating." And finally he feared that the domestic results would be a rise in the cost of living and increased unemployment. Under such circumstances, he argued that the abstention of 20 Conservative MPs would bring the government down and with no chance for re-election. Thus deferring Robot, with the hope that existing measures and the budget would enable the country to get over "the hump" and bring the "economy to the self-supporting basis which is now contemplated."[326] That same day Butler prepared what he titled "An Alternative Plan" which strongly resembled the options supported by Salter and others the previous day.[327]

The cabinet finally discussed Robot on the evening of 28 February and twice the following day. The minutes of the three meetings in 24 hours only recorded who attended, including Salter, with no information other than the fact that "The Cabinet held a discussion on the current economic situation."[328] However, the "Confidential Annex" to the conclusions detailed Butler's concerns about the ongoing drain on the gold and dollar reserves of the sterling area, leading soon, in his words, to its possible "collapse." He then outlined a complex plan designed to protect the currency. He advocated a variable rate of exchange, fixed since September 1949, at £=$2.80, to be held with the help of the Exchange Equalisation Fund within a range of $2.40-$3.20. In addition, "all foreigners' sterling balances would be blocked, except for Canadian and American accounts already convertible into dollars." He wished to see 10% of these balances classified as "external sterling" which, together with any sterling earned subsequently, "would be convertible into gold, dollars, or other currencies at the current rate." Finally not less than 80% of the sterling balances held by other sterling area countries would be held in "funded form," and the London gold market would be re-opened so as to "provide a free market against external sterling" and would fluctuate freely. Butler explained that such measures would enable the strain on the balance of payments to fall, not on the reserves, but on the exchange rate. He conceded that the plan involved serious risks and would shock Commonwealth members of the sterling area, disrupt the European Payments Union, be regarded suspiciously by the Americans, and lead to a rise both in the cost of living and unemployment. In contrast, Cherwell argued that such "a violent reversal of policy" was premature. He wished existing remedial measures, taken in November and those promised as a result of the Commonwealth Finance Ministers Conference, be given further time to take effect, along with greater cuts in imports and an expansion of exports. Salter similarly opposed the scheme, indicating it would not resolve the balance of payments question. He also feared the pound would fall even below $2.40 and thus exhaust reserves. In theory, he added, he was in favour of a floating rate, "but not from a position of great weakness." Churchill's summary of the discussion was to note that, given the clear division of opinion, it would be "hazardous to implement so violent a change of policy." Instead, plans went ahead to frame a severe budget, including cuts in imports and defence production and an increase in bank rate to 4%. Robot was thus not to be included in the budget, but any final decision about its eventual implementation was deferred.[329]

This initial attempt to restructure British finance and the economy, limit government controls, and correct the balance of payments by the price mechanism of the exchange rate thus ended. It was apparent that Salter had played a pivotal role in the discussions leading to the plan's demise. Robert Hall afterwards blamed the proponents for trying to get the plan approved before the budget, leaving time scarce to build a consensus.[330] In the aftermath, Butler, who regarded the whole thing "as his own child to save the country," called a meeting "and practically upbraided Salter and Plowden."[331] For his part Salter produced a document, entitled "The B Plan, Personal Note as to Reasons for Opposing Adoption and Announcement with Budget." He reaffirmed the arguments he had advanced in cabinet regarding Robot, adding that the net effect would have been to create "shock and resentment" in numerous quarters, worsen the balance of payments position, and make the £ worth less than $2.40. He remained convinced that "import reductions, a severe Budget [and] an increase in Bank Rate" would obviate the need for the "B Plan." He concluded that there was a reasonable chance of getting over the hump, and ending the year without a fatal exhaustion of reserves.[332]

A cabinet meeting on 10 March finalized the budget and on the following day Butler presented it to the House. Its main features were cuts in imports and food subsidies, and an increase in bank rate from 2.5% to 4%.[333] On 12 March Salter responded on behalf of the government to various criticisms from the Opposition. His primary contention was that the "austerity and restrictions" found in the budget supplemented previous measures, such as the November cuts and those projected by the Commonwealth Finance Ministers. Together these were designed to deal with the balance of payments crisis and the drain on reserves. He commended Butler's budget as "courageous," with the advantage of "combining both realism and hope."[334] The Manchester Guardian afterwards noted that Salter's speech "would have made an article for a quarterly review. But in reading it will be found to be a comprehensive vindication of the Budget."[335] Both before and after the budget, Salter was in constant touch with Butler on these related issues. In his view, and one sharply critical of the prior Labour governments, as well as the methods used to make economic forecasts, Salter suggested:

> As we are now proceeding to an economy in which the price mechanism and competitive private enterprise play a larger part in determining economic adjustments, the old method of guessing economic developments and purporting to base policy on arithmetic conclusions from them become fantastically inappropriate.[336]

Salter's prominence and parliamentary performance were targeted in an acerbic portrait by Michael Foot in The Daily Herald on 21 March. "Man with a Past" described Salter as "a mild little man who seems to wear a perpetually aggrieved look on his otherwise placid countenance." Foot went on to remind readers of Salter's previous career as an Independent, liberal and strongly supportive of public ownership and greater state intervention. And not for the first time was the Ivar Kreuger episode rehashed.[337]

For some time issues other than convertibility preoccupied Salter. These included the problems of growing unemployment in the textile and clothing industries, and the thorny issue of returning the road transport industry, nationalized in 1947, to private enterprise. Salter later sat on a committee preparing the transport bill which had a stormy passage until becoming law in May 1953.[338] He also attended the OEEC's Ministerial Council meetings in Paris during the last week of March.[339] Agreement was there reached to increase production, particularly of coal, as Salter had often previously urged. There was also further discussion on the future both of the OEEC and of the European Payments Union. Afterwards Salter thought the meeting had produced a useful debate on Europe's economic problems.[340]

Even as parliament continued to debate the budget and other parliamentary issues, the controversy over convertibility persisted. This was raised several times in the Commons on 17 March with arguments for and against.[341] Behind the scenes, and once again shrouded in secrecy, the question of "Setting the Pound Free," or as one memorandum put it, "Robot Walks Again," continued to preoccupy officials at the Bank of England, the Treasury and the Economic Section of the Cabinet Office.[342] Cherwell cautioned Churchill against reviving the question before the sterling area was in surplus and had rebuilt its reserves.[343] On 24 April Salter answered a question in the Commons on the issue, noting that the objective was still to achieve convertibility, but only "by progressive steps."[344] Behind the scenes he was playing an active part in the ongoing discussions on convertibility, a subject which Bank of England officials continued to press. On 9 April Butler had advised the cabinet that "we cannot afford to let matters drift while the reserves dwindle."[345] Nevertheless, he did explore the possibility of "half-way steps that might be taken towards ROBOT." Such a compromise was not regarded favourably either by the Bank of England nor the Treasury.[346] As discussion continued, attention was increasingly focused on Commonwealth sterling balances and in particular the role of Australia. This was made more pressing with an expected visit to London by its prime minister, Sir Robert Menzies. As both a gold producer and the holder of the second largest sterling balance, it was regarded as vital for that country to remain in the sterling area. On 25 April Sir Leslie Rowan suggested that a senior Treasury official should tour Commonwealth countries both to discuss Robot and canvass opinion prior to the reconvening of Salter's Working Party on Convertibility in June.[347] Salter's response was that such consultations, before the cabinet had come to conclusions on the subject, were "highly undesirable and dangerous." What he feared most of all was the possibility of a leak somewhere on the long tour, forcing the cabinet into a hasty decision. However, he was all in favour of Menzies getting a full briefing.[348] That too was the view of Cobbold and Bridges and the tour never took place.[349] On 6 May, worried by the increasing tempo of discussions, Salter wrote to Butler urging more study of the probable consequences of Robot before its submission to the cabinet. In his view any approval must be informed by the political will to weather "the re-emergence of the present crisis under worse conditions" and defeat of the government in the Commons and in the country. Thus he asked Butler to gather expert financial and economic opinion on the fallout so that the cabinet would be better informed when it came to make a decision.[350]

The arrival of the Australian prime minister in London on 24 May for a three-week visit enabled discussion about what emerged as Robot II to advance.[351] On the one hand, Menzies spent much time rationalizing Australia's recent cuts in British imports to help preserve its own overseas balances.[352] Salter attended a meeting of cabinet ministers on 28 May when Menzies explained that with Australia's current sterling deficit, due in part to falling prices for wool and a poor wheat harvest, it was impossible to withdraw the cuts.[353] In the House Salter placed these cuts in context, reminding MPs that it was part of the strategy, adopted by the Commonwealth Finance Ministers Conference in January, to get the entire sterling area to balance its accounts.[354] However, on 10 June Menzies was in fact briefed by Cobbold on current thinking about Robot and the latter "without in any way committing himself was clearly in favour of a step on these lines." As a result and having revised the original Robot proposal, Cobbold again approached Butler and the expected flow of memoranda, minutes and cabinet papers ensued.[355] On 12 June Butler cautioned the cabinet that "there were signs of a renewed loss of confidence in sterling."[356] Once more, Plowden and Hall provided Salter with copies of their memoranda, again very critical of Robot II, with the former describing it as a "leap in the dark."[357] In an undated manuscript note, written in June, Salter again detailed his opposition to what he described as an "irrevocable step" which would lead to large-scale unemployment. His own preference was for further restrictions of dollar imports, cuts in housing and defence expenditure and a possible further increase in interest rates. He also observed that the Bank of England's prediction that if Robot was not implemented there would be a serious loss in the reserves did not come true.[358] Salter followed this with another assessment on 24 June, this time directed to Butler. In this he questioned whether the loss of confidence was indeed so serious as to make the exhaustion of the reserves inevitable, unless Robot was adopted. After reiterating his familiar economic and financial reservations, he argued that not enough was known about the reaction of other countries around the world and the political impact in Britain, where he predicted convertibility would bring down the government. He concluded, "after all, the Bank may be mistaken – and has been in the past in assessing the confidence factor." Butler's brief response, the same day, read, "I am much obliged, all these avenues must be pursued."[359] The fact of the matter was that Salter's views had "shaken" Butler.[360] The chancellor immediately solicited a response to Salter's critical arguments from the Bank of England whose comments, naturally, reaffirmed the arguments for proceeding with Robot.[361]

Thus reassured, Butler produced on 28 June a memorandum for the cabinet which argued that the respite in the losses of gold reserves was only temporary and that a renewed crisis of confidence in sterling was inevitable without the adoption of Robot. The current version, according to Butler, "is a combination of a floating rate of exchange, convertibility of sterling in the market for people outside the sterling area, and holding action on the sterling balances." Its main difference, he continued, was that it "contains no provision for the formal funding of sterling balances of sterling area countries," and included reductions in spending on defence and housing and cutting imports.[362] On 30 June Cherwell produced his response, declaring that nothing had occurred since Robot's first rejection in March to justify its acceptance in June.[363] Salter's last recorded contributions to the discussions at this stage were contained in two memoranda, the first on 27 June and the second on 30 June. These summarized his thinking on Robot, namely, that while convertibility was ultimately desirable, it was too dangerous to proceed when confidence was absent and there was a large deficit in balance of trade and payments. As well, he pointed out that most economists and others who approached the issues "from the point of view of the economy (trade, employment) rather than the currency" were opposed to Robot.[364] On the evening of 30 June a select group of ministers, not including Salter, met for an informal discussion of Robot with the result that on 2 July Butler withdrew the plan.[365] He accepted there was resistance "to change the mechanism of our external financial system at the present time" and instead went ahead with plans to right the balance of payments along lines advocated by anti-Robot advocates.[366] On 8 July the cabinet heard Churchill declare that "there was unlikely to be any large body of opinion in the cabinet in favour of undertaking at the present time the hazardous operation of setting sterling free at a floating rate of exchange." However, as part of the planning for a Commonwealth Economic Conference in November, he urged ministers to find ways of "working as rapidly as possible towards the convertibility of sterling."[367]

Looking back at this period in his career, Salter took issue with the claim made afterwards that, but for Cherwell's solitary opposition, Robot might have been implemented.[368] He called this an "innocent but mistaken accusation," and in his <u>Slave of the Lamp</u>, based on his own private papers from 1952, he expanded on the role that he and others had played "to kill the project." With evident approval he finally quoted a comment made by Churchill at the time: "I don't know much about these technical financial questions myself, but I can't help feeling that when Cherwell and Salter agree there must be something in what they say." On another occasion, Churchill told Salter: "'You did a great public service in that affair about sterling last year – and Rab now knows you are right.'"[369] Later Salter and Cherwell exchanged letters on the subject, with Cherwell writing, "On one occasion at least, I am sure neither of us have anything to reproach ourselves with in the line we took."[370] Both Hall and Plowden averred that in later years Butler had admitted to them that he was "wrong" about Robot. However, in his own memoir, Butler maintained that "In the long term the decision not to free the pound was a fundamental mistake."[371] According to Aubrey Jones, who obviously followed these events closely, Salter "was embarrassed at having opposed and defeated his superior minister."[372] Indeed, some time later Salter wrote to Butler that he had enjoyed working together, and admitted, "It was very painful to me to find that on one important question I could not take the same view & that I thought it my duty to state what I thought even where you differed. But I was very careful to limit the expression of my views to those with whom I was bound to discuss them."[373] Many years later, Butler noted, "I fear I should have been kinder to him in my book," and added, "I myself thought Salter made much sense & was a dear character."[374]

Nothing Salter did in the following weeks rivaled the intensity of the Robot discussions. Much of his time was spent answering parliamentary questions on subjects ranging from the possible reevaluation of the price of gold to progress with regard to the balance of payments.[375] A brief respite from this was offered when on 18 and 19 July he chaired a special ministers' meeting of the OEEC in Paris. Under discussion was a report on financial stability drafted by a team of international experts and aimed at Britain, France, Belgium and the US. Among its many recommendations was that monetary policy should be used to fight inflation and that currency convertibility should be generally restored. Salter naturally greeted the latter recommendation with "reserve" and suggested that many factors affecting the balance of payments would have to be settled before convertibility "comes into sight." A further informal meeting of representatives from the US, Belgium and France, again presided over by Salter, was held in London on 29 July. However, any action on the report was deferred until a meeting in October of the full Ministerial Council of the OEEC.[376]

On 2 August Salter and Lady Salter left London for a three-week stay at the Suvretta Hotel in St. Moritz. "It will be marvelous to get away," Lady Salter wrote on 29 July to Frances Perkins.[377] However, during their absence, Butler sent a telegram to Salter, explaining that he could not attend the seventh annual meeting of the Governors of the International Bank for Reconstruction and Development and the International Monetary Fund in Mexico City from 3 to 12 September. Preparations for the November Commonwealth Economic Conference, announced by Churchill on 29 July, required his presence in London. The cabinet, therefore, had agreed on 7 August to send Salter.[378] Notifying the President of the International Bank of this change, Butler wrote, "You know him and his high qualities and he will play a worthy part in your discussions." Butler informed Salter that he considered it important that Britain be represented by "someone of your calibre." Salter replied at once, "Will willingly take your place in Mexico." Thus forced to cut their holiday short, the Salters returned to London and then sailed aboard the *Queen Elizabeth* on 28 August to New York from where Salter proceeded directly to Mexico.[379] Given the fact that the meetings were regarded as routine, with no items of great importance, the press readily accepted the change in British representation.[380] Indeed, the meetings of the 51 member nations proved largely uneventful, devoted to such routine business as discussing the Bank's annual report. It was generally regarded that the two institutions were beginning to fulfil their roles in strengthening national currencies, encouraging international trade and providing development loans. During the course of the discussions, Salter urged that creditor nations should assume greater responsibility for the solution of debtors' problems. Furthermore, he argued that the International Monetary Fund "might do something to make resources more readily available." He also confirmed that Britain had reached the point where "we can hold our reserves fairly steady."[381] Certainly, the impression left after the meeting was that the International Monetary Fund's future was secure and that it was moving towards the reserve bank of the non-Communist world. Further, it remained the case that Britain was bound to move towards convertibility on current account sterling.[382] A member of the British delegation, Roy Harrod, wrote that "Salter made a most magnificent impression here in Mexico. His performances have been most polished and perfectly adjusted to his audience. This is, of course, his milieu. He has really done splendidly, and revived the British reputation."[383]

A return to London meant for Salter attendance at the Commons, and as usual answering questions on Butler's behalf. He still continued to attend meetings of the Economic Policy Committee of the cabinet. In fact, on 1 October he submitted to the Committee an analysis of "The Conversion Value of Exports of Goods Containing Steel" with the intention to resolve the issue of Britain's shortage of steel with its balance of payments problems.[384] He was present on 8 October at the Lord Mayor's annual banquet for bankers and merchants of the City to hear Butler declare that Britain's economy was "a good deal less inflationary than it was a year ago."[385] A somewhat less sanguine message was delivered by Salter when he accompanied Eden to Paris for a meeting of the Council of the OEEC on 20 October. In his address to the Council the following day, Salter focused on the issue of the "dollar gap," arguing that it was the most serious of all economic difficulties. In his view "high tariff barriers, import restrictions and export subsidies" continued to widen the gap.[386] On 30 October in the House of Commons, he was forced to admit that the 3% increase in industrial productivity, a cornerstone of the March budget, had failed to materialize, adding to the country's economic woes. The statement received a good deal of press on both sides of the Atlantic, with The Financial Times declaring "Uncertain Outlook," and The New York Times writing of "the gloomy picture" Salter had projected.[387]

During a major debate on economic affairs on 5 November, Salter made just one minor intervention and contributed little when he attended a cabinet meeting on 11 November.[388] That same day, in the Commons, it was Butler who touted the success of the measures he had introduced in his 11 March budget. He pointed to the improvement in the balance of trade, the increasing strength of sterling, and to reserves that had reached "some state of stability." When asked about the issue of convertibility, he referred only to the statement on the subject made after the Commonwealth Finance Ministers' meeting on 21 January.[389] In reality, the issue of convertibility, after its abandonment in early July, had never in fact disappeared. Its advocates in the Bank of England and the Treasury reconfigured Robot into a new scheme called the "Collective Approach to Convertibility." This envisaged that both sterling and European currencies, possibly with American support in the form of stabilization funding, would opt for convertibility along with a floating exchange rate.[390] The Collective Approach was privately aired on 23 September with the intention to present it to the Commonwealth Prime Ministers Conference in November. Salter was only marginally involved in these renewed deliberations. However, in two critical memoranda, he pointed out that this most recent proposal "was less specific than what had been previously discussed." It contained no target date and discussions had revealed differences of opinion "as to a 'floating' against a fixed rate." There was also doubt about the value of a plan involving convertibility for residents outside the sterling area, but not inside. Finally, he was adamant that the plunge into convertibility should only be made after negotiations with key OEEC countries and the US. Butler initialled Salter's memoranda, adding it was interesting but required no further comment.[391] The Collective Approach soon faded into obscurity, and was finally abandoned in March 1953. Full convertibility did not come, in fact, until December 1958.

On 25 November the press carried the news that in a cabinet reshuffle Churchill had appointed Salter as Minister of Materials. Lord Swinton had previously held that portfolio along with the office of Chancellor of the Duchy of Lancaster. Salter was to become the first minister to hold the former office separately, while Swinton took over Commonwealth Relations.[392] It was noted at the time that Salter's position as Minister of State for Economic Affairs was allowed to lapse and instead Reginald Maudling was appointed as Economic Secretary to the Treasury but with similar duties to those exercised by Salter. All these changes indicated that the collaboration between Butler and Salter had not proven entirely successful. Salter later graciously averred that his relations with Butler had been "friendly."[393] In contrast, Butler recalled that Salter was "'very trying, because he didn't really agree with very much I did.'"[394] More generally, Salter's performance had given rise, in the words of The Manchester Guardian, to "stupid press clamour" directed at him personally.[395] As well, there was a certain amount of Conservative backbench opinion critical of Salter's performance in the Commons.[396]

The Ministry of Materials had been created by the previous Labour government on 12 July 1951, in order to insure that the country's rearmament programme and economic recovery was not hindered by the lack of industrial raw materials.[397] Salter undertook his new duties as an ongoing gesture of loyalty to Churchill and with the clear knowledge that these were terminal. With the end of the Korean War, the demand for, and the price of raw materials declined. His task, therefore, was "to liquidate most of the controls on materials then in force and prepare the way for the abolition of the Ministry."[398] He set to work at once, receiving on 25 November at his request, a mass of briefing papers setting out the details of the organization and functions of the ministry and those raw materials falling under its responsibility.[399] He retained his place on the Economic Policy Committee which he attended, in his new capacity, the following day. At its request, he completed his first memorandum as Minister of Materials, approving the allocation of steel for a new shipbuilding yard in Newport, Monmouthshire.[400] On 27 November, in his capacity as the new Minister of Materials, he provided the first of many written answers to questions posed by MPs.[401] On 3 December, however, in a surprise announcement, he revealed that the decline in some commodity prices would force him "to seek fairly large supplementary provision for the trading activities of the Ministry of Materials for the current financial year." He added that supplementary estimates, including funding needed for the strategic reserve purchases, would be presented to the Commons in the near future.[402]

These were the issues Salter faced as the House of Commons reassembled on 20 January. The question of supplementary estimates was debated on 26 January when Salter requested parliamentary approval for an additional sum of £33 million for expenditure on trading services and assistance to industry. He pointed out this extra funding was due to trading losses as a result of falling world prices for publicly traded materials. Most of these, he explained, had been purchased when supplies were scarce and hence expensive. With world prices of most of the publicly traded materials falling, supplies were ample, and hence the losses. Under questioning, he reminded the House that the government's policy was "to get out of public trading" wherever it could. The motion approving the supplementary sum was passed, as was a related motion to approve an additional £20 million for the procurement of strategic reserves.[403] Salter's comments about restoring private trading, and by implication reviving London commodity markets, were interpreted as helping to explain the strengthening of the value of the pound.[404] However, the ongoing strategy of the Chancellor of the Exchequer was to continue to reduce expenditure in such areas as defence, the social services and food subsidies. As well, Butler proposed drastic reductions in expenditure for the strategic stockpiles. This was, he noted, despite the appeal from Salter who had the responsibility for stockpiling, for a significant increase in purchases in the coming year.[405] The cabinet meeting on 3 February attended by Salter, discussed Butler's memorandum on supply, with general approval. The only dissenting voice was Salter's who made a futile plea for increased expenditure to build up strategic stocks. In his view, these stocks could be regarded as supplementing the gold and dollar reserves.[406]

As Minister of Materials, Salter was constantly answering questions in the Commons. At times these were of a policy nature, as when on 16 February and subsequently, he restated the view that it was government policy "to revert to private trading, except where and when there are special reasons for its remaining in public hands." Thus his Ministry had returned to private trading zinc, lead and timber, but still imported and distributed copper, aluminum, magnesium, tungsten ore, jute and imported jute goods, sulphur and pyrites. He also pointed out that his Ministry had other duties such as ensuring adequate stocks of strategic war materials.[407] On other occasions, it was a question of a specific product. For example, the Lancashire cotton industry had been in decline for some time and looked to the government for assistance. Salter pointed out that same day in the Commons that raw cotton was not purchased by the government but by the Raw Cotton Commission, albeit a state-sponsored cotton buying agency established in January 1948, or by individual spinners if they opted out of its monopoly.[408] Indeed, there was mounting pressure to finally break up the monopoly of the Raw Cotton Commission, or at least change its responsibilities. At issue was the question of insurance "cover," which the government provided during fluctuations in the price of cotton. A cabinet paper, co-authored by Salter and Peter Thorneycroft, the President of the Board of Trade, recommended both the continuation of cover for another year and that a committee re-examine the complex questions involved. It was considered premature, because of balance of payments issues, to reopen the Liverpool Cotton Exchange. In effect this would be a return to free dealings in futures with the inevitable result of a substantial drain on dollar reserves. These proposals were approved when discussed by the cabinet on 19 February.[409]

Over the next several weeks Salter and Thorneycroft met deputations representing various textile interests, such as the Liverpool and Manchester Cotton Associations, the Master Spinners' Federation and the textile trade unions. These were exploratory discussions in order to plan for the future of the dual system of Raw Cotton Commission and private cotton buying interests.[410] The results of these consultations, announced in the House of Commons on 5 March, were continuing insurance cover against fluctuations in the prices of raw cotton for another year. As well, a Cotton Import (Review) Committee was to be set up to examine both the role of the Raw Cotton Commission and the provision of cover for the cotton industry.[411] It was to be some time before the Review Committee submitted its report which Salter and Thorneycroft brought to the cabinet. The Review Committee recommended a general continuation of previous arrangements, except with regard to cover. Some technical changes were suggested in order to reduce the risk of public funds being used to provide cover for private trade. Salter and Thorneycroft recommended acceptance of the report, its publication and immediate study of how private funding could provide cover.[412] The recommendations of both the Review Committee and the two ministers were accepted by the cabinet on 17 June and the next day laid before parliament.[413] It was only in 1954 that the Liverpool Cotton Exchange was finally re-opened.

Salter also continued his several efforts to return commodities and trading activities to the private sector. Thus on 1 April he attended the cabinet, as a member of the Economic Policy Committee, to recommend the termination of the steel distribution scheme. He pointed out that steel supplies were generally adequate and no longer needed government allocation. However, special measures were still required to control the distribution of steel plate required by the shipbuilding industry. These were approved by the cabinet without reservation.[414] A day before, Salter had recommended to the Economic Policy Committee, a first for him as Minister of Materials, to end public trading in copper. Zinc and lead had already been restored to private trading in October 1952 and January 1953 respectively. With copper as the only metal holding up the full restoration of the London Metal Exchange, he wrote that the arguments in favour of its return to private trading outweighed any risks involved. The Economic Policy Committee discussed this on 1 April. Salter explained that as part of the government's policy of freeing the economy, and with copper as the last of the non-ferrous metals to remain under government control, the re-establishment of the London Metal Exchange would increase the country's invisible earnings and secure copper supplies at the lowest possible price. The proposal, despite Butler's support, resulted in several objections, including the need to give Southern Rhodesian copper producers, a major supplier, adequate notice of the ending of British bulk buying. To this Cherwell added his authoritative voice, saying that he had "grave doubts about the wisdom of the proposal." He considered that the risk of losing dollars through trading in foreign exchange on the London Metal Market was underestimated. As a result, the cabinet concluded that no action was to be taken until there was further examination of Cherwell's proposal "of prohibiting the re-export of dollar copper except for dollars," and that the issue and government intentions should be kept entirely secret.[415]

It was not until 29 April that the subject returned to the agenda of the Economic Policy Committee. Although Cherwell held his ground, and asked "to have his dissent recorded," the familiar arguments made by both Butler and Salter, in favour of resuming private trade in copper, prevailed and agreement was reached to do so and reopen the London Metal Exchange. Salter was also authorised to announce this decision in the Commons as soon as possible.[416] This he did on 4 May, informing MPs that the London Metal Exchange would reopen on 5 May for trading, including copper, and that this notice had been given to Commonwealth [417] Buoyed by his success, Salter continued to work to free other resources and materials from public control wherever possible. In some instances, for example, timber by-products such as plywood and newsprint, he was criticised for not moving fast enough, for not scrapping his department, and for being too "high-handed."[418] In his defence, he argued that copper, in terms of value, had constituted over half of his Ministry's imports. As well, part of his ongoing duties concerned not only public trading, but also "the supply, distribution, and use of materials needed by industry and for the strategic stockpile." Even with the end of the Korean War, he pointed out, the stockpile of strategic raw materials would continue as an essential part of Britain's defence structure.[419] Nonetheless, he was able to announce on 22 June the relaxation of some controls over newsprint, allowing certain categories of weekly newspapers to print as many pages as they wished.[420] He also announced that the government had decided to turn over trading in aluminum to private enterprise as of 1 July, and that under agreement with the major supplier, the Aluminum Company of Canada, a price reduction had also been secured.[421] On 1 July, at a dinner given by the British National Committee of the International Chamber of Commerce, Salter proudly announced that seven commodities had been returned to private trading since 1951 (softwood, fertilisers, lead, plywood, zinc, copper and aluminum). He explained that this constituted a total reduction of 84% in public trading since June 1951. Among the commodities Salter's ministry still controlled were jute and imported jute goods which constituted 57% of those remaining. While eager to return this to public trading, he wished to see special protection for the Dundee jute manufacturers against cheaper Indian imports.[422] On 8 July the Economic Policy Committee, unable to reach a decision on Salter's recommendation, could agree only to study the matter further.[423]

Salter was also questioned continuously in the Commons about a variety of issues, including how he intended "the orderly disposal" of stocks of materials, such as plywood, not required for the strategic reserve.[424] A culmination came on 20 July when he was on his feet no less than 12 times to answer a series of questions ranging from the number of officials employed by his Ministry (1,018) to measures he was taking to encourage the use of salvaged waste paper. He also faced several taunts about being too slow in dismantling state trading, termed a "hoary relic of Socialism," that he should disband his ministry at the earliest possible moment and that he was treating the House in a "flippant, irresponsible manner."[425] More of the same followed for the rest of the month, with questions eliciting minor details about the Ministry of Materials' work, including the running down of stock of sawn softwood.[426] On 30 July, on what was to prove to be Salter's last contribution to a debate in the Commons, the Cotton Import (Review) Committee's report on future of the Raw Cotton Commission, laid before parliament on 18 June, was reviewed and approved. Winding up for the government, he generously complimented the expertise on the subject displayed by some speakers and the "constructive criticisms" voiced by contributors to the debate.[427]

The reality of Salter's situation, which he only later revealed to Churchill on 2 September, was that a resignation letter he had written on 27 June had not been sent, because he had heard Churchill had suffered a stroke. In tendering this resignation, "at some time this year, at the moment most convenient to you," Salter explained:

> My present office is very interesting and comparatively unexacting. But I find the combined strain of division duties in the House at night added to departmental duties by day very heavy. My second reason is that I think that such personal contributions as I can make to the work of the Ministry of Materials can soon be completed. By August nearly nine-tenths of the public trading activities in which my Department was engaged when we came into office will have been handed back to private enterprise (two-thirds of this change having been made since the beginning of this year). Other essential duties remain of course, including in particular the stockpiling of strategic materials, in which I

have a special interest through my association with shipping in both wars; but here again I think that such personal contribution as I can make can be made within the next few months.

Salter continued that after his resignation he wished to leave the House. Although he greatly valued his experience of the last two years, he admitted, "I am conscious too that, though I have been an M.P. for fifteen years, I am not really a House of Commons man. I am much more at home in a Department, in office work."[428]

Equally evident was that Salter was most content when he could think at leisure, provide analyses of current issues and tender advice. In fact, Churchill had long admired these qualities in Salter and in 1953 had continued the previous practice of asking him to provide "from time to time, brief (2 page) notes on developments affecting our economic prospects, for personal use." On 29 April Salter had provided Churchill with such a note on "Raw Material Prices," suggesting that while falling prices had helped the UK balance of trade and the cost of living, they could also threaten the earnings of the sterling area.[429] This evoked no response from the prime minister. However, on 19 June another such note followed "on steps to counter a depression if and when we should run into one." Salter argued that the only satisfactory way to forestall it was by maintaining "our competitive position (in price, quality and delivery dates) before a loss of exports brings a depression." Churchill considered this issue serious enough to ask Cherwell for comments and the latter replied that "Salter is quite right to stress the dangers of an American recession."[430] The underlying reasons for this exchange were fears expressed by both Salter and Cherwell about a revival of Robot. On 23 July Salter wrote to Cherwell "that, while there is formal acceptance of the fact that the old Robot scheme is impossible for a long enough period to make an interim policy imperative, the development of the latter may be seriously impeded by the influence of those who still regret the decision not to try Robot last year and subordinate everything to the desire of returning to it." Cherwell responded on 30 July: "I also agree wholeheartedly that we must guard against premature convertibility. There is still a danger, I believe, that the old Robot scheme might be brought in by a side-wind."[431]

Even as he contemplated resignation, Salter continued to offer economic advice to the prime minister and put in long hours at the Ministry of Materials and the House of Commons. Lady Salter was concerned: "Arthur is very tired – which worries me," she had written to Felkin on 13 May and continued, "I pray he feels better when he does not have to walk through lobbies in the H. of C. for two weeks."[432] Salter himself confided to Violet Markham, "By the time I get to bed nowadays I'm usually pretty tired. This double business of an office day & being lobby fodder at night is inhuman."[433] Thus during the parliamentary recess, from 22 May to 9 June, they vacationed at Hôtel des Trois Couronnes in Vevey, Switzerland, before returning to London for a series of engagements surrounding the Coronation of Elizabeth II. In anticipation, Lady Salter noted, "Life is hectic for us. I shall wear a borrowed tiara four times – dinner and evening reception at Buck Palace." On 30 May the Salters attended a government reception at the National Gallery, followed by a garden party on 31 May given by Lord and Lady Salisbury at Hatfield. On 2 June, Coronation morning, Lady Salter wrote:

> I was up at 4.45 a.m. I had to be fully dressed and also help Arthur get into his uniform before the hair-dresser came to put on the tiara just after 6. Arthur looked very nice in a blue-black silk velvet with cut steel buttons, lace breeches and long black silk stocking, pumps with cut steel buttons – a cocked hat which he held under his arm and a sword of which alas the great beauty did not show as it was in a scabbard. He wore the silver gilt (before the war solid gold) chain of the Grand Cross of the British Empire Order (G.B.E.) with badge, tied with white satin bows, the G.B.E. Star, the K.C.B. (Knight Commander of the Bath) ribbon and order around his neck and the K.C.B. star below the other on the left breast with the miniature decorations above. We got to the Abbey quite comfortably just before 8. Owing to our wonderful seats we could see all the intimate ceremony which was not shown on the films.

The following night the Salters attended the state banquet at Buckingham Palace and the evening reception on 5 June. Lady Salter wrote, "The dinner was the most beautiful sight of that sort I have ever seen. We all assembled, 240 people about on this occasion, around 8 p.m. in the long gallery where many of the best pictures of the Royal Collection are hung. The Queen, Duke of Edinburgh and the Queen Mother assembled in one of the adjoining drawing rooms and we were the presented to each. They shook hands with all of us, I curtseying as well as my groggy knees would allow and Arthur bowing deeply." Lady Salter found the throne room where the banquet was held "a fairy-like scene." Over the next days, further events included a party at the zoo, a gala performance at Covent Garden, the 9 June Thanksgiving Service at St. Paul's, where Lady Salter found the music "more gorgeous than even at the Coronation Service in the Abbey," the Trooping of the Colour on 11 June and finally the Naval Review at Spithead on 15 June. "The only flaw in the actual Coronation celebrations," she observed, "was the weather that week."[434]

Parliament adjourned on 31 July for the summer recess and was scheduled to reassemble on 20 October. On 30 July the Salters left London for an Austrian vacation, and afterwards Lady Salter joined her sister Marchesa Louise de Rosales for a month, first in Florence and then Bavaria.[435] When Salter returned to London on 1 September, awaiting him was an unexpected, but not unwelcome letter from Churchill. "Since the time is approaching when we shall be able to distribute the continuing functions of the Ministry of Materials among existing departments it is I think no longer necessary to have a full time Minister of Materials," Churchill wrote. "I should therefore be grateful if you would let me have your resignation. I am most grateful to you for all the work which you have done since I persuaded you to come forward for Ormskirk. Your advice and influence have been most valuable." Churchill then offered Salter a peerage, noting that "Your high academic and economic attainments and your long public service make this in every way fitting. In the House of Lords you would be able to speak freely on the major economic issues on which you are a master." On 2 September Salter responded in writing, revealing he had drafted a letter of resignation (and enclosed a copy) in June but had delayed sending it because of Churchill's stroke. In that letter, Salter emphasized, he too believed the remaining functions of the Ministry of Materials did not require a full time minister.[436]

Salter went to see Churchill at Chequers on 2 September to discuss the formalities of the resignation and to agree on an exchange of letters to be published in the press. As a result, Churchill redrafted his 1 September letter, beginning now, "I accept your view that the time has come when other arrangements can suitably be made for the Ministry of Materials. I have therefore submitted your resignation to the Queen." This revision, at Salter's request, gave the rightful appearance that he had taken the initiative to wind up the work of the Ministry of Materials. At the same time he accepted the submission of his name for a peerage. The exchange of letters appeared in the press on 4 September. Salter's letter noted, "I think that such personal contribution as I can make has now been practically completed. By last month about nine-tenths of the 'public trading' activities in which my Department was engaged when we came into office had been handed back to private enterprise. Other essential duties remain, of course, but for the Ministerial supervision of these other arrangements could, I suggest, now be made." He then revealed his intention to resign in June and concluded, "It is with feelings of gratitude and continuing loyalty that I now submit my resignation." Churchill's response agreed with Salter's view on winding up the Ministry of Materials and concluded, "I shall always be grateful to you for the excellent advice you have given us on many difficult questions and for the efficient discharge of your administrative duties. I hope you will long continue to give us the benefit of your mastery of economic and financial problems."[437] In a following, unpublished, letter to Churchill on 4 September, Salter formally accepted the peerage. As for timing, he thanked the prime minister for allowing him to return briefly to the Commons as an MP, thus giving the Conservative Association in Ormskirk time to select a candidate.[438]

Salter kept Lady Salter, still on the continent, informed about the turn of events. On 3 September he wrote:

I have today been to the country house (Chequers) & spent the afternoon there. The announcement will be made on Friday morning. The position is substantially the same, but there are two differences. The form will give the initiative to me (based on my letter in June) & there will be no reference to the second proposal of immediate resignation. This doesn't mean a real difference of substance, but the announcement of this part has been postponed at my request partly because I don't want to appear to have run away as I should If I didn't appear next month, & partly to give time for a new selection locally. But all was cordial & in substance all is for the best. I must expect a few disparaging comments but that won't matter & will soon be over. It will involve the loss of certain things I shall (& I expect we both will) miss, but it will have many great advantages.

Thank you for a perfect holiday – it was lovely wasn't it? Rest & sleep & eat & come back to a life of 'greater freedom & less responsibility.' It will be lovely to have you back, but don't shorten your stay by a day – I'm doing very well.[439]

On 4 September Salter paid his last visit to the Ministry of Materials in Horse Guards Avenue, Whitehall. In a letter to members of his staff, he thanked them for their services and concluded, "I have found the work of this office exceptionally interesting and the standards of competence of those engaged in it exceptionally high."[440] He also sent a letter to his successor, Lord Woolton, congratulating him and enclosing a note about the principal issues which required action. To Woolton, as to many others who wrote him, he confessed, "I didn't want another winter of the combined strain of departmental duties by day and division obligations at night."[441] On 4 September, he wrote twice to Lady Salter on the events of the day. "The press has on the whole taken the changes as a minor affair – as indeed they are. The office is I think rather sorry to lose me – & they are of course anxious about their future." He concluded, "I do hope that you are having an enjoyable & restful time, in good weather & that Louise is now safely with you."[442] His second letter continued:

The close of such a chapter – a long one for it is nearly 49 years since I entered the public service – can't come without a pang or two. You will be interested to know that when I said goodbye to W[inston] yesterday he walked to the door to see me off & his last word were 'you did great public service last year in averting a disaster' – which pleased me very much. It will be lovely when you're back. But there's not the least reason to come back sooner than you had intended. I'm getting on fine – very busy as you may imagine, & I expect I shall be over the next few days. I thought, however, of going to All Souls on Saturday night, & I must see the Kidlington family if I do.[443]

From friends came letters of encouragement and comment, including Harold Macmillan who wrote on 5 September, "I thought the exchange of letters read very well. It is very sad to lose you from the team – but I know you will always be ready to help. It seems a long time since we first worked together in All Souls, over the Five Year Plan. There is a lot to be done (and to be left undone.)" Salter replied, "I suppose I have known you longer and better than anyone else now in the Government, and worked with you for a time more intimately. I appreciate what you say the more."[444] On 6 September he wrote to Lady Salter from All Souls, continuing to update her and reflect:

> The week-end press makes very little reference to the changes. The Evening Standard was characteristically vulgar in that (while making no adverse comment) they remarked that the loss of salary would mean no financial problem, because I have family interests in Salter Bros. (that I think is rather humorous in the circumstances) which have made boats for the Oxford crews (in fact it's many years since they made one) & because I have quarters at All Souls. They add that I married an American & have a house at Chelsea. Well, one little spice in life will now, I suppose, come to an end, as neither the Express, Sunday Express, nor E. Standard will have any more interest in me.

On 7 September he wrote again about his and their future together:

> I realize how lucky I am. I never felt lonely in all the years when work was pressing upon me. But I should certainly be lonely if I were alone in the time to come. We don't often tell each other what we mean to each other, but I think you know in your heart what you mean to me. I am, as you know, in personal relations inexpressive.
>
> The kind of work which I think I should attempt now – there are some things I should like to write & think I ought to – will not be remunerative. This of course has consequences. On the whole, since our marriage, my current income, though not expenditure from income & capital together, has been equal to or somewhat greater than yours. But my income that is independent

of current earning is small (& this means of course that my capital too is very limited) & it is unlikely that I could increase it much. However, we must talk over all this when you get back. I don't of course like my contribution to common expenditure being as small proportionately as it will necessarily be on our present standard of living, unless I draw on my capital at a rate which would exhaust it very rapidly. Indeed, I only mention this now because you said you didn't want, any more that I do, to seek work now purely for its financial reward. I am quite busy now with letters, & am seeing a number of people.

On 9 September Salter wrote to Lady Salter saying he had the previous day lunched with Aubrey Jones and dined with the Keith Josephs. He continued:

It is lovely to think of you being back so soon; & I will of course meet you on Sunday afternoon if your plans hold. I'm very well indeed & getting on well in every way. And all is well with the house. I am dining with Violet to-night. I have said I will run up to Ormskirk on Thursday next (17th), to meet the committee, staying with the Lumbys that night & returning the next morning.

As planned Lady Salter returned from Bavaria on 13 September and Salter met with the local Conservative Association on 17 September. Having apprised his Ormskirk supporters of his acceptance of a peerage, and hence of the need to schedule a by-election, an announcement was forthcoming. Salter had originally wished to sit once more and briefly in the Commons. However, with the reassembly of parliament scheduled for 20 October, his elevation to the Lords went ahead earlier, and the press carried the news on 30 September that, on the previous day, Queen Elizabeth II had approved the conferment of a barony on Salter. On 16 October he had an audience with the Queen where she officially conferred upon him "the name, style and title of Baron Salter of Kidlington."[445] On 21 October, introduced by Lords Sandford and Brand, Salter "took the oath and subscribed the roll" as the newest member of the House of Lords.[446]

When Churchill had offered Salter a peerage he noted that this would enable the latter to speak freely on a variety of subjects. There is no doubt that Salter relished this return to "independence" and from the outset took this very much to heart. In his maiden speech in the Lords on 5 November, he lauded the fact that "good management," for which he took a "modest" responsibility, and "good luck" had enabled the country to improve its balance of payments. He then turned to praise the recent efforts by the government to promote and develop the work of the OEEC and the European Payments Union. However, he also reaffirmed his long held view that a full customs union was "not possible in the immediate, or even foreseeable future" for Europe, still less for Britain dedicated to maintaining Imperial Preference. He believed OEEC represented a stage in the evolution of "a partial customs union" that in time would encompass Britain, Western Europe and the Commonwealth. His maiden speech was generously praised by his fellow peers as "remarkable" and "admirable and lucid."[447] His next interventions from 8 to 10 December ranged over topics such as the powers of the Tate Gallery and the National Gallery to dispose of works of art in their possession to encouraging the government to find replacements for the aging merchant fleet.[448] Much later, looking back at his entry into the House of Lords, Salter wrote, "I realized that my official life was at an end. The days of ministerial or official responsibility were over."[449]

Endnotes

1. Salter to Rowse, 2 Aug. 1945, Rowse Papers, EUL MS113/3/1/Corr.S.
2. Salter to Cecil, 8 Aug. 1945, Cecil Papers, ADD MSS 51113, vol. 43, fol. 119.
3. The Times, 4, 7 Aug. 1945.
4. The Times, 16 Aug. 1945.
5. H.C. Debs., vol. 413, 16 Aug. 1945, cols. 101-104, The Observer, 19 Aug. 1945.
6. "The United Nations and the Atomic Bomb," International Conciliation, no. 417(Jan.1946), 42.
7. H.C. Debs., vol. 413, 22 Aug. 1945, cols. 694-701.
8. H.C. Debs., vol. 413, 23 Aug. 1945, cols. 861-870, 878-879, 944-955. Salter had declined the position of assistant secretary general of the United Nations' Department of Economic Affairs. Trygve Lie, In the Cause of Peace: Seven Years with the United Nations (1954), 48.
9. The Observer, 26 Aug., 2 Sept. 1945.
10. The Times, 18 Sept. 1945.
11. Arthur Bullard to Mrs. Bagg, June 1913 [sic], 17 Dec. 1916, Bullard Papers, MC008.
12. Salter to Lamont, 26 Apr. 1945, Lamont Papers, 129-14, 1937-1947, Perkins to Salter and Lady Salter, 4 May 1945, Perkins Papers, Personal "S".
13. http://www.britishlistedbuildings.co.uk/en-203797-west-house-35-chelsea.
14. Joyce Newton Thompson, The Story of a House (Cape Town, 1968), 129.
15. "The United Nations and the Atomic Bomb," International Conciliation, no. 417(Jan.1946), 40-48, The Times, 9 Oct. 1945, The Manchester Guardian, 9 Oct. 1945, "Importance of the Moscow Meeting," The Listener, 34(20 Dec. 1945), 723.

16. The Times, 10, 22, 25, 26 Oct. 1945, Record of a Meeting, 25 Oct. 1945, Documents on British Policy Overseas, Series 1, vol. 5, M.E. Pelly and H.J. Yasamee, eds., (1990), 273-279.
17. H.C.Debs., vol. 414, 26 Oct. 1945, cols. 2351-2454. In response to the notice of Salter's motion, Smith had prepared a cabinet paper on the subject. See "Food for Europe," C.P. (45)237, 22 Oct. 1945, NA-UK, CAB129/3. Salter, Memoirs, 299, admits he erred with regard to wheat stocks which were in fact somewhat depleted.
18. The Times, 29 Oct. 1945.
19. Letter to the editor, The Spectator, 175(9 Nov. 1945), 436.
20. "The Relief of Europe," Contemporary Review, 168(Nov.1945), 257-261.
21. The Manchester Guardian, 27 Nov. 1945.
22. H.C. Debs., vol. 415, 30 Oct. 1945, cols. 340-342.
23. The Economist, 99(3 Nov. 1945), 618-620, 623.
24. H.C. Debs., vol. 415, 5 Nov. 1945, cols. 1012-1013.
25. H.C. Debs., vol. 414, 26 Oct. 1945, col. 2380.
26. H.C. Debs., vol. 415, 16 Nov. 1945, cols. 2570-2616.
27. H.C. Debs., vol. 416, 23 Nov. 1945, cols. 787-792, 844, The Manchester Guardian, 29 Nov. 1945. In the New Year, Salter added his support to a proposal to set up a National Research Development Corporation to fund new scientific discoveries likely to lead to the creation of new industries. It found no favour with the government. The Manchester Guardian, 27 Feb. 1946, The Economist, 150(9 Mar. 1946), 384.
28. See H.C. Debs., vol. 416, 5 Dec. 1945, cols. 2317-2318, H.C. Debs., vol. 417, 19 Dec. 1945, col. 1473.
29. Salter to Noel-Baker, 2 Jan. 1946, Noel-Baker to Salter, 23 Jan. 1946, NA-UK, FO371/58076, UR459/154/850.
30. Minute, C. Crowe, 21 Jan. 1946, NA-UK, FO371/57933, UR785/247/53, minute, K. McGregor, 21 Jan. 1946, NA-UK, FO371/57933, UR785/241/53.
31. H.C. Debs., vol. 418, 4 Feb. 1946, cols. 1351-1352.
32. The Economist, 150(26 Jan. 1946), 124-125.
33. H.C. Debs., vol. 418, 5 Feb. 1946, col. 1541, The Times, 7 Feb. 1946.
34. H.C. Debs., vol. 418, 7 Feb. 1946, cols. 1927-1933, The Economist, 150(16 Feb. 1946), 250-251, Beveridge to Salter, 18 Feb. 1946, Beveridge Papers, BEV2B/45/5.
35. H.C. Debs., vol. 423, 23 May 1946, cols. 579, 583-585, 590.
36. "The Summing Up," in The Way Ahead: The Strange Case of the Friendly Societies, John A. Lincoln, ed., (1946), 66-68, The Times, 1 July 1946.
37. H.C. Debs., vol. 419, 14 Feb. 1946, cols. 563, 583, 595-607.

38. "The Hunger of the World," The Observer, 17 Feb. 1946. The idea of a Supreme Economic Council received support in the US. See The Washington Post, 13 Mar. 1946.
39. H.C. Debs., vol. 419, 20 Feb. 1946, cols. 1135-1136, vol. 420, 4 Mar. 1946, col. 35, vol. 421, 25 Mar. 1946, col. 40.
40. Minutes, Cabinet Meeting 29(46), 1 Apr. 1946, NA-UK, CAB128/5, "Draft White Paper on the World Food Shortage," C.P. (46)1271 Apr. 1946, NA-UK, CAB129/8, The World Food Shortage, April 1946, Cmd. 6785, Salter Papers, File 16, European Relief, May 1946.
41. H.C.Debs., vol. 421, 4 Apr. 1946, cols. 1402-1504.
42. "The Shadow of World Famine," The Listener, 35(11 Apr. 1946), 453-454, "Can We Prevent Famine," Picture Post, 4 May 1946, The Times, 16 Apr. 1946. The Economist, 150(20 Apr. 1946), 629, endorsed Salter's proposal.
43. H.C. Debs., vol. 422, 9 May 1946, col. 1224.
44. British Security: A Report by a Chatham House Study Group (1946), 7-176.
45. H.C.Debs., vol. 423, 24 May 1946, cols. 724-727.
46. Hubert Howard to Salter, 11 April 1946, RIIA Papers, "The Control of Nuclear Energy and the Development of International Relations, 21 Mar. 1947," Sir Charles Webster Papers, 19/13, AE51, BLPES, London, reprinted in Atomic Energy: Its International Implications (1948), 91-101.
47. "The Atomic Bomb and World Security: A Discussion Between Sir Arthur Salter and Sir George Thomson," The Listener, 36(1 Aug. 1946), 131-132.
48. Salter, Memoirs, 300-301, Salter, Slave of the Lamp, 211-213. Both accounts are chronologically inaccurate.
49. Salter to Sir Orme Sargent, 2 Apr. 1946, NA-UK, FO371/57545, U3623/120/73.
50. "Diary, Visit to Germany, 12-20 May 1946," Salter to Lady Salter, 12, 14, 16 May 1946, Salter Papers, File 15, Diary of Visit to Nuremberg, May 12-20 1946.
51. H.C. Debs., vol. 430, 14 Nov. 1946, col. 315.
52. Salter to Sargent, 22 May 1946, NA-UK, FO371/57545, U3623/120/73.
53. H.C. Debs., vol. 423, 20 May 1946, col. 25, 23 May 1946, col. 547, 3 June 1946, col. 1618, 7 June 1946, col. 2387, letter to the editor, The Manchester Guardian, 7 June 1946. He returned to the subject in the Commons on 18 July. H.C. Debs., vol. 425, 18 July 1946, col. 1380.
54. H.C. Debs., vol. 419, 14 Feb. 1946, col. 598, H.C.Debs., vol. 423, 22 May 1946, col. 328.
55. "Famine and the Planners," The Observer, 26 May 1946.
56. The Times, 28 May 1946.

57. H.C. Debs., vol. 423, 31 May 1946, cols. 1527-1535, The Times, 1 June 1946, Salter, Memoirs, 305-308.
58. See e.g., H.C. Debs., vol. 424, 18, June 1946, col. 60.
59. The Times, 29 June 1946.
60. H.C. Debs., vol. 424, 3 July 1946, cols. 2171-2237.
61. H.C. Debs., vol. 425, 18 July 1946, cols. 1522-1528, Second Review of the World Food Shortage, July 1946, Cmd. 6879, Salter Papers, File 16, European Relief, May 1946.
62. Noel-Baker to Salter, 1 Aug. 1946, NA-UK, FO371/57768, WR1871/32/48, Salter to Noel-Baker, 14 Aug. 1946, NA-UK, FO371/57768, WR2360/32/48. It was not until 15 October that Salter was informed that what was in effect a temporary "freezing order" had been lifted. See Hector McNeil to Salter, 15 Oct. 1946, NA-UK, FO371/57770, WR2615/32/48.
63. Salter to James Langham, 27 Aug. 1946, BBC WAC, R. Cont. 1, Salter Talks, File 1, 1926-1948.
64. H.C. Debs., vol. 427, 18 Oct. 1946, cols. 1235-1236. Salter made the same point during a debate on 9 December regarding the Exchange Control Bill. H.C. Debs., vol. 431, 9 Dec. 1946, cols. 802, 805, 893-899.
65. H.C. Debs., vol. 427, 21 Oct. 1946, col. 1302.
66. H.C. Debs., vol. 430, 14 Nov. 1946, cols. 312-321, 18 Nov. 1946, col. 24.
67. H.C. Debs., vol. 430, 20 Nov. 1946, col. 883, vol. 431, 17 Dec. 1946, cols. 1808, 1815, 1846, 18 Dec. 1946, cols. 2012-2021, 2071.
68. Salter to Lamont, 5 Dec. 1946, Lamont Papers, 1 29-14, 1937-47.
69. Salter to Churchill, 7 Dec. 1946, Churchill to Salter, 11 Dec. 1946, Salter Papers, File 17, Correspondence: Salter-Churchill, 1946-1957, Salter to Churchill, 28 Oct. 1947, Churchill Papers, CHUR 2/375.
70. "'L.G': An Appreciation," The Spectator, 174(1945), 287-288, "Maynard Keynes," The Spectator, 176(1946), 421-422.
71. Geoffrey Faber to Spencer Curtis Brown, 16 Jan., 20 Feb. 1947, Brown to Faber, 8, 27 Jan., 1947, Salter to Faber, 7 Feb. 1947, Margaret Sweeting to Salter, 27 Feb. 1947, Faber and Faber Ltd Papers, London.
72. Personality in Politics: Studies of Contemporary Statesmen (1947), 9-253.
73. The Times, 17 Jan. 1947. Among the members were Amery, Boothby, Curtis, Layton, J.J. Mallon and Gilbert Murray.
74. Curtis to Salter, 22 Jan. 1947, Curtis Papers MSS 40, fol. 98.
75. The Times, 6 Feb. 1947, "The Role of the Dominions in Imperial Policy," United Empire: Journal of the Royal Empire Society, 38(Mar.-Apr. 1947), 77-80. Lionel

Curtis thought so highly of Salter's admission that Britain could no longer afford to defend the Commonwealth as a whole, that he published the speech in pamphlet form, with a Preface that stated the speech had opened "a new epoch." Salter also contributed to a discussion the Society held on 7 May on US foreign policy. See United Empire: Journal of the Royal Empire Society, 38(July-Aug. 1947), 179-180.

76. H.C. Debs., vol. 432, 5 Feb. 1947, cols. 1838-1845.
77. The Manchester Guardian, 8 Feb. 1947.
78. H.C.Debs., vol. 433, 14 Feb. 1947, cols. 761-764.
79. The Times, 21 Feb. 1947.
80. H.C. Debs., vol. 433, 26 Feb. 1947, cols. 2135-2146.
81. On Salter's intervention, see e.g., The Manchester Guardian, 12 Feb. 1947, The Financial Times, 12, 19, 21, 25 Feb. 1947, The Economist, 152(15, 22 Feb. 1947), 30-31, 307.
82. H.C. Debs., vol. 434, 3 Mar. 1947, cols. 93-98, Minutes, Cabinet Meeting 28 (47), 13 Mar. 1947, NA-UK, CAB128/9.
83. Salter, Memoirs, 210, H.C. Debs., vol. 434, 8 Mar. 1947, cols. 744-749. For Salter's further reflections on India, see "Talking About India No. 8," 22 May 1947, and "Between Ourselves," 16 Apr. 1949, BBC WAC, Salter Scripts.
84. H.C. Debs., vol. 435, 19 Mar. 1947, cols. 472-478.
85. H.C. Debs., vol. 436, 16 Apr. 1947, col. 214.
86. H.C. Debs., vol. 436, 22 Apr. 1947, cols. 844, 847-852, The Times, 23 Apr. 1947.
87. H.C. Debs., vol. 436, 23 Apr. 1947, col. 117, 24 Apr. 1947, col. 128, 25 Apr. 1947, cols. 1420- 1421, 1426-1429, 1465, 1489-1492, The Sunday Times, 4 May 1947.
88. See The Economist, 152(29 Mar. 1947), 12, The Times, 28 Apr. 1947.
89. H.C. Debs., vol. 436, 29 Apr. 1947, cols. 1822-1824, 1854-1858, 30 Apr. 1947, cols. 1977-1978, 2035-2036, 2043, The Financial Post, 1 May 1947.
90. H.C. Debs., vol. 437, 5 May 1947, cols. 37, 39, 70-78, 89-90.
91. The Manchester Guardian, 16 May 1947. The same issue was addressed in The Sunday Times, 14 Dec. 1947.
92. H.C. Debs., vol. 437, 6 May 1947, col. 340, 12 May 1947, col. 1073, 22 May 1947, cols. 2557-2558, 23 May 1947, col. 2767.
93. H.C. Debs., vol. 419, 26 Feb. 1946, col. 1716, vol. 437, 23 May 1947, cols. 2701, 2718.
94. H.C. Debs., vol. 438, 10 June 1947, cols. 841-842.
95. H.C. Debs., vol. 438, 11 June 1947, col. 1057, H.C. Debs., vol. 458, 19 Nov. 1948, cols. 778-781.

96. Letter to the editor, The Times, 5 June 1947.
97. The Sunday Times, 15 June 1947.
98. H.C. Debs., vol. 438, 19 June 1947, cols. 2241-2246, 2332.
99. The Observer, 22 June 1947.
100. "Mr. Marshall's Policy For Reconstruction in Europe," 1 July 1947, RIIA Papers.
101. H.C. Debs., vol. 446, 29 Jan. 1948, col. 1283.
102. H.C. Debs., vol. 439, 3 July 1947, cols. 1553, 1577-1585, 1632.
103. The Economist, 153(12 July 1947), 75-76.
104. Salter to Archie Gordon, 15 May 1947, BBC WAC R Cont. 1 Talks File 1, 1926-1948, The New York Times, 16, 23 July 1947.
105. The Times, 17 Sept. 1947, International Bank for Reconstruction and Redevelopment, Second Annual Meeting of the Board of Governors, London, September 11-17, 1947 (Washington, DC, 1947), 18, 21, The Washington Post, 29 June 1948.
106. Note by Salter, 15 Sept. 1948, encl. in M.M. Mendels to Herbert Hoover, 20 Sept. 1948, Hoover Papers.
107. Note by Salter, 25 Feb. 1948, encl. in Mendels to Hoover, 18 Apr. 1949, Hoover Papers.
108. International Bank for Reconstruction and Redevelopment, Third Annual Report to the Board of Governors, 1947-1948 (Washington, DC, 1948), 31, "First Advisory Council Meeting," World Bank Archives, http://go.worldbank.org/VABY48FC90, International Bank for Reconstruction and Redevelopment, Fourth Annual Report to the Board of Governors, 1948-1949 (Washington, DC, 1949), 39.
109. International Bank for Reconstruction and Redevelopment, Fourth Annual Meeting of the Board of Governors, September 13-16, 1949, (Washington, DC, 1949), 18-19, 24.
110. "The International Bank and How It Works," The Rotarian, 74(Apr. 1949), 10-12, Salter, Memoirs, 335-336.
111. The Manchester Guardian, 20, 27 Sept., 1, 7 Oct. 1947, A.P. Wadsworth to Salter, 11 Dec. 1947, The Guardian Archive, B/523/6.
112. Salter to Raymond B. Fosdick, 4 Feb. 1948, Fosdick Papers, Box 2.
113. Extracts from reviews of Personality in Politics, Faber and Faber Papers, 1947-1948.
114. The Times Literary Supplement, 6, 13, 20, 27, Dec. 1947, 624, 645, 661, 675, 3 Jan. 1948, 9.
115. Saturday Review of Literature, 31(31 July 1948), 434.

116. Salter to J.B. Condliffe, 9 May 1949, J.B. Condliffe Papers, BANC MSS C-B 901, Bancroft Library, University of California, Berkeley, CA.
117. H.C.Debs., vol. 443, 27, 29 Oct. 1947, cols. 533, 1010, The Times, 2 Jan. 1948, letter to the editor, The Times, 20 Mar. 1948.
118. H.C. Debs., vol. 443, 3 Nov. 1947, col. 1420.
119. Lady Salter to Winant, 16 June 1946, 20 Jan. 1947, Winant to Lady Salter, 24 June 1946, Winant Papers, 248, Sa 1946-1947.
120. Winant to Salter, 5 Feb. 1947, Winant Papers, 248, Sa 1946-1947, Bernard Bellush, He Walked Alone: A Biography of John Gilbert Winant (The Hague, 1968), 226-227.
121. Winant, A Letter from Grosvenor Square, 180-183, Interview with Salter, 9 July 1951, Bernard Bellush Papers, Franklin D. Roosevelt Papers, Hyde Park, NY.
122. H.C. Debs., vol. 445, 2 Dec. 2011, cols. 318-321, 3 Dec. 1947, cols., 418-423, The Manchester Guardian, 4 Dec. 1947, The Financial Times, 4 Dec. 1947.
123. H.C. Debs., vol. 445, 4 Dec. 1947, cols. 594-608, 10 Dec. 1947, col. 1089.
124. H.C. Debs., vol. 446, 29 Jan. 1948, cols. 1225-1284, The Manchester Guardian, 30 Jan. 1948.
125. "Great Britain's Dollar Problem," The Listener, 39(19 Feb. 1948), 283-285.
126. The Times, 31 Jan. 1948. The constituencies were Cambridge, Combined English Universities, London, Oxford, Queen's Belfast, Scottish Universities and Wales.
127. Salter to Wadsworth, 10 Feb. 1948, The Guardian Archive, B/523/6. On 14 Feb. 1948 The Manchester Guardian carried a very critical editorial on the issue, based on Salter's letter to Wadsworth.
128. H.C. Debs., vol. 447, 12 Feb. 1948, cols. 574-576.
129. The Times, 17 Feb. 1948, H.C. Debs., vol. 447, 16 Feb. 1948, cols. 864, 919-927.
130. H.C. Debs., vol. 447, 17 Feb. 1948, cols. 1015-1016, 1117.
131. The Manchester Guardian, 11 Mar. 1948.
132. H.C. Debs., vol. 448, 16 Mar. 1948, cols. 1896-1959.
133. The Times, 19 Mar. 1948, The Economist, 154(20 Mar. 1948), 448-449.
134. The Observer, 21 Mar. 1948.
135. Salter, Memoirs, 327-334.
136. Herbert, Independent Member, 397.
137. "Tribute," in Ruskin: Prophet of the Good Life, J. Howard Whitehouse, ed., (1948), 20-22. Salter again addressed the Ruskin Society on 8 Feb. 1950. The Times, 9 Feb. 1950.
138. Salter to Wadsworth, 6 Dec. 1947, The Guardian Archive, B/S23/3a-b.

139. See BBC WAC, R Cont 1, Salter Talks, Files 1 and 2, 1926-1970 for details of his numerous contributions to BBC broadcasts.
140. Salter to C.J. Curran, 1 Sept. 1949, BBC RAC, R Cont 1, Salter Talks File II 1949-1970.
141. "Introduction, The Impact of Broadcasting on Great Britain's Life and Outlook – I," The B.B.C. Quarterly, 3(Apr. 1948), 1-7, "Concluding Comments, The Impact of Broadcasting on Great Britain's Life and Outlook – II," The B.B.C. Quarterly, 3(July 1948), 103-108.
142. The Times, 23 Dec. 1947, H.C. Debs., vol. 448, 22 Mar. 1948, cols., 2609-2613, 2623.
143. H.C. Debs., vol. 449, 8 Apr. 1948, cols. 389, 407-415.
144. Letters to the editor, The Times, 14 Apr., 28 Apr. 1948.
145. The Times, 20 Jan. 1948.
146. The Times, 13 Mar. 1948, H.C. Debs., vol. 448, 18 Mar. 1948, cols. 2302-2303.
147. H.C. Debs., vol. 450, 5 May 1948, cols. 1335, 1351-1358.
148. The Times, 17 Apr. 1948, The Manchester Guardian, 17 Apr. 1948.
149. The Financial Times, 10 May 1948.
150. Salter to Wadsworth, 13 May 1948, The Guardian Archive, B/S23/7, The Manchester Guardian, 17 May 1948, "Economics and Peace," International Student Service Review, 3(1948), 14.
151. "Report from Britain," 10 May 1949, BBC WAC, Salter Scripts.
152. The Meaning of the Marshall Plan (1948), 3-19, revised and reprinted from The National Provincial Bank Review, no. 2(May 1948), 1-8, The Manchester Guardian, 5 Oct. 1948.
153. Salter to Hamilton Fish Armstrong, 31 March 1948, Hamilton Fish Armstrong Papers, MC002, Department of Rare Books and Special Collections, Princeton University Library, Princeton, NJ, Salter to Wadsworth, 13 May 1948, The Guardian Archive, B/S23/7.
154. H.C. Debs., vol. 451, 3 June 1948, cols.1255-1259, 1261, 1271-1272, 1279-1281.
155. The Observer, 13 June 1948.
156. H.C. Debs., vol. 452, 14 June 1948, cols. 185-193, 201.
157. The Times, 17, 18 June 1948, "Western Union," C.P. (48)162, 24 June, NA-UK, CAB129/28.
158. "Notes on the Proposed Assembly," n.d., encl. in R.W.G. Mackay, MP to Churchill, 27 June 1948, NA-UK, FO371/73096, Z5743/4416/72.
159. H.C. Debs., vol. 453, 5, 6 July 1948, cols. 61, 255, 293-301.

160. C.P. Mayhew to Mackay, 17 July 1948, NA-UK, FO371/73096, Z5743/4416/72, draft letter, Attlee to Churchill, encl. in Attlee to Bevin, 28 July 1948, NA-UK, FO371/73096, Z6439/4416/72.
161. The New York Times, 15 July 1948.
162. Salter to Stimson, 21 Sept. 1948, Stimson Papers.
163. The Times, 1 Nov. 1948.
164. H.C. Debs., vol. 457, 1 Nov. 1948, cols. 536-550. On Salter's evolving views on Labour economic policy, see "Questions of the Hour: Planning," 19 Feb. 1948, BBC WAC, Salter Scripts, "Maxims for Planners," The Listener, 39(4 Mar. 1948), 368-369.
165. The Financial Times, 2 Nov. 1948, The Manchester Guardian, 2 Nov. 1948.
166. Author's interview with Lord Salter, 5 May 1970.
167. The Times, 19 Nov. 1948.
168. H.C. Debs., vol. 458, 25 Nov. 1948, col. 1460.
169. The Financial Times, 10 Dec. 1948. For the aims of the Industrial Co-partnership Association, see The Times, 22 Apr. 1948.
170. "European Recovery: A Look Ahead," Foreign Affairs, 27(1949), 289-301.
171. See Cmd. Paper 7572, H.C. Debs., vol. 460, 27 Jan. 1949, cols. 1111-1123.
172. The Times, 4, 10 Feb. 1949.
173. See The Times, 21 May 1949.
174. H.C. Debs., vol. 463, 23 Mar. 1949, cols. 415-418.
175. The Times, 22 Mar. 1949.
176. H.C. Debs., vol. 463, 31 Mar. 1949, cols. 1501-1509, 1559, 1 Apr. 1949, cols. 1579-1667.
177. H.C. Debs., vol. 463, 7 Apr. 1949, cols. 2233, 2336, 11 Apr. 1949, col. 2511.
178. See H.C. Debs. vol. 464, 9 May 1949, cols.1502-1616.
179. R.G. Hawtrey, Western European Union, The Implications for the United Kingdom (1949).
180. "Western Union," 28 Apr. 1949, RIIA Papers.
181. H.C. Debs., vol. 464, 12 May 1949, col. 2129.
182. "Western Union," 28 Apr. 1949, RIIA Papers.
183. H.C. Debs., vol. 464, 5 May 1949, cols. 1280-1285, 1346-1347.
184. "The Best Route to Western Union," United Empire: Journal of the Royal Empire Society, 40(July-Aug. 1949), 195-199.
185. The Times, 26 May 1949, Salter to Murray, 30 May 1949, Murray Papers, vol. 370, ff. 189-192.
186. Curtis to Violet Markham, 9 July, 9 Aug., 15 Aug. 1949, Markham Papers, 25/73.
187. The New York Times, 14 July 1949.
188. Violet Markham Itinerary, Mackenzie King Papers, p. 605.

189. William M. Chadbourne to Herbert Hoover, 16 Aug. 1949, Hoover Papers.
190. "Notes on Devaluation," encl. in Salter to Churchill, 22 Sept. 1949, Churchill Papers, CHUR 2/91. Churchill declined Salter's offer to return at once by air to London. Salter to Churchill, 21 Sept., Churchill to Salter, 21 Sept. 1949, Churchill Papers, CHUR 2/85A.
191. H.C. Debs., vol. 468, 27 Oct. 1949, cols. 1576-1583. For further details on Salter's critique of the economy, see "The Economic State of the Nation, I-VI," 4 Nov.-10 Dec. 1949, BBC WAC, Salter Scripts
192. General Problem of the Dollar Shortage, Lecture on November 8, 1949, Institute of Bankers, (1949), 2-19. See also his "Prospects and Policy: Britain's Problem in Outline," National Provincial Bank Review, no. 11(Aug. 1950), 1-14.
193. Fish Armstrong to Salter, 24 Oct. 1949, Fish Armstrong Papers, MC002, 54/26, "After Devaluation: The Common Task," Foreign Affairs, 28(1950), 215-230.
194. Salter to Aldrich, 17 July, 21 Oct., 30 Nov.1949, Aldrich to Salter, 24 Oct. 21 Nov. 1949, Winthrop W. Aldrich Papers, 1949-1951, Box 199S, Baker Library, Harvard Business School, Boston, MA, Salter, Memoirs, 336.
195. Salter to Aldrich, 30 Nov. 1950, Aldrich to Salter, 13 Dec. 1950, Aldrich Papers, 1949-1951, Box 199S.
196. Salter to Aldrich, 10, 26, Jan.1950, Aldrich Papers, 1949-1951, Box 199S.
197. H.C. Debs., vol. 470, 1 Dec. 1949, cols. 1349, 1357, 1387, 1394-1404.
198. H.C. Debs., vol. 468, 27 Oct. 1949, col. 1583.
199. H.C. Debs., vol. 470, 1 Dec. 1949, cols. 1415-1416, 1421.
200. Salter to Aldrich, 30 Nov. 1949, Aldrich Papers, 1949-1951, Box 199S.
201. "The Changing Parliamentary System," Britain To-day, no. 159(July 1949), 8-14, The Manchester Guardian, 21 Jan. 1950, "Cabinet and Parliament," in Parliament: A Survey, Lord Campion, ed., (1952), 105-120. The latter resulted from a series of lectures offered at the University of London, 18 Jan.-22 Mar. 1950.
202. The Manchester Guardian, 4 Feb. 1950.
203. The Times, 2 Feb. 1950.
204. The Oxford Mail, 15 Feb. 1950.
205. The Sunday Times, 12 Feb. 1950.
206. Author's interview with Douglas Jay (Lord Jay), 20 June 1980.
207. The Times, 4 Feb. 1950.
208. Salter to Wadsworth, 13 Feb. 1950, The Guardian Archive, B/S23/8, The Manchester Guardian, 18 Feb. 1950. For Salter's further critiques of nationalization and the policies of a future Conservative government, see "The Crux of Nationalization," The Political Quarterly, 21(1950), 209-217, and "British Conservatism Today," The Yale Review, 41(Sept. 1951), 1-12.

209. The Times, 20 Feb. 1950.
210. Salter to Aldrich, 1 Mar., 23 Mar. 1950, Aldrich Papers, 1949-1951, Box 199S.
211. Salter to Churchill, 1 Dec. 1949, Churchill Papers, CHUR 2/176A. Copy in Salter Papers, File 17, Correspondence Salter-Churchill, 1946-1957.
212. Salter to Churchill, 27 Feb. 1950, Churchill to Salter 1 Mar. 1951, minutes by E.G. [sic], 28 Feb., 8 Sept. 1950, Churchill Papers, CHUR 2/90B. On 7 July 1950 Salter sent to Churchill, for the latter's war memoir, a copy of his note, "The American Shipping Achievement, Apr. 1941-June 1943," Churchill Papers, CHUR 4/263.
213. Salter Papers, File 30, Author's London Draft of Salter Biography.
214. Salter, Memoirs, 337-338.
215. See NA-UK, FO953/861 for the itinerary, etc.
216. The Times, 10 May 1950.
217. The Times, 16, 17 May 1950.
218. Salter to Curtis, 24 May 1950, MSS Curtis 61, fol. 127.
219. Curtis to Lt. Col. H. Nugent Head, 22 May 1950, MSS Curtis 61, ff. 120-121, Curtis to Salter, 13 June 1950, MSS Curtis 61, fol. 179.
220. Lionel Curtis, The Open Road to Freedom (Oxford, 1950), v-viii, Curtis to Salter, 20 June 1950, MSS Curtis 61, ff. 192-193, Salter to Curtis, 27 July 1950, MSS Curtis 62, ff. 37-38.
221. Salter to Aldrich, 7 July 1950, Aldrich Papers, 1949-1951, Box 199S.
222. Salter to Curtis, 21 Aug. 1950, Curtis to Salter, 23 Aug. 1950, MSS Curtis 62, ff. 80-81.
223. The Times, 18, 19, 21, 24, 25 Aug. 1950. On 12 April 1951 the Commons was informed that the government was already doing this stockpiling. See H.C. Debs., vol. 486, 12 Apr. 1951, col. 1199-1200.
224. Salter to Allen Dulles, 15 Aug. 1950, Allen Dulles Papers, Box 50, Folder 8, Princeton University Library, Princeton, NJ.
225. See e.g., Liddell Hart to Salter, 18 Aug. 1950, Salter to Liddell Hart, 21 Aug. 1950, Liddell Hart Papers, LH5/1.
226. The Financial Times, 12 Sept. 1950. He returned to the subject several months later. See The Financial Times, 21 Feb. 1951.
227. Salter to Curtis, 21 Sept. 1950, MSS Curtis 62, fol. 124, Curtis to Salter, 25 Sept. 1950, MSS Curtis 62, fol. 125.
228. Salter to Curtis, 28 Sept. 1950, MSS Curtis 64, fol. 151, Curtis to Salter, 3 Oct. 1950, MSS Curtis 64, fol. 152.
229. Salter to Curtis, n.d., MSS Curtis 62, fol. 97, Curtis to Salter, 29 Nov. 1950, MSS Curtis 63, fol. 148.

230. Curtis to Salter, 5, 8 Dec. 1950, encl., draft letter, MSS Curtis 63, ff. 193-195, 222, Salter to Curtis, 7 Dec. 1950, MSS Curtis 63, fol. 209.
231. See e.g., Salter to Curtis, 25 July 1951, MSS Curtis 67, fol. 82.
232. Salter to Aldrich, 27 Jan. 1950, and encl., "Foreign Investment," Aldrich to Salter, 2 Mar., 27 Mar. 1950, Aldrich Papers, 1949-1951, Box 199S.
233. Salter to Aldrich, 6 Apr. 1950, and encl., "Britain's Experience as a Creditor Nation," Aldrich Papers, 1949-1951, Box 199S.
234. Salter to Aldrich, 9, 14, 15 June 1950, Aldrich to Salter, 14,15 June 1950, Aldrich Papers, 1949-1951, Box 199S.
235. Memorandum by Arthur W. Page, 11 Sept. 1950, Salter to Adrich, 15 Nov. 1950, Aldrich Papers, 1949-1951, Box 199S.
236. Foreign Investment: Essays in International Finance, No. 12 (Princeton, NJ, 1951), 1-56.
237. Arthur M. Johnson, Winthrop W. Aldrich: Lawyer, Banker, Diplomat (Boston, 1968), 316-322, Salter to Aldrich, 25 Apr. 1951, Aldrich Papers, 1949-1951, Box 199S.
238. Salter to Aldrich, 25 Jan. 1951, Aldrich Papers, 1949-1951, Box 199S.
239. Salter, Memoirs, 338.
240. Churchill to Salter, 4 Dec. 1949, Salter to Churchill, 6 Dec. 1949, Salter Papers, File 17, Correspondence: Salter-Churchill, 1946-1947.
241. Salter, Memoirs, 338-339.
242. Salter to Curtis, 3 Feb. 1951, MSS Curtis, 60, ff. 124-126.
243. Salter to Churchill, 6 Feb. 1951, Churchill Papers, CHUR 2/90A, Churchill to Salter, 11 Feb. 1951, Salter to Churchill, 12 Feb. 1951, Salter Papers, File 18, Ormskirk By-Election, Feb.-Apr. 1951 and Election, 25 Oct. 1951.
244. Churchill to Henry Lumby, 11 Feb. 1951, Churchill Papers, CHUR 2/90A.
245. Lumby to Salter, 19 Feb., Salter to Lumby, 20 Feb. 1951, Salter Papers, File 18, Ormskirk By-Election, Feb.-Apr. 1951 and Election 25 Oct. 1951.
246. Salter to Aldrich, 3 Mar. 1951, Aldrich Papers, 1949-1951, Box 199S.
247. The Times, 3, 16, 19 Mar. 1951, The Manchester Guardian, 5, 12 Mar. 1951, Salter to Lumby, 23 Mar. 1951, Salter Papers, File 18, Ormskirk By-Election, Feb.-Apr. 1951 and Election, 25 Oct. 1951.
248. Salter to Churchill, 20, Mar. 1951, Salter Papers, File 18, Ormskirk By-Election, Feb.-Apr. 1951 and Election, 25 Oct. 1951, Woolton to Churchill, 20 Mar. 1951, Churchill Papers, CHUR 2/90B.
249. "Constituency Plan A," Salter Papers, File 18, Ormskirk By-Election, Feb.-Apr. 1951 and Election, 25 Oct. 1951.

250. Salter to Churchill, 25 Mar. 1951, Churchill Papers, CHUR 2/90AB, Churchill to Salter, 28 Mar. 1951, Salter Papers, File 18, Ormskirk By-Election, Feb.-Apr. 1951 and Election, 25 Oct. 1951, The Times, 29 Mar. 1951.
251. Salter to Churchill, 30 Mar. 1951, Churchill Papers, CHUR 2/90B.
252. "To the Electors of Ormskirk," Salter Papers, File 18, Ormskirk By-Election, Feb.-Apr. 1951 and Election, 25 Oct. 1951.
253. The Manchester Guardian, 31 Mar. 1951.
254. The Manchester Guardian, 30 Mar. 1951.
255. Churchill to Salter, 6 Apr. 1951, Churchill Papers, CHUR 2/90B, The Manchester Guardian, 7 Apr. 1951.
256. Lady Salter to Rowse, 28 Apr. 1951, Rowse Papers, EUL MS113/3/1/Corr.S.
257. Salter to Amery, 9 Apr. 1951, Amery Papers, AMEL1/7/63.
258. Salter to Rowse, 30 Apr. 1951, Rowse Papers, EUL MS113/3/1/Corr.S.
259. H.C. Debs., vol. 486, 9 Apr. 1951, col. 660, Salter, Memoirs, 339.
260. H.C. Debs., vol. 486, 12 Apr. 1951, cols. 1199-1200, 1204, 1233-1248, 1281-1282, 1301-1302, 1308, The Times, 13 Apr. 1951. Salter added further analysis in The Sunday Times, 22 Apr. 1951.
261. See H.C. Debs., vol. 486, 12 Apr. 1951, cols. 1199-1200.
262. H.C. Debs., vol. 486, 20 Apr. 1951, cols. 2156-2161.
263. H.C. Debs., vol. 487, 27 Apr. 1951, cols. 719-722, 734, 769.
264. Salter to Perkins, 25 Apr. 1951, Perkins Papers, Personal "S".
265. Salter to Aldrich, 25 Apr. 1951, Aldrich Papers, 1949-1951, Box 199S.
266. "Exports to China, Notes on the Facts," in Salter to Churchill, 9 May 1951, Churchill Papers, CHUR 2/117A, Churchill to Salter, 14 May 1951, Salter Papers, File 17, Correspondence: Salter-Churchill, 1946-1957.
267. The Times, 2 June 1951.
268. H.C. Debs., vol. 488, 6 June 1951, cols. 1096-1107, 1157-1158.
269. H.C. Debs., vol. 488, 8 June 1951, cols. 1440, 1453-1460, 1481-1483, vol. 489, 3 July 1951, cols. 2202-2226.
270. H.C. Debs., vol. 489, 3 July 1951, col. 2149.
271. H.C. Debs., vol. 491, 26 July 1951, cols. 756-765, 766-767.
272. The Economist, 161(11 Aug. 1951), 326-327.
273. Salter to Churchill, 21 Sept. 1951, Churchill Papers, CHUR 2/117A.
274. See e.g., The Times, 15, 18 Oct. 1951.
275. "To the Electors of Ormskirk," Salter Papers, File 18, Ormskirk By-Election, Feb.-Apr. 1951 and Election, 25 Oct. 1951.
276. Salter to Aldrich, 30 Oct. 1951, Aldrich Papers, 1949-1951, Box 199S.

277. Salter, Memoirs, 339, Salter, Slave of the Lamp, 216, Salter to Aldrich, 16 Nov. 1951, Aldrich Papers, 1949-1951, Box 199S. The office had been created by the Labour government on 1 Mar. 1950 and was first filled by Gaitskell. See "Note for Record," 3 Mar. 1950, NA-UK, T199/208.
278. Lord Butler, The Art of the Possible (1971), 156.
279. The Economist, 161(3 Nov. 1951), 1014-1015, The Manchester Guardian, 1 Nov. 1951.
280. The Times, 6 Nov. 1951.
281. Lord Moran Churchill, Taken from the Diaries of Lord Moran: The Struggle for Survival (1966), 497.
282. Author's interview with Aubrey Jones, 5 June 1980.
283. Cabinet Secretary's Notebook, 2 Nov. 1951, NA-UK, CAB195/10.
284. H.C. Debs., vol. 493, 7 Nov. 1951, cols. 191-306, vol. 494, 22, Nov. 1951, col. 80, 27 Nov. 1951 cols. 1110-1111, entries of 5, 7 Nov. 1952, The Robert Hall Diaries, 1947-1953, Alec Cairncross, ed., (1989), 177-178.
285. The Times, 10, 16 Nov. 1951, The Times, 10 Nov. 1951.
286. H.C. Debs., vol. 494, 21 Nov. 1951, cols. 425-430, 469-471.
287. Economic Policy Committee, 21 Nov. 1951, E.A. (51)1, NA-UK CAB21/5001.
288. The Times, 23 Nov. 1951.
289. H.C. Debs., vol. 494, 23 Nov. 1951, cols. 739-835, 27 Nov. 1951, cols.1112-1114.
290. H.C. Debs., vol. 494, 28 Nov. 1951, cols. 1678-1679.
291. H.C.Debs., vol. 494, 30 Nov. 1951, col. 1981, The Times, 1 Dec. 1951.
292. Entry of 29 Nov. 1952, Robert Hall Diaries, 1947-1953, 185.
293. John Boyd-Carpenter to the author, 25 June, 17 July 1979, author's archive.
294. Foreign Office to Strasbourg, 19 Nov. 1951, NA-UK, FO371/94420, M584/161, Strasbourg to Foreign Office, 24 Nov. 1951, NA-UK, FO371/94420, M584/164.
295. Minute by E.A. Berthoud, 21 Nov. 1951, NA-UK, FO371/94421, M584/175, T.W. Garvey to I. Radice, 23 Nov. 1951, NA-UK, FO371/94420, M584/167.
296. Minute by Berthoud, 29 Nov. 1951 NA-UK, FO371/94421, M584/176, minute by Berthoud, 30 Nov. 1951, NA-UK, FO371/94421, M584/181.
297. "Address by Salter," 5 Dec. 1951, NA-UK, FO371/94421, M584/188, The Times, 6 Dec. 1951.
298. Consul General, Strasbourg, to Foreign Office, 6 Dec. 1951, NA-UK, FO371/94421, M584/188, The Manchester Guardian, 7 Dec. 1951.
299. Salter, Memoirs, 343.
300. "Sterling Area Policy: Report of a Confidential Chatham House Study Group," 4 Jan. 1952, RIIA Papers, Salter, Slave of the Lamp, 216, 219-220, John Fforde,

The Bank of England and Public Policy, 1941-1958 (1992), 426-427. The Study Group included Crowther, Macadam and Professor Lionel Robbins of the London School of Economics.

301. Minutes, Preliminary Meeting of Officials, 8 Jan. 1952, F.M.(O)(52), NA-UK, T236/3067.
302. Minutes, Economic Policy Committee, Sub-Committee on the Economic Situation, 10 Jan. 1952, E.A.(E)(52) 1st Meeting, NA-UK, CAB134/856.
303. Memorandum by Butler, Commonwealth Finance Ministers Meeting, Cabinet Paper [CP] 3(52), 5 Jan. 1952, NA-UK, CAB129/49.
304. Minutes, Cabinet Meeting 2(52), 10 Jan. 1952, NA-UK, CAB128/24. That same day, during a meeting of officials preparing for the forthcoming Commonwealth Finance Ministers meeting, convertibility was discussed as a possible antidote to "the chronic nature of the deficit." Minutes, Preliminary Meeting of Officials, 10 Jan. 1952, F.M.(O)(52), NA-UK, T236/3067.
305. Memorandum by Butler, Commonwealth Finance Ministers Meeting, CP 3(52), 5 Jan. 1952, NA-UK, CAB129/49, Minutes, Meeting of Commonwealth Finance Ministers, 15 Jan. 1952, F.M.(52), NA-UK, T236/3067.
306. Minutes, Meeting of Commonwealth Finance Ministers, 18 Jan. 1952, F.M.(52), NA-UK, T236/3067.
307. Minutes, Meeting of Commonwealth Finance Ministers, 21 Jan. 1952, F.M.(52), NA-UK, T236/3067, The Times, 22 Jan. 1952.
308. Minutes, Cabinet Meeting 4(52), 17 Jan. 1952, NA-UK, CAB128/24.
309. Minutes, Cabinet Meetings 5(52), 22 Jan., 6(52) 24 Jan. 1952, NA-UK, CAB128/24, Memorandum by Butler, The Economic Situation, CP 8(52), 19 Jan. 1952, NA-UK, CAB129/49.
310. H.C. Debs., vol. 495, 29 Jan. 1952, cols. 40-48.
311. H.C. Debs., vol. 495, 30 Jan. 1952, cols. 210-221.
312. F.M.(C)(52)1, Meeting of Working Party on Convertibility, 23 Jan. 1952, NA-UK, T230/217. The minutes can also be found in NA-UK, T236/3069.
313. Memorandum by Salter, "Some General Notes on Convertibility," 24 Jan. 1952, NA-UK, T230/217. The Working Party included British departmental representatives and Commonwealth experts from Australia, New Zealand, South Africa, India, Pakistan, Ceylon and Southern Rhodesia. The Canadian representative, not a member of the sterling area, was present as an observer.
314. F.M.(C)(52)3 (Final), Working Party on Convertibility and Related Problems, Interim Report, 11 Feb. 1952, NA-UK, T230/217.
315. Salter to Butler, 19 Feb. 1952, minute by Butler, 19 Feb. 1952, NA-UK, T236/3069.

316. F.M.(C)(52)4, Communique, 8 Feb. 1952. NA-UK, T236/3069, The Times, 20 Feb. 1952, The Financial Times, 13 May 1952.
317. H.C. Debs., vol. 496, 22 Feb. 1952, cols. 567-570, 642-657.
318. The name Robot may have been derived from the names of the three main proponents: Sir Leslie **Ro**wan, head of the Overseas Finance Division of the Treasury, Sir George **Bol**ton, an executive director of the Bank of England, and Richard W.B. 'O**tt**o' Clarke. See Edmund Dell, The Chancellors: A History of the Chancellors of the Exchequer, 1945-90 (1996), 166-167.
319. Memorandum, "Convertibility," 25 Jan. 1952, NA-UK, T236/3249, Cobbold to Butler, 13 Feb. 1952, NA-UK, T236/3240. See also minute by Clarke, "E.S.P.: Causes and Consequences," 26 Feb. 1952, NA-UK, T236/3241.
320. Churchill to Eden, 21 Feb. 1952, NA-UK, PREM11/137.
321. Minute, Bridges to Butler, 26 Feb. 1952, NA-UK, T236/3241. The phrase "Bank scheme" appeared in that minute.
322. Draft Memorandum by Butler,"External Action," 26 Feb. 1952, NA-UK, T236/3241. This 17 page memorandum provided a very detailed rationale for Robot.
323. Minute, Hall, "External Action," 23 Feb. 1952, Plowden to Butler, 25 Feb. 1952, Plowden, "External Action," 26 Feb. 1952, minute, Plowden to Butler, 27 Feb. 1952, Salter Papers, File 19, "Robot," Top Secret, Jan.- Dec. 1952, Hall, "Note For Record," 4 Mar. 1952, NA-UK, T236/3245.
324. Entries of 20, 29 Feb. 1952, Robert Hall Diaries, 1947-1953, 205-206, Edwin Plowden, An Industrialist in the Treasury: The Post-War Years (1989), 149.
325. Notes of a Meeting of Ministers Held at 10 Downing Street, 27 Feb. 1952, NA-UK, T236/3241.
326. Memorandum by Salter to Butler, "External Action," 28 Feb. 1952, Salter Papers, File 19, "Robot" – Top Secret, Jan.-Dec. 1952.
327. Memorandum by Butler, "An Alternative Plan," 28 Feb. 1952, NA-UK, T236/3241.
328. Minutes, Cabinet Meeting, 28(52), 29 Feb. 1952, CAB128/24. The secrecy was urged upon Churchill by Sir Norman Brook, the Cabinet Secretary. See minute, Brook to Churchill, 27 Feb. 1952, NA-UK, PREM11/138.
329. Minutes, Cabinet Meeting, Confidential Annex, 28, 29 Feb. 1952, NA-UK, CAB128/40, Secretary's Notebooks, Minutes, Cabinet Meeting 23(52), 28 Feb. 1952, Cabinet Meeting 24(52), 29 Feb. 1952, NA-UK, CAB195/10, Plowden, An Industrialist in the Treasury, 144.
330. Hall, "Note For Record," 4 Mar. 1952, NA-UK, T236/3245.
331. Entry of 4 Mar. 1952, Robert Hall Diaries, 1947-1953, 206.

332. "The B Plan, Personal Note as to Reasons for Opposing Adoption and Announcement with Budget," 4 Mar. 1952, Salter Papers, File 19, "Robot" – Top Secret, Jan.-Dec. 1952.
333. Minutes, Cabinet Meeting 28(52), 10 Mar. 1952, NA-UK, CAB128/24.
334. H.C. Debs., vol. 497, 12 Mar. 1952, cols. 1495-1508.
335. The Manchester Guardian, 13 Mar. 1952.
336. "Defence of the Budget," 24 Mar. 1952, NA-UK, T171/423.
337. The Daily Herald, 21 Mar. 1952.
338. Butler, "Textile Industry," CP 117(52), 7 Apr. 1952, NA-UK, CAB129/51, Lord Woolton, "Reorganization of Road and Rail Transport," CP 83(52, 20 Mar. 1952, NA-UK, CAB129/50, Minutes, Cabinet Meeting 33(52), 25 Mar. 1952, NA-UK, CAB128/24, "Transport Bill," CP 204(52), 19 June 1952, NA-UK, CAB129/53.
339. The Financial Times, 28 Mar. 1952.
340. The Financial Times, 28 Mar. 1952, The Times, 27, 29, 31 Mar. 1952, H.C. Debs., vol. 502, 12 June 1952, col. 43.
341. See H.C. Debs., vol. 497, 17 Mar. 1952, cols. 1932-2062.
342. Memorandum by Clarke, 11 Mar. 1953, NA-UK, T236/3241.
343. Cherwell to Churchill, 18 Mar. 1952, NA-UK, PREM11/137.
344. H.C. Debs., vol. 499, 24 Apr. 1952, col. 30.
345. "The Balance of Payments Position," CP 111(52), 9 Apr. 1952, NA-UK, CAB129/51.
346. Rowan to Bridges, 1 May 1952, memorandum by Sir Herbert Brittain,"ROBOT – Interim Measures," n.d., Salter Papers, File 19, "Robot" – Top Secret, Jan.-Dec. 1952.
347. See memorandum by Rowan, "ROBOT – Discussion with the Commonwealth," 25 Apr. 1952, Salter Papers, File 19, "Robot" – Top Secret, Jan.-Dec. 1952.
348. Minute, Salter to Butler, 3 May 1952, Salter Papers, File 19, "Robot" – Top Secret, Jan.-Dec. 1952. Also in NA-UK, T236/3243.
349. Rowan to Bridges, 29 Apr. 1952, Salter Papers, File 19, "Robot" – Top Secret, Jan.-Dec. 1952. Also in NA-UK, T236/3243.
350. Minute, Salter to Butler, "Robot – Next Steps," 6 May 1952, NA-UK, T236/3243.
351. See Hall, "External Sterling Plan, Note on Brief for Mr. Menzies," 27 May 1952, Salter Papers, File 19, "Robot" – Top Secret, Jan.-Dec. 1952.
352. See The Times, 26, 27, 28 May, 6, 10 June 1952, Minutes, Cabinet Meeting, 60(52), 17 June 1952, NA-UK, CAB128/25.
353. The Financial Times, 29 May 1952.
354. H.C. Debs., vol. 501, 29 May 1952, cols. 187-188.
355. Fforde, The Bank of England and Public Policy, 463, 467.

356. Minutes, Cabinet Meeting 59(52),12 June 1952, NA-UK, CAB125/25.
357. See memoranda Plowden to Butler, 24 June 1952, Hall to Butler, 25 June 1952, Salter Papers, File 19, "Robot" – Top Secret, Jan.-Dec. 1952.
358. "Manuscript Note on Timing of Robot," June 1952, Salter Papers, File 19, "Robot" – Top Secret, Jan.-Dec. 1952.
359. Minute, Salter to Butler, 24 June 1952, Salter Papers, File 19, "Robot" – Top Secret, Jan.-Dec. 1952. For Butler's annotations, see the copy of this minute in NA-UK, T236/3244.
360. Entry of 1 July 1952, Robert Hall Diaries, 1947-1953, 233.
361. Clarke to Rowan, "Questions on Robot," 28 June 1952, NA-UK, T236/3244.
362. Memorandum by Butler, "External Financial Policy," 28 June 1952, CP 217(52, NA-UK, CAB129/53.
363. Memorandum by Cherwell, "External Financial Policy," 30 June 1952, CP 221(52), NA-UK, CAB129/53.
364. "Robot – Summary," 27 June 1952, "Robot – Summary of Issues," 30 June 1952, Salter Papers, File 19, "Robot" – Top Secret, Jan.-Dec. 1952. The latter paper can also be found in NA-UK, T236/3244. It is not evident what circulation these two papers had. In his thinking, Salter was assisted by two memoranda from Professor Lionel Robbins. See "Notes on a Certain Plan and Suggestions for Alternative Actions," Salter Papers, File 19, "Robot" – Top Secret, Jan.-Dec. 1952.
365. Diary entry, June 30-July 4 1952, MSS Macmillan, dep. d. 11, Harold Macmillan Papers, Bodleian Library, Oxford.
366. "External Financial Policy," CP 223(52), 3 July 1952, NA-UK, CAB129/53.
367. Minutes, Cabinet Meeting, 66(52), 8 July 1952, NA-UK, CAB128/25, Minutes, Cabinet Meeting Confidential Annex, 8 July 1952, NA-UK, CAB128/40.
368. See Birkenhead, The Prof in Two Worlds, 285.
369. Salter, Slave of the Lamp, 222-224. In a footnote, Salter noted that after he defeated Cherwell at the Oxford by-election in 1937, they "had for many years after differed on most things." Salter, Slave of the Lamp, 223.
370. Salter to Cherwell, 11 Nov. 1953, Cherwell to Salter, 16 Nov. 1953, Cherwell Papers, A73/f1-2. When Cherwell died, Salter paid him an obituary tribute in the Lords on 4 July 1957. The latter quoted with satisfaction Churchill's comments about finding Salter and Cherwell in rare agreement. H.L. Debs., vol 204, 4 July 1957, cols. 652-653.
371. Entry of 30 Dec. 1953, Robert Hall Diaries 1947-1953, 281, Plowden, An Industrialist in the Treasury, 157, Butler, Art of the Possible, 158.
372. Aubrey Jones, Britain's Economy: The Roots of Stagnation (1985), 11.

373. Salter to Butler, n.d., Dec. 1953, Lord Butler Papers, RAB G24[106], Trinity College Library, Cambridge.
374. Butler to the author, 14 Dec. 1979, 28 Jan. 1980, author's archive.
375. H.C. Debs., vol. 503, 10 July 1952, cols. 1513-1514, 17 July 1952, cols. 163, 2306-2307.
376. The Financial Times, 2, 19, 30 July 1952, The Observer, 20 July 1952, The Times, 19, 21, 26 July 1952.
377. Lady Salter to Perkins, 29 July 1952, Perkins Papers, Personal "S".
378. Minutes, Cabinet Meeting 76(52), 7 Aug. 1952, NA-UK, CAB128/25.
379. Foreign Office to Berne, 8 Aug. 1952, Berne to Foreign Office, 9 Aug. 1952, NA-UK, FO371/99021 UEE159/9G, UEE159/8, Treasury to Washington, 11 Aug. 1952, NA-UK, FO371/99021, UEE159/10, The Financial Times, 28 Aug. 1952. For a list of briefs taken by Salter to Mexico City, see NA-UK, FO371/99022, UEE159/19.
380. See e.g., The Financial Times, 13 Aug. 1952, The Economist, 164(16 Aug. 1952), 411.
381. The New York Times, 5 Sept. 1952, The Financial Times, 6 Sept. 1952.
382. The Financial Times, 17 Sept. 1952, The Manchester Guardian, 20 Sept. 1952.
383. Quoted in Lady Rhys-Williams to Churchill, 18 Sept. 1952, Churchill Papers, CHUR 6/2.
384. "Report on the Conversion Value of Exports of Goods Containing Steel," E.A.(52)117, 1 Oct. 1952, CAB134/842.
385. The Financial Times, 8 Oct. 1952.
386. The Financial Times, 22 Oct. 1952.
387. H.C. Debs., vol. 505, 30 Oct. 1952, cols. 2104-2106, The Financial Times, 1 Nov. 1952, The New York Times, 21 Oct. 1952.
388. H.C. Debs., vol. 507, 5 Nov. 1952, col. 179, Minutes, Cabinet Meeting 95(52), 11 Nov. 1952, NA-UK, CAB128/25.
389. H.C. Debs., vol. 507, 11 Nov. 1952, cols. 768-784, 857-858.
390. See "Steps Towards Convertibility, Draft Report by a Working Party," W.P.S.C.(52)1, 27 Aug. 1952, NA-UK, T230/217.
391. "'Collective Approach," Oct. 52 [sic], "Commonwealth Conference and After," Nov. 52 [sic], Salter Papers, File 19, "Robot" – Top Secret, Jan.-Dec. 1952. This same file contains a detailed "Top Secret, Summary of Developments: Robot and the Collective Approach," Dec. 1952, by A.H.M. Mitchell (Salter's private secretary).
392. The Times, 25 Nov. 1952.

393. Salter, Slave of the Lamp, 216.
394. Quoted in Anthony Seldon, Churchill's Indian Summer: The Conservative Government, 1951-1955 (1981), 158.
395. The Manchester Guardian, 25 Nov. 1952.
396. See John Boyd-Carpenter, Way of Life (1980), 97-98, Lewis Baston, Reggie: The Life of Reginald Maudling (Stroud, 2004), 90.
397. Minute by Richard Stokes, 10 July 1951, NA-UK, BT161/240. The materials included lead, zinc, aluminium, copper, magnesium, hemp, sulphur, tungsten, leather, timber, jute and cotton.
398. Economic Policy Committee, E.A.(53)1, 1 Jan. 1953, NA-UK, CAB134/847, Salter, Memoirs, 343
399. H.O. Hooper to Salter, 25 Nov. 1952, "Ministry of Materials: History, Organization, Staff and Functions," n.d., NA-UK, BT161/243.
400. Economic Policy Committee, E.A.(52)30, 26 Nov. 1952, NA-UK, CAB134/842, Memorandum by the Minister of Materials, E.A.(52)142, 3 Dec. 1952, NA-UK, CAB134/845.
401. H.C. Debs., vol. 508, 27 Nov. 1952, col. 98.
402. H.C. Debs., vol. 508, 4 Dec. 1952, col. 508.
403. H.C.Debs., vol. 510, 26 Jan. 1952, cols. 726-750.
404. See e.g., The Times of India, 31 Jan. 1953.
405. Memorandum by Butler, "Supply Expenditure," CP 31(53), 30 Jan. 1953, NA-UK129/58.
406. Minutes, Cabinet Meeting 6(53), 3 Feb. 1953, NA-UK, CAB128/26.
407. H.C.Debs., vol. 511, 16 Feb. 1953, cols. 865-866, 23 Feb. 1953, cols. 1697-1700.
408. H.C. Debs., vol. 511, 16 Feb. 1953, col. 864.
409. Memorandum by Salter and Thorneycroft, "Cotton: Importing and Marketing Arrangements," CP 63(53), 16 Feb. 1953, NA-UK, CAB129/59, Minutes, Cabinet Meeting 13(53), 19 Feb. 1953, NA-UK, CAB128/26.
410. Entry of 4 Apr. 1952, Lancashire and Whitehall: The Diary of Sir Raymond Streat, vol. 2, 1939-1957, Marguerite Dupree, ed., (Manchester, 1987), 636-638, The Manchester Guardian, 24, 27, 28 Feb. 1953, The Times, 28 Feb. 1953, The Financial Times, 28 Feb., 3 Mar. 1953.
411. H.C. Debs., vol. 512, 5 Mar. 1953, cols. 56-57.
412. Memorandum by Salter and Thorneycroft, "Cotton: Importing and Marketing Arrangements," CP 164(53), 3 June 1953, NA-UK, CAB129/61.
413. Minutes, Cabinet Meeting 35(53), 17 June 1953, NA-UK, CAB128/26, H.C.Debs., vol. 516, 18 June 1953, cols.1158-1160.

414. Memorandum by Duncan Sandys, Minister of Supply, and Salter, "Termination of the Steel Distribution Scheme," E.A.(53)50, 21 Mar. 1953, CAB134/847, Minutes, Cabinet Meeting, 24(53), 1 Apr. 1953, NA-UK, CAB128/26.
415. Memorandum by Salter, "Private Trading in Copper," E.A.(53)55, 30 Mar. 1953, NA-UK, CAB134/847, Economic Policy Committee, E.A.(53)12, 1 Apr. 1953, NA-UK, CAB134/846.
416. Economic Policy Committee, E.A.(53)14, 29 Apr. 1953, NA-UK, CAB134/846.
417. H.C. Debs., vol. 515, 4 May 1953, cols. 35-36.
418. The Financial Times, 15 June 1953.
419. H.C. Debs., vol. 515, 4 May 1953, cols. 3-5, vol. 516, 18 June 1953, col. 84.
420. H.C. Debs., vol. 516, 22 June 1953, cols. 114-115.
421. H.C. Debs., vol. 516, 22 June 1953, cols. 116-117.
422. The Financial Times, 23 June 1953. The Times, 24 June 1953.
423. Memorandum by Salter, "The Jute Industry," E.A.(53)82, 26 June 1953, NA-UK, CAB134/848, Economic Policy Committee, E.A.(53)20, 8 July 1953, NA-UK, CAB134/846. On 30 December the Economic Policy Committee agreed to find some form of protection for the Dundee producers. "Protection of the Jute Industry," E.A.(53)164, 30 Dec. 1953, NA-UK, CAB134/849.
424. See, H.C. Debs., vol. 517, 30 June 1953, col. 204, *vol. 517, 6 July 1953, cols. 855-856, vol. 517, 13 July 1953, col. 1697-1698.*
425. H.C. Debs., vol. 518, 20 July 1953, cols. 1-17.
426. See e.g., H.C. Debs., vol. 518, 27 July 1953, cols. 98-99.
427. H.C. Debs., vol. 518, 30 July 1953, cols. 1661-1665.
428. Salter to Churchill, 27 June 1953, [Not sent] Salter Papers, File 20, Resignation from Ministry of Materials, June-Sept. 1953.
429. "Raw Material Prices," encl. in Salter to Churchill, 29 Apr. 1953, Salter Papers, File 17, Correspondence, Salter-Churchill, 1946-1957. Also in NA-UK, PREM11/521.
430. Salter to Churchill, 19 June 1953, minute by Cherwell, 3 July 1953, NA-UK, PREM11/521.
431. Salter to Cherwell, 23 July 1953, encl. "Two Notes on Economic Policy," Cherwell to Salter, 30 July 1953, Cherwell Papers, J129/2-21.
432. Lady Salter to Felkin, 13 May 1953, Felkin Papers, AEF/3/1/220.
433. Salter to Violet Markham 18 June 1953, Markham Papers, 25/73.
434. Lady Salter to Felkin, 13 May 1953, Felkin Papers, AEF/3/1/220, Lady Salter to Perkins, [?] June 1953, Perkins Papers, Personal "S".
435. de Rosales to Felkin, 11 July 1953, Felkin Papers, AEF/3/1/220, Lady Salter to Violet Markham, 23 July 1953, Markham Papers, 25/73.

436. Churchill to Salter, 1 Sept. 1953, Salter to Churchill, 2 Sept. 1953, Salter Papers, File 20, Resignation from Ministry of Materials, June-Sept. 1953.
437. Salter to Churchill, 2 Sept. 1953, Churchill to Salter, 2 Sept. 1953, Salter Papers, File 20, Resignation from Ministry of Materials, June-Sept. 1953, The Times, 4 Sept. 1953. This file also contains notes on Chequers letterhead of the draft prepared there by Salter.
438. Salter to Churchill, 4 Sept. 1953, Salter Papers, File 20, Resignation from Ministry of Materials, June- Sept. 1953.
439. Salter Papers, File 30, Author's London Draft of Salter Biography.
440. "Circular Letter," 4 Sept. 1953, Salter Papers, File 20, Resignation from Ministry of Materials, June-Sept. 1953.
441. Salter to Woolton, 4, 7 Sept. 1953, Salter Papers, File 20, Resignation from Ministry of Materials, June-Sept. 1953.
442. Salter Papers, File 30, Author's London Draft of Salter Biography.
443. Salter Papers, File 30, Author's London Draft of Salter Biography.
444. Macmillan to Salter, 5 Sept. 1953, Salter to Macmillan, 9 Sept. 1953, Salter Papers, File 20, Resignation from Ministry of Materials, June-Sept. 1953.
445. The Times, 30 Sept. 1953, The London Gazette, 16 Oct. 1953, 5498.
446. The Times, 22 Oct. 1953.
447. H.L. Debs., vol. 184, 5 Nov. 1953, cols. 145-151, 165, 188.
448. H.L. Debs., vol. 184, 8 Dec. 1953, col. 1102, 9 Dec. 1953, cols. 1125-1130.
449. Salter, Memoirs, 343.

CHAPTER 8

"THE LESS EXACTING CHAMBER," 1954-1975

Shortly after he entered the House of Lords, Salter observed, "I don't want myself to retire completely just yet, but it will certainly be a very different life from what it has been the last two years, with office all day & the Commons most of the night."[1] He also noted, "If I can be of any help, e.g. in the 'special mission' form for an appropriate job I should be happy too. But with some experience of few Departments of state, I don't think the likelihood very great, and I am not attracted by the run of the mill 'Royal Commission' invitations that usually come along."[2] Little did he realize at that point how short-lived would be his absence from work for which he was so experienced. Nor could he have foreseen that with the passing of years, he would became largely inactive in the Lords, lonelier as his contemporaries passed away and, after the death of Lady Salter in 1969, increasingly frail. Finally, he also could not have anticipated that as he entered his 73rd year, there still lay ahead years filled with participation in a variety of public institutions, a renewed interest in the affairs of All Souls College, and an unchanging routine of continental vacations alternating with three month stays at Hickory Farm.

The "special mission" came Salter's way sooner that he might have expected or desired. On 21 January 1954 John Boyd-Carpenter, Financial Secretary at the Treasury, wrote to Salter that the government of Iraq had asked the International Bank for Reconstruction and Development to nominate a candidate for a new position of Economic Adviser to the Iraq Development Board. The Board, set up in 1950, was responsible for planning and implementing economic development with funding coming from 70% of the royalties paid by foreign oil companies operating in Iraq. The Iraqis were searching for an "international figure" to assist and advise the Board, Boyd-Carpenter explained. Given that Britain imported much of its oil from Iraq, "we have therefore a keen interest in seeing that her economy is developed along sound lines. It might be very serious if she turned for advice to the wrong quarters."

Salter replied on 25 January that he thought the work would be of interest and agreed to his nomination, with final agreement depending on the precise conditions of the mission.[3] On 4 February the Iraqi Minister of Development, Arshad Al-Umari, indicated that Salter's name had been approved and over the course of the following two weeks, the conditions and the terms were agreed upon. It was understood that Salter was to pay two visits to Iraq. The first in mid-March was, in his words, "exploratory with preliminary consideration of alternative schemes in relation to the general economy of Iraq." Thereafter, Salter proposed, he would consult widely on the mission, with a second, longer visit scheduled for the fall, when he would offer his "considered opinions" to the Board. The Iraqi government agreed to the remuneration both for him and a personal assistant, Stanley Payton, a Bank of England specialist in Middle Eastern economic affairs, and also to provide accommodation for both and for Lady Salter. In Salter's view, her presence was necessary "because of her exceptional personal contacts useful for the kind of external consultations that will be required."[4] In its final form, Salter's mandate was to examine the existing development programme and projects in order to co-ordinate them and thus ensure they proceeded smoothly and made the best use of resources, especially scarce ones such as skilled labour. He was also to examine the administrative and executive structure of the Ministry of Development and the Development Board.[5] As he prepared for the visit, Salter wrote on 23 February to the British Ambassador in Baghdad, Sir John Troutbeck, that "I expect that the work on which I might be most useful would involve delicate conversations with some of those concerned with both Iran and Iraq oil developments." He added that he was consulting with various officials, studying relevant documents and getting inoculations both for himself and Lady Salter. Anticipating his departure on 16 March, he continued, "I find myself, as I think over the possible developments, getting very interested. It may all fall through or fail of course. But some of the wider implications are rather exciting." To which Troutbeck replied, "There is so much that they [the Board] would like to do and it is so easy to squander money unless there is a well thought out plan to work on."[6]

Once in Baghdad, and settled in an extensive suite at the Tigris Palace Hotel, Salter and Payton set to work to study the various development programmes both planned and in operation. By 8 April Salter was ready with a series of proposals in which he defined his task as "to give advice as to the timing and balance of the different projects of the Development Board, and their co-ordination with action by other authorities." He anticipated his suggestions would likely result in a modification of the current list of projects. As the modifications were discussed by the appropriate authorities, he anticipated that "a general plan of development and also a specific programme of action, with defined priorities, should emerge." Salter's proposals were unanimously accepted on 14 April at a full meeting of the Development Board.[7] One unexpected task which he undertook on 21 April was to broadcast on the BBC home service an appeal, on behalf of the Baghdad Flood Relief Fund, for contributions to assist Iraqi victims of the extensive flooding. "I am speaking from Baghdad," he began. "I flew over the city. Almost in every direction and as far as my eye could see, there was a vast expanse of water over what a few days before had been fertile lands and little villages."[8]

The Salters left Baghdad on 27 April, with Payton returning directly to London, while they vacationed for a week in Rome. On their return to London, Salter at once wrote to Cobbold to express his appreciation for the loan of Payton. "I could not possibly have wished for anyone better as regards both his work and personal qualities," Salter noted. "He was the greatest possible help and also a charming companion."[9] To Troutbeck he confirmed that "I think I made a reasonably good start in establishing personal relations with those most concerned in Iraq's development, and acquiring the necessary information for studying the problem." Salter continued, "But, not for the first time, I find that having to tackle an economic problem I found that, standing in front of any practicable economic policy was the problem of the administrative machine, and that everything was conditioned by the political background." As an example, he pointed out that between February and April there had been four Ministers of Development.[10] Salter brought back to London a massive amount of printed materials, and he quickly embarked on a period of intense study and personal consultations. The latter included meeting with experts on water systems and flood control, land tenure and land taxation, and irrigation. He also consulted on plans for the utilization of natural gases from the Kirkuk and Basra oil fields, as well as a chemical plant to produce ammonia and fertilizer. Even as he studied the issues, there emerged a concern that he shared with Eugene Black, President of the International Bank for Reconstruction and Development. Writing to him on 26 July Salter observed, "In Iraq the economic opportunities are of course immense; but they are dependent upon reasonably efficient administration and that in turn on political stability. These conditions are at present far from being attained."[11]

On 27 July he and Lady Salter left for a month's vacation at Wörthersee and Bad Gastein in Austria. On their return on 2 September, Salter continued his busy round of consultations. As he pushed ahead with his preparations, he was apprised by Troutbeck, in a letter on 14 September, of the recent political changes in Iraq. With Nouri el Said installed as prime minister, with the opposition silenced, and with a new Minister of Development appointed, Abdul Majid Mahmud, the sixth appointee since the ministry was formed in July 1953, Troutbeck concluded, "The Development Board at the moment seems to be rather in the doldrums." In his reply and in response to the Iraqi political situation, Salter urged "action, on a sufficient scale, to use some of the development money for quickly visible results (e.g. on housing) to curb potential public unrest." He added that he was very much aware of the precarious authority of most Iraqi ministers. This he regarded as the root of the problems on which he had been asked to advise. He continued, "It is comparatively easy to work out the economic policy which would be in Iraq's interest. But it cannot be implemented successfully without a reasonably efficient administrative machine; and that in turn depends for its creation – and maintenance – on the political authority behind it."[12] Even as he made final preparations for a second visit, Salter was not overly optimistic. On 18 October he wrote, "I think it is unlikely that I shall have got much further in this visit than I had hoped to have reached before I went."[13]

On 28 October the Salters, once again accompanied by Payton, returned to Baghdad and to the Tigris Palace Hotel. The purpose of his first visit to Iraq, in Salter's own words, had been to work "on the problem of the timing, balance and co-ordination of the development project." His second visit was to discover "just what actual work has been accomplished and is in progress; what decisions have been taken by the Board; what action has been taken to implement them; what commitments have been made, etc." On 16 November he complained that he was having great difficulty in proceeding, because it was so difficult to find the person with the relevant information.[14] An order issued by the Minister of Development to provide full cooperation soon enabled Payton, in charge of research, to proceed with the collection of the necessary materials.[15] Thereafter, the study and consultations progressed steadily over the next three months, including visiting sites vital to the development programme. Payton later noted, "Before the Mission ended we had travelled from Mosul in the north to Basra in the south, and visited many places in between." Payton also recalled the role played by Lady Salter during the mission:

> She spent her days happily by rising late and then usually visiting what she called 'the beauty shop.' Here she not only had her hair dressed but picked up a great deal of gossip of what was going on in Baghdad which enlivened our dinner conversation in the evening. She read the airmail copies of "The Times," which were usually several days old, thoroughly and kept her husband up to date (or nearly) with what was going on in London – everything from the Court Circular to the obituaries. In the afternoon she undertook visits which had been arranged for her or rested. She developed a lively interest in everything that was going on, particularly court circles, and also visited schools, hospitals and a convent as the guest of various Iraqi ladies related to the Royal family.[16]

By the end of February sufficient materials had been gathered to justify a return to London and the writing of the report. On 9 March Salter noted, "I got back last week, after nearly 4 months in Iraq & 12 heavenly days in Rome en route for London.

Ethel went on to Germany from there for a fortnight while I came on here."[17] He immediately threw himself into preparing his report, working long hours and with the assistance of several further experts in such areas as hydrology and health.[18] Pressure to complete the report came from the new British ambassador to Iraq, Sir Michael Wright, as well as Nouri el Said, both of whom asked Salter for an advance copy.[19] On 31 March Salter informed Rowse, "I'm still plunged very deep in my Iraq work, but hope to be past the worst in a few days."[20] By mid-April the report, <u>The Development of Iraq: A Plan of Action</u> by Lord Salter, Assisted by S.W. Payton, was finished. Salter reminded his readers that the report was rooted in the quite limited terms of reference agreed to by the Development Board on 14 April, namely the timing, balance and co-ordination of projects. "I am an adviser on the actual and unresolved issues of development policy," he observed.

Thereafter, the report was divided into two parts: the first gave a general picture of the development policy recommendations; the second consisted of facts and figures, and the detailed arguments underlying the recommendations. Regarding development policy, he observed that too much emphasis had been placed on building dams for flood protection and not enough on planning for the use of stored water for irrigation. With regard to health and education, he thought the Board had paid too much attention to capital investment and not enough to human investment. Similarly, he was critical of development plans which did not bring quick enough results, such as might be obtainable by providing housing for the poor and improvements in agriculture. Finally, he made a plea for efficient administration which was at the heart of successful development. "More than once in my experience," he wrote, "I have been invited to advise a country on economic policy, and have found that the heart of the problem is the reform or creation of an administrative system capable of carrying it out." The main impediment to the success of development in Iraq could be the efficiency of the administrative machine. Among the further recommendations in his <u>Plan of Action</u>, Salter proposed curtailing the construction of large dams, concentrating instead on flood control, irrigation and drainage, increasing agricultural production, and finding an appropriate system of land tenure and taxation. Improved systems of communications, rail, air and port facilities were vital, as were as an extended road, and the construction of a new standard gauge railway, from Baghdad to Basrah. He also recommended a new housing authority to oversee large-scale house building, funding for preventive medicine and more vocational training. He advised industries should be limited to those based on local raw materials, thus assured of a domestic market and for which skills were available. "One of the most difficult, and one of the most important problems of a development policy," he observed cautiously, was "the creation of an efficient administration to carry it out." Thus he suggested that the Board act as "a general planning and allocating authority" with administrative responsibility transferred to the requisite government departments or special institutions. In conclusion, he pointed out that, while he liberally drew on numerous reports of previous advisers in Iraq, he was attempting to provide a renewed "coherent pattern of policy." His final words were that, granted wise administration, peace and stability, "Iraq now has a prospect of a rapid advance in national prosperity and individual welfare which has been rarely equaled in history."[21]

Although Salter thought it "highly undesirable" that the report be published, it appeared almost a year later. He was then lauded for having "contributed a notable document to the literature of economic planning." In June 1956, the Iraqi parliament approved a new five-year plan which closely followed Salter's recommendations for greater flexibility and diversity.[22] Salter described his experience in Iraq as "the most intriguing and exciting" of all he had undertaken, over a period of 30 years, regarding post-war reconstruction or economic development in underdeveloped countries. He noted, "I shall retain a pleasant memory of a year's unexpected experience."[23] The Salters also met and became well acquainted there with the archeologist Max Mallowan, working at various sites in the country, and his wife Agatha Christie. On Mallowan's recommendation Salter became President of the British School of Archaeology in Iraq and served until 1965. In turn Salter championed the successful appointment of Mallowan as a Fellow of All Souls in 1962.[24]

Salter had the occasion to draw on his experience in Iraq on several further occasions. On 21 February 1956 he gave a talk at Chatham House on the subject of "Development in Under-Developed Countries." He elaborated, and with numerous anecdotes, on his personal experience since 1919 as an adviser on economic and financial development in foreign countries. He then touched on his recent mission to Iraq, drawing the lesson that there was no single "formula or prescription for development. The whole nature and character of procedure, and approach and plan differs according to the particular country with which one is dealing."[25] This was to be his final talk at Chatham House although he remained a member until he resigned in August 1970.[26] On 17 July 1956 he also made his last contribution to the Overseas Service of the BBC and was still optimistic that Iraq could emerge as a model oil state in the Middle East.[27] A year later in an unpublished note, he wrote hopefully that Iraq's development was "bringing real and important benefits to the people."[28] Finally, in the House of Lords on 20 July 1959, when discussing the question of making loans to under-developed countries, and on the basis of his experience in Iraq, he stressed the importance of having an administration that spent wisely, and had a sufficiently stable government.[29] In retrospect, however, he remained convinced that larger expenditure on projects that would have been immediately visible and of obvious benefit might have avoided the July 1958 revolution, which bought down the Hashemite dynasty, the career of Nouri el Said and the many recommendations in his report.[30]

Reflecting on the completion of his work in Iraq, Salter observed that "my own practical and responsible experience ended in the year 1955."[31] While that was the case, his public life continued under various guises. When appointed to the House of Lords in 1953, Salter had initially made several contributions to its debates before year's end. However, due to his preoccupation with the Iraq mission he was absent from the Lords throughout 1954 and only returned on 29 June 1955. Although he later indicated that he was a frequent contributor to its debates, the record shows that he was selective in his attendance, making his final speech in the chamber on 29 June 1970. As well, the subjects he chose to discuss were those about which he felt either committed, knowledgeable or where he could bring to bear the experiences of his long career. With regard to his performance there, a colleague observed that "Salter was respected and loved, but not feared in the House."[32]

Environmental issues had been an area of ongoing concern for Salter. Thus on 29 June, after his long absence from the Lords, he contributed to a debate on how to relieve urban congestion and how green belt areas should be established to prevent further urban sprawl. He claimed that distant "dormitory towns" were "time consuming, life-consuming, soul-destroying factors in our economy." The only way to stifle their further growth, in his opinion, was to encourage industries to relocate there and become a magnet to attract people and supporting infrastructure.[33] Another issue which had interested him for some time, and quite naturally, was that of traffic congestion in and around his Oxford. As early as 6 June 1936 he had observed that in his life thus far he "had seen the outskirts of Oxford industrialised, the roads motorised, the countryside suburbanised, and the approaches ribbonised," and made a plea for greater future planning.[34] On 26 February 1946 he had spoken in the Commons on the need to curb industrial development in Oxford which was leading to even greater traffic congestion.[35] He then served as chairman of the Council and later President of the Town and Country Planning Association. He also was a Trustee of the Oxford Preservation Trust from 1943 to 1965 and chairman from June 1957 to June 1959.[36] Hence, on most occasions, when environmental issues relating to Oxford were debated, Salter would repeat his connections to the city:

> I was born in Oxford; my father and my uncle were both Mayors of Oxford; I was educated both as a boy and as an undergraduate in Oxford; I became a professor in Oxford; I was for thirteen years, with my Sir Alan Herbert as my

colleague, a Member for Oxford University. I am at this moment a Fellow, technically, and not infrequently also, actually resident in Oxford. I have had a deep love for Oxford for something like eighty years, which is rather more than the normal span of human affection.[37]

With the support of many fellow peers on 13 February and 2 July 1957, Salter spoke against a contentious plan to relieve traffic congestion in central Oxford, by building a southern relief road that would run though Christ Church Meadow, closing The High to traffic. In his 15 June 1957 address as chairman of the Oxford Preservation Trust, he spoke in favour of completing a comprehensive ring of by-pass roads as a solution to the traffic issues.[38] The debates evoked a government commitment to hold a new inquiry into the issue, to be held under the 1947 Town and Country Planning Act. The results of two further inquiries were debated in the Lords on 26 June 1961 and 3 March 1966. Salter, along with many other peers, continued to voice his objections to the Meadow road and that proposal was finally vetoed on 26 January 1966 by Richard Crossman, Minister of Housing and Local Government.[39]

As would be expected, Salter retained his lifelong interest in economic and financial matters. However, he now spoke without the access to private information which he had enjoyed for several decades. His comments, while often general and drawing on his previous experience, still remained trenchant. It was not until 8 March 1956 that he intervened for the first time in the Lords during a debate on the economy. He cautioned that Britain's economic situation was parlous and that both Labour and Conservative governments since 1945 were equally responsible. In his view, the danger to the country, as in years past, was its dependence upon imported food and raw materials, its failure to increase exports, largely because of increased inflation, and the ongoing impact this had in draining the reserves. He then warned of "the evils and dangers" of wage inflation, occasioned by the large wage settlements in nationalized industries. With regard to the effectiveness of monetary policy, he admitted that, while high interest rates were useful at certain stages of an inflationary period, they should be combined with a regulator such as "hire purchase," tightened in case of a boom and eased in case of Depression. Salter acknowledged that many in the House referred to the necessity of "recovering the dynamic character" of British civilization. He offered the view that the priorities were to get past the critical drain on reserves and to increase productivity. "You should first create your wealth and then decide how to share it."[40] He next spoke on 8 May and found much to support in the 17 April budget, a so-called "savings budget," from the new Chancellor of the Exchequer, Harold Macmillan. In particular, he liked the decision "to retain the large surplus for the purpose of disinflation instead of giving it away in tax concessions." And yet again he offered dour warnings about the dangers of the ongoing imbalance between imports and exports. He noted that if a future historian were to analyse the decline and fall of Britain, the cause would be the failure "to restore and revive again the dynamic energy on which the greatness and power of this country have in the past been founded." It is not surprising that Salter was taken to task for his views on history.[41]

When Salter returned to the subject of the economy almost a year later, it was again to address the continuing issue of inflation and the need to encourage investments and increase incentives.[42] A further economic crisis in the fall of 1957 saw the government backing away from another devaluation, but resorting to raising the bank rate from 5% to 7%. Salter spoke to this issue in the Lords on 6 November, and characteristically admitted that his comments were disjointed and based only on limited knowledge. He then suggested that increasing the bank rate was an inadequate policy and should only be a temporary measure. What was required in the long run was a united nation which, translated, meant an agreement between "the forces of unionised labour and Government policy."[43] In the coming months the stability of the pound and further inflationary conditions continued to be a major concern. The House of Lords again discussed this subject on 4 February 1958, and Salter reaffirmed his prescription that a permanent solution depended on "co-operation between the power exercised by Her Majesty's Government and the power of organized labour." On related issues, and again citing his lack of relevant information, he confessed that it was not clear whether the primary objective should be to curb inflation or safeguard against possible deflation. However, he stood firm on the necessity to avoid another devaluation of the pound similar to 1949.[44]

As he continued to observe the economic situation both domestically and internationally, Salter briefly grew somewhat more sanguine. On 28 March 1961 in the Lords, he welcomed what he perceived as a new development, namely, complementary action as "surplus countries" assisted those with balance of payments problems. He cited the recent upwards re-evaluation of the mark by Germany as one such example.[45] However, during another Lords debate on 17 May, one peer referred to the "depressing" outlook for the British economy. As a result Salter, returning to his usual plea, argued that it was urgent to increase exports to improve the country's external balance of trade. It was not just a case of adding to the reserves, he contended. Failure to do so would make it impossible to continue overseas investments and would harm the country's world-wide influence. Ultimately, failure would also have a domestic impact, because the inability to pay for raw materials for British industries could lead to massive unemployment. On this occasion, Salter turned for the first time to the issue of the Common Market. He was critical of the government's initial approach to membership, when British participation would have been welcomed.

"We were inflexible in demanding both full entry and freedom to deal separately with such British issues as Commonwealth Preference." In urging a rethinking of the advantages of membership for Britain, he emphasized the economic benefits of access to a rapidly expanding market, and the stimulus this competition would have on British industry. "It is of the utmost importance that the Government put an end to this long shilly-shallying process," he continued, "and should make up their mind what they are going to do and to act quickly." He thus urged a genuine attempt at membership, otherwise further delay would mean "we may get the worst of both worlds."[46] Salter's exhortation did not finally come until May 1967 when Britain resubmitted its application for membership.

Other areas of concern for Salter, illustrated by his contributions to House of Lords debates, were foreign and colonial policies. Among his most poignant contributions were those he made in the wake of Egyptian President Nasser's nationalization of the Suez Canal, announced on 26 July 1956. The Salters heard this news while sailing to the US for their annual summer holiday. As Salter followed the crisis from a distance, he became increasingly concerned that an invasion of Egypt was projected, an action he regarded as "criminally foolish." He decided to fly back to England and, after consulting with various ministers and officials in Whitehall, on 13 September made his first contribution to the debate on the ongoing crisis.[47] He agreed that the Egyptian action was "inadmissible in International Law, and inconsistent with the generally accepted code on international conduct." To date, he admitted, he regarded the government's response as "correct and skilful." However, anxious nonetheless about future British intentions, he urged Prime Minister Anthony Eden to refer the dispute to the Security Council of the United Nations. It should be made clear he stated, "that we should never use force except in the cases and under conditions prescribed or allowed in the United Nations Charter, by which we are bound." He then presciently cautioned that a successful outcome required "that America should be with us and be known to be with us." In the interim he advised, the best policy was to play for time and refer the dispute to the Security Council with force a last resort.[48] Salter wrote later that he "flew happily" back to Hickory Farm, convinced that a peaceful outcome was certain. In early October, while staying at the River Club, William Tyler, then working in the US Foreign Service, hinted to Salter that the UK and France were being less than honest about their intentions. Tyler noted that Salter was distressed by the thought.[49] On returning to Britain, however, as the Salters sailed along the Solent observing a long line of military vessels, Salter recalled that he had been "deceived."[50]

On 29 October Israeli forces crossed into the Sinai Peninsula followed by a combined Anglo-French attack against Egypt on 31 October. The House of Lords met the following day, without detailed military information save that operations were ongoing in Egypt. Rising to speak, Salter shied away from any criticism. Instead, he focused on the future in terms of what was "politically desirable and morally right." He wanted every effort be made to repair the damage done by the invasion to Britain's relationship with the Commonwealth, the US and the Arab world. He also urged Eden to clarify the short- and long-term objectives of the military operation.[51] On 6 November, with mounting opposition both domestically and abroad, Britain and France accepted a ceasefire. In its aftermath, Salter rose in the Lords, where criticism of the operation ran deeply, to suggest that armed force was only an option in the event the Security Council could not agree because of a veto by one of its members.[52] Opposition to the Suez adventure continued to animate the House of Lords, with Salter contributing again to the debate on 12 December. In the absence of full disclosure of the facts, he focused again on the future rather than the past. The first "unpalatable" lesson he drew was that "we are not now strong enough to act without the support of the United States of America." Secondly, Britain must be willing to modify its foreign policy in order to carry along its friends and Allies, while at the same time he urged greater consistency in American foreign policy. Thirdly, Britain must accept it was no longer the leading western power in the Middle East. With regard to future Middle Eastern policy, he contended that it was both an exaggeration and "a great mistake to say that the Canal was a matter of life and death to us." What was vital was the political stability of the region and the need "to reverse the present trend towards either anarchy or communism." To this end he urged, in the short term, that the United States join the 1955 regional defensive Baghdad Pact of Britain, Iraq, Turkey, Iran and Pakistan and help thwart the further penetration of Soviet influence into the Middle East. In the longer term, he hoped for a time when the borders of Israel would be guaranteed both against invasion and expansion. Even if British power was diminished, Salter concluded, he expected that its experience, traditions and its association with so many countries and races still had much to offer to the international community.[53]

It was not until 1965 that another overseas issue so seized Salter's attention. On 11 November 1965 the Southern Rhodesian Prime Minister Ian Smith issued a Unilateral Declaration of Independence [UDI] from Britain. The British Prime Minister Harold Wilson, in turn declared this move illegal, imposed sanctions and for the next 14 years efforts at a settlement continued. From the outset, Salter took an interest, beginning on 25 November, when he admitted that he had "no special knowledge and no special authority," but condemned the UDI as "both illegal and unwise." No doubt, he continued, among the minority white settlers were those who believed in the illusion that they could perpetuate their monopoly on power. While he believed that a hasty transition from colonialism could lead to "chaos and tyranny," he regretted that the Rhodesian authorities should not have made preparations to share and then transfer power. Salter's friend Lord Molson interpreted his comments as support for a "bi-racial Constitution" as a possible solution.[54] As sanctions in the following months intensified, Salter was among those who feared these might lead to war with Rhodesia, but later voiced his relief that the British government had in effect ruled out the use of force.[55] With a resolution nowhere near and with the passage of time, he was among the first in the Lords who raised the question of the economic impact of the crisis. On 8 December 1966 he stated that his greatest concerns were the negative impact on the balance of payments and the strain on the reserves. These economic difficulties, he asserted, had been occasioned by military and naval movements and the loss of trade, particularly with South Africa, second only in volume to the US. Fearing the possibility of yet another devaluation of the pound, he concluded that "the damage of the past has already been immense; the danger of the future is immensely greater and beyond all calculation – and it may be fatal."[56] When further sanctions followed in the New Year and with negotiations deadlocked, on 21 June 1967 Salter again underlined the enormous economic price Britain was paying. Particularly, he highlighted the borrowing to support the pound, the loss of the South African market, and the fact that other countries, despite sanctions, were continuing to trade with Rhodesia. For the first time he then stated, in view of the damage being done to the British economy, that he favoured the option of granting Rhodesia independence first, to be followed by majority rule at a fixed date. He added, perhaps unconvincingly, "I also believe that the present regime is more acceptable than any other practicable alternative to the resident African majority."[57] When he returned to the subject a year later, it was to focus again on the negative impact that the Rhodesian affair was having on the British economy, and in particular the external balance of payments.[58] In his last substantive intervention on the Rhodesian issue, on 17 June 1969, he continued to dwell on the impact on the balance of payments, and called for an immediate end to sanctions.[59] In the event, he did not live to see the end of the Rhodesian government and a transfer of power to majority rule in 1980. However, his last letter to the editor of The Times on 1 March 1969, co-written with Lord Clitheroe, remained critical of the damage done both to the British economy and to the place of sterling in the world.[60] Salter's very last speech in the House of Lords was to join in an appeal to have Rudolf Hess released from Spandau Prison after 28 years of solitary confinement.[61]

With the increased leisure he now enjoyed, Salter also turned his attention to All Souls College, where he had enjoyed a long and varied association. Although he no longer had an academic profile there, he was still a Fellow with rooms described by a visitor as "astonishingly spacious, numerous and well-appointed."[62] In term he still spent weekends at All Souls and continued to take an interest in its affairs. Over the course of the years, for example, he had occasion to suggest an Oxford D.C.L. be given to such figures as R.H. Tawney, Sidney and Beatrice Webb, who had "done more than any living people to contribute to the study of social sciences," J. A. Spender, Sir John Anderson and A.P. Herbert who "did more than anyone else to establish the tradition that University members should be Independents."[63] Such suggestions proved unavailing, with the result that on 22 February 1950 Salter wrote to the Vice-Chancellor of the University, John Lowe. He criticised both the process and the selection of recipients of honourary degrees, contending that the selection should be free of political or academic "prejudice." Lowe's response strongly denied that there ever was any political prejudice and that controversy was inevitable following the choice of recipients.[64]

Over the years, as well, Salter had enjoyed a close relationship with such Wardens of All Souls, as W.G.S. Adams, 1933 to 1945 and with John Sparrow elected in 1953. In fact, Salter gave the memorial address for Adams on 19 March 1966 in the College Chapel and Sparrow often consulted Salter on College affairs.[65] In the late 1950s and throughout the 1960s Salter kept up a stream of letters to College officials with one consistent theme. Beginning in November 1958, and again on subsequent occasions, he wrote to complain about the declining quality of candidates for election as All Souls Fellows. To this was tied his view that the College was failing "to form a bridge between the academic and public life (its most distinctive function in respect of which the College is unique among educational institutions in Oxford or elsewhere) to anything like the same extent as in the inter-war years." He recalled such names as Amery, Simon, Cosmo Lang, Archbishop of Canterbury, Halifax, Geoffrey Dawson and Wilfred Greene as eminent Fellows, as well as the four highest ranking British civil servants in Washington during the war – himself, Halifax, Butler and Brand. Among his suggestions for change was that the Fellowship examination should be less academic and specialized, and more reflective of intellectual quality. He also suggested that more publicity be given to the variety of available Fellowships. He advocated inviting "distinguished foreigners," not only academics, to partake in College life, given its prestige and material resources for such hospitality. He considered it might be possible to guide research done by Prize Fellows toward "current public problems," and reduce their elected term from seven to five years to measure productivity before re-election. Indeed, Salter went so far as to write that it was "difficult to justify the use of the College's rich resources for purely academic work of the kind it now encourages."[66] Sparrow sympathised on the issue of achieving greater balance in the College between the academic and the non-academic, but admitted a solution was difficult.[67] On 22 October 1974, and fittingly at the initiative of Sparrow, Salter was informed that the College had conferred upon him "the rare distinction of an Honorary Fellowship."[68]

No other issue, rooted directly and indirectly at All Souls College, caused Salter more unhappiness than the succession in 1952 to the position of Warden. B.H Sumner who had been Warden since 31 July 1945, an election at which Rowse had proposed Salter, died on 25 April 1951. He was succeeded on 10 June by Salter's friend, the economist Hubert Henderson, who resigned on medical advice on 26 January 1952, suddenly leaving the position of Warden suddenly vacant.[69] What followed in the upcoming election, unfortunately, had a profound impact on the relationship between Rowse and Salter. Their friendship went back to the early 1930s, and over the years that relationship had grown more intimate, based at its core on mutual respect and deep affection. As Salter later wrote to Rowse, "Your friendship has meant much to me in the last 20 years, & I should be sorry if it should be lost."[70] The relationship was challenged as a result of the election for Warden of All Souls in early 1952. Rowse, as sub-warden by rotation, and according to his own account, allowed his name to go forward as a future Warden. However, questions about his suitability, his irascible personality, the divisive nature of loyalties and politics of All Souls Fellows, and his own uncertainty about his talents for administration finally led to the election on 1 March of John Sparrow. Rowse called his defeat "an agonising experience," and accused Salter of being "a false friend at the crisis of my life."[71] It marked a turning point both in his career, leading to his spending the winter months at the Huntington Library in Pasadena, California, and impacted profoundly on his friendships. Particularly affected was his relationship with Salter who had voted for Sparrow, but had not at the time spoken to Rowse about his choice. As a result, in the following several years Salter and Rowse ceased almost entirely to communicate in writing or upon meeting at the College. It was Salter who took the initiative to rekindle this friendship, writing on 31 December 1955:

> I have been sadly conscious that recently our personal relationship has not been what it used to be. I am not conscious of anything I have said or done to contribute to this. But, as you once told me, I forget personal things more easily than you do & it is possible that I have been guilty of something which I have now forgotten: if so I'm sorry. There is of course the old question of the wardenship.

Salter then pointed out that Rowse did not have that "'impersonal' attitude" necessary for the position and therefore he voted for Sparrow, "quite as much in friendship to you as from the point of view of the College." Salter continued, "the great work you have done would have been handicapped rather than helped by your becoming either an M.P. (as you had once contemplated) or responsible for academic-administrative duties. Cannot we recover our old relationship?" He concluded, "I am conscious myself of certain defects in myself which have some times been a handicap in personal relationships – a reserve & absence of any forthcoming quality – & it is not without difficulty that I have written this letter."[72] On a later occasion, and further in his defence, Salter wrote, "As an Anglo-Saxon, a temperamental 'liberal' and an official by professional training, I am inclined to be both less emphatic & less personal, & less articulate & inhibited in expression."[73]

Over time Salter and Rowse occasionally spoke and corresponded, but the rift remained. After what Salter described once as an "inconclusive" conversation, he again tried to befriend Rowse. He recalled that when Rowse first indicated his willingness to be considered for the position as warden, he felt "both disturbed & uncertain." He then frankly noted that because of Rowse's temperament, not the kind that "lowers the temperature," divisions among the Fellows about his suitability, and his many literary commitments the position "was not your real job." As to Rowse's grievance that at the time he offered no comments, Salter added, "I did not – unasked – proffer advice or tell you all that was in my mind." He then accused Rowse of a similar lack of candour. He recalled that, after a period of "personal adjustment" created by his resignation and acceptance of a peerage in 1953, and at their first meeting after the election, when he greeted Rowse, "you in effect cut me publicly" and offered no explanation for the incident. Salter concluded, "I am not, I think, quick to take offence or temperamentally inclined to let a hurt fester. I have, like everyone else in the rough and tumble of a public life, had many slights & wounds which have hurt for the moment. I can now not remember most of them, & such feelings as I may have had have faded away. So it will be, on my side, if we can now close this unhappy chapter. What of you?"[74] In his brief response, Rowse still was aggrieved that at the time Salter offered "not a word, nor a letter, not even of moral support or sympathy." [75]

On 12 January 1957 Rowse sent Salter a lengthy letter, complimenting his generosity and kindness, and wrote, "I know you to be a good man." However, he also admonished Salter for being "rather obtuse and tactless" and revealed that "I never did want to be Warden even at the time." In response, Salter admitted that he regretted not sharing his thoughts with Rowse in the moment. However, he was prepared to accept their future relationship as acquaintances rather than friends.[76] Following this exchange, Salter and Rowse did remain good acquaintances. With the publication of each new book, Rowse always sent Salter a copy to which the latter unfailingly responded in generous terms.[77] After reading <u>A Cornishman at Oxford</u>, Salter wrote to Rowse, "I thought at one time that I understood you & your psychology pretty well, but this book reminds me of the limits of my perception. I realize too that the 'unforgetting' quality is an essential element in the strength of will & determination which has driven you through so many obstacles."[78] In addition, Salter provided Rowse, who was spending even more time in the United States, with information about College affairs and gossip.[79] They met occasionally at the River Club or the Century Club in New York in the fall, prior to the Salters' return to London, and with Rowse on his way to the Huntingdon. In his diaries Rowse described these New York encounters in less than generous terms, with occasional humour but more often with unkind references to Lady Salter. During an early October 1965 visit with the Salters at the River Club, Rowse noted in his diary, "Arthur impressed on me how exclusive it is and how difficult to get into, with a long waiting list. And how wonderful Ethel is, gets the best suite in the Club every year for their departure from New York, when they throw a farewell party to their friends. I was duly impressed: a cul de sac, no traffic, looking out over the East River; within, opulent good taste, Sèvres, satinwood furniture, quiet drawing room."[80] Some time later Rowse wrote in his pen portrait of Salter, "I was excessively hard, and am sorry." In 1990, he added, "I still have a sense of guilt about my old friend and often dream about him, where it comes out."[81]

Another integral part of Salter's life was his writing, always in longhand and in pen. "He set his thoughts down rapidly in his small and elegant handwriting," a former colleague noted, "which was beautiful to look at but almost impossible to decipher."[82] Beside a prodigious amount of official material relating to the various positions he held both at home and abroad, books, forewords to books, pamphlets, essays, articles and journalism had poured from his pen. Periodical articles no longer interested him with one exception; an invitation on 7 January 1958 from Hamilton Fish Armstrong, editor of <u>Foreign Affairs</u>. Given, in his words, Salter's "unusual combination of practical common sense and statesmanlike vision," Fish Armstrong suggested an analysis of the economic strategy needed by the West to challenge the Soviet Union. Salter agreed on 18 January and the article was completed on 3 April, the eve of his departure with Lady Salter for a two-week stay in Italy.[83] In the article he surveyed some of the economic history of the inter-war years, and pointed out that few lessons applied to the post-1945 period. He agreed that "tonics and tranquillizers," such as deficit budgets and the supply of easy money, eased the impact of recurrent recessions. For the rest he concentrated on his prevailing concern for "the disequilibrium between the dollar and the non-dollar world," and the negative impact of the imbalance of trade. Domestic solutions, he suggested, were necessary to meet the external challenges posed by the Communist world. Here he recommended a combination of government overseas financial assistance coupled with expert advisers, as well as encouraging greater private investment. It was his hope that in the long term, if a phased reduction of atomic armaments could be achieved, the United Nations might become the central organ for the distribution of both western and Soviet aid to the underdeveloped world.[84]

When forwarding a copy of the article to Rowse, Salter noted that it was "an indication that my recent indolence has not been quite complete." With his usual modesty, he also described it as "a stodgy article."[85] Lecturing too had been an integral part of Salter's public persona, but in this area he contributed little after his elevation to the House of Lords. In March 1957 he delivered the annual memorial lecture to the David Davies Memorial Institute of International Studies. In answering the question as to what was to be done with the United Nations – "Reform, Replace or Supplement?" – he argued the novel case that "When a world system of collective security fails to function, a free word system of collective defence is needed to supplement it." Thus he recommended, as a complement but not as a substitute for the United Nations, that NATO, the Baghdad Pact and SEATO be enlarged and greater communication established. In an article discussing the faults of the UN charter, The Times considered Salter's proposal "a possible line of advance."[86] When sending a copy of his lecture to Walter Lippmann, and providing some context for his thoughts, Salter wrote, "It seems to me that we are reaching an impossible situation there."[87]

During this time Salter increasingly turned his mind to personal writing. In July 1956 he completed a typescript which he titled Anecdotes and Incidents. "As one looks back over a long life," he wrote in the preface, "memory presents a kaleidoscope of incidents and events." This lengthy but never published piece of writing contained almost 100 such anecdotes, many relating to "great men" and others detailing significant encounters in Salter's career. All displayed his eye for telling detail, his quiet humour and vivid insight into personality and politics.[88] Soon afterwards, he turned his attention to drafting what was to become his first volume of memoirs, Memoirs of a Public Servant. In the preface, dated 15 March 1961, he justified the book on the grounds that the world of a civil servant, working in "cloistered secrecy," was little known to the public. Furthermore he added, "I have seen official life from within as a civil servant, in both national and international work, and from without as a writer, academic teacher and Minister." He hoped his book would go far towards bridging this gap. The manuscript was submitted on 25 November 1960, with proofs ready by March and then circulated to potential reviewers. Salter followed his usual practice of closely collaborating with his publisher, Faber and Faber, on aspects of production, publicity and the search for serialisation, which ultimately proved futile. He confessed that "I'm not a T.V. personality (present or potential)" and preferred more traditional avenues of publicity, such as book reviews.[89]

Publication date for Memoirs of a Public Servant was fixed for 13 October and the reviews, mostly favourable and many from former colleagues, soon followed.

Alexander Loveday described the book as "an absorbing record of a very exceptional and brilliant career of public service," and noted Salter was "an ideal boss."[90] W.A. Robson wrote, "This is an interesting account by an interesting man of an interesting life." He also observed that aside from his official positions, Salter "became an influential free-lance writer and speaker" in the 1930s.[91] Lord Longford pointed out that "In his variety of distinction and achievement Lord Salter stands alone," and found the memoir "deeply instructive."[92] Lord Altrincham was impressed that Salter "does not lay bare his soul, as some writers affect to do, but his reticence is more honest than any amount of egotistical gush."[93] Almost uniformly, reviewers complimented Salter's skill at personal sketches, his "humour and humanity," "frank self-analysis," and "the idealism that has been the driving force" of his long career.[94] Despite such enthusiastic reviews and a glowing note from Rowse quoted in advertisements, Salter remained disappointed that the book could not find an American publisher. In the five months after publication only 1300 copies were sold.[95]

Salter continued, nonetheless, to actively pursue his writing and desire for further publications. He had tried, unsuccessfully, to get Penguin Books to issue an edition of <u>Personality in Politics</u>, and in 1966 he asked Faber and Faber, also unsuccessfully, to reprint both that and <u>Memoirs of a Public Servant</u>. By that point Salter was already engaged in yet another project which he informally described as "trying to write from a different angle."[96] In his foreword to <u>Slave of the Lamp: A Public Servant's Notebook</u>, which he completed on 15 March 1967, his 86th birthday, he noted, "This is a personal narrative, but not an autobiography." He wished to offer "the reader a seat in the wing to watch some of the dramas of the period and a portrait gallery of some of its great figures." All this would be conveyed through the experience of the civil servant, working in secrecy in Whitehall, but determining what becomes visible in Westminster and through Fleet Street. Noting that the book contained a mixture of anecdotes, comments and reflections, he conceded that this discursive method required a connecting thread. In his view this was provided through a combination of personal experiences and reflections. In his preface, he further explained that he had an exceptionally varied career "as a British Civil Servant, in peace and war, an international official, an Oxford Professor on political institutions, an adviser to several foreign governments, and later as a Minister." Salter thus wished to share with the reader his experiences in public service and hence he had borrowed Churchill's description of such individuals as "slaves of the lamp." The chapters that followed were of two kinds: those intended to make a specific contribution to history, such as the one on the shipping mission to wartime United States and his contribution to Robot; and those offering glimpses of people such as Churchill, Monnet, Royall Tyler and Neville Chamberlain.[97]

What the British press immediately picked up, after publication on 9 November, were Salter's revelations regarding Robot which added to those in Lord Birkenhead's 1961 biography of Cherwell.[98] The reviews which followed publication were few and marginally complimentary. The Observer thought the book betrayed "a note of world-weariness," while The Economist singled out the very long chapter on the shipping mission to Washington and called it Salter's "finest hour."[99] The Times Literary Supplement described the book as "a collection of postscripts to twentieth century history."[100] Salter remained bitterly disappointed by the book's poor reception, in contrast to the private warm tributes from his former colleagues. Rowse did his part by sending a review to The Sunday Telegraph in which he praised Salter as "a great public servant" and the book as making "a distinctive contribution" to contemporary history.[101] Salter took some comfort from the review and, when thanking Rowse, confirmed the view that the book would provide source material for future historians.[102] In a further letter to Rowse on 12 December Salter observed, "Nothing has been written by anyone in the press who understands anything about the period or what I am writing about." In part he blamed poor publicity by the publisher, Weidenfeld and Nicolson, but after speaking to George Weidenfeld discovered that the latter was also surprised and disappointed at the poor reception.[103] As his final words of Slave of the Lamp had noted, "It is enough. It is time to stop."[104]

In the two decades following his elevation to the House of Lords, the Salters' social lives followed an annual pattern. "February is the time to get away from London, fogs & damp & rain," was Lady Salter's view. They usually travelled to the continent, staying at familiar places such as Hôtel des Trois Couronnes in Vevey, or Haus Hirt in Bad Gastein in the Austrian Alps.[105] A return to London inevitably meant attending receptions for visiting foreign dignitaries or those honouring former colleagues. The annual routine also found either or both attending the dinners and meetings of the Pilgrims Society, the Town and Country Planning Association, the British School of Archaeology in Iraq, the English-Speaking Union of the Commonwealth or the St Cecilia's Festival sponsored by the Musicians' Benevolent Fund at the Savoy Hotel. July signalled the large garden party hosted by the Salters at West House. This was recalled by some guests as a "very grand affair" where "one met so many of one's friends in the Diplomatic Service and Society."[106] Another recalled, while attending this "vast and distinguished annual cocktail party," overhearing the comment about the guests – "My God! The whole Establishment of the 1930s!"[107] Yet another wrote of Lady Salter on these occasions: "She had a warm, expansive, generous personality. The chain of dry martinis one was compelled to drink was the only drawback to her hospitality."[108] Following this were elaborate preparations required before travelling on the "Queens" to New York, and from there to spend the summer at Hickory

Farm. Though not one to complain, Salter once confided that "the last week before we sail is fearfully cluttered up."[109] A witness described the proceedings as "a minor pageant." Up to the last minute Lady Salter spent her time packing some 14 huge trunks, despatched by truck to the docks on the day of departure. Besides the two staterooms reserved for her and Salter, another held all the trunks.[110]

Summer at Hickory Farm was always relaxing, with visits from friends both local and abroad. To the small converted farm house, once described by Salter as "primitive but not barbaric," there was added for Salter's work a study in the barn. For exercise he "roamed the countryside with interest and a real love for it," or swam in the natural pool behind the house, its only user.[111] Their box at the Tanglewood Music Festival provided diversion for themselves and their numerous visitors. The Labour Day weekend witnessed the annual garden party where up to 75 people attended, with endless rounds of martinis and abundant flowers from the extensive gardens. A close neighbour and friend observed, "They arrived bringing delight and departed leaving regret."[112] On rare occasions Salter could be coaxed to address the local Rotary Club or contribute a book review to The Berkshire Eagle.[113] Before the return to London in October, there was always "a farewell cocktail party" for American friends at the River Club in New York.[114] This was usually followed by a side trip to Washington to visit with Lady Salter's lifelong friend, Coleman Jennings, and then the return to New York to board ship for England.

The round of receptions, dinners and entertaining at West House continued into the New Year. This routine, however, was gradually curtailed due to Lady Salter's failing health and the advancing age of both. On 2 December 1963 Salter wrote to Rowse, "We are both well though a bit slowed up (or at least I am.)"[115] In reality that was hardly the case. The summer visit to Hickory Farm in 1961 was "somewhat marred by an accident & health troubles," Salter wrote. Lady Salter fell and gashed her head which left her with dizzy spells, but as Salter noted it "was a narrow escape from something worse."[116] This was followed by another such accident, this time a fall in the bath on 15 December 1964, resulting in lingering dizzy spells, although Salter wrote that Lady Salter "retains her zest for life though now with less energy to satisfy it." On 14 August 1965 he informed Rowse that "Ethel is not quite clear of the consequences of her two accidents."[117] This was followed by surgery later that year with resulting complications. In addition her angina pectoris intensified and in the winter of 1969 a severe bout of pneumonia almost proved fatal.[118] Weakened as she was, however, she insisted on making the "valiant effort" required for the annual visit to Hickory Farm which proved to be her last.[119] When saying good-by to her New York friends, she candidly remarked: "This is my last farewell."[120] She died peacefully in her sleep on 13 October 1969 aboard the *Queen Elizabeth* while returning to England. In an obituary tribute in The Times, James Pope-Hennessy wrote that "she belonged to that older generation of Americans who were not, in the Jamesian sense, expatriates, but to whom the fading epithet 'cosmopolitan' could be most properly applied." Those who knew her, he continued, "will chiefly remember her for her quite exceptional warmth of heart, her alert interest in her friends, and for her dry and realistic sense of humour. Her views on many subjects were formed and fairly inflexible, but they were in no sense old-fashioned."[121] In a typical act of generosity she left Hickory Farm to Walter de Kay Palmer, the nephew of her friend Rosamond Gilder.[122]

In his declining years Salter was fortunate to remain in general good health. On 28 October 1966 he wrote to Gertrude Caton Thompson, "So long as the mind lasts one can find happiness. For myself I hope that when that goes I shall have gone too. At present, though I'm nearer 80 than 85 [sic] I find life still very enjoyable."[123] Two years later he noted, "For myself (now 87), I have been conscious of the disabilities of age for the last two years – but not till then – & regard myself as one of the luckiest men with more unmerited good fortune than anyone I have known."[124] In his memorial address for W.G.S. Adams, on 19 March 1966, Salter had stated, "As we look back we think first of the losses of friends we have long known and cared for, each loss as poignant as in earlier days but now each year more frequent."[125] Salter experienced an almost never ending period of lamenting the passing of friends and colleagues. Attendance at memorial services became a regular activity, as did the writing to The Times of obituary tributes for former friends and colleagues. These included, *inter alia*, the Earl of Perth, Lionel Curtis, Viscount Waverly, William Rappard, Violet Markham, J.J. Mallon, Pierre Comert, Frances Perkins, Lord Layton, E.M.H. Lloyd and Guy Wint.[126] His last attendance at a memorial service and obituary tribute was for Sir Leslie Rowan in May 1972.[127] The previous year, dining at an All Souls Gaudy on his 90th birthday, Salter remarked, "90 was a good age to have reached, but not a good age to be at."[128] Lord Hailsham recalled the speech, "exhilarating for its length," one hour, with an outline of a plan of work for the next 20 years.[129] During the final period of his life, Salter lived in comfort and ease at West House, enjoying being what he termed "excessively lazy."[130] He still had a full staff of chauffeur, cook, cleaner and an assistant that for a time included his niece, Anne Vestey.[131] He noted at that time that "The most terrible thing about growing old is watching your friends die."[132] On 10 February 1975 he suffered a stroke which left him incapacitated and in deteriorating health. He finally slipped into a coma and three days later, in the early evening of 27 June 1975, died peacefully at the age of 94, at the time the oldest member of the House of Lords.[133]

On 2 July a funeral service for Salter was held at Oxford Crematorium, followed by a memorial service in St Mary's Church, Kidlington. His ashes were afterwards scattered in the churchyard. A lengthy obituary in The Times, originally written by

Layton in 1962 and later brought up to date by its obituary editor, highlighted Salter's "important contribution to victory through his work in connexion with the control and allocation of shipping." Then, after surveying Salter's career, firstly his public service at home and abroad, and secondly, as professor, member of parliament, cabinet minister, journalist and author, it concluded that "Like Keynes, Salter found that his years in the corridors of power sharpened his interest in his fellow human beings, and his comments on contemporary statesmen showed the closeness with which he had watched them in action."[134] In one of two obituary tributes, the Warden of All Souls, John Sparrow, recalled Salter's long association with the College, to which he was "devoted." Sir Richard Powell wrote at length about the shipping mission in Washington which he regarded as Salter's "most important contribution to the affairs of the nation." He praised Salter as "a skilled and pertinacious negotiator," possessing "the clearest and most ingenious of minds, and was fertile in devising solutions to the most esoteric of problems." Because of his "short, stocky and determined figure," Powell added, Salter was known as "Little Arthur."[135] On 22 July a memorial service for Salter was held at St Margaret's Westminster where the address was given by Lord Hailsham, also a Fellow of All Souls, to a small gathering of relatives, friends and former colleagues, including Harold Macmillan. Hailsham described Salter as "sociable but never frivolous, serious but not pompous, courteous but never familiar, public spirited but without the appearance of emotionalism, rational but not materialistic." Hailsham concluded, "Eternal Rest would not be quite appropriate to our friend, but light perpetual will surely shine upon him."[136]

Endnotes

1. Salter to Felkin, 9 Nov. 1953, Felkin Papers, AEF/3/1/220.
2. Salter to Macmillan, 9 Sept. 1953, Salter Papers, File 20, Resignation from Ministry of Materials, June-Sept. 1953.
3. Boyd-Carpenter to Salter, 21 Jan. 1954, Salter to Boyd Carpenter, 25 Jan. 1954, Salter Papers, File 21, Mission to Iraq, Jan.-Oct. 1954.
4. Draft Communication to Iraq from Salter, 8 Feb. 1954, Salter Papers, File 21, Mission to Iraq, Jan.-Oct. 1954. Payton was later appointed the first Governor of the Bank of Jamaica on 13 June 1960.
5. Summary of Telegrams about Lord Salter, February 4-March 1, 1954, Salter Papers, File 21, Mission to Iraq, Jan.-Oct.1954.
6. Salter to Troutbeck, 23 Feb. 1954, Troutbeck to Salter, 28 Feb. 1964, Salter Papers, File 21, Mission to Iraq, Jan.-Oct. 1954.

7. "Memorandum by Lord Salter Circulated to Development Board on April 8th and Discussed at Board on April 14th," Ali H. Sulaiman, Acting Minister of Development, to Salter, 26 Apr. 1954, Salter Papers, File 21, Mission to Iraq, Jan.-Oct. 1954.
8. The Times, 21 Apr. 1954. For the text of the broadcast see Salter Papers, File 21, Mission to Iraq, Jan.-Oct. 1954.
9. Ali Mumtaz Al-Dafteri, Minister of Finance, to Salter, 28 Apr. 1954, Salter to Cobbold, 12 May 1954, Salter Papers, File 21, Mission to Iraq, Jan.-Oct. 1954.
10. Salter to Troutbeck, 14 May 1954, Salter Papers, File 21, Mission to Iraq, Jan.-Oct. 1954.
11. Salter to Black, 26 July 1954, Salter Papers, File 21, Mission to Iraq, Jan.-Oct. 1954.
12. Troutbeck to Salter, 14 Sept. 1954, Salter to Troutbeck, 24 Sept. 1954, Salter Papers, File 21, Mission to Iraq, Jan.-Oct. 1954.
13. Salter to F.F. Haigh, 18 Oct. 1954, Salter Papers, File 21, Mission to Iraq, Jan.-Oct. 1954.
14. "Note to Vice-Chairman H.E.Taha al Hashimi," 16 Nov. 1954, Salter Papers, File 21, Mission to Iraq, Jan.-Oct. 1954.
15. See Payton, "Correspondence with the Ministry about Basic Information Required for Study," n.d., Memorandum by the Minister of Development, n.d., Salter Papers, File 21, Mission to Iraq, Jan.-Oct. 1954.
16. Payton to the author, 19 June 1979, author's archive.
17. Salter to Gertrude Caton Thompson, 9 Mar. 1955, author's archive.
18. See e.g., M.G. Ionides to Salter, 7 Mar. 1955, Salter to Ionides, 8 Mar. 1955, Salter Papers, File 22, Mission to Iraq, 1955-64.
19. Wright to Salter, 9 Mar. 1955, Salter to Wright, 17 Mar. 1955, Salter Papers, File 22, Mission to Iraq, 1955-64.
20. Salter to Rowse, 31 Mar. 1955, Rowse Papers, EUL MS113/3/1/Corr.S.
21. Lord Salter, Assisted by S.W. Payton, The Development of Iraq: A Plan of Action (April 1955), 1-252.
22. Salter, The Development of Iraq, 9, The Times, 24 Nov. 1955, The Manchester Guardian, 19, 21 June 1956.
23. Salter, Memoirs, 348, Salter to K.G. Fenelon, 27 Apr. 1955, Salter Papers, File 22, Mission to Iraq, Jan.-Oct. 1954. On 24 May 1955 the Salters were both elected members of the Anglo-Iraqi Society. C. Young to Lord and Lady Salter, 25 May 1955, Salter Papers, File 22, Mission to Iraq, 1955-64, M.M. [Max Mallowan], "Obituary, Lord Salter," Iraq, 37(Autumn, 1976), 77-78.

24. Author's interview with Lord Salter, 13 July 1971, Max Mallowan, Mallowan's Memoirs: Agatha and the Archaeologist (1977), 292-293, The Times, 7 Nov. 1956.
25. "Development in Under-developed Countries," Chatham House Meeting, 21 Feb. 1956, RIIA Papers.
26. Dorothy Hamerton to the author, 8 Aug. 1979, author's archive.
27. "This Day and Age, The Development of Iraq," 17 July 1956, BBC WAC, Salter Scripts.
28. Note, "Development in Iraq," n.d., Salter Papers, File 22, Mission to Iraq, 1955-64.
29. H.L. Debs., vol. 218, 20 July 1958, cols. 247-251.
30. Salter, Memoirs, 348. The Report became a resource for historians and others writing about Iraq in the 1950s and later. See e.g., Fahim I. Qubain, The Reconstruction of Iraq, 1950-1957 (New York, 1958), Matthew Elliot, Independent Iraq: The Monarchy and British Influence, 1941-1958 (1996),
31. Salter, Slave of the Lamp, 240.
32. Lord Clitheroe to the author, 2 Aug. 1979, author's archive.
33. H.L. Debs., vol. 193, 29 June 1955, cols. 366-369.
34. The Manchester Guardian, 8 June 1936.
35. H.C. Debs., vol. 419, 26 Feb. 1946, col. 1716.
36. The Times, 16 June 1949, The Oxford Preservation Trust, 19th, 30th, 31st, 32nd and 39th Reports (Oxford, 1946, 1957, 1958, 1959, 1966).
37. H.L. Debs., vol. 273, 3 Mar. 1966, cols. 857-858.
38. H.L. Debs. vol. 201, 13 Feb. 1957, cols. 811-815, 851-852, vol. 204, 2 July 1957, col. 540, vol. 210, 2 July 1958, col. 1121, 16 July 1958, col.1121, The Oxford Preservation Trust, 31st Report to 14 June 1958 (Oxford, 1958), 5-7. See also, Salter to Beveridge, 2 Nov. 1956, Beveridge Papers, BEV VII 32, Salter to Cherwell, 21 Mar. 1957, Cherwell Papers, B164/5.
39. H.L. Debs., vol. 232, 26 June 1961, cols. 906-909, vol. 257, 29 Apr. 1964, cols. 961-962, vol. 273, 3 Mar. 1966, cols. 857-861.
40. H.L. Debs., vol. 196, 8 Mar. 1956, cols. 244-254.
41. H.L. Debs., vol. 197, 8 May 1956, cols. 239-247.
42. H.L. Debs., vol. 202, 6 Mar. 1957, cols. 310-313.
43. H.L. Debs., vol. 206, 6 Nov. 1957, cols. 81-86.
44. H.L. Debs., vol. 207, 4 Feb. 1958, cols. 378-386.
45. H.L. Debs., vol. 230, 28 Mar. 1961, cols. 85-92.
46. H.L. Debs., vol. 231, 17 May 1961, cols. 678-685. As early as 7 Oct. 1956 Salter had signed a statement urging Britain to participate in the early formation of

the Common Market. See The Times, 8 Oct. 1956. In March 1957 he attended a three day conference in Paris on Euratom and the Common Market. The Times, 18 Mar. 1957. On 25 May 1961 he added his signature to a petition, signed by more than 100 other eminent personalities from the "Common Market Campaign," urging the government to join the European Common Market. The Times, 26 May 1961.

47. Salter, Memoirs, 349-350, Slave of the Lamp, 229-230.
48. H.L. Debs., vol. 199, 13 Sept. 1956, cols. 772-778, 853.
49. William Tyler to the author, 1 Mar. 1980, author's archive.
50. Salter, Slave of the Lamp, 230.
51. H.L. Debs., vol. 199, 1 Nov. 1956, cols. 1319-1321.
52. H.L. Debs., vol. 200, 8 Nov. 1956, col. 143.
53. H.L. Debs., vol. 200, 12 Dec. 1956, cols. 1087-1093.
54. H.L. Debs., vol. 270, 25 Nov. 1965, cols. 1077-1080, 1084. See also Salter's letter on the subject in The Times, 29 Nov. 1965.
55. H.L. Debs., vol. 271, 21 Dec. 1965, col. 981, 22 Dec. 1965, cols. 1166-1167.
56. H.L. Debs., vol. 278, 8 Dec. 1966, cols. 1276-1280.
57. H.L. Debs., vol. 287, 21 June 1967, cols. 1444-1448.
58. H.L. Debs., vol. 293, 17 June 1968, cols. 455-456.
59. H.L. Debs., vol. 302, 17 June 1969, cols. 966-969.
60. The Times, 1 Mar. 1969.
61. H.L. Debs., vol. 308, 25 Mar. 1970, cols. 1467-1468.
62. Thomas W. Childs, "Notes on Lord Salter for S. Aster," 29 Oct. 1979, author's archive.
63. Salter to Beveridge, 28 Feb. 1938, Salter to K.C. Wheare, 7 Feb. 1950, Salter to Halifax, 2 Jan. 1957, Salter to J.C. Masterman, Salter Papers, File 23, All Souls College, 1934-1974 (1).
64. Salter to John Lowe, 22 Feb. 1950, Lowe to Salter, 6 June 1950, Salter Papers, File 23, All Souls College, 1934-1974(1).
65. See William George Stewart Adam, CH, A Memorial Address given in the College Chapel, 19 Mar. 1966, Oxford, 1966.
66. "Note," Nov. 1958, "Development of College Policy," May 1959, "Note," Dec. 1959, "The Future of All Souls," 1962, "The Changing Character of All Souls," 1963, Salter Papers, File 23, All Souls College, 1934-1974(1).
67. Sparrow to Salter, 16 Jan. 1960, Salter Papers, File 23, All Souls College, 1934-1974(1).
68. Neill to the author, 3 Apr. 1980, author's archive.

69. Geoffrey Hudson to Rowse, 14 Jan. 1945, Rowse Papers, MS 113/3/1/Corr.H, The Times, 1 Aug., 26 Apr. 1951, 15 Jan., 25 Feb., 3 Mar. 1952.
70. Salter to Rowse, 13 Oct. [sic], Rowse Papers, EUL MS113/3/1/Corr.S.
71. "Private Lives of the Fellows of All Souls," John Sparrow, Rowse Papers, MS 113/1/2/4, vol. 2, "Private Lives of the Fellows of All Souls," Arthur Salter, Rowse Papers, MS 113/1/2/4, vol. 4, Rowse Diary, typescript, Rowse Papers, MS 113/2/2/13/1.
72. Salter to Rowse, 31 Dec. 1955, Rowse Papers, EUL MS113/3/1/Corr.S.
73. Salter to Rowse, 4 Apr. 1961, Rowse Papers, EUL MS113/3/1/Corr.S.
74. Salter to Rowse, 13 Oct. [sic], Rowse Papers, EUL MS113/3/1/Corr.S.
75. Salter to Rowse, 13 Oct. [sic], Rowse to Salter, 17 Oct. [sic] Rowse Papers, EUL MS113/3/1/Corr.S.
76. Rowse to Salter, 12 Jan. 1957, Salter to Rowse, 15 Jan. 1957, Rowse Papers, EUL MS113/3/1/Corr.S. Rowse's biographer reprinted the letter of 15 Jan. 1957 to Salter as an appendix. See Richard Ollard, A Man of Contradictions: A Life of A.L. Rowse (1999), 323-327.
77. See e.g., Salter to Rowse, 23 Nov. 1956, 8 June 1961, 21 Nov. 1962, 21 Sept., 28 Nov. 1963, 4 Oct. 1964, 5 Jan. 1965, Rowse Papers, EUL MS113/3/1/Corr.S.
78. Salter to Rowse, 5 Jan. 1965, Rowse Papers, EUL MS113/3/1/Corr.S. See also "Portrait of Ethel, Lady Salter, pp. 1-10, Rowse Papers, MS Box 70.
79. See e.g., Salter to Rowse, 18 Oct. [sic], 21 Nov. 1968, 3 Mar. 1969, Rowse Papers, EUL MS113/3/1/Corr.S.
80. Journal, Sept. 1965-1974, Rowse Papers, MS113/2/2/26, typescript, pp. 8-14, 329-330.
81. "Private Lives of the Fellows of All Souls," Arthur Salter, Rowse Papers, MS 113/1/2/4, vol. 5 (typescript).
82. Obituary tribute by Sir Richard Powell, The Times, 22 July 1975.
83. Fish Armstrong to Salter, 7 Jan. 1958, Salter to Fish Armstrong, 18 Jan., 3 Apr. 1958, Fish Armstrong Papers, Series 1: Box 54, Folder 26.
84. "Economic Strategy of the West," Foreign Affairs, 36(1958), 618-632.
85. Salter to Rowse, 22 July 1958, Rowse Papers, EUL MS113/3/1/Corr.S.
86. The, Reform, Replace or Supplement? Annual Memorial Lecture, March 1957, David Davies Memorial Institute of International Studies (1957), 3-19, The Times, 31 May 1957.
87. Salter to Lippmann, 22 Mar. 1957, Lippmann Papers, MS 326, Box 100, Folder 1877.
88. Salter Papers, File 1, Anecdotes and Incidents, Jan. 1956.

89. See Salter to Charles Monteith, 24, 26 Nov. 1960, 10, 14 Apr., 8 July, 15 Nov. 1961, Monteith to Salter, 13 Apr. 14, 22 Sept. 1961, Faber and Faber Papers.
90. International Affairs, 38(1961), 242-243.
91. The Political Quarterly, 33(1962), 90-92.
92. The Times Literary Supplement, 27 Oct. 1961, 777.
93. The Observer, 15 Oct. 1961.
94. See e.g., The Economist, 201(11 Nov. 1961), 545-546, The Times, 26 Oct. 1961, The Sunday Times, 5 Nov. 1961. Lord Layton wrote the review for The Economist. See Layton Papers, 10[88(1)].
95. Monteith to Salter, 5 Mar. 1962, Faber and Faber Papers. Rowse's note to Monteith, n.d., used in advertisements for the book, stated "Lord Salter has been a great public servant. Modest, observant, authentic, this book offers us a significant cross-section of the life of our time." Faber and Faber Papers. In response, Salter wrote to Rowse, "I'm glad you liked my memoirs & appreciate the letter you wrote to Charles Monteith." Salter to Rowse, 29 Dec. 1961, Rowse Papers, EUL MS113/3/1/Corr.S.
96. Monteith to Salter, 18 July 1958, 1 Apr. 1966, Salter to Monteith, 3 Apr. 1966, Faber and Faber Papers.
97. Slave of the Lamp: A Public Servant's Notebook (1967), vi-xii, 1-302. Chapter 7, "Shipping Mission to Washington," had in fact been written in 1960 and was intended to be a stand-alone essay. See Salter to Monteith, 3 Nov. 1960, Faber and Faber Papers.
98. See The Manchester Guardian, 9 Nov. 1967, The Times, 6, 7 Dec. 1967.
99. The Observer, 14 Jan. 1968, The Economist, 225(2 Dec. 1967), 3.
100. The Times Literary Supplement, 18 Jan. 1968, 54.
101. The Sunday Telegraph, 19 Nov. 1967.
102. Salter to Rowse, 21 Nov. 1968, 3 Mar. 1969, Rowse Papers, EUL MS1113/3/1/Corr.S.
103. Salter to Rowse, 12, 23 Dec. 1967, Rowse Papers, EUL MS1113/3/1/Corr.S.
104. Salter, Slave of the Lamp, 291.
105. Lady Salter to Perkins, 13 Feb. 1960, Perkins Papers, Personal "S".
106. Robert V. Adamson, "Recollections of Lord and Lady Salter," n.d., author's archive, Sir Edmund B. Ford to the author, 15 Sept. 1979, author's archive.
107. H.V. Hodson to the author, 31 Aug. 1979, author's archive.
108. John Pope-Hennessy, Learning to Look (1991), 135.
109. Salter to Layton, 3 July 1962, Layton Papers, 10[86].
110. Author's interview with Augusta Cobbold, 2 Mar. 1971, author's archive.

111. Quoted in Pope-Hennessy, Learning to Look, 128, Lithgow Osborne, "Memoirs of Arthur Salter," June 1979, author's archive.
112. Mary D. Kierstead to the author, 21 Sept. 1979, Dr. Rustin McIntosh to the author, 8 July 1979, and John McLennan to the author, 9 Mar. 1980, author's archive.
113. The Berkshire Eagle, 3 Sept. 1960, 22 Aug. 1963.
114. Salter to Lewis Douglas, 25 Sept. 1964, Lewis Douglas Papers, AZ290, Box 334, Folder 3.
115. Salter to Rowse, 2 Dec. 1963, Rowse Papers, EUL MS113/3/1/Corr.S.
116. Salter to Monteith, 18 Sept. 1961, Faber and Faber Papers.
117. Salter to Perkins, 1 Jan. 1965, Perkins Papers, "Personal "S", Salter to Rowse, 14 Aug. 1965, Rowse Papers, EUL MS113/3/1Corr.S.
118. Salter to Gertrude Caton Thompson, 11 Jan. 1966, author's archive, Salter to Douglas, 18 June 1963, 28 July 1967, Douglas Papers, AZ290, Box 334, Folder 3, Salter to Rowse, 23 Dec. 1967, 13 Mar. 1969, Rowse Papers, EUL MS113/3/1Corr.S.
119. Rosamond Gilder to Salter, 31 May 1969, courtesy of Rosamond Gilder.
120. Author's interview with Lord Salter, 10 Nov. 1970.
121. The Times, 21 Oct. 1969. On Lady Salter, see also John Pope-Hennessy to Peter Quennell, n.d., Sir John Pope-Hennessy Papers, Box 49, Getty Research Institute, Los Angeles, CA. Lady Salter's sister, Marchesa Louise de Rosales, had predeceased her on 25 Aug. 1958. The Times, 26 Aug. 1958. She died at Garmisch and was buried in the cemetery at Genthod, Switzerland.
122. Rosamond Gilder to the author, 20 Jan. 1980, author's archive, Last Will and Testament, Lady Salter, 7 Oct. 1969, Probated 3 Sept. 1970, Pittsfield, MA.
123. Salter to Gertrude Caton Thompson, 28 Oct. 1966, author's archive.
124. Salter to Joyce Newton Thompson, 31 July 1968, Newton Thompson Papers, BC 643 B22.18.
125. Memorial Address for Walter George Stewart Adams, 19 March 1966 (Oxford, 1966), 1-7. The phrase was borrowed by Salter from the "Penultima" to his Memoirs, 352.
126. The Times, 19 Dec. 1951, 7 Dec 1955, 7 Jan., 2 May 1958, 4 Feb. 1959, 14 Apr. 1961,19 Mar. 1964, 18 May 1965, 16 Feb. 1966, 31 Jan. 1968 and 21 Jan. 1969.
127. The Times, 6, 18 May, 1972.
128. Douglas Jay to the author, 26 July 1979, author's archive.
129. Author's interview with Lord Hailsham, 24 June 1981, author's archive.
130. Salter to Rowse, 26 Dec. n.d., Rowse Papers, EUL MS113/3/1/Corr.S.
131. I am grateful to Anne Vestey (Anne Lady Vestey) for her recollections of this period. Anne Vestey to the author, 7 Sept. 1979, author's archive.

132. Author's interview with Lord Salter, 13 Oct. 1970.
133. Gillian Watson to the author, 15 July 1975, author's archive.
134. The Times, 30 June 1975. For Layton's draft obituary and the related correspondence, see Layton Papers, 10[89-96].
135. The Times, 5, 22 July 1975. A shorter obituary in The Daily Telegraph, 30 June 1975, recapitulated the highlights of Salter's career.
136. "James Arthur Salter, 1881-1975, An Address Given on 22 July 1975 in St. Margaret's Church, Westminster by the Rt. Hon. Lord Hailsham."

Bibliography

Given the lengthy span of Lord Salter's career, 1904-1975, it would be impractical to provide an adequate bibliography. This would extend to hundreds of pages. Instead, what follows is an inventory of papers of individuals which yielded Salter documentation. Listed afterwards is a number of libraries, depositories and archives which held relevant materials. Finally, there is a list of Lord Salter's annual publications, attesting to his astonishing productivity, even though hand written with pen and ink.

Private Papers

Lady Aberdeen	Courtesy of Lord Aberdeen[1]
Winthrop W. Aldrich	Baker Library, Harvard Business School, Boston, MA
Lord Allen of Hurtwood	University of South Carolina Library, Columbia, SC
Lady Allen of Hurtwood	Author's Archive[2]
Allen and Unwin Ltd.	Courtesy of Rayner Unwin
Sir L.S. Amery	Churchill Archives Centre, Cambridge
Sir Norman Angell	Ball State University, Muncie, IN
Hamilton Fish Armstrong	Department of Rare Books and Special Collections, Princeton University Library, Princeton, NJ
Will Arnold-Forster	Courtesy of Jake Arnold-Forster
Lady Astor	Special Collections, University of Reading, Reading
Lord Astor	Special Collections, University of Reading, Reading
Frank Ayedelotte	Presidential Papers, Friends Historical Library, Swarthmore, PA
Lady Baldwin	Courtesy of Lady Baldwin
A.J. Balfour	British Library, London
Edward Price Bell	Newberry Library, Chicago, IL
George Bell & Sons	Ltd Special Collections, University of Reading, Reading
Eleanor Belmont	Columbia University Library, New York
Adolf A. Berle	Franklin D. Roosevelt Library, Hyde Park, NY
R.B. Bennett	University of New Brunswick, Fredericton, NB
Bernard Bellush	Franklin D. Roosevelt Library, Hyde Park, NY
Lord Beveridge	British Library of Political and Economic Science, London
Robert and Mildred Bliss	Harvard University Archives, Cambridge, MA
Roland Boyden	Houghton Library, Harvard University, Cambridge, MA
W.J. Brathwaite	British Library of Political and Economic Science, London

---

1. "Courtesy of" indicates *copies* have been provided from privately held papers for use by the author.
2. "Author's Archive" indicates that *original materials* have been permanently deposited with the author.

Lord Brand	Bodleian Library, Oxford
Ekaterina Breshkovskaia	Columbia University Library, New York, NY
Arthur Bullard	Princeton University Library, Princeton, NJ
Lord Butler	Trinity College Library, Cambridge
Harold E. Caustin	Courtesy of Harold Caustin
Lord Cecil	British Library, London
Sir Sydney John Chapman	British Library of Political and Economic Science, London
Lord Cherwell	Nuffield College Library, Oxford
Thomas W. Childs	Courtesy of Thomas W. Childs
Sir Winston S. Churchill	Churchill Archives Centre, Cambridge
William Clark	Bodleian Library, Oxford
G.D.H. Cole	Nuffield College Library, Oxford
Lady Colefax	Bodleian Library, Oxford
J.B. Condliffe	Bancroft Library, University of California, Berkeley, CA
W.P. Crozier	The Guardian Archive, John Rylands University Library, University of Manchester, Manchester
Lionel Curtis	Bodleian Library, Oxford, and Chatham House, London
Sir Hugh Dalton	British Library of Political and Economic Science, London
Lord Davies	National Library of Wales, Aberystwyth
Joseph S. Davis	Author's Archive
Norman H. Davis	Library of Congress, Washington, DC
Lewis W. Douglas	University Libraries, University of Arizona, Tucson, AZ
Allen and John Foster Dulles	Princeton University Library, Princeton, NJ
Elliott Felkin	King's College Archive Centre, Cambridge
E.M. Forster	Berg Collection, New York Public Library, New York, NY
Raymond B. Fosdick	Department of Rare Books and Special Collections, Princeton University Library, Princeton, NJ
Renée de Lucy Fossarieu	Author's Archive
A.G. Gardiner	British Library of Political and Economic Science, London
J.L. Garvin	University of Texas Library, Houston, TX
Huntingdon Gilchrist	Library of Congress, Washington, DC
Helena de Kay Gilder	Lilly Library, Indiana University, Bloomington, IN
Rosamond Gilder	Courtesy of Rosamond Gilder
G.P. Gooch	Courtesy of Bernard Gooch
Lord Hailsham	Churchill Archives Centre, Cambridge
Mary Agnes Hamilton	Courtesy of R.V. Adamson
Lord Hanworth	Bodleian Library, Oxford
Frank Hardie	Bodleian Library, Oxford

Averell Harriman	Library of Congress, Washington, DC
Basil Liddell Hart	Liddell Hart Centre for Military Archives, King's College, London
Jennifer Hart	Bodleian Library, Oxford
Hubert D. Henderson	Nuffield College Library, Oxford
A.P. Herbert	Courtesy of John Herbert.
Herbert Hoover	Herbert Hoover Library, West Branch, IA
Harry L. Hopkins	Franklin D. Roosevelt Library, Hyde Park, NY
Charles P. Howland	Yale University Library, New Haven, CT
Manley Ottmer Hudson	Harvard Law School Library, Cambridge, MA
Per Jacobsson	British Library of Political and Economic Science, London
Frederick P. Keppel	Columbia University Library, New York, NY
William Lyon Mackenzie King	Library and Archives Canada, Ottawa, ON
Sir John Maynard Keynes	King's College Archive Centre, Cambridge
Sir Basil Kemball-Cook	Imperial War Museum, London
Thomas G. Lamont	Baker Library, Harvard University, Boston, MA.
Rear Admiral Emory S. Land	Library of Congress, Washington, DC
Lord Layton	Trinity College Library, Cambridge
Herbert H. Lehman	Columbia University Library, New York, NY
Sir Norman Leslie	Churchill Archives Centre, Cambridge
Walter Lippmann	Yale University Library, New Haven, CT
E.M.H. Lloyd	British Library of Political and Economic Science, London
Sir David Lloyd George	House of Lords Library, London
Lord Lothian	Scottish Public Record Office, Edinburgh
Sir Harold Macmillan	Bodleian Library, Oxford
Arthur Marder	University of California Library, Irvine, CA
Violet Markham	British Library of Political and Economic Science, London
Vincent Massey	University of Toronto Archives, Toronto, ON
James G. McDonald	Columbia University Library, New York, NY
Mary Agnes Craig McGeachy	Library and Archives Canada, Ottawa, ON
James Edward Meade	British Library of Political and Economic Science, London
Marie M. Meloney	Columbia University Library, New York, NY
Jean Monnet	Jean Monnet Foundation for Europe, Lausanne
Henry Morgenthau, Jr.	Franklin D. Roosevelt Library, Hyde Park, NY
Dwight W. Morrow	Amherst College Archives and Special Collections, Amherst, MA
Paul Scott Mowrer	Newberry Library, Chicago, IL
Gilbert Murray	Bodleian Library, Oxford

Joyce Newton Thompson	Special Collections, University of Cape Town Libraries, Cape Town, SA
Beverley Nichols	University of Delaware Library, Newark, DE
Nichols-Shurtleff Family	Schlesinger Library, Harvard University, Cambridge, MA
Sir Harold Nicolson	Balliol College Library, Oxford
Lord Noel-Baker	Churchill Archives Centre, Cambridge
Sir Montagu Norman	Bank of England Archive, London
Oral History Collection	Memoirs by Thanasis Aghnides, Sir Normal Angell, Paul Appleby, Bernard Gladieux, Carl Hamilton, Commander Sir Robert Jackson, Emory S. Land, Branko Lukac, Frances Perkins, George Rublee, Henry Self, Henry Wallace, James P. Warburg, Meredith Wood, (Book-of-the Month Club), Butler Library, Columbia University, New York, NY
Sir Frederic J. Osborn	Welwyn Garden City Central Library, Welwyn Garden City
Frances Perkins	Columbia University Library, New York, NY
Lord Pethick-Lawrence	Trinity College Library, Cambridge
Sir Horace Plunkett	Plunkett Foundation, Oxford
Frank L. Polk	Yale University Library, New Haven, CT
Sir John Pope-Hennessy	Getty Research Institute, Los Angeles, CA
Eleanor Rathbone	Liverpool University Library, Liverpool
Franklin D. Roosevelt	Franklin D. Roosevelt Library, Hyde Park, NY
A.L. Rowse	University of Exeter Library, Exeter
Sir Michael Sadler	Bodleian Library, Oxford
C.P. Scott	John Rylands University Library, Manchester
James T. Shotwell	Columbia University Library, New York, NY
Sir E.L. Spears	Churchill Archives Centre, Cambridge
Sir Josiah Stamp	Courtesy of Lord Stamp
Henry H. Stimson	Yale University Library, New Haven, CT
Arthur Sweetser	Library of Congress, Washington, DC
Frank Swinnerton	University of Arkansas Library, Fayetteville, AR
Gertrude Caton Thompson	Author's Archive
Royall Tyler	Courtesy of William Tyler
Elisina Tyler	Courtesy of William Tyler
Euan Wallace	Bodleian Library, Oxford
Sir Charles K. Webster	British Library of Economic and Political Science, London
Beatrice Webb	British Library of Political and Economic Science, London
Sidney Webb	British Library of Political and Economic Science, London

H.G. Wells	University of Illinois Library, Urbana-Champaign, IL
John Gilbert Winant	Franklin D. Roosevelt Library, Hyde Park, NY
Lord Woolton	Bodleian Library, Oxford
Sir Alfred Zimmern	Bodleian Library, Oxford

Other Libraries, Archives, etc.

British Broadcasting Corporation Written Archives Centre, Caversham Park, Reading
Centre national des archives diplomatique, La Courneuve Cedex
Council on Foreign Relations, New York, NY
Faber and Faber Ltd., London
Fabian Society, Nuffield College Library, Oxford
Federation of British Industries, Modern Records Centre, University of Warwick Library, Coventry
Institute of Politics, Williams College Archives, Williamstown, MA
League of Nations Library, Geneva
League of Nations Union, British Library of Political and Economic Science, London
Library and Archives Canada, Ottawa, ON
Morley College Archives, London
The National Archives, London
The National Archives, Washington, DC
Oxford Preservation Trust, Oxford
President's Office, Yale University Library, New Haven, CT
President's Office, University of California, Bancroft Library, Berkeley, CA
Royal Institute of International Affairs, Chatham House, London
Stanley Unwin Publishers, London
UN Relief and Rehabilitation Administration, United Nations Archives, New York, NY

Publications by Lord (Sir Arthur) Salter

Books:
Salter's Guide to The Thames, with J.H. Salter, 13th ed., Oxford, 1910ff
Allied Shipping Control: An Experiment in International Administration, London, 1921
Recovery: The Second Effort, London, 1932
The United States of Europe and other Papers, W. Arnold-Forster, ed., London, 1933
China and Silver, (Economic Forum), New York 1934
Security: Can We Retrieve It? London, 1939 [Trans. Italian, Chinese, Dutch,

Turkish]
Personality in Politics: Studies of Contemporary Statesmen, London, 1947
Memoirs of a Public Servant, London, 1961
Slave of the Lamp: A Public Servant's Notebook, London, 1967

Shorter Books:
Europe's Recovery: What It Means to World Peace, New York, 1924
The Role of the Dominions in Imperial Policy, Oxford, 1947
General Problem of the Dollar Shortage, London, 1949
Foreign Investment: Essays in International Finance, No. 12, Princeton, NJ, 1951. Reprinted in Foreign Trade and Finance: Essays in International Economic Equilibrium and Adjustment, William R. Allen and Clark Lee Allen, eds., New York, 1959, and Issues and Insights on International Investment, Mira Wilkins, ed., New York, 1977

Contributions to Books (including annuals, encyclopaedias, etc):
"Economics and Finance," in The League of Nations Starts: An Outline by its Organizers, London, 1920
"Preface," to Currencies After the War: A Survey of Conditions in Various Countries, London, 1920
"Economic Conflicts as the Cause of War," in Valentine Chirol, Yusuke Tsurumi and James Arthur Salter, The Reawakening of the Orient and other Addresses, London, 1925
"The Progress of Financial Reconstruction in Europe," in The Europa Year-Book, 1926, Michael Farbman, et al., eds., London, 1926
"League of Nations: The Work of the First Six Years," Encyclopaedia Britannica, 13th ed., vol. 30(1926)
"Control: Inter-Allied," Encyclopaedia Britannica, 13th ed., vol. 29(1926)
"The Economic Conference," in The Europa Year-Book, 1927, Michael Farbman, et al., eds., London, 1927
"Introduction: The League's Contribution," in The Economic Consequences of the League, The World Economic Conference, London, 1927
"Note," in League of Nations Union, World Prosperity And Peace: Being The Report of a Conference Held by The League of Nations Union at the Guildhall, E.C. 2, December 13th-15th, 1927, on the Work of the International Economic Conference, London, 1928
"Allied Maritime Transport Council," Encyclopaedia Britannica, 14th ed., vol. 1(1929)

"Preface," to Eugene Havas, Hungary's Finance and Trade in 1929, 3rd ed., London, 1930

"John Stuart Mill," in The Great Victorians, H.J. and Hugh Massingham, eds., London, 1932

"Foreword," to Alfred Plummer, The World in Agony: An Economic Analysis, London, 1932

"The Economic Causes of War," in The Causes of War: Economic, Industrial, Racial, Religious, Scientific and Political, Arthur Porritt, ed., London, 1932

"Introduction," to Documents on International Affairs, 1931, John W. Wheeler-Bennett, ed., London, 1932

"Preface" to H.V. Hodson, Economics of a Changing World, London, 1933

"World Government," in Leonard Wolfe, Lord Eustace Percy, Mrs. Sidney Webb, W.G.S. Adams and Arthur Salter, The Modern State, London 1933

"World Government," in The Causes of War and the Possibilities of Peace, Sukeo Kitasawa, ed., Tokyo, n.d.

"Foreword," to Viscount Astor and Keith Murray, The Planning of Agriculture, London, 1933

"The Economic Factor," in In Pursuit of Peace: Ten Lectures Delivered at Oxford July, 1933, G.P. Gooch, ed., London, 1933

"Foreword," to Wallace McClure, World Prosperity as Sought Through the Economic Work of the League of Nations, New York, 1933

"A New Framework for the Economic System," in The Obligation of Universities to the Social Order, H.P. Fairchild, ed., New York, 1933

"World Without War," in Essays and Addresses Toward a Liberal Education, A. Craig Baird, ed., London, 1934

"Presidential Address," in League of Nations, Sixth International Studies Conference, A Record of a Second Study Conference on the State and Economic Life, London, May 29 to June 2, 1933, London, 1934

"Introduction," to William Martin, Understand the Chinese, London, 1934

J. Hilton, J.J. Mallon, S. Mavor, B.S. Rowntree, A. Salter and F.D. Stuart, Are Trade Unions Obstructive? An Impartial Inquiry, London, 1935

"Planned Socialization and World Trade," in The Burden of Plenty? Graham Hutton, ed., London, 1935

"Introduction," to Eugene Staley, War and the Private Investor: A Study in the Relations of International Politics and International Private Investment, New York, 1935

"A New World Order," in Leadership in a Changing World, M. David Hoffman and Ruth Wanger, eds., London, 1935

"Practical Suggestions for Reform," in The Future of the League of Nations, The Record of a Series of Discussions Held at Chatham House, London, 1936

Arthur Salter, Lord Allen of Hurtwood, et. al., The World Foundation: A Proposal for Immediate Action on a World Basis, Oxford, 1936

"The Need for a New Economic System," in A Modern Reader: Essays on Present-Day Life and Culture, Walter Lippmann and Alan Nevins, eds., London, 1936

"Foreword," to G. Lowes Dickinson, The International Anarchy, 1904-1914, London, 1937

"Economic Nationalism: Can It Continue," G.D.H. Cole, A. Salter, Wickham Steed, Sidney Webb, P.M.S. Blackett and Lancelot Hogben, What is Ahead of Us? London, 1937

"Foreword," to An Atlas of Far Eastern Affairs, G.F. Hudson and Marthe Rajchman, eds., London, 1938

"China's New Unity," in China: Body and Soul, Ernest Richard Hughes, ed., London, 1938

"The Challenge to Democracy," in Constructive Democracy, Sir Ernest Simon, et. al., London, 1938

"Foreword," to Ruskin College Oxford: Activities of Some Former Students, London, n.d.

"Semi-socialized Economic Systems," in Études dédiées a la Mémoire d'André M. Andréadès, K. Varvaressos, ed., Athens, 1940

"Modern Mechanization and Its Effect on the Structure of Society," in Science and Social Change, Jesse E. Thornton, comp., Washington, 1939

"Introduction," to Brig.-General Sir Osborne Mance, The Road and Rail Transport Problem, London, 1940

"Preface," to Advisory Bodies, A Study of their Uses in Relation to Central Government 1919-1939, R.V. Vernon and N. Mansergh, eds., London, 1940

"Forward," to An Explanatory Atlas of the Far East, G.F. Hudson and Marthe Rajchman, eds., London, 1942

"The Summing Up," in The Way Ahead: The Strange Case of the Friendly Societies, John A. Lincoln, ed., London, 1946

"The Control of Nuclear Energy and the Development of International Institutions," in Atomic Energy: Its International Implications, Chatham House Study Group, London, 1948

"Tribute," in Ruskin: Prophet of the Good Life, J. Howard Whitehorse, ed., Oxford, 1948

"Cabinet and Parliament," in Parliament: A Survey, London, 1952

"Foreword" to Moral Foundations of Citizenship, M. Alderton Pink, ed., London, 1952

"The Crux of Nationalization," in Problems of Nationalized Industry, William A. Robson, ed., London, 1952

"Foreword," to The Economist Intelligence Unit, The Commonwealth and Europe London, 1960

Books: Official Publications:

"Preface," The Settlement of Greek Refugees: Scheme for an International Loan," League of Nations, Geneva, 1924

"General Survey" in The Financial Reconstruction of Hungary, General Survey and Principal Documents, League of Nations, Geneva, 1926

"Introduction," Scheme for the Settlement of Bulgarian Refugees, League of Nations, Geneva, 1926

"General Survey," The Financial Reconstruction of Austria, League of Nations, Geneva, 1927

"General Survey," The Financial Reconstruction of Hungary, League of Nations, Geneva, 1926

"Note," Guide to the Documents of the International Economic Conference, Geneva, May 1927, League of Nations, Geneva, 1927

"The League's Contribution," in The Economic Consequences of the League: The World Economic Conference, London, 1927

A Scheme for an Economic Advisory Organization in India, Government of India, Calcutta, 1931

Ministry of Transport, Report of the Conference on Rail and Road Transport, 29 July 1932, London, 1932

China and the Depression: Impressions of a Three Months Visit, National Government of the Republic of China, Nanking[?], 1934

The Development of Iraq: A Plan of Action, Iraq Development Board, Baghdad, 1955

Statistics and the Public, private circulation, London, Dec. 6th, 1939

Lectures and Addresses:

"Problems of International Administration," in The Development of the Civil Service, Lectures delivered before the Society of Civil Servants, 1920-21, London, 1922

"Reconstructing Austria: An Address by Sir Arthur Salter," International Chamber of Commerce at Rome, Italy, March 24, 1923

Europe's Recovery: What It Means To World Peace. New York: Reprinted by the League of Nations Non-Partisan Association, 1924

"The World Economic Conference of May, 1927, How to Secure Practical Results," Address Delivered to the Congress of the International Chamber of Commerce at Stockholm, July 1st, 1927, Stockholm, 1927

"The Progress of Economic Reconstruction in Europe," The Problems of Peace, Lectures Delivered at the Geneva Institute of International Relations, August 1926, London, 1927

"Economic Policy: The Way to Peace and Prosperity," <u>Problems of Peace, Second Series, Lectures Delivered at the Geneva Institute of International Relations, August 1927</u>, London, 1928

"The First Results of the World Economic Conference," <u>Problems of Peace, Third Series, Lectures Delivered at the Geneva Institute of International Relations, August 1928</u>, London, 1929

Foreign Policy Association, <u>Prosperity, Economic Nationalism or Internationalism</u>, Discussed by Joseph M. Pavloff, David Friday and Sir Arthur Salter, February 16, 1929, New York, 1929

<u>Some Reflections on the World Economic Depression</u>, Prepared for the Biennial Congress of the International Chamber of Commerce, 4 May 1931, Washington, 1931

<u>The World's Economic Crisis and the Way of Escape, The Halley Stewart Lectures, 1931</u>, by Arthur Salter, Josiah Stamp, J. Maynard Keynes, Basil Blackett, Henry Clay and W.H. Beveridge, London, 1932

<u>Political Aspects of the World Depression, Burge Memorial Lecture, 1932</u>, Oxford University Press, London 1932. Reprinted in Ernest Barker, et al., <u>Burge Memorial Lectures, 1927-1933</u>, Oxford, 1933

<u>Modern Mechanization and Its Effects on the Structure of Society</u>, Second Massey Lecture, McGill University, 18 Apr. 1933, Oxford University Press, Oxford, 1933

<u>The Framework of an Ordered Society</u>, The Alfred Marshall Lectures, 22, 23, 24 Feb. 1933, Cambridge, 1933

"Presidential Address," in League of Nations, <u>A Record of a Second Study Conference on the State and Economic Life, Held in London, May 29 to June 2, 1933</u>, Paris, 1934

"Peace and the Colonial Problem," in National Peace Council, <u>Peace and the Colonial Problem</u>, London, 1935

<u>World Trade and Its Future</u>, Swarthmore College Lectures, Philadelphia, 1936

<u>The English Speaking Peoples and World Peace</u>, Second Jonathan Peterson Lecture, League for Political Education, New York 1936

<u>Economic Policies and Peace</u>, Merttens Lecture, 1936, Day to Day Pamphlets, no. 34, London, 1936

<u>Letter to the Electors of Oxford University: Oxford University By-Election 1937</u>, Oxford, 1937

"Inaugural Address," in <u>Nutrition and Public Health, Proceedings of a National Conference on the Wider Aspects of Nutrition, April 27-29, 1939</u>, London, 1939

"Address," <u>Proceedings of the American Society of International Law, April 30-May 1, 1943</u>, Washington, DC, 1943

The Role of the Dominions in Imperial Policy, An Address to the Royal Empire Society, 5 February 1947, Preface by Lionel Curtis, Oxford, 1947

General Problem of the Dollar Shortage, Lecture on November 8, 1949, Institute of Bankers, London, 1949

The United Nations, Reform, Replace or Supplement? Annual Memorial Lecture, March 1957, David Davies Memorial Institute of International Studies, London, 1957

Pamphlets:

Toward a Planned Economy, The John Day Pamphlets, no. 40, New York, 1933

Is It Peace? The Nettle and the Flower, The Spectator, London, 1938

The Dual Policy, Oxford Pamphlets on World Affairs, no. 11, London, 1939

The Meaning of the Marshall Plan Now and in 1952, London, 1948

William George Stewart Adam, CH, A Memorial Address given in the College Chapel, 19 Mar. 1966, Oxford, 1966

Articles:

1911

"Citizenship in Stepney," The Toynbee Record, 24(Dec. 1911), 33-36

1923

"The Financial Reconstruction of Austria," The American Journal of International Law, 17(1923), 116-128

"The Reconstruction of Austria," Young Men of India, 34(1923), 201-209

"Austria: Saved or Duped?" The New Republic, 35(1923), 359-361

1924

"The Reconstruction of Austria," Foreign Affairs, 2(1924), 630-643

"The Reconstruction of Hungary," Journal of the British Institute of International Affairs, 3(1924), 190-202

"The League of Nations Program for the Financial and Economic Rehabilitation of Hungary," The Economic World, 113(1924), 809-811. Originally published in the New York Evening Post, 30 May 1924

1925

"Good Work in Greece," Headway, 7(Jan. 1925), 5

"Paving the Way to Europe's Recovery: The Financial Work of the League of Nations," The Manchester Guardian Commercial, (29 Jan.1925), 33

"Reconstruction: Five Years of Work by the League of Nations," Journal of the British Institute of International Affairs, 4(1925), 313-314

"War Risks in Economic Conflicts," The Yale Review, 14(1925), 683-698

1926

"The Reconstruction of Hungary," Foreign Affairs, 5(1926), 91-102

Hungary Stabilized, New York, 1926, reprinted from The Financial News, 13 Sept. 1926

1927

"The World Economic Conference," Round Table, 17(1927), 267-286

"What's Wrong With the World: The League Tackles Tariffs and Cartels," Headway, 9(April 1927), 67

"The Economic Conference and After," The Nation and the Athenaeum, 41(1927), 328-330

"The World Economic Conference of May 1927," Nineteenth Century and After, 102(1927), 15-27

"La Conference Economique Internationale de 1927," Bibliothèque universelle et Revue de Genève, (July 1927), 60-70

"Progress and Economic Understanding," Central European Observer, 3(1927), 44-47

"The Economic Conference: Prospects of Practical Results," Journal of the Royal Institute of International Affairs, 6(1927), 350-367

"Are We Getting Richer or Poorer?" Radio Times, 17(1927), 239

"The Contribution of the League of Nations to the Economic Recovery of Europe," The Annals of the American Academy of Political and Social Science, 134(1927), 132-139

"World Economic Problems and Trade Barriers," Manchester Chamber of Commerce, Monthly Record, 38(Feb. 1927), 47-51

1928

"The League of Nations, Economic Policy: The Next Stages," The Spectator, 140 (1928), 189

1929

"The Coming Economic Struggle," The Yale Review, 18(1929), 505-519
"The United States of Europe," Round Table, 20(1929), 79-99
"The League of Nations," The Spectator, 143(1929), 15

1930

"The Economic Work of the League," The Nation and the Athenaeum, 47(1930), 587-588
"Trade Within the Empire – II," The Listener, 4(1930), 729-730, 762
"The Economic Organization of Peace," Foreign Affairs, 9(1930), 42-53
"Where is Europe Going?" Round Table, 21(1930), 1-16
"World Finance and Economics: The Next Step," The Spectator, 145(1930), 770-771
"The League of Nations in Action: An Actual Example of How a War was Stopped," The Highway, 23(Oct. 1930), 8-11

1931

"The Silver Problem," Political Science Quarterly, 46(1931), 321-334
"Chatham House Annual Dinner," International Affairs, (1931), 592-596
"The Future of the Pound," The Spectator, 147(1931), 800-801
"The World Financial Crisis," The Yale Review, 21(1931), 217-231
"What I Would Do with the World – I," The Listener, 6(1931) 567-570, 599-560

1932

"China, Japan and the League of Nations," Contemporary Review, 141(1932), 279-288
"The Technique of Open Diplomacy," The Political Quarterly, 3(1932), 58-70
"The Prospects of World Settlement," The Listener, 7(1932), 37-38, 72
"I – The Problem of World Government: Transport and Telegrams Transform the World," The Listener, 7(1932), 291
"II – "The Clash Between Frontiers and Trade," The Listener, 7(1932), 298-299
"III – "Must National Sovereignty Go?" The Listener, 7(1932), 329-330, 361
"IV – The Structure of World Government," The Listener, 7(1932), 376-377
"V – Referee or Super-State?" The Listener, 7(1932) 436-437
"VI – A World Purged of War," The Listener, 7(1932), 466-467
"Disarmament – the Prospects," The Listener, 8(1932), 577-579

"What America Thinks of the War Debt Settlement," The Listener, 8(1932), 928
"Ottawa and the World," The Spectator, 148(1932), 821-822
"Ottawa and the World," The Spectator, 149(1931), 438-439
"The Conferences of This Year: Geneva, Lausanne, Ottawa, London," The Political Quarterly, 3(1932), 467-488
"The Road to Recovery," The Highway, 25(1932), 4-5
"Past, Present and Future," Lloyd's Bank Review (Supplement), 3(1932), 54-73
"Geneva in Retrospect," Index, 7(1932), 287-301
"The Future of Economic Nationalism," Foreign Affairs, 11(1932), 8-20
"A Year and A Half of Crisis," The Yale Review, 32(1932), 217-233
"Address at Chatham House Annual Dinner," International Affairs, 11(1932), 849-851
"The Shanghai Crisis," International Affairs, 11(1932), 171-173
"England's Dilemma: Free Trade or Protection?" Foreign Affairs, 10(1932), 188-200
"Disarmament," Round Table, 22(1932), 532-551
"The Forthcoming Conferences," The News-Letter: The National Labour Fortnightly, 1(11 June 1932), 7-10

1933

"War Debts," International Affairs, 12(1933), 147-167
"International Studies Conference on the State and Economic Life," International Affairs, 12(1933), 535-546
"A New Economic Morality" Harper's Magazine, 166(1933), 641-649
"Obsolete Jobs Not Obsolete Men," Fortune, 3(Apr. 1933), 60-63
"Why Mr. Keynes is Right," The Spectator, 150(1933), 417-418
"Steps Toward Recovery," Proceedings of the Academy of Political Science, 15(1933), 126-135
"The Nations at the Crossroads," The New York Times Magazine, (11 June 1933), 1-2, 18
"America's Chance to Lead Again," The New York Times Magazine, (16 Apr. 1933), 1-2, 13
"The Way Out: Internationalism?" The New York Times Magazine, (2 July 1933), 1-2, 14
"Planning the Future Economic State," The New York Times Magazine, (10 Sept. 1933), 3, 16
"The Week Abroad." The Listener, 9(1933), 402-403
"The Nazi Revolution," The Listener, 9(1933), 461
"From East to West," The Listener, 9(1933), 480-481
"Internationalism: Necessity or Delusion?" The Listener, 9(1933), 517-518, 549
"The Economic Conference: Progress Up-to-Date," The Listener, 10(1933), 10

"Obsolete Jobs, Not Obsolete Men," Fortune, 3(Apr. 1933), 60-63

"How Recovery May Come," Speech at The Canadian Club, 24 Apr. 1933, http://www.canadianclub.org/SearchResults.aspx?IndexCatalogue=SearchIndex&SearchQuery=Salter

"Is a World Government Possible?" Saturday Night, 48(7 Oct. 1933), 15, 24

1934

"Back To the League," The Spectator, 153(1934), 156-157

"National and World Recovery," Co-Partnership: The Organ of the Industrial Co-Partnership Association, 43(1934), 10-11

"The Social Work of the League," The Listener, 12(1934), 434-436

"Poverty in Plenty - Planned Socialisation and World Trade," The Listener, 12(1934) 978-979

"Toward a Planned Economy," The Atlantic Monthly, 153(1934), 31-38

"International Aspects of Recovery," Academy of Political Science, Proceedings, 16(1934), 117-124

"Recovery: The Present Age," The Yale Review, 24(1934), 217-236

"China in 1934," The Canadian Forum, 14(1934), 293-294

"China and the Depression," Supplement to The Economist, 118(1934), 1-16

"China and the World Depression," Round Table, 24(1934), 531-547

1935

"Real Sanctions or None," The Spectator, 155(1935), 347-348

"The Anniversary Postbag," The Yale Review, 25(1935), 12-13

"The Economic Legacy of the Peace Treaties," The Listener, 13(1935), 956-958

"Foreign Investments in China," Economic Journal, 45(1935), 141-142

"Stabilization and Recovery," Foreign Affairs, 14(1935), 12-25

"A Progressive Policy: II, Planned Socialization," The Spectator, 154(1935), 39-40

1936

"Reform of the League," The Political Quarterly, 7(1936), 465-480

"The Future of the League: V, Immediate Policy," The Spectator, 156(1936), 1071-1072

"World Trade Awaits Stable Money," The Rotarian, 49(1936), 9-11, 60-62

"British Monetary Policy, A Symposium," The Economist, 125(14 Nov. 1936), 297-298

"The European Cauldron," The Listener, 16(1936), 11

"Auto-Obituary VI, A Civil Servant's Career," The Listener, 16(1936), 346
"The Direction of Shipping in Time of War," The Listener, 16(1936), 794-797
"America and the Manchurian Affair," The Spectator, 157(1936), 462
Salter, et al., "Proposals for the Reform of the Covenant of the League of Nations," New Commonwealth Quarterly, 2 (Sept. 1936), 216-241
"The League and the Problem of Change: A Suggestion," The New Outlook, 10 June 1936, 22-25
"Oxford University By-Election: Sir Arthur Salter on His Candidature," The New Outlook, 12 Nov. 1936, 3-5

1937

"Did We Starve Germany?" The Spectator, 157(1937), 117-118
"What Lies Ahead for Britain's Vast Empire?" The New York Times Magazine, (16 May 1937), 3, 25, 27
"Broadening the Foundations of Peace," The Rotarian, 50(1937), 8-11, 64-65
"Economic Nationalism Today," The Listener, 18(1937), 59-60
"An All-Party Policy," The Spectator, 158(1937), 256-257
"Europe Looks Towards America," The Political Quarterly, 8(1937), 467-481
"The Perils of Recovery," The Yale Review, 27(1937), 217-234
"The Oxford Election," The Spectator, 158(1937), 397-398
"Food Storage for Defence," The Economist, 129(1937), 12-16
"Peace and Economic Policy," Peace, 5(July-Aug. 1937), 62-64
"The Far Eastern Crisis," The Democrat," 1(Dec. 1937), 3-4

1938

"British Policy Now – II," The Spectator, 161(1938), 643-644
"The Adventure of the Twentieth Century," California Monthly, (May 1938), 6-7, 42, 44
"Who Should Own our Mines? IV – A Consumer's View," The Listener, 20(1938), 816
"Have We Duped America?" John O'London's Weekly, 19(10 June 1938), 350-351

1939

"What Are Our Aims," Picture Post, 5(28 Oct.1939), 47
"Saving Needed for National Welfare," National Savings, no. 16 (1939), 2-3
"The Public and the Air Menace," New Statesman, 17(1939), 238-239
"War Purposes and Peace Aims – I," The Spectator, 163(1939), 575-576
"The Economic Strategy of the War," Contemporary Review, 156(1939), 641-651

"Depressions Breed Revolutions Unless –," The Rotarian, 54(June 1939), 8-11
"The Right League Policy for Great Britain," Headway, 1(July 1939), 2-4

1941

"The Presidency," Time, 37(1941), 17-18

1943

"Pressing the Fight for Freedom," Proceedings of the Academy of Political Science, 20(1943), 74-84

1944

"From Combined War Agencies to International Administration," Public Administration Review, 4(1944), 1-6

1945

"Conference on International Administration: Concluding Remarks," Public Administration: Journal of the Institute of Public Administration, 23(1945), 1-2
"Dumbarton Oaks: The Future of Security," The Listener, 33(1945), 339-341, 352
"Importance of the Moscow Meeting," The Listener, 34(1945), 723
"'L.G': An Appreciation," The Spectator, 174(1945), 287-288
"Problems of Germany," The Spectator, 175(1945), 436
"The Relief of Europe," Contemporary Review, 168(1945), 257-261
"The Task in Europe," The Spectator, 174(1945), 426-427
"Post-War Britain," London Calling: The Overseas Journal of the BBC, no. 284(18 Mar. 1945), 4, no. 285(25 Mar. 1945), 6, no. 286(1 Apr. 1945), 4, no. 287, (8 Apr. 1945), 4, no. 288(15 Apr. 1945), 8, no. 289(22 Apr. 1945), 4, no. 290(29 Apr. 1945), 13, no. 291(6 May 1945), 6, no.292(13 May 1945), 17, no. 293(20 May 1945), 6, 18, no. 294(27 May 1945), 8, no. 295(3 June 1945), 12-132
"A Collective and Constructive System," Headway, 7(March 1945), 10

1946

"The United Nations and the Atomic Bomb," International Conciliation, 417(1946), 40-48
"The Atom Bomb and World Security," The Listener, 36(1946), 131-132

"Can We Prevent Famine?" Picture Post, (4 May 1946), 10-12
"The Shadow of World Famine," The Listener, 35(1946), 453-454
"Maynard Keynes," The Spectator, 176(1946), 421-422

1947

"The Role of the Dominions in Imperial Policy," United Empire: Journal of the Royal Empire Society, 38(1947), 77-80

1948

"Great Britain's Dollar Problem," The Listener, 39(1948), 283-285
"Maxims for Planners," The Listener, 39(1948), 368-369
"Maynard Keynes, I, "Pioneer of the New Economics," Britain To-day, no. 143(Mar. 1948), 11-16, II, His Influence in World Affairs," Britain To-day, no. 144(Apr. 1948), 11-15
"Introduction, The Impact of Broadcasting on Great Britain's Life and Outlook – I,"The B.B.C. Quarterly, 3(1948), 1-7
"Concluding Comments, The Impact of Broadcasting on Great Britain's Life and Outlook – II," The B.B.C. Quarterly, 3(1948), 103-108
"Economics and Peace," International Student Service Review, 3(1948), 9-14
"The Marshall Plan: Its Wider Implications," National Provincial Bank Review, no. 2(May 1948), 1-8

1949

"European Recovery: A Look Ahead," Foreign Affairs, 27(1949), 289-301
"The Best Route to Western Union," United Empire: Journal of the Royal Empire Society, 40(1949), 195-199
"The Changing Parliamentary System," Britain To-day, no. 159(July 1949), 8-14
"The International Bank and How it Works," The Rotarian, 74(Apr. 1949), 10-12

1950

"The Crux of Nationalization," The Political Quarterly, 21(1950), 209-217
"Lew Douglas," The Spectator, 185(1950), 505
"After Devaluation: The Common Task," Foreign Affairs, 28(1950), 215-230
"Prospects and Policy: Britain's Problem in Outline," National Provincial Bank Review, no. 11(Aug. 1950), 1-14

1951

"British Conservatism Today," <u>The Yale Review</u>, 41(1951), 1-12
"British Government Since 1918," <u>The Political Quarterly</u>, 22(1951), 137-141

1958

"Economic Strategy of the West," <u>Foreign Affairs</u>, 36(1958), 618-632

1963

"Lord Beveridge 1879-1963," <u>The Proceedings of the British Academy</u>, 49(1963), 417-429

CPSIA information can be obtained
at www.ICGtesting.com
Printed in the USA
LVOW03s1425120416
483250LV00024B/332/P